THE PRINCIPLES OF TEACHING-METHOD

THE
PRINCIPLES OF
TEACHING-METHOD

With Special Reference to Secondary Education

By

A. PINSENT M.A. B.Sc.

FORMERLY
SENIOR LECTURER DEPARTMENT OF EDUCATION UNIVERSITY COLLEGE
OF WALES ABERYSTWYTH
AND FORMERLY HEADMASTER HANDSIDE SCHOOL
WELWYN GARDEN CITY HERTS

THIRD EDITION REVISED AND ENLARGED

GEORGE G. HARRAP & CO. LTD
LONDON   TORONTO   WELLINGTON   SYDNEY

First published in Great Britain 1941
by GEORGE G. HARRAP & CO. LTD
182 High Holborn, London, W.C.1

Reprinted: March 1945 ; *March* 1946 ; *March* 1947 ;
September 1949 ; *December* 1952 ; *May* 1955 ; *July* 1956 ;
October 1958

Second edition, revised, 1962

Reprinted: 1964 ; 1965

Third edition, revised and enlarged, 1969

© *A. Pinsent* 1962, 1969

Copyright. All rights reserved
SBN 245 59397 7

Made in Great Britain. Printed by J. & J. Gray, Edinburgh

PREFACE TO THIRD (REVISED) EDITION

In this third revision the chapter on transfer of training has been completely rewritten and expanded. Discussions on topics which have recently aroused much interest in professional circles, namely, creativity, originality, and productive thinking, comprehensive secondary education, and programmed learning, have been added. In order to make room for the new material, the last chapter in the original edition has been omitted.

As before, in presenting the new material, the aim has been to select certain psychological principles which seem particularly relevant to the contemporary educational situation and to relate them as clearly as possible to problems of everyday teaching practice.

It is hoped that the new material may suggest ways of combining instruction with education.

I wish to record my indebtedness and thanks to Miss M. E. Jones and Mr J. R. Morrison for reading parts of the revised material and for discussions and suggestions in connexion therewith.

A.P.

CONTENTS

SECTION I.   INTRODUCTION

SECTION I
INTRODUCTION

CHAPTER I

WHAT IS SECONDARY EDUCATION?

ALL education is, primarily, a process through which the adults of one generation transmit to the next oncoming generation the knowledge, skills, attitudes, and opinions necessary to ensure the survival of a tribe, clan, social class, or nation. Naturally, the knowledge, skills, attitudes, and opinions will be those which appear most desirable in the conditions of a particular historical period. Schools are built, teachers trained, text-books written, opinions propagated, to conform with the interests of the dominant classes, ecclesiastical and secular.

However, institutions, once firmly established, tend very tenaciously to persist unchanged—educational institutions particularly. Some cynic has said, with reference to universities, that they are organized on the principle that in academic affairs nothing must ever be allowed to happen a first time. The late Professor Archer was perhaps somewhat nearer the truth when he said that English people are very reluctant to believe in the possibility of anything of which they have had no experience.

At the same time economic and social conditions undergo radical changes. School buildings, curricula, teaching methods, text-books, and educational opinions of one historical period get out of touch with the next. Then follows a verbal (and financial) conflict : the modern generation criticizes the existing conditions and demands reform ; the establishment resists. The conflict continues until some crisis forces a change. Even then, in most cases, the new dispensation is influenced to a marked extent by stereotyped traditional ideas and values. The human race persistently tries to pour its new wine into old bottles.

The post-1944 period in England and Wales is no exception. In 1944 a Bill was passed raising the school-leaving age to 15, with a promise of an additional rise to 16 at a later period, and making *secondary education compulsory for all pupils.*

9

This enactment created an entirely novel set of problems for educational administrators and teachers. Immediately three questions urgently required answers—namely, (*a*) what, in fact, is secondary education when *every* pupil of secondary-school age must be provided for according to the terms of the Act (different ages, abilities, and aptitudes) ? (*b*) What curricula and methods of teaching were indicated for the new dispensation (particularly if practical instruction and training appropriate to respective needs were to be incorporated) ? (*c*) In what type or types of school should the new secondary education be organized ?

Question (*c*) is likely to be solved, eventually, on social rather than educational principles. We are more closely concerned here with questions (*a*) and (*b*). Question (*b*) involves, among other considerations, the definition of ' liberal,' ' cultural,' and ' general,' which traditionally, have been deemed to be distinct from and altogether superior to ' technical ' or ' vocational ' education ; it involves also the place, if any, of technical, vocational subjects in a secondary education properly so-called.

Some of the topics in this chapter will be discussed again in more detail later in the book. The intention now is to present a conspectus of the problems in the new dispensation in the light of the historical development of education in this country, and to suggest some revisions of traditional attitudes with regard to the content and methods of secondary schooling which seem to be indicated if the new synthesis of secondary education is to be accomplished success-fully. In short, what should be our objectives in the post-1944 period ?

What is Secondary Education ?

Strange as it may seem, even in 1944 there was no generally accepted concept of secondary education. Interested parties, both professionals and laity, interpreted it in terms of traditional practices, particular vested interests, and stereotyped habits of thought. Just as the Schools Inquiry Commission had recommended in 1868 that Latin should be included even in the curriculum of their proposed third-grade schools with a leaving age of 14–15, so in 1944 many people assumed as a matter of course that the new compulsory secondary education for every pupil would be that currently practised in the secondary grammar schools, even though ' every pupil ' now meant every pupil down to the intellectual level of the just-not-certifiably-feeble-minded ! Looked at from this point of view, the assumption is patently absurd. Indeed, as we hope to show later, the existing grammar-school regime seems unsuitable for some of the pupils already in it, to say nothing of the large majority of pupils of secondary-school age who are not considered to be grammar-school type. If we are not to repeat the mistakes of past generations it is necessary to approach this problem of compulsory secondary education with due regard for post-1944 conditions. To do this we need to glance back over the history of schools and educational ideas in England and Wales.

In the first place, secondary education has been organized on a social-class basis. The authors of the Spens Report,[1] in a comment on the Schools Inquiry Commission (1864–68), say :

> The constructive recommendations of the Commissioners in respect of curriculum show clearly the influence of that class idea of education which held the field in England till the end of the nineteenth century. Education was envisaged in terms of social classes, one education for the less affluent class, another for the middle classes of society and a third for the upper classes. There was no machinery for passing from one grade to another though a boy of exceptional ability might succeed in doing so. The type of education which a boy received depended on the wealth and social position of his parents, the career marked out for him and the age at which he would like to embark on it.

Secondly, the curriculum of the grammar schools since their inception has been heavily biased in favour of the classical languages, mainly Latin.

There were several reasons for this. The first grammar schools were established by the Catholic Church in a period when Latin was the language not only of the Scriptures but also of affairs. It was a necessary qualification for university studies and the learned professions. More than that ; as A. F. Leach describes it,

> the diplomatist, the lawyer, the civil servant, the physician, the naturalist, the philosopher, wrote, read and to a large extent spoke and perhaps thought in Latin. Nor was Latin only the language of the higher professions. A merchant, or the bailiff of a manor wanted it for his accounts ; every town clerk or guild clerk wanted it for his minute book. Columbus had to study for his voyages in Latin, the general had to study tactics in it. The architect, the musician, everyone who was neither a mere soldier nor a mere

---

[1] *Secondary Education with Special Reference to Grammar Schools and Technical High Schools*, p. 32.

handicraftsman wanted, not a smattering of grammar but a living acquaintance with the tongue as a spoken as well as a written language.[1]

At that time Latin was an essential *vocational* qualification and Latin grammar the essential preparation for any but the labouring classes.

When conditions changed during and after the Tudor period Latin was no longer necessary except for candidates for the universities. The demand then was for the vernacular languages, mathematics, accountancy, astronomy, geography for use in the expanding foreign trade, in banking, in diplomacy and new types of warfare.[2] The new dominant classes of Renaissance Europe, nobility, bankers, and merchants, demanded new types of knowledge and skills.[3]

The grammar schools failed to respond to these new demands. Their teachers were not competent in the new subjects. Their deeds of endowment enacted that the business of the schools was teaching the grammar of the classical languages ; the endowed schools were prevented by law from doing anything else. As late as 1805 the governors of Leeds Grammar School were prevented by a ruling in the Court of Chancery from using school endowments for teaching modern subjects. Consequently, the endowed grammar schools declined. Their place was taken by private academies. Nevertheless, entrenched in the universities, perpetuated by school endowments, and required by the ecclesiastical authorities for training priests, the classics persisted. Moreover, Greek and Latin were the repositories not only of the Scriptures but also of physical science, medicine, Greek philosophy, Roman law, principles of political science, and ethics of the period. They were still indispensable sources of knowledge for scholars, priests, and statesmen. Again, while the vernacular languages were comparatively crude forms of expression, the classics were outstanding examples of clear exposition, literary style, logical argument, poetic expression, and dramatic art. They could be, and have been, defended on the grounds that they were by far the most valuable instruments for training the

---

[1] *English Schools at the Reformation*, p. 105.

[2] It is interesting, in view of post-1945 developments, that much of the scientific research of Leonardo da Vinci and Galileo was closely concerned with gunnery and the behaviour of ballistic missiles.

[3] See in this connexion : F. Watson, *The Beginnings of the Teaching of Modern Subjects in England* ; J. W. Adamson, *A Short History of Education*, particularly Chapter 8 ; A. Von Martin, *Sociology of the Renaissance*.

logical powers of the mind, inculcating high standards of literary expression and taste as well as setting out the principles of law and good government.

The classical literatures provided Western Europe with a concept of an ideal man—scholar, man of affairs, soldier if need be, patron of literature and the arts, with courtly manners, impeccable taste, able and willing to devote himself to the disinterested pursuit of truth and beauty and to *voluntary* participation in local and national government, with an alert, flexible mind able to apply itself successfully to any problem which happened to arise. This concept developed in the city states of Greece, in which a free-born aristocracy ruled the community while technology, trade, and menial labour were the exclusive lot of slaves.

The ideal education was that which appeared most likely to produce this ideal man. We get, thus, concepts assumed to be fundamentally important in estimating educational values and priorities—namely, those of a liberal, cultural, general as opposed to a technical and vocational training sufficient for the menial work of artisan and tradesman.[1]

When the classical languages ceased to have a direct vocational value they were justified as subjects of study by their supposedly liberal, cultural, and general values. Moreover, these values fitted, admirably, the economic and social structure of the eighteenth century, when this country was governed by a landowning aristocracy, a leisure class, the daily work being done by labourers and small tradesmen for a mere subsistence wage often in shocking conditions.

The subjects and their justifications persisted through the nineteenth century and later. The values in question became identified exclusively with the study of classical literature, while technical or vocational training was identified with menial, manual labour. The former type of education had a very high academic and social prestige ; the latter no prestige at all. It was regarded as educational slumming.

Meanwhile, throughout the nineteenth century industry,

---

[1] Detailed discussions of these concepts may be found in the Spens Report, Chapter I, " Historical Sketch " ; *General Education in a Free Society*, Report of the Harvard Committee (Harvard University Press, Cambridge, Massachusetts, 1946), Chapter II, " Theory of General Education " ; *Liberal Education in a Technical Age* (published for the National Institute of Adult Education by Max Parrish and Co., Ltd, London, 1955).

commerce, and methods of *national defence* were being revolutionized by the impact of the physical sciences. This scientific revolution has proceeded at an increasingly rapid pace through the twentieth century. Physical science now enters into every aspect of industry and commerce. Biological science is transforming medicine and public health. Technology—that is, applied science—is essential for industrial progress, national prosperity, and national defence. Whether we like it or not, we owe to science and technology our rising material standards of living and our security. Vast sums are spent on research not only in universities and technical colleges, but in the laboratories and workshops of the great industrial combines, and this up to university level.

Roles in industry and commerce have been inverted in importance and in public estimation. The skilled artisan, miner, technician, now may have better pay than the clerk, the minor civil servant, and the teacher. Industry and commerce are no longer necessarily menial occupations, and are carried on in many cases in vastly improved working conditions.

There have been corresponding changes in social mobility. Whereas it was extremely difficult a century or so ago for a youth no matter how intellectually gifted to rise from one social grade to another, nowadays such change is commonplace. This mobility has been accelerated by the impact of total war. Now that a whole nation, including women, may be conscripted into military service as civilian-soldiers, the feeling has grown that equality of sacrifice deserves equality of opportunity, in education as well as elsewhere.

These changes have been reflected in criticisms of the grammar schools and their curricula. Science was taught scarcely at all in the public schools—the accepted models for the grammar type of education—and even then only perfunctorily ; technology, not at all. When public pressure during the nineteenth century induced education authorities to organize the teaching of science and vocational subjects it was carried on in Higher Grade Schools, 'Central' Schools, Day Trade Schools, and Junior Technical Schools, *all offshoots of the elementary-school system having no connexion whatever with the recognized secondary education.*[1]

When in 1902 Local Education Authorities were given the responsibility for all State-supported schools an opportunity was presented to bring secondary education more into touch with modern conditions. Instead, the new county and municipal second-

[1] See the Hadow Report, Chapter 1.

ary schools were modelled on the ' public ' schools. It is true that ' modern ' subjects—for example, science, history, geography, modern languages—were introduced into the new grammar-school curricula, but they were taught by formal methods in preparation for a matriculation examination and university entrance. Pre-vocational studies were excluded altogether. In a comment on this the authors of the Spens Report said :

> The most salient defect in the new Regulations for Secondary Schools issued in 1904 is that they failed to take note of the com-paratively rich experience of secondary curricula of a practical and quasi-vocational type which had been evolved in the Higher Grade Schools, the Organized Science Schools and the Day Tech-nical Schools. *The new regulations were based wholly on the tradition of the Grammar Schools and the Public Schools. Furthermore, the concept of a general education which underlies these Regulations was divorced from the idea of technical or quasi-technical education though, in reality, much of the education described as ' liberal ' or ' general ' was itself vocational education for the ' liberal ' professions . . . an unreal and unnecessary division was introduced between secondary and technical education.*[1]

In summary, we may say that the terms ' liberal,' ' cultural,' ' general,' as distinct from ' technical ' and ' vocational,' education are no longer indicative of genuine educational values. This is not to say that they are meaningless. They represent ideas of funda-mental educational importance. But in their traditional inter-pretation they have become symbols of outworn academic and social status. They need re-interpretation if we are not to repeat in the modern synthesis of secondary education the errors of 1902.

Relevance—A Criterion of Educational Value

Instead of approaching the problem of secondary education in terms of liberal, cultural, general, technical, vocational, there is much to be said for adopting the hypothesis that *education must be relevant*—relevant, that is, to the essential needs and aspirations of the community as an economic and social organization ; relevant to the nature, needs, and aspirations of the individual learners.

In summary form, the needs and aspirations of the community can be stated thus :

(*a*) The need to survive ; a dead community has no needs or aspirations.

[1] Report, pp. 66–67. Italics in original.

    (b) Aspirations to improve standards of living.
    (c) Needs for social stability, efficient government, a moral code,
        and a common purpose.

From the point of view of the community the primary purpose of the schools and other educational institutions must always be the training of sufficient personnel with the necessary knowledge, skills, and attitudes to ensure the satisfaction of these economic needs and social aspirations. In other words, *the primary function of the schools is vocational.* In a vigorous community so soon as the dominant classes feel convinced that the schools are not fulfilling this primary function there is a demand for change. Sooner or later, if the community is sufficiently vigorous, the schools will have to conform. If they do not, then not only the schools but the community also will degenerate and die out. Ample evidence for this principle may be found in a study of history.

What has not been so clearly recognized is that educational institutions must satisfy also the nature, needs, and aspirations of the individual learners.

The learners' needs, impulses, and aspirations may be summarized as follows :

    (a) Care, guidance, security, *affection* during childhood.
    (b) Adequate opportunities for exercise and expression—physical, mental, emotional, social.
    (c) The impulses of curiosity with respect to natural things and events ; persistent tendencies to probe, explore, experiment, to learn what seems relevant to personal interests.
    (d) Even in childhood, but more intense in adolescence, the wish to *understand* the universe around them and their place in it.
    (e) Again, particularly in adolescence, the aspiration to grow up, to become adult, to achieve independence, which means, in practice, getting acquainted with the professions, industry, and commerce—the technical and vocational environment in which future careers must be found.
    (f) Need for a purpose in life ; some sufficient reason for living and striving for improvement, in the absence of which an individual ceases to strive.

In addition to the above, the human race, both children and adults, has revealed apparently irresistible impulses towards various forms of personal and communal expression—expressing ideas, for example, in words or concrete symbols ; decorating, elaborating, beautifying ; satisfying emotions in music and dancing ; and all this to a great extent undertaken as a form of play, for sheer pleasure and personal satisfaction rather than for utility or profit.

We shall try to show that the true meaning of a liberal, cultural, or general education must be sought within this context of the learners' needs, impulses, and aspirations. ' Liberal,' ' cultural,' ' general,' indicate qualities of mind and personality which can be cultivated or destroyed *by the way in which the subjects of the curriculum and activities of the school are organized rather than by the subjects or activities themselves, classical or otherwise.* It may be, therefore, that subjects and activities which are technical and vocational from the community point of view may at the same time be ' liberal,' ' cultural,' and ' general ' in their effect on the learner. The artificial distinction between secondary and technical education noted in the Spens Report may turn out in fact to be unreal and unnecessary and generally unfortunate for the learner and the community.

EDUCATIONAL ABILITIES

One insistent criticism of grammar schools' curricula and methods is that they are unsuitable for even a proportion of the supposedly grammar-school type already selected for grammar-school places, much less for the great majority of secondary-school age who have been excluded, but who must now receive a secondary education.

The grammar schools always have been and, in many cases, still are dominated by university-entrance requirements. Pupils are treated, both in subject-matter and in method, as if they were going on to an honours degree. In other words, say the critics, the majority are being sacrificed to the interests of a minority.

There is evidence for this complaint. In *Education in 1958,* the Report of the Ministry of Education, we find the following statistics :

During the school year ending July 31, 1958, out of 99,545 pupils who left maintained grammar schools in England and Wales, 12,856 were 15 years old or less (*i.e.*, 12·9 per cent.) ; 54,556 were 16 or under (54·8 per cent.) ; only 12,283 went to a university (12·3 per cent.) ; only 30,303 went to some institutions for full-time higher education, including universities—that is, rather less than one in three of the grammar-school leavers. The total population in maintained secondary grammar, technical, and modern schools in

1958 was 2,331,063. Of these only 608,034 were in grammar schools or grammar ' streams ' (26 per cent.).[1] This 26 per cent. had been selected by various means as the grammar type—most likely, that is, to succeed in grammar-school work. Yet, in a recent survey of a sample of grammar schools in England, the authors say :

> Our sample shows that in order to secure from the bottom third of the intake three pupils who will do very creditably in a grammar school it has been necessary to accept five who will do pretty badly.[2]

> And again : The academic results for the lowest third of the grammar school intake are so poor relatively—even in the most favoured social group one in three becomes something of an academic failure by the age of 16.[3]

At the same time there is evidence of a considerable reserve of relatively high-grade ability among the 74 per cent. of ' non-grammarians.'[4]

The range of subject-matter in grammar schools has indeed been widened by the introduction of modern languages, history, geography, mathematics, and science. In addition, there are domestic science, handicrafts, and art. There should be, therefore, something for everybody in this range of studies. The statistics indicate that there is not. The conclusion seems to be that grammar-school methods are too abstract ; the subject-matter, as it is presented, too remote from their interests and too difficult for the majority of learners, the practical subjects not taken seriously. In approaching the problem of secondary education for everybody, therefore, account must be taken of the nature of educational ability, and its distribution in the secondary-school population.

Grammar, Technical, and Modern ?

It seems to have been assumed as part of the nature of things that the three traditional divisions of schooling—namely, grammar, technical, and elementary—would persist in the new regime. The Act of 1944 stated merely that the secondary schools in each Local

---

[1] Report, Table 5, pp. 148–149, and 4, p. 144.
[2] *Early Leaving*, Report of the Central Advisory Council for Education, p. 14.
[3] *Ibid.*, p. 21.
[4] *15 to 18*. Report of the Central Advisory Council, Vol. II, pp. 116 and following. See also B. Simon (ed.), *New Trends in English Education*.

Authority area must be sufficient in number, character, and equipment to afford for all pupils opportunities for education·offering such variety of instruction and training as may be desirable in view of their different ages, abilities, and aptitudes—including practical instruction and training appropriate to their respective needs. There is no mention whatever of different types or grades of secondary schools. The question was prejudged, however, in the White Paper (1943), which stated, quite categorically, " such then will be the three types of secondary schools to be known as grammar, technical and modern schools."[1]

The pundits on the Norwood Committee were even more explicit. Not only did they assume that there would be three types of secondary schools ; they went on to divide the school population into three types of mentality and ability—grammar type, technical type, and the rest.[2]

These suggestions seem to be in reality a rehash of the social-class distinctions of the Schools Inquiry Commission noted above, rather than indications of sound psychological evidence. There has been a widespread belief that academic and practical-manual abilities were complementary, as if Nature had rewarded those unfortunate enough to be lacking in ' brains ' by giving them more than usually skilful ' hands.' Given the truth of this belief, the distinction between an academic and a technical type would seem to be a logical consequence.

Since the invention of the Binet tests of intelligence in France soon after 1900 numerous studies of abilities have been made by means of standardized tests. The evidence provided by these investigations contradicts the notion of complementary endowments or distinct mental types. It has been found, for example, that performances in a wide range of subject-matter, *including practical activities*, are positively related. *When the population as a whole is considered* those who excel in academic subjects tend to be above average in other types of activity, and they learn more quickly. Psychological investigations strongly support the view that there is a general ' factor ' or aptitude, whether we call it ' intelligence ' or general educational potential, which enters into all kinds of mental activity. Along with this general educational potential are several more restricted aptitudes—for example,

[1] *Educational Reconstruction*, para. 31, p. 10.
[2] *Curriculum and Examinations in Secondary Schools*, Chapter I : " What is Secondary Education ? "

linguistic, mathematical, mechanical, and practical, among others. The general factor ' g ' determines the level of difficulty at which the learner can work successfully ; the ' group factors ' help to determine in which direction the learner's major interests are likely to lie. The actual course of a pupil's career will be determined, in the main, by his endowment of the general and group factors *and the opportunities or restrictions provided by the local environment.* The position is summarized as follows by Professor P. E. Vernon. With regard to the existence of types, the theoretical or academic and practical abilities are not opposed. They are independent *only when the influence of the general factor is ignored.*

> Thus, in fact, the majority of children who are superior educationally are also above average in mechanical ability, in doing things with their hands, even, in physique, because of the common influence of ' g '. The Norwood Report's separation of academic and practical-technical types of children is unsound for several reasons but chiefly because the child with high ' g ' who is likely to do well at a grammar school would also do well at a technical school.[1]

There is, therefore, no psychological justification for separating academic from technical education.

This general factor of educability is associated with powers of logical argument and logical classification ; quickness to perceive relationships of a logical nature ; problem-solving ; the application of experience to novel situations, as opposed to rote memorizing ; ability to deal successfully with abstract theoretical studies. This general factor is distributed in the population as a continuous function like height. People vary in degree from a few very highly gifted individuals to a few very poorly gifted, but there is no break in between, just as people of the same race vary in height from very tall to very short. There are no gaps anywhere, as, for example, between 5 ft. 9 in. and 5 ft. 6 in. The great majority of the population cluster around the average. This means that most pupils possess some powers of logical reasoning and understanding relationships, but the lower down in the scale of general educational ability they are, the simpler must be the problems and the more concrete

---

[1] P. E. Vernon, *The Structure of Human Abilities*, p. 34. See also C. L. Burt, " The Education of the Young Adolescent : the Psychological Implications of the Norwood Report," in *British Jnl. Educational Psychol.* Vol. XIII (1943), pp. 126–140.

the studies and activities in which they can succeed. Thus the psychological evidence supports the contention that the relatively abstract theoretical studies of the grammar school and university are unsuitable for that proportion of the population insufficiently endowed with the general factor.

SECONDARY-SCHOOL CURRICULA AND METHODS

It is a matter of common observation that continued failure in any enterprise induces frustration followed by indifference or avoidance, and finally aversion. Failure in school studies is no exception to this rule. Failure blunts curiosity, damps down active learning, and leads to intellectual stagnation, rather than progress either liberal or cultural. At the same time, individuals are endowed with varying degrees of the group factors mentioned above. Their major interests will differ. At any given level of ability some will prefer linguistic studies, others mathematical, or mechanical, or practical, or artistic, or various combinations of these. It follows, therefore, that if the new secondary schools are to conform to the principle of relevance they must provide curricula *sufficiently graded in level of difficulty and sufficiently wide in range* to satisfy the nature, needs, and aspirations of the pupils concerned.

This principle is recognized and acted upon by some Education Authorities. In both their grammar and secondary modern schools alternative courses—alternative, that is, to the normal academic studies—have been organized—for example, engineering, agriculture, commerce. These alternative courses introduce pupils to some of the principles and skills involved in local industries.[1] This practice is by no means universal, however. The report on " Early Leaving " states that in the sample of grammar schools investigated one only of the boys' schools had a course with a vocational bias (in economics, for banking). In mixed schools the alternative courses were followed almost exclusively by girls. Thus, for nearly all boys at about the age of 16 the choice is between starting an advanced academic course and leaving school.[2]

It also follows that methods of teaching and organization must be adapted to the needs of individual pupils or small groups, as opposed to formal class teaching. The following actual examples

[1] See *The Secondary Modern School*, a report published by the Cheshire Education Committee ; Introduction, Chapter V, Chapter VII.

[2] *Early Leaving*, pp. 30–32.

illustrate the range of variation which may be found in a secondary modern school at age 11-plus :

SCHONELL VOCABULARY TEST

VOCABULARY AGE	NO. OF CASES	VOCABULARY AGE	NO. OF CASES
15	1	10	22
14	3	9	16
13	2	8	8
12 (normal)	5	7 or less	33
11	21		Total 111

SCHONELL READING COMPREHENSION TEST

READING AGE	NO. OF CASES	READING AGE	NO. OF CASES
15	0	10	20
14	0	9	25
13	2	8	21
12 (normal)	1	7 or less	30
11	12		Total 111

This represents a yearly intake of approximately the same chronological age, but ranging in vocabulary age from a 15-year-old level down to less than 7 years, and in reading comprehension from less than 7 years up to 13 years. In a multilateral or comprehensive school the range would have been even greater. It is obvious that such a situation cannot be dealt with successfully by mass methods of teaching.

The example also emphasizes the great importance of standardized tests of attainment in the new secondary schools for purposes of diagnosis and guidance.

In summary, our contention is that throughout their long history the main grammar-school objectives have been, primarily, technical and vocational rather than liberal and cultural, and that the distinction between liberal and vocational is unreal and unnecessary. This is not to say that the critics of the grammar schools despise this liberal, cultural education. Quite the contrary. What they do believe is that school exercises in Latin, French, English or Welsh, history, geography, chemistry, physics, biology, and the like, pursued to the Ordinary or even to the Advanced level of the General Certificate of Education only, and *taught within the prescribed syllabuses with a view to the questions likely to appear in the next examination paper*, have little or no *necessary* liberal or cultural value. As evidence they can point to a rather alarming number of students in our universities and training colleges, as well as to the products of grammar schools in further education courses, who have read little or nothing outside their prescribed texts, who show little interest in literature, and who cannot even write simple sentences grammatically, much less express clear ideas in straightforward prose. The claim that snippets of Latin, French, English literature, or history, taught as they are for examination purposes, have some magic powers of mental cultivation not possessed by activities such as handicrafts, rural science, or domestic science, for example, is contradicted by experience. It is founded on psychological notions of the mind which are demonstrably false, and on traditions quite out of touch with present-day realities. There are better grounds for the belief that the liberal and cultural values depend not so much on the subject-matter or activity itself as on the way in which it is presented to the pupils ; by the effect it has on their interests and aspirations, standards of taste and of morality ; by the extent to which they can appreciate its purpose and value in relation to the conditions in the community in which they live, and by the degree of intellectual and emotional satisfaction they find in its pursuit. It is possible to teach any of the so-called cultural subjects in such a way that the pupils rapidly acquire a profound distaste for them, a feeling of intolerable frustration and boredom and attitudes of surreptitious or open resistance. On the other hand, domestic science, home management, handicraft, and other pre-technical or pre-vocational activities which have been regarded as unworthy of serious study in the traditional grammar schools can be taught in such a way that the pupils' interest is aroused, their imagination stimulated, their capacity for planning strengthened, their standards of taste and intellectual honesty raised. In which case does the liberal or cultural virtue reside ?

The case has been expressed with admirable precision by the

authors of the Bryce Commission Report (1895). They said that the difference between technical and secondary education is not one of kind or character, but of emphasis.

> We are aware that there are some who would limit the term education to the discipline of faculty and the culture of character by means of the more humane and generous studies and who would deny the name to instruction in those practical arts and sciences by means of which a man becomes a craftsman or a breadwinner. But this is an impossible limitation as things now stand. We have just seen that the training in classics may have as little liberal culture in it as instruction in a practical art ; modern literature may be made a field for as narrow and technical a drill as the most formal science. Education becomes, inevitably, more and more practical, a means of forming men not simply to enjoy life but to accomplish something in the life they enjoy. . . . All education is development and discipline of faculty by the communication of knowledge, and whether the faculty be the eye and hand or the reason and imagination and whether the knowledge be of nature or art, of science or literature, if the knowledge be so communicated as to evoke and discipline faculty the process is rightly called education. . . .
>
> Secondary education may be described as a modification of this general idea. It is the education of the boy or girl not simply as a human being who needs instruction in the mere rudiments of know-ledge, but a process of intellectual training, and personal discipline conducted with special regard to the profession or trade to be followed. . . . *no definition of technical instruction is possible that does not bring it under the head of secondary education, nor can secondary education be so defined as absolutely to exclude from it the idea of technical instruction.*[1]

Topic and Project Methods

The term ' general ' education has been mentioned and needs some definition. It may mean the study of abstract theoretical subject-matter which deals primarily with principles of wide logical generality, such as physics, mathematics, or philology. On the other hand, it is often used to indicate studies of a *wide range* of subject-matter—for example, some combination of the mother tongue, history, geography, physics, chemistry, biology, mathematics, and a foreign language. It can be said in its favour that the abstract,

[1] *Report of the Royal Commission on Secondary Education*, pp. 135-136. Italics mine.

theoretical subject-matter represents a coherent body of knowledge the parts of which are logically related to each other and to a single comprehensive purpose. On the other hand, the separate subjects, taught as they are in most grammar schools by specialist teachers for examination purposes, can, and only too often do, exist in the minds of the pupils as separate, exclusive areas of information having no connexion with each other or with the world of affairs in which the learner lives. At the same time, there are practical as well as psychological reasons for desiring that what pupils learn shall represent an understandably coherent whole, rather than a collection of unrelated bits. But this introduces a difficulty. The abstract, theoretical general principles of mathematics or physical science are beyond the capacity of the majority of pupils to understand. Must these, then, be condemned to learn the collection of unrelated bits.

This problem has emphasized the desirability of the ' topic ' and ' project ' methods of organizing subject-matter, particularly for learners of average ability.

Thus, instead of learning bits of mathematics, science, history, geography, as separate subjects having separate periods on the time-table, a topic or project is undertaken which will require the acquisition of items from a range of subject-matter, but which must all be related to the topic or project in question. The terms ' topic ' and ' project ' are sometimes used more or less interchangeably. In other cases the ' project ' is a more practical undertaking, such, for example, as managing a school garden. A useful short description of these methods is given in *The New Secondary Education* :

> One of the most promising lines of solution in the modern school is indicated by what has been called the project method, that is, the relation of a whole body of work in several fields to a central core of interest such as the soil, the town, transport, tools . . . or any other large-scale and many-sided topic which can give a unity to a large variety of investigation and discoveries undertaken by the pupils . . . it must allow for variety of treatment so as to provide full play for various kinds as well as various degrees of ability and aptitude. If the topic can emerge from the children's own free occupations and interests so much the better. There should be historical and geographical possibilities ; there should be scope for ' technical investigation ' ; above all there must be aspects of the topic that are familiar to the children in their ordinary lives to provide the first-hand experience that will fire their curiosity and start the trail of research. . . . The pursuit and tabulating of inform-ation will inevitably involve a great deal of reading and writing of

a very varied kind. It will be surprising if mathematics does not crop up. The need for requisite advances in technical skill (whether in writing, calculating, manipulating, constructing, sketching or painting) will be appreciated and the necessary drudgery will be tackled with the vigour and determination that result from a recognition of the relevance.[1]

THE TEACHERS IN THE NEW SECONDARY SCHOOLS

The argument in this chapter, so far, has been a warning against the dangers of approaching the new situation in secondary education with traditional concepts of values, curricula, and methods in mind. New attitudes are necessary, particularly in the teachers concerned. There is a marked tendency among university graduates to regard anything other than sixth-form work in a grammar school as beneath their dignity. They tend to forget that the education of the remainder of the population of secondary-school age is a matter of urgent national importance.

Again, some teachers even when interested in and well disposed towards the new secondary education have misgivings : they are dubious about their ability to succeed in it. To a specialist teacher teaching a specialist subject at grammar-school level is comparatively straightfoı ward work. It consists of training the more intellectually able minority of pupils in knowledge and skills essentially the same as his own, in the form in which he has himself learned them in school and university. The subject-matter is the primary factor in the process.

On the other hand, the university-trained graduate teaching in the secondary modern schools needs to revolutionize his ideas about subject-matter. Now, the individual pupil, his interests, and abilities are the crux of the situation. The subject-matter must be modified to suit the pupil. Clear-cut subject divisions may no longer be appropriate. Moreover, the topic or project method may lead into regions of knowledge and practices quite unfamiliar to the university specialist. They will, in all probability, require the teacher to begin his own education all over again. As the authors of *The New Secondary Education* say, these methods will not appeal to every teacher. They are not easy to bring off successfully. They

---

[1] *The New Secondary Education*, Ministry of Education Pamphlet No. 9 (1947). The whole pamphlet deserves careful study. More details of topics and projects can be obtained from references in the bibliography.

demand a rather special measure of imagination and mental alertness. While he has to adopt the role of supervisor and counsellor
rather than instructor, the teacher must at the same time ensure
that the work is co-ordinated and purposeful, and that progress is,
in the long run, sufficiently systematic. At the same time, the new
requirements present an enterprising teacher with a challenge.

To a great extent, any teacher's success depends on the confidence he has in the methods used, and confidence comes only with
experience. One way out of this difficulty is to study other people's
records of the new methods and conditions.[1] An even better way is
to undertake for oneself some actual projects or topics and get the
feel of this method of learning and its peculiarities. This is a matter
for the training departments and training colleges to take up.

Another consideration more important in secondary education
now than formerly is the necessity to *understand* the individual
pupils. This is important in any kind of teaching, but particularly
important in the non-grammar sections. In the grammar sections
of the schools the pupils will come, for the most part, from the same
type of social environment as the teachers. Their objectives will be
the same ; their interests and their attitudes similar. This is
certainly not the case in secondary modern schools in lower-class
districts. These neighbourhoods represent a ' sub-culture ' of their
own, with objectives, attitudes, values, moral codes, quite different
in many cases from those of the teachers. Understanding the pupils
in many secondary modern schools means understanding their
home and neighbourhood backgrounds, and being prepared to deal
with these pupils without condescension. Tolerance and sympathy
as well as intellectual awareness are necessary.

To sum up. The new secondary education is the education—
spiritual, mental, moral, and physical, to quote the Act of 1944—of
all pupils of secondary school age—that is, 11 or 12 up to 15, 16, or
18 years. This period follows on and should be integrated with the
education in the primary period. In that period the pupils should
have learned the tools of learning—the elements of reading, writing,
and number—and have made acquaintance with their physical and
social environment—that is, the beginnings of the studies of history,
geography, and science.

The secondary period, in England and Wales from age 11-plus to
15, 16, or 18 years, represents a transition period in human development from childhood to adulthood. So far as subject-matter is

[1] See the bibliography.

concerned, it must include studies and activities corresponding in range and difficulty with the wide variations in natural endowment of the pupils. It must widen and deepen the pupils' knowledge of their environment. In the secondary modern schools particularly the methods of teaching must be such as will stimulate the curiosity and inspire the imagination of the pupils, raise their standards of conduct and taste, and, in the later years of school life, include at least some material of a pre-technical and pre-vocational character which will lead the pupils to a closer acquaintance with the affairs of industry and commerce in which they must seek their careers and to which their interest and aspirations turn increasingly as they approach school-leaving age.

BIBLIOGRAPHY

This bibliography is selected with particular reference to the secondary modern schools. They represent the most insistent problems in the post-1944 organization of secondary education. For an introductory survey the following books are recommended : Dent, *Change in English Education : A Historical Survey* ; Dent, *Growth in English Education*, 1946–52 ; Dent, *Secondary Education for All* ; Dent, *Secondary Modern Schools* ; Dempster, *Purpose in the Modern School* ; Loukes, *Secondary Modern* ; Ministry of Education Pamphlet No. 9, *The New Secondary Education* ; Glassey and Weekes, *The Educational Development of Children* ; Rowe, *The Education of the Average Child* ; Pedley, *Comprehensive Schools To-day*.

All the above are comparatively short books. Also recommended for a preliminary reading is A. D. C. Peterson, *A Hundred Years of Education* (Duckworth, 1952), a readable conspectus and shrewd commentary about the development of educational ideas, methods, and organization, with a direct bearing on some of the problems discussed in this chapter.

I. *General History of Education*

  CURTIS, S. J. : *History of Education in Great Britain* (University Tutorial Press, fourth edition, 1957).

II. *History of Secondary Education*

  WATSON, F. : *The Old Grammar Schools* (Cambridge University Press, 1916).

ARCHER, R. L.: *Secondary Education in the Nineteenth Century* (Cambridge University Press, 1921).

DENT, H. C.: *Secondary Education for All: Origins and Development in England* (Routledge and Kegan Paul, 1949). *Secondary Education*, The Spens Report (H.M.S.O., 1938).

III. *History of Elementary Education*

JONES, M. G.: *The Charity School Movement* (Cambridge University Press, 1938).

SMITH, F.: *A History of English Elementary Education, 1760–1902* (University of London Press, 1931).

Education of the Adolescent, The Hadow Report (H.M.S.O., 1926). See particularly Chapter I.

IV. *Educational Organization and Administration*

LESTER-SMITH, W. O.: *Education: An Introductory Survey* (Pelican Books, 1957). An outline for the general reader, with special reference to fundamental issues in education to-day.

ARMFELT, R. N.: *The Structure of English Education* (Cohen and West, 1955). A survey of post-1944 organization, with notes on historical development.

DENT, H. C.: *Growth in English Education, 1946–52* (Routledge and Kegan Paul, 1954). See particularly Chapter 3: " Experiment in Secondary Education."

NEWSOM, J. H.: *The Child at School* (Pelican Books, 1950). Chapter on secondary education, including reference to grammar and modern schools.

DENT, H. C.: *Change in English Education: A Historical Survey* (University of London Press, 1952). A short account of post-1944 problems considered against the background of English traditions from 1700. Motives for educational reform as well as against it.

V. *Secondary Modern Schools: General Principles*

DENT, H. C.: *Secondary Modern Schools: An Interim Report* (Routledge and Kegan Paul, 1958). Descriptions of work in some secondary modern schools. Discussion of problems of secondary modern schools.

DEMPSTER, J. J. B.: *Purpose in the Modern School* (Methuen, 1956).

LOUKES, H. : *Secondary Modern* (Harrap, 1956). Valuable discussion of fundamental principles. Strongly recommended in view of some prevailing prejudices about secondary modern schools.

Report : *The Secondary Modern School* (University of London Press, 1958). Report of a Committee set up by the Cheshire Education Committee. Notes on spiritual, moral, mental, emotional, physical development ; preparation for home-making and parenthood ; citizenship ; employment ; dull and backward children.

VI. *Secondary Modern Schools : Detailed Studies*

Ministry of Education Pamphlet No. 9 : *The New Secondary Education* (H.M.S.O., 1947). Notes on grammar, technical, and modern schools and on the Project Method.

GREENHOUGH, A., AND CROFTS, F. A. : *Theory and Practice in the New Secondary Schools* (University of London Press, 1949). Notes on testing ; activity groups ; experiments in methods (English, arithmetic, art, social studies). Detailed practical suggestions.

CHAPMAN, J. V. : *Your Secondary Modern Schools* (College of Preceptors, 1959). Notes on organization, curriculum, methods. Suggestions for text-books and readers.

DEMPSTER, J. J. B. : *Education in the Secondary Modern School* (Pilot Press, 1947). Short account of secondary modern problems, with suggestions for teaching methods.

KNEEBONE, R. M. T. : *I Work in a Secondary Modern School* (Routledge and Kegan Paul, 1957). Descriptions and suggestions about plans ; time-tables ; curriculum ; teaching methods ; clubs and societies.

ROWE, A. W. : *The Education of the Average Child* (Harrap, 1959). Valuable discussion of principles and methods. Details of a ' job-card ' method of organizing secondary modern school work (an adaptation of Project Method, Dalton Plan, and Parents' National Educational Union system for individual work).

VII. *Testing, Diagnosis, Problems of Slow and Retarded Learners*

DUNCAN, J. : *The Education of the Ordinary Child* (Nelson, 1942). Notes on testing for intelligence, attainments, and aptitudes.

GLASSEY, W., AND WEEKS, E. J. : *The Educational Development of Children* (University of London Press, 1950). Notes on elementary statistics ; intelligence tests ; attainment tests ; special aptitudes and interests ; qualities of disposition ; keeping school records. Bibliography of tests.

TANSLEY, A. E., AND GULLIFORD, R. : *The Education of Slow-learning Children* (Routledge and Kegan Paul, 1960). Appendix on diagnostic and attainment testing.

HIGHFIELD, M. E. : *The Education of Backward Children* (Harrap, second edition, 1951).

BURT, SIR CYRIL : *The Causes and Treatment of Backwardness* (University of London Press, second edition, 1953).

FERNALD, G. M. : *Remedial Techniques in Basic School Subjects* (McGraw-Hill, 1943).

KIRK, S. A., AND JOHNSON, G. O. : *Educating the Retarded Child* (Harrap, 1952).

SCHONELL, F. J. : *Backwardness in the Basic Subjects* (Oliver and Boyd, fourth edition, 1948).

————— *The Psychology and Teaching of Reading* (Oliver and Boyd, third edition, 1951).

————— *Diagnosis and Remedial Teaching in Arithmetic* (Oliver and Boyd, 1957).

————— *Diagnosis of Individual Difficulties in Arithmetic* (Oliver and Boyd, 1937).

————— *Diagnostic and Attainment Testing* (Oliver and Boyd, fourth edition, 1960). Includes a manual of tests.

————— *Essentials in Teaching and Testing Spelling* (Macmillan, 1932).

VIII. *Sociological Background*

JEPHCOTT, A. P. : *Girls Growing Up* (Faber and Faber, 1942). Case studies of adolescent girls.

REEVES, M. : *Growing Up in a Modern Society* (University of London Press, fourth edition, 1956). Problems of young people in a mass society.

BRAITHWAITE, E. R. : *To Sir, With Love* (Bodley Head, 1959). One teacher's experience in a tough secondary modern school. Emphasizes the need for knowledge of the school neighbourhood.

IX. *Comprehensive Schools*

PEDLEY, R., AND OTHERS : *Comprehensive Schools To-day* (Councils and Education Press, 1955). Contains articles both for and against.

SYMPOSIUM : *Inside the Comprehensive School* (Schoolmaster Publishing Company, 1958). Accounts of comprehensive schools. Illustrated. Contains an exhaustive bibliography of reports, books, pamphlets, and articles on these schools.

SIMON, B. (ED.) : *New Trends in English Education* (Mac-Gibbon and Kee, 1957). Articles on secondary modern and comprehensive schools. Suggestions for common syllabuses and methods of organization in English, history, science, mathematics, and languages.

CHAPTER II

LEARNING AND TEACHING

THE previous chapter dealt with problems created by the policy of secondary education for everybody irrespective of intellectual ability. This chapter will deal with learning, the learners, and teaching, and the relations between them. Some of the topics will be treated in more detail later. At the moment it seems desirable to get an over-all view of learning and teaching in the context of contemporary education. Our main concern will be the secondary-school period, although much of what follows is applicable to primary and further education.

I. LEARNING

1. WHAT IS LEARNING ?

Meanings of words carry over from one historical period to another, while the conditions to which they refer change radically. Consequently, it is difficult to think clearly about present-day affairs when the words we habitually use are loaded with meanings carried over from centuries ago. This is the case with learning and teaching. An attempt to clarify meanings, therefore, is a practical necessity for clear thinking, rather than mere pedantic verbal hair-splitting.

Learning is used either for a process or for the result of the process. In the *Concise Oxford Dictionary* we find the following definitions :

" learn (verb). Get knowledge of (subject) or skill in (art etc.) by study, experience, or being taught ; commit to memory (esp. *by heart* or *rote*) ; become aware , be informed, ascertain ; receive instruction.

" learning (noun). Esp. (possession of) knowledge got by study, esp. of language or literary or historical science ; studies, esp. of Greek, introduced into England in the 16th c.

" learned (adjective). Deeply read, erudite ; showing profound knowledge."

These definitions emphasize verbal knowledge got by instruction, study, and rote memory. They evoke a mental picture of the medieval scholar poring over his manuscripts, seldom, if ever, that of a scientist in a modern laboratory, or of an engineer superintending the building and maintenance of complicated machinery, or of a highly skilled craftsman.

To call these ' learned ' seems to many people quite incongruous. Yet they are learned in modern knowledge and affairs.

Unfortunately these ' stereotypes ' derived from the Middle Ages or earlier dominate much thinking and discussion about educational values and teaching methods, particularly in secondary education.

To the psychologist learning refers either to a *process* which produces progressive series of changes in behaviour and experience, or a *result*—the sum-total of all such changes in the learner.

Strictly speaking, we can observe only the results of learning in the form of changes in behaviour and experience. The underlying process is a matter of intelligent guesswork. That learning depends on the brain and nervous system is obvious. What happens, exactly, in the brain and nervous system during learning is as yet by no means well understood, nor do the experts agree about it.[1]

The course of learning in the psychological meaning of the term can be observed from the outside. The young baby can perform a few actions with some degree of precision soon after birth, such as sucking, swallowing, grasping an object laid in the palm of its hand. As time goes on the patterns of behaviour change. The growing child sits up without support, crawls, stands, walks. It shows signs of recognizing familiar objects and people. It begins to talk, to ask and answer questions, to make deliberate choices. It acquires more complex skills, enlarges its vocabulary, approximates to more adult forms of expression ; conforms (more or less) to the accents, manners, opinions and attitudes of its home, neighbourhood, and social class.

We can also describe learning in terms of mental awareness. Strictly speaking, each individual can enjoy (or suffer) only his own particular private experience. However, various modes of communication indicate that different learners in the same environment are aware of similar experiences. These experiences include *perceptions*—perceptions of objects ; of qualities such as colour, sound, weight, texture ; of relationships such as bigger–smaller, same–different, cause–effect ; of meanings. We experience *images* in the absence of the corresponding objects. We are aware of *feelings*—likes, dislikes, pleasure, anger, anxiety, frustration ; of *cravings, desires, intentions.* As time goes on we can realize changes in our

---

[1] See, for example, B. H. Bode, *Conflicting Psychologies of Learning* (Heath, Boston, 1929) ; E. R. Hilgard, *Theories of Learning* (Appleton-Century, N.Y., 1948).

mental life : experiences accumulate, become inter-related in increasingly complex patterns, tastes develop, judgments and opinions are modified, desires change, understanding improves.

In short, learning, the process, is revealed by progressive changes in behaviour and experience ; learning, the result, is the sum of these progressive changes.

2. SOME CONDITIONS OF LEARNING

(i) *Learning depends on Environment*

Negatively, absence of contact between learner and environment prevents learning. This happens in the case of children born deaf or blind. Positively, a particular environment determines what is learned. Children in different language areas acquire the local speech, accent, manners, and attitudes.

The richer the environment in physical and social stimulation, and the more varied the opportunities for educative activity, the more effective is the learning. Conversely, *deprivation has a very detrimental effect, particularly on attainment in language, and, in consequence, on the full development of intelligence and personality.*

Dr A. F. Watts reported that several thousand children who worked his Vocabulary Tests were divided into two groups representing poor and relatively well-to-do districts. At ten years of age the more well-to-do pupils had scored an average of 50 per cent. more marks than the others.[1]

Surveys in London, Northumberland, Scotland, and Wales have shown that school attainments are affected by the environment as estimated by the occupational status of fathers.[2]

It may be argued that inherited capacity is sufficient to account for these observations. There is evidence, however, that the effects of environment are greater than might be expected by reason of inherited capacity alone.

In an American survey the general development of a number of young babies in a foundling hospital was compared with that of samples

---

[1] A. F. Watts, *Language and Mental Development of Children*, p. 25.

[2] C. Burt, " Ability and Income," *British Jnl. Educ. Psych.*, Vol. XIII, pp. 82–98 ; J. H. Duff and G. H. Thomson, " The Social and Geographical Distribution of Intelligence in Northumberland," in *British Jnl. Educ. Psych.*, Vol. XIV, pp. 192–197 ; W. R. Jones, *Bilingualism and Intelligence* ; Scottish Council for Research in Education, *Social Implications of the 1947 Scottish Mental Survey*.

B

from a poor isolated fishing village, from professional families in a city, and from the nursery of a penal institution for young delinquent mothers. Average development quotients for the first four months after birth were : professional, 133 ; village, 107 ; penal nursery, 102 ; *foundling hospital*, 124. Corresponding quotients for the last four months of the first year were 131, 108, 105, *and* 72. The foundling-hospital babies showed serious retardation. The other babies were reared in environments offering social stimulation and opportunities for normal play. The hospital babies were reared in what amounted to solitary confinement (although the hygienic conditions were satisfactory).[1]

A survey of children in a Birmingham institution revealed that the proportion of dull children in the sample was higher, that of bright children lower, than among schoolchildren generally. Backwardness in language was larger than in reading attainment or intelligence. In reading *comprehension* it was at least twice as great as in the ordinary school population.[2]

In a survey of Aberdeen children commenced at the age of transfer to secondary schools and continued during their subsequent school career, it was found that among children *with equal educational capacity* as estimated by intelligence tests, those from better home conditions were more successful at school.[3]

Similar trends are recorded in the report on " Early Leaving,"[4] in the Crowther Report,[5] in investigations of canal-boat and gipsy children in England[6] and children in isolated rural communities in America. In tests of 3000 children attending mountain schools in Tennessee the average I.Q.'s decreased progressively from 103 at age six years to 81 at fifteen. Conversely, orphanage children who attended a well-equipped and staffed nursery-school for periods of six to eighteen months registered advances in I.Q., while comparable children who remained in the orphanage, deteriorated. Moreover, these studies have revealed that the progress or retardation increases the longer the children remain in the more, or less, favourable environments.[7]

Even size of family affects intelligence-test scores. In the Scottish

---

[1] R. A. Spitz, " Hospitalism," in *Psychoanalytic Study of the Child*, Vol. I, (1945), pp. 53–74. The meaning of development quotients will be explained later ; see p. 66.

[2] M. L. Kellmer-Pringle and V. Bossio, " A Study of Deprived Children," Part II : " Language Development and Reading Attainment," *Vita Humana* (Basle), Vol. I, No. 3/4 (1958).

[3] E. Fraser, *Home Environment and the School*.

[4] See Chapter VI : " Influence of the Home."

[5] *15 to 18*, Vol. II (Surveys), Chapter I.

[6] H. Gordon, *Mental and Scholastic Tests among Retarded Children*. Board of Education Pamphlet, No. 44 (1924).

[7] G. G. Thompson, *Child Psychology*, p. 418.

Mental Survey (1947) children from smaller families scored higher marks on the average than did those from bigger families.[1]

It may be argued that tests normally used for estimating intelligence are not suitable for deprived children. However, investigations have shown a similar trend in widely different localities. Moreover, not all children in rural districts are retarded. The *quality* of the environment, particularly the social and cultural quality, is a factor. Whether or not the environment affects the innate bases of intelligence is a moot point. What is certain is that children reared in conditions of deprivation score steadily less on various types of intelligence tests as they grow older. Most probably lack of stimulation, of educative exercises, of opportunity for social contacts, of encouragement, depresses their ability to express themselves, and thus to utilize efficiently whatever intellectual aptitudes they may have had originally. Moreover, the deadly monotony of their environments damps down their *eagerness* as well as their ability to learn.

This evidence has been noted at some length on account of its bearing on the interpretation of intelligence-test scores and intelligence quotients in the course of educational guidance, particularly in non-selective schools.

(ii) *Learning depends on Maturation*

As well as a favourable environment, organic development (maturation) is involved in learning. By maturation is meant the internally determined aspects of development.

For example, constant stimulation and encouragement will not teach a six-month-old baby to walk, talk, count, add two and two, or read. Yet these accomplishments will be ' picked up ' at a later phase of development by normally gifted children in a favourable environment without any special coaching *when a necessary degree of maturity has been reached.*

More important for schooling is the fact that premature training may improve performance, but only with considerable waste of time and effort.

Gesell and Thompson used two identical twin girls. At 46 weeks old one twin was trained on six days a week for six weeks in climbing stairs. After six weeks' training she could climb the stairs in 26 seconds. At 53 weeks of age the other twin climbed the stairs *at the first practice session, although she had had no training and no opportunity at all to*

---

[1] J. D. Nisbet, *Family Environment* ; Scottish Council for Educational Research, *Trend of Scottish Intelligence.* See Chapter VII : " Intelligence and Family Size."

practise. She took 45 seconds at her first attempt, but at age 55 weeks, after only two weeks of training, she climbed in 10 seconds. Thus at 55 weeks the second twin's performance was far superior to that of her sister, although the latter was trained seven weeks earlier and three times longer. The authors suggest that the maturity advantage of three weeks of age must account for the superior performance.[1]

Other experiments have yielded similar results in both children and animals.[2]

The influence of maturation can be studied with much greater precision in animals reared in controlled conditions. In a report by an American psychologist he states :

> Both observational and experimental findings indicate that visual responsiveness to detail appears rather suddenly between the eighth and tenth days of life in individual monkeys. Associated with this development there is a burst of exploratory-manipulatory activity to detailed stimuli, and we are convinced that these behaviour patterns are dependent on maturation rather than learning. Researches being conducted show that the eight-to-ten-day-old macaque monkey suddenly becomes able to solve a black-white discrimination problem, and the first of these which it then faces it solves rapidly. Other data indicate that the ability to discriminate between a triangle and a square matures a few days later.[3]

(iii) *Learning Readiness*

Apparently, training and practice are not equally effective at all times. In some cases an ability appears without previous training.

Before learning can proceed with maximum efficiency the learner must have reached a necessary degree of maturity. These degrees of maturity represent periods of ' readiness ' for learning when a minimum of training and practice will produce the greatest returns in achievement.

The bearing of these results on the most favourable time to begin *systematic* teaching of reading, writing, and arithmetic, for example, is obvious. Chronological age is not an accurate indicator of readiness ; children develop at different rates. A favourable environment offering opportunities for spontaneous learning will encourage the onset of

---

[1] A. Gesell and H. Thompson, " Learning and Maturation in Identical Twins," Chapter XIII in *Child Behaviour and Development.*

[2] See L. Carmichael (ed.), *Manual of Child Psychology*, pp. 380–390.

[3] H. F. Harlow, " Experimental Analysis of Behaviour," in *American Psychologist*, Vol. 12, No. 8 (August 1957), p. 488.

readiness ; deprivation will delay it. Certain indications of the onset of readiness are useful. The pupil shows a more lively and sustained spontaneous interest in the activity in question ; practice is undertaken, often voluntarily, with greater zest and concentration ; progress is more rapid.

Thus, learning as the psychologists see it is an organized system of progressive changes in behaviour and experience due to maturation of body, brain, and nervous system in intimate contact with a favourable physical and social environment.

3. MODES OF LEARNING

Five modes of learning are noteworthy for teaching purposes—namely, exploration and observation, imitation, suggestion, trial and error, and logical analysis.

In exploration and observation the learner is active. Prompted by sheer curiosity or some other need to be satisfied, the learner *seeks* new experiences by an expedition, or an experiment ; by reading ; by asking questions. Incidentally, we can seek mentally, for example, when we strive to recall some temporarily forgotten item of information.

Imitation is the act of making a copy. It can take place at different levels of awareness. Some imitation is unwitting. Accents of speech, mannerisms, prejudices, attitudes, are acquired, chameleon-like, from the local surroundings. The learner may be completely unaware of these habits until he goes into a different neighbourhood or social class. This tendency to unwitting imitation makes the ' tone ' of a school important.

Imitation may be reproducing a model arbitrarily imposed on the learner. This is a time-honoured method of teaching and learning which has persisted almost unchanged from pre-history till now. The teacher says, " Say this after me," or " You must do it this way," or " Copy this from the blackboard," or " Learn this declension." The learner's self-activity is at a minimum. In too many cases the words and movements copied have no intelligible meaning and no recognizable purpose. The learning may be done in passive indifference or intolerable boredom. This type of imitation, by itself, is not an efficient way either of teaching or of learning.

Learning is more effective when a model is copied deliberately because the learner wants to copy it, whether it be arithmetical tables, declensions, skill at football, or the dress and deportment of the latest film star. Whatever the objective, the learner is interested and active, and copies with intent to make a good reproduction.

Suggestion is a process by which a learner accepts statements and beliefs as true and adopts attitudes without any critical consideration, and in the absence of any logical justification. Modern advertising and political propaganda are good examples of teaching and learning through suggestion.

By trial and error and logical analysis we learn to overcome difficulties and solve problems. Trial and error may proceed at different intellectual levels. At a low level is the apparently random activity of an animal trying to get out of a cage. Neither the nature of the problem nor any method of solution is clearly perceived. At a higher level the learner has some notion of the result he wants, but knows no effective method of achieving it—for example, a non-mechanical amateur whose car refuses to go—a case of trying one possibility after another in the hope that something will happen, somehow, some time. Or the learner may know a number of possible procedures, but, baffled by an unfamiliar difficulty, he is uncertain which available procedure is appropriate to this particular case—a recently qualified professional man facing his first difficult problem.

Trial and error is a form of exploration. It takes place in scientific research when a new problem is met the nature of which is not yet clearly known. The process can be carried on mentally. In preliminary planning, for example, when the end to be achieved is clearly realized, possible arrangements are called to mind, their implications reviewed in relation to the objective and to prevailing conditions, inconsistencies or ' snags ' revealed, the suggested operation rejected, and the sequence repeated until an arrangement is envisaged which appears to be free of contradictions or impossibilities. This arrangement can then be put into practical operation, much waste of time and expense in useless effort having been avoided.[1]

Mathematical and scientific problems are often solved in this way by a process of logical analysis, really a refined form of mental trial and error.

Learning usually proceeds by means of some combination of these modes. Which will predominate in school will depend on the teacher, on the resources of the school, and on the educational aim. As we shall see later, active exploration of the environment is a necessary basis for further learning. It should take precedence over words and symbols ; otherwise the words and symbols have no meaning. As the learner gets older, verbal communication may be substituted for direct experience, particularly in the case of the intellectually able pupils. Too often, however, imitation and verbal

---

[1] Consider, for example, planning the conveyance of a large, very heavy, and awkwardly shaped piece of machinery from a factory in the Midlands to a site in the interior of Africa.

communication have been substituted for exploration and observation before an adequate range of direct experience has been aquired. In any case, with slow learning pupils exploration is likely to be more effective than exposition even in the secondary school. This is one justification for the 'Project' method of teaching and learning.

II. THE LEARNERS

1. PATTERNS OF DEVELOPMENT

(i) *Rates and Upper Limits of Development*

Rates and upper limits of development, physical and mental, vary widely in different individuals. Therefore some knowledge of these facts is necessary for teaching practice and educational guidance, particularly in non-selective schools.

(ii) *The Over-all Pattern of Development*

Sequences of development tend to be constant in individuals of the same species. While there are no abrupt changes in a normal course of development, a succession of phases showing characteristic features is recognizable—for example, infancy, early childhood, later childhood, puberty, and adolescence. These phases correspond roughly with the pre-school, nursery and infant school, junior school, and secondary school period.

Certain subsidiary aspects can be distinguished within the over-all development pattern—skeletal, neural, lymphoid, genital, and mental, each with its own characteristic 'time-table':

Skeletal aspect—bones, chest-cavity, muscles—development is rapid during the first year, followed by a relatively steady advance till puberty. Then the rate is accelerated, to be followed again by a steady advance till full maturity is reached.

Neural aspect—brain, spinal cord, nerves—development is very rapid during the later fœtal period, infancy, and early childhood. At age two the normal child's brain has reached 60 per cent. of its adult size ; by age seven it is very near the adult limit.

Lymphoid aspect—lymphatic glands, tonsils, thymus gland— development is rapid during childhood, slower up to puberty, followed by a relative decrease.

Genital aspect—the genital organs develop slowly in infancy, are almost stationary from about two to about ten years, then mature rapidly during puberty and early adolescence.

MENTAL DEVELOPMENT

The facts about mental development are important because beliefs about it have influenced educational practice very markedly.

One set of beliefs was derived from the assumption that mental development was analogous to stratification. ' Faculties ' supposed to be non-existent up to a certain age suddenly emerged. Each faculty was, as it were, laid down, then consolidated, to be followed in due course by another, ' higher ' faculty, to be consolidated in its turn. Thus, during the first year the primitive senses appear, due, it was supposed, to a faculty of perception. This phase is followed by one in which muscular activity is predominant. Next in order appears a faculty of mechanical memory, to be followed during the adolescent period by the emergence of the faculties of imagination and logical reasoning.

If these beliefs were true, then it would be good practice to organize school work around motor activity in the infant school, mechanical imitation and memorizing in the primary school, leaving exercises in imagining and logical reasoning to the secondary stages. This educational organization was, in fact, typical of much traditional practice.

Other assumptions were that each individual recapitulates in a rapid and abbreviated form the evolution of the human race—an analogy derived from the doctrine of organic evolution. Or, alternatively, a child's mental development recapitulates the phases or ' culture epochs ' in the development of civilization from primitive to modern times. This ' culture-epoch ' hypothesis was used by the followers of Herbart as a guide to the sequence in which topics could be introduced profitably for teaching purposes.

None of these views is borne out by more recent, experimental studies of the actual mental development of children. The belief in faculties appears to be mistaken.[1] The beliefs in recapitulation and culture epochs are based on dubious analogies too vague to be reliable guides even if they were true.

Children's responses to progressive series of tests—the Binet–Simon or Terman–Merrill series, for example—indicate that all the main aspects of intellectual activity—perception, recognition, imagery, memory, apprehension of relationships, reasoning—appear in their simpler forms quite early and develop at a fairly constant rate until adolescence. The development is not of separate faculties, but of a fund of experiences and the capacity to deal with progressively more complex situations and more subtle relationships.

It would seem, therefore, that instead of the junior-school period being devoted almost exclusively to imitation, repetition, and

[1] See Chapter IX.

memorizing, as was the case only too often in the past, it should include activities calculated to encourage all the mental powers, *but suited to the junior pupils' levels of maturity and intellectual capacity.* The same principle is indicated in the cases of slow learners in secondary modern schools.

Another feature of mental development indicated by more recent studies is the relative influence of the general educational capacity (the ' g ' factor) compared with that of the group factors. Differences in mental capacity in the primary-school period seem to be due mainly to the influence of the ' g ' factor. During the second half of the secondary-school period interests begin to specialize into preferences for linguistic, numerical, mechanical, scientific, practical-manual, artistic, musical studies. It is becoming increasingly evident that secondary schools need to provide a wider variety of courses than those offered by the traditional grammar school, and to allow the older pupils some freedom to follow their preferred subjects. Reports from comprehensive and secondary modern schools where this has been arranged tell of work being done at a higher standard with greater enthusiasm, and of mprovement in the attitudes of some hitherto difficult pupils towards schooling as a whole.

(iii) *Development during the Secondary-school Period, Puberty and Adolescence*

Changes during the secondary-school period can be studied conveniently under three aspects : physical and organic ; intellectual ; emotional.

Puberty, the achievement of sexual maturity, happens at about age twelve in girls and fourteen in boys, though there are considerable variations in the age of onset even in normally healthy individuals. More recently, observers here and in America have reported a general tendency towards earlier sexual maturity.

At or near puberty there is a period of accelerated skeletal growth, followed in later adolescence by increase in muscular development and sheer physical strength. This accelerated growth, particularly in the long bones, may cause some temporary clumsiness in rapidly growing pupils. Later, however, muscular control increases, making possible high standards of precision and technical achievement.

It has been suggested that there is a tendency for children who mature late physiologically to be somewhat retarded in school attainment. An American observer remarks that " late starters," " slow maturers," or " late bloomers " tend to appear with greater frequency from families showing delay in maturing. He adds that teachers will do well to be patient and avoid making premature decisions about the future achievements of such children. In more than purely chance numbers some of them will cause surprise by their later and mature accomplishments.[1]

In this country reports from secondary modern schools have recorded cases of pupils who, after failing the 11+ examinations, have gone on, *given the opportunity*, to pass the Ordinary and Advanced level G.C.E. examinations, and in some cases, to achieve honours in university degrees.[2] It is possible, of course, that some pupils have been bored by primary-school methods and have found a new interest and zest for learning in the more flexible organization of good secondary modern schools. Whatever the ultimate explanation, there is no doubt about the emergence of these late developers—a matter of importance in educational guidance.

The main characteristics of *intellectual* development in the adolescent period seem to be :

(a) While experience and wisdom may grow until comparatively late in life, sheer intellectual capacity seems to reach its peak in later adolescence.

(b) The capacity to think in words and symbols improves, together with ability to deal with situations involving greater complexity of relations, particularly in pupils of more than average intelligence. This goes with greater ability to understand abstract general principles and to tolerate more formal instruction.

(c) Critical acumen increases.

(d) As we have already noted, the group factors in intellectual aptitude become more prominent.

As to the *emotional* aspect, feelings are intensified ; interest in matters of sex, particularly the opposite sex, increases. The adolescent is more preoccupied with the self—physical attractiveness ; sexual competence ; effect of the self on other people ; opinions of other people, particularly ' teenagers,' about the self. The adolescent wants to be accepted by a congenial group. He/she tends to resent criticism from adults, particularly if it is sarcastic.

---

[1] W. C. Olson, *Psychological Foundations of the Curriculum*, U.N.E.S.C.O. Publication No. 26 (Paris, 1957). See pp. 12 and 28.
[2] See B. Simon (ed.), *New Trends in English Education*.

This is wounding and painful to the expanding ego, which is striving desperately for adult status and independence.

Many adolescents, normally attractive and well-grown physically, reared in congenial home circumstances, trained in social *savoir-faire*, and tolerated by parents, pass through this period without much difficulty. A minority, less fortunate, may suffer intense emotional conflicts.

The period, generally, is apt to be one of uncertainty and anxiety. The changes in puberty may be profoundly disturbing to young people who have had no psychological preparations for them. Any suspicion of physical imperfection or abnormality, or social *gaucherie*, may be extremely painful, causing feelings of inferiority. These may lead to over-compensation in the form of rudeness; impudence; aggressiveness; loud, silly, apparently aimless horseplay, occasionally destructive. On the other hand, some adolescents retreat within themselves, become sullen, morose, subject to phases of depression, violently critical of their surroundings, permanently dissatisfied, unwilling to attempt any social contacts for fear of being rejected.

Adolescence is a period of transition. Within it the youth aspires to adult status and independence without normal opportunity for satisfactory hetero-sexual relations, and without the experience necessary for successful adjustment. The period calls for tolerance, tact, and sympathetic guidance on the part of parents and teachers. Uncertainty is intensified by the absence too often characteristic of contemporary urban conditions of a generally accepted moral code and system of ethical values. Secondary schools must accept some responsibility for guidance. The case has been well stated in the Crowther Report :

> If the schools have been doing their job properly, boys and girls will have grown up in a society which has, without fuss or preaching, taught them to respect and practise a way of living certainly higher than much of that with which they are familiar through the world of entertainment ; and, unfortunately in many instances also, better than a good deal of what they meet in the streets and even at home. . . . If the schools are to do their duty of moral education efficiently—and one strong strand in the tradition of English education even sees this as their main duty—they must come into the open with a full and frank treatment of ethical problems. . . . Adolescence is a period of uncertainty, unwelcome uncertainty about life as a whole and about man's place in the universe, about what is real and true, what is the purpose of it all, and

what matters. . . . The adolescent needs help to see where he stands but it must be given with discretion and restraint. He does not want to be ' told.' He wants a guide who will be honest in not over-stating a case. There is no period of life when people more need what the Education Act means when it refers, perhaps rather unhappily, to ' religious instruction,' and no period when it is more difficult to give. What is true of ethics is also true of politics. The fact that politics are controversial—that honest men disagree—makes preparation for citizenship a difficult matter for schools. But it ought to be tackled and not least for the ordinary boys and girls who now leave school at fifteen and often do not find it easy to see any argument except in personal terms.[1]

2. ADOLESCENT INTERESTS

The adolescent period is one of intensified and diversified interests.

In a study of 196 boys and girls, of average intelligence, aged 14 to 17 years, Dr W. D. Wall records the following reported increases in interests :[2]

	Boys	Girls
	%	%
Personal appearance :		
dress, hair, face, figure, deportment, etc. . .	66	86
Impression made on others by :		
personal appearance	50	60
manner of speaking	40	54
things you can do	41	54
manners and behaviour	55	61
Going on expeditions away from parents . .	56	56
Sport, athletics, physical training . . .	72	56
Opposite sex	70	73
Social activities	59	79
Future careers	60	63
Books and reading	51	69
Music	33	72

[1] *15 to 18*, Vol. I (Report), p. 114. See also in this connexion W. D. Wall, *The Adolescent Child* (Methuen), pp. 113–119. Quotations by kind permission.
[2] *The Adolescent Child*, p. 102.

The differences between sexes are worth noting.

Sex differences in educational preferences appear in another of Dr Wall's surveys. A group of 135 adolescent industrial workers aged 14–16 reported the following:[1]

SUBJECT	LIKED		DISLIKED	
	Boys	Girls	Boys	Girls
	%	%	%	%
Cookery	0	77	100	10
Needlework, dressmaking . .	0	63	100	21
Dancing	22	90	73	7
Dramatics	0	24	93	43
Music (general)	11	67	76	16
Shorthand	4	65	91	26
Typewriting	6	68	89	22
Handicrafts (various) . . .	62	35	29	48
Workshop drawing . . .	46	0	31	92
Use of workshop tools . .	63	1	20	93
Study of machinery . . .	58	1	27	93
Workshop calculations . .	57	0	22	94
Arithmetic	51	11	31	68
Elocution	11	34	76	49

The preferences may be due in some degree to innate factors associated with sex. It is most probable that, in addition, they are determined by traditional expectations of what a boy or a girl *ought* to be interested in doing. These young people were all products of elementary schools. Dr Wall points out that in this group no subject was liked " very much " or " quite well " by two-thirds of the boys, and only four (cookery, dancing, music, and typewriting) by two-thirds of the girls. Twenty-eight activities in all were surveyed, and the figures which showed the proportions who registered some dislike of all the items are a shrewd index of the failure of education to make appeal to such youth.

The table brings out strikingly *the practical and non-verbal nature of the preferences of both girls and boys of this particular intellectual and educational background.* In the boys' list there is no subject into which verbal mastery enters to any great extent. . . . In the girls' list, though in view of the known verbal superiority of girls one might have expected differently, *there is a similar predominance of practical non-verbal activities.* The only subjects which could be said to have a marked verbal bias are two of a vocational nature—typing and shorthand—in which manual and perceptual skills are paramount ; and dramatics, which relies for its appeal (mainly) on impulses of display and identification with adult characters. . . . The entire absence from the boys' list and the scanty representation in the girls' of any subject of aesthetic appeal is striking, and there is in neither any indication that social or political awareness has been aroused at school.[1]

In surveys by Professor Valentine and Professor Olive Wheeler groups of university students and young adult workers recorded intensified interests in nature, music, art, poetry, religion, games, and reading.[2]

These results are suggestive for the provision of a variety of alternative courses, particularly in secondary modern schools, in which the pressure of examination requirements is less intense.

In a study of some 8300 replies to a questionnaire by secondary-school pupils aged 11+ to 16+ years R. A. Pritchard noted six prominent interests reported by the group : a craving for self-activity as opposed to lessons in which a teacher talks all the time ;[3] a feeling of satisfaction in proving things ; pleasure in discussion and argument ; need for variety ; desire that school work shall be relevant to everyday life ; a tendency to look for human interest wherever possible.[4]

Pritchard's survey has an obvious bearing on teaching methods and modes of learning.

An informative study of adolescent needs and interests arose out

[1] Italics mine.
[2] C. W. Valentine, " Adolescence and Some Problems of Youth Training," in *Brit. Jnl. Educ. Psych.*, Vol. XIII, Part II (1943) ; O. A. Wheeler, " Variations in the Emotional Development of Normal Adolescents," in *Brit. Jnl. Educ. Psych.*, Vol. I, Part I (1931).
[3] A case of exploration rather than exposition !
[4] R. A. Pritchard, " Relative Popularity of Secondary School Subjects at Various Ages," in *Brit. Jnl., Educ. Psych.*, Vol. V (1935), pp. 157 and 229. My own experience when teaching chemistry accords with the sixth item in this list. Pupils showed a lively interest in biographical details of people who had made notable chemical discoveries. If I omitted to mention such details the pupils asked for them.

of a convention arranged by the American Progressive Education Association in 1930. The objective was the improvement of American secondary education. Many suggestions were put forward and approved, but against almost every one it was urged that the reform could not be carried out without jeopardizing the students' chances of gaining admission to college. This the schools were not prepared to do.

The difficulty was overcome by an agreement with college authorities that they would accept students from thirty selected secondary schools on the results of the students' school records and the schools' recommendations.

The Association then appointed expert committees to review curricula and teaching methods from the point of view of adolescent interests and needs rather than that of college regulations.[1]

Of immediate interest in this report for our purpose is a list of the major interests and concerns of American adolescents. It includes the following :

Establishing personal relationships with own sex, other sex ; desire for congenial companionships and for popularity and how to achieve them ; concern about social behaviour (particularly in relation to the opposite sex) ; confusion arising from conflicting standards in society ; anxiety about achieving successful marriage.

Establishing independence—leaving home, independent income, freedom of choice.

Understanding human behaviour, particularly in connexion with difficulties in personal relationships.

Establishing self in society—desire to be accepted at adult level, to feel important, to excel in some skill.

Concern about normality in physical growth, appearance, sexual functions, mental ability.

Anxiety with respect to overpowering impulses and uncontrollable emotions and guilty feelings about them.

Understanding the universe : marked increase in sensitivity to beauty ; interest in natural laws ; urge to create (*e.g.*, in writing or art) ; desire for security in a universe very imperfectly understood ; desire to establish a philosophy of life.

---

[1] The experiment is described in detail in five volumes entitled *Adventure in American Education* : I. " The Story of the Eight-year Study " ; II. " Exploring the Curriculum " ; III. " Appraising and Recording Student Progress " ; IV. " Did they succeed in College " ; V. " Thirty Schools tell their Story " (Progressive Education Association Publications, Harper and Bros., New York and London). The whole work deserves careful study, particularly Volumes II and III.

III. Teaching in relation to Learning. Teaching Processes and Teaching Methods

Traditionally, the learner has been regarded and treated as a passive receiver of instruction. Teaching has been conceived as a process of making impressions on passive pupils, " hammering in the facts." When asked why they wanted to teach, applicants for acceptance into a training department have said, quite frequently, that they felt under some obligation to pass on to the pupils the knowledge they themselves had acquired. In this identification of teaching and education with erudition they were following a long tradition, and were prompted, probably, by their own training in school and college.

This attitude is held in less esteem now than formerly. Given favourable opportunities, the normal healthy child is active and alert during most of his working day ; eager to explore, experiment, ask questions, demand information, acquire skills which promise to realize his purposes. He can, and does, learn much by his own activities out of school without any formal instruction. Even in school only the child himself can learn. Nobody else can learn for him.

What, then, is the function of teaching if not to hand on information ? It is, in a more general context, to facilitate the processes of learning.

Here we may profitably turn back to the dictionary. It defines a ' process ' as a course of action, a method of operation. ' Method ' is defined as a special form of procedure. With these definitions in mind we propose to distinguish between teaching processes and teaching methods.

TEACHING PROCESSES

Learning can be facilitated by means of some quite well-known and commonly used processes :

(i) The provision and arrangement of selected experiences of educative value : *directly*—e.g., by taking pupils to places of interest ; collecting and displaying specimens, models, pictures, apparatus ; *indirectly*, at second hand, as it were, through the medium of oral communication or books (which pupils should be trained to use).

(ii) Guidance. Inexperienced, untutored learners are apt to follow blind alleys in the search for experience and information, thus wasting time and energy to little advantage and getting anxious or frustrated as a result. They ' pick up ' inefficient work habits which hinder future performance. They tend to be satisfied, in the absence of good standards, with levels of performance below their real capacities. Guidance can be given by demonstrating correct methods of work ; by suggestion, advice, recommendations ; by questions and discussion which serve to encourage active thinking and analysis, directing attention to significant aspects of experience ; by setting good standards of performance, and of behaviour.

(iii) Motivation—encouraging zeal and strengthening the will to work. For this we can relate work to pupils' interests and needs (relevance to everyday life) ; adapt tasks to pupils' rates of development, degrees of maturity, and present attainment, thus increasing the probability of success and building up confidence ; help when help seems necessary ; appeal to self-respect, exhort, and, on occasion, bring some judicious pressure to bear on too indolent or careless pupils. Some degree of anxiety is quite a useful spur to effort.

Incidentally, there is a difference between guidance and direction. As the words are used here, in guidance, suggestion and advice are *offered* when they seem needed. The pupil can accept or not. In direction the teacher instructs, commands, insists on being obeyed exactly, in detail. The pupil obeys whether he likes it or not. Some direction may from time to time be necessary, but as a process in constant use it has unfortunate results. The strong-willed, independent, intelligent pupils rebel. The weaker ones lapse into indifference or submission, being unwilling or afraid to take any intellectual initiative. In both cases learning is impeded—unless it be learning to evade instructions or to indulge in sabotage.

(iv) Testing and correcting. Internal tests (as distinct from external examination) are essential in teaching. They reveal errors and weaknesses needing extra attention to both teachers and pupils. Given at regular intervals, they provide a measure of progress. Tests within the pupils' competence which can be attacked with a reasonable chance of success act as a challenge and an incentive.

In short, teaching is best regarded as a complex process of co-operation and inter-communication between teacher and learners, not as a one-way traffic in information from teacher to learner.

TEACHING METHODS

The teacher acts as an intermediary between the curriculum, which is what some authority or other decides is necessary for the schools to teach, and the pupils. The curriculum is arranged for teaching purposes in sequences and units deemed to be appropriate to the pupils' degrees of development and to the educational aim to be attained. This selection and arrangement of elements of the curriculum and the various ways in which they are introduced to the pupils, is the more specialized meaning of teaching method.

A teaching method may be a form of play (a classroom shop, for example, as an aid to learning simple arithmetic) ; memorizing and subsequent recitation by the pupils ; exposition (' chalk and talk ') by the teacher ; an object lesson ; a lecture-demonstration ; practical work in laboratory, workshop, or school garden. It may be working through a project. Subject-matter may be arranged inductively, going from particular cases to general principles, or deductively, going from general principles to particular cases, or by combining the two. Reading may be taught by a phonetic method or by ' look and say,' or a mixture of the two ; language by grammar-book exercises or by the ' Direct Method.' Children may be set to learn by manipulating self-corrective didactic apparatus, as in the Montessori method. Nowadays schools can use the devices of broadcasting, cinema films, and television. Again, instead of the teacher giving oral lessons to a class, the syllabus can be subdivided into convenient units each of which is set out on cards together with some directions for guidance. These ' assignments ' are then made available, and books and material provided for individual pupils to work through at their own pace, as in the Dalton Plan and the ' job-card ' method. Teaching can be carried on by correspondence, as in the Parents National Educational Union system or the correspondence-college organizations.

In all these instances the teacher selects subject-matter with or without suggestions from the pupils, makes experiences possible, acts as guide, encourages zeal, maintains standards, tests progress. The specific methods determine the emphasis which shall be given to particular teaching processes and modes of learning. In the Dalton and job-card methods the teacher relies less on exposition and becomes to a much greater degree a guide. The methods also determine the amounts and, by implication, the relative importance of pupil activity as distinct from that of the teacher.

IV. The Practical Teaching Situation. Some Conditions and Limitations

Hitherto we have dealt with learning processes, with the learner, and with teaching processes without reference to the conditions of everyday teaching practice. It is necessary now to take the practical teaching situation into account.

The history of teaching methods is a record of attempts of pioneer educators—clerics, doctors, philosophers, aristocrats, much more frequently than professional teachers—to reform traditional teaching practices. From time to time a new method (often an old method rediscovered and refurbished) is introduced, becomes a fashion, is accepted with uncritical enthusiasm as the one universally most efficient way to facilitate learning. Some of the propaganda for and against these methods has been based on philosophical and theological principles, unverified assumptions, and dubious analogies. It is not surprising, therefore, that attempts have been made more recently to test the value of different methods by controlled experiment.

What has emerged from much of the experimental work is that a given teaching method is not equally effective in all conditions. In fact, the efficiency of a method may depend on who uses it, who learns by it, what is taught, in what particular conditions, and for what purpose. It is as important to know the conditions as the method in pronouncing judgment on the effectiveness or otherwise of any proposed teaching method.

Teachers, even very good teachers, have not complete freedom of action. In practice, teaching is necessarily a compromise between an ideal and certain limitations of time, place, and human nature in the shape of pupils, teachers, parents, and society generally. A glance at some of the more important of these limitations is desirable.

(i) *The Learners*

Mention has already been made of the effects on scholastic attainment of home circumstances, housing conditions, neighbourhood standards, previous schooling, levels of maturity, rates of development, educational capacity. All these need to be taken into account most particularly in a non-selective school. Chronological age is not a good guide for educational organization and teaching practice.

Moreover, even if pupils are classified and treated on the basis of mental age they will still vary in relative *rates* of physical and mental development, in temperament, and in predominant imagery—visual, auditory, kinaesthetic—as well as in special talents and preferred subjects. Different pupils do not all learn and think in the same way, *nor do they all learn and think necessarily in the same way as the teacher*. Some degree of allowance must be made for these differences. It is not good practice to take for granted that all pupils remember by visual images, or that they will all use exactly the same thinking process in arriving at the answer to an arithmetical problem.

Professor Humphrey, after summarizing a number of experimental investigations into the processes of abstracting and generalizing, remarks that they practically all record individual differences in the people taking part in the experiments. There is no such thing as a determinate type of observer. There is, even, variation from day to day in the predominant methods used. He goes on to say that no method of abstracting or generalizing has been demonstrated which is constant in rate, or general psychological procedure, or imagery employed. There is a suspicion that this variation obtains not only from person to person, but even in the same person on different occasions and using the same material. Nowhere is the difference between psychology and logic better illustrated. Logic shows the rules by which thinking ought to proceed. Psychology shows different individuals working according to these constant formal rules in a bewildering multiplicity of ways.[1]

This is, most probably, one reason why experimental investigations into the relative efficiency of different methods of learning and teaching have produced apparently conflicting results.

Chronological age, and the status that goes with it, is a limiting factor in teaching method. It has been found, for example, that secondary-modern-school pupils with the physical stature of a twelve-year-old and a mental age of nine or less may not take kindly to infant-school methods of treatment.

One of the most difficult problems at the present time is to provide for wide individual differences within a practicable school organization. ' Streaming ' according to mental age or scholastic attainment, organization of ' sets ' within forms, sixth-monthly instead of yearly promotions, individual methods, have all been tried without being universally successful.

(ii) *Economic Conditions*

Economic conditions affect teaching practice very markedly. The money the community is prepared to provide will limit school buildings, furniture, books, pictures, apparatus, laboratories, and workshops, as well as the supply of teachers. If schools are built to accommodate the greatest number of pupils in the smallest possible space with the least expense, then classes will be large, classrooms overcrowded and, maybe, badly heated, lighted, and ventilated ; materials will be scarce. In these circumstances activity methods,

[1] G. Humphrey, *Thinking: An Introduction to its Experimental Psychology*, p. 304.

individual methods, project methods, however effective they may be in good school conditions, are almost impossible. Teachers are forced to rely mainly on imitation, repetition, recitation, and ' chalk and talk.' Even the chalk part is difficult with about a square yard of blackboard and a class of forty or more children.[1] It does not follow that a competent teacher cannot teach to some purpose a class of forty to fifty children if the classroom is big enough and there is an ample supply of books, apparatus, writing materials, and room to move about. What is clear is that in the absence of books, materials, and space the teacher is forced into verbal communication and mass methods whatever critics may say about them. The monitorial schools were a case in point.

Economic conditions will limit the training as well as the supply of teachers.

Economic conditions will limit the length of school life and the time available for learning. If some prescribed objective—an examination, for example—must be achieved in the shortest possible time, then cramming and ' spoon-feeding ' are inevitable. As a result, much of what has been acquired in the process will be even more speedily forgotten. Learning is a process which takes time. Each increment of information needs to be incorporated within a system of knowledge. For this to happen opportunity for discussion, for quiet thought, browsing, contemplation, is necessary. What applies to pupils in this connexion applies also to teachers in training.

Teachers are not free to choose by psychological or educational criteria alone what they will teach. The curriculum in most schools is determined by pressure groups—parents, employers, professional associations, universities—and by the predominant needs of social classes, industry, and national defence. When classics was an essential vocational qualification classics was a staple school subject. When mathematics, or science, or engineering, or theology are vocational necessities, then the schools have to teach them or go out of operation.[2] Up to about 1900, school arithmetic was the arithmetic of accountants, bankers, book-keepers, and shopkeepers.

---

[1] According to the Ministry of Education statistics for 1958, there were still, in England and Wales, in January 1958, 28,734 classes in primary schools with more than forty pupils per class. See *Education in 1958*, Table 8, p. 154.
[2] See, for example, N. Hans, *New Trends in Education in the Eighteenth Century*.

Since about 1928 it has become the arithmetic of engineers and craftsmen, but the change has been accepted as *educational* progress. Perhaps it is.

Examination requirements exert a powerful influence, in primary schools by the 11+ grammar-school entrance tests ; in secondary schools by university regulations and standards operating through the Ordinary and Advanced levels of the General Certificate of Education and university scholarship papers. Since the real business of the primary schools is to get as many pupils as possible into the grammar schools, and of the grammar schools to get as many as possible into the universities, the schools cannot take the risks of failure. Careers depend on examination results ; parents and pupils expect the schools to make sure of credits, distinctions, and scholarships. Consequently, the teaching is done with a view to the questions in the next examination ; strict concentration on the prescribed syllabuses and set books is demanded ; the predominant methods are formal exposition, dictated notes, memorization, and reproduction. This may not matter quite so much in the case of intellectually gifted pupils. Many pupils not so gifted are driven by cramming to attempt to reach a minimum level of attainment for a pass. The results may be boredom, failure, resistance to any further schooling, not to mention the waste of time and effort and public money.[1] In addition, as the Crowther Report puts it :

" There is a tendency of long historical standing in English educational thought to concentrate too much on the interests of the abler pupils in the group and forget the rest."[2] Examination pressure intensifies this tendency.

It is, of course, to the national advantage to make the most of the abilities of the abler students (although whether driving them through academic examinations is, in fact, making the most of them is doubtful. The State Scholarship results are not reassuring). It is equally in the national interest to develop the reserves of ability in the rest of the school population, much of which is now being wasted

---

[1] The ratio of passes to subjects attempted tells its own tale—59 per cent. at Ordinary Level, 68 per cent. at Advanced Level, in 1958. Even more significant are the later achievements of State scholars, the academic *crème de la crème* of the grammar-school output. In 1958, out of 2009 scholars, 564 got third-class Honours or worse, or did not complete a university course ; rather more than 1 in 4. See *Education in 1958*, pp. 178, 180, and 240. At the time of writing it has been announced that the Ministry of Education proposes to abolish the award of State Scholarships.

[2] *15 to 18*, p. 87.

by too short a school life and by unsuitable curricula and methods.[1]

This is not intended to be a plea for the total abolition of examinations. It is an argument in favour of attempts to improve the conduct of public examinations, to make them less mechanical and impersonal. The General Certificate of Education examination is not the only or necessarily the best way of testing the ability of students. It is most certainly an argument for providing more facilities for higher education which would, to some extent at least, mitigate the inhuman drive to secure what places are available.

(iii) *Teachers*

That teachers are a limiting factor in teaching processes and methods is not so often acknowledged, not merely because they are too few, or insufficiently trained either academically or professionally, but because of their temperaments and their convictions about human nature, teaching methods, and educational aims. Teachers who believe devoutly that children should be seen and not heard ; that purposeless drudgery is an essential factor in mental discipline ; that Latin is the most perfect medium for mental development and culture just because it can be made superlatively difficult ; who demand unquestioning obedience ; who will not tolerate any intellectual initiative or independent thought in their pupils— these authoritarian classroom despots will emphasize learning processes and teaching methods consonant with their temperament and convictions. They will, quite honestly, believe that activity methods, projects, attempts to enlist the interests and co-operation of pupils, are academically crazy or morally reprehensible.

Again, most people teach most easily what they have learned in the way they have learned it. They do not feel comfortable or secure in using a ' new-fangled ' method. Teachers whose inclinations are strongly in the direction of intellectual system and strictly logical thought-processes may find real difficulty in dealing with what seem to them to be grossly untidy, sloppy methods of learning —projects, for example. It has been suggested that whatever success was achieved by the American Eight-year Plan was due as much to the conversion of the teachers as to any reform of school organization and curriculum. Not all the schools responded equally well to the new dispensation.

[1] See, for example, the report on " Early Leaving."

(iv) *Subject-matter*

The nature of subject-matter imposes limitations on teaching methods. It is not good practice to deal with appreciation of poetry or art in the same way as one would with accuracy in spelling or arithmetical computation. The difference in the results hoped for as the outcome of the learning makes necessary a difference in the methods employed in the teaching.

(v) *Ultimate Aims and Educational Values*

Here we touch upon topics about which there are profound differences of opinion. Educational aims and values are related to such problems as what knowledge is of most worth, what qualities should the educative process produce in the individual to be educated. The difficulty lies in agreeing about the purposes to which knowledge and education should contribute. Worth for what purpose ? What *ought* to be the ultimate aim of education ? The present complaint about demands for scientific and technological subjects is a case in point. What is the correct relation between technical as opposed to liberal or cultural subjects ? Or, from a religious point of view, how important is success in this life as against salvation in the next ?

At one extreme are the people who believe that the individual is all important. The late Professor T. P. Nunn wrote a book whose purpose, he said, was to reassert the claim of Individuality to be regarded as the supreme educational end. He believed that " educational efforts must be limited to securing for every one the conditions under which individuality is most completely developed—that is, to enabling him to make his original contribution to the variegated whole of human life as full and as truly characteristic as his nature permits ; the form of the contribution being left to the individual as something which each must, in living and by living, forge out for himself."[1] At the other extreme are the people who hold a fanatical belief in the absolute value of the State or Party or Social Class or Creed, and in what Nunn called the " deadly doctrine that the State can admit no moral authority greater than its own, and the corollary that the educational system, from the primary school to the university, should be used as an instrument to ingrain these notions into the soul of a whole people."[2]

The problem is intimately connected with teaching and school organization. If individuality is the supreme aim pupils will be

---

[1] *Education : Its Data and First Principles*, p. v and p. 5.
[2] Book cited, p. 3.

encouraged to act independently, to follow their impulses. Any form of external direction and teacher domination will be reduced to a minimum, or even abolished altogether. If strict conformity to State, Party, or Creed is the supreme aim external direction and teacher domination will predominate. Strict subservience to established authority will be rigidly enforced. Intellectual initiative and independent activity, if any, must be exercised strictly within and for the service of State, Party, or Creed, otherwise they will be treated as deviations from the true paths, to be suppressed at all costs. Even neutrality is dangerous and objectivity positively wicked.

The doctrine of Individuality, if carried to its logical, or illogical, extreme, must inevitably end in anarchy and chaos. Motor traffic on congested roads is a case in point. Complete individual licence is impossible in real life. Apart altogether from social relationships, the material environment imposes its own limits on action. The most successful farmers and hunters, other things being equal, are those who understand and conform most thoroughly to conditions of soil conservancy, plant growth, and animal behaviour. Successful craftsmen must obey the limitations imposed on their activity by the nature of their implements and materials. Nunn, in the book referred to, went on, after stating his aim, to qualify it in various ways.

On the other hand, systematic indoctrination and exploitation of individuals in the interest of State, or Party, or Ideology, or Industrial Organization, seem to lead, ultimately, so far as can be judged by historical events, either to revolt or to intellectual stagnation, complacence, or apathy. In that case any value there may be in intellectual adventure, initiative, and moral responsibility is lost.

If one believes with conviction that intellectual adventure, initiative, moral responsibility, and personal integrity are valuable and should be encouraged, then the educational problem is to discover a school organization and teaching methods which will foster self-realization *within the limits imposed by the need for social order and effective conditions for learning.*

Much has been said, particularly in America, about adjustment as the aim of education. According to this principle, the individual must be taught to settle sociably into the life of the community, adopt the community manners, and avoid making himself a nuisance. The difficulty with this concept is, of course, that young people may be persuaded in the interests of what has been called the Establishment to adjust themselves to forms of living which are already obsolete. If there is one lesson rather than any other to be learned from world history since the Middle Ages it is that our world—economically, politically, socially—does not remain constant. Change rather than fixity is the rule, and change which accelerates as time goes on. If pupils are to be trained to adjust themselves the adjustment should be towards the world as it is likely to be when they are adult rather than what it is now. Even so, the question is still left open as to which of the possible changes which may happen is the one, if any, to which people *ought* to adjust themselves and train children to do so.

The view suggested in this chapter is that normal, healthy children and young people, *given the opportunity*, are physically active, intellectually curious, and in various degrees capable of independent thinking and adventure. All the evidence accumulated so far supports the view that *learning is most efficient when the characteristics of the individual learner are respected and allowed for ; when school work is relevant to the nature and purposes of the pupils.*

At the same time the evidence seems equally certain that children and young people dislike uncertainty, confusion, and chaos. They do not welcome being left to their own resources without guidance. The case has been stated very clearly by the Head of the original Rugby Day Continuation School. This pioneer adventure in adolescent education was commenced in 1920. The first intention of the staff was to provide an organization free from adult domination and with the greatest possible liberty of action for the pupils. The results are best expressed in the Head's own words :

> Those who from the comfortable clean warm sunny atmosphere of our temples of learning plan attractive schemes for the education of working youth and who speak and write so fluently and persuasively about the service of youth may find realistic reminders of ordinary human weaknesses disturbing or even depressing. But if they are overlooked *when the whole and not a small picked proportion of working youth is conscripted for school*, the experiences which will follow will bring as great a shock to society as did the evacuation in 1939. The young people themselves did not care much for a time-table given over to interesting tasks ; they did not like handicraft work which came easily to them, mathematical problems which they could always solve and science demonstrations which were prepared for them ; they felt vaguely that all was not well. . . . . The absence of the usual familiar landmarks,

graded class lists, marking schemes, examinations, competitions, rewards and punishments, added to the strangeness and gave to the organization a cloudy vagueness.[1] . . . Sympathetic understanding, freedom from restraint, self-expression, interesting pursuits and the usual stock-in-trade of well-meaning enthusiasts we soon found from experience are not in themselves universal solvents for the difficulties of youth, although over a period of time they can contribute towards a solution and in occasional cases provide striking results. After struggling for a short time with the new order which did not seem somehow to meet the situation, we received perhaps the unkindest cut of all when one of our most efficient, most popular teachers at the end of a period in which he had been struggling heroically to radiate kindness all round received from one of his best groups of students the retort " But, sir, you are not strict enough with us." This is not unlike the plaintive retort of another class to a teacher in another school where free discipline was the order of the day, as they started the day with " But, sir, must we do as we like again to-day ? "

The Head goes on to say that when the staff took control of all daytime activities and adopted a classroom technique such as is common anywhere where learning is earnestly pursued, calling for orderly, reasonable response, the effect was immediate and striking. The pupils responded far better to a clarion call to work than to an invitation to play, and in this way they found that confidence, satisfaction, and thrills replaced the former nausea, which resulted from too much ease and comfort.[2]

We seem to have reached an impasse. Psychological considerations support the principle of respecting pupils' interests, tolerating individual idiosyncracies, and encouraging individual initiative. Experience suggests that these attitudes are not always or necessarily effective when translated into practice.

However, there may be, in fact, no contradiction. In the Rugby scheme the ' playway ' was *imposed* on those adolescent pupils just as certainly as a traditional authoritarian regime could have been imposed. The pupils had had no opportunity of revealing their preferences. They did this later by a process of passive resistance. Moreover, it does not follow that any given teaching method or school organization will be equally effective in all cases. What may

[1] As the Head described it—like playing a game of football without goalposts and boundary-lines.

[2] P. I. Kitchen, *From Learning to Earning* (Faber). Quoted by kind permission. p. 44. Italics mine.

be admirable in an infant school or a special school for emotionally maladjusted pupils may not be equally suitable for a normal secondary school. Interests and purposes change with age. If adolescents, particularly working-class adolescents, are given the opportunity they may choose, voluntarily, to work ; to be treated seriously commensurate with their adolescent status ; to be given an orderly organization and guidance in line with their needs and aspirations. They may rebel against having all the responsibility for their schooling thrust upon them. Their attitude may quite well be "What are these teachers paid for, anyway ? " H. C. Dent recalls that, in a school which would correspond with a present-day secondary modern school, when the boys were offered the choice of alternative courses one group *insisted* on being allowed to take a course, including Latin, in preparation for the School Certificate Examination. What is more, they pursued it successfully.

So, we repeat, the cult of individuality is not, in itself, sufficient. Some degree of social order is essential for effective freedom. Pupils must acknowledge some reasonable authority, accept some necessary regulation, conform to some elements in tradition, and tolerate facts. Otherwise they are unteachable. They cannot even teach themselves.

So far as the schools are concerned, the resolution of the conflict between self-realization and society seems to lie in imposing as few regulations as possible, making the regulations and the need for them clearly understood, allowing discussion about points of dispute, directing attention when pupils are sufficiently mature to the function of tradition as a stabilizing factor in social change and to aspects of tradition which should be accepted and acted upon after critical consideration, and, perhaps most important of all, training pupils to recognize and accept facts when they meet them.

The schools need to provide opportunities for the pupils to accept responsibilities and be trained in the techniques of social administration through the organization of clubs and societies, for example. Freedom is not merely an opportunity to insist on rights and privileges. It is also the result of the recognition and voluntary acceptance of duties and obligations. So far as the welfare of society is concerned, this training in social co-operation is at least as important as academic and technical attainments. Freedom in practice must be found in a compromise between personal expression and initiative, and social obligation. The ideal solution may lie in personal expression and initiative through social obligation.

The more any society is democratic, the greater is the need for self-control and enlightened, disinterested leadership.

It may be argued, of course, that any sort of social training is a form of propaganda and indoctrination. The distinction between legitimate training and illegitimate propaganda (illegitimate, that is, on educational grounds) lies in the intention with which the process is undertaken, and whose interest the result is calculated to promote. If party, or sectarian, or some exclusive economic advantage is the objective, then the persuasion is propaganda and the training indoctrination. If the objective is genuinely the well-being of individuals and community and the method persuasion, the process may legitimately be regarded as education. The same principle applies to the distinction between technical and liberal studies. If the object of the studies and practical training is the production of specific skills necessary for some industrial or commercial process that is technical education, and the place for it is the technical high school or college of further education, or apprenticeship, not the secondary school. If the objective is to use the vocational interest and vocational subject-matter to provide experience, to train habits of clear thinking and expression, skill in planning, appreciation of good design and sound workmanship, to encourage the realization on the part of the pupils of the function of vocation in the life and prosperity of the community, and the acceptance of vocation as in some way a form of social service, then handicraft, machine-drawing, building construction, nursing, home management, and domestic science, for example, as well as classics, can be the media for a liberal education.

Learning includes more than book knowledge. It includes knowledge and practice of the conditions for physical health,[1] knowledge and practice of the conditions for social health. The educated person should be equipped for marriage, family life, civic responsibility, and leisure, as well as vocational competence. Desirable social manners and attitudes ; a moral code ; skills in discussion and democratic procedures ; a practical working compromise between critical thinking, independent judgment, and acknowledgment of necessary authority ; some acceptance of ethical values—all these are aspects of learning within the meaning of the term as it is used here. The aim of education should be not merely a ' scholar ' with a head full of classics, or an engineer with a

[1] See, for example, Herbert Spencer's Essay on Physical Education (Everyman Edition, Dent).

head full of technology, or a craftsman with highly skilled hands, but a balanced personality. The proper function of educational administration is to foster an economic, social, and scholastic environment likely to produce this result, and of teaching to use it to the best advantage.

V. Educational Guidance

Guidance has already been mentioned as one of the processes of teaching. In the context of Section III above the term referred to a personal relationship between teacher and pupil by means of which the pupil is helped in the course of everyday schooling by demonstration, explanation, advice ; by suggestion and example. Guidance in that context was contrasted with the arbitrary imposition of instructions, regulations, directions, commands, which have to be obeyed, willy-nilly.

Educational guidance to be discussed now is a different matter. A familiar example will illustrate what is meant.

School reports often include such remarks as " Does not try hard enough " ; " Is not taking the work seriously " ; " Must pay more attention " ; " Is not doing his best " ; " Lacks concentration." These statements may describe the appearances with some accuracy. They give no indications, however, about the reasons why the pupil is behaving in the manner described. They are useless, therefore, for suggesting any appropriate remedial treatment. A doctor who reported merely that a patient had a high temperature, or a rash, or a cough, and omitted a prescription or any suggestion for treatment would soon be out of work.

Educationally, it is important not merely to report signs and symptoms of unsatisfactory conduct or progress, but to make some diagnosis of the underlying difficulty. Is the pupil really not trying hard enough ? Why is he not taking the work seriously ? Is he, *in fact*, not doing his best ? Why does he lack sustained effort ? Why is he inattentive ? These are the vital questions. If they can be answered with some degree of accuracy, remedial treatment may be introduced with some likelihood of curing or at least improving the defect.

The pupil may be doing the best *of which he is capable*, but his best may not be good enough for the tasks he is required to do. What, exactly, is the best he can be expected to do ? He may have missed some essential explanation or demonstration without which it is impossible to understand further work. If a pupil's language development has been neglected, if his vocabulary is inadequate, if his reading abilities are defective, then *all* his work will suffer.

The pupil may be ill, or undernourished, or overtired, or constitutionally timorous, or anxious about some difficulty outside the classroom or the school. He may be emotionally upset, or suffering from some hitherto unsuspected physical defect, bad eyesight, imperfect hearing, or some earlier environmental deprivation which has hindered normal development.

The pupil may not take his work seriously because it is not worth taking seriously. He may be too intelligent and despise it as " kid's stuff " ; bored with the subject and the teaching. At the other extreme he may be frustrated by continual failure or what he considers unfair nagging. He may see no point in the work. He may be trying deliberately to be annoying on account of some real or imaginary grievance. What he does in school may be ridiculed by parents, neighbours, and friends. It is not beyond the limits of possibility that the teaching is incompetent. What, exactly, is the difficulty, and what, if anything, can be done, in school, about it ?

These are the questions with which educational guidance in schools is concerned. Its objectives (as distinct from the work of special psychiatric clinics) are the discovery of the probable underlying causes of unsatisfactory behaviour or scholastic retardation and the application of appropriate remedial measures. Such gu dance is desirable at all stages of schooling. It is particularly important in the secondary-modern and comprehensive schools, with their unselected populations ; their wide range of individual differences ; the wide variations in teaching methods in the primary schools from which the pupils have come and the types of neighbourhood in which they live. In some areas, for example, there are about as many methods of teaching primary arithmetic as there are primary schools and primary teachers !

Much difficulty has been caused in the past by the custom of classifying pupils according to chronological age and assigning to each age, on a more or less arbitrary basis, standards of attainment which ought to be reached by all pupils at that age. This has been unfortunate for two reasons at least. The less able pupils were driven, only too often with merciless efficiency, to reach the standard assigned to their age-group in time for the next inspection or examination. The abler pupils who could reach the required standards with ease and would pass anyway were left to their own devices, bored to desperation, and tempted to indulge in various kinds of mischief, not because of original sin or youthful ' cussedness,' but simply as a relief from the tedium of aimless schooling.

Thanks largely to the experimental work of more recent times, a good deal is now known about the course of child development and the conditions of effective learning. If schooling is to realize its maximum efficiency these conditions, as well as subject-matter, chronological age, and purely examination requirements, must be taken adequately into consideration in organizing school work.

THE USE OF STANDARDIZED TESTS IN EDUCATIONAL GUIDANCE

Teachers interested in pupils as well as in subject-matter do attempt to fit the work to the pupils as far as conditions permit. However, subjective impressions may be misleading. They tend to be determined by local conditions. If, for example, a class or group is on the average, bright intellectually, then any pupil below the group average will appear to be retarded. On the other hand, if the group is, on the whole, backward, the same pupil would appear to be bright in comparison. For a similar reason it is difficult to compare the results in two or more different schools, particularly if they differ in social status.

To obviate these difficulties standardized tests have been constructed. These allow any given pupil's rank in capacity and attainment to be estimated by comparison with a large *unselected* population of the same chronological age.

Several types of standardized tests are available—tests of *general educational capacity* (' *intelligence* ') ; tests of *scholastic attainment*, in arithmetic, vocabulary, reading, for example.

Some tests are designed for use with *individual* pupils, such as the original Binet–Simon series and the Terman–Merrill revision. Other tests can be given to a whole class simultaneously—*group* tests. Since language is a factor in testing intelligence, *non-verbal* tests have been constructed in which the influence of language is reduced as far as possible to a minimum. Non-verbal tests may be *performance* tests, in which the pupil is required to perform some practical activity such as threading a maze, assembling a jigsaw puzzle, or manipulating blocks ; or they may be ' *pencil and paper* ' tests, in which the problems are presented in the form of pictures or geometrical patterns. Non-verbal tests are useful for children in bilingual areas.

Scales of physical development, mental development, and scholastic attainment can be constructed in the following way. The intention is to arrive at development ages, mental ages, or attainment ages based on experiment rather than on personal impression, subjective judgment, or what some authority decides is desirable.

Suppose attainment in arithmetic is to be surveyed. Questions typical of processes in mechanical or problem arithmetic are assembled and tried out on groups of pupils *representative of the child population for whom the test is intended.* As a result of these trials, unsatisfactory questions are amended or discarded. The final series of questions is then given to a sufficiently large unselected sample of pupils. From these scores an average (or median) score can be calculated for each month of chronological age. This will represent the *most probable score* to be expected *from an average pupil in that population, in that area,* at the given chronological age. As an example, the following items have been abstracted from a Schonell Mechanical Arithmetic Age Scale :

Marks obtained	Arithmetic Age
3	7 years 0 months
4	7 ,, 2 ,,
5	7 ,, 5 ,,
20	10 ,, 0 ,,
31	12 ,, 0 ,,
42	14 ,, 6 ,,

Thus if a pupil is 10 years old and scores 20 marks he has an arithmetic age of 10 ; if 31 marks, his arithmetic age is 12 ; if only 3 marks, his arithmetic age is 7. In other words, at a chronological age of 10 years his arithmetical attainment is equivalent to that of an *average* pupil of 10, 12, or 7 years respectively. The arithmetical age represents his upper limit of *achievement at the time* and, *in the conditions of the test.*[1]

If the arithmetic age is divided by the chronological age the *quotient* represents the attainment reached in a given time. It is an estimate of *rate* of progress. In the example given the respective quotients would be 10/10, 12/10, or 7/10. It is usual to multiply the quotients by 100. They would be given as 100, 120, 70.

In a similar way, development ages and development quotients can be constructed for height, weight, bone development (carpal age), dentition, general educational capacity, or intelligence (mental age), as well as for attainments in arithmetic, vocabulary, and reading comprehension, for example.

The very wide range of attainment ages and rates of progress which may be expected in a secondary modern school was illustrated on p. 22 above.

[1] The qualifications in italics should be noted carefully.

C

INTERPRETATION OF STANDARDIZED TEST RESULTS

Care is needed in interpreting scores on standardized tests.

(i) Tests are not precision instruments. They yield *estimates of the most probable* levels and rates of development and scholastic progress. They must not be taken absolutely literally.

(ii) Judgments should be based on more than one test. The same children may vary somewhat on similar tests at different times. Periodic testing is desirable, particularly in the case of backward children.

(iii) Attainment ages must on no account be thought of as upper limits of attainment which all pupils of a given chronological age ought to be made to reach. They give the best possible estimates of what may be expected of an *average* child at the given chronological age. If 20 marks is the standard score for a chronological age of 10 years it does not at all follow that every ten-year-old pupil *must* score 20 marks. Each pupil's score will be determined by aptitude for arithmetic, general educational capacity, experience, and the quality of the teaching. Most people would agree, at once, that if the *average* height of English schoolboys in a given area is 5 feet at age 12 it would be absurd to put every twelve-year-old who is less than 5 feet on a rack and stretch him to size.

(iv) Standardized tests give valid estimates *only when they are used in conditions similar to those in which they were originally standardized, and when they are administered strictly according to the directions given by the operation manuals.*

Tests of aptitude or capability, intelligence, for example, represent a rather different problem from tests of attainment. Arithmetical attainment or vocabulary can be tested directly in terms of speed, accuracy, number of words understood, or arithmetical operations successfully performed. Aptitude on the other hand, can be measured only indirectly in terms of a performance of some kind. But performance depends on previous experience, practice, special coaching, and schooling, as well as innate capacity. Somehow these environmental aspects of the performance must be discounted if the object of the test is to get an estimate of *sheer capacity or intellectual power.* If the test is to be fair, then all the pupils to be tested must be *equal in terms of educational opportunity, schooling, and general experience.* Test constructors have tried to make fair tests by confining the questions to such experience and skills as every child in the population in that environment might be expected to have acquired in the ordinary course of living ; or, alternatively, by using problems which require ingenuity, logical reasoning, and intellectual initiative, rather than memorized information and automatic habit. In so far as the results of schooling and other environmental influence can be discounted, it would seem to follow that those pupils who are most successful in the tests are the most naturally able. As we have seen, however, surveys have revealed that scores on intelligence tests are affected by environmental differences, early deprivation, for example, and home conditions. If mental age is accepted as an estimate of a pupil's *present* level of development and the intelligence quotient (I.Q.) as an estimate of rate of intellectual development *up to the present*, no great harm is done. The difficulty arises when the I.Q. is used to predict *future* development. There is no guarantee that future conditions will be the same as in the past, or that development will continue during adolescence at the same rate as hitherto. Favourable or unfavourable home conditions, and later spurts in intellectual development after puberty and the emergence of new interests, do affect future scholastic progress. These considerations must be taken into account in any attempt to estimate from a pupil's I.Q. at age 11 what his scholastic attainment will be at 16 or 18 years. It is not likely that a pupil with a correctly estimated I.Q. of 70 will ever change to an I.Q. of 140 plus or vice versa. It is much more difficult to predict the future of pupils with I.Q.'s in the region of 100.

With these qualifications in mind estimates of mental age and intelligence quotient can be employed in educational guidance.

It is useful to distinguish between pupils who are *backward* because they are generally dull and those who are *retarded*—that is, whose attainment age is significantly below their mental age. If, for example, a pupil whose mental age is 8 achieves an arithmetic age of 8, then he is *working up to the limit of his capacity* whatever his chronological age may be. He is doing his best in spite of appearances to the contrary. If such a pupil is driven to attempt work in arithmetic suitable for a mental age of 10 or more, then behaviour difficulties—inattention, apathy, anxiety, lack of concentration— are very likely to follow. If a pupil with a mental age of 10 achieves no more than an attainment age of 8 he is a case for further investigation. What particular difficulty is holding him back ? Again, if a ten-year-old pupil has a mental age of 14, but is kept working at an attainment level of 10, he is being retarded. He is capable of doing more difficult work, and may very well be bored, inattentive, and mischievous.

The main purpose of educational guidance in everyday school work, as distinct from the special child-guidance clinic, is to adapt the level of the work to the level of intellectual capacity and rate of development. Any serious discrepancies call for more detailed investigation. Quite often, when a successful compromise has been arranged between work and capacity, the general behaviour and attitude of the pupil improve.

VI. TEACHER-PUPIL RELATIONSHIP. RAPPORT

We can observe the behaviour of other people, but we are directly aware only of our own private experiences. However, we can relate our own experiences to our own behaviour. This is important in teaching. Much of a teacher's success both as instructor and guide depends upon his ability to " read his pupils' minds "— that is, to guess what they are thinking or feeling or intending from how they behave.

This sensitivity, or social perceptiveness, or intuitive insight, can be improved by practice and by the study of relevant literature. Ultimately, however, it depends on a teacher's own self-awareness. We have to guess from what the pupil does to what he is probably experiencing, in terms of what we ourselves have experienced when we behave in a similar way. This sensitive relation between teacher and pupil (or between physician and patient) is known as *rapport*. It is the quality more than any other that distinguishes the ' born ' teacher, if teaching capacity can be regarded as innate !

Sympathy, interest, guidance, are necessary in teaching, but by themselves they are not sufficient. One needs in addition to be able to realize *in a particular case* what is the most favourable moment to give help or suggestion or advice, and what sort of help and suggestion and advice is most likely to be effective. It is equally desirable to realize when *not* to give help or make suggestions, or offer advice; when a pupil must be left to conquer his difficulties himself, or when some crisp admonition or even pressure is indicated ; when to encourage, when to curb.

This sensitivity is doubly valuable in dealing with adolescents when ill-timed help or tactless criticism may be equally unwelcome.

It follows that the more the pupils' experiences, environment, and attitudes differ from those of the teacher the more difficult it is to establish this *rapport*—a fact to be kept in mind when dealing with pupils of a different nationality or social class. Knowledge of the environment as well as observation of the pupil is necessary.

VII. A WARNING TO NOVICES

At the end of their period of professional training, students should have developed some ideals of professional practice, and made acquaintance with modern methods of teaching and school organization. There is a danger that they may approach their first permanent post full of enthusiasm and determination to reform everything and everybody. It is well to remember that teaching in practice may be different from descriptions in professional text-books. If practical professional difficulties are not approached sensibly a period of disillusion, even cynicism, may follow in which any ideals or interest in reform are dismissed with contempt.

It is desirable, therefore, to realize that some difficulties may be inevitable and to be prepared to meet them. We have already stressed that teaching processes and teaching methods are limited by local conditions. Only too often school conditions are the reverse of perfect. School buildings may be out of date ; classes large ; pupils improperly graded ; work too difficult or too easy or lacking in relevance ; apparatus, books, materials, meagre in quantity or absent altogether.

Moreover, pupils themselves may be—indeed, often are—difficult. They may have been unwisely treated at home, and transfer their annoyance with parents to any representatives of authority, including teachers. They may have been reared in a neighbourhood in which attitudes towards schooling, morals, sex, are quite different from those of the teachers. Their interests and tastes with respect to music, books, reading, may seem appalling, their manners uncouth. If they are to be managed with any degree of success both they and their neighbourhood must be understood, and to some degree at least accepted.

Again, it must be remembered that schools are the products of centuries of tradition. Tradition (rather like a fly-wheel in a machine) has both momentum and inertia. School organization and teaching methods have been evolved by generations of teachers as the best compromise that could be made with the conditions prevailing at some particular time (the monitorial school, for example). It may not be possible, or even desirable, to destroy a tradition in a day. The result may be chaos. It may not be sound practice, therefore, to condemn all tradition and all existing conditions outright. It is better to try to sort out what is valuable in the tradition and discard what is now an incumbrance. In some cases new methods cannot be introduced with any degree of success until the educational organization as a whole is improved. The extension of the school life till 15 has made possible a number of changes in secondary-school practice. Compulsory schooling till 16 with adequate provision for further education till 18 will make possible even more radical reforms.

The most sensible proceeding is to get some clearly envisaged ideals of professional practice, to realize that they will have to be adapted in some degree to existing conditions, and then to attempt to achieve the ideals to the extent that is possible in practice. In this way one can meet difficulties without too much disillusion and cynicism. And it is always possible to work for what seem desirable reforms.

REFERENCES FOR FURTHER READING

I. *Adolescence*

> WALL, W. D.: *The Adolescent Child* (Methuen, second edition, 1955).
>
> LANDIS, P. H.: *Adolescence and Youth* (McGraw-Hill, second edition, 1952). A general introduction from an American point of view.
>
> FLEMING, C. M.: *Adolescence: Its Social Psychology* (Routledge and Kegan Paul, 1948).
>
> FLEMING, C. M. (ED.): *Studies in the Social Psychology of Adolescence* (Routledge and Kegan Paul, 1951). See Chapter VIII: Attitudes of adolescents towards their own development.
>
> WHEELER, O. A.: *The Adventure of Youth. The Psychology of Adolescence* (University of London Press, second edition, 1950).
>
> JEPHCOTT, A. P.: *Girls Growing Up* (Faber, 1942).
>
> REEVES, M. E.: *Growing Up in a Modern Society* (University of London Press, fourth edition, 1956).

II. *The Curriculum*

> Olson, W. C.: *Psychological Foundations of the Curriculum* (U.N.E.S.C.O. Publication No. 26, Paris, 1957). A concise summary of curriculum problems in relation to child development.
>
> DENT, H. C.: *Secondary Modern Schools* (Routledge and Kegan Paul, 1958). See Part I, Chapter IV: " Development out of the Interests of the Children "; Chapter V: " Special Courses "; Part II: " Problems New and Old."
>
> *Secondary Education* (Spens Report) (H.M.S.O., 1938). Chapter IV: " The Curriculum of the Grammar School "; Appendix II: " Concept of General Liberal Education ";

Appendix III : " Secondary School Curricula " ; Appendix
IV : " Faculty Psychology " ; Appendix V : " Transfer
of Training."

III. *Development*

Secondary Education (Spens Report) (H.M.S.O., 1938).
Chapter III : " Physical and Mental Development from
11+ to 16+."

The Primary School (H.M.S.O., 1931). Chapters II and III
and Appendix III.

STONE, C. R. : " The Factor of Maturation," Chapter 8 of
Handbook of General Experimental Psychology (Clark
University Press, 1934).

CARMICHAEL, L. : *Manual of Child Psychology* (Chapman and
Hall, 1954). Chapters on growth, maturation, learning,
language development, adolescence, character development, emotional development.

BRECKENRIDGE, M. E., AND VINCENT, E. L. : *Child Development : Physical and Psychological Growth through the School
Years* (W. B. Saunders, third edition, 1955). A comprehensive account of various aspects of development.

BUHLER, C. : *From Birth to Maturity* (Kegan Paul, 1935).

BARKER, R. G., KOUNIN, J. S., AND WRIGHT, H. F. (EDS.) :
Child Behaviour and Development (McGraw-Hill, 1943).
Thirty-five detailed studies of aspects of development.

THOMPSON, G. G. : *Child Psychology* (Harrap, 1952).

IV. *Educational Aims and School Government*

CLARKE, F. : *Freedom in the Educative Society* (University of
London Press, 1948).

SPENCER, H. : *Essays on Education and Kindred Subjects*
(Everyman Edition, Dent, 1919).

NUNN, T. P. : *Education : Its Data and First Principles*
(Edward Arnold, third edition, 1945).

REEVES, M. E. : *Growing Up in a Modern Society* (University
of London Press, fourth edition, 1956).

MACKAY, A. L. G. : *Experiments in Educational Self-govern-
ment* (Allen and Unwin, 1931).

WHITEHEAD, T. N. : *Leadership in a Free Society* (Oxford University Press, second edition, 1950).

PANETH, M. : *Branch Street* (Allen and Unwin, 1944). A description of an attempt to run a children's club in a tough London district on freedom principles. Useful study of influence of neighbourhood on behaviour and attitudes.

KITCHEN, P. I. : *From Learning to Earning* (Faber, 1944). An account of the first Day Release School (Rugby).

SYMPOSIUM : *Education in Citizenship* (Oxford University Press, 1950). Aims and methods.

BANTOCK, G. H. : *Freedom and Authority in Education* (Faber, 1952).

V. *Psychology of Learning*

HILGARD, E. R. : *Theories of Learning* (Appleton-Century-Crofts, New York, 1948).

PEEL, E. A. : *The Psychological Basis of Education* (Oliver and Boyd, 1956). Chapters on learning, intelligence (including tests), general and group factors, individual differences, intellectual development, emotional development, personality, school examinations, record cards.

FLEMING, C. M. : *Teaching : A Psychological Analysis* (Methuen, 1958). Sections on learning, development, testing.

RUSSELL, R. W. : " How Children Learn—Contemporary Psychological Theories of Learning," in *Bearings of Recent Advances in Psychology on Educational Problems* (Studies in Education No. 7, University of London Institute of Education ; Evans, 1955).

MILLER, N. E. AND DOLLARD, J. : *Social Learning and Imitation* (Kegan Paul, 1945)

YOUNG, K. : *A Handbook of Social Psychology* (Kegan Paul, 1946).

RUSK, R. R. : *An Outline of Experimental Education* (Macmillan, 1960). See particularly Chapters VII to X.

VI. *Educational Guidance, Tests and Testing*

GLASSEY, W., AND WEEKS, E. J. : *The Educational Development of Children* (University of London Press, 1950).

SYMPOSIUM : *The Educational Guidance of the School Child* (Evans, 1946). Suggestions for the use of cumulative records.

FLEMING, C. M. : *Cumulative Records : Notes on their Content and Use* (University of London Press, 1945). Useful concise summary with bibliographies.

WALKER, A. S. : *Pupils' School Records* (Newnes, 1955). Survey of nature and use of cumulative records in England and Wales.

MILNER, M. : *The Human Problem in Schools* (Methuen, 1938). An experimental study in a girls' grammar school, with advice on educational guidance.

BURT, C. L. : *Mental and Scholastic Tests* Staples, third edition, 1949).

───── *Handbook of Tests* (Staples, second edition, 1948).

KNIGHT, R. : *Intelligence and Intelligence Tests* (Methuen, fifth edition, 1956).

HUNT, E. P. A., AND SMITH, P. : *A Guide to Intelligence and Other Psychological Testing* (Evans, 1947).

DANIELS, J. C. : *Teachers' Handbook of Test Construction, Marking and Records* (Crosby Lockwood, 1949). Short introduction, including elementary statistics.

DREVER, J., AND COLLINS, M. : *Performance Tests of Intelligence* (Oliver and Boyd, fourth edition, 1946).

FREEMAN, F. N. : *Mental Tests : History, Principles, Application* (Harrap, 1939).

TERMAN, L. M., AND MERRILL, M. A. : *Measuring Intelligence* (Harrap, 1949). A guide to the administration of the New Revised Stanford-Binet Tests of Intelligence.

VERNON, P. E. : *The Measurement of Abilities* (University of London Press, second edition, 1949). A more advanced statistical treatment.

───── *The Standardization of a Graded Word Reading Test* (Scottish Council for Research in Education, Publication XII ; University of London Press, second edition, 1939). A concise description of the standardization of an attainment test.

Details of available tests may be had from :

G. G. Harrap and Co., Ltd, 182 High Holborn, London, W.C.1.

Newnes Educational Publishing Co., Ltd, Tower House, Southampton Street, Strand, London, W.C.2. Publishers of tests produced by the National Foundation for Educational Research.

Oliver and Boyd, Ltd, Tweeddale Court, 14 High Street, Edinburgh, and 39a Welbeck Street, London, W.1.

University of London Press, Ltd, Little Paul's House, Warwick Square, London, E.C.4.

VII. *Sex Education*

BIBBY, C. : *Sex Education* (Macmillan, second edition, 1948).

VIII. *Influence of Environment*

Scottish Council for Research in Education Publications, University of London Press :

Social Implications of the 1947 *Mental Survey.*

Educational and Other Aspects of the 1947 *Mental Survey.*

Trends of Scottish Intelligence. See Chapter VII : " Intelligence and Family Size."

City and Rural Schools (A. S. Mowat).

Home Environment and the School (Elizabeth Fraser).

NISBET, J. D. : *Family Environment* (Cassell, 1953).

IX. *Further References on Development*

HUNT, J. McV. : *Intelligence and Experience* (Ronald Press Co., New York, 1961).

ISAACS, N. : *The Growth of Understanding in the Young Child* (Educational Supply Association, 1961). A brief introduction to Piaget's work.

LOVELL, K. : *The Growth of Basic Mathematical and Scientific Concepts in Children* (University of London Press, 1961).

MUSSEN, P. H. : *The Psychological Development of the Child* (Prentice-Hall Inc., New Jersey, 1963).

PIAGET, J. : *The Origin of Intelligence in the Child* (Routledge and Kegan Paul, 1953).

TANNER, I. M. : *Education and Physical Growth* (University of London Press, 1961).

—— : *Growth at Adolescence* (Blackwell Scientific Publication, 1953).

X. *Teacher-Pupil Relationship*

ARGYLE, M. : *The Psychology of Interpersonal Behaviour* (Pelican, A853, 1967).

SECTION II

MOTIVATION AND INTEREST

CHAPTER III

MOTIVATION

SOME understanding of human motives is indispensable for success-ful teaching. The teacher's best work will not be done unless pupils are actively interested and pursue the work with zest. This applies particularly to monotonous repetitive work which is inseparable from the acquisition of a high degree of skill in games and occupations like writing shorthand or using a typewriter at high speeds. The study of motivation is therefore very important for teachers of technical subjects. In addition, good school-government and class control are best established upon a basis of interest and goodwill in pupils.

Some of the teacher's difficulties are due to apathy arising out of a general low level of vitality and interest. Many more, however, arise from a conflict of interests, the pupils being much keener on outside activities than on school-work.

There are, of course, two rough-and-ready methods of inducing interest in school-work. One is to make the pupils so averse to painful punishment that they turn to their work as the lesser evil. This produces at best only a grudging effort, usually accompanied by evasion and a growing dislike for any form of education. The other is to allow all pupils to do what they please when they please. This also is open to serious objections. It is not practicable in a normally conducted school. It is not conducive to a sane discipline, either moral or mental. Further, it is educationally unsound. Children are not always good judges of educational value. They tend to choose the easiest tasks which seem most profitable at the moment. In education a long view is often essential. What is easiest at the moment, like counting on the fingers or using a typewriter with a finger and thumb, may be positively harmful in later years when a high degree of skill is needed. Moreover, it is very doubtful whether we ought to remove all difficulties from a child's occupations. Effort is essential for full development. Difficulties conquered bring pleasure and confidence, and help to build up self-respect.

In this section we shall consider the sources of human effort and try to discover how children can be induced to attack their work with zest.

The doctrines of human motive have had a long and chequered history. It has been suggested that the one universal motive is the desire to gain pleasure and avoid pain. Common observation will show that this principle is by no means universally true. If it were, it is difficult to understand how some very brave but at the same time very dangerous enterprises are ever begun. It has been suggested that we all seek to realize imagined future pleasures, and to avoid imagined future pains. This is true of a good deal of the behaviour of sophisticated adults, but it is certainly not true of young children. It has been suggested that ideas act as forces and so determine our motives and interests. This was the Herbartian theory of motive and provided the basis for the Herbartian system of teaching-methods. If it were true it would be ideal for teachers, since it would follow immediately that a teacher could determine the interests of all his pupils by the simple expedient of organizing their ideas. Unfortunately for this 'teacher's psychology' the study of hypnotism and the practice of psycho-analysis have shown, without doubt, that ideas are effects rather than causes. It is necessary to explain ideas in terms of motive rather than motive in terms of ideas. This must be so, since young babies seem to have motives before they have had time to develop ideas.

The most recent fashionable explanation of human motive is that in terms of instinct. On examination, however, this explanation seems even less profitable than the others. In the first place, no two authorities seem able to agree about what an instinct is. The whole topic is chaotic with confusion. In the second place, in normal human life we seldom see any really instinctive behaviour, and if we do, we regard it as childish or brutish, look upon it with repugnance, and endeavour to modify it or suppress it as soon as possible. The instinct doctrines of motive have little value for educational theory. They are misleading even in the study of animal behaviour.

All these historical suggestions suffer from the same defect. They all endeavour to give one simple, all-inclusive answer to a problem which does not admit of a simple solution. They are all partly correct, and all partly wrong. Each has selected one significant factor in motivation and made that into a complete explanation of all behaviour. Present-day students have the advantage of a great deal of patient and accurate physiological and psychological investigation. Here we shall endeavour to give a more comprehensive theory of motive without committing ourselves to any one traditional school of thought. We can best begin by trying to describe the *facts* of behaviour.

STRIVING AND CONATION

As we have said above, we can study behaviour from two different but related points of view :

(*a*) That of an *external observer* noting changes in the behaviour of other people.

(*b*) That of an *internal reporter* noting changes in our own experience and correlating these with movements we make ourselves, and with movements we observe in other people.

On the basis of our personal experiences as we feel them, and our corresponding behaviour, we can then examine other people's behaviour and *infer* their probable experiences. In this way we can interpret their behaviour and their probable motives in terms of our own. In addition we can use observations of animal behaviour.

External observation indicates three main types of activity :

(i) Quick, more or less stereotyped non-rhythmic muscular movements, *e.g.*, turning the head following a sudden sound ; sneezing if the nostrils are tickled.

(ii) Continuous rhythmic movements of various internal organs, *e.g.*, expansion and contraction of lungs, heart, stomach, and intestines.

(iii) Persistent activity of the whole creature towards some end-point. This persistent activity is maintained with variations in the form of the activity until either a result favourable to the creature is achieved, or it is overcome by fatigue.

Internal report reveals the following types of experience :

Awareness of objects and situations in the external environment, or of disturbances within our bodies, when the sense-organs are stimulated.

A feeling of interest, that is, a feeling that *what is experienced concerns us, or has some kind of value for us.*

Feelings of pleasure or its opposite, unpleasure; elation or depression; surprise; satisfaction; complacence; nausea; anger; fear (among others).

A feeling of urge or ' drive,' a feeling that something must be done with regard to the experience noted. This varies from a generalized uneasy restlessness to a well-defined determination to achieve some clearly anticipated result.

We shall now try to co-ordinate these external observations and internal experiences into coherent patterns. Observation of ourselves and of other people and animals indicates that these movements and experiences are connected and ordered with respect to certain fundamental needs of the living organism. The living organism is a *self-regulating system*, the direction of the regulation being determined by the needs. It is this concept of regulation in accordance with needs which supplies the key to the understanding of motives and behaviour. This concept may be understood by reference to just one or two of the needs.

One of these needs is for food. We must eat to keep alive. However, the amount and kind of food eaten is important. Food is required for two main reasons:

To provide the material for building up and then maintaining the tissues of the body.

To provide energy. Part of this energy is used in maintaining the body at a suitable temperature. Part of it is expended as physical movement and mental activity.

Now there is a definite quantitative relation between the amount and kind of food we eat, and the rate of growth of tissue and the energy expended in action. Hence the amount and kind of food required by the body will vary from time to time. We shall require more food during periods of rapid growth. We shall require more food during periods of intense work. We shall require more food during spells of cold weather when heat escapes more quickly from the body to the air around it. Conversely we shall require less food in proportion as growth ceases, activity slows down, and the external temperature increases. All these facts can be corroborated by common observation. For example, the best way of starving in comfort, so to speak, is to retire to bed, cover oneself with blankets, and lie still.[1]

---

[1] This principle has been discovered empirically by many permanently unemployed workmen, who confirm its truth without knowing the reasons for it.

It follows from the above that for successful existence an *equilibrium must be maintained* between the amount and kind of food eaten and the changing conditions of the organism. If we do not eat enough the vitality of the organism decreases. If we eat too much the body mechanisms are clogged with surplus material and again vitality is depressed. *How then is this essential equilibrium maintained ?*

When the food reserves in the body begin to be depleted we feel a hunger. Food-hunger begins as an obscure barely localized uneasiness and intensifies into a gnawing unpleasant pain.[1] *This food-hunger is accompanied by interest in food, or in any signs of food.* We cannot rest. If food is not immediately available we seek it. We *strive* to find it and the striving increases in intensity with the increase in hunger. The sense-organs—particularly smell —become more susceptible to signs of food. We are alert and disposed to pay attention to such signs. If the first efforts to obtain food fail, the striving continues. We keep on seeking, but vary our efforts according to what we can remember of past situations of a similar kind.

If we are still unsuccessful we experience anxiety, then fear. These feelings deepen into despondency and finally despair.

If we find food we eat, using both learned habits, such as handling a knife and fork, and primitive reflexes, such as biting, chewing, and swallowing. Having found food we are elated. Tasting it gives us at first intense pleasure ; the greater the hunger, the more intense the pleasure. As we eat and approach repletion, pleasure in the eating subsides, the drive to eat diminishes, satisfaction supervenes, and finally we become *complacent* towards food. We have no further interest in it.

Now suppose we eat too much, or that food is forced upon us. We pass beyond the complacent condition. We begin to feel unpleasantly uneasy, and depressed. If the forced feeding continues, the unpleasure and depression increase accompanied by pain, nausea, and disgust. We now *strive to get away from* even the sight and smell of food. *In extremis* we ease the tension by sickness. When the tension is eased, we feel pleasure and some degree of elation, finally reverting to the mid-point of satisfied complacence with respect to food.

We can trace a similar cycle of events in connexion with several

---

[1] It has been shown that the pain is caused by increased activity of the rhythmic expansion and contraction of the stomach muscles.

other vital needs such as the needs for water, or for a correct body-temperature. Further, each sense-organ seems to have an optimum degree of stimulation which produces satisfaction. If the light stimulation in the eyes is too intense we seek to reduce it, if it is too feeble we seek to raise it. Each time the object of the striving is to re-establish the conditions in which we feel comfortable and satisfied.

It is noteworthy that this striving towards the conditions of satisfaction goes on both at a sub-conscious and a conscious level. The striving for a satisfactory intensity of light-stimulus is a good example. If the intensity of the lighting decreases slightly, the eye-mechanisms adjust themselves involuntarily. The pupils of the eyes are enlarged. The eyes are opened more widely, and the person concerned peers ahead more intently. If the lighting increases the pupils decrease, eyelids are partially closed, the eyeballs retracted slightly, and the person withdraws from the source of light until adequate compensation has been achieved. These slight compensatory adjustments operate without the explicit knowledge of the person concerned. They are achieved by involuntary reflex processes. If, however, the involuntary compensatory adjustments fail to restore the conditions of satisfactory illumination we begin to *feel* discomfort and our *interest and attention are directed* towards the unsatisfactory situation. We then try various ways of alleviating the difficulty. At a still higher level of analytic thinking we seek the causes of the difficulty by the use of scientific knowledge and thus attempt to remove it.

THE BEHAVIOUR-CYCLE

We can express this striving behaviour in a general formula—a behaviour-cycle—which gives us a clue to an explanation of motive and interest. The cycle can be described as follows:

The normal condition of the living organism is one of complacent satisfaction. In this condition we are not interested in ourselves or our immediate environment. We do not pay attention and are not disposed to exert any effort. Physical and mental activity are at a minimum. The organism is in equilibrium with its environment.

Then the equilibrium is disturbed by changes either within or outside the body. The disturbance may take place in two directions, *e.g.*, towards depletion or surplus. The disturbance is followed first by an unconscious striving which tends to restore the equilibrium.

If this fails we become conscious, feel interest, pay attention to the situation, and strive with more or less deliberate intent to restore the condition of equilibrium.

When this condition has been successfully re-established, interest, attention, effort diminish again to a minimum and we resume the normal state of complacent satisfaction.

We can represent this behaviour-cycle diagrammatically (see Fig. 1).

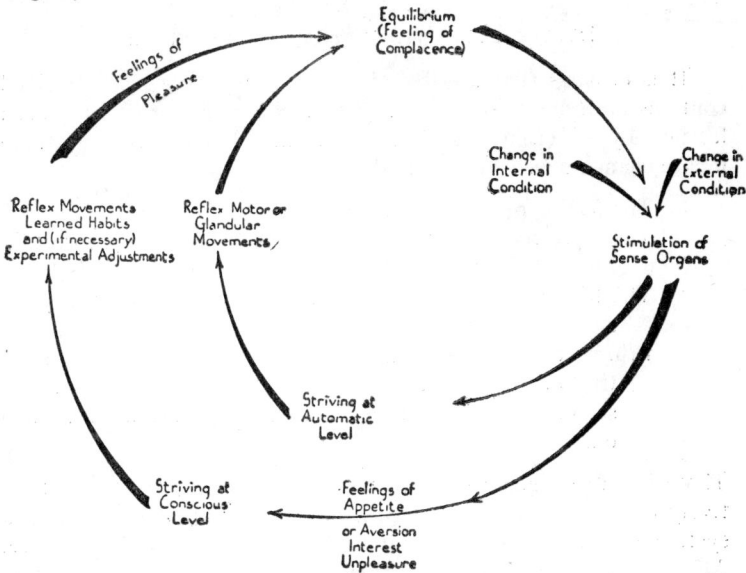

FIG. I

In the next chapter mention will be made of other equilibria necessary for successful existence. At the moment we are concerned to clarify this view of the living organism as a self-regulatory system, striving continuously to maintain certain constant internal conditions against changes in the environment. This view enables us to give a clearer and more satisfactory description of motivation. It is the striving of a living organism to maintain the conditions necessary for its continued existence. The striving may be either unconscious, or conscious and deliberate. When striving is conscious it is called *conation*.

Motives are experienced in two forms either as *hungers* or *aversions*.

THE RELATION BETWEEN STRIVING AND LEARNING

These behaviour-patterns involving hungers and aversions are, for the educator, the most important features of human life because *learning proceeds most quickly and efficiently under the influence of the drives of hunger or aversion.* In fact, we can say that in the absence of hungers or aversions learning does not occur.

INNATE ELEMENTS IN HUMAN BEHAVIOUR

It is obvious that this behaviour-cycle we have just described contains both innate elements as well as elements which have been learned by experience, such as ideas and habits. Among these innate elements we can detect :

The feeling of drive or urge.

The mere tendency to pay attention to objects of a certain kind related to the need of the moment.

The feelings of interest, pleasure-unpleasure, elation-depression, nausea, anger, fear.

Primitive reflexes such as biting, chewing, swallowing, spitting out, wiping the lips after tasting something nasty, secretion of saliva, movements of eyes and limbs, and so on.

These innate elements of feeling and reflex response remain relatively constant throughout healthy life, no matter how elaborate a system of knowledge and skill may be built up by experience. Also, whenever the educated human being is in conditions of desperate need, or danger, acquired knowledge and skill are temporarily swept aside and behaviour reverts to primitive patterns. In disease and insanity this reversion may be permanent.

To some extent therefore it is legitimate to speak of instinctive tendencies in human behaviour if we mean by this term certain innate propensities for feeling and acting which do not depend upon learning.

SOME SUBSIDIARY PRINCIPLES OF BEHAVIOUR

Having established the fundamental principle of motive and interest we must now glance at certain subsidiary principles of human behaviour which are relevant to the practice of teaching and school government.

PRINCIPLE OF LEAST ACTION

The human organism is an energy-system which has at its disposal only a limited supply of energy. As such it tends to obey a principle of least action. That is, it tends to behave in such a way that no more energy is expended in any given situation than is required to cope with the immediate difficulty.

This principle is exemplified in unconscious and conscious striving. Any disturbance of an equilibrium condition is countered first by primitive localized unconscious compensatory responses. Not until these fail do the more intense and varied conscious efforts to restore the equilibrium begin to operate.

This principle of energy-economy is met with frequently in school-work. Pupils are disinclined to use any higher mental processes so long as habitual conduct will satisfy their needs. Moreover, *any artificial demand for attentiveness and effort beyond the apparent need is resented and resisted by the pupils.*

We may note this peculiarity frequently in connexion with attentive observation. This function varies in intensity according to the needs of the organism at the moment. A full-fed animal does not notice food. Normal human beings select for observation just those details in the environment which are necessary for their particular task at the moment and they neglect the rest, *e.g.*, people neglect to count the buttons on their coats, or the steps in a familiar flight of stairs.

Claparède, a Swiss psychologist, has reported that he once asked a group of university students a question concerning some details of a large window on the main stairway in the college building. The majority of the students denied that the window was there at all, and only a few were able to answer the question. The students' need was to find their way to and from the lecture-room. The stairway itself was the means of satisfying the need. The window, although intrinsically as striking an object as the stair, was *irrelevant* to the need and therefore escaped attentive observation.

This point is important in school-practice because the question of improving the powers of observation by special artificial training is raised by education authorities from time to time. Some enterprising business man discovers with horror that pupils from the neighbouring primary and secondary schools have not noted some detail or other to which he himself attaches great importance because it happens to concern him. Then the schools are accused of gross inefficiency because they are said to have failed to train the pupils' powers of observation. Some school inspectors (who should have known better) adopted a habit some years ago, of asking small children questions about how many lamps or trees there were in the school street, or their home street. When the children could not answer, it was concluded either that the pupils were feeble-minded, or that the teachers could not teach. Hence there was a search for artificial ways of training powers of observation.

What is true of observation is equally true of remembering, imagining, and reasoning. These more complex mental processes require greater effort and more energy than habitual responses which will go on almost automatically. Hence there is a disinclination to use them deliberately *unless they are required by the organism in response to a need*. Therefore if we wish pupils to remember, imagine, or reason with concentrated effort, we must arrange the educational environment in such a way that the effort is *worth while and satisfying to the pupils*.

CHANGES IN THE LEVEL OF COMPLACENCE

The level at which complacence is established is a most important factor in connexion with interest and effort. According to the principle of least action, striving, and with it interest, attention and effort, are at a minimum in the complacent condition. While that condition remains, learning will not take place, since there is no sufficient reason whatever why it should take place.

It is important therefore to consider how the level of complacence with respect to any particular need changes. It is altered both by training and by maturation.

An interesting example of the first occurs in the training of athletes. One of the most important results of athletic training is the raising of the level at which oxygen-hunger begins. The normal level depends upon body-build, and different untrained individuals have different levels.

When athletes begin to train, comparatively little exertion disturbs the oxygen-equilibrium and they quickly feel air-hunger, distinct unpleasure, and a strong desire for increased breathing. There is also an aversion to further exertion. As training proceeds, the level of the oxygen-equilibrium is raised. Exertions which previously would have produced laboured breathing, nausea, and aversion to further effort, now scarcely alter the breathing-rate. The exertions can be maintained over a much longer period and continue to be pleasurable.

Conversely, lack of exercise, sedentary occupation, illness may lower the level of the oxygen-equilibrium.

The influence of maturation on the level of complacence is shown by changes in appetite for food which accompany normal growth. As a child grows, both the quantity and the quality of food necessary for complete satisfaction must be changed progressively.

The fact that spontaneous changes[1] in the complacence-level are induced by increasing maturity is important in education. The result is that the growing organism not only receives from the environment what is necessary for its present needs, but *it is constrained to seek what will satisfy it at the next approaching phase of development.* It is as if the organism were continually preparing, a little in advance, for what it will become. It has already been pointed out that by noting spontaneous changes in interest the teacher can to some extent anticipate future needs and consequently arrange an environment which shall be favourable to the development of the organism at the next succeeding phase of development.

When any physical or mental function approaches maturity, its exercise produces pleasure and elation. These feelings stimulate more energetic and repeated activity which in turn reacts favourably on the maturing function, assisting further growth until full maturity is established.

In addition to maturation and deliberate training, the general social environment may modify the level of complacence both upward and downward.

Consider the example of a skill-hunger. Suppose a healthy, well-grown boy or girl of eleven years old leaves his small village school and goes to a secondary school in another district. He will have been adjusted to the skill-level of his first envrionment. Arriving at the secondary school, he finds himself in an environment with a higher level of skill in games and athletics. Another type of hunger (which will be specified in more detail later) now comes into play to reinforce the movement-hunger of the boy. He compares his own achievements (with which he was previously quite satisfied) with the standards existing in the new school and he becomes dissatisfied. He seeks a higher degree of skill and endurance. This spurs him to increased effort and extended practice until his achievements produce satisfaction at the new complacence-level.

---

[1] *I.e.*, changes arising from within the system of the organism, as opposed to external stimulation.

Conversely, by attending a school with lower standards than his own, the skill-hunger tends to operate about a lower level of complacence.

We may anticipate at this point a later stage of our discussion and indicate another important implication of this condition of complacence. Since the human being has several needs he can experience several varieties of hunger and aversion. Thus a person may experience food-hunger, thirst, hunger for fresh air. He may also experience hunger for knowledge and skill. Now the teacher must depend for success in learning and teaching upon the pupils' hungers for knowledge and skill. But if the pupil is at the same time hungry for food, or warmth, or free movement, these hungers will conflict with those for the knowledge and skill which the teacher desires to impart. Hence, the teacher must contrive as far as possible *to satisfy the hungers for food, warmth, and free-movement, and establish a feeling of complacence with respect to them* while at the same time he disturbs deliberately the pupils' complacence with respect to further knowledge and skill. Some devices for doing this will be discussed later.

THE FUNCTION OF PLEASURE-UNPLEASURE FEELING-TONE IN MOTIVATION

Pleasure and unpleasure feeling-tones are not primary motives in that they do not *initiate* striving. Obviously, since striving commences below a conscious level, and in some cases does not reach the conscious level, it cannot be initiated by feelings of pleasure or unpleasure. At the same time these feelings do play an important part as *regulators of the duration of the striving*. We tend to prolong, or repeat, any process or condition which produces pleasure. We tend to cut short, and avoid repeating, any process or condition which produces unpleasure. The more intense the feeling-tones, the greater is their regulative influence.

The pleasure-unpleasure pair of feeling-tones appears to have no specific local reference. It accompanies a great variety of conditions and experiences and can be recognized over and above the specific qualities of each experience. One may be aware of an aromatic or savoury smell of a particular kind, *e.g.*, smell of benzene or of roast beef. At the same time as one experiences the smell one may also find it pleasant or unpleasant. Similarly, a harmony is pleasant, a discord unpleasant.

Pleasure-unpleasure depends upon the course of a process.

Generally speaking, *any situation which is developing towards satisfaction is found to be pleasant. Any situation which is developing away from satisfaction is unpleasant.*

Thus it follows that we may be suffering some unpleasant experience, but at the same time find the total situation pleasant. In music, we may be listening to a series of discords, each of which taken by itself would be judged unpleasant. However, from the form of the successive discords we anticipate that the end point will be a harmony. In so far as the individually unpleasant discords tend as a series towards an end-point of harmony, we find the situation as a whole *increasingly* pleasant.

Again, a person may be in a condition of considerable physical pain, yet at the same time suffused with a feeling of intense pleasure, *e.g.*, a badly injured soldier who has just been awarded the V.C. and cheered to the echo by his comrades. Here again the effects of the physical injuries themselves would be very unpleasant. However, in so far as the *total situation* ends in public recognition, it is capable of producing keen pleasure.

Conversely, similar relations may be detected between process and unpleasure.

It is important to note that although pleasure and unpleasure are not motives, at the same time they may become powerful *incentives, i.e.,* end-conditions towards which we strive. We begin, quite early in life, to asssociate pleasure and unpleasure with the objects and situations which produce them. If then we have a choice we tend to strive towards pleasure-producing situations, and to avoid unpleasure-producing situations.

THE FUNCTION OF EMOTIONS IN MOTIVATION

The term ' emotion ' is used very loosely even in technical psychology and still more so in current speech and literature. It is used sometimes to cover a whole range of feeling-tones. In this book we shall restrict the use of the term to cover *experiences of anger and fear only*, together with the physiological changes which accompany them.

Both anger and fear are distinct from elation-depression and pleasure-unpleasure in that they have no corresponding partner. They do not tend towards a mid-point. Both arise from a zero intensity and increase positively to a maximum intensity.

In both conditions, the individual undergoes extensive physiological changes, particularly associated with the sympathetic nervous system and the ductless glands. There are changes in rate and depth of breathing, in the pressure and distribution of the blood. The heart beats more quickly, blood is fed to the muscles and certain of the vital organs and withdrawn from others. Sugar (the muscle-food) is fed at an increased rate into the bloodstream. The adrenal glands secrete substances which have a tonic effect upon the heart and muscles, and which increase the tendency of the blood to coagulate.

The physiological effect of anger and fear is *enormously to increase the energy* at the disposal of the creature. This increased energy is then available for aggression or flight according to the demands of the situation.

Psychologically, the effect of anger and fear is to intensify the striving and thereby constrain the angry or fearful individual to put forth and to maintain a maximum effort. Thus they facilitate attempts to overcome opposition or to escape from danger. They play the same rôle in the human mechanism as does the supercharger in an internal-combustion engine.

Anger and fear also are correlated with the course of action. If the behaviour of the individual is leading without hindrance towards satisfaction the emotions are quiescent. If satisfaction is withheld, anger and fear increase in proportion to the degree of opposition or of danger.

The emotions are less important than the feelings in the learning-process. A *mild* degree of anger or fear intensifies effort and attention and therefore to that extent may aid the learner. If a pupil is angry with himself after having made a careless mistake, or after having failed to complete a task successfully, he will be the more inclined to resist making the error again, and will put forward more intense efforts to succeed.

Again, if the pupil is afraid of the consequences of error and failure, he will be the more inclined to work for success.

However, when the emotions pass beyond a mild degree of intensity, they seriously interfere with the poise and efficiency of the person concerned. Anyone who is thoroughly angry, or thoroughly afraid, becomes ' possessed.' He is occupied with but one intention, namely, to destroy the cause of his anger, or fly from what he fears. Past experience fades from consciousness. The critical, reasoning powers of the person are superseded. In the last stage he is a blindly ferocious maniac, or a horror-stricken paralytic.

The thoroughly angry or fearful person reverts to a primitive level of existence. He loses his acquired skills. Even speech fails. His behaviour becomes most definitely anti-social.

In addition, extreme anger and fear are *very expensive of energy.* By the nature of things the angry or fearful person is using up his reserves of energy at a very rapid rate. After a paroxysm of rage or fear the sufferer is left limp and exhausted, and is incapable of further effort until the energy reserves have been replenished.

It is obvious, therefore, that any intense conditions of anger and fear are definitely harmful to the learning-process as well as to the individual himself, and every precaution should be taken to ensure that these emotions are not aroused beyond a mild degree in school conditions.

THE FUNCTION OF IDEAS AND HABITS IN MOTIVATION

Ideas and habits have also been claimed to be sources of motive. Again, this claim seems to be incorrect, since ideas and habits do not in the first place *initiate* striving. They accompany it, and *are developed in the service of the hungers and aversions.*

The function of ideas is (*a*) to direct the striving more effectively, and (*b*) to increase the range and variety of responses by which satisfaction may be achieved.

Through the medium of ideas we can recall previous experiences of striving, the situations involved, and successes or failures. When similar situations occur again we can anticipate the probable course of events, select suitable responses, and reject unsuitable responses. By the association of ideas we can compound simpler into more complex responses. By means of logical analysis we can apply successful responses to novel situations.

By the development of ideas we are able to anticipate future needs, imagine future possibilities, and apply the cumulative experience of the race in order to satisfy those needs and realize the possibilities.

The function of habits is to capitalize successful responses. Under the spur of a persistent hunger we vary our responses when primitive measures fail to bring satisfaction. All new responses are tentative, slow, and inaccurate at first. At each repetition of a *successful* response it becomes swifter, more accurate, more economical of energy, and it requires less and less concentrated attention. By repetition the successful responses become automatic, thus stabilizing the individual's ways of obtaining satisfaction, and freeing the attentive thinking-processes for newer and more complicated tasks.

However, although ideas are not primary motives, they become, in the course of learning, closely associated with and organized around primary motives. Thus pictures, words, and signs, and their corresponding mental images, can stimulate a dormant motive —food-hunger, thirst, and sex, for example. This fact is used in modern commercial advertising. Such stimuli exert the most powerful effect when some corresponding hunger is in a phase of increasing intensity.

TOPICS FOR FURTHER CONSIDERATION

1. Follow up the discussion of instincts in McDougall's works, e.g., Social Psychology, The Outline of Psychology, The Energies of Men. Summarize his descriptions of human instincts. Compare and contrast his descriptions and explanations of human motives with those developed in the present chapter.

2. Repeat Exercise 1 but substituting Thorndike's account of motives as it is set out in the Psychology of Learning (Vol. I).

3. Analyse and record carefully your own experiences and behaviour during a typical behaviour-cycle.

4. Can you describe in your own case any example of a change in the level of complacence? What conditions caused the change? (Note the effects of coming to college as an example.)

Compare notes with friends on this topic.

EXERCISES

1. How much 'instinctive' behaviour can be observed in children at 3 years, 7 years, 16 years of age? How much in the normal adult?

2. Note the conditions, in the case of children and adults, in which behaviour approximates to 'instinctive' responses.

3. From your observations in Exercises 1 and 2, discuss the value of the terms 'instinct' and 'instinctive' for a theory of behaviour.

Books for Further Reference

CANNON, W. B. : *The Wisdom of the Body* (Kegan Paul, 1932). Studies in bodily self-regulation.

FREEMAN, G. L. : *The Energetics of Human Behaviour* (Cornell University Press, New York, 1948).

GREEN, D. R. : *Educational Psychology* (Prentice-Hall Inc., New Jeısey, 1964).

HART, B. : *The Psychology of Insanity* (Cambridge University Press, fifth edition, 1956).

McDOUGALL, W. : *Outline of Psychology* (Methuen, thirteenth edition, 1949). See Chapters V, VI, VII, and IX.

———— *Energies of Men* (Methuen, eighth edition, 1950).

MURPHY, G., MURPHY, L. B., AND NEWCOMB, T. M. : *Experimental Social Psychology* (Harper, New York, 1937). See Part II, Chapters III and IV, and Part III.

MURRAY, E. J. : *Motivation and Emotion* (Prentice-Hall Inc., New Jersey, 1964).

PETERS, R. S. : *The Concept of Motivation* (Routledge, 1958). A critical review of theories of motivation.

ROSS, J. S. : *Groundwork of Educational Psychology* (Harrap, second edition, 1935).

RAUP, R. B. : *Complacency : The Foundation of Human Behaviour* (Macmillan, New York, 1925).

THORNDIKE, E. L. : *Educational Psychology*, Vol. I (Teachers' College, New York, 1921).

———— *Educational Psychology : Briefer Course* (Teachers' College, New York, 1917).

TROTTER, W. ; *Instincts of the Herd in Peace and War* (Oxford University Press, 1953).

YOUNG, K. : *Handbook of Social Psychology* (Kegan Paul, second edition, 1946). See Chapter IV : " Drives and Emotions."

CHAPTER IV

CLASSIFICATION AND DESCRIPTION OF MOTIVES

In the previous chapter we showed that motivation and interest are connected with processes of regulation by means of which the human organism maintains conditions essential to healthy existence.

Motives assume distinguishable forms—hungers and their corresponding aversions—each hunger and aversion being connected with some biological need.

We find also that learning takes place most effectively under the drive of these hungers and aversions. In the absence of some kind of hunger or aversion no learning occurs.

Now, if the purpose of teaching is to facilitate learning in the most efficient way, it follows that we must be able to harness the energy represented by the drives of hungers and aversions and direct it into educationally and socially useful channels. Our aim all the time should be not to impose facts, figures, and habits upon passive pupils, after the manner of Dickens' famous (or infamous) characters, Gradgrind and McChoakumchild, but to encourage in the pupils active hungers for facts and figures and the various kinds of skill needed by the educated person. If we can do this the actively interested pupil will educate himself. Hence, we must try to find what hungers and aversions are available for the teacher's work in school and everyday life.

For a thoroughly scientific psychology it would be necessary to analyse the complex strivings of living creatures and sort out elementary modes of striving in terms of which all complex behaviour and experience could be expressed. This nicety of analysis is impossible at present simply because methods of analysis of sufficient accuracy and validity have not yet been perfected. Indeed, it is only within the past generation that any adequate *quantitative* methods of factor analysis in psychology have been elaborated. In what follows therefore any classification of hungers will be put forward, not with a view to precise scientific analysis, but for practical professional guidance.

94

Nomenclature presents some difficulty. Here ' need ' and ' drive ' will refer to the physiological ·tensions which accompany excess or depletion. ' Craving,' ' desire,' ' longing,' ' appetite,' ' hunger,' ' aversion,' ' interest,' indicate the feelings experienced when under the influence of some tension. For purposes of description and classification ' hunger ' and ' aversion ' seem the most convenient terms to use. Experience of motive seems to be reducible to a hunger-aversion pattern. Deprivation sets up hungers ; excess, aversions.

For teachers and social workers a convenient classification of hungers may be made with respect to the main reference. Thus we have :

(a) A class of hungers having special reference to the maintenance of general bodily well-being and security.

(b) A class having special reference to the maintenance of personal status in a physical and social environment.

The hungers in group (a) serve to maintain the conditions necessary for physical existence. The more important are :

Food hunger.
Thirst.
Hunger for fresh air.
Hungers for general bodily well-being and security.
Hunger for *free* physical movement.
Hungers for excretion.
Hunger for rest, and sleep.

The more important hungers in group (b) are :

Hunger for companionship (gregariousness).
Hunger for sex-experience.
Hunger for self-enhancement.
Hunger for intellectual free movement (leading to exploration and experiment). This hunger seems to be what is signified by the term ' pure curiosity.'
Hunger for routine and system.
Hunger for explanation (that is, for the resolution of novel and mysterious events into terms already familiar).

One item in group (a) needs further elaboration. The hungers for general bodily well-being and security form a group all of which are connected *with specific conditions of normal stimulation*. These are the conditions best suited for the security and well-being of the creature. Any considerable departure from these conditions signifies danger. A newly born child will make defence-responses against stimulations of the kind which produce pains in an adult *e.g.*, pinching, pricking, scalding, burning, irritation of the skin, etc. It also reacts strongly to being tilted or lowered quickly, and to loud, sudden noises. If the reflex defence-responses do not bring satisfaction, and the abnormal conditions continue, the child will strive violently in the attempt to seek the normal comfortable stimulation-level.

As the child grows up, and learns by experience, a great variety of abnormal conditions of stimulation become associated with danger and arouse a hunger for the conditions the child associates with security. Two cases of abnormal under-stimulation are darkness and dead silence. Many adults never lose their aversions to these two conditions.

Also, the hunger for self-enhancement seems to include several distinguishable components, *e.g.*,

> Hunger for personal domination—power over other people, over animals, and over the inanimate objects and forces of the physical environment.
>
> Hunger to excel (without domination).
>
> Hunger for perfection.

Experience presents three elementary qualities :

(*a*) Qualities conveyed by specific sense-organs in vision, hearing, touch, etc. These give rise to perception, imagery, ideas, and the complicated systems of knowledge built upon them. This aspect of experience is known as *cognition*.

(*b*) Qualities of feeling—pleasure-unpleasure, elation-depression, and the complex feelings such as confidence, hope, anxiety, despondency, grief, sorrow, joy, etc. This aspect of experience is called the *affective-tone, affection,* or *affect.*

(*c*) Qualities of striving, craving, urge, desire. These are called *conation.* Conation is conscious striving.

CHARACTERISTICS OF SOME HUNGERS COMMONLY OBSERVED IN CONNEXION WITH SCHOOL LIFE

In a boarding-school the institution becomes for the time being the home of the pupils. The teachers perform *two* functions. They act as tutors in the normal work of a school, and they act as substitute-parents. Therefore they can control the life of the pupil much more completely, and they are responsible for the satisfaction of the hungers for food, drink, security (out of school-hours), and general well-being. In our discussions we shall be concerned mainly with the teacher as tutor acting within the normal day-school organization, and only by implication with the teacher acting as substitute-parent (or real parent !).

For this purpose it is desirable to note the characteristics of certain of the hungers which provide the motives directly or indirectly involved in learning in classroom conditions. The hungers in question are :

Hunger for fresh air.
Hunger for conditions of optimum stimulation.
Hunger for physical free movement.
Hunger for rest.
Hunger for companionship.
Hunger for self-enhancement.
Hunger for intellectual free movement.
Hunger for routine and system.
Hunger for explanation.

HUNGER FOR FRESH AIR

If people are confined for some length of time in a badly ventilated room, they begin to show signs of uneasiness, and later of distress. They complain of drowsiness, lassitude, headache, nausea. The outward signs are drooping postures, yawning, slow response, general lack of alertness, and lapses of attention.

These symptoms have been shown to be due to insufficient *fresh air*. Contrary to general opinion the discomfort is due not to deficiency in oxygen, or excess of carbon dioxide, but to increase in temperature and humidity of the *stagnant* air. Flugge, at Breslau (1905), placed some people in an air-tight box. When the atmosphere became oppressive, he allowed them to breathe fresh air from outside the box, through tubes, but found that their discomfort was not reduced. On the other hand, people in the fresh air outside the box who breathed through tubes the vitiated air from inside the box showed no signs of distress.

For optimum comfort and efficiency a *steadily renewed supply* of fresh air at the correct temperature and humidity is required. In rooms heated by coal fires the convection currents set up by the fires maintain a stream of air through the rooms. When central heating is used, the air is apt to become stagnant unless there is a mechanical system of ventilation.

When a class of pupils becomes drowsy, listless, inattentive, and slow to respond to questions or instructions we should first inspect the temperature and ventilation conditions and make sure that the air in the classroom is fresh. If the ventilation is faulty it is obviously useless to submit the class to a course of five minutes vigorous physical exercise, inside the room, as some teachers do, in order to ' smarten up ' the pupils. This practice will merely make the bad conditions worse. It is much more sensible to correct the bad ventilation and *thereby satisfy the pupils' hunger for fresh air*. They will then have more appetite for lessons.

HUNGERS FOR CONDITIONS OF OPTIMUM STIMULATION

These hungers are connected with the maintenance of general physical well-being and security. They are set up by any conditions of over- or under-stimulation. Several types of such conditions frequently occur in school-classrooms, *e.g.*,

Minor ailments—toothache, headache, cuts, abrasions, bruises, *aches caused by badly fitting desks*.

Classroom too hot, or too cold ; pupils sitting too near a fire, stove, or radiator ; pupils sitting under an open window in cold weather.

Presence of foul, pungent, or acrid smells (as sometimes is the case in a laboratory or in a classroom near a factory or cesspool).

Lighting too intense, *e.g.*, pupils sitting in direct rays of sun ; pupils seated so that they look directly towards a window ; maps and blackboards ' shining ' or situated near a window instead of opposite to it ; artificial lights badly placed.

Lighting not strong enough, *e.g.*, pupils sitting in dark corners ; blackboard, pictures, maps, specimens too far from pupils to be clearly seen ; pupils attempting to read in fading daylight.

Sounds too intense, or conflicting, causing distraction—teacher shouts continuously with harsh, strident voice ; teacher's voice too high-pitched ; miscellaneous noises outside classroom ; too much noisy movement within classroom ; teacher stamps or shuffles about unnecessarily while talking.

Sounds not intense enough, or indistinct—teacher's voice weak, or hoarse ; teacher ' mumbles ' ; talks to blackboard and maps instead of to class ; talks in unfamiliar accent, or with jerky delivery ; *pupils answer questions indistinctly, so that remainder of class cannot follow the discussion.*

Teacher shows threatening bullying manner, or uses excessive punishment (particularly if liable to sudden unaccountable fits of irritation and temper).

Teachers just beginning their professional work are apt to become immersed in the presentation of their lessons, and to neglect entirely these important classroom-conditions. The more conscientious the teachers, the more frequently does this happen. Then, when the pupils become restless and inattentive, instead of noting the classroom conditions, they redouble their efforts to make their material impressive and thereby intensify the bad conditions. It should be made an invariable practice to ensure that the *pupils are as comfortable and happy in their classroom environment as the classroom arrangements permit.* If a teacher's voice and manner are unfortunate, it is usually possible by practice to improve it. With regard to voice, diction, and delivery the teacher should be as much as possible an artist. Generally speaking, the pupils do not elect to go to school. Their presence is enforced by parents and by the State. When conditions are bad the unfortunate children cannot walk out. They have to sit and bear with their misfortune without the option of criticism or complaint, and they acquire very strong aversions to school, teachers, and work.

It may be objected that if the teacher's manner is unfortunate, his speech indistinct, his blackboard summaries chaotic and illegible, and other pupils' answers inaudible, that the pupils will adjust themselves to these conditions without worrying unduly about the waste of time. This may be true of some pupils. Even so it is not a good argument for maintaining such conditions. In other cases, however, pupils may be conscientious, anxious about passing a test, questioned at home by over-anxious parents who are concerned with their children's future careers. In such cases bad school-conditions can, and frequently do, set up anxiety-states in the pupils, making them thoroughly unhappy, reducing their efficiency, and sometimes leading to nervous breakdown.

It is particularly necessary for teachers to maintain a strict supervision of classroom conditions because they themselves are in the most favourable position to make satisfactory adjustments. If there is a nasty cold draught, or an irritating sun-glare, the teacher can remove himself out of it and forget that it still remains. He can always see the blackboard, apparatus, or pictures because

D

he stands quite near to them. If they are not clear he goes closer. Having thus satisfactorily adjusted himself it is very easy to forget that the pupils are still badly adjusted.

Many pupils associate schools with habitual discomfort, and their aversion to the classroom-conditions spreads, by conditioning, to the subjects of instruction.

HUNGER FOR FREE MOVEMENT

The conditions which set up this hunger are :
(i) Forced movements.
(ii) Continued rigidity of posture.

What is meant by forced movement may be understood by considering the mechanical structure of the body. An arm or leg swinging freely in its socket-joint resembles a compound pendulum. The trunk turning freely to and fro about the waist resembles a balance-wheel. If a pendulum or balance-wheel is allowed to swing freely, it will do so at a natural period (*i.e.*, the time occupied by one complete swing) which is characteristic of it. The period depends upon several factors but mainly upon the length of the pendulum, or the radius of the wheel. If allowed to maintain its natural period the system will continue to move rhythmically and will require a minimum of energy to keep it going. If we try to force the movement at a rate faster or slower than this natural period, much more energy is required, and the system resists the change. It seems as if it were striving to resume its natural rhythm.

Many human movements are rhythmic—swinging arms and legs, turning and bending the trunk, walking, running, skipping, etc. Any of these movements, when made freely, will be found to proceed at a characteristic period *depending upon the body-build of the individual performer*. At this periodic rate, the movement feels most comfortable and can be kept going easily for a considerable time without fatigue. If we attempt to depart from this natural rhythm we have to pay special attention to the movement, and deliberately apply energy very much in excess of the amount required for free movement. So soon as the attention is withdrawn the limbs tend to revert to their natural rhythmic period. To maintain a forced movement is very fatiguing and *irritating*, aversion being rapidly induced. The more the natural period is altered, the greater will be the additional energy required, and the greater the fatigue and aversion.

Individuals of different body-build have different optimum rates of movement.   In physical training, gymnastics, games, or using tools a heterogeneous class of pupils cannot be expected to work at exactly the same rates.   An average rate of movement will be too fast for some and too slow for others.

The second condition which sets up hunger for free movement is rigidity of posture.   It seems to have been assumed by many people that sitting or standing in one position needs no effort. Actually it requires very considerable expenditure of energy, leading to rapid local fatigue, and to strong aversions in the person concerned.   From this point of view, the practices of the teacher who was considered a model disciplinarian were thoroughly unsound. It is not good practice to keep classes of pupils standing in a straight line, or sitting bolt upright with arms behind their backs for periods of thirty to forty-five minutes.   For young children this is torture. When it is necessary for children to be seated (for an oral lesson, for example), they should be allowed to adjust themselves comfortably at the outset, and allowed reasonable opportunity to change their posture from time to time.

One type of rigidity is noteworthy—namely, that with which the learner grasps a new tool.   This can be noted in any beginner learning to write with a pen, to ride a bicycle, or drive a car.   For this reason, the first practice-periods (particularly for young pupils) should be short, and *opportunity for complete relaxation allowed immediately after the practice.*

If the difficulties of forced movement and rigidity of posture are ignored in school the craving for free movement and relaxation will soon *set up conflicts in the pupils' attention-processes* which prevent any effective concentration upon the school-work.   In making time-tables, care should be taken that lesson-periods in which there has been forced movement or rigidity should be followed by periods in which change of occupation, or relaxation is possible.   When the forced movements involve a restricted set of muscles (as in writing with a pen), a complete change of occupation is as good as a rest.   New sets of muscles are then brought into play and the tired muscles relieved from strain.   The most effective change is from an occupation involving a restricted set of muscles, to one involving the larger muscle groups of the whole trunk and limbs.

One frequently used classroom-practice needs careful supervision in view of this hunger for free movement and relaxation, that is, the showing of hands in response to a question. Some students-in-training ask a question of their pupils, and these respond by holding up their hands. The students have probably been warned that they must keep a strict eye upon the lazy members of a class. Therefore they request an answer from some pupil whose hand is down. There may be no answer, or a foolish one. Unwilling to pass this over, they proceed conscientiously to extract an answer from the dumb pupil or to correct the foolish one. During all this time the others dutifully keep up their hands until their shoulders ache with fatigue. If it happens that a correct answer is delayed, and the teacher needs to attend to some individual pupil, the remainder of the class should be asked pleasantly and quietly to put down their hands for the time being. Then at the appropriate time the question can be asked again, and the pupils saved much needless strain and strong aversion.

HUNGER FOR REST

Alternating with the hunger for free movement is the hunger for rest and sleep. The intensity of this hunger varies from one individual to another. It depends also on a person's health and the conditions of growth, more rest being needed during periods of rapid growth.

The hunger is connected with the need for the body to recuperate after periods of active exercise or illness. Continuous driving of the human body, particularly if the expenditure of energy is excessive, is very dangerous. It is necessary to recognize this in dealing with adolescent boys and girls.

Adequate rest and sleep are as necessary for growing children as is food. Some authorities believe that lack of sleep is as potent a cause of poor development as malnutrition, particularly in the case of children living in the over-crowded noisy conditions of large towns. Before reprimanding such children for laziness and inattention in school we need to discover first that the difficulty is not due to a craving for sleep.

HUNGER FOR COMPANIONSHIP

The great majority of the human race are gregarious. They show a strong tendency to herd together. This hunger for the presence of other people is probably associated with security. At the same time it exists in situations where no danger is likely to arise. The desire to be with other people may be quite irrational, *i.e.*, it may serve no useful purpose. Some persons do not wish to co-operate, talk, or play with others. At the same time they feel impelled to mingle with a crowd.

This hunger tends to a mid-point of complacence. We can have too much even of companionship, and most people pass through periods in which there is a more or less definite aversion to crowds and a desire for comparative solitude.[1]

The hunger varies in intensity in different individuals partly owing to the interplay of other interests. The busy craftsman or professional worker, absorbed in his work, feels, at the moment, no hunger for companionship. Nevertheless the hunger appears during periods of relaxation. It is most improbable that the popularity of scientific, educational, and political conferences is due entirely to a pure interest in knowledge and affairs. The social element is also strong.

Feeling-tones are intensified by the presence of a crowd. Pleasure is increased, terror, sorrow, and despair are more intense. We are so made that signs of feeling and emotion in others arouse, directly, experiences of the same feeling and emotion in ourselves. In the presence of a crowd the tendencies to imitate and accept suggestions are particularly strong.

Children appear to pass through characteristic behaviour-phases with respect to gregariousness. The young child shows little tendency for active co-operation. He likes the presence of other people to take the form of a neutral or admiring background for his occupations. A normal child will play happily with his toys by himself for considerable periods while he knows or believes that there are other people within reach. He will be considerably disturbed, however, if he realizes that he is really alone.

Towards the age of eight years (approximately) children develop a much more active interest in other children and in people generally. They show a tendency to form co-operative groups. Team-games and gang-play become popular. The junior-school period (approximately eight to twelve years of age) has been called by some writers the gang-age.

During adolescence, many young people show a marked preference for solitude, or for intimate companionships. This phase passes later into the normal adult's gregariousness.

The hunger for companionship may be turned to good account

[1] Consider the following extract from the journal of a civilian prisoners' camp : " Only to be out of this crowded desert, just for ten minutes to be on a solitary mountain top . . . anywhere even where danger lies to be away from the sight and sound and smell of mankind and to be able to think one's own thoughts."

in school-work, particularly after the infant-school phase is completed. The heightened pleasure in being with others may be used advantageously by arranging group-work. It is noteworthy in music and dramatics, in fact in any pursuit which involves feeling and emotion.

The fact that in the presence of others, imitation and suggestion are strong, helps in maintaining good class-order and school-tone. Pupils tend to fall into line with the majority. Hence the presence of a group of other children happily at work is, often, a quite sufficient reason for an individual pupil to join in, and set to work himself. It sometimes happens that a certain pupil does not like the work particularly, but he prefers to do it rather than be left out of the group.

At the same time this hunger to be like and do like other people constitutes a potential danger. It tends to reduce physical and mental activity to the crowd-level of mediocrity, thus acting as a brake upon original thinking and progressive social organization. The schoolmaster's aim must be to exploit the useful aspects of the tendency while discouraging the dangers by promoting free discussion and sane experiments. It is also true that by joining a community with higher standards of living, an individual tends to rise to that level, and *vice versa*.

HUNGERS FOR SELF-ENHANCEMENT

This group of hungers is connected intimately with the maintenance of the individual's position with respect to his physical and social environment. The hungers are satisfied by success, mastery, domination, and excellence. The corresponding aversions are caused by failure, *forced* subordination, inferiority.

The term 'self-enhancement' has been used advisedly. It is awkward, but it signifies an essential factor in the operation of these hungers. They are all forms of self-assertion. The term 'self-assertion,' however, covers rather the 'behaviouristic' aspect of the activity. Coupled with self-assertion in all but the most crude types of activity is an element of *self-valuation*. The mere fact of successful self-assertion may be profoundly unsatisfactory to the person who asserts. The robust schoolboy of twelve years or so may jump over a hurdle a foot high, or spank an 'infant' of seven years. This is evidence of mastery, but it brings no particular elation. *It does not count in the development of his personal valuation.* On the other hand, to break the school high-jump record or thrash the school bully does produce tremendous elation and vastly increases the self-valuation.

In every aspect of life this group of hungers plays a most influential part. As motives they enter into almost every type of behaviour and purpose. Prestige is, on occasion, a stronger determinant of the national policy of a State than even economic factors.[1] ' Face-saving ' seems to be one of the major aims of industrial and political diplomacy. In human sex-relations two *motifs* constantly appear, namely, the wish to possess the loved one exclusively, and the wish to be loved for oneself alone. Again, sex-jealousy contains a strong prestige component. The anger of the jilted or neglected lover arises, not so much from frustration of the satisfaction of sex-hunger, as from the implication that *another person is judged to be superior.* The usual reactions of the rejected lover are either to injure the favoured one, or to achieve some outstanding success in another field. In both cases the reaction is one which confirms the rejected one's personal worth and restores, to some extent at least, the damaged self-valuation. This is aptly illustrated by a case quoted by Burt.

Harry, a dullard of sixteen, rejected by his youthful sweetheart, goes straight from his wooing and commits his first burglary. " I couldn't get her," he explains, " so I got old Ikey's cashbox." [2]

Many cases of petty delinquency turn out, on examination, to be compensations for damaged self-esteem. When the offender is placed in conditions such that satisfactory adjustment is possible, and the self-valuation thereby established at a higher level, the delinquent tendencies disappear.[3]

Mastery and success of some kind seem indispensable for the building up of strong character and stable personality. Without them self-respect is impossible. They encourage the attitudes of confidence and hope, and are essential elements in true courage. Habitual failure and inferiority produce despondency and despair, choke any positive effort, and end in the disintegration of personality with its accompaniment of mental disease.[4] This principle is of the greatest importance in teaching and school-organization.

[1] *E.g.*, the German demands for colonies after the peace-settlement of 1918. Note also how often Welsh nationalists speak of insults to Wales.

[2] *The Young Delinquent*, p. 451.

[3] See Burt, book cited, pp. 323 and *ff.*

[4] This is one of the social dangers of permanent unemployment.

The hungers for self-enhancement and their corresponding aversions are connected with the need of the living creature to maintain the integrity of its organism in face of environmental difficulty and opposition. In this connexion we can distinguish two aspects of the environment—physical and impersonal ; and social. Corresponding with these we can observe two ends for which people strive : (a) domination and mastery over physical situations and impersonal difficulties (such as a problem in mathematics) irrespective of the presence of a real or potential audience ; and (b) a position which, in some respect or other, is a mark of superiority over other people.

The following are some common manifestations of these hungers :

(a) (i) Striving for domination, e.g., performance of feats of brute strength which have the effect of bending the environment to one's will.

Manipulating powerful tools, e.g., guns and other weapons, machinery, motor-cars.

Mastering intellectual problems and moral difficulties.

In this connexion the presence of an audience, or the possibility of recounting the feats to a potential audience, enhances the elation and satisfaction, but the striving is directed primarily to mastery of the opposition itself.

(ii) Striving to achieve an impersonal standard of excellence.

The desire to excel may be due in the first place to a desire to surpass one's fellows. With the development of experience and intelligence, however, the complacence-level at which a performer is satisfied rises as ability and confidence increase. The performer then compares his present standard not with that of other people, but with his own previous performances and with a possible future performance which can be envisaged but is not at present realized.[1] What the *ideal* will be depends upon the performer's special aptitudes and training. It may be ideal skill in games or athletics ; ideal physical perfection and beauty ; designing and constructing an ideal building or a Utopia (an ideal society) ; achieving ideal moral excellence.

This striving to achieve perfection is the real spur to what is commonly called ' disinterested ' effort. As such it should be exploited to the full in any general education.

[1] *Cf.* p. 150.

(b) (i) Striving for domination over people, *e.g.*, political and industrial exploitation (not always due to economic necessity).

Carrying one's point in debate, thus impressing one's own opinion upon other people.

(ii) Striving for public approbation.

This is very often one partial motive for the production of works of art, for making scientific discoveries, for engaging in public work. In fact, it occasionally happens that the actual work is valued by the performer only as a means for securing the social fruits of success—a school pupil passing an examination to secure a publicly awarded prize ; or a wealthy adult practising philanthropy to achieve a knighthood (" for public services " as it is phrased in the honours lists).

(iii) Striving for ostentation, *e.g.*, eating off gold plates ; wearing more diamonds than anybody else ; inventing bizarre fashions ; [1] arranging superlatively expensive weddings (and funerals).

In connexion with the hungers for self-enhancement it is important to note that the level at which satisfaction is experienced is represented by a standard which may involve both qualitative and quantitative factors. Thus, satisfaction may depend upon quantitative achievement, *e.g.*, amount of wealth, degree of ostentation, batting average at cricket, etc. On the other hand, the level of satisfaction may be estimated in terms of value. Wealthy people may live simple unostentatious lives because they hold the conviction on rational, social or religious grounds that this type of living is socially more valuable and therefore more dignified. Similarly, one may meet a cricketer who is far more satisfied with an innings of fifty runs made without a flaw on a difficult wicket than he would be with an innings of a hundred runs, including several ' flukes,' on an easy wicket.

Thus the level at which complacence is stabilized will depend upon :

The general standards of living, both material and cultural, in the social group with which the individual identifies himself.

The variety of experiences of different social groups and standards of life enjoyed by the individual.

Degree of personal maturity.

Intelligence, *i.e.*, powers of logical analysis and comprehension of rational principles of value.

Quality of self-valuation.

---

[1] *Cf.* keeping pigs or tiger-cubs as drawing-room pets.

What makes this group of hungers so pervasive and powerful in personal development is the fact that the complacence-level is, in effect, a *level of aspiration* towards which the individual is strongly, sometimes irresistibly, attracted. A person's ' style ' of living is, very largely, the expression of his level of aspiration together with the directions in which the hungers for self-enhancement and their corresponding aversions have been determined by his native aptitudes and environmental opportunities.

The presence of a level of aspiration can be observed in many children at an early age, and it provides a continuous and powerful dynamic factor in their motivation, particularly when the level is skilfully adjusted to their abilities by the teacher. Experimental evidence of this fact will be submitted in the next chapter.

The above indicates a most important indirect educative function of schools and universities. By bringing together pupils and students from different local communities they make comparisons possible, even inevitable, and thus lead to a critical discrimination of values. Further, at their best, they represent a community with broad high standards of excellence to which the complacence-levels of the pupils may approximate. In particular the educative institutions should make available critical constructive guidance enabling the pupils to distinguish the impersonal and ideal standards of excellence from other less worthy standards.

By raising and refining standards of complacence a good school may leaven a whole community.

These hungers for self-enhancement have the two-directional quality. The person who is, or believes himself to be, in a position below his complacence-level will experience an aversion to his present situation and strive to reach the higher position. On the other hand, a person may find himself in a position surpassing his complacence-level. He also will experience an aversion, but will strive to return to the lower level. A young player may perform exceedingly well in a second team and be promoted there and then to the first team. Here the standard of play may be very much higher and the player find himself quite out of his ' class.' The resulting failure is a blow to his self-esteem and may be followed by a strong desire to return to a lower standard. The same difficulty may arise in a too rapid scholastic promotion of a promising but immature pupil. The danger is that the shock to the pupil's self-esteem may be severe enough to destroy his self-confidence and establish a *permanent* aversion against rising to a higher level. Therefore when any questions of promotion of younger pupils arise, either to a higher grade in academic work, or to a position of responsibility in the school social organization (*e.g.*, house captain, prefect), the staff should be as certain as possible that the pupil will be able to carry on with *at least average success* at the new standard.

THE FEELING OF SELF-ABASEMENT

One feeling-tone of considerable importance in school-work is that of self-abasement. It is a component of the complex feelings of awe, humility, gratitude, admiration, and it is invariably present in the attitude of a disciple towards his teacher or master.

During the presence of the feeling-tone the person experiencing it is much more than usually prone to imitate and to accept suggestions from the person admired. Self-abasement is an element in crude faith.[1] Such faith with its tendency towards uncritical subservence has its dangers. Nevertheless, some admixture of self-abasement makes learning easier. A completely self-assured, hyper-critical pupil may be as unprogressive as an unduly subservient pupil. He who criticizes everything believes nothing, and therefore does nothing of a positive nature. He criticizes the good as well as the bad and feels superior to both.

Fortunately, there is a golden mean between undue subservience and undiscerning criticism. The pupil can be encouraged to learn how to discriminate, and at the same time be encouraged to develop self-respect in due proportion. His self-valuation then keeps pace with his power of discrimination, and he will always be *willing to learn* from a proved and trustworthy authority.

Self-abasement is distinguishable from a feeling of mere inferiority.[2] The latter is unpleasant and sets up aversions, whereas self-abasement may be accompanied by deep satisfaction.[3] In self-abasement there is a tendency for the person concerned to *identify his personality with what is contemplated.* That being so,

[1] We may believe because we know that the object of belief is demonstrably true. We may believe without any sort of factual evidence or demonstration being considered necessary. The latter is crude faith.

[2] The reason is that self-abasement implies the presence of a ' sentiment,' whereas inferiority need not.

[3] As in the case of the devout worshipper contemplating the Divinity.

he feels absorbed within the powerful object of contemplation, and, seeming to be a part of it, he shares its might, and satisfies his wish for power or greatness indirectly.

One special set of inferiority-conditions needs careful note, namely, *physical disabilities*. Persons afflicted with lameness, hunchback, deformed limbs, squint, abnormal clumsiness, marked shortness of stature are usually very painfully aware of these disabilities and suffer an agonizing feeling of inferiority. The painful feeling is increased when public notice is attracted by the disability, and particularly when the person is the object of ridicule or contempt.

People afflicted in this way are often irritable, and unduly aggressive.[1] They attempt to compensate for their disability by constant attempts at domination. In some cases the sufferer makes intense efforts to achieve superiority in some form of learning or skill.

Teachers should make it an invariable rule never to call attention to a physical disability which is not the fault of a pupil. Ridicule of any kind is indefensible in such cases. Every effort should be made to render such a pupil happy in his surroundings, and to provide him with opportunities and encouragement to achieve success in directions compatible with the disability.

We now come to a group of hungers of immense importance in intellectual progress. They are :

Hunger for intellectual free movement.
Hunger for routine and system.
Hunger for explanation.

HUNGER FOR INTELLECTUAL FREE MOVEMENT

This hunger leads to what might be called adventures in ideas. It is a spur for practical experiment, theoretical speculation, and æsthetic creation. It is obvious that much scientific investigation as well as literary and other artistic activity is carried on in the direct service of other hungers. This will be appreciated if we attempt to discard all the work and knowledge connected with the production and distribution of food, water (in some form or other), and clothing ; the organization of efficient conditions of shelter, protection, warmth, coolness, ventilation, light, cleanliness, and sanitation ; the production of materials for adornment and

---

[1] One potent cause of behaviour-problems during puberty.

aids to beauty ; provision of opportunity for physical exercise and amusement, both individual and social ; and the satisfaction of sex-hunger.

However, after we have made due allowance for all this directly or indirectly *useful* work and knowledge, there remains a highly significant residuum which owes little if anything to immediate or even ultimate utility. This residuum is motivated by an urge to experience something new—what may be called ' pure curiosity.' This striving to encompass the unknown is admirably described in the well-known passage from St Paul's adventures in Athens.[1]

> Then certain philosophers of the Epicureans, and of the Stoics encountered him. And some said, " What will this babbler say ? " [2] Others said, " He seemeth to be a setter forth of strange gods." And they took him and brought him unto Areopagus saying, " May we know what this new doctrine, whereof thou speakest, is ? For thou bringest certain strange things to our ears ; we would know therefore what these things mean." (For all the Athenians and strangers which were there, *spent their time in nothing else but either to tell, or to hear some new thing*.)

The Apostle, being thus invited, began by saying, " As I passed by and beheld your devotions I found an altar with this inscription—TO THE UNKNOWN GOD."

This hunger for new experience *for its own sake* is strongest when all other needs are satisfied, that is, in times of peace, prosperity, and security. Also it bears a definite relation to the degree of intelligence of the individual who shows it. One of the most distressing features, from the teacher's point of view, of backward and mentally deficient children is the very low degree of this curiosity which they show. So soon as their primitive animal wants are satisfied they lapse into complacent lethargy. The hunger is particularly characteristic of normal children between the second and the sixth or seventh years, during the period when the world is new to their developing intelligence. Some people show a persistent hunger for new experience throughout life. Speaking of Sir Francis Galton, a writer says :

> In his wealth of novel ideas he is indeed without a parallel in the whole of modern psychology ; but his genius was of a roving rather than a persevering order. His insatiable curiosity constantly attracted

---

[1] Acts of the Apostles, Chapter xvii, verses 18–23. (The italics are mine.)

[2] Note the obvious implication of intellectual superiority in the natives over the foreigner. (*Cf*. Hunger for Self-enhancement.)

him to new problems, to each of which in turn he brought to bear his characteristic energy, originality, and courage. . . . From fashions to finger-prints, from the geographical distribution of female beauty to the application of statistics to prize-giving, from weight-lifting to the future of the race, nothing lacked interest to this ingenious, versatile, and all enquiring mind.[1]

In the majority, unfortunately, the appetite for new know-ledge is beginning to abate by the time they reach the secondary school, partly because their hunger has been satisfied—they know enough for their immediate needs—more particularly because the schools have been very slow in studying and discovering ways of encouraging this extremely valuable hunger. If we may use such an analogy, the schools have specialized in supplying chaff instead of bread !

Nevertheless, the hunger does persist to some degree in a majority of people, and can be developed by the use of suitable incentives. It is important to note that the most powerful incentive is *not the unknown, but the partially known.* If the presented situation be absolutely novel, it will be passed by unnoted, for the simple reason that it will not be connected in any way with the observer's past or present experiences.[2] The possibility of pro-ducing new species of grasses which shall be more palatable, more nutritive, earlier to appear in spring, faster to grow and later to cease growing, is not a problem for sheep although it concerns them closely. It is not a problem to a townsman on a country walk. He believes there is only one kind of grass and therefore does not envisage the possibility of rearing others. It is a problem and therefore an incentive to the scientific agriculturist who *has noted varieties of grasses* and who begins to wonder at their variety and how they arise, and who realizes that some are more prolific than others.

Before a situation arouses this intellectual curiosity we need to possess some knowledge relevant to it and to suspect there is other possible knowledge not yet discovered.

A simple example is afforded by observation of a loose end of a rope. If we walk alongside a high wall and see a rope-end dangling over it we experience a strong tendency to follow the rope visually. We infer the existence of the remainder of the rope, but cannot verify

---

[1] J. C. Flugel, *A Hundred Years of Psychology*, p. 126.
[2] *Cf.* Chapter VI.

the inference directly. *The tendency to follow the rope visually is checked before the conation is satisfied.* Then we adopt a questioning attitude and wonder what is on the other side, and feel a desire to look over the wall to find out.

Any departure from a normal expected sequence of events, any real or apparent contradictions are occasions for the display of this hunger.[1]

HUNGER FOR ROUTINE AND SYSTEM

When we have gathered more unrelated experiences than we can comprehend together we begin to feel some aversion to further exploration. We want a system. We desire to group the experiences into some sort of order which can be grasped easily and used with a feeling of mastery. Having made a system both in our ideas and our material environment, we can reduce thinking and behaviour to a routine which represents a condition of least action.

Hunger for routine may be observed quite early in child-development. Young children insist on being dressed in a prescribed way. Their games must be played strictly according to a formula. Stories must conform strictly to the letter of the originals.

In adults we find a strong aversion to a haphazard, constantly shifting environment. Such a condition demands continuous alertness. It sets up conflicts in the attention-process. It is extremely tiring and consequently very unpleasant. We begin to experience a hunger for rest and peace. So soon as we find ourselves in a state of chaos, we set about creating a stable system. This applies to political and religious beliefs as well as to office and school-management.

This desire for routine and system seems to be connected with (a) the tendency of any physical system to adjust itself so that there is the least possible expenditure of energy, (b) the increasing facility which habit gives to performance, (c) the hunger for mastery and domination.

What we can do easily and skilfully gives us the feeling of mastery and satisfies that hunger. This fact constitutes a danger to progressive learning. We prefer the first routines which satisfy our needs. To depart from them promises disorder, unpleasantness, and a feeling of inferiority which we desire to avoid. For progressive learning we must steer a middle way between chaos and complete systematization.

[1] See N. Isaacs' appendix on *Epistemic Questions* in *Intellectual Growth of Young Children.*

This tendency to cling to habits which, while relatively inefficient, are easy to acquire at first and therefore bring premature complacence is important for teachers of technical processes (*e.g.*, shorthand, typewriting, playing a musical instrument). It is very desirable to train the pupils from the outset in efficient methods before they have developed the inefficient habits. Too early complacence is thereby prevented and there is not the same distressing tendency for the pupils to resist further training.

HUNGER FOR EXPLANATION

This is a variant of the hunger for routine and system. It arises whenever we experience an event, or receive an idea which does not fit into its environment. A novel experience disturbs our system of habits and beliefs. We seek to incorporate the novel event within our established systems. When the novel event can be restated in terms of already familiar experience it is thereby ' explained ' and we are satisfied.

The completeness of the explanation varies with the intelligence and knowledge of the observer. The small child will accept any likely analogy as a sufficient explanation, *e.g.*, the moon is a glass globe with an electric bulb inside it. The scientific worker is more exacting. He demands that the novel experience shall be *demonstrated logically* to be a particular case of an already established general law (*e.g.*, Newton's explanation of the motion of the moon). In both cases, achieving the explanation brings great satisfaction.

Here again the hunger for system and explanation is so strong that even well-educated people are constrained to adopt, *and cling to*, the first hypothesis or the easiest hypothesis which appears in any way to fit the case. Thereupon, the satisfaction aroused by the relief of unpleasant tension, and by securing an apparently sound foundation for belief and action, is so intense that not only is further research and analysis stopped, but *it may be resisted altogether* by the interested parties. This is a common occurrence even in scientific research.

SOME SUBSIDIARY PRINCIPLES OF MOTIVATION

Having differentiated and described the characteristics of the hungers of most importance in teaching and school-organization, we must now take note of certain subsidiary principles which govern the working and interaction of these hungers.

1. SUBSTITUTE-SATISFACTION OF HUNGERS—SUBLIMATION

It may happen that *direct* satisfaction of a hunger is prevented by social conditions. It is necessary to consider how *substitute-satisfaction* may be possible.

Such satisfaction is desirable, since the hungers represent a flow of energy directed towards the means of satisfaction. This energy arises from physiological processes within the organism, and it resembles a flow of energy in any physical system. In particular it obeys the law of conservation. This implies that the energy *cannot be destroyed*. It may be dissipated and, from the point of view of useful work, wasted. It may also be directed from its normal course into alternative channels.

Young children crave for mastery over their environment. This latter, however, has been organized mainly for the convenience of full-grown adults. Consequently, the child's small stature, limited strength, and crude skill are quite inadequate to enable him to behave towards his environment as adults can. Since the adult's behaviour signifies mastery to the child, he craves to behave like an adult but cannot obtain *direct* satisfaction for his craving.

The hunger for free movement is very strong in children. They want to run, jump, dance, throw stones, shout, and so forth. But any direct satisfaction of this hunger may be extremely inconvenient in a well-organized [1] and expensively furnished house, garden, or school.

Hunger for sex-experience is strong in later adolescence. Direct satisfaction of this hunger is difficult in normal civilized economic and social conditions. Premature and promiscuous sexual intercourse lead to consequences which the community in general finds intolerable.

These three examples have been chosen because they frequently occur in everyday educational and social conditions. They are, however, only typical of many other situations in ordinary life. The problem now arises—what should be done when circumstances make impossible or socially intolerable the direct satisfaction of a hunger.

The first response of an unreflective adult community (*i.e.*, parents, teachers, elders of the Church, local government authorities) is to ignore the hunger and assume that it is not a fact. Ignoring the hunger, however, does not remove it. Sooner or later, it may be manifested in grossly anti-social behaviour. This is then met by prohibitions enforced by punishment.

[1] Well-organized, that is, from the adult point of view.

Prohibition and punishment do not remove the hunger. Aversion from the punishment may be strong enough temporarily to prevent any *direct* satisfaction, but it has the effect of ' bottling up ' the energy at the service of the hunger, *making the craving for satisfaction even more intense.* The repressed energy will then force outlets in the form of *substitute-satisfactions.*

If we will bear in mind that we are using an analogy and not stating a fact, it is convenient to compare the repression of the satisfaction of a hunger with the damming up of a stream of running water. The energy of the stream is not destroyed by the dam, although the normal *course* of the stream is stopped. The energy accumulates behind the dam. To maintain the stoppage, the dam must be made continually bigger and stronger. Even so, the water will finally overflow in some other direction, or make for itself devious subterranean outlets. Hence, in building dams, engineers invariably provide controlled channels through which the water may escape, and, in so doing, they can often *use its accumulated energy in useful work.* Or they provide some means of escape which though economically useless, is at the same time harmless.

This analogy is useful, for it suggests that the teacher and social worker can apply the engineers' principles to the control of human behaviour. Substitute-satisfactions may take various forms. Some of these are socially undesirable ; some even may be secret and dangerous perversions. At the same time, others are socially harmless, and still others may be personally and socially useful.

Consider the examples cited. The young child craves for mastery over his environment. His very immaturity effectively prevents his mastery in an environment designed for adults. The child may seek a substitute-satisfaction in *day-dreaming.* He imagines what he will do when he grows up. He dreams himself into a kind of fairyland in which his craving for mastery would be satisfied. This is one form of secret, ' subterranean ' outlet for the hunger-energy. It is socially harmless, but may be personally dangerous. The child's fairyland may be, in fact usually is, a very distorted version of the actual reality he will meet when he does grow up. His day-dreams may not issue in action at all. Therefore he will derive from them no adequate training for the future. Further, the day-dreams may be so seductive that the dreamer gets into the habit of seeking his satisfaction in them and retreating from the reality when he finds it difficult in some respect.

In a reflective progressive community, the child's craving for mastery is acknowledged. In this case, realizing that full direct satisfaction is physically impossible, and that day-dreaming is a not altogether desirable substitute, the adults endeavour to create an artificial environment *which will provide a substitute-satisfaction and at the same time guide the hunger energy into socially useful channels.* In other words, the child's physical environment is reduced in scale so that he can effectively master it. In the modern infant school-room we find miniature armchairs and tables. There are real pegs for hats, coats, and school-bags, but they are placed within easy reach of the child's arms. There are real cupboards, but low enough for infants to use without the indignity of having to be lifted by an adult, or having to stand on tiptoe on a chair.

In this miniature environment the child does not obtain full and direct satisfaction for his craving for mastery. He is not yet an adult, and he is not dealing with the adult's environment. Nevertheless, in his miniature environment he can behave *as if he were an adult,* and since the two environments are similar, the child in mastering his miniature environment is learning *valuable habits of social skill which will be applicable in the real adult environment later.* A well-conducted modern nursery-school approximates very closely to a miniature social system in which the adults present play only an unobtrusive rôle. The feature of such schools most frequently noted by lay observers is the dignity of the young persons who make up the community and the serious way in which they carry out their miniature social responsibilities. *They have achieved the status of persons.*

The child in the dead-silent classroom of the traditional school seeks satisfaction for his hunger for free movement in day-dreams. That means that his attention is diverted from the school-work. In addition he becomes fidgety and irritable under the irksome restraint and this leads to difficulties of class-order. Indiscipline is always liable to break out. Moreover, the child develops a strong aversion from the school and school-work and strives to avoid it.

In modern educational practice systematic attempts have been made to harness the energy of the hunger for free movement *by making the school-work itself a source of substitute-satisfaction. School-subjects are presented as activities.* Familiar examples are practical manipulation and measurement in arithmetic and geometry ; experimental science ; gardening ; field work in botany, zoology, geography ; dramatization in literature ; constructive art and craft work ; physical training, dancing, eurhythmics, **organized games.**

It should be noted that these subject-activities do not all provide *direct* satisfactions for the hunger for *free* movement. Measurements, experiments with scientific apparatus, constructive art and handwork, physical training, and even organized games have to be carried out according to definite rules and with instruments or tools which impose their own restrictions upon the operators. Hence any formal instruction and practice in these activities must not be undertaken too soon in the child's school life ; and no matter how full of *organized* activity and games the school programme may be, some time must be allowed for each pupil during which he is as free as possible from any artificial restriction on his natural movements and rhythms. In this respect probably the most directly satisfying school-activities are eurhythmics and informal dramatization. In these the pupil imposes his own interpretation upon the music or words.[1]

Nevertheless, the subject-activities mentioned in the previous paragraph do provide controlled channels for the expenditure of the energy of free movement and make a very good substitute for direct satisfaction. In the light of this principle of substitute-satisfaction we can appreciate more fully Dr Ballard's assertion [2] that where handwork has been introduced into the curriculum, problems of class-order disappear and the pupils' whole attitude towards the school and school-work is changed.

The adolescent's ' subterranean ' outlet for the energy of sex-hunger is erotic day-dreaming and various forms of self-abuse. These substitute-satisfactions are both personally and socially undesirable. Several types of healthy substitute-satisfaction are available. We may note the study of romantic literature ; the presentation of stage-plays, particularly tragedies, in which the ' love-interest ' is shown in relation to wider problems of social life ; sane discussion of sex-problems ; study of reproductive processes in scientific biology ; attempts by pupils at creative work in art and craft ; dancing ; ' mixed ' games, such as tennis and badminton ; organized social functions in which members of both sexes take part. By participating in these activities adolescents not only find substitute-satisfactions for sex-hunger, but they may also learn something of the courtesies and responsibilities which will be indispensable in their adult lives.

[1] There are also percussion bands for young children and country dancing for everybody.
[2] See *Handwork as an Educational Medium*.

The concepts of energy-flow and substitute-satisfaction are fundamental in psycho-analytic literature. There the energy represented by the various hungers is called 'libido,' and when energy is diverted from the normal course of direct satisfaction into channels of substitute-satisfaction it is said to be *sublimated*. The concept of sublimation is most important in social development.

This principle of substitute-satisfactions raises a point of great importance in general social education. The school must fulfil a wider social function than that of providing academic *instruction* in subject-matter and professional skill only. It is essential that the school shall organize, in addition, a variety of healthy satisfactions and make those pleasures habitual. The more the pupils find interest in literature, science, arts and crafts, music and dancing, dramatics, organized games, the less will they be inclined to seek satisfaction in the cruder pleasures of eating, drinking, sex, and personal domination by brute strength. Particularly does the school owe this duty to those pupils whose home-life is drab and restricted. Education in substitute-satisfactions is essential for the growth of well-balanced personalities and stable social organization. This seems to be the essential significance of 'education for leisure.'

II. MUTUAL INTERACTION OF HUNGERS

We have discussed distinguishable hungers as if they acted in isolation. In actual life this is never the case. There we find, always, *some person who experiences* more or less clearly recognizable hungers.

Occasionally we are not quite clear about what kind of a hunger it is that we experience. It is possible to feel a vague restlessness, an indeterminate want or aversion. We cannot locate the source of it, nor determine what exactly we wish to do about it. We just feel a mild wish to do something.

However, when the conation becomes definite and we realize what we are hungry for, the hunger does not operate in isolation. It is influenced by the general condition of the organism and by other hungers which may be more or less active at the same time. In this way, human motive is almost invariably complex. This fact has certain important implications for the teacher.

When a hunger is active it controls for the time being the

interest of the person and makes him prone to attend only to those signs in the situation connected with the satisfaction of the hunger. We may ask, therefore, what is likely to happen when two or more hungers are active simultaneously. Two alternatives are possible : (a) the hungers will co-operate and reinforce the motive ; (b) the hungers will conflict, thereby competing for control of the attention-process, and the use of habit systems and ideas. The connexion of these two alternatives with interest and success in school-work is obvious.

Hungers co-operate and reinforce motive

Consider a food-hungry child who is averse to darkness. Suppose he is about nine or ten years old and his hunger for self-enhancement is strong. The food he desires may be in a dark pantry, at night. His food-hunger drives him towards the dark pantry. His aversion from darkness keeps him away. He oscillates between going and staying away. At the same time he wants to think of himself as strong, brave, and manly. He is averse to weakness and cowardice. The two motives food-hunger and hunger for self-enhancement reinforce each other and together may be stronger than the aversion to darkness. Then, although the boy may go with a shudder, and return in an undignified hurry, nevertheless he does go to get the food, and satisfaction in eating is intensified by the satisfaction of his hunger for self-enhancement. He has proved his courage in the act of getting food.

This principle is important in that some school-work is both necessary, and at the same time inherently uninteresting to some pupils. The teacher must seek to induce his pupils to attack this kind of school-work by arranging conditions so that several partial motives in favour of the work are compounded together, finally becoming strong enough to overcome the aversion against the work.

Conversely, of course, two or more aversions may be compounded to overcome an undesirable hunger.

Hungers may conflict and dissipate motive

In this case oscillating indecisive behaviour ensues until either the individual is exhausted or one hunger becomes so intense that it takes priority over the other and thus determines the conflict in its favour.

Consider the food-hungry child at the age of about three years, before the desire to be considered manly has been well differentiated. He may approach the dark place. As he gets nearer, his aversion to darkness increases till it is stronger than the food-hunger and he retreats.[1] As he retreats, his hunger for security is temporarily satisfied and the food-hunger takes control. Again he approaches the dark place. If the child is intelligent and circumstances are favourable he may resolve the conflict satisfactorily by varying his methods. He may take a light into the pantry. He thus removes his aversion to the darkness, and makes it possible to satisfy his food-hunger also. He may persuade an older person to go with him. If he is very intelligent he will persuade the older person to go and get the food for him.

This competition for the attention-process is always liable to arise in pupils during school-hours. The teacher's problem is not to make the pupils interested. It is to ensure that they shall be *so much more interested in school-work than in outside pursuits* that they will spontaneously attend to the school-work. Further, having induced the pupils to attend, the teacher must be careful not to allow other conflicts for attention to arise until the work in hand is completed.

III. ORDER OF PRIORITY OF HUNGERS

It is important to note an approximate order of priority of the hungers. Those of our first group (p. 95) will claim priority, in case of conflict, over the hungers in the second group. Of those in the first group, the hungers for food, drink, fresh air, and excretion will claim priority over the others in the same group, if a conflict is continued to extreme limits. These basic hungers are essential for the immediate welfare of the creature.

This order of priority bears directly upon problems of interest-control and class-order. In most schools as they are at present constituted, the subject-matter of instruction directly or indirectly satisfies the hungers in group (*b*). The pupils in school, however, cannot be separated from the same pupils as they exist out-of-school. They are not intellectual abstractions, or machines for registering dates and formulæ, and performing habits of reading, writing, and calculating. The effects of the pupils' social and economic circumstances will be carried into the classroom.

Now suppose, as is only too frequently the case in distressed

---

[1] *Cf.* the timid adult with a toothache trying to decide to go to the dentist.

areas, that pupils are ill-nourished ; insufficiently clad ; verminous ; or suffering from some minor but distressing ailments. Pupils may be tired, due to insufficient sleep in over-crowded living conditions, or having to work at home ; or (as in some rural areas) travelling long distances to school. Some pupils may be anxious for their immediate security. They may have been threatened with a ' hiding ' by an irate parent or older pupil. On the other hand some pupils may have been fed unwisely and too well. They have stomach-aches and feel sick.

These conditions will set up primary hungers and aversions which will control the pupils' attention-adjustments to the exclusion of school-work. If the teacher attempts to force the attention of these pupils, instead of achieving his aim he merely makes things worse by adding further basic aversions to reinforce those already working against school-interest.

Fatigue due to a hard day's work frequently prevents evening-school students and adults in extra-mural (University Extension, or Workers' Educational Association) classes from concentrating their attention upon their studies. Such students crave sleep.

Before such pupils are capable of paying adequate attention to their school-work they must have their primary hungers and aversions satisfied. They must be adequately fed, reasonably clean, sufficiently clothed and rested, and free from minor ailments. They must also be comfortable and secure in school.

The power of primary hungers to control the attention-process has not met with sufficient recognition, partly because teachers and education authorities generally belong to the more fortunate section of society whose lives are well ordered. They seldom, if ever, find themselves in conditions of extreme privation.

The effect of constant hunger and great muscular exertion is well described by Major Priestley.[1] He says that the diet of a man-hauling sledge party in Polar exploration " leaves the party with a craving which nothing can allay but the next meal, and that, but for all too short a time. The effect of this hunger upon the waking mind is to *concentrate the thoughts upon every variety of savoury food that the individual has known*. Its effect in sleep is to *lead to a succession of food dreams* which carry the dreamer from one paradise of the gourmand to another until he awakes to find the craving for food almost unbearable. The normally constituted party talk food, think food, dream food." [2]

---

[1] " The Psychology of Exploration," *Psyche*, Vol. II, No. 1, 1921. (The italics are mine.)

[2] See also Koestler, *A Spanish Testament*.

Unfortunately, the teacher has no direct control over the satisfaction of these hungers. That depends upon the condition of parents, upon the general economic conditions and social conscience of the community. It has slowly dawned upon successive governments and public education authorities that any kind of organized instruction is merely an expensive waste of time and money unless the pupils are in a fit condition to concentrate upon their studies. Hence, in spite of many vociferous protests from vested interests of all kinds, education authorities now make some attempts at least to supplement the distressed pupils' food and clothing ; to provide adequate school-buildings and furniture ; to maintain a system of medical inspection, and treatment for dental and other minor ailments. Also children are prevented by law from undue employment out-of-school ; protected from serious neglect or harsh treatment by parents ; and, when schools are re-organized, transported at public expense to and from school.

One rather frequent cause of exploitation is often forgotten, namely, the custom of expecting girls of school-age to do more than their share of the domestic work of the house. Many girls, even in secondary schools, are unpaid domestic servants as well as school-pupils.

Those classroom-conditions listed on p. 98 will arouse primary hungers which compete successfully for the attention-processes and thereby interfere with a pupil's progress. In such conditions pupils strive to escape instead of striving to master the work, and no matter how the teacher may threaten or persevere the aversions will win in the end. Some of these bad conditions are due to poor buildings and equipment and are beyond the teacher's immediate control. Others, however, depend directly upon the teacher himself and can be remedied.

Exercises

1. Analyse your own motives in such cases as the following :
   (a) Choosing your favourite subject.
   (b) Choosing a profession.
   (c) Attending a particular lecture.
   (d) Going (or not going) to church on Sundays.
   (e) Studying a ' dry ' subject instead of idling (or not doing so as the case may be).
   (f) Putting on your best clothes to go to a dance.

Compare notes about the same topics with other people.

How far are your statements real reasons, or merely excuses ?

2. Study some cases of combination and conflict of motives both in literary examples (novels, biography, drama) and in real life.

3. Students of literature may consider how far ' tragedy ' is the portrayal of an irresolvable conflict of hungers within a personality. (Cf. *Kristin Lavransdatter, Gone with the Wind, Hamlet*.)

4. Follow up the concept of conflict of hungers and consequent competition for the attention-processes by studying the conditions which lead to lapses of memory, and the causes of insanity. (See, for example, Hart, *The Psychology of Insanity*.)

5. Collect examples of sublimation both in school and in social affairs.

How far can war be avoided by organized sublimation of the hunger for mastery ?

6. Note actual examples in school-pupils and fellow-students of each of the hungers (and the corresponding aversions) listed in this chapter.

7. Compare this classification and description of hungers with McDougall's list of " primary instincts " and Thorndike's " original satisfyers and annoyers."

Books for Further Reference

See Bibliographies at ends of Chapters III and V

CHAPTER V

ORGANIZING INTEREST IN SCHOOL-WORK

We have now to consider how the principles of motivation set forth in the two previous chapters can be applied in the practical work of organizing interest. The principles are quite general. They apply to children of various ages as well as to adults, and can be used in social and industrial problems as well as in normal teaching. Here we must restrict the discussion more particularly to the problems of teachers in primary and secondary schools. The section on motivation of monotonous repetitive work is important for teachers of technical subjects involving a high degree of skill.

Before discussing practical procedures in detail we must glance at one or two preliminary problems.

WHAT IS INTEREST ?

In the psychological meaning of the term, interest is a condition of a living creature when experiencing a hunger or aversion.

Interest is revealed in *consciousness* as feelings of urge, want, desire, appetite, craving, and wonder. When we are interested, the object of interest is felt to concern us, to have a value for us, to be worth striving for.

Interest is revealed in *behaviour* by such signs as the following :
Tense, eager alertness.
Readiness to act.
Anticipation of the next phase of a developing situation. (*Cf.* animal hunting its prey.)
Persistent effort towards a given end-point with varying means.
Actions which indicate impatience and irritation when the end-situation is delayed.
Teachers need to observe children and note carefully the external signs of interest (and of its absence !). The external signs are indications of the pupils' inner condition.

OUGHT WE TO MAKE SCHOOL-WORK INTERESTING ?

So far we have taken for granted that it is desirable to make school-work interesting. This assumption is by no means universally accepted. It is said that " the play-way boy makes the work-shy man " and " to teach children through interest is to lead them along the broad and easy path of self-indulgence." The real objection behind these views is that teaching through interest is not conducive to either intellectual or moral discipline, for which some measure of difficulty and persistent effort are essential.

The fallacy in these objections to what is called " soft pedagogy " consists in identifying interest with self-gratification. The people making them have failed to distinguish between *interest* and *interests*.

Interest is the *subjective feeling of value* which we experience when striving. This feeling implies some end-point, an object or situation in which we are interested, and for which we strive. Such objects or situations are the interests.

Now we can distinguish between two broad classes of interests : (a) those in which the objective sought is some form of self-gratification ; and (b) objectives other than self-gratification. This distinction may be seen in the case of food-interest. If we are food-hungry the primary objective is the food itself. The pleasure in eating is incidental, serving merely to prolong the process of eating until sufficient food has been eaten. However, some kinds of food are more pleasant than others. By reason of our intellectual equipment we can distinguish the pleasure of eating from the process of eating itself. Then we tend to establish a scale of pleasures, and the pleasure to be derived from some kinds of food may become the primary object of eating, the food itself becoming incidental. We may eat, that is to say, merely to secure delightful perceptions of taste and smell.

Eating for self-gratification may become a real danger. It is a well-known fact that we become adapted (*i.e.*, complacent) to a given degree of pleasure. Thereupon we cease to feel pleasure. The stimulation has lost its ' kick ' as we say in our elegant modern phraseology. Therefore if our objective is self-gratification we seek ever more intense forms of pleasure. This constitutes the danger, since, *if we choose our food for its pleasure-producing qualities only, it soon ceases to have any due relation to the primary needs of the body as a whole.* The food-hunger is perverted. At its logical (or illogical) extreme the process ends in the eater trying to subsist on Worcester Sauce and jam. This inevitably ends in digestive disorders, disease, and loss of physical and social efficiency.

The objections to systematic self-gratification are evident.

The process has *moral* and *social* implications. The physical degeneration which inevitably follows systematic self-gratification offends our ideal of what a healthy individual should be. In the second place, the unhealthy and degenerate person is economically inefficient and becomes a liability to his family and the community. Other people, as well as himself, suffer from the unfortunate consequences of his self-gratification.

What is true of food-hunger is equally true of all the other hungers. Therefore there is a very good ground for the objections to interests of self-gratification. However, so soon as we realize the fact that some interests (what we may call objective interests) do not involve self-gratification, the objections against teaching through interest break down.

By teaching through interest we shall mean here encouraging objective interests in the pupils. This process is not only quite compatible with moral and intellectual discipline but inseparable from it. We shall see later that difficulty itself is quite often a strong incentive to persistent effort.

Educationally, the most valuable interests are those which involve creating things. It matters little (from an *educational* point of view) whether the thing made is a drawing, a toy, a working model, literary composition, scientific hypothesis or moral character. Even making money is better than making nothing at all. What is actually made will depend on the intelligence, skill, maturity, inclination, and training of the person concerned. The educational importance lies in the striving to create something, the effort put into the making, and the gains in knowledge and skill which result from the process.

PROMOTING INTEREST ELIMINATES DRUDGERY BUT NOT HARD WORK

By drudgery is meant monotonous work performed under external compulsion, when the worker has no realization of the ends to be achieved by it. It has, therefore, no value for the worker and produces strong aversions.

Actually, drudgery is the most fertile cause of self-gratification. Life without some degree of pleasure is intolerable for human beings. If the pleasure is not attainable through constructive intellectual or physical work it will inevitably be sought in self-gratification. It is common knowledge—out of school at least— that the happiest people, and the people least prone to seek self-gratification, are those who have clearly realized objective and constructive interests in life. On the other hand, people without such interests are prone to nervous and physical disorders, and all kinds of perversions. Self-gratification of some kind is their only hope of satisfaction.

When interest in some constructive end is present, much monotonous and tiresome work will be undertaken with vigour, *without external compulsion*, because the end in view is valued by the learner, and the connexion between work and end is clearly realized.

IMMEDIATE AND MEDIATE INTEREST

Actually there are not several kinds of interest but it is convenient for teaching-purposes to note two ways in which objects and situations (including school-subjects) may become interesting :

(*a*) Interest may arise because the object or situation is the appropriate means of satisfying a hunger, *e.g.*, food is interesting to the food-hungry person. In this case the interest is said to be *immediate* or *direct*.

(*b*) Interest may arise because the object or situation has been associated with a directly interesting experience, *e.g.*, a restaurant-sign may be, in itself, a perfectly indifferent object, but it becomes interesting to a food-hungry person because of its probable association with food. In this case the interest is said to be *mediate*, *indirect*, or *derived*.

PRACTICAL PROCEDURES FOR ORGANIZING INTEREST

We can best begin our main discussion by summarizing the conditions of interest, namely :

We deal in practice with a person who is interested

It is essential to keep this apparently obvious but frequently forgotten fact clearly in view in all our thinking about interest. In psychological discussion we have to consider interest and attention as abstractions, but in actual life they are *always functions of the person as a whole*. From this fact follow certain important corollaries :

Interest will be determined not only by conditions at the moment in school, but also by conditions of the pupils' out-of-school lives, by their previous life-histories, and by their native endowments.

Hungers may co-operate and reinforce interest.

Hungers may conflict and cancel out interest. In this case certain hungers will claim priority over others in the competition for the available attention-adjustments, action-systems, physical and mental energy.

If direct satisfactions are not available the interested person will seek and accept substitute-satisfactions.

Interest will spread by subconscious ' conditioning,' and by conscious association, from directly interesting objects or situations to otherwise indifferent details which may happen to be connected with them.

Ideas and the motor mechanisms of action are developed in the service of the hungers. This is equivalent to saying that knowledge and skill are accumulated in the course of satisfying hungers or removing aversions. In the absence of any kind of hunger or aversion, knowledge and skill have neither value nor meaning.

Direction of Striving

We strive for any object or situation which seems likely to satisfy a hunger, or remove an aversion, either directly or indirectly.

We are complacent towards and tend to ignore :

> Any object or situation not connected directly or by association with satisfying a hunger, or removing an aversion.
>
> Any situation in which a hunger has been satisfied for the time being.
>
> Any situation which remains constant and shows no likelihood of developing (*cf.* monotonous repetitive tasks, monotonous conditions of stimulation, ' plateauperiods ').

We are averse to and strive to avoid :

> Conditions of over- and under-stimulation.
>
> Conditions of over- and under-satisfaction.
>
> Conditions of constraint in which we are *forced* to maintain a period of rest or activity unduly.

PRACTICAL PROCEDURES CLASSIFIED

We can now make a convenient classification of the practical procedures available for organizing interest in school-work. They are :

> **Removing aversions by organizing suitable conditions in school and classroom.**

Selection of subject-matter and educational activities which will provide either direct or substitute-satisfaction for hungers.

Skilful presentation of subject-matter and arrangement of exercises for practice.

Organizing incentives when work is intrinsically uninteresting.

REMOVING AVERSIONS DUE TO SCHOOL AND CLASSROOM CONDITIONS

This group has been placed first because the general school and classroom-conditions are a constant background for all the positive educational activities. Further, many teachers, both beginners and others, get so immersed in the details of their subject-matter that they neglect these conditions.

It is no exaggeration to say that most children have associated schools first and foremost with aversions, and this is equivalent to saying that they have been in explicit or sub-conscious conflict with school-conditions. The ideal school would be a place to which pupils enjoy going. This ideal has actually been achieved by some schools, particularly nursery and infant schools. However, even if this ideal cannot be reached, it is possible to make every school which is fit for human habitation a place to which children are not unwilling to go.

The most frequent aversions can be classified into three groups according as they are connected primarily with (1) buildings and equipment ; (2) the teacher ; (3) school-regulations.

BUILDINGS AND EQUIPMENT

Here we are concerned with conditions of over- and under-stimulation and physical constraint. The chief difficulties arise from poor ventilation, bad lighting, incorrect room-temperatures, unsatisfactory seating-accommodation, and lack of sufficient space for some degree of free movement (change of posture and of occupation).

We should cultivate a habit of attending to the pupils' physical comfort before commencing each lesson, and during the lessons. The aim should be to arrange the conditions of normal stimulation which induce in the pupils a feeling of physical satisfaction, general well-being, and security. All their mental activity can then be concentrated upon their work without the competition of primary hungers which are soon set up by bad conditions.

Some difficulties, of course, will be beyond the teacher's control. Lighting, heating, ventilation, classroom-space, playgrounds, and equipment depend largely upon the provision which the Local Education Authority is able or willing to make. Nevertheless an intelligent teacher, careful for the welfare of the pupils, can often mitigate the effects of bad conditions by making the best use of the facilities available. It is wise to enlist the co-operation of the pupils themselves in arranging expedients. This helps to promote social consciousness and public spirit, and the very fact that the teacher is interested in their welfare will often remove the bitterness felt by children on account of the bad conditions, even if it is impossible to remove them.

THE TEACHER

Personal characteristics and manner

In every social situation outside schools charm of manner is a highly credited characteristic considered to be well worth taking some pains to cultivate, while in school it is frequently conspicuous by its absence. Yet children of all ages are particularly susceptible to the influence of a pleasant, kindly, dignified, humorous, and tolerant personality and respond eagerly even though they may not find his subject-matter particularly fascinating. Many children, in well-to-do homes as well as in slums, are treated with indifference or even regarded as nuisances. Such children are often pathetically eager for friendship, sympathy, and encouragement.

Conditions have improved very much since 1900, but one still detects a tendency to make schools feel like prisons and penitentiaries, with the teachers acting as warders or officers of correction. Now the pupils are required to attend school, and they are not in a position openly to criticize the teacher's manner and his method of conducting class-work. They feel this disability and it makes their real or fancied injustices the harder to bear without resentment. Hence we should seek at the outset to establish a happy personal contact with the pupils, such as will exercise a civilizing and liberalizing influence upon their lives.

It is not denied that most children, if they are robust and healthy, are mischievous, and a few are vicious, perverted by bad hereditary endowment or unwise treatment. It is necessary to be firm and establish reasonable class order. The fact is, however,

E

that firmness and order are welcomed by children when connected
with a teacher whom they trust and respect. Moreover, reproof
from such a teacher has much more influence on their conduct
than punishment from one whom they dislike.

Some points to note in this connexion are : cultivate a pleasant
voice with clear diction, and avoid monotony in delivery ; avoid
unnecessary mannerisms and noisy movements ; *look at, and speak
to the class as though personally interested in each pupil* ; avoid
sarcasm, superior aloofness, and disdain. In particular do not
punish for faults made in ignorance. Generally speaking, treat
pupils with the consideration and courtesy due to them as persons.
This encourages the development of their self-respect.

Methods of Presentation

All really good teachers are ' artists,' and their lessons have a
distinct entertainment value. Teaching should be serious in its
purpose, but that is not identical with dulless in presentation. It
is a great gain if pupils are attracted by the lessons, even if they
do not like the subject.

In particular we should avoid long oral expositions and
academic lectures, and provide a reasonable variety of occupation.
This keeps pupils busy and reduces boredom.

SCHOOL-REGULATIONS

Regulations are inevitable. The school-authorities must
organize a stable routine in which pupils can ' settle down ' comfortably and know what is expected of them. Again, the great
majority of children prefer an ordered habitual routine which at
the same time allows them a reasonable freedom of choice and
inclination.

Regulations should be made the means to an end, the end
being social economy and efficiency. If the purpose of the
regulations is simply and clearly indicated even young children
can understand their necessity and value, and will accept them
willingly.

The practical problem is to steer a middle way between under-
organization which inevitably leads to slackness, chaos, and
frustration, and meticulous over-organization in which every
detail of every minute is prescribed and carried out by numbers.
This latter condition breeds very strong aversions and leads
inevitably to evasion or open rebellion.

The regulations should be as few as possible and clearly worded. They must be administered impartially and *must be honoured by the staff* as well as obeyed by the children. A dual code of rules providing exceptions for the staff is a potent source of aversion, particularly in secondary schools.

Before leaving this topic we must note certain conditions which influence the interest of pupils in school-work, but which are beyond the immediate control of the teachers. Bad housing and overcrowding, malnutrition and unwise feeding, insufficient clothing, minor ailments neglected, and chronic disease—all these factors disturb the pupils' equilibria and set up conflicts which interfere with interest in school. Such factors are due to poverty, prejudice, and ignorance. With respect to these, teachers can assist in the education of public opinion in the direction of good mental and physical hygiene. One approach to public opinion on these matters is by way of the children themselves. Through the teaching of physical exercises and domestic science sound knowledge of the conditions of healthy feeding and living can be given. Adolescent pupils discuss these topics at home, and since they will be the citizens and parents in the next generation good attitudes permanently inculcated in school will bear fruit in an improved public opinion later. For the rest, teachers can co-operate with the school medical authorities, assist in the organization of school-meals, and make every possible use of local voluntary efforts for alleviating the worst consequences of extreme poverty. In spite of vociferous objections from vested interests, school authorities have been forced by the facts into recognizing that the provision of schools and trained teachers is so much waste of public money unless the pupils are in a fit state to profit by the education organized for them.

SELECTION OF SUBJECT-MATTER

In the actual selection of subject-matter for instruction, practising teachers may have little power of choice. In the first place, any given subject-matter is introduced into school-curricula because it is judged by the community to be socially or economically necessary. Secondly, the work of teachers in primary and secondary schools is hedged about by the requirements of entrance-scholarship and school-leaving examinations. In any case a full discussion of the principles of selection would take us too far afield for our present purpose.

It can be taken for granted that, whatever the particular variations may be in any given case, the school-curriculum will include the following broad classes of subject-matter : language and literature (including the accessory skills of speaking, reading, writing, and spelling) ; pure and applied mathematics ; pure and applied science ; humanistic subjects (geography, history, economics, civics) ; handicraft and art ; physical training and games. This will be true, in a general way, of all types of school from the infant school to the secondary and technical high school.

The problem then, for the practical teacher, is not so much the choice of subjects for the school curriculum as the varying emphasis which ought to be placed upon different aspects of the subject-matter at different stages in school life, and the ways in which the various topics and exercises should be arranged and presented to the pupils, in order to secure the fullest interest and effort on their part.

Referring again to the conditions of interest, we see that subject-matter may be directly interesting because it offers direct satisfactions for certain human hungers ; and it may also be indirectly interesting because it is the means whereby other hungers may be satisfied and aversions removed. Hence we may regard subject-matter in two ways :

(*a*) As an *end* in itself. In this case it will appear as actual experience and activity which the pupil lives through *and enjoys*— intellectual food, physical and mental exercises needed by the growing powers of the child.

(*b*) As a *means* to various ends. Here the subject-matter will appear as organized knowledge and skill which must be acquired for efficiency in theoretical and practical pursuits.

From the point of view of interest and educational value, schools have erred in placing undue emphasis, at too early a stage, on the indirect value of subject-matter (*i.e.*, the technical knowledge and skill required for adult academic and vocational purposes) while the direct value as experience and activity to be enjoyed has been in many cases almost, if not entirely, neglected. We can get a better perspective if we consider certain hungers connected with school-work. These are :

Hungers for physical and mental free movement.

Hungers for rhythm, routine, and system.

Hunger for self-enhancement.

To these may be added hunger for group-activity and, in the adolescent phase, hunger for substitute sex-satisfaction.

We have noted that, as human physical and mental powers approach maturity, the individual concerned feels a craving for the appropriate exercise. Hence we may expect in the earlier phases of development a craving for experience through all the sense-organs and for free activity of the larger muscle co-ordinations. Throughout school-life we shall find curiosity, with its accompanying tendency for physical manipulation and exploration, and fantasy (that is imaginative adventure) ; and the hungers for self-enhancement.

Thus in the infant and junior schools when conducted with a view to interest and good human development, the subject-matter *must be presented as experience and activity.* The children will dramatize various situations—keeping house ; keeping a shop or a post-office ; running a ' farm ' of pets or a flower and vegetable garden ; going on a journey ; living in an Eskimo igloo, or an African kraal. Their craving for physical activity is satisfied by the action involved, by the help they can give in improvising dresses and scenery, and making simple models required for the dramatic play. They will listen to and later read stories and thus dramatize in imagination. They will manipulate, draw, paint, play musical games, and dance. During this earlier phase knowledge and skill are incidentally acquired in the course of the experience and activity.

Beside the direct value of this experience and activity in terms of enjoyment, the child will find the satisfaction of self-enhancement. Successful use of the natural powers brings a feeling of mastery and confidence. The child frequently says, with elation, " I can do this." He also finds that success brings approbation. He says, " See what I can do," and strives to master various activities in order to gain praise. Further, he wants to do something better than other pupils, and finds the opportunity for rivalry in the school-work.

After the transition to the secondary stage of schooling, certain kinds of subject-matter will still have direct value as experience and activity. Music, pictorial and dramatic art, constructive practical work, literature of the more romantic kind, dancing, games, are all directly interesting. Further, the hunger for system will lead to classification of knowledge gained incidentally in the earlier stages and to logical order. The more intelligent pupils will begin to enjoy the æsthetic aspects of order—the simplicity and elegance of a mathematical proof, a scientific hypothesis, a sonnet, or a classical piece of prose. These latter, intellectually satisfying aspects of knowledge and skill should be given due prominence in secondary work, particularly in dealing with the more intelligent pupils.

In this later period of schooling, however, academic and vocational needs make necessary the introduction of a much larger proportion of theoretical conventional knowledge and skill which has only an indirect interest-value for the majority of the pupils. At the same time, the pupils themselves are in a better condition to appreciate the indirect value. In the first place, the necessity for economic self-support and a career becomes insistent. The young child's hungers for food, shelter, protection, and general well-being were satisfied (in the majority of cases) by parents or guardians. The adolescent begins to realize that he himself will have to provide for the satisfaction of these primary needs. In addition, developing sex-consciousness and its relation with marriage emphasizes the economic value of a good career. In the second place, the growth of the power of comprehension enables the pupil to envisage more distant objectives and to grasp more easily the connexions between what must be learned now in order to secure some benefit in the future.[1]

From the point of view of interest and spontaneous effort, the teacher's main problem in the secondary period is how to encourage the fullest possible interest in these indirectly valuable aspects of the work. Assuming that aversions due to factors specified on p. 98 above have been removed, the solution of the problem can be achieved by skilful presentation of subject-matter and good grading of exercises for practice.

PROCEDURES IN PRESENTATION OF INDIRECTLY INTERESTING SUBJECT-MATTER, AND GRADING OF PRACTICE EXERCISES

We may recapitulate briefly to make quite clear the exact problem to be discussed. We find that in the secondary stage (and to some extent in the primary stage) subject-matter must be introduced which is not directly interesting to the majority of the pupils because it does not offer them any direct satisfaction.

[1] *Cf.* Chapter II : Adolescent Interests, p. 46.

Much of this indirectly interesting material is conventional, and theoretical. It may be required for examination purposes, or for specific vocational tasks, in the future. Examples are grammar, the numerical aspects of mathematics, theoretical science, constitutional history, economic geography. These subjects may, of course, be entrancingly interesting to a few adult academic scholars, but they are not directly interesting to the normal school-pupil. At the same time some parts of such subject-matter must be mastered, and our problem is to present it in such a way as to encourage the greatest possible interest on the part of the pupils.

To do this we can take advantage of the fact that interest spreads by association ; and we can organize the work in such a way that it provides some degree of satisfaction for the hungers for free movement, exploration, system and explanation, and self-enhancement. The practical procedures can be classified according as they serve to fulfil one or other of these aims. We will consider them in the order named.

MAKE THE WORK PURPOSEFUL

Here we attempt to use the fact that interest spreads by association. We can show how grammar is necessary for communication, and for the expression of clear meaning. We can emphasize the social value of good grammar and indicate its economic value as an aid to passing examinations, and securing posts. In many professional pursuits the ability to speak and write readily, clearly, and grammatically is essential. In the same way we can associate theoretical mathematics and science [1] with practical craftwork, domestic science, field-work, and practical laboratory work.

Occasionally it is quite effective to give pupils a problem they cannot do because they lack a specific item of knowledge or skill, then when they realize the need, introduce the item concerned and show how it helps in the solution.

The value of this procedure is enhanced if we note what subjects and activities have a strong appeal to individual pupils and then, whenever an opportunity presents itself, associate the indifferent subject-matter with these special direct interests.

[1] See, for example, Hogben, *Mathematics for the Million* ; Hadley, *Everyday Physics*.

Making the school-work purposeful is the keynote of the Topical Method of teaching science, and of the Project Plan of organizing school-work.[1]

UTILIZE THE HUNGER FOR FREE MOVEMENT

Interest can be enhanced if the subject-matter is presented in such a way that it provides *sufficient opportunity for pupil-activity*. Teachers must at all costs avoid doing all the work in the classroom while the pupils remain passive listeners and watchers. Pupil-activity is automatic in well-conducted science and craftwork. But it is equally necessary in teaching mathematics, languages, geography, and history. Pupils can answer questions, prepare short reports, make drawings, learn to make their own notes, demonstrate on the blackboard. It is often possible to turn a lesson into a class-discussion instead of an exposition by the teacher alone. In preparing lessons, students-in-training should use every possible opportunity to *organize the active co-operation of the pupils*. Perhaps the worst fault of the average student is his tendency to model lessons upon the lines of a college lecture.

In language-teaching it is most desirable, in the junior forms at least, to organize a *variety of occupation* within one lesson-period. In a forty-minute period a single topic or text-book exercise will admit the use of phonetic drill, oral reading and translation, question and answer, written translation, or dictation. Less ground may be covered, but from a learning point of view this is an advantage, since interest is enhanced, boredom reduced, and memorizing made more efficient.

APPEAL TO CURIOSITY AND THE DESIRE FOR EXPLORATION

This can be done in the following ways :

Organize an anticipatory interest relevant to the topic or exercise before it is introduced. Some teachers find it profitable to put up a list of the topics which will be dealt with during the next month. The attention of the class may be called to current events which are relevant to the topic to be introduced (*e.g.*, an accident to a submarine warship may enhance the interest in the topic of buoyancy in physics).

---

[1] See Brown, *Teaching Science in Schools* ; Van Buskirk and Smith, *The Science of Everyday Life* ; Collings, *An Experiment with a Project Curriculum* ; Rugg and Shumaker, *The Child-centred School*.

Arrange a striking introduction

This may take the form of an anecdote or amusing joke, or an arresting sensory stimulation.

In using this device, however, we must take care that the striking introduction leads directly into the topic to be considered. A spurious interest which does not develop merely sets up a conflict of interest which may destroy the value of the lesson. Thus introducing a lesson on reindeer by dressing up as Santa Claus would defeat its purpose since instead of the presents associated with Santa Claus the teacher could only deliver information about reindeer. On the other hand, a loud explosion would be a most apt introduction to certain topics in the chemistry of combustion, since it leads directly towards the theoretical work involved.

Bring clearly before the pupils any striking contradictions, inconsistencies, or peculiarities in the subject-matter or in related experience which lead to the questions " Why ? " or " How ? " Then follow this up by showing how the subject-matter to be studied helps to resolve these queries.

This device is the characteristic of the Socratic dialogue which can be studied in the dialogues of Plato. An excellent example of the device applied to everyday teaching is described in Adams' *Primer on Teaching.*[1]

Make free use of problems and puzzles

This is particularly applicable in teaching mathematics and science. There, instead of presenting topics as material to be memorized, they can be presented as problems to be investigated. The work then becomes an adventure.

Thus we could tell a class that the circumference of a circle is $3\frac{1}{7}$ times longer than its diameter and then let them repeat the fact till it is learned by heart. It is much more interesting to say, " How many times is the circumference of a circle longer than its diameter ? " and let the class suggest ways of finding out. Teaching through problem-solving puts a premium on imaginative ingenuity and is most attractive to many able pupils.

Problems are useful for recapitulation as well as for introductions. After studying the chemical and physical properties of water, the pupils can be presented with three or four samples of colourless fluids and be required to apply tests to discover which

[1] J. Adams, *Primer on Teaching*, Chapter VII.

of them is pure water. Recapitulation then becomes a little game in detection.

Make the subject-matter develop

At the secondary stage it is desirable to begin the systematic treatment of subject-matter, particularly where it has a logical structure (as in mathematics, science, physical and regional geography), or when it reveals some type of evolution (as in the history of human institutions).

In these cases the problems or topics which constitute the subject-matter are connected by logical relations, or relations of cause and effect. Then one topic arises inevitably out of the previous topic and leads forward to its successor in the series. Thus, by carefully articulating the syllabus and bringing out the connexions as vividly as possible, the material can be made into a medium for *continuous exploration* and each topic becomes an introduction for the next. By emphasizing the fact of connexion the abler pupils can be encouraged to adopt the attitude of expecting connexions and development, and of actively searching for these.

When dealing with a syllabus which allows of this continuous development, it is advantageous to divide the material into topics and sub-topics, each of which is a comprehensible unity, at the end of which reference may be made to the next following topic, giving rise to anticipatory curiosity. Teachers can often take a leaf out of the book of the publishers of serial stories and makers of screen-serials and close each episode at an intriguing and exciting juncture, whetting the appetite of the pupils for the next topic.

UTILIZE THE HUNGER FOR ROUTINE, SYSTEM, AND EXPLANATION

This hunger is extremely powerful throughout life, and is expressed in the ready formation of any habits, both physical and mental, which will reduce the uncertainty of existence and thus minimize the need for continual alertness. The hunger is an example of the tendency of the human organism to obey the principle of least action.

One finds many examples of disorderly material in school-work, *e.g.*, lists of exceptions to conjugations, declensions, and rules of syntax in Latin. Somehow or other these apparently illogical and arbitrary items must be committed to memory, and in the absence of connexions the task seems insuperable. Much aversion is prevented and satisfaction enhanced if the items can be arranged in an easily memorizable order.   An excellent example of this device is the series of rhyming jingles to be found in certain Latin grammar text-books.   (These were almost the only part of Latin the present writer ever found tolerable.)   The satisfaction in these mnemonic routines is considerably enhanced by rhythm.

The beauty and relative simplicity of system is well revealed in theoretical science.   Note the attractiveness of the Periodic Classification of the elements in chemistry, and of the reduction of many branches of physics to the concept of wave motion.

Hence, at the more advanced levels of study particularly, the systematic nature of certain kinds of subject-matter should be emphasized, and the main principles of the system made as clear as possible.   The present book is actually an attempt to reduce the multifarious details of everyday school-practice to a comprehensive system.

The value of an intellectual system is enhanced when it affords an explanation of puzzling facts in everyday experience.   Explanation consists in referring some particular fact to a logical system, thus enabling us to understand it.   The delight afforded by modern theories of evolution in biology arises mainly from the fact that they resolve so many otherwise incomprehensible contradictions presented by the study of the varieties of living things.

This interest in system is so strong that it may become an intellectual danger.   We are prone to accept the first system we can invent, and we are so satisfied by it that we cease to question its probable correctness, and resist any attempt to revise it.

UTILIZE THE HUNGER FOR SELF-ENHANCEMENT

This hunger is satisfied by domination and a position of superiority.   These results bring elation and increased self-valuation. Conversely, being beaten, or suffering a position of inferiority causes intense aversions and loss of self-valuation.   School subject-matter may be the means to a position of domination and superiority.   A problem solved is a problem dominated and beaten.   Competition for class-positions is one way of obtaining superiority.   The very fact that a topic is clearly understood, and can be applied successfully in further studies produces a feeling of mastery, confidence, and elation quite apart from any intrinsic interest in the subject-matter itself.   Even more important is the fact that what is apprehended obscurely and not understood produces intensely unpleasant feelings of helplessness, anxiety, and frustration, particularly when the pupil is required to apply his knowledge in answering questions or solving problems. His failure then becomes public and may lead to penalties. Thus any interest is destroyed and effort damped down. To proceed with the work is equivalent to inviting further humiliation.

Hence we must attempt to *organize success and minimize the liability to failure* in school-work of all kinds. What practical procedures are available for this purpose ?   We have :

Selection

In selecting topics for instruction and materials, tools, and exercises for practical work, we must adjust the difficulty involved to the degree of maturity, and the aptitudes of the pupils.

Too difficult work, which is beyond the pupils' native intelligence, or which has been introduced before they are ripe for it, will inevitably cause failure and the resulting aversions. On the other hand, too easy work, which can be accomplished with nonchalance, will be despised as childish and will bring no increase in self-valuation. This need for adjusting the difficulty of the work emphasizes the importance of the study of general and intellectual development. The course of general development has been touched upon in Chapter II. A detailed discussion of intellectual development will be given in Section III later.

It follows from this rule that if the school-organization is to be really successful, there must be either some degree of individual treatment for different pupils,[1] or careful grading and the arrangement of homogeneous classes or groups with appropriate modifications of the syllabus to suit each group.[2]

If a heterogeneous group of pupils, particularly at the secondary stage, is taught as a class, then the amount of material introduced and the rate of progress will be too great for some pupils and too small for others. The result will be either frustration or boredom.

Presentation

(a) In presenting the subject-matter we must take every precaution to make it clearly apprehended and thoroughly under-

[1] As in the Dalton Plan.
[2] Note the ' triple-stream ' and ' double-stream ' systems of grading ; the so-called ' vertical ' classification ; and the public-school system of teaching ' sets.'

stood. For this purpose we must be guided by the course of intellectual development. This will be appreciated more clearly after reading Section III. For the moment we will anticipate that section by stating a few obvious rules :

Begin the treatment of a new topic by using concrete examples already made familiar by experience, and proceed through these to abstract principles and formal definitions. Principles and definitions are the end-points of instruction—not the beginning.

Relate new knowledge clearly to knowledge already mastered.

Illustrate the unknown and obscure, in terms of what is familiar and clear.

(*b*) Avoid presenting more material at any one time than can be assimilated comfortably by the pupils. Overloading lessons is a frequent error.

(*c*) Introduce only one new difficulty at a time, particularly in mathematics. (But the rule applies also to other subjects.)

(*d*) Present the successive steps in the lessons in some order, that is to say, present what is required to make the next step clear before proceeding to it. In all subjects with a logical structure (*e.g.*, grammar, mathematics, and science) the order of presentation is an essential factor in clearness.

In the past this rule was frequently broken in teaching fractions. The rules for addition, subtraction, multiplication, and division of fractions were taught before the notion of the equivalence of fractions had been thoroughly mastered.[1] Until this key-principle of fractions is understood the rules for computation must remain so many arbitrary mysteries.

Even in story-telling the point of the story depends upon the orderly development of the plot. Nothing is more tiresome than having to listen to a recital during which the narrator keeps saying, " Oh ! I forgot to say that. . . ."

(*e*) Treat one topic sufficiently thoroughly to make it clear before proceeding to the next. Perhaps the most effective way of confusing children whose powers of comprehension are not fully mature is to get half-way through a topic, then introduce another topic, and before that is satisfactorily completed return to finish off the first. Actually this practice is by no means infrequent and the unfortunate pupils detest it.

(*f*) Avoid harrying and driving the pupils. Mental assimilation

[1] *I.e.*, $\frac{2}{8}=\frac{4}{8}=\frac{10}{15}$; $\frac{1}{2}=\frac{2}{4}=\frac{4}{8}$, etc.

does not occur instantaneously any more than does physical digestion. It needs time. Hence allow sufficient time for reflection during which the mental organization is accomplished.

(g) Introduce sufficiently frequent and regular recapitulation, and revision, to keep the salient points in the course of study already covered, fresh in the pupils' minds. This ensures that the new knowledge is continuously associated with the old.

Grading of Exercises for Practice

Practice is an essential factor in the mastery of many kinds of school-work, and it is usual to provide opportunity for it by arranging special exercises.

Success can be emphasized by careful grading. Thus we should commence with the easiest possible exercises which illustrate the point at issue. Much work in mathematics and grammar is made unnecessarily forbidding to the pupils because the early exercises are too abstract and difficult.

The pupil should continue with the exercises until the feeling of mastery is felt.

In correcting exercises we should emphasize success by marking somewhat more leniently and criticizing less severely in the early stages of practice. The standards can be raised progressively as proficiency and confidence develop. To mark and criticize savagely at the beginning is like pinching out the top of a tender young plant.

This last rule was well exemplified in a learning-experiment undertaken by a number of American university students. One section of the students believed that they had reached the limit of their ability to improve, and, more or less unwittingly, ceased to try further. The supervisor thereupon ' arranged ' the scores of that section to show an apparent increase. At once the students concerned renewed their efforts and went on to catch up and actually beat the artificial improvement.[1]

RELATION BETWEEN HABIT AND MASTERY

Habits facilitate the ease, speed, and accuracy of recall and performance. They are therefore an essential factor in mastery. In many cases new work is interfered with seriously and progress prevented if certain preliminary ideas and processes have not been made habitual. It is doubtful whether a pupil can ever arrive at

[1] Book, *Economy and Technique of Learning*, Chapter VIII, Section III.

the ability to read the literature of a foreign language with enjoyment and full profit unless he can recall meanings of words,
interpret idioms, and follow the grammatical constructions
automatically. The same principle is obvious in skilled crafts.

There has been a tendency to react from the earlier insistence
upon verbal repetition in learning by going to the opposite extreme
and decrying all habit-formation. Such an extreme reaction is
psychologically unsound. It leads to sloppiness, vagueness,
inaccuracy, and waste of time, and since these shortcomings
prevent adequate mastery in the pupils concerned, interest in the
subject-matter remains superficial and is always liable to be
cancelled out by the irritation of failure. Habits may be bad
masters but they are extremely good servants.

RELATION BETWEEN APTITUDE, ABILITY, AND INTEREST

The efficient utilization of the hunger for self-enhancement in
promoting interest in school-work introduces a topic not sufficiently
well recognized in educational psychology and school-organization,
namely, the relation between aptitude, ability, and interest.

By ability we mean here actual facility in some given performance, e.g., writing shorthand at the rate of 80 words per minute ;
running 100 yards in 10 seconds ; solving problems of a given
degree of difficulty in mathematics. Each ability presupposes,
beside practice, certain corresponding aptitudes. Without aptitude
practice is ineffective, and without practice aptitude remains latent.

Now, it is obvious that interest will tend to generate ability,
since the interested person will practise more frequently and with
greater zest in proportion to the interest.

At the same time it is true that aptitude tends to generate
interest. The person with good aptitude succeeds more quickly
on taking up a new task which involves the aptitude in question.
His practice produces more rapid results which in turn produce
elation and confidence, and this pleasure arising from success leads
to further practice, more skill, renewed pleasure and continued
interest. Other things being equal we tend to continue our
successful performances. The success makes them interesting.

This relation between aptitude and motivation suggests certain
points of importance for school-practice.

It should be a function of the school to *discover aptitudes* as
well as train them. For this reason, premature specialization in
either academic or industrial pursuits is most undesirable. It

tends to stereotype an individual before his aptitudes are given a favourable opportunity for expression.

Once a pupil's predominant aptitudes are discovered, the school-work should be organized as far as possible in relation to them. In this way interest will spread by association.

There should be, in a good school, a sufficient variety of activities to allow every pupil some degree of success. Psychological tests have shown that different pupils, even those with good intellectual capacity, vary widely in their individual aptitude endowment. Hence it is unlikely that they will all obtain adequate opportunity for success and therefore attain full interest in school-work if the curriculum is restricted to one type of subject-matter only, *e.g.*, the linguistic-mathematical type in which the traditional secondary school has specialized almost exclusively.

The desirability of organizing opportunities for *successful* work by every pupil is the psychological and educational justification for a multi-lateral secondary-school system, or for schools with alternative courses.[1]

MOTIVATION OF MONOTONOUS REPETITIVE WORK : ORGANIZING INCENTIVES

When a very high degree of skill is required for professional pursuits long and arduous practice is essential. At the beginning of the work progress is usually rapid, and the success keeps up sufficient interest to maintain the effort. However, the initial success is often followed by a temporary period of no improvement (a ' plateau- ' period) although the practice is maintained. The learner may pass through several of these periods before approaching the physiological limit of skill and speed at which practice produces no further improvement.

The difficulty in monotonous repetitive practice is to maintain sufficient interest in the task to overcome the strong aversions set up by the monotony, particularly during periods of no improvement. This concerns closely the teachers of technical subjects, but it may arise also in other subject-matter in normal school-work. What can be done to encourage and maintain interest in this case ?

The aim must be to organize a number of positive incentives in connexion with the work so that the compounded effects of several partial motives will eventually become strong enough to overcome the aversion caused by the monotony.

[1] See Board of Education, *Report on Secondary Education.*

An incentive is any objective for which a person is willing to strive. Again we shall find it possible to utilize the hunger for self-enhancement, and most of the procedures indicated below owe their value to the operation of that hunger.

We will assume again that the classroom-conditions are good, that there is a satisfactory co-operation between pupils and teacher, that the nature of the task to be accomplished has been set forth clearly by the teacher and understood by the pupils.

We can utilize the following procedures :

Arrange rewards (and if necessary, penalties)

In vocational training it is possible at times to arrange for material rewards (e.g., money-payments, increases in pay, bonuses for improvement). In school-work these are seldom practicable. There the rewards must be prizes, marks, privileges, positions of responsibility ; and the penalties, the withholding or loss of these.

Praise and blame constitute effective incentives if given by a respected teacher in a judicious and not too lavish manner. Also praise or blame in public adds to the incentive.

The effects of praise and blame were investigated experimentally by an American teacher. Four groups of children equivalent in age, sex, and ability were required to work standardized tests in arithmetical addition for fifteen-minute periods on each of five days. The first group did the work in a separate room under normal conditions, and no comments were made on their work. Groups two, three, and four worked in one large room. The members of group two were called by name before beginning to work and praised publicly for what they had done in the previous test. Members of group three were publicly reproved. Group four was ignored.

The results showed that, taken by groups, the order of improvement was (i) highly praised, (ii) reproved, (iii) ignored, (iv) control group (first group mentioned above). When the results shown by individual pupils were considered it was found that reproof was more effective with boys than girls, and with children of superior ability.[1] The children of inferior ability were motivated more strongly by praise than reproof.[2]

Objections have been raised against rewards as incentives. There is a danger that the reward and not the work will become the primary object of interest. Now, in normal conditions, where the work is valuable and interesting in itself, such a result is

[1] Probably they were complacent with respect to praise.
[2] Hurlock, Journal of Educational Psychology, Vol. 16, 1925, p. 145.

harmful. But in the particular case we are considering the work
is by its nature intrinsically uninteresting and when progress is
slow or has stopped, the work cannot possibly be its own reward.
A more powerful objection concerns the conditions of award. If
the rewards are given for actual success, then the pupils with the
best native endowment will always get them and the others will
cease to try. Rewards should be given for steady work and
conscientious effort as well as for success. Then every pupil has
a chance of winning.

Introduce an element of rivalry and competition

Again there have been serious objections to competition, and
some people have tried to eliminate it altogether from school-
work. This undiscriminating attitude seems both unwise and
unnecessary. If the work is so organized that the rivalry is the
only incentive then the system may be harmful, particularly as it
tends to arouse animosity and encourage the taking of unfair
advantages. This objection, however, is against the abuse rather
than use of competition. Also, however much one may deplore the
fact, there are people, adults as well as children, who will not do
any tedious work unless they are competing against others.

The rivalry need not be for individual advantage only. Competitions can be arranged between teams, classes, and ' houses.'

Utilize biographical material

There are numerous examples of people—skilled at sport or
artistry of some kind—whose success is due in part at least, to
monumental patience and assiduity in practice. The fact that
some well-known person has had to practise and has overcome
difficulties thereby may be very stimulating to some pupils,
particularly when they are on the point of giving up in disgust or
despair. The school-library should contain some accounts of
distinguished people who have owed some of their success to
assiduous work.[1]

Arrange definite objectives which the learners believe to be within their capacity to achieve

This procedure is most valuable in providing incentives. It
can be accomplished in the following ways :

(i) Prescribe *in advance* a definite limit for the period of practice
and do not allow it to be exceeded.

[1] *Cf.* Pritchard's report, p. 48.

Compare the effect of the two following instructions :

This work is not particularly interesting, but it must be done. Work as hard as you can at it until I tell you to stop.

This work is not particularly interesting but it must be done. Work as hard as you can at it for fifteen (twenty, etc.) minutes, and then you will be able to rest.

In the second instruction the definite limit restricts the work within a period which is recognized by the worker as being not really long, and the rest at the end of the period is a definite reward worth striving for. The first instruction indicates no such definite objective.

The time-limit must be fixed according to the difficulty of the work and the capacity for endurance of the learners. In any case the work should be stopped while the learners are still fresh. It is necessary to prevent the discomforts of fatigue from reinforcing the other aversions to the monotonous work.

(ii) Prescribe *in advance* a finite task within the pupil's capacity to achieve. Indicate exactly what is to be done.

In the case of a bad speller, choose say five words only which he frequently misspells and limit the task to the learning of just those five words. This is much more effective than requiring him to learn all the mistakes he made in his last piece of dictation. The very wording of this instruction makes the task seem indefinite and relatively enormous. Even if ' all the mistakes ' amount only to five, it feels easier to learn five than all of them. This rule is also valuable in vocabulary and grammar work in a foreign language.

It has been well said that in teaching we should be not only definite, but finite.

(iii) Secure a definite undertaking to finish the work within the time prescribed.

It is useful with a wavering pupil to encourage him to make a definite declaration, in public if possible, that he will accept responsibility for some definite piece of work, or that he will finish the work in a definite time. Most pupils have a crude sentiment of honour manifested in a desire to ' keep to one's word.' Among themselves they dislike those who will not keep a declared promise. Therefore persuade the unwilling waverer to give a definite affirmative promise. Do not accept evasions and half-promises such as, " I'll think about it, " or " I'll let you know to-morrow," etc. Make your active help and encouragement conditional upon a definite declaration.

This principle has been used in the 'contract' system incorporated within the Dalton individual work plan. Pupils undertake to complete all their assignments within a month, or whatever is the specified time, and not to proceed to the next month's assignments until all the current work is satisfactorily completed. In this case, the desire to get on to the next assignments in the more interesting parts of the work is an added motive for completing the less interesting present tasks.

(iv) Set a definite standard of work to be aimed at.

If the learner has before him, clearly, a standard of achievement, he can compare his own merits with the standard. If he falls short, his desire for self-enhancement is still unsatisfied. If he reaches or surpasses the standard he enjoys the pleasure of success.

The standard may be one of quality or quantity (*i.e.*, speed).

It follows from our principles of motivation that the standard prescribed must advance *proportionately with the learner's aptitude and improvement* if this incentive is to maintain its full efficiency. We have seen that if the learner cannot achieve the standard, he feels frustrated and begins to doubt his capacity. That feeling quickly damps out effort. Therefore he must be allowed to reach the prescribed standard quickly enough to prevent the feeling of frustration and futility. On the other hand, when the standard has been surpassed, satisfaction supervenes and that means that no further effort is needed. The learner leans back and takes his ease. Hence, for continuous practice a *moving* standard is necessary.

The value of a moving standard has been investigated by C. A. Mace.[1] (Incidentally, Mace's experiments afford a convincing demonstration of the correctness of some of the principles of motivation set out in this and the two previous chapters.)

Mace tried to discover an incentive which would increase in value as the practices proceeded, thus cancelling out the accumulating effects of familiarity and boredom.

The first experiments involved university students. They worked complicated routine arithmetical computations for ten-minute periods, four days per week, during six weeks. Group A were told to *beat their own previous records*, *i.e.*, the average number of correct computations

---

[1] *Incentives, Some Experimental Studies,* Industrial Health Research Board Report No. 72, H.M. Stationery Office, 1935.

completed by them in a ten-minute period during the previous week. Group B were told to *attain and if possible surpass a definite absolute standard*, namely, 70 correct computations in a ten-minute period.

Groups A and B were equal in initial ability but the results showed a small superiority in favour of group B. It was noted, however, that the workers in group B showed a rapid improvement *just when the standard*—70 correct computations in a ten-minute period—*was nearly attained*. This suggested that the effect of the prescribed standard as an incentive would be continuously maintained at a maximum intensity if the standard were arranged so that it was always just within the learner's reach.

This suggestion was tested in a second series of experiments. Two groups of boys, aged 11½ years, worked arithmetical computations for twenty-minute periods on five consecutive days, Monday to Friday, during two weeks. Both groups were given pocket-money—3d. per week for regular and conscientious work, and special bonuses.

Group A worked first. In addition to the reward-incentive they were instructed to beat their own previous best performance. From the results of this trial, an estimate was made of the number of correct computations which could be expected from a typical good, medium, and poor worker. This estimate was then used to set the moving standard for group B.

The latter worked under the same conditions as A, except that a definite standard adjusted to the initial ability of the worker was prescribed *at the beginning of each work period*. The instructions were to attain or surpass this standard which moved upward along with the worker's improvement.

Group B showed a striking superiority over group A. Moreover, the improvement was *continuous*. Usually, largely owing to the unwitting easing up when one's previous best record has been surpassed, improvement shows a series of reversals in performance. The ability falls off for a time. In Mace's second series of experiments, every worker in group A showed *two or more* reversals, during the first ten-days' practice. In group B, only one worker showed as many as two reversals, seven showed only one, and two, none at all.

(v) Keep the learners informed about the results of their work.

Practice has very little effect on improvement if the learners are kept in ignorance of their results. Hence frequent assessment is needed. In another experiment by Mace [1] a group practised throwing darts for thirteen periods during which they were informed about their scores, and for thirteen periods during which the results were withheld. They continued to improve up to the

[1] Same Report, p. 26.

end of the first thirteen periods and then began to deteriorate. A second group reversed this procedure, being informed of their progress after the thirteenth period. In this group it was found that the immediate effect of giving information about the results was greater than that produced by the thirteen previous practice-periods.

COMBINING INCENTIVES

The effect of all these incentives can be compounded together. Thus :

Express confidence in the pupil's power to succeed if he tries.

Let him know that you expect him not to let himself, and you, down by failure to try.

Call attention to other pupils who have succeeded without having any greater aptitude than his own.

Praise improvements, and spells of conscientious effort.

Organize the work so that he gets definite tasks within his capacity, and early success.

Prescribe definite and advancing standards.

In addition note the predominate temperamental traits of each pupil and modify your attitude accordingly. The lazy ones may need more supervision and some penalties. Pugnacious, aggressive pupils react favourably to a little judicious and calculated bullying. It brings out their pugnacity. Timid, cautious pupils respond best to kindly encouragement and praise.

EXERCISES

1. What is your favourite (a) subject, (b) game, (c) leisure-occupation ? Analyse the reasons for your preference in each case.

2. Collect instances of aversion to school-work changing to positive interest as ability increases or when some particular cause of lack of understanding has been removed.

3. Collect instances from your own case and that of fellow-students in which aversion to some subject or topic can be traced to a teacher who taught it. What traits in the teacher aroused the aversion ?

4. Compare the attitude of pupils to (a) a game, (b) a story, (c) a handwork lesson, (d) an exposition lesson. Are all the pupils equally interested ? If not, what type of pupil seems most interested

in each case ? How far is interest in games and handwork related to ability therein ?

5. Compare an interesting book of your acquaintance with a dull book in the same subject. What differences in manner and order of presentation seem to account for the difference in interest-value ?

Compare two lectures (or lecturers) from the same points of view.

Apply the results of your study to your own case in teaching.

6. Compare the spontaneous interests of (a) a group of bright children, (b) a group of dull children, of approximately the same age, sex, and environment. What similarities, differences, do you note ?

7. Compare the play-interests, and school-interests of a group of girls and a group of boys of approximately the same age, ability, and environment.

8. Ascertain the subject-preferences of a group of boys, and girls, at different ages.

Which seem to be the most interesting, least interesting subjects at a given age ?

What changes occur with advancing age ?

Are there any significant sex differences ? (E.g., compare attitudes of boys and girls to language-study, history, the sciences, handicraft, mathematics.)

What bearing has your study upon (a) differentiation of the curriculum according to sex of pupils, (b) organization of curriculum for different ages of pupils ?

9. Study the effect of various incentives upon pupils (a) of different temperaments, (b) of different grades of general ability.

10. Try to obtain by observation, careful questioning and discussion a record of the aversions felt by (a) a number of bright pupils, and (b) a number of dull pupils, in school.

Analyse these aversions and find out (i) which are related to the school-buildings ; (ii) which to the teacher ; (iii) which to the school-organization ; (iv) which to the school-work.

Compare the aversions of the bright pupils with those of the dull pupils. What differences do you find ?

Consider how some of these aversions can be removed. Try to carry out your suggestions practically and find out whether the aversions diminish or disappear.

Think back to your own school-days and compare your own aversions with those you collect from the pupils.

Note.—When asking children questions about their interests, preferences, aversions, do not forget that some children always try to tell you what they believe you would like to know without regard to the strict truth. Hence pupils' assertions need to be corroborated by repeating the questions on other occasions, and by independent observations of their activities when they do not know they are being observed.

Also in asking the questions care must be taken to avoid suggesting possible answers.

BOOKS FOR FURTHER REFERENCE

SCHOHAUS, W. : *The Dark Places of Education* (Allen and Unwin, 1932). Some first-hand accounts of aversions to school and school-work.

KITCHEN, P. I. : *From Learning to Earning* (Faber, 1944). Autobiographies often contain references to the genesis of interests and the interplay of motive and incentive.

ARGYLE, M. : *The Psychology of Interpersonal Behaviour* (Pelican Books, 1967).

SECTION III

INTELLECTUAL DEVELOPMENT

THE AIM OF INTELLECTUAL EDUCATION—ERUDITION OR WISDOM

THROUGHOUT educational history one finds educational reformers criticizing schoolmasters for producing men who are merely learned instead of being wise. The difference is very significant in every-day life as opposed to school-work. In general terms we may say that the merely erudite person possesses a great deal of technical information or skill, but cannot use it in circumstances not immediately connected with his learning. He is a reproducer, not an originator or even an adapter. On the other hand, the wise man can successfully apply his knowledge (or skill) in a variety of circumstances not immediately connected with his learning.

Thus, education may be specific or general. General education may imply that :

(a) The knowledge and skill gained cover several branches of human activity.

(b) Knowledge and skill learned in one branch can be applied with success to other related but not identical activities.[1]

If the second meaning is intended, the person so educated must possess a just appreciation of the value of his knowledge and skill, good judgment of the requirements of a problem, and power of adaptation. The essential difference between wisdom and erudition is the difference between intellectual power and ability to memorize.

The difference is important even in modern industrial and commercial work, in spite of the tendency to reduce all such activity to a standardized routine. When the routine breaks down the most valuable people are those who can size up the new situation quickly and accurately, and act wisely on their own initiative. It is important above all in matters of citizenship and home life where complete standardization of routine is neither possible nor desirable.

On the whole, secondary schools, particularly of the grammar

[1] *Cf.* Chapter IX.

and technical types, have put most stress on erudition (including specific skills as well as specific knowledge). This has been due to several causes. Examinations have set the standards in these schools, and it is easier to examine erudition than wisdom. Employers of labour like a certain amount of initiative in their employees but not too much. The teachers themselves tend to be erudite. They are the most successful products of the school-system in question.

It is desirable that we should define our aim in teaching, particularly since the secondary period is the one most favourable for the systematic training of pupils. We need to aim at both the acquirement of knowledge and skill and the training for intellectual power up to the limit of any given pupil's native aptitudes. Both these aims can be realized through the medium of school-activities, provided that the aims are clearly formulated and the value of school subjects in relation to both aims is realized. In any particular case, realization of the aim selected will depend mainly upon the way in which the subject-matter is presented to the pupils. We can teach mathematics as a series of tricks for working commercial and technical calculations. Each particular trick and its common uses can be presented and learned *as a separate unit.* On the other hand, mathematics can be presented as the study of *general principles of number and magnitude.* Viewed in this way many tricks of calculation which would seem at first sight to be quite different processes are now seen to be only variants of a single general principle. Moreover, exercises in mathematics can be used either as instances of methods of calculation or as problems requiring clear thinking and sustained logical reasoning.

If the more general and more desirable aim is to be realized, we must have a clear appreciation of two things—the nature of the aptitudes and thinking-processes involved in intellectual power, and the characteristics of the various branches of subject-matter. Such clear appreciation is essential since it is possible to achieve a result without being able to describe how, or explain why we can do it. A person may reason successfully even without knowing he is reasoning. However, before a teacher can train pupils how to observe, or reason, he must first realize clearly what these processes are, and the conditions in which they can best be carried on.

In the present section of the book we shall endeavour to analyse the more important mental processes involved in the development of intellectual power. In a later section we shall try to show how the results of that analysis can be applied to the problem of improving practical teaching.

This analysis of the course of intellectual development is directly connected with the principles of motivation and interest discussed in the previous section. We there found that mastery and understanding of the subject-matter are factors in interest, and are more likely to be achieved if the material is presented to the pupils in accord with the course of their development.

CHAPTER VI

EXPERIENCING—BECOMING ACQUAINTED WITH THE ENVIRONMENT

A. Experiencing at First Hand

PERCEPTS AND PERCEPTION

In a familiar situation the adult observer recognizes a large number of objects. Each object is individualized and named. It appears to stand out *as an object* distinct from a vaguer background. Also, objects seem to be ordered and related with respect to the observer, and to one another. The mental experience of any particular object or related group of objects is called a *percept*.

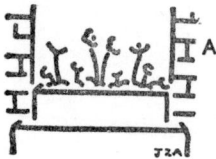

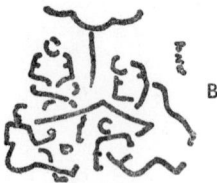

To an adult the recognition of a familiar object seems to be a simple and instantaneous process. It is possible to show, however, by experiments that perception is a complex activity, and that each percept has its own history in the mental development of the observer.

Look carefully at the drawings *A*, *B*, and *C* in Fig. 2. With respect to each one try to answer the question, " What does this represent ? " At the same time try to observe as carefully as possible what mental processes are going on in yourself.

Most readers will find that they are aware, immediately, of a series of black marks on a white background. This bare immediate awareness *via* a sense-organ is the sensory stimulus, or sensation. Over and above this bare sensory awareness we feel puzzled. We say to ourselves, " What is this ? " or " What does it mean ? "

FIG. 2

At the same time we find ourselves *trying to fit a meaning upon this sensory pattern*. We try to think of some object it might possibly represent, and then we test whether the imagined object fits the sensory pattern. Usually at first we are not satisfied. Something seems wrong. We imagine a second possibility and try that. We may again be unsatisfied and try yet a third time, and so on. This process of trial and error goes on until either we find a solution which seems satisfactory, or we get tired, and bored, and give up the puzzle. As an example, object *C* might possibly be a pincushion on the corner of a shelf, a tree behind the corner of a wall, the shell of a sea-urchin.

Now comes an interesting question. From where do we get these possible meanings? It is clear that they are derived from our past experience of objects which resemble the sensory pattern in the puzzle-picture.

We may ask then, why we do not feel any puzzlement when observing a familiar object. Actually we do so *if the object is seen in an unfamiliar position or unfamiliar surroundings.* For example, Fig. 3 represents an object perfectly familiar to nearly everybody, yet few people can correctly interpret the picture at first glance.

Tests such as these indicate quite clearly that perception involves two related functions:

(*a*) Immediate response to a set of sensory stimuli (which may be received through any one of several sense-organs).

(*b*) *An activity of construction* which seems to change the sensory stimulus into something beyond its immediate sensory character. In other words, the sensory stimulus is *interpreted* in this constructive process by means of ideas derived from our past experience. In familiar circumstances the interpretation appears to be instantaneous. The significance of the sensory

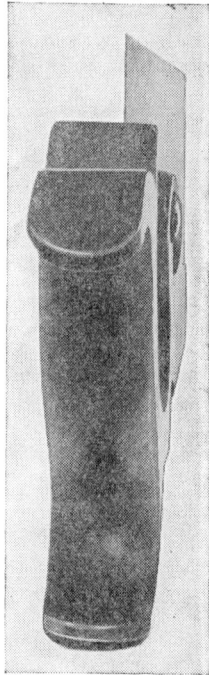

FIG. 3

A common object viewed from an uncommon angle. What is the object represented?

pattern seems to be given with the appearance of the pattern itself. Normally, we act upon the interpretation and the act is successful, that is, the interpretation fits the environmental situation. It is not until we are faced with unfamiliar circumstances that we falter, and then the distinction between sense-impressions, and the interpretation we put upon them, becomes clearly apparent.

The operation of this constructive interpreting process in perception can be illustrated in many ways. Here are some examples :

Most people are aware that we have a ' blind ' spot in each eye, just at that point on the retina where the optic nerve cable passes inward to the brain. If the left eye be closed, the spot *A* fixated steadily with the right eye,[1] and the book brought from a distance of a foot towards the eyes, a position can be found at which the spot *B* will completely disappear. The area blotted out by this blind spot can be quite considerable in distant vision. For example, I find that by putting the paper flat on the table, and fixating *A* with the right

A   B

Fig. 4

eye held vertically above it at a distance of twelve inches, a halfpenny with its centre 3·8 inches to the right of *A* just completely disappears. The blind spot, in that position, therefore blots out an area *one inch in diameter*. Yet in normal vision, *even with one eye*, we are not aware of blank spaces in the visual field. The area covered by the blind spot cannot actually be seen, however. The details it covers are *constructed* by the interpretative activity of the perceptual process.

The perceptual process can be analysed by the use of an instrument called a tachistoscope. This exposes objects or diagrams for a fraction of a second only, thus removing the sensory impressions before the interpretative process is completed. Using this apparatus Bartlett showed a diagram like that in Fig. 5.[2] After the short exposure, observers named what they believed they had seen, and then attempted to draw it.

For our present purpose, the significant result was that the drawings resembled much more *the object named* than the diagram actually seen. It was called a ' pickaxe ' and drawn with pointed prongs ; a ' turf-cutter ' and drawn with a rounded blade ; a ' key,' ' anchor,' ' shovel.' Only one

Fig. 5

observer correctly reproduced the point in the middle of the blade, and he had called the figure a " prehistoric battle-axe."

This experiment thus reveals another feature important for a later discussion, namely, that the interpretative ' schemas ' or ' stereotypes ' as they are sometimes called (*i.e.*, the pattern of ideas we try to fit over the sensory impression), are habitually associated with a name. Thus the name serves to recall the whole complex arrangement of ideas we habitually associate with it.

The interpretations are not, of course, only visual. They can be

---

[1] The observer must look *steadily* and continuously at the spot *A*.

[2] See *Remembering*, p. 19.

derived from the experiences of all our sense-organs. Thus a steel object viewed at a distance ' looks ' heavy, smooth, cold, hard. These descriptions, ' heavy,' ' smooth,' ' cold,' ' hard,' do not represent actual observations. They are *suppositious* drawn from past esperiences of obiects which look similar to the one now observed. If a piece of cardboard be made to look like a solid cube of copper, then when we lift up the supposed cupper cube the hand seems to fly into the air and we experience a feeling of surprise. The cardboarb cube has been interpreted as a heavy object and we put forward the amount of effort usually necessary to lift such an object.

The process of interpretation in perception is often the cause of serious errors and distortions in observation. The paragraph previous to this contains five spelling mistakes. How many of these were noted by readers ? Glaring errors may pass unnoted because the attention of the reader is concentrated upon the meaning of the sentences. This being so, we actually appear to observe, not the spelling of the printed words on the page, but the spellings which would be needed to make the meaning of the passage sensible.

PERCEPTION A CONATIVE PROCESS. STRIVING AFTER MEANING

There has been a tendency to assume that perception is a process in which an impression is made by an external influence upon a *passive* recipient, in much the same way as a pattern is imprinted upon a sensitive photographic film. This view is quite misleading and most unfortunate from a teaching point of view. It is easy to demonstrate that perception has a considerable component of striving in it. When we are presented with a stimulus-pattern which is not immediately intelligible, we experience a restless dis-satisfaction and we try to fit first one then another possible interpretative schema on to the sensory pattern in order to establish a meaning for it. The unpleasant feeling-tone, and the striving to fit a meaning to the pattern persist until we have found one which seems correct—that is, one which satisfies us. This conative process—striving after meaning—in unfamiliar or ambiguous situations is an important factor in curiosity.

PREPERCEPTION AND APPERCEPTION

The systems of ideas derived from past experience, and associated with names, which we bring to bear upon the sensory impressions presented to us by the environment, are called ' pre-percepts.'

Thus, when we attend to an object, or situation, two sets of influences are mutually active. The present experience modifies existing pre-perceptual schemas. If the object is a variant of some familiar type the corresponding schema is made more comprehensive, being reorganized to assimilate the new experience. At the same time *the already existing schema determines to some extent the way in which we shall perceive the new object.*[1] The incoming sensory impressions seem to be fitted into an existing mould.

Consider again the drawings in Fig. 2. Note the changes which occur in your experience of the patterns when descriptive titles are given. Drawing *A* is called " The Week-end in the Garden." The puzzling pattern of lines now resolves itself into a window-box containing flower plants. The horizontal lines at the sides of the picture take on the appearance of bricks. The flat pattern seems to fill out and become more solid. A pleasant feeling of satisfaction takes the place of doubt, suspense and further striving.

B is entitled, " The Week-end out of Doors." It now becomes unmistakably a representation of a picnic-party.[2] *C* is a cutting from an advertisement of those popular sweetmeats, " Liquorice All Sorts." Readers familiar with this brand will be able now to ' place ' the drawing, which, previously might have seemed to represent a tree on the top of a wall, or a colony of soap-bubbles, a pincushion, or possibly a biological specimen! These diagrams serve to illustrate how the pre-perceptual schemas suggested by the titles " The Week-end out of Doors," etc., *mould* the sensory patterns. Note also the feeling of satisfaction when we have finally got our interpretations correct.[3]

This *mutual* influence of immediate experiences and pre-percepts is called ' apperception.' It is, as it were, the growing point of mental life.

DISTORTION AND ERROR IN PERCEPTION

We can now understand more clearly the source of that common difficulty in school-work—errors and distortion in perception due to faulty apperception. Several types may be noted :

(*a*) Gross error in perception of sense-impressions.

Any very strong expectation or belief may produce an illusion of actual experience. This is shown in science-work. If a substance is given to a student to be chemically analysed and some person quietly yet firmly suggests to him that a particular chemical

---

[1] *Cf*. the failure to note the spelling errors on p. 161.

[2] Showing four people sitting or reclining round a cloth spread under a tree.

[3] Frequently one gets amusing (and instructive) interpretations from young children. One small boy, aged about two years, on seeing the sea for the first time exclaimed, " Look ! a big bath."

element is present, it is difficult for the analyst not to see the signs of that element in the course of the analysis. Strong expectations arising from such suggestions will produce illusions of colour, smell, and taste definite enough to appear unmistakable facts. Scientific workers must guard against the possibly distorting influence of anticipation on observation. Research work needs to be repeated by different observers with different expectation patterns and different past experience, so that errors due to personal idiosyncrasy may be cancelled out.

(b) Distortion due to *selection* of certain aspects only from a total situation and consequent omission of other aspects which do not fit the particular pre-percepts used in interpretation. A person not interested in geology, and having no knowledge about it, will fail to note the deep scratches on the rocks at the bottom and sides of an old glacier valley, while the expert geologist sees them so clearly that it seems to him impossible for anyone to overlook them. If a geologist, a botanist, and a practical farmer be taken through the same stretch of countryside, and then each is asked to record what he has observed, it is usual to find each one reproducing a list of observations *characteristic of his own individual interests and expert knowledge.* What is noted readily by one may be completely ignored by the others.

(c) ' Howlers '

We can find examples of mistaken interpretations, usually of auditory sense-impressions, in the often amusing schoolboy ' howlers.' A pupil, when asked recently what was the meaning of ' bosom friend,' replied, " A friend you go to the public house with." The teacher had pronounced ' bosom ' as ' boosom ' and the phrase was interpreted by the child as ' boozing friend.' [1]

The effect of many amusing anecdotes depends upon the fact that a wrong interpretative schema is deliberately suggested in advance to the listener.[2]

[1] During a recent conversation, a speaker said that she could never understand, when a child, why ' bacon powder ' should be put into flour for cooking purposes.

[2] Consider the following :

GRANDMA (*to Dorothy, aged ten years, who has just entered the room*). Hello ! Where have you been this afternoon ?

D. I've been for a walk with some visitors. Grandma, you ought to have seen the ' Devil's Gorge.'

G. Hush, Dorothy ! How can you be so rude ? I'm certain it was only healthy appetite.

F

THE CONDITIONS OF CLEAR AND ADEQUATE PERCEPTION

It follows from the previous discussion that perception may be clear with respect to the reception of sensory impressions, but at the same time inadequate with respect to the interpretation and comprehension of their significance. In Fig. 2, the lines of each diagram may be perceived clearly while its significance remains vague. Hence for satisfactory perception, two sets of conditions must be fulfilled :

Physical Conditions

(*a*) Sense-organs in good working order.

If sense-organs are impaired then the material presented to the would-be observer for interpretation is obscure, or partial (as in colour-blindness).

(*b*) Experience must be apprehended through a full complement of sense-organs.

This is a most important condition. The traditional five senses, touch, taste, smell, hearing, and sight, by no means exhaust the range of sensory apparatus known to modern psychologists. In the skin there are receptors for touch, pain, and temperature (heat and cold). The ears contain sense-organs for indicating the position of the head and direction of turning, as well as those for hearing. The former are located in the semicircular canals and play an essential part in maintaining body-balance. In the muscles, tendons, and joints are located the kinæsthetic sense-organs which enable us to perceive the positions of the limbs, the amount and direction of movement, and muscular strain. The kinæsthetic sense enters into all kinds of skilled movement, and helps in the perception of distance, size, solidity, and weight.

For adequate perception it is essential that *all the range of appropriate sensory apparatus shall have been exercised.* Too often school-work is confined to experience obtainable through eyes and ears alone. The result is that school-experience feels ' thin.' It lacks the variety and massive quality of out-of-school experience in which the whole sensory apparatus is usually active, including the kinæsthetic senses. Children should be able to move themselves, to manipulate common objects and come into contact with their environment by means of as great a variety of sense-impressions as possible.

(*c*) Good health and physical tone.

Malnutrition, excessive fatigue, inflammation of mucous membranes, adenoids, septic conditions of eyes and ears, all prevent clear perception and retard mental development. Mental retardation due to bad sight and hearing is sometimes confused with feeble-mindedness. In so far as systematic physical training and organized games raise the general physical fitness of the body, including the nervous system, they contribute to a great extent to mental development also. Good health increases alertness.

Mental Conditions

(*a*) Interest in the situation observed.

This depends primarily upon primitive hungers and needs. The interest produces alertness, organizes attention-adjustments, lowers the threshold of sensitivity of sense-organs, and leads to the direction of mental activity upon specific details of the situation to be observed.

(*b*) Specifically directed mental activity.

This condition for correct and adequate perception is most important in teaching. Unless attention is directed specifically towards them details will not be noted although the sensory stimuli are present. This is shown by the non-perception of errors in spelling when attention is directed towards the meanings of the words, instead of towards their appearances.

(*c*) Organized knowledge about the situation perceived.

The more varied and well-organized the observer's knowledge about the situation observed, the more adequate will be the perception in any given case. In the first place, since names play an important part in observation, the more names known by the observer, the more details will he be able to search for (see condition (*b*) above).[1] In the second place, the greater the amount of organized experience possessed by the observer, the more exact and full will be the interpretation of the significance of each detail noted.

(*d*) A correct and adequate mental ' set ' in relation to what is observed.

By a mental ' set ' is meant the system of ideas most active in the mind at the moment of observation.

I had been reading in a newspaper about the League of Nations, then glanced at a book-review on the same page. I interpreted the

---

[1] *Cf.* Fox's experiments on observation, p. 244.

book-title as " Warning to Nations." The review, however, had no
relation whatever to international politics, so, puzzled, I looked again
more carefully at the title. This time it appeared as " Warning to
Wantons."

The influence of mental set upon interpretation of significance is
illustrated frequently by the headings in ' tabloid ' journalism. " Tie
for Golf Prize " might mean that the successful competitor had been
presented, for his pains, with a neck-tie ; or that two competitors had
made the same score. Which interpretation occurs will depend upon
the system of ideas uppermost at the time of reading.

SIGNIFICANCE OF THE ANALYSIS OF PERCEPTION FOR TEACHING-PROCESS

It is obvious that the analysis of perception just completed
has a close connexion with methods of teaching. The first duty
of the teacher in encouraging intellectual development is to make
the child's world as fully as possible *intelligible* to him. In other
words the child must be able, quickly and accurately, to interpret
a large number of common objects when these are met with in
everyday life and in school.

We have seen how correct and adequate interpretation depends
upon the variety and extent of the observer's *first-hand acquaintance*,
through the sense-organs, with the material environment. Hence
*the basis of all intellectual development must be a rich and varied
first-hand experience.* There is no possible substitute for this, but
unfortunately it is just in this respect that most of our traditional
junior and secondary schools are lacking. Modern infant-school
teaching and equipment are far in advance of those of the junior
schools in this respect. If the foundations of first-hand experience
have been well and truly laid in the infant and junior stages, such
experience is not so necessary in the secondary stages. Nevertheless, even there, the orthodox school is much too verbal in its
methods of presentation.

In the second place, it is equally obvious that since correct
interpretation depends upon the pupil having a correct mental
set at the time of observation, the teacher must at all times take
pains *to induce the correct mental set in the minds of his pupils at
each stage in his lesson-development.* We shall merely note the
importance of this fact here. How the mental set can be induced
will be indicated in a later chapter.

Thirdly, among the most frequent and extensive classes of
objects a school-pupil is called upon to interpret are those artificial

conventional objects we call words (both spoken and printed), maps, and diagrams. This brings us naturally to the consideration of the psychological processes involved in such interpretation, which will be undertaken in the next section.

B. Experiencing at Second Hand. Interpretation of Words, Diagrams, and other Conventional Symbols

SUBSTITUTE-EXPERIENCE

One great difficulty in teaching is caused by the fact that some school-subjects must deal with situations which are outside the range of the pupils' possible first-hand experience. This is particularly the case in history, since all but a minute fraction of historical events have happened either before the birth of the learner or outside the range of his experience at the present time. It is impossible, therefore, to give the present-day pupil any direct experience of them. The same difficulty exists in connexion with geography. Many primary- and secondary-school pupils have never travelled beyond the boundaries of their own county, and the majority have never been to any foreign country. It is still possible to find children in remote hilly districts who have never seen a train, and many in the midst of large towns who have never seen the sea. It is obvious that with the best will in the world, geography teachers cannot bring the Arctic Regions, or China, or the South Sea Islands into the classroom. Nor can they take all their classes to these places. To a less extent the same difficulty presents itself in the teaching of natural history. Lions, tigers, elephants, whales, tropical forests, foreign birds, and so forth, cannot be had even for the asking. It is true that some more fortunate children can visit zoological gardens, and dead specimens may be seen occasionally in museums. Even so, many pupils cannot enjoy so much as these restricted substitutes.

When immediate first-hand experience is impossible the teacher may in some cases present *substitute-experience*.

The most satisfactory forms of substitute-experience are provided by pictures[1] and models. Excellent pictures for history, geography, and nature-study may now be obtained. Also, there is an increasing number of educational cinema-films at the disposal of education authorities. These aids should be considered as a *necessary* part of school-equipment ranking much higher in importance in the earlier stages of learning than books.

[1] Particularly cinema-films.

One still finds the impression that a stock of pictures, moving or still, and the means to store and display them effectively, constitute a luxury which may be indulged in with strict economy if any funds are left over from what are thought to be the essentials of school-equipment. Very frequently we find schools which possess a piano used for playing march-tunes to keep the pupils in step when they enter and leave the classrooms, hymns for morning assembly, and songs for the music periods once or twice a week. This is considered to be eminently satisfactory, but a small cinema projector or epidia-scope, which could be obtained for the price of a piano, is looked upon as an impossible luxury. One suspects that we have not yet rid ourselves of the opinion that looking at pictures is a sinful waste of time to be tolerated on Sundays when no real work should be done.

Models, again, are essential parts of school-equipment par-ticularly valuable for history, geography, and the less accessible aspects of nature-study and science. A good deal of the more advanced work in biology, chemistry, and physics is concerned with things too minute to be observed with the naked eye. In some cases they are difficult or impossible to follow even with powerful microscopes. Pictures or models which magnify the natural objects many times and display them for class-teaching purposes are therefore desirable.

A word of warning is indicated here concerning these forms of substitute-experience. They are not direct first-hand experiences, and in the absence of a background of actual first-hand experience, pictures (even cinema-pictures) and models may not be intelligible to pupils. This point may be tested by noting the reactions of younger children to pictures and models. The picture and model are seldom life-size. The picture is a two-dimensional, flat representation of solidity. Hence the picture and the model need interpretation.

This is particularly the case with historical material. Even ruins (*e.g.*, of a feudal castle) may be quite ineffective as a teaching-device, unless the pupils have a general educational background sufficient to enable them to imagine the ruin in the setting of its contemporary historical situation. Without adequate preparation, a ruin may convey to pupils no more than the experience of a bewildering collection of crumbling blackened walls having no further significance.

INTERPRETATION OF WORDS AND SYMBOLS

Even if he possesses a rich supply of pictures and models and easy access to a well-equipped museum, the teacher still must depend for communication between himself and his pupils upon *words* in the form of narrative, description, and verbal illustration. Much of the pupil's school-time is spent in the perception of spoken and written words, that is, of conventionalized sounds and shapes. It is important therefore to realize the conditions which govern this aspect of perception.

Consider carefully the following descriptive passage [1] and try to note the mental processes which accompany the reading.

> The Fanö women have a practical but peculiar costume ; the thickly pleated skirt has a bright coloured border, while the close-fitting bodice is adorned with embroidery and pretty antique buttons. A folded cotton kerchief and accordion-pleated apron give a daintiness to the whole dress. The headdress, however, gives the most singular finish to the costume. A dark, check-bordered handkerchief tied over a stiff, cambric frame entirely envelops the head. The four ends of this handkerchief are tied in an odd way, two being left upstanding like rabbits' ears.

What meaning does this convey to the reader ? In other words, how are the signs—the printed words—interpreted ?

Each individual has his own particular modes of interpretation. What is true of one individual in detail may not be true of another. I will therefore indicate my personal reactions to the description. I find myself aware of a succession of images, mainly visual. First there comes a directive mental ' set ' or anticipation produced by ' women ' and ' costume ' in the first sentence. This indicates in advance, in a general way, what is to follow. Consequently, I have a vague image of a woman's figure, a kind of outline sketch, lacking detail. Then details emerge and materialize, as it were, within this sketchy outline as the descriptive words are read. " Thickly pleated skirt " with " bright coloured border," " close-fitting bodice adorned with embroidery," " pretty antique buttons," —all these phrases *reactivate some definite experiences I myself have lived through in the past.* When I read " thickly pleated skirt," I have an image of nuns walking (a frequent experience in my case as there is a convent in the neighbourhood). " Close-fitting bodice " and " pretty antique buttons " bring to mind some old family portraits depicting relatives dressed in the fashions of the 1880s in England. I imagine also a hotel page-boy in his short, close-fitting jacket adorned with a vertical row of bright buttons.

---

[1] Taken from M. P. Thomson's *Peeps at Many Lands—Denmark*, p. 70, by permission of the publishers, Messrs A. and C. Black, Ltd.

" Accordion-pleated " suggests the appearance of the bellows of a concertina, and this image is followed by the image of a type of skirt sometimes worn formerly by young women when playing at tennis.

These memories are assembled, under the guidance of the author's description and analogies, into a kind of composite ' picture ' which is, for me, the significance of this descriptive passage. It is interesting to note that in order to make the significance more certain in detail the author deliberately guides the image-formation by suggesting standard analogies such as " accordion-pleated," " upstanding like rabbits' ears." It is taken for granted that every reader will have experienced actual examples of accordions, and rabbits' ears.

Not all the images are visual. For example on reading " entirely envelops the head " I not only imagine a nun's headdress, but also feel as if I were pulling a piece of cloth round my own head and imagine my head inside it. Again, " four ends . . . tied in an odd way " recalls motor images—the feeling of actually tying knots, and " folded cotton kerchief " produces more motor imagery.

The following points of importance for our purpose emerge from this analysis :

(a) The imagery which conveys the meaning of the passage read, is derived, ultimately, from actual *first-hand experiences through which I have lived*. These experiences range over a long period, some being recent, others dating from childhood.

(b) In the absence of an adequate supply of such lived experiences, the passage read would be perceived *merely as a succession of visual signs on a sheet of paper, together with the slight movements of inner speech during the reading*. No interpretation and therefore no meaning would be possible.

(c) Before any reader can respond adequately to the passage above, he must first have lived through a set of experiences which correspond with those described therein.

(d) These pre-perceptual systems upon which the interpretation of the printed signs depends, composed as they are from details derived from each reader's own personal experiences in a given locality, will resemble only approximately, the first-hand experience of the author. Hence it is almost inevitable that there will be, in every case, some degree of distortion in the interpretation due to the purely individual character of each person's experience. The synthesis of imagery which constitutes this experiencing at second hand can never be more than an approximately-correct substitute for direct first-hand experience.

Note also the fact, frequently experienced, that one or two vivid images, recalled in response to the opening phrases of a descriptive passage, may so absorb the attention and form the nucleus for so vivid and obstinate a picture that all or nearly all the subsequent description is either ignored completely, or moulded according to these dominant images. This fact emphasizes the need for the careful analysis by the teacher of the passage (prose or poetry) in question, to bring out clearly all the significant items, and also a careful *following-up* of the reading or speech to discover what interpretation has been made by the pupils.

The following-up process in teaching will be discussed at a later stage.

Adult students will find it expedient, after reading or listening, to follow up for themselves by deliberately going through the passage in question, item by item, to check up their first impressions and, if necessary, to correct misinterpretation.

(*e*) *There will be as many different interpretations as there are individuals reading the passage, since each one's personal experience is unique.* This fact is important for all kinds of inter-personal communication. How then can we communicate at all by way of speech or writing ? Only when all the parties to the communication refer the same word-sounds or shapes correctly to standard experiences which all have shared in common.

Differences in individual interpretation occur in arguing at cross-purposes. I listened on one occasion to an acrimonious exchange of opinion in a philosophical discussion. One speaker had made an assertion which another speaker immediately described as "nonsense." Then the fun began. Actually the first speaker interpreted 'nonsense' as being equivalent to 'ridiculous' or ' silly,' whereas the second merely intended to indicate that the assertion was non-sense, that is, logically impossible.

It should be noted that we have taken for granted certain other factors in perception, particularly in second-hand experience, namely, the ability to choose from among a great variety of possible images, those which most nearly fit the incoming sense impressions, and also the ability to comprehend, that is to hold together mentally, a number of different details and synthesize them into a coherent whole. The point we wish to emphasize here is the impossibility of *adequate* perception of word-sounds or word-shapes in the absence of the essential first-hand experience, even though the observer's capacities to discriminate, select, and comprehend are adequate.

The statements (*a*), (*b*), and (*c*) above can be confirmed by means of another descriptive passage, with which, it is hoped, readers will be quite unfamiliar.   Here it is:

> The olivo-cerebellar tract arises from the inferior olive, crosses to the opposite side in the inter-olivary space, penetrates the other olive without effecting functional connection with it, and then enters the cerebellum through its inferior peduncle. The cerebral cortex sends large descending cortico-pontile tracts to the pons of the same side. Here there is a synapse in the pontile nuclei whose neurons discharge into the opposite cerebellar hemisphere through the tractus ponto-cerebellaris in the middle cerebellar peduncle. The efferent path from the cerebellum to the red nucleus contained within the superior cerebellar peduncle decussates in the cerebral peduncle before entering the red nucleus.[1]

This second passage has been chosen for purposes of illustration, because in spite of its formidable appearance, it is just a straightforward descriptive account of matters of fact comparable with our first illustration on p. 169.   Readers partly familiar with the technical jargon of neurology will gather that it has to do with the topography of the central nervous system. They will be able to interpret common verbs, adjectives, adverbs, prepositions : for example, ' arises,' ' crosses to the opposite side,' ' penetrates,' ' here there is,' and so forth.   However, even the apparently familiar words such as ' olive,' ' tract,' ' arises,' ' discharge,' ' red nucleus ' are likely to reactivate pre-perceptual schemas which are quite inadequate to interpret the intention of the words as used in this context.   For the rest, the technical terms remain mere words to lay readers. They have a thin foreign ' feel ' about them.   They seem strange and repellent.   No imagery arises in response to their stimulation.   We feel puzzled and dissatisfied with the passage.

It may be noted in passing that this state of mind is more common than we are willing to admit in many unfortunate pupils in our primary and secondary schools during a considerable proportion of their school-time.   In addition, one suspects that it is not unknown even in university students.

This state of mind is very dangerous from an educational point of view since it indicates aversion. Not only is the meaning of the words obscure or non-existent, but the obscurity or blankness is annoying. We tend very strongly to turn away from any further perusal of the passage if it is too difficult and obscure.

---

[1] Herrick, *Introduction to Neurology*, p. 215.

In a case like this, voluntary attention is comparatively useless. If we force ourselves to pay attention we experience only word-shapes, or word-sounds, together with an intolerable feeling of strain and boredom. We get a headache instead of a meaning. There is only one way by which a layman could be prepared adequately to interpret the technical description just quoted, that is, by undertaking an extensive training in dissection of human and animal nervous systems, examining specimens of tissue under the microscope, and associating the conventional technical terms with the first-hand experience thus gained. This illustrates the noteworthy fact that a dictionary may be quite a useless piece of apparatus for a child until he has acquired the minimum foundation of first-hand experience necessary for the correct interpretation of the words in the dictionary definitions.

An intelligent boy about ten years old asked me on one occasion for the meaning of some abstract noun in which he was interested. I told him to consult a dictionary. He said he had already done so and it was quite useless, because he had to look up definitions of all the individual words in the dictionary definition itself, and then all the words in each of those definitions and by the time he had followed all those up he would have read most of the dictionary. He added that he was too busy to do all that so would I kindly produce the explanation myself.

The only satisfactory dictionaries for younger children are picture-dictionaries.[1] For schoolroom use these can be made in the form of a card-index.

PERCEPTION AND INTERPRETATION OF DIAGRAMS

What applies to words applies equally well to diagrams. Consider diagrams *A* and *B* in Fig. 6. Every reader will respond to diagram *A* by saying or believing that it represents a man running. Some readers interested in wireless telephony will interpret diagram *B* as representing a wireless circuit. Experts in wireless will at once be able to identify and name the particular type of circuit represented and to picture valve, crystal receiver, variable resistance, variable condensers, reaction coils, telephones, and batteries as they would appear on a bench in the laboratory or workshop. Those entirely unfamiliar with wireless apparatus will perceive some straight lines, some wriggly lines, a circle, and two arrows. They cannot translate the conventional technical signs into direct first-hand experiences of actual apparatus.

[1] See MacMunn, *The Child's Path to Freedom*, p. 109.

Both diagrams represent matters of fact. Diagram *A* is just as much, or as little, like a man running, as diagram *B* is like an actual wireless set. *B* is as easy to interpret as *A* if the observer has adequate pre-perceptual schemas derived from first-hand experience with wireless apparatus.

In teaching-practice, the most careful precautions are necessary in the use of conventionalized diagrams, *including maps*, until their

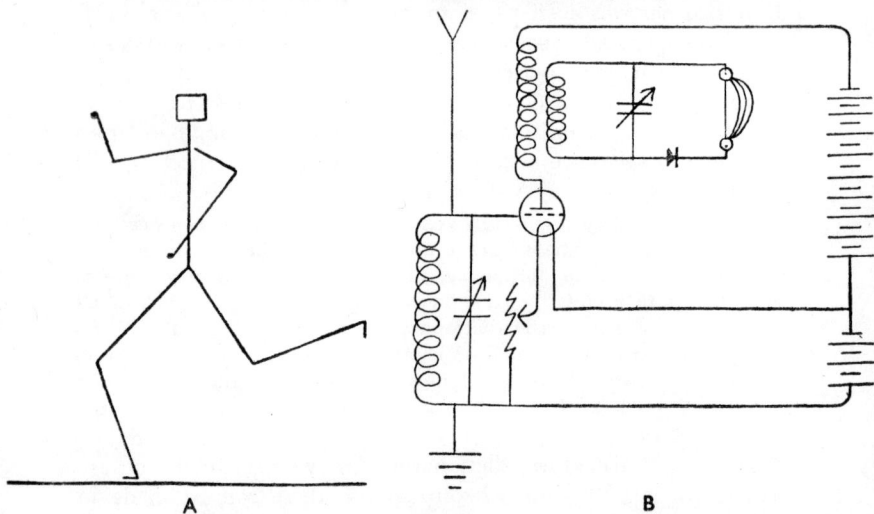

A   B

FIG. 6

language has been learned adequately. We may note the following warnings :

(*a*) Never use diagrams as *substitutes* for first-hand experience. Diagrams are useful to *represent and summarize experiences which have already been apprehended directly.*

(*b*) Conventionalized diagrams are quite unsuitable for young pupils. If appropriate first-hand experience is not available for them, pictures should be used.

VERBALISM

Summarizing the discussion in the previous section we may say that :

(*a*) Words (spoken and written) and diagrams are conventional-ized objects used to indicate actual experiences. By means of words and diagrams we can communicate (within limits) our experiences to other people, including pupils.

(b) Before words and diagrams can fulfil this purpose of communication adequately, the persons to whom they are addressed must first have enjoyed *at first hand* experiences similar to those indicated by the words. If this condition is not fulfilled the perception of a word or diagram is merely the perception of a sound or shape having no further significance.

Now we can understand what is meant by verbalism. It is a kind of mental disease particularly prevalent in schools and colleges. It is a condition in which experience consists entirely of words and diagrams, for which there exist in the minds of the observers no corresponding associates in terms of things and relations in real life.

The condition arises because pupils are able to memorize accurately, if given sufficient practice, successions of words and diagrams which can be reproduced in the same order as that in which they were learned. Hence, so long as these pupils are required to reproduce the same succession of sounds or shapes, they can give apparently correct answers to questions, and they can simulate intelligence.

Verbalism is dangerous because the sounds and shapes have no significance in terms of real everyday life. They cannot be translated, when necessary, into concrete experiences. *Hence the words and diagrams cannot be applied and used successfully outside of the particular school-context in which they have been memorized.* This difficulty is aptly illustrated by the following story.[1]

A visitor to a certain school found the pupils ' studying ' geography. She was invited by the headmaster to question the class. After glancing at the subject of the lesson she put this question : " If I could dig a very deep hole right down into the inside of the earth, would it be hotter at the bottom of the hole than it is up here ? " There was no response. The class was perplexed, and dumb. The headmaster, anxious for his reputation, intervened and said he feared that the visitor had not asked the question correctly. He was quite certain the children knew the answer. He therefore begged that he might be allowed to put the question himself. He said, " Now, children ! In what condition is the interior of the globe ? " The class responded immediately, " The interior of the globe is in a condition of igneous fusion."

---

[1] Believed to be due to the psychologist, William James.

In verbalism, the word-shapes and -sounds instead of referring to first-hand experience of things become themselves the only first-hand experience the pupil possesses. Since he cannot interpret it, such experience is valueless to him. An extreme case of verbalism would be one in which a pupil repeats mechanically the word-sounds of a foreign language without in the least apprehending the meanings of the words. This extreme form of verbalism is always liable to arise in bilingual areas [1] where the pupils speak their native language in their homes, and at play, while the school-teaching is carried on in another language.

LITERARY VERBALISM

Verbalism is not restricted to the subject-matter of geography, history, or science. It can arise in connexion with the study of grammar and literature. A child eight years old can memorize a catechism such as the following without in the least understanding its import :

On the Genitive Case

QUESTION : Define the genitive case ?

ANSWER : Tne genitive is the case which qualifies nouns like an adjective. It is also used as the direct object of nouns and adjectives, and as the indirect object of certain verbs.

QUESTION : Distinguish between the subjective and objective genitive ?

ANSWER : The subjective genitive is a genitive dependent on a substantive, and regarded as the subject from whence that substantive proceeds, as Amor Dei, *the love of God*, that is the love which *God* has *for us* (where God is the subject who loves). The objective genitive is etc., etc.[2]

Such memorizing can be done before the young learner has any insight into the reasons why there should be a genitive case at all, to say nothing of the reasons why it should be necessary to distinguish between a subjective and objective genitive ! Pupils in this condition are in much the same difficulty as those previously referred to who could repeat that the interior of the globe is in a state of igneous fusion, but who had no notion at all that the interior of the earth is so hot that even rocks and metals melt in it.

[1] *E.g.*, in rural districts in Wales, and in the Flemish area of Belgium, where the official language of school-instruction used to be English or French,
[2] See J. B. Allen, *An Elementary Latin Grammar* (Oxford University Press, 1931).

In the natural order of development, people learn to speak, and then to write a language because they need speech and writing to express their wants, and their feelings, because they must communicate with one another. They do not begin to *reflect* about formal grammar until a later stage when accuracy of meaning and fitness of expression become important. At this later stage the need for a study of the rules of correct speech, and the benefits to be obtained by classifying and systematizing the rules, is realized.

Similarly the adequate study of literature must be rooted in first-hand experience. A good novel or play is a description of people, their reactions to one another and to the physical and cultural environment. The author portrays ambitions, successes and failures ; joys, hopes, fears, and despair. His success (from a literary standpoint) depends upon the accuracy with which he portrays human personalities and their interplay. But, before the reader can enjoy and appreciate a novel or play, he must, to some degree, have lived through, enjoyed, and suffered experiences comparable to those portrayed in the literary work. One's own inner life is therefore the essential first-hand experience in the study of literature. It follows that literary subject-matter, both prose and poetry, should be chosen to suit the age and experiences of the pupils.

The appeal of poetry is two-fold. The sounds and rhythm of metrical speech are themselves intrinsically interesting. Also, the poem, if successful, arouses in the hearer or reader feelings and attitudes similar to those experienced by the poet himself.

Hence we cannot expect full appreciation of poetry until pupils are mature enough to have experienced in some degree the subjective feelings as well as objective situations depicted.

If the study of language and literature is to have real educational value, and particularly if it is to stimulate pupils' imaginations, the following conditions must be fulfilled :

(*a*) The grammar must arise out of, and be closely connected with, the need for clear expression and communication of thoughts and feelings.

(*b*) The literary works studied at any stage of the course must have sufficient connexion with the pupils' own experiences of life.

(*c*) First-hand acquaintance with a *variety* of literary works of merit must precede any treatment of the principles of criticism and canons of literary style.

In science and craftsmanship, first-hand observation of natural objects and events, or actual practice in the making of things provides the essential foundation for reflection about principles. Similarly in literature, original works of writers of merit must be the foundation of study. *The essays, novels, poems, are the facts of literature.* It is necessary to stress this point since it is not uncommon to find secondary-school and university students preparing for examinations in literature by memorizing, in a sweat of anxiety, neat little text-books *about* Keats, Shelley, Goldsmith, and the like, wherein are set down the date of the author's birth, his school, his family relations, when his works were published, and what Mr X (the author of the text-book) has been able to gather concerning what the various experts in literary criticism believe that Keats, Shelley, etc., meant to say, and what students ought to believe about the merits or demerits of the work. Apparently, reading the original works is quite superfluous ; or one gathers that it is allowable only if the student can find the time for it without interfering with his real work !

REVOLT AGAINST VERBAL INSTRUCTION

This is expressed in the time-honoured slogan—" Things before words."

It must not be supposed that the revolt against verbalism is modern. It is one of the recurring refrains of educational history. A history of teaching-method would be an account of a struggle between a few outstanding reformers and the mortifying institutionalism of school-systems. Schools and schoolmasters—as a class—have seemed fatally predestined to settle into a rigid linguistic conformity with tradition. The Renaissance, in so far as it affected educational principles and practice, was a revolt against linguistic pedantry which had reached a fatuous limit in the practice and theory of the so-called Ciceronians, who wished to remove from the school curriculum everything which did not admit of being discussed in Cicero's recorded words ! [1]

As an alternative to this, Vittorino da Feltre (1378–1446) organized a ' modern ' school in Mantua in which he taught the literature, history, and civilization of the Romans instead of the mere form of their language : literature dominating while dialectic and grammar were subordinate.[2]

[1] See Monroe, *Text-book in the History of Education*, p. 372 ; Adamson, *Short History of Education*, p. 126.
[2] Monroe, work cited, p. 376.

Comenius (1592–1671) wanted children to study things before words and indicated in his *Great Didactic* how this could be done. However, the most shattering attack on verbalism was launched by Rousseau. " The pedagogues," he wrote, " what do they teach ? Words ! Words ! Words ! " [1]

THINGS WITHOUT WORDS

Largely due to the influence of Rousseau's doctrines, attempts have been made to introduce more and more activity and first-hand experience into educational practice. Pestalozzi and Froebel attempted to implement Rousseau's ideas in the teaching of young children, and a notable, but not so frequently noted contribution to the same movement was made by the Edgeworths.[2] Seguin and Itard, two French medical psychologists, pointed out the value of practical activities in the education of the feeble-minded, and their work was the direct inspiration for Madame Montessori. Dewey, an American philosopher, has developed systematically the principle that we should not merely introduce some activities into education but that activity is education.[3]

As usual, the intensity of the reaction from verbalism in teaching has led to extreme views in the opposite direction. Rousseau asserted " Give your scholar no verbal lessons. He should be taught by experience alone." [4] Some more modern enthusiasts for the ' heuristic ' method have tried to make their unfortunate pupils find out everything for themselves.

Thus from nothing but words, pedagogues have tried to use no words at all. But it is just as foolish to try to teach by experience alone as by words alone. As we shall see in the next chapter, experience and words are both essential, in due proportion, in intellectual development. Without words the pupil is prevented from transcending his immediate, concrete, perceptual experiences. He cannot proceed to well-developed abstract ideas and general principles, without which science and mathematics as well as ethics are impossible.

Hence we must aim at developing an adequate vocabulary along with perceptual experience. At all times the pupil should be able to translate mentally his experiences into words and

---

[1] *Emile* (Everyman's Library edition), p. 37.
[2] See *Practical Education.*
[3] *Democracy and Education* and *New Schools for Old.*
[4] *Emile*, p. 56.

symbols, and his words and symbols into experiences when such translation is necessary. When the child with sufficient mental aptitude can generalize his experiences and represent the generalizations by appropriate words, it is just as bad practice educationally to make him continue to use concrete materials as it is to make the backward child try to think in abstract terms.

WORDS AS FIRST-HAND EXPERIENCES

Before closing this section we must note certain cases in which words themselves are objects of perception, having definite characters and relations as important for certain branches of study as the characters and relations of material objects are for natural science.

Words are first-hand experience for the student of phonetics. In this case the sound-characters are the significant elements. The expert in phonetics studies word-sounds, and endeavours, among other things, to formulate scientific principles concerning the evolution of word-sounds and the changes which occur in common pronunciation (*e.g.*, Grimm's Law).

Words are first-hand experience of immense interest to the literary stylist. In this case the interest lies in selecting words not only because they have a meaningful significance relative to the theme which is developed by the author, but because they have different sound- and stress-values. Therefore care must be taken to choose words which harmonize in sound and rhythm with their context. Word-sounds and stresses are as important to the literary artist as colours to the painter, and characteristics of different materials to the sculptor.

Words are first-hand experience to the etymologist. Etymology is in some respects a natural history of words. It deals with their origin and evolution, just as natural history of animals deals with the origin and evolution of modern forms of living creatures. A collection of specimens such as *fenestra* (Latin), *finestra* (Italian), *fenster* (German), *fenêtre* (French), and *ffenestr* (Welsh) is as interesting to the etymologist as a collection of five similar but not identical beetles is to the entomologist. Moreover, it raises similar problems of origin, development, and connexion. It is interesting to note that there are fossil words, as well as fossil plants and animals.[1]

---

[1] See Trench, *The Study of Words*, Chapter I.

Exercises

1. Make a study of a set of typical ' howlers ' and endeavour to diagnose the probable cause of the mental confusion exemplified by each. What is the bearing of your study upon presentation in teaching ?

2. Collect and analyse errors, omissions, and distortions in children's perceptions of objects and words.

3. Compare the imaginative picture you have made from descriptions concerning some person, building, sea-side resort, etc., with the actual experience of the object or place obtained later.

4. Collect some instances of verbalism in school-pupils and fellow-students. Can you find any instances in your own case ?

5. Note as carefully as you can all the mental processes which you experience when some one asks you, " What is the meaning of justice (life, motion, Mendelian inheritance, spiritual, quanta, etc., etc.)." How do you ' explain ' the meanings ?

Books for Further Reference

Bartlett, F. C. : *Remembering* (Cambridge University Press, 1932)

Chase, S. : *The Tyranny of Words* (Methuen, seventh edition, 1950).

Fiske, D. W., and Maddi, S. R. : *Functions of Varied Experience* (Dorsey Press Inc., Illinois, 1961).

Gombrich, E. H. : *Art and Illusion* (Phaidon Press, 1960).   A study in the Psychology of Pictorial Representation.   The rôle of perception in the interpretation of pictures.   Useful reading for teachers of art.

Hochberg, J. E. : *Perception* (Prentice-Hall Inc., New Jersey, 1964).

Hunt, J. McV. : *Intelligence and Experience* (Ronald Press Co., New York, 1961).

James, W. : *Principles of Psychology* (Macmillan, 1890).   See Vol. II, Chapters XVII, XIX, XX.

Katz, D. : *Gestalt Psychology* (Methuen, 1951).   Short introduction.

McDougall, W. : *Outline of Psychology* (Methuen, thirteenth edition, 1949).   See Chapter VIII : " Perceptual Thinking."

Montessori, M. : *The Montessori Method* (Heinemann, 1914).

Rousseau, J. J. : *Emile, or Education* (Everyman's Library, 1921).

Stout, G. F. : *Analytic Psychology* (Allen and Unwin, 1918).   See Vol. II, Chapters V to VIII.

Sumner, W. L. : *Visual Methods in Education* (Blackwell, Oxford, 1956).   Chapters I to IV.

Trench, R. C. : *On the Study of Words.*

Vernon, M. D. : *Visual Perception* (C.U.P., 1937).

—— : *A Further Study of Visual Perception* (C.U.P., 1952).

CHAPTER VII

ORGANIZATION OF EXPERIENCE

In actual life, mental activity seems to be continuous, like a 'stream.' Normally, the stream is not chaotic. It ' flows ' in certain directions with some sort of order and system. What, then, is the nature of this connectedness ? What determines the direction of flow, the order and the system ? Grains of sand can make up a stream. The familiar hour-glass is an example. Is the stream of mental life like a stream of sand, or is it more like a stream of water ?

To discover the correct answers to these questions is the real purpose of theories of learning. However, many practical people are suspicious of theory. Of what practical use is it ?

A theory is another name for a set of established principles which seem to explain in a reasonable way the observable events in everyday life. *Its real purpose is to justify beliefs and actions*, and these, most emphatically, have practical importance. In so far as a theory is correct it indicates rules for action. The atomic theory in chemistry, the theory of genes in biology, are cases in point. If the true nature of mental activity can be demonstrated we shall be so much nearer to knowing what is the truth about learning processes and to settling questions about the treatment of subject-matter for teaching purposes. In addition, we shall have the only acceptable basis for a teaching profession. A profession without a system of established principles to profess is an absurdity. These are very good reasons for considering theories, including theories of learning.

There are two main theories of learning—namely, the Associationist theory and the Gestalt or configuration theory—both having direct connexion with practical teaching.

THE ASSOCIATIONIST THEORY OF LEARNING

One way of reducing a complex situation to some sort of order and thereby explaining it is to seek apparently constant ' elements ' in it which by themselves or in combination will account for the observed events.

Thus it was supposed, centuries ago, that there were only four primary qualities—wet, dry, hot, cold ; four elements—earth, air, fire, water ; four humours (or liquids) out of which human bodies are made—blood, phlegm, black bile, yellow bile—the excess or defect of any of which would account for diseases and also for temperaments (sanguine, phlegmatic, melancholic, choleric). Nearer to our own time chemists have analysed all sorts of materials into the atoms and molecules of about a hundred elementary substances, each of which is capable of undergoing chemical reactions and of being recovered, later, apparently unchanged. Physicists resolved colours, sounds, heat, ' wireless,' X-rays—in fact, all kinds of radiations—into waves. Later, they supposed that energy is distributed in ' quanta,' rather like bullets out of a machine-gun. Psychologists have analysed abilities into ' factors.' Whether actual abilities are really combinations of general and group and specific factors or unitary abilities, whether the physical world is made up of molecules and atoms, waves, and quanta, is a moot point. What is important for psychologists and physical scientists is that abilities and the physical world behave as if they were made up of such elements.

In view of this persistent search for elements it is not surprising that, quite early in the history of knowledge, mental events were analysed into apparently simple, constant parts—namely, *sensations* and *reflex actions*. In this context a sensation refers to such apparently simple, constant items of experience as a glimpse of a pure colour, a momentary pure sound, a taste, a smell, a pain—in fact, an element of whatever type of experience is acquired through a single sense-organ. The reflexes were supposed to be simple actions due to the stimulation of a sensory nerve-ending causing an impulse which was then conveyed to the brain or spinal cord via a sensory nerve, whence it was conducted via a motor nerve to a muscle or a gland. These sensations and movements were assumed to be the simple, constant elements out of which could be organized all our percepts, thoughts, and habits ; all our intellect, in fact.

The perceiving mind has been likened to a wax tablet, or a sheet of white paper on which ' impressions ' could be registered.[1] These impressions when recalled in the form of images could then act as carriers of meanings linking up the past with the present and making possible the continuity of mental life.

In a series of lectures to teachers on the theory and practice of

---

[1] This notion might be regarded as a justification for hammering in the facts !

education, delivered in 1880, the late Professor James Ward gave the following account of this Associationist doctrine :

> Let us turn to our own minds. What have we there ? Nothing but sensations and movements and complexes of these . . . nothing, I believe, except the mind which is conscious of having all these, together with the pleasure or pain it receives from them.
>
> Is it possible that our noblest thoughts and aspirations are nothing but complexes of sensations and movements ? Suppose you reflect awhile on the saying ' virtue is its own reward.' Such a state of mind is enormously complex, as you will at once realise if you imagine yourself expounding the maxim to a boy of twelve. ' Virtue ' stands for virtuous acts, or for a life of such, and this, finally, has to be pictured out in detail by means of what the boy has himself seen and done in the past. . . . Try, if you choose, for yourselves and see if you do not find that the material of all that can be presented to our minds is reducible to sensations and movements just as the materials of all the vast variety of substances on the earth can be reduced to some one or more of the chemical elements.[1]

However, even if this doctrine as stated by Ward were true, it was still necessary to explain how the sensations and movements are connected to form the stream of awareness. For this purpose certain laws of association were described. The recollected sensations and movements appeared as ideas. Ideas were then associated by *contiguity* and *similarity*. Thus items experienced in one act of observation either together or in immediate succession would be registered together or in sequence and then recalled in that contiguity and order on a subsequent occasion.

For example, the sound of a step or a voice will call up an idea of the person to whom they belong. That idea may call up the scene of the last occasion on which the person was met, what he/she was wearing, what was talked about, the place where the meeting occurred, thence to other details of the situation. If we see or hear the word ' white ' it may suggest an idea of snow, or whitewash, or a white dress, or white paper—associations due to some form of similarity.

In the case of movements it was supposed that any particular reflex would activate the movement which had been learned next to it

---

[1] James Ward, *Psychology applied to Education*, p. 21. It is necessary to add that in a later book (*Psychological Principles*) Ward repudiated this Associationist doctrine and developed a description of intellectual activity much more in line with modern conceptions.

in a habitual series. We put a hand into a pocket, draw out a bunch of keys, select the key for the door we want to open, put it into the lock, turn it, open the door, withdraw the key, put the bunch back into the accustomed pocket, and close the door. Having performed this series in (apparently) the same way and the same order many times until it has become habitual, we find that as soon as we stand before the familiar door the sequence of movements begins and then goes on without our having to think about it. We can go through the series quite efficiently while carrying on a conversation or thinking about some other problem having nothing whatever to do with opening the door.

It may be asked, what about ideas of classes, general ideas ? Educated people think about trees, animals, cattle, mammals, insects, and so on without necessarily recalling images of particular objects. The Associationists explained this by supposing that each subsequent experience of a dog, for example, leaves an impression on the original image, much as one might imagine a series of snapshots of different faces superimposed on the same photographic film. This generalized image then represents the class or generalization.[1]

Again, we do not recall equally readily every detail we experience. The Associationists accounted for this by supposing that, other things being equal, we recall most readily what has been experienced most recently, what has been repeated most frequently, what was most vivid and impressive, and what was most satisfying.

This neat explanation of mental activity was attractively simple, and in one form or another has held the field until the present day. Under the influence of physiological psychology, ideas and images have gone out of theoretical fashion, their place being taken by conditioned reflexes. Nevertheless, the modern reflexology, as it has been called, is another form of Associationist theory.

ASSOCIATIONIST THEORY, LEARNING, AND TEACHING

The Associationist theory of mental activity with its sequences of sensations and reflexes could be used as a justification for the traditional methods of teaching languages and the ancillary arts of reading and writing.

[1] So long as a class of the same animals is concerned this might be a plausible supposition. However, carried to its logical conclusion, the image for ' animal ' would have to be the generalized image of the dog superimposed on a generalized image of the horse, and these on generalized images of rats and tigers and elephants and fishes, and so on. This would appear to raise more problems than it solves.

In systematic teaching, as opposed to the informal, easygoing instruction which a child enjoys at home or at play, there is a syllabus to be covered. The syllabus represents the kind and amount of information which learners should have acquired by the time schooling ends. Paradoxically, the teacher begins at the end of the academic programme. He has then to decide what is the most suitable order in which to introduce this end-product, the syllabus, to the pupils. Even the most hardened academic disciplinarian realizes that it is not satisfactory to begin teaching, even languages, at the university level to children who cannot yet read. Somehow or other the subject-matter must be simplified. One way of simplifying reading, writing, and composition would be to analyse language into its ' elements.'

Language as written or printed is composed of words, words of syllables, and syllables of letters. The letters represent a few simple elements which, put together according to certain rules, make up syllables and words. In that case, since the letters are the simplest elements of the written language, why not teach children to read by teaching them the letters first, then making letters into syllables and syllables into words ?

In literary composition words are combined into clauses, clauses into sentences, sentences into paragraphs, and paragraphs into continuous prose. Why not begin the study of grammar and composition by learning the parts of speech and their names in what would appear to be the most convenient order ? One learned, therefore, the declen-sions of nouns, then of adjectives, then of pronouns. One conjugated verbs ; after which one dealt with adverbs, prepositions, conjunctions, and the remainder of the bric-à-brac of Latin, including the ineffably tiresome exceptions to every rule, memorizing on the way meaningless ditties like that on the genitive case already quoted. When all these elements of language had been put together according to the authorized rules of syntax one then started at the other end and unravelled (construed) the prose or verse of some long-dead author back again into its constituent parts of speech, parsing in great detail on the way.

Similarly, one learned to write by making strokes and ' pothooks,' which were then combined into letters and words. Woodwork was introduced by exercises in sawing, planing, making joints, before the pupils were allowed to make an intelligible object. History was a succession of facts and dates learned in chronological order ; geography a collection of names of towns, counties, mountain-ranges, rivers, capes, bays, imports, and exports.[1]

---

[1] These are descriptions from actual life, not figments of the author's imagination. I began to learn the ' elements ' of Euclid's system of geometry by memorizing the postulates and axioms, presumably on the principle that since they came first in the book they should be ' learned ' first. Fortunately for me, my real education went on much more realistically out of school.

SOME DIFFICULTIES, EDUCATIONAL AND PSYCHOLOGICAL

This method of teaching had its advantages. So long as the purpose of schooling was ability to perform routine computations in arithmetic, or to write Latin prose in the words and style of Cicero or Caesar, or to memorize the Catechism and the creeds, or to reproduce text-book history and geography, the method worked, up to a point. It had the additional advantage that teachers need not *understand* their subject-matter. It was sufficient for them to be able to read the text-book in order to test the accuracy of the pupils' memorizing processes.

Out of school, however, it was less successful and aroused much criticism. This mechanical learning of simple elements and rules of association might be intelligible to philosophers ; *it was meaningless to children.* They had to be driven to the scholastic tasks by exhortation and punishment, whereas out of school the same children would learn easily, quickly, and with apparent satisfaction, whatever captured their interest or served their purposes. Moreover, the mechanical repetition of rules seemed to have no influence on what the learners did apart from their memorizing. It has been a perennial complaint that children who could recite rules of grammar perfectly still talked and wrote, out of school, in quite ungrammatical ways. Even worse—the method did not help the pupils to solve problems or adapt themselves to new conditions. What was memorized by this method could be used only in the form in which it had been learned. Taught in this mechanical way, children who had memorized a geometrical proof have been known to fail to reproduce it if the figures were lettered P, N, Z ; X, L, D instead of the customary A, B, C ; D, E, F ; or, in reply to the question, " What are 7 times 9 ? " they had to repeat *sotto voce* the appropriate table from the beginning ; or, if asked to find how many times 256 could be taken from 12,345, they performed a long series of subtractions, instead of dividing.[1] If planning, foresight, adaptability, discovery, were needed the mechanically associated material was not merely useless, it was a positive hindrance.[2]

Modern methods of justifying a theory depend more on experimental investigation than logical analysis. During the second half

[1] Some instructive cases of failure to adapt what has been learned by rote to altered conditions are given in *Productive Thinking*, by Max Wertheimer (Harper, 1945). See Chapters I to III. Incidentally, some university students' minds appear to work according to Associationist principles !

[2] *Cf.* the example about igneous fusion quoted above (p. 175).

of the nineteenth century dissatisfaction with Associationist doctrine stimulated experiments to find whether mental activity did, in fact, consist of sequences of images and movements in association by contiguity and similarity, particularly in problem-solving.

The reports of these experimental studies indicated that in dealing with problem situations what is perceived and recalled and thought about depends not exclusively on associations of contiguity or similarity, but also on the nature of the problem to be solved, on the instructions given to the subjects of the experiments, on what the subject had been doing before the task in question was undertaken, and on the environmental conditions at the time. Humphrey, in a statement quoted previously, says that the experiments revealed no constant process of generalizing, or thinking. There were variations not only from person to person, but in the same person on different occasions even when using the same materials.[1] Images may be present during thinking, but as learning proceeds and thinking becomes more habitual imagery tends to disappear. Much thinking can and does go on without any observable imagery at all.

THE GESTALT OR CONFIGURATION THEORY OF LEARNING

When the Associationist principles had been questioned numerous examples of non-associationist mental activity were noted.

Identical stimuli are apprehended in different ways according to their context. The same medium-grey strip of paper will be perceived as tinged with red or green or blue on a green or red or yellow background respectively. It will appear dark grey on a white background and light grey on a black background. The illusion may be so strong as to suggest convincingly that there are two different strips of grey paper. The lengths and directions of lines, sizes and shapes of figures, can appear distorted by the presence of other lines and shapes. In one demonstration what is apprehended cannot possibly be due to the presence of specific sensations. If two slits in a backcloth are illuminated successively the distances between the slits and the time-interval between the illuminations can be arranged so that an observer ' sees ' not two separate slits, as the Associationist doctrine would suggest, but a *band of light moving from one slit to the other.*

The effect of context on meaning is obvious in speech. The words ' chaste ' and ' chased ' sound exactly alike when spoken, but the sounds convey very different meanings if the topic is virtue rather than pursuit.

---

[1] See Chapter II, p. 54, above.

The same meaning can be conveyed by quite different sets of 'sensations.' " Papa ka okoku esubit bala toto ka (akoku) " means the same in an African dialect as " Father is to son as mother is to (daughter) " in English.

Relationships (i.e., meanings), not stimuli or movements, are the constant 'elements' in thinking. The Associationist doctrine will account for some of the facts of learning. It is useful, up to a point. The Morse signalling code dot-dash, short-long, must be learned by associating letters of the alphabet with arrangements of dots and dashes. However, when these arbitrary associations have been learned in the form of printed signs . . . — — — . . . (SOS), for example, the letters can be recalled by an intelligent operator if the signals are given by flags, or flashes of light, or taps on a board, or taps on the skin, or sounds on a buzzer, and this without previous practice in the new medium. Conversely, the letters can be signalled by a sender by wagging flags, manipulating a lamp or a mirror, or tapping a key. Any arrangement which produces the correct configuration or pattern of short-long intervals can be substituted for any other without altering the message or preventing the performance.[1] Here again neither the stimuli nor the movements are constant, only the meaning. In cases like these what is learned cannot be merely connexions between specific sensory and motor nerves, or between particular images. It must be a *pattern or configuration in the central nervous system.*

This principle of a *Gestalt* or configuration or pattern in the central nervous system appeared in a series of experiments on rats. K. S. Lashley trained rats to traverse a maze. When the performance could be accomplished without error, the animals were operated on surgically, different areas of the brain being put out of action in such a way that the original stimulus-response connexions were destroyed. Nevertheless, the operated rats went through the maze without errors and without random variations, but they used sets of movements entirely different from those in which the habit had been learned. As the investigator said, " One drags himself through with his forepaws ; another falls at every step but gets through with a series of lunges ; a third rolls completely over in making each turn but manages to avoid rolling into a cul-de-sac and makes an errorless run. . . . If the customary series of movements employed in reaching the food is rendered impossible *another set not previously used in the habit constituting an entirely different motor pattern, may be directly and efficiently substituted* without any random activity." [2] If, it is said, this may be true for rats,

---

[1] *Cf.* the substitution of one set of letters for another in the mechanical reproduction of a geometrical proof.

[2] K. S. Lashley, *Brain Mechanisms and Intelligence* (Chicago, 1929), p. 137. My italics.

but not for human beings, the answer is that similar results have been observed in people suffering from brain injuries.[1]

'HIGHER' AND 'LOWER' LEVELS OF THINKING AND ACTING

Neither the Associationist nor the Gestalt theory provides a complete explanation of mental activity. Both are exemplified in a complex performance. Whether the activity takes the form of mechanical association or association by meaning and relationships seems to depend to a marked degree *on the conditions under which the learning and thinking are done.* We do associate by contiguity in memorizing the alphabet, or the Morse Code, or the names and dates of the battles of the Wars of the Roses. In such cases we are concerned with memorizing and reproducing a series of conventional symbols in some arbitrary order. There is a minimum of connexion by meaning. (Even so, it usually happens that the intelligent learner searches around for some sort of meaningful connexion, a mnemonic, for example, in order the better to fix the associations.[2] Moreover, the Associationists' laws of recall—recency, frequency, vividness, and satisfaction—do account for some of the vagaries of recollection, as we shall find in Chapter XI. Nevertheless, meaningful associations are learned much more quickly and retained longer than nonsense materials. When problem-solving, planning, trial and error, discovery—that is when *adaptability*—is required from the learner, then the Associationist principles do not work. Thinking and acting at a higher level than mechanical reproduction are required. In these cases we seem to be dealing not with simple associations between sensations and images, or with reflex actions arranged in contiguous series, but with relatively stable configurations or patterns of intelligible relationships which are mediated by relatively stable arrangements in the central nervous system. These, in some way not clearly understood as yet, are capable of being aroused into action by a variety of sensory stimuli or ' cues,'[3] and of setting off a variety of actions. In this way a variety of situations or problems can be recognized as belonging to the same type, and if one course of action is prevented or fails to achieve the purpose in

---

[1] See, for example, H. Head, *Aphasia and Kindred Disorders of Speech* ; D. Katz, *Gestalt Psychology*, Chapter 3 : " The Plasticity of Motor Processes " ; D. O. Hebb, *The Organisation of Behaviour.* Chapter 7 : " Higher and Lower Processes Related to Learning."

[2] *Cf.* the mnemonic described on p. 525, below.

[3] *Cf.* the suggestions of a prompter to the actors during a stage-play.

view, other courses can quickly be substituted. The system of Morse signals is a good example. In a similar way, the National Anthem is recognizable by anyone who is not tone deaf whether it is sung by one performer or by a crowd, or played on a piano, or organ, or violin, or trumpet, in a variety of keys and speeds. The sound qualities may be totally different, the time-intervals shorter or longer, but so long as the *pattern* of sounds and intervals remains the same the melody is recognizable. The melody can be recalled if the pattern of intervals is tapped out on a table or on the back of one's hand. Reasoning by analogy appears to be another way of learning by recognizing a pattern. It occurs frequently in scientific discovery. The fall of an apple is said to have suggested the principle of gravitation to Newton. Harvey solved the problem of the circulation of the blood when he thought of the heart as a pump forcing blood through the system of arteries and veins.

During recent years teaching methods have changed from Associationism towards Gestalt principles. So far as circumstances permit, learning has been made more purposeful, subject-matter has been more closely connected with the experience and interests of the pupils; apprehension of meanings and relations is substituted for rote memorizing. In teaching by topics, or projects, techniques—*i.e.*, skills of various kinds—are learned in the service of the project, and take their meaning and ' worthwhileness ' from it, instead of being acquired as a series of mechanical connexions.

It has been increasingly recognized that thinking and acting are closely connected, that in the early stages of learning, relationships are best apprehended by practical activities—for example, in arithmetic and geometry. Memorizing is postponed until relationships are apprehended. As the learner matures and gathers a wider knowledge of meanings and relations, words and symbols can then take the place of practical activities, particularly in the case of intellectually brighter pupils. Slower pupils may still find learning through practical activities most effective—*e.g.*, learning the principles of mechanics through experience with machinery, or principles of biology through gardening and keeping small animals.

Again, it is increasingly recognized that childhood is not exclusively the period for rote memory, and adolescence the period for reasoning. All the processes involved in learning are already present quite early in life. They may exist in embryonic form and make progress together. The difference between the infant-school child and the grammar-school adolescent is not a difference between a mechanical memorizer and a logical reasoner, but rather between the amount of experience available and the mental skills involved in dealing with more and still more complex systems of relationships. Intelligent children can be more adaptable than unintelligent adults. Quality of brain and the conditions in which learning takes place are more significant than chronological age.

ADAPTABILITY AND INTELLIGENCE

It is generally agreed that brighter children can apprehend relationships more easily, make inferences more readily and correctly, think more easily in words and symbols, and build up more complex systems of relationships, and are therefore more adaptable than duller children. In fact, there is a strong tendency to identify intelligence with capacity for apprehending relationships. This tendency has influenced, very markedly, the form of tests of intelligence.

Many items in intelligence tests are phrased in such forms as the following :

Finger is to Hand as Toe is to ?

Warmth is to Stove as ? is to Knife.

Worse is to Bad as Better is to (Excellent, Best, Good, Inferior).

Write the next two items in the following series : 1, 4, 9, 16, 25, ? ?

Underline two of the following words that do not belong to the same class or category as the rest : Oil, Quicksilver, Bladder, Lead, Boat, Cream, Cork.

In each case the correct answers depend on the recognition and application of relationships.

Professor Spearman proposed three principles of cognition in his work on the nature of intelligence :

(i) Any lived experience tends to evoke immediately a knowing of its characteristics and the experiencing subject.

(ii) Mentally presenting any two or more characters (simple or complex) tends to evoke immediately a knowing of a relation between them.

(iii) The presenting of any character together with any relation tends to evoke immediately a knowing of a correlative character.

In the above, ' to evoke ' means to call up, to bring to awareness ; ' a character ' is any distinguishable feature of the objects or situations observed ; ' correlative ' means ' corresponding.' Thus, in the test items illustrated above, Finger and Hand, Warmth and Stove, Worse and Bad, are characters between which there are relations—for example, of part to whole, of attribute or quality, of relative conditions. In Spearman's system, characters (or fundaments) can be themselves relations, and then we have a higher-order relationship—namely, a relation between relations—e.g., between worse, bad, good.[1]

Spearman's principles illustrate a further objection to Associationist doctrine. The Gestalt psychologists believe that the juxtaposition of two ' sensations ' cannot give rise to awareness of relations between them, one reason, among others, being that we never, in actual life, apprehend single simple sensations. On the contrary, even the simplest experience imaginable is already a system of relations. For example, a black dot on a sheet of white paper is not apprehended merely as a black dot. It is a black dot *on a background* and is therefore already an item (or a character) in a relation. Thus, the order of development of the intellect on Gestalt principles is directly opposite to that according to the Associationists. The Associationists implied that knowledge began with an empty space, as it were, which was then filled in with impressions—a sort of additive process. The Gestalt psychologists believe that we begin with whole experiences whether of objects or situations consisting of characters and relations already constituted. At first we apprehend these wholes of experience vaguely. Intellectual development then proceeds by a gradual bringing of these implicit characters and relations to ever clearer awareness. The process is illustrated by the series of children's drawings on pages 199 to 200. Inspection of one's own mental processes seems to support this. One's first acquaintance with a new building or a complicated machine feels vague, with a few prominent details standing out against a relatively undifferentiated background. That being so, the question now arises, how do we ' unravel ' the original complex but vague experience and arrive at clear knowledge ?

How Characters and Relations are grasped clearly. Implicit and Explicit Cognition—Attending, Abstracting, Naming

In so far as the account just given is correct, characters and relations are the analytical mental ' elements ' into which our total perceptual experiences must be resolved before we can begin the process of generalizing and systematizing experience into knowledge. How, then, do we perform the necessary analysis ? Three processes seem to be involved—namely, *attending*, that is concentrating and

---

[1] *The Nature of Intelligence and the Principles of Cognition.*

directing mental activity towards details ; *abstracting* ; *naming*. We shall see as the argument develops how associations as well as analysis are involved.

That the analysis of perceptual experience is not automatic, instantaneous, or complete is already sufficiently obvious from the discussion on perception. The environment presents us continually with an enormous number of possible characters and relations. Of these, we *realize explicitly* only comparatively few and ignore the remainder. Mental activity is selective. The very fact that we bring some particular sense-organ to bear upon one aspect of the environment means that other aspects must be ignored. In addition, we have already noted the principle of least action. Our attention-adjustments are controlled by our hungers, and these again are related to our needs. As soon as a need is satisfied, hunger gives way to complacence, during which observation is at a minimum. Hence in normal circumstances we *never proceed with the analysis of our perceptual experience into characters and relations further than is required for the satisfaction of our need at that moment.*

How many pedestrians (not expert motor-engineers) who see cars hundreds of times in a day, can draw accurately from memory the details of any well-known brand of saloon car ? (Readers might amuse themselves by trying to draw a typical Rover, or Daimler, or Ford, without reference to an actual car or picture. It might be made into a competition to find who can include the greatest number of correct details.)

The need of the average pedestrian is either to ride in cars, or, more frequently, to avoid being squashed flat by them. For these needs the recognition of one or two outstanding characters and relations is ample.

It is more striking to note that many people cannot analyse out characters and relations correctly even when they are observing an actual situation. Give some untrained pupils a map to copy, or a spray of flowers to draw, and note how the result, with which they are satisfied, corresponds with the original. Almost invariably gross errors are recorded, showing that certain characters and relations in the objective situation observed have not been noted explicitly at all, although the original is in front of the observers all the time.

People can, and do, react correctly in a practical way to relations without realizing exactly what the relations in question are. For example, a verbally untrained adult may possess a settee, a sofa, and chairs. If asked to do so he will point out each correctly, but may be quite at a loss to say what is the significant *logical difference* between these three common objects. A person can walk along a busy street while talking to a friend or thinking about what he will do when he arrives at his destination. If the neighbourhood is familiar he proceeds in the correct direction, avoids vehicles and other walkers, steps up and down kerbs at the correct moment. All this activity implies that the person concerned is reacting correctly to perceptual relations of space, time, colour, sound, etc., yet the relations need not be explicitly realized. These details of the journey may be quite forgotten by the time the destination is reached.

Hence we must take account, particularly for teaching-purposes, of the difference between *implicit* and *explicit* cognition. In ordinary experience, even of educated adults, many details of a perceptual experience remain bound, as it were, within the total situation. They are implicit in the experience and not consciously realized (or explicit). Clearly these implicit characters and relations are useless for intellectual development since by the very nature of things they cannot be organized by the learner. Therefore we must inquire how implicit cognition can be changed into explicit cognition. This change is the essential factor in intellectual development and, as we shall see in Chapter IX, in the transfer of the effects of training.

ATTENDING

The first phase in the passage from implicit to explicit cognition is *attending*.

Attending is the name we give to the complex set of physiological and mental adjustments which bring the sense-organs into the most favourable position for receiving stimuli clearly, and which concentrate the mental activity upon a specific objective (mental or physical).

The result of attending with alertness is a more intense and clear cognition.

How the attending can be started and controlled will be considered later.

COMPARING, CONTRASTING, ABSTRACTING

The second phase is that of comparing and contrasting the fundaments (which may be objects, characters, or relations) and

G

abstracting the item concerned (which may be a character or relation).

When a character or relation has been singled out and made explicitly conscious it can be thought of as a character or relation in abstraction from the particular perceptual experience in which it was originally embodied. Thus a trained person can think of ' white ' without at the same time thinking also of a piece of white chalk, or a snowfield, or a swan in which he may have noted the character in question originally. In the same way a relation, *e.g.*, ' a distance of twelve inches,' can be thought of without imagining a particular twelve-inch ruler.

Any character or relation which can be thought of apart from the concrete perceptual situations in which it may be embodied is called an *abstraction*.

Comparison and contrast facilitate the process of abstracting. Thus, at first, the whiteness of a piece of chalk seems to belong to the object very persistently. It is conceivable that if we saw no other white objects but pieces of chalk, the abstraction of the character ' white ' would be most difficult or even impossible. However, when the perception of a piece of white chalk is followed by that of a sheet of white paper, a swan, an expanse of snow, white flowers, etc., the fact that the white character is common to all these situations while all of the other characters differ, serves to emphasize the white character and depress the others, particularly if the mental activity is directed specifically to the whiteness. At the same time the whiteness of any given white object can be intensified in cognition by presenting it in close conjunction with other objects not white.

Comparison and contrast are facilitated by presenting the characters and relations in question in close proximity. Separating the fundaments may prevent explicit cognition. (See account of Line's experiments, p. 209.)

It is worth noting for teaching-purposes that in comparison we direct mental activity towards and emphasize similarities ; in contrast, differences.

NAMING

The process of abstracting is completed (fixed as it were) by naming the character or relation abstracted. Behaviourist psychologists call this naming ' verbalization,' a word of which they are very fond. For the orthodox Behaviourist there is no such process as thought, only the repetition of word-habits.

How do We arrive at a Knowledge of Logical Classes and Generalizations ?

We have followed in some detail the processes by which we arrive at explicit awareness of elementary characters and relations. Now we have to inquire how these elements are reorganized into logical classes and generalizations.

We can study the process by means of a simple example.

Experience presents us with a multifarious *collection* of living things. We begin our mental organization by noting certain striking and predominant characters. Some of the things move, others remain fixed in one place. The first we call animals; the second, plants. Some animals walk on two legs (*e.g.*, human beings and birds), others on four legs. Each broad class includes characters between which we note relations of similarity and difference. We begin to assemble sub-classes of like creatures. Then these creatures, when compared within their class, reveal *significant* differences. Differences in size may not be significant. Some rabbits are bigger than some dogs. Closer examination shows that the rabbits are all vegetable-eaters while no dogs are vegetable-eaters. This difference is *critical*. It serves to distinguish completely all rabbits from all dogs. Then we find that this critical difference is *invariably correlated with* other characters, *e.g.*, kind of teeth, type of digestion, and so on.

Thus, by comparing and contrasting the original objects in the multifarious collection and isolating (abstracting) characters and relations *always manifested by certain only of the individuals and never by the others* we can organize the original collection into a number of mutually exclusive logical classes to each of which we give a name.

To each name there corresponds a definition, that is, a specification of the *essential* characters and relations appropriate to that class.

We classify more than objects. Thus, ' a distance of one foot ' is a class of relations. ' Boiling,' ' running,' ' thinking ' represent classes of activities or processes. ' Poor,' ' rich,' ' healthy ' are classes of conditions.

Having arrived at a knowledge of classes, we can note relations between classes. For example, rabbits, sheep, deer are grass-eating animals. Cats, lions, wolves are flesh-eating animals. All are quadrupeds. Animals and plants are all living things.

Thus, by this process of logical classification we reduce the bewildering multiplicity of our perceptual world to an ordered arrangement which can be organized and reorganized *mentally*. Clarification and organization of the items of experience *proceed concurrently in two directions*, namely, (a) the analysis into more and more circumscribed sub-classes each with its own special characteristics ; and (b) the re-synthesis of many sub-classes into broader groups according to some common feature possessed by all in the group.

Some very clear cases of classification and generalization are presented by grammar (classes of words and sentences) ; logic (classes of propositions) ; and the various branches of natural science, *e.g.*, zoology, botany, geology, chemistry, and physics.

SUMMARY

The organization of experience involves two main processes : analysis and synthesis.

In analysis complex perceptual experience is resolved into elementary characters and relations. These elements are brought into explicit awareness by selective attending, and are then abstracted and named.

Concurrently with analysis goes synthesis. Objects (both simple and complex) having the same characters are grouped into classes.

THE ACTUAL COURSE OF INTELLECTUAL DEVELOPMENT IN LIVING CHILDREN

We have considered the processes of intellectual development in abstraction, as if they occurred singly. This is never the case in actual life, and to get a truer picture of the teacher's task we must try to make a survey of the normal living pupil in action.

The child's perceptual world is, at first, what psychologists call a ' presentational continuum ' or , as William James much more picturesquely phrased it, " one big blooming buzzing confusion." Out of this continuum there emerge first, striking sense-impressions—bright colours, loud sounds, movements. These serve to objectify things with which they are habitually associated.

Thus the first stage of intellectual development is the recognition of individualized objects by means of some striking characteristic which commands the child's attention. The first names are usually descriptions of objects in terms of the predominant character, *e.g.*, dogs are 'wow-wows'; ducks 'quack-quacks'; carts, motor-cars, perambulators, 'go-go's.'

The predominating mental activity in early childhood is sorting out the perceptual continuum into more clearly defined objects. The object seems to be noted as a crude whole at first, and advance consists of bringing to explicit awareness a constantly increasing nicety of detail. This is very well shown in Figs. 7 to 12.[1] Thus

FIG. 7

Drawing of Bear, Monkey, and Human Being,[2] by child aged 4 years 3 months

FIG. 8
Drawing of a House.[3]
Age, 4 years 9 months.

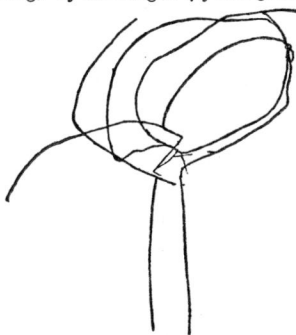

FIG. 9
Drawing of a Tree.[4]
Age, 5 years 8½ months.

[1] Reproduced from *The Psychology of Children's Drawings*, Helga Eng, by permission of the publishers, Messrs Kegan Paul, Trench, Trubner and Co. Ltd.
[2] Work cited, p. 41.   [3] Work cited, p. 46.   [4] Work cited, p. 57.

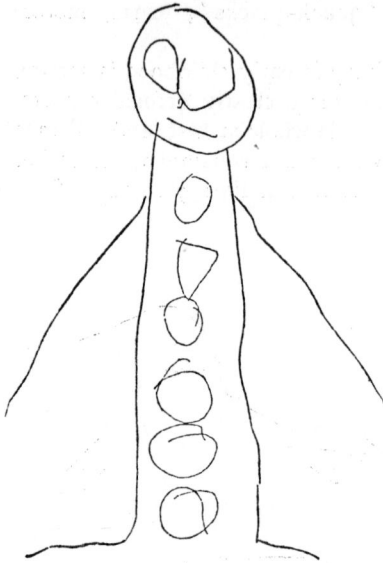

FIG. 10
Drawing of a Lady.[1]
Age, 4 years 7 months.

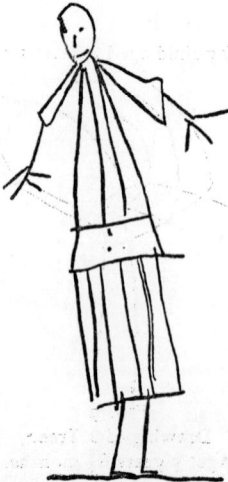

FIG. 12
Drawing of a Girl playing Ball.[3]
Age, 7 years 10½ months.

FIG. 11
Drawing of a Lady.[2]
Age, 6 years 2½ months.

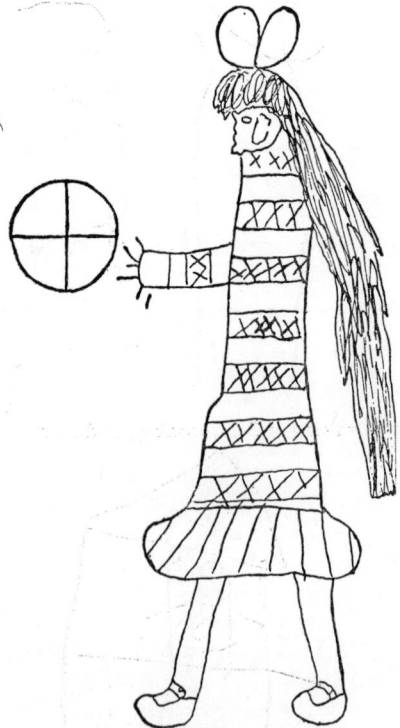

[1] Work cited, p. 45.   [2] Work cited, p. 76.   [3] Work cited, p. 176.

the direction of intellectual analysis is from crude wholes of experience to finer and still finer details. These details are not just added together in a mechanical way. They emerge or unfold from the original continuum as the powers of analysis improve and as observation is supplemented by memory and habit.

True classification is a rather later phase than analysis although it has usually begun before the normal child is ready to enter the infant school. The child's first groups are collections of objects rather than classes. In the process of classification, the young child's first perceptual objects represent types. Thus, if the first object seen is the domestic dog, then all similar animals will be called dogs—horses and donkeys will be big dogs ; rabbits, little dogs. This again illustrates the fact that the child at this stage perceives wholes (compare the drawings of the bear, monkey, and human being on p. 199).

Here again progress goes from crude undefined wholes to clear details. The types recognized by a general-outline similarity give place gradually to logical classes arranged according to one or a few common elementary characters.

The Relative Importance of Practical Activity and Language in Intellectual Development at Different Stages of School-life

We have seen that the essential mental processes in both analysis and classification are first, concentrated attending, and second, the to-and-fro direction of the attention adjustments (comparison and contrast) which serves to bring different objectives within the same mental field. From the practical teaching point of view we need to realize clearly what conditions determine this alert attending, comparing, and contrasting and how the processes can be directed by the teacher.

In the very first stages of development, attending is stimulated by striking and massive changes in the environment. This reflex attending continues throughout life, but more important for systematic learning is the attending which is motivated by a hunger or aversion.

Needs in the young child lead directly to practical, manipulative activity, the aim of which is to satisfy the need. Now, so long as the practical activity is successful, resulting in satisfaction, attending remains at a low level of intensity. The learner is just sufficiently aware of the total situation to react successfully in an habitual way. This is the condition of implicit cognition.

The practical, manipulative activity, however, frequently ends in some *difficulty* which prevents further progress towards satisfaction. Then we get *mental arrest* accompanied by some degree of emotion (anger, fear, surprise) and a reinforcement of the hunger or aversion which prompted the activity. The mental arrest and the rise in intensity of conative and affective experience concentrate the mental activity and direct it towards the specific cause of the difficulty, giving rise to *more intense cognition* and *increased clearness* of apprehension.

Thus, a small child in a Montessori school may be provided with a form-board in which holes of various sizes and shapes are cut. Into these holes he is required to fit wooden insets. Suppose he begins with a circular hole. He may pick up a square or hexagonal inset without noting specific features of its shape, and endeavour to force this into the hole. It will not fit. Thereupon he twists it about, possibly hammers it. Still it will not go in. The arrest produced by this difficulty concentrates attention upon the detailed differences between the shape of the hole and of the wrong inset. Thereupon the process is repeated with a second inset—the trial-and-error type of learning.

In normal circumstances social intercourse plays a significant part in the development of a situation like this. The baffled and disappointed child goes to an older pupil or to the teacher. The latter has two alternatives, *depending on the vocabulary of the pupil.* He can point to the root of the difficulty, and then demonstrate the correct solution by doing the trick himself. As he performs the actions he *names* the significant items and thus intensifies the process of abstraction.

At a later stage when the pupil's vocabulary is sufficiently well developed, a description or verbal instruction will serve the same process as practical pointing, and demonstration. A pupil may have drawn a map of Great Britain in which the details are grossly out of proportion. The teacher may say, " Look at England on your map. Now look at Wales. Which is bigger ? Now look at England and Wales on your atlas. What is wrong with your drawing ? "

Thus mental activity can be directed *either* by practical manipulative activity on the pupil's part, and by pointing, pantomime, or demonstration on the teacher's part, *or* by using words. In actual practice these two sets of processes are combined, but it is important for teaching-purposes to note their *relative* importance at different stages in intellectual development. It is very obvious that practical activity by the pupil and practical guidance by the teacher must predominate in the early stages of development, since words then have a minimum of significance. Verbal direction of mental activity is useless until an effective vocabulary has developed. This fact is an additional justification for the predominance of practical manipulative activity as an educational medium in infant and junior schools, and among the more backward seniors.

WHAT ARE THE FUNCTIONS OF LANGUAGE IN INTELLECTUAL DEVELOPMENT ?

The importance of verbalization merits a more detailed discussion of the topic. What are the main connexions between intellectual development and the development of a language ?

Words act as vehicles for meanings.

Intellectual development depends upon the analysis of first-hand experience into elementary characters and relations. These when abstracted from the concrete objects of experience are the ideas, properly so-called. Now, ideas are elusive. They fade quickly from consciousness. They may re-emerge spontaneously from time to time but are often quite difficult to recall voluntarily. Yet if we are to continue the organization of experience beyond first-order relations and crude classifications we must be able to maintain ideas in the ' focus of consciousness ' sufficiently long for adequate contemplation.

Again, so soon as a related system of objects is broken up, the relations in question cease to exist. In the absence of any vehicle for the relations it would be impossible to contemplate them again without reconstituting the precise objective system in an identical way. This is frequently difficult, and it may be impossible (in the study of history, for example).

Hence, for intellectual development beyond the crude stage of perceptual experience we need an efficient vehicle for the perpetuation and mental control of abstract ideas. This is provided very efficiently by words.

Words, both spoken and written, are themselves perceptual objects with the sensory vividness and intensity of material things.

Written and printed words are permanent and relatively constant in appearance, being easily recognized. The motor-mechanisms of speech and writing persist for long periods as habits enabling the trained learner to reproduce a great variety of words at will. Further, by the use of a conventional alphabet, an almost infinite variety of new words can be invented to keep pace with the advance of fresh discovery and analysis.

If, then, we learn associations between abstracted characters and relations (the meanings) and corresponding words, and make the associations habitual, we can by organizing the words also organize the corresponding ideas to a very high degree of complexity and subtlety.

It is a commonplace of observation that if we are looking or listening intently for some object, or trying to solve a complicated problem, we tend to repeat and stress the appropriate words either aloud or in inner speech. Also, the more difficult and elusive the ideas are, the more intently do we stress the words. This motor-activity serves to maintain the corresponding ideas in the focus of consciousness. Occasionally a problem which has resisted solution during quiet contemplation can be solved if the thinker attempts to expound the difficulty to an audience.

It is easy to see that a language made permanent by writing and printing accumulates the wisdom and knowledge of many past generations of thinkers. An intelligent child who can read ' stands on the shoulders ' of his predecessors. The extraordinarily rapid progress of mathematics and physical science within recent years would have been quite impossible in the absence of a written language.

A developing language facilitates increasing nicety of characterization and subtlety of relation-eduction (that is, growth in the depth of intellect).

The fact that words are distinct and easily distinguishable objects, facilitates discrimination between two similar but not identical experiences. This function has been very well depicted by William James.

> How does one learn to distinguish claret from burgundy ? Probably they have been imbibed on different occasions. When we first drank claret we heard it called by that name, we were eating such and such a dinner, etc. Next time we drink it a dim reminder of all these things chimes through us as we get the taste

of the wine. When we try burgundy, our first impression is *that it is a kind of claret*,[1] but something falls short of full identification and presently we hear it called burgundy. During the next few experiences, the discrimination may still be uncertain—" Which," we ask ourselves, " of the two wines is this present specimen ? " But at last the claret-flavour recalls pretty distinctly its own name ' claret,' " that wine I drank at So and So's table," etc. ; and the burgundy-flavour recalls the name ' burgundy ' and some one else's table. . . . After a while the tables, and other parts of the setting besides the name, grow so multifarious as not to come up distinctly into consciousness. But along with this, the adhesion of each wine with its own *name* becomes more and more inveterate, and at last each flavour suggests instantly and certainly its own name and nothing else. The names differ far more than the flavours and help to stretch these latter farther apart. Some such process as this must go on in all our experience. Beef and mutton, strawberries and raspberries, odour of rose and odour of violet contract different adhesions which reinforce the differences already felt in the terms.[2]

This process of ' pinning down ' each newly developed idea as it emerges during the process of analysis resembles to some extent the practice of the biological student dissecting a complicated animal structure. As each component is isolated clearly from the original complication it is pinned down and labelled, making future identification more accurate and rapid.

If we learn words for characters and first-order relations, then these words help to keep in mind the first-order relations so that second-order relations between them are more easily grasped. These, expressed in words, form the fundaments for third- and higher-order relations. Without the aid of words it is doubtful whether these subtle higher-order relations could be held in mind sufficiently long to make them clear. One frequently finds in considering a new problem that, by pondering over the relations already clarified, more subtle relations emerge, at first very vaguely. They represent more of a feeling than a developed thought. Unless these fleeting subtle higher-order relations can be expressed in words immediately, they are apt to fade from consciousness and are exceedingly difficult to recall.

[1] Italics mine, *cf.* p. 201, second para.
[2] William James, *Principles of Psychology*, Vol. I, p. 511. Reprinted by permission of the publishers, Messrs Macmillan & Co., Ltd.

A developing language extends the span of comprehension, i.e., *it favours growth in breadth of intellect.*

The span of attention is measured by the number of objects which can be perceived successfully at a single rapid glance or act of listening. This span is strictly limited, most people being unable to encompass more than six or seven different objects. In children, the span is usually less than this. If more objects are displayed than can be encompassed by the mental activity of the observer, the observation breaks down, as it were, and instead of the normal six or seven objects being recalled, only one or sometimes none at all can be thought of.

What is true of objects is much more true of ideas. It is difficult to think of more than one idea at a time. If we concentrate upon a second idea, the first quickly fades from explicit consciousness. If we must relate a number of disparate ideas, we must be able to hold them together mentally sufficiently long for the relations to emerge clearly. This can be done by speaking the corresponding words intently, or better still by writing the words down. Thus, since the written words remain permanently, each associated with the corresponding idea, the mental activity can be directed to the words as often as is necessary and the corresponding ideas related in a system. Again the words can be rearranged in various patterns making the rearrangement of the ideas, with the consequent emergence of new relations, more easy. Thus words favour breadth of comprehension.

Words offer a means of ' exploring ' mentally a complicated situation more effectively.

Words can act as probes, as it were. Armed with a battery of appropriate words which have been associated with certain characters and relations *and memorized,* the learner can approach a new situation, apply the words to it in some definite order, and thus *direct his mental activity to corresponding features in the situation.* Observation of the presence or absence of specific characters and relations is thereby improved. This fact has been demonstrated experimentally by Fox (see p. 244).

Instead of words, conventional symbols may be used for the same purposes. This has been done most extensively in mathematics and those physical sciences capable of mathematical expression. The discussion in this section can be illustrated very clearly by a mathematical example :

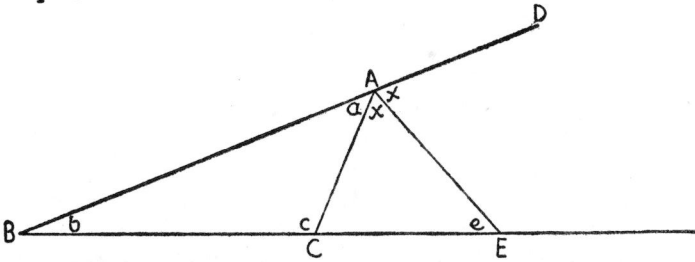

ABC is a triangle of which the side *BA* is produced to *D*. *AE* bisects the angle *CAD* and cuts the side *BC* produced, at *E*. It is required to show that the angle *AEB* is equal to half the difference between two angles of the triangle *ABC*.

In this example we have a fairly complicated figure manifesting many possible relations, and a rather vague problem. We have therefore to explore the situation first, isolate a number of possible relations, think them over, arrange and rearrange them until we get a system which is relevant to this particular demonstration.

Suppose we represent each angle by a letter. Previous experience suggests that out of all the possible relations shown in the diagram, the solution will depend on the fact that the exterior angle of any triangle is always equal to the sum of the interior opposite angles. (Note the process of supplementation by memory.)

Now we can write down some relations, *e.g.*,

$$2x = b + c.$$
$$c = e + x.$$
$$x = \tfrac{1}{2}(b + c).$$

By combining these equalities and rearranging the terms we can arrive at the relation required, thus :

$$e = c - x$$
$$= c - \tfrac{1}{2}b - \tfrac{1}{2}c$$
$$= \tfrac{1}{2}c - \tfrac{1}{2}b$$
$$= \tfrac{1}{2}(c - b).$$

I.e., angle *AEB* is equal to half the difference between angles *ACB* and *ABC*.

Finally, to test the value of the words and symbols in working out the demonstration, readers are invited to solve the problem *without using any words or symbols* either spoken or written.

Thus intellectual development goes on concurrently with the development of a conventional language.[1] The language serves as

[1] *Cf.* the relation between language development, intelligence, and scholastic attainment, Chapter II, p. 35, above.

a vehicle for the analysis and synthesis of experience, and at the same time it fixes and preserves the gains of mental activity. Conversely, the developed language favours the active exploration of new situations, thereby providing more fundaments out of which further systems of relations and an increasing vocabulary may be evolved.

The educational value of language is therefore immense, *always provided that the language develops along with the active analysis and synthesis of real experience.* If language is taught mechanically without its corresponding ideas its educational value is nil. The result is a fatuous verbalism which hinders rather than helps further intellectual development. (*Cf.* p. 175). Hence it is essential in teaching for intellectual development, to follow these rules :

(*a*) Appropriate words should be provided for every new character and relation which has been grasped explicitly by the pupils.

(*b*) The ideas and the associated words must be memorized together *so that the association becomes habitual.* Then the words can be used as carriers for the ideas.

(*c*) Constant careful training in the accurate use of words is indicated.

Clearness of expression is evidence of clear thought but also the effort to express thoughts clearly encourages the development of clear thinking. The two abilities are inter-related. Hence the value of calling attention to ambiguities of speech and giving practice in word discrimination.

In this connexion the learning of a second language is valuable *for those pupils who have sufficient intelligence to profit by it.* There are many ambiguities and inaccuracies in English which are not realized explicitly until a pupil begins to learn a second language with a different idiom. In colloquial English we say, " I am going away for a holiday next week." The absurdity of this common usage is not realized explicitly by the average pupil until he learns that the French always use the future tense of the verb to express the corresponding idea.

The effectiveness of the comparison and contrast of word-meaning and grammatical structure is likely to be the greater, the more the two languages differ in idiom. This is the real psychological and educational reason why Latin or Greek may be a better medium *for linguistic discipline* than a modern Western European language, for English pupils.

The arguments in this section dispose of the contention of some **non-language** specialists that the teaching of English is not their concern in school. Actually, no subject can be taught effectively, even mathematics and science, unless careful attention is paid to the need for clarity of expression in both spoken and written speech. The fact is that every teacher is to some extent necessarily a teacher of language if he does his work efficiently. Contempt for grammar and accuracy of speech encourages the spread of ' journalese ' in many schools, which is as offensive in its lack of style as it is ineffective for the purpose of expressing clear meaning. We may well pray to be delivered from the modern ' tabloid ' newspaper-headline mode of speaking and writing, and the absence of clear thinking of which it is the outward manifestation.

MEANING OF CONCEPT

Books on the psychology of knowledge and theory of education frequently contain the term ' concept.' It is desirable therefore to know exactly what the term signifies.

The dictionary meaning of ' concept ' is " an idea of a class of objects, a general notion." However, classes of objects, from a logical point of view, can only be established mentally by the abstraction of characters and relations. Any abstracted character or relation must of necessity be general, e.g., white, red, square, a length of 12 inches, one pound weight, an angle of 90 degrees. Their generality is established by the fact that any such character or relation is necessarily constant and applies to any object or set of related objects which embody that character or relation.

Hence, using the analysis developed in the previous section, we may say that a concept is any character or relation which has been abstracted mentally.

Concepts may represent very different degrees of subtlety and complication.

EXPERIMENTAL INVESTIGATION OF THE GROWTH IN CHILDREN OF THE POWER TO EDUCE RELATIONS

Some experimental evidence concerning the growth in children of the power to educe relations has been obtained by Line.[1] The evidence is not only valuable from a psychological point of view, but useful for practical teaching-purposes.

Line set out to find answers to the following questions : At

[1] " Growth of Visual Perception in Children," *British Journal of Psychology*, Monogr. Supplement, 15, 1931.

what age does the power to educe relations emerge ; what type of relations can children of a given age recognize ; what connexion exists between power of educing relations in the visual test material employed in the investigation and intelligence (as measured by a standard mental test) ; is progress continuous or does it proceed by jumps ?

The experiments included some 1500 children from two and a half to sixteen years of age. The tests were restricted to the eduction of relations of similarity and difference between colours, shapes, and lines.

The tests were so arranged that they included increasing orders of complication and difficulty. Some tests involved only *first-order* relations, *e.g.*, the relation ' same ' or ' different ' between two colours. Other tests involved *second-order* relations. Thus the child was presented with a card bearing two figures similar in shape and colour. He was next presented with a card bearing two figures similar in shape but different in colour. Now, the task is to compare the relation (similar) between the first pair, with the relation (different) between the second pair, and apprehend a *second-order* relation (different) between the two relations.

Relation-systems can be complicated to almost any degree. The process can be represented diagrammatically as follows :[1]

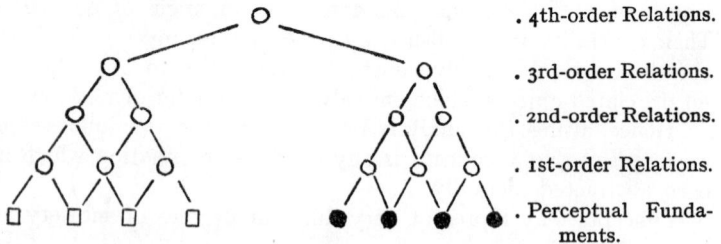

. 4th-order Relations.

. 3rd-order Relations.

. 2nd-order Relations.

. 1st-order Relations.

. Perceptual Fundaments.

The most important findings in this investigation for our purposes were the following :

1. The scores in these visual tests showed a high degree of correlation with the scores made by the same children in a standardized verbal ' intelligence ' test (Spearman's *Measure of Intelligence for Use in Schools*).

[1] In this diagram the open squares and black circles are intended to represent characters derived from observation of perceptual details. The open circles represent relations apprehended between corresponding characters or relations. It is possible to apprehend relations between relations, and relations between systems of relations, in increasing order of complexity.

This fact suggests that the same aptitude (or aptitudes) were involved in both performances. At first sight it might be supposed that Line's test-material involved only visual perception of shapes and colours while the intelligence test involved knowledge of abstract word-meanings and ability to reason. Thus the two types of test were related to each other as perception is related to thinking (or reasoning), and there has been a strong tendency on the part of psychologists and teachers to believe that these two activities were quite distinct and separate. Line's investigation indicates that what we commonly call perceiving and thinking have very much in common.[1]

Incidentally, this result is significant for the study of bilingual problems since it indicates the possibility of estimating the actual mental development (or intelligence) of bilingual children by means of non-verbal tests. It is obvious that *verbal* intelligence tests are useless in bilingual work since they take for granted the very factor they are supposed to investigate.

2. The eduction of relations begins very early in life.

3. Improvement in power to educe relations with increasing age is revealed in two ways : by a rise in the order of the relations grasped correctly ; and by an increase in the number of fundaments which can be comprehended (*i.e.*, held together mentally) within the same situation. This may be likened to an increase in depth or subtlety, and in breadth or complication.

Taking average ages, three-year-old children passed first-order tests successfully. Between three and five years the ability remained at about the first-order level, but improvement consisted in relating more fundaments together.

Second-order tests were passed completely at about five years, and the period five to eight years was occupied with another increase in breadth of comprehension.

Third-order tests were passed completely at eight to nine years, and fourth-order tests at about eleven to twelve years.

These averages give some indication about the ability which may be expected in the normal school pupil at the ages mentioned. The moral is, do not present multiple-order relations too early.

4. Cognitive development obeys two rules which we have already noted about development in general, namely :

---

[1] In this connexion see the sections on observation, reasoning, factorial analysis of ability in Chapters VIII and IX below.

(i) Eduction of relations between objects as wholes, occurs more easily and at an earlier age than eduction of relations between details within each object. Progress, that is, goes from broad to increasingly finer discrimination of details, an important factor in determining choice of subject-matter and materials for practical activity at different ages.

(ii) Eduction of relations takes place at different orders of subtlety at the same time, and improvement takes place at all levels simultaneously.

The following results abstracted from one of Line's tables illustrates this point.[1]

Years	6	9	12	15
1st-order tests . . .	5·0	7·6	8·1	9·5
2nd-order tests . . .	3·2	6·4	6·8	9·0
3rd-order tests . . .	2·3	4·8	5·2	6·8
4th-order tests . . .	1·3	2·3	4·0	5·4

The numbers in the above table represent *average* scores on tests of a given order, made by children at the ages indicated.[2] It will be seen that six-year-old children while most successful on first-order tests showed some degree of ability even on fourth-order tests. Also the improvement continues on all four levels simultaneously. That implies that there is *no sudden jump in ability* at any given age, and therefore it is not necessary for the child to become perfectly proficient at first-order relations before it can attempt to educe second-order relations. This point again is important in choice of materials for instruction and the organization of syllabuses.

In addition to the facts presented about the development of relation-eduction with increasing age, Line also showed two further facts of great educational importance.

(a) Separation, both in space and time, of the fundaments between which a relation is to be educed makes the realization of the relation much more difficult. Realization is easiest when the fundaments are presented in close proximity, and it may be prevented altogether if they are widely separated. This indicates another important principle in lesson-presentation and guidance.

[1] Work cited, Table A, Appendix II, p. 125.
[2] A score of 10 would represent complete success in any given test.

(*b*) There is a distinction between ' as ' and ' that ' cognition. In other words a person at any age can react to characters as related to each other without realizing explicitly *that* they are related. This point has already been mentioned in the discussion of implicit and explicit cognition.

NOTE ON THE CONDITIONS OF EFFECTIVE ATTENDING

Alert critical attending is necessary for analysis of experience and the eduction of relations.

The process of attending consists in making a complex set of adjustments which serve to produce the best conditions for the reception of certain sensory stimuli and to direct the mental activity towards certain specific impressions or ideas at the expense of others.

Books on educational psychology and teaching-method used to show elaborate classifications of ' attention ' as though there were several different types. Actually there is only one process of attending, but this may be started, and maintained, in different ways :

Involuntary attending is caused by a sudden intense change in some sensory quality of the environment, *e.g.*, loud sound, flash of light, pain. In this case certain hungers for security and well-being are aroused and the person *cannot help but attend* until the situation becomes normal again.

Spontaneous attending is caused by the presence of an unsatisfied hunger. It is maintained until the hunger is satisfied. Involuntary attending is really a special case of spontaneous attending in which the process is maintained for a short period only.

Voluntary attending happens when the person *decides* to attend, and actively maintains the attitude of attending. This mode of attending is characteristic of a mental conflict during which there is a competition for the available mental activity. The direction of activity oscillates, being distracted between two or more objectives. In order to determine the conflict, motives derived from the hunger for self-enhancement are brought in to reinforce one side of the conflict at the expense of the other. This happens when the wavering or distracted person decides, " Now I must (or will) attend to this object instead of that."

In teaching-practice no difficulty arises during spontaneous attending. Then mental activity is continuously directed towards the satisfying objectives. This is the best condition for learning. However, it frequently happens that school-activities do not arouse spontaneous attending. Or, in other cases, distractions are inadvertently introduced into the situation either by changes within the attending person, or by events in the local environment. Since distraction due to conflict is not conducive to effective learning, it is desirable to note some of its causes in order to prevent it as far as possible.

SOURCES OF DISTRACTION AND COMPETITION FOR MENTAL
ACTIVITY

1. Conflicting sense-impressions, particularly if intense and lasting.
Refer to Fig. 13. If the mental activity is concentrated on the
printed words, the figure underneath is not adequately perceived, and
vice versa.

UTOMATI

ENTILATIN

CO. LTD.

factory is complete unless it
isfactorily ventilated.

fans, no moving parts. Wor
enty-four hours a day at no co
ntilation for: Pantries, Larde
throoms, Basements, Cella
nemas, etc., wherever air con
ning is required.

OTATIONS GIVEN FOR COMPLE
TALLATIONS ON THE AUTO VEI
SYSTEM.

FIG. 13

2. Hungers and aversions in conflict.
Examples of this have already been noted. When any strong
motive is active it determines what sensory impressions and ideas
shall be favoured. Hence during a conflict of motive there will be a
corresponding distraction as between two sets of impressions or ideas.
3. Any emotional disturbance interferes with alert steady attending. When one is angry or afraid it is difficult to attend to anything
else but the source of anger or fear. If one tries to read, or work a

calculation, the process is disturbed by the intrusion of ideas and feelings associated with the emotion.

4. Perseveration.

This is the name given to the tendency for mental activity once it is started in some particular direction to persist by its own momentum, so to speak. Different individuals experience this tendency in widely different degrees, but most are familiar with the experience of a tune or refrain which keeps intruding into the ' focus of consciousness ' and displacing ideas already there.

Some causes of distraction commonly found in class-teaching are :

1. Showing too many objects, or presenting too many ideas at the same time.

2. Presenting badly grouped sensory impressions or ideas, including the case in which the mental objects to be contemplated are separated too widely in space or time.

Examples :

Chaotic disarrangement of words and sketches on a blackboard.

Performing experiments while the demonstration table is littered with miscellaneous odds and ends of apparatus.

Having striking pictures or diagrams on the wall of the classroom facing the class during a lesson for which they are not appropriate.

Giving out several conflicting instructions. Presenting items of information too quickly and in bad order.

Some more subtle sources of distraction are :

1. Competition between the appearance of an object and its significance. This happens in reading words. If one attends closely to the appearance of the words one neglects their meaning and *vice versa*. (*Cf.* p. 161).

2. Competition of aims. This would occur if we told pupils to listen to the plot of a story and at the same time to pick out as many nouns as possible in the narrative.

3. Competition between a situation or object as a whole and the details which constitute it, *e.g.*, in a page of print, if we attempt to visualize it as a whole we neglect the individual words. The same thing holds good for pictures, maps, models, scientific apparatus. Occasionally some striking detail monopolizes the mental activity at the expense of other details and of the object as a whole. This is one frequent cause of distorted perception. (*Cf.* drawings on p. 199).

In presenting complex objects for teaching-purposes, it is desirable to call attention first to the object as a whole, then direct the mental activity to the desired details, lastly *relate the clearly apprehended details to each other and to the whole.*

A special case of this type occurs when a striking illustration, joke, or story is more interesting than the lesson of which it is a part. If such an item is introduced in a lesson, care must be taken to allow the immediate interest to subside before proceeding further.

4. Competition between the process of attending itself, and the object of attending.

This frequently occurs in attending to obscure stimuli. We strain to attend and in doing so become preoccupied with the strain and fail to note the object itself.

This is one difficulty of voluntary attention. A bored student may try to drive himself to attend by repeating in inner speech, " I must attend to this." In consequence he attends to the process of attending and forgets for the time being what it is he is trying to concentrate upon.

In presentation, particularly to younger pupils, we should take pains to make all the stimuli clear so that no distraction is caused by the effort to attend.

OTHER CONDITIONS AFFECTING CLEAR ATTENDING

1. Facilitation due to familiarity and habit.

When any character or relation has been clearly apprehended it is easier to note the same item on a subsequent occasion. Hence, other things being equal, we tend to note familiar details and neglect the novel aspects of a situation, which may, of course, be the more valuable.

Also, we tend to note most readily the items for which names are known.

2. Fatigue and boredom prevent alert attending.

3. Oscillation.

It has been shown that intensity of mental activity and with it clearness of apprehension tends to rise and fall in a periodic rhythm. The intensity oscillates from a high to a low degree of intensity about an average level. This oscillation seems to be independent of fatigue.

4. Span of attention is limited.

We cannot attend to an indefinitely large number of items at the same time. If we attempt to do so the mental activity is dissipated and we do not attend clearly to any one of the items in question.

We can, however, attend to as many groups of objects as single items. This is illustrated by the following diagram :

Practice and familiarity increase the span to some extent. Fatigue and novelty decrease it. It is usually less in children than in adults.

The bearing of these facts upon lesson presentation is obvious.

CONCLUSION

All these cases emphasize one essential point, namely, *the process of attending is selective.* Concentrating mental activity on one item in the field of awareness drains it away from otner items which are for the time being ignored.

It follows therefore that *we cannot take any particular act of attention for granted*, especially in teaching younger pupils. It is always desirable to *direct specific attention to significant elements* in the lesson-material. This can be done by (*a*) giving clear instructions to attend to some specified detail, (*b*) asking questions and setting problems which cannot be answered until the appropriate observations have been accurately made, (*c*) pointing or using manipulative activity if the pupil's vocabulary is not adequate.

Further, *any presentation should be followed up* to test whether the necessary observations have been made accurately. (*Cf.* p. 547).

Finally, since pupils can attend effectively to only one thing at a time, make sure that all pupils are attending before giving instructions or proceeding with a lesson. If pupils are busy at work either in classroom or laboratory, and it is necessary to give some instruction, first call for silence, have apparatus and writing materials put down in a safe place, and *wait till all are ready to listen*. Then say what is necessary ; make sure that it has been noted, allow a few seconds for it to ' sink in,' then let the work proceed.

When pupils move from room to room between lessons, a period of two or three minutes is necessary for settling down before beginning the lesson. In this case train pupils to take out just what books they require for the present lesson, put them conveniently on their desks, put away their bags, etc., and dispose themselves comfortably and quietly to listen. Make a point of not beginning until all are ready to listen. Students-in-training frequently spoil what would have been a good lesson by beginning before order has been established in the classroom.

EXERCISES

1. Examine critically the value of different types of questions and problems as tests of intelligence. Accepting the definition of intelligence as the ability to realize and use relevant characters and relations, state what must be the essential features of a good test of general intelligence. Compare various standard intelligence tests from this point of view.

What bearing has your exercise on the framing of oral and written questions for the purposes of (*a*) lesson-development, and (*b*) scholarship examinations ?

2. By means of a vocabulary test explore the differences between a group of very bright pupils and a group of backward pupils of the same chronological age.

3. Illustrate the progressive analysis of a complex situation

into characters and higher-order relations by examining carefully and noting the stages by which you become acquainted with :

(a) a complicated building such as your college building.

(b) a strange town.

(c) a new class of pupils in school.

(d) a book dealing with some subject for study.

In the above, note carefully the function of intense and massive sensory impressions ; the effect of interest and purpose (use) ; the effect of difficulty and mental arrest ; the function of words, symbols, and maps ; the function of memory.

What bearing has your exercise upon the introduction of a new topic or a new skilled method of working to a class of pupils ?

4. Collect instances of correlate-eduction which are made by pupils during a science, mathematics, or history lesson.

5. Show in detail how the attempt to suggest a correct ' atmosphere ' for the study of (a) pre-historic Britain ; (b) an Anglo-Saxon village in the time of Alfred the Great ; (c) Wat Tyler's Rebellion ; (d) the Civil War in the reign of Charles I ; requires the process of correlate-eduction in the pupils. How can this process be encouraged by the teacher ? What part does the local environment play in the process ? What precautions are necessary ? What practical aids are likely to be useful (e.g., pictures, models, visits to ruins, dramatization, etc.) ? What is the function of these practical aids ?

6. State in detail the differences between a logical generalization and a summary.

7. Try to arrange a class of pupils in an order of merit according to some trait (e.g., general intelligence ; ability in history ; cheerfulness of disposition ; industry ; trustworthiness) without using any words or symbols either spoken or written.

Why is it so much more difficult to perform the above exercise for the traits mentioned than it would be for height ? Explain in terms of characters and relations.

Use the above exercise as an illustration of the function of words in mental activity.

8. Collect a number of drawings (not memory-drawings) of the same object (e.g., a man, woman, dog, motor-car, tree, house) made by children from about three years to fourteen years of age. Compare the drawings from the point of view of nicety of analysis, grasp of relations, errors, and distortions.

What insight does the collection afford into the nature and

direction of intellectual development ?   Make a note of the types of details usually noted, and of those usually ignored.   Apply your findings to the problem of directing attention.

9. Repeat Exercise 8, but with memory-drawings of familiar everyday objects by adults.   Compare these with the occupations and interests of the adults.   What details are noted, what omitted or distorted ?   How does your collection illustrate the law of least action in mental activity ?

10. Collect instances, in your own experience and from the work of pupils, in which some character or relation has remained implicit and unnoted until pointed out specifically, or until it has emerged in the course of a discussion.

(Watch for the expression, " Oh !   Of course !   I can see it quite clearly now ! ")

11. Write down the steps by which a child passes from the experience of a collection of objects to logical classification and generalization.

Try to detect the steps as they happen in actual pupils whom you teach.

How far does the progress seem to develop spontaneously ?

BOOKS FOR FURTHER REFERENCE

BARTLETT, F. C. : *Thinking: An Experimental and Social Study* (Allen and Unwin, 1958).

BRUNER, J. S., GOODNOW, J. J., AND AUSTIN, G. A. : *A Study of Thinking* (J. Wiley and Sons, 1961).

CARROLL, J. B. : *Language and Thought* (Prentice-Hall Inc., New Jersey, 1964).

DEWEY, J. : *How We Think* (Harrap, 1933).

HEBB, D. O. : *The Organisation of Behaviour* (Chapman and Hall, 1949).   A neuropsychological theory.

HILGARD, E. R. : *Theories of Learning* (Appleton-Century-Crofts, New York, 1948).

HUMPHREY, G. : *Thinking: An Introduction to its Experimental Psychology* (Methuen, 1951).   Chapters I, VI–IX.

HUNT, J. McV. : *Intelligence and Experience* (Ronald Press Co., New York, 1961).

220   THE PRINCIPLES OF TEACHING-METHOD

ISAACS, N. : *The Growth of Understanding in the Young Child* (Educational Supply Association, London, 1961). A brief introduction to Piaget's work.

——— : *New Light on Children's Ideas of Number* (Educational Supply Association, London, 1960). The work of Professor Piaget.

KATZ, D. : *Gestalt Psychology* (Methuen, 1951).

KOFFKA, K. : *The Growth of the Mind* (Kegan Paul, 1924). An introduction to child psychology.

KOHLER, W. : *The Mentality of Apes* (Pelican Books, 1957).

LOVELL, K. : *Growth of Basic Mathematical and Scientific Concepts in Children* (University of London Press, 1961).

McDOUGALL, W. : *Outline of Psychology* (Methuen, 1949). Chapters VIII, IX, X, XV.

PEEL, E. A. : *The Psychological Basis of Education* (Oliver and Boyd, 1956). Chapters I–X.

——— : *The Pupil's Thinking* (Oldbourne Press, London, 1960).

PIAGET, J. : *Judgment and Reasoning in the Child* (Routledge and Kegan Paul, 1962).

SPEARMAN, C. : *The Nature of Intelligence and the Principles of Cognition* (Macmillan, 1923).

STOUT, G. F. : *Analytic Psychology* (Allen and Unwin, 1918). Vol. II, Chapters V, VII, VIII, IX, X.

SYMPOSIUM : *Some Aspects of Piaget's Work* (National Froebel Foundation, London).

THOMAS, F. C. : *Ability and Knowledge* (Macmillan, 1935). An exposition of Spearman's principles.

VINACKE, W. E. : *The Psychology of Thinking* (McGraw-Hill, 1952).

WARD, J. : *Psychology Applied to Education* (Cambridge University Press, 1926).

WERNER, H. : *Comparative Psychology of Mental Development* (Science Editions (Paperback), New York, 1961).

WERTHEIMER, MAX : *Productive Thinking* (Enlarged Edition, Social Science Paperbacks, Tavistock Publications, 1966).

CHAPTER VIII

CONTINUOUS MENTAL ACTIVITY—THINKING AND OBSERVATION

So far we have discussed perceiving, attending, apprehending characters and relations, abstracting, correlate-eduction, and memorizing as if they were separate processes. Such treatment is a device necessary for exposition. In normal waking-life our mental activity flows in a continuous complex stream of which the more elementary processes just mentioned above are only aspects. Which aspect will be predominant at any moment will depend upon our environmental circumstances, needs, and interests.

There has been a tendency in the past to emphasize distinctions between mental and physical activity. This has been marked in the case of perception and conception. There is, however, no hard and fast distinction between the two. Perceiving is not exclusively a physical activity, nor is conceiving exclusively a mental activity ; neither is perceiving exclusively a childish activity and conceiving an adult activity. The two types of experience represent the extremes of a scale of activity, physical qualities predominating at one end and mental qualities at the other. Both occur at all ages. So soon as the young child realizes some simple outstanding character of an object or apprehends a simple first-order relation the conceiving activity has begun. These simple concepts form the groundwork upon which the abstract theoretical systems of adult knowledge will be built.

It is merely a convenient device to abstract thinking from perceiving. If we attempt to divorce the two in the practice of teaching, we are prone to encourage a one-sided development of the pupils. We tend either to restrict the training to first-hand experience, *i.e.*, practical activity with concrete things ; or to feed the pupil entirely upon words, *i.e.*, definitions, ready-made generalizations, and logical arguments divorced from the practical situations of which they are the logic. In the first case the pupil may be practically skilful in simple concrete problems but unable to think in general terms. In the second case, he will memorize words and formulæ without realizing their significance. Enrichment of practical experience should go hand in hand with conceptual development.

With this proviso, we shall now consider the characteristics of four modes of thinking important in school-work :

Reproductive Imagination.
Fantasy (Day-dreaming or Reverie).
Constructive or Inventive Imagination.
Reasoning.

REPRODUCTIVE IMAGINATION

This is the process involved in the recovery of a series of past experiences, either (a) in the space-time sequence in which they were originally enjoyed, or (b) in some order which is conventionally correct.

An example of the first type is when we recount the details of a journey, enumerating the places we passed through, and the events which happened, in the space- and time-order in which they occurred.

Examples of the second type are the reproduction of tables of weights and measures ; spellings of words ; theorems in geometry, or pieces of poetry ; drawing diagrams of mathematical figures, or scientific apparatus.

The reproduction is usually effected *in the first place* by means of some form of imagery. That is, we seem to see, hear, or feel something which represents the actual experience as we had it originally. If the original experience was very striking and exciting, after we have been through it once we can recover it in imagery, often very clearly, on a subsequent occasion. Even if the experiences are relatively mild, and free from emotional accompaniments, the subsequent imagery may be very distinct, approximating in some cases to hallucination.

Recently, studies have been made of what has been called *eidetic* imagery. The investigations have been concerned mainly with visual imagery in children. The subject of the experiment is seated at a table with his back to a window. A screen of dark grey paper is placed at a distance of half a yard from the eyes. Coloured papers, pictures of animals, houses, trees, or silhouettes rich in colour and detail are exposed to the gaze of the child. In some experiments toys and other solid objects are shown. The objects are exposed for a short time, then removed, and the child asked to report what he can then ' see ' upon the screen. Some children have been discovered who can report with great fidelity minute and even meaningless details. Allport states [1] that individuals capable of reproducing these eidetic images can report without effort the precise number of buttons on a pedestrian's pocket, the letters composing a word in a *foreign* language on a poster in the background, the length and direction of the lines of shading in a stretch of roadway, the number of whiskers on a cat's lip. The case of an Italian child has been reported who could, without special effort, reproduce Hebrew words, or symbols taken from the Phœnician alphabet. The presentation of a picture for thirty to sixty seconds may be sufficient for obtaining accurate eidetic images after some months or even a year. [2]

The phenomenon seems fairly common among children, but disappears with advancing age, probably owing to an increased tendency to think in words which represent *generalized experiences or classes*.

Obviously the possession of such clear imagery as has been reported in some of the experiments is an aid to reproduction. On the other hand, since the imagery is so distinct and concrete (*i.e.*, concerned with particular cases) *it may be a disadvantage* in that, if it persists, it may prevent the more rapid and effective thinking in words and general propositions which is so necessary in mathematical and scientific pursuits of all kinds.

Some kinds of experiences, usually second-hand experiences of words and symbols, need repeated reproduction before they can be retained accurately ; nonsense syllables, strings of digits, spellings of words, for example. In this case the reproductive imagination shades off into a motor habit, and the imagery tends to disappear *so long as the habit is successful*.

For example, if I am asked to give the answer to 6 × 8 the words ' forty-eight ' occur immediately, without the accompaniment of any kind of imagery that I can detect. Similarly, if asked to spell ' cat ' I say ' c-a-t,' again without being able to detect any imagery. If, however, the test word is a ' teaser ' like ' phthisical,' or ' psychiatrist,' I cannot depend upon habit. The letters have not been repeated sufficiently often in that order. In such a case I have first a feeling of hesitation and doubt, then visual and motor images begin to arise. I imagine what the word looks like, and what it feels like if written. I also emphasize the words strongly in subvocal speech, and this

[1] *British Journal of Psychology*, 1924, Vol. 15, pp. 99–120.
[2] Kluver, *Eidetic Imagery*, Handbook of Child Psychology, Chapter XVII, p. 699.

appears to strengthen the visual images. If I get into difficulties I have to concentrate more intently upon the visual image. If this is not successful I usually write down a few possible alternatives and then select the one which looks most satisfactory.

Imagery seems to be very much of a personal idiosyncrasy. It differs in different individuals both in kind and degree of intensity.[1] There was a tendency at one time to suppose that children (and adults) could be divided into pure types, according to their dominant imagery, namely, a visual type, an auditory type, and a motor or kinæsthetic type. Careful investigation shows that examples of a pure type are seldom found. Most people possess and use images of several kinds. We may, and usually do, have a preferred kind of imagery, on which we depend most often for mental reproduction, but when this fails we fall back upon any other kind which will serve the purpose.[2]

Readers can get a rough insight into their own preferred imagery by attending carefully to the way in which they remember how to spell words, or reproduce figures, diagrams, or definitions of which they are not quite sure.

Another indication is given by the way in which one remembers a stage play, particularly an opera. People who are, on the whole, visualizers, will reproduce it mentally by imagining what it looked like. Images of colours, shapes, spatial arrangements of stage, furniture, scenery, the appearance of the characters in the play, will come to mind most readily, attended by kinæsthetic and auditory elements as subsidiaries. People who prefer auditory images will reproduce the sounds, noises, melodies most readily, with kinæsthetic and visual elements as subsidiaries.

The kind of imagery we use for mental reproduction is governed also by the way in which we have lived through the actual experiences. If our school-training was exclusively oral, we shall reproduce spellings and definitions by auditory-motor rather than visual images whatever may be the kind we prefer.

Since we shall require pupils to retain the significant items of

[1] See Galton, *Enquiries into Human Faculty*, Everyman Edition, p. 57 *ff.*

[2] For myself, I depend mainly upon a combination of visual and motor images, but in certain cases I can detect, quite distinctly, mental reproductions of sounds of letters and words, mechanical noises or melodies. However, I cannot, no matter how much I concentrate upon it, mentally reproduce (*i.e.*, imagine) a sound without making some movements of tongue, lips, and larynx which would produce an imitation of it.

experience presented to them in school, and be able to recall the corresponding ideas and images, we must take care in presentation to ensure that the experiences in question make as massive and vivid appeal as possible.

Generally speaking, visual impressions are most effective, and the majority of pupils possess visual imagery. Nevertheless, any group of pupils may contain individuals in whom visual imagery is relatively weak, and who rely more on sound and movement (kinæsthetic) impressions.

Also, co-ordinated impressions through several sense-organs at the same time reinforce one another.

Therefore, in presenting experiences for educative purposes, we should make an appeal to as many sense-organs as possible. It is desirable in teaching a new word for the teacher to pronounce it, write it on the blackboard, allow the pupils to pronounce it and write it for themselves. Thus eyes, ears, and muscles in motor speech and writing, all contribute their quota to the total impression.

FANTASY, REVERIE, DREAMING

By fantasy we mean the kind of ' thinking ' which occurs in dreaming, both while we are awake and asleep. In some ways this is the most interesting and practically important type of thinking, since it leads to the creation of original thought-patterns and therefore is an essential feature in discovery and invention.

The motive for fantasy is an unsatisfied hunger. The ' castles in Spain ' which we construct in a day-dream are wish-fulfilments. They provide us with substitute-satisfaction for hungers which cannot be fully satisfied in the everyday world of affairs. Many fairy stories, romantic novels and plays with happy-for-ever-after endings, idealized situations in painting, are all the objectified manifestations of fantasy. The imagery is usually vivid and concrete, and the process strongly tinged with feeling-tone and emotion.

What makes fantasy so interesting and practically important is the *kind of association* characteristic of it. In a day-dream we get an inconsequential succession of images giving thought-patterns which are sometimes bizarre in the extreme. For a while we may review some past experience—a journey or a conversation. The images pass along in the space-time sequence in which we enjoyed the experiences. Then quite suddenly, and sometimes apparently inexplicably, the sequence breaks and a new set of associations begins. A personal example will illustrate this peculiarity.

I read a poem by D. H. Lawrence which describes with amusing and malicious accuracy a ride on a decrepit old electric tramway somewhere in the English Midlands. The poem started a day-dream, and I passed in review the thrills and discomforts I actually experienced on one memorable ride on this very tramway. In the day-dream the noisy old tram lurches and bumps along till we reach the town of H——. Then without any apparent reason or warning, suddenly I imagine myself in the reading-room of the British Museum. The change is so abrupt and apparently nonsensical that I stop to examine it. What connexion has H—— with the British Museum reading-room? I think carefully about details of the reading-room and *after some time* find myself in imagination talking to a friend O—— whom I met there unexpectedly on my last visit. Now the puzzling hidden association emerges. O—— was a schoolmaster at H—— before he joined the army in 1914.

The psychological significance of these abrupt, puzzling breaks in the sequence of images lies in the fact that we are *not necessarily conscious of the association*. There is no immediate association by contiguity, succession, or similarity. The associations in question are analytical, that is, one detail in the first series of images is connected with a detail of the second series. In the example described above, by thinking round the images of the British Museum reading-room and analysing out various details connected with that situation, I was able *after some time* to discover the active significant association, although I was quite unable at first to account for the sudden transition.

This example was commonplace and yielded easily to analysis. Many of the obscure connexions in both dreams and day-dreams remain persistently hidden from consciousness, but are at the same time *active in determining the sequence of images* experienced by the dreamer.

The *doctrine* of psycho-analysis is an attempt to formulate a rational explanation of such unconscious association processes, and psycho-analytic *method* is a practical procedure used more or less systematically by medical psychologists for analysing out and making the hidden connexions explicitly conscious to the thinker.

These analytical associations are important in medical psychology, being causative factors in mental disease. If the connexions remain unconscious they are beyond voluntary recall, and therefore not controllable by the thinker. They are strong and persistent in many cases, and may arouse frightful or shameful images which cause the patient much anxiety. The very fact that the associations recur and that the connecting links cannot be discovered or controlled may in itself be disconcerting and exasperating. Normal constructive thought-processes are disrupted, energy dissipated, and fatigue produced. In this way alone, by disrupting the normal mental organization they may produce a condition of mental ill-health. If the images recalled by the hidden connexions are frightful or shameful (as in some dreams) they arouse fear and disgust in addition to the exasperation due to the feeling of helplessness and mystery, and their disruptive influence upon mental organization is correspondingly stronger. In some mental diseases, the essential step in the cure of the patient is the analysis of the hidden connexions which cannot be recovered voluntarily. When the hidden connexions are made explicitly conscious, the patient can gather up the dissociated elements in his mental organization and bring the whole again under his voluntary control. The function of the psycho-analyst is to uncover the hidden connexions by the use of his ' method,' thus enabling the patient to reconstitute his disrupted personality.

The importance of fantasy for practical invention and theoretical speculation is due to this possibility of analysing experiences and images into elements which can then be recombined into thought-patterns never actually experienced. The synthesis may represent anything from a comic strip or a new form of gargoyle to an abstruse hypothesis in physics.

Fantasy may be both an advantage and a danger. It is an advantage in that *the imagery represents a mental trial-and-error experiment* which can be carried on without the necessity for overt action. When our desires are baffled by difficulties, we imagine our problems solved, and thereby devise ways and means of solving them. In the day-dream, events are represented as happening in the way we desire them to happen. We can compare our present condition with conditions in the past, and project ourselves into a possible future. The images in a day-dream are manageable in ways our actual experiences are not. We can exaggerate the value of some details, and ignore others. We can split up a total experience, fix upon certain details, and combine these with details from other experiences, and do all this without the expenditure of time and labour which would be necessary to perform the operations in our actual world.

Children continually perform these mental experiments. They imagine themselves as what they would like to be when they grow

H

up. Many small boys and girls dramatize their fantasies in play. They invent companions, play at being parents, soldiers, sailors, drivers of buses and trains. This may seem to the adult a rather foolish procedure. Actually it enables the child to experiment in personalities and in various ways of living ; to put himself into the position of other people, and thus widen his contacts with life. In so far as the child tends to objectify his fantasies in play he is widening his experience and acquiring new knowledge. Incidentally, he learns in the most effective way to distinguish what is actual, and possible, from what is merely a vagary of the imagination. Thus fantasy is an indispensable instrument of individual and social progress. If we imagined no ambition as individuals, and did not dream of the possibility of standards of living and a level of social happiness at present beyond our realization, we should be content to remain at a crude stage of living. The construction of an ideal in fantasy in response to a feeling of need is often a necessary preliminary to the realization of an advance in actual life.

Fantasy becomes a danger, only when the imaginary world is accepted as a satisfactory substitute for reality. If a person refuses to face his difficulties and retires within himself to seek substitute satisfaction in a day-dream, then the latter acts as an opiate and stifles effort. Such an individual loses his grip on life, and becomes socially and intellectually ineffective.

The motive operative in fantasy is, as we have seen, some unsatisfied hunger. The hunger may be due to some specific lack which is clearly recognized by the person in question—lack of food, water, freedom of movement. On the other hand, a fruitful source of fantasy in the growing individual may be the pressure of a newly maturing function for expression, before the knowledge and skill necessary for adequate expression have been gained. Day-dreaming may be a kind of mental play and the activity of dreaming itself a source of satisfaction to the growing organism, just as the physical play of a child is a source of satisfaction for the needs of his maturing bodily organs. Thus, the day-dream may reveal, both to the pupil and to an observant teacher, a natural bent of the individual and indicate the lines along which his future development may best be planned.

This possibility makes it undesirable to over-organize a child's activities. Some time ought to be allowed, and opportunity provided for the pupil to browse unfettered by examination requirements or vocational demands.

CONSTRUCTIVE OR INVENTIVE IMAGINATION

This is the mode of thinking characteristic of invention and problem-solving.

In the day-dream no objective conditions are imposed upon the thinker. His aim is some kind of personal substitute-satisfaction in which objective demands of time and space are not important. In fact, fantasy is a device for circumventing the awkward conditions which the physical environment imposes upon the dreamer.

On the other hand, in constructive imagination the products of the thought-process must accord with certain objective conditions which are implied by the nature of the problem to be solved. Hence this mode of thinking must include a critical attitude and some form of logical demonstration, *i.e.*, reasoning.

Any simple problem-solving situation will illustrate the way in which reproductive imagination, fantasy, and logical demonstration are incorporated in constructive imagination. In a crossword puzzle one clue given was, " Made in more senses than one by successful carpet-manufacturers." There was no indication of the first letter, but the word must have four letters.

Here the imposed conditions are clear—the word must have four letters and represent two meanings both connected with carpets.

We begin to *recall* what we know about carpets. Nothing seems to fit. We find ourselves *thinking rather aimlessly* about carpets ; rooms in which we have seen or walked on carpets ; rich, gorgeous carpets ; walking on velvet. Then, quite suddenly, the word ' pile ' pops up, as it were, from nowhere. This word has four letters. It is made by successful carpet-manufacturers. It also fits the second meaning indicated in the clue, since the successful manufacturer makes a ' pile ' of money.

We then *check the cross references* (demonstration). These indicate that the second letter must be ' i ' and the fourth ' e.' The problem is now completely solved.

Mechanical invention and scientific investigation are not entirely precise and calculated processes. The element of fantasy is essential.[1]

It is said that the ' key idea ' of a mechanical sewing-machine was revealed in a dream. All the sewing-needles known hitherto had had the eye at the end opposite to the point. The inventors tried for a long time to make a machine which would reverse the needle after passing it through the material to be sewn, but no practicable method of doing this could be found. So long as the eye of the needle was kept at the end opposite to the point, a workable sewing-machine was mechanically impossible. When at the stage of despair, one inventor dreamed that he was tied to a stake, about to be executed by a band of savages. The executioner stepped forward holding a spear in which there was a hole *near the point*. This provided the missing clue. Needles were manufactured with the eye near the point and the sewing-machine became an accomplished fact.

Progress in scientific theory and practice depends very much upon imaginative constructions of the possible or probable nature of things. Hypotheses are essentially fictions arrived at through the operation of fantasy, sometimes years before they can be verified by experimental test. One of the most striking instances of the ' fantastic ' origin of a hypothesis was the suggestion of the ring-formula for benzene. Chemical analysis had established the fact that the benzene molecule contained six carbon atoms and six hydrogen atoms, but chemists could not conceive how these atoms could possibly be arranged in space. They were baffled, in the same way as the inventors of the sewing-machine were baffled, because they tried to solve their difficulty by the use of familiar knowledge, whereas an original construction was necessary. Up to that period, chemists had thought of the atoms in a molecule of an organic substance as if they were arranged in a line, something like an open string of beads. Kekulé, the inventor of the new hypothesis, thus describes how it occurred to him :

> I was sitting, writing at my text-book ; but the work did not progress ; my thoughts were elsewhere. I turned my chair to the fire and dozed. Again the atoms were gambolling before my eyes. This time the smaller groups kept modestly in the background. My mental eye, rendered more acute by repeated visions of the kind, could now distinguish larger structures of manifold conformations ; long rows all turning and twisting, in snake-like motion. But look ! What was that ? One of the snakes had seized hold of its own tail and the form whirled

---

[1] See Montmasson, *Invention and the Unconscious.*

mockingly before my eyes. As if by a flash of lightning I awoke ; and this time also I spent the rest of the night in working out the consequences of the hypothesis.[1]

That dream led to the foundation of the modern theory of benzene and its derivatives, which has played so important a part in many branches of industry.

One gets a false picture of scientific thinking if it is represented as consisting exclusively of observation and experiments with real apparatus. The function of observation and experiment is, first, to reveal difficulties which prevent us from realizing desires ; second, to provide us with accurate experience and relations relevant to the problem ; third, to *test* the fitness of the guesses which are produced by constructive imagination. In between gathering the knowledge about the problem and testing a possible solution, the solution itself must be formulated in a period of brooding reflection. If the scientific worker has not been gifted with an aptitude for this imaginative phase he remains what T. H. Huxley called, rather contemptuously, a hodman of science. He laboriously hews out and collects facts, but can do nothing more with them.

The ' mechanism ' of constructive imagination seems to be correlate-eduction. Consider the case of the benzene formula. Chemical analysis proved that a benzene molecule contained six carbon atoms and six hydrogen atoms. These were the theoretical fundaments which had to be related into a system. The chemists also knew the kind of chemical relation which could exist between carbon and hydrogen atoms. In all other carbon-hydrogen compounds known at that time each carbon atom was joined chemically to other carbon atoms and one or more hydrogen atoms, *e.g.*,

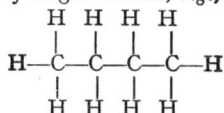

$$
\begin{array}{c}
\text{H} \quad \text{H} \quad \text{H} \quad \text{H} \\
| \quad | \quad | \quad | \\
\text{H—C—C—C—C—H} \\
| \quad | \quad | \quad | \\
\text{H} \quad \text{H} \quad \text{H} \quad \text{H}
\end{array}
$$

Each carbon atom thus required four chemical ' bonds ' and each hydrogen atom only one. Hence the relation between the atoms was indicated. The problem was, given six carbon atoms and only six hydrogen atoms and the normal chemical relations between them, to educe a theoretically correct correlate.

The difficulty which prevented the eduction of the appropriate correlate was caused by the influence of past experience.

Incorrect correlates in the shape of chain formulæ (as shown above)

---

[1] Reprinted from the article on " Chemistry," *Encyclopædia Britannica*, Vol. V, p. 372, by permission of the publishers.

obtruded themselves by the process of reproduction, thus obscuring the development of a better alternative. The correct correlate which satisfied the system of chemical relations was found to be:

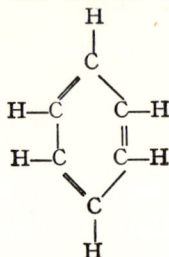

$$
\begin{array}{c}
\text{H} \\
\text{C} \\
\text{H—C} \quad \text{C—H} \\
\text{H—C} \quad \text{C—H} \\
\text{C} \\
\text{H}
\end{array}
$$

in which some of the carbon atoms were joined together by a ' double bond.' This was the correlate suggested to Kekulé in his ' day-dream ' by the analogy of a snake thrusting its tail into its mouth. When tested by further experiment the correlate was found to fit all the facts of the case then known.

REASONING

Reasoning is the mental process used in argument, demonstration, or proof. J. S. Mill defined it in the most extensive meaning of the term as " inferring a proposition from a previous proposition or propositions ; giving credence to it or claiming credence for it as a conclusion from something else." [1]

The formal reasoning described thus in the standard treatises on logic, and set out in those rather forbidding logical formulæ or syllogisms with which such books are so liberally decorated, seldom happens in everyday life. People, even young children, reason *without realizing explicitly that they are doing so.*

The dog which goes to the door on seeing his master put on a coat and hat performs a simple act of reasoning. So does the small child who on hearing a familiar step outside looks expectantly at the door, waiting to greet the person whose appearance he anticipates.

At a somewhat higher level of reasoning we find the thought-process of a person who digs up a piece of hard yellow substance and says, " This is gold." The same process appears at a still higher level of abstraction in such a case as the following. A physicist sends minute rays of light through two narrow slits placed very close together. These two rays fall upon a screen and the observer sees, not a continuous band of light, but alternate

[1] *System of Logic*, Book II, Chapter I.

light and dark bands. He then concludes that light must in some way resemble waves.

In all the above cases some experience is presented to the observer, and on the ground of this experience he bases a belief (conclusion). However, the antecedents need not be first-hand experiences. Facts or beliefs may be asserted in the form of verbal propositions from which conclusions can be drawn, *e.g.*, a person says, " I am fifty years old." If the year in question were 1900 then we should conclude that he must have been born in 1850.

The essential process in reasoning is *inferring*. In this process we pass mentally from the apprehension of something given—a datum—to the apprehension of something related in some way to the datum.[1]

What is the nature of this relation of inference ?

In the case of the child mentioned above, certain experiences have been followed by others so frequently as to become customary—a characteristic step is usually followed by the appearance of father or mother at the door. By virtue of the power of comprehension these happenings can be held together mentally in a simple system—sound-of-step-followed-by-appearance-at-door.

On a subsequent occasion, sounds of steps are perceived. Together with this fundament comes awareness of a relation supplied by memory, namely, " similar to the sounds usually followed by the appearance of father at that door." This enables the child to educe the correlate, namely, the appearance of father. Thus reasoning depends on the three noegenetic principles supplemented by memorization.

It is scarcely necessary to say that the child need not and does not repeat this explicit form of words. Neither does an adult *in familiar circumstances*. The whole process from experiencing the fundament, through reaction to the relation, up to the behaviour appropriate to the anticipation of the correlate is fused into one complex experience in which the various aspects are implicit. After repeated experiences of the same kind the process becomes a perceptual habit which does not require any verbalization.

Verbalization begins when the child is asked to say why he behaves in that way. Later, the reasoning-process becomes explicitly realized and verbalized *when a difficulty which does not yield to an habitual solution is critically argued out*. In the lives of many people in well-ordered circumstances with no theoretical

[1] See Stebbing, *A Modern Introduction to Logic*, p. 210.

interests, this explicit reasoning-process happens but seldom. Here we meet another instance of the law of least action.

VALID REASONING

It is obvious that inferences are not always correct. The familiar step is not always followed by the expected appearance. Similarly, the person who says, " This stuff is gold," may be quite wrong. On the other hand, *some inferences are invariably and necessarily correct and the anticipated conclusions always follow.* Inferences based upon these *necessary* relations are called *implications.* Valid reasoning must employ the relations of implication between antecedents and consequents.

Relations of implication are provided by exact experiment, logical classification, and definition. For example, chemical analysis has revealed that different kinds of material have constant characteristic attributes. One particular kind of yellow substance always has a specific gravity of 19·2. It is very malleable and can be hammered into sheets of incredible thinness. It exhibits certain characteristic chemical properties. Furthermore, in this one kind of substance *all* of a certain group of characters are found by repeated experiences to go together. The characters have to the substance the relations of attribution and constitution. This being so, we can define this unique constant system of characters and relations and represent it by a name—' gold.'

Now, the statement (proposition), " This is gold," *implies* the presence of any or all of the characteristic attributes of gold. Therefore we can say, " If this is gold, then its specific gravity will be 19·2." Conversely, we can say with perfect assurance, " If the specific gravity of this yellow substance is *not* 19·2, then it is not gold." This latter aspect of the reasoning process indicates how it can be used for the purposes of testing, demonstrating, and proving.

In certain cases we do not discover fundamental characters and relations by experiment, but we *agree upon a convention.* Thus we agree to call any group like this ● ● ' two ' and any group like this ● ● ● ● ' four.' We then agree that ' plus ' shall stand for a specified relation of conjunction. We further agree that any group of the type ● ● ● ● ● ● or ● ● ● ● shall be called ' six.' Then when these conventional definitions have been agreed upon by everybody concerned, we can assert with perfect assurance that " Two plus four equals six." This is bound to be correct, since we have made it so by agreement.

It is worth noting that these propositions which depend on arbitrary definitions *cannot be proved*. They are merely accepted. It is easy to see that by adopting some other definitions of ' two,' ' four,' and ' plus ' we might just as easily arrive at the convention, " Two plus four equals twelve."

Thus we find that valid reasoning depends upon :

(*a*) The apprehension of correct facts by the analysis of experience.

(*b*) Connecting these correct facts by means of relations which are found in experience, or made by convention, to be invariably the same, *i.e.*, universally true.

Hence it is clear that reasoning may be *invalid* or *fallacious* in two ways :

(*a*) The facts of the case have not been correctly apprehended.

(*b*) The relations used are not implications, *i.e.*, they are not universal in nature, or agreed upon by convention.

Errors in reasoning due to the first cause are called *material* fallacies ; errors due to the second cause *formal* fallacies. Both sources of error should be searched for in examining a logical (or illogical) argument.

It follows from this that even a good logician may reason accurately in form but arrive at quite wrong conclusions for practice if he is not familiar with the material facts of the case. Hence the danger of getting a lawyer to advise you about medicine, and a doctor to advise you about law.[1]

LOGIC

Formal logic is very much of a mystery to many people. Actually it is merely the accurate study of the characters of and relations between all the possible kinds and combinations of propositions which will give valid conclusions. Just as the chemist studies the characters and chemical relations of elementary substances, and the biologist studies the characters and relations of different types of plants and animals, so the professional logician studies the characters and relations of elementary [2] propositions,

[1] This principle is recognized in every calling but teaching, and in that case everybody seems to know more about education than the teachers !

[2] ' Elementary ' means here, not ' easy to understand ' but ' logically simple.' *i.e.*, not capable of any further sub-division (*cf.* chemical elements).

classifies them, and thereby organizes the practice of reasoning into a science. By reducing all forms of valid reasoning to a few comprehensive formulæ, the professional logician can, on applying his formulæ, quickly detect fallacies in complicated arguments.

It is not necessary to have studied the principles of logic in order to be able to reason. If that were so there would be even fewer logical arguments in speeches and newspapers than there are now. However, if we wish to teach pupils how to reason, it is necessary to make them *explicitly aware* of the commoner forms of good and bad reasoning. This is not likely to happen unless the teachers themselves are *explicitly aware* of the forms of good and bad reasoning, and can use them deliberately. Hence, some knowledge of the elements of logic is essential for really efficient teaching, particularly at the more advanced levels of instruction.

THE FUNCTION OF REASONING

Many people believe that reasoning is a method of discovery. This is quite false. Discoveries and inventions are made by careful examination of first-hand experience followed by contemplation of the significance of the facts disclosed. The real function of reasoning is that of testing, demonstrating, or proving. This is evident if we consider the mental processes involved in mathematical or scientific demonstration. It is also revealed in simple planning. In planning we are presented with certain conditions which must be obeyed, and we have to find a method of procedure which will be practically sound. The procedure itself is imagined. Then it has to be tested to find if it is likely to work.

Bad planners just try to put into practice the first plan which occurs to them. This is usually a wasteful process.

For example, it is said that on one occasion a heavy gun was sent by ship to a distant port. On arrival it was found that no crane sufficiently powerful to lift the gun out of the ship was available. Thereupon the ship returned with the gun to procure a crane. The crane was packed underneath the gun and away went the ship a second time. Arriving at the port of destination, it was impossible to get the crane out because the gun was on top of it. They had to bring both back again to have them repacked.

To prevent a fiasco such as this it would be necessary to work out a plan beforehand, or, in other words, *make a mental experiment*. This involves first selecting certain facts, then stating corresponding implications. These implications indicate correlative facts which can then be tested either by seeking already existing knowledge or by making a test-experiment.

Thus, in our example, if the gun weighed 50 tons (fact), this implies that there must be a crane capable of lifting at least 50 tons at the port of destination. Is there such a crane available? This can be tested by sending a telegram, or by looking up the detail in an authoritative book of reference.

'METHODS' OF REASONING: INDUCTION AND DEDUCTION

It is commonly believed that there are two general methods of reasoning—induction and deduction. Induction is said to be the method by which we pass, mentally, from the examination of particular cases to the assertion of a generalization about them. Conversely, in deduction we are said to pass, mentally, from a universal proposition to an assertion about a particular case.

Further inspection suggests, however, that induction in this significance is rather a case of classification than of reasoning, and deduction the enlargement of a class by the addition to it of another particular instance.

In teaching children the elements of parsing we might call their attention to a number of sentences like the following :

> The boy is *near* the fire.
> The book is *on* the table.
> John stands *beside* Tom.
> The dog sat *under* the table.
> He jumped *over* the brook.
> Etc., etc.

Inspection of the words in italics shows that they all perform a similar function, namely, they indicate a relation between the things named by two other words, either nouns or pronouns, in the sentence. We give the name ' preposition ' to this class of words. We arrive thus at a generalization by induction.

Suppose now we meet another word not previously known, such as ' through,' in the sentence " The brick fell *through* the roof." Inspection shows that ' through ' indicates a relation between brick and roof. We conclude that it is a preposition.

Thus we use the previously established generalization to classify a new particular case. Reasoning is used in this classification process. Fully expanded, the argument can be expressed in syllogistic form :

> All words indicating a relation between things named by other words in a sentence, are prepositions.

This word ' through ' indicates a relation between things named by other words in a sentence.

Therefore ' through ' is a preposition.

Deduction, strictly speaking, is a process in which we accept certain propositions (which may be statements of general principles, definitions, or even assertions about particular cases) as data and then work out the implications which follow from these data.

Mathematical reasoning is almost entirely a deductive process of the type just described. Consider the following. In going home I can travel by bus to the terminus, then walk by a direct road $2\frac{1}{4}$ miles. From the terminus, however, I may choose an indirect route, which means that I must wait 16 minutes for a second bus, travel by it for 20 minutes, and then walk half a mile. I get home at the same time by either method. At what speed do I walk ?

We examine the data presented and work out certain relations implied by them. Thus, the time taken to walk $2\frac{1}{4}$ miles must be equal to 16 minutes, plus 20 minutes, plus the time taken to walk half a mile. But the time taken to walk the half mile is assumed to be the same in each case. Therefore it is *implied* that the walker can cover $1\frac{3}{4}$ miles in 36 minutes. This deduction enables the speed of the walker to be calculated.

The method of induction, obviously, can never lead to absolute certainty, except in rare cases when it is possible to examine *all* the particular instances available and we know for certain that no other instances exist, or will be discovered in the future. Usually, induction gives only a measure of probability.

SCIENTIFIC REASONING. THE METHOD OF EXPERIMENTAL INVESTIGATION

It was supposed, largely through the erroneous opinions of Sir Francis Bacon,[1] that physical science was exclusively founded upon induction. For the reasons just stated in the previous paragraph, many logicians have denied that experimental science has any logical value. However, while the professional logicians have been gnashing their teeth, so to speak, the experimental scientists have gone blissfully onward from one spectacular success to another. This raises a question about the real nature of scientific thinking, and since science is commonly recommended in schools and colleges because it is supposed to train the ability to reason, it is desirable to realize explicitly the thinking-processes involved.

---

[1] See his *Novum Organum.*

A clear understanding of scientific thinking is an essential preliminary to teaching science effectively.

A very clear example of the investigatory method used in scientific research is provided by the work of Lavoisier, a celebrated French chemist, on the nature of combustion.

It was known that a number of substances when burned or heated in air increased in weight. The problem was to discover exactly what caused the increase.

Before any actual experiments were carried out for this purpose, Lavoisier imagined certain alternative possibilities which he stated in the form of *hypotheses*, namely :

(i) Matter from the flame and fire penetrated the pores of the containing vessel and entered the substance burned.[1]

(ii) Some portion of the surrounding air joined with the substance burned.

Now the problem was to decide which of these alternative hypotheses seemed the more correct. To do this Lavoisier stated the implications of each hypothesis in such a form as could be tested by experiment. Thus :

(i) If the increase were due to fire-matter, then if a known weight of substance were heated in a hermetically sealed vessel, the total weight of substance plus containing vessel would increase during the experiment.

(ii) If increase were due to air joining with the substance burned, then the total weight of the apparatus would remain constant, but the increase of weight of the substance would be equal to the decrease in weight of the air contained within the vessel.

Both these implications could be tested by experiment. The weights contradicted the first hypothesis and confirmed the second.

This investigation illustrates the course of all scientific demonstration. In the first place a practical or theoretical difficulty is presented. To begin with, *the facts of the case are confirmed.* This is an essential preliminary, since if the facts have been wrongly observed and asserted there may be no problem to solve. Next, by reflection upon the facts as confirmed certain possible solutions or explanations are constructed imaginatively. These are the hypotheses. Thirdly, each several hypothesis is considered and an implication which follows from it is asserted in the form : If hypothesis x is true then y is implied. The implication y is then tested by reference to facts already ascertained, or by experimental investigation. If y is found to be demonstrated then the hypothesis is accepted for the time being as correct. If not, it is rejected and a further hypothesis framed and tested.

[1] The work was performed between 1772 and 1774, at which period such a notion seemed quite reasonable.

Hypotheses are conjectured by fantasy in constructive imagination. The scientist endeavours to think himself into the 'nature' of the universe of which he can actually perceive only the outward signs, the events as they happen. He expresses this imaginative world in terms of tentative guesses or hypotheses. So far there is no difference in form between scientific and primitive thinking. The primitive man's gods serve exactly the same purpose as the scientist's electrons and forces. They are *possible* explanations of the actual events observed. The primitive man, however, accepts his hypotheses because they are personally satisfactory to himself. His hypotheses remain dreams. The scientific thinker goes on to *test* his hypotheses. This is the phase in which reasoning, properly so-called, enters.

REASONING BY ANALOGY

In practical life, and quite often in theoretical studies, reasoning is based on analogies. We argue that since x resembles y, therefore it must be y.[1]

Educational theory contains quite a number of examples, such as the recapitulation theory, culture-epoch theory, idea-forces acting as motives.

Primitive races and children generally are particularly prone to this kind of reasoning.

Most scientific hypotheses involve analogies. The falling apple is said to have suggested to Newton the notion that the moon also was falling towards the earth and this led to the formulation of the general theory of gravitation. Students of physics cannot fail to note the similarity between the structure of the solar system and modern models of the structure of the atom (planetary electrons revolving round a central nucleus).

If the similarities are correctly observed, and, in particular, if the analogies selected are *significant*, then reasoning by analogy may be a powerful instrument for research. However, these two criteria are difficult to apply and all arguments based on analogies need careful, critical scrutiny.

DEVELOPMENT OF REASONING-ABILITY IN CHILDREN

At what age do children begin to reason? The answer to this question depends on how we define reasoning. If we confine it strictly to the explicit use of implications in formal arguments

[1] *E.g.*, this stuff looks like gold. Therefore it must be gold.

then it is likely that a child does not realize *full* reasoning-powers until the period of adolescence. This was the type of reasoning assumed by the 'faculty' theorists when they denied that the reasoning-'faculty' ripened before puberty. If we consider the reasoning-process from a *psychological* point of view, then it may include any kind of inference. There is no doubt that children begin to make perceptual inferences at a very early age. They begin to pass mentally from the apprehension of a given event to the expectation of some consequence, not immediately perceived, which is likely to follow the first event. Evidence has been presented above [1] to show that children can educe relations even between relations themselves (*e.g.*, likeness and difference) at an early age, and act correctly upon their judgments. Further, Burt has found, as a result of an extensive application of standardized reasoning-tests, that the commoner simpler relations of space, time, number, quantity, similarity, difference, and the like, can all be grasped *before the age of seven, if only the material presented to the child is sufficiently simple, familiar, and adapted to his limited knowledge and powers of comprehension.* The young child's inability to reason is caused, not so much by an inability to apprehend logical connexions, as by an inability to *comprehend* (*i.e.*, hold together mentally in a single system) many different relations presenting *a high degree of complexity.*[2] Burt considers that all the elementary mechanisms essential for formal reasoning are present before the normal child leaves the infant department, that is, before the age of seven or eight years. Even logical criticism and the detection of absurdities is within the powers of normal children of eight years old if the instances are sufficiently glaring, and if the pupils have had some practice and understand what they are required to do.[3]

It appears that the growth of reasoning-ability follows a course similar to that already noted several times in connexion with the growth of other physical and mental functions. Growth begins in embryo at an early age. There are no sudden changes, and no gaps, in the development. The advance proceeds from coarsely defined activity through continuously increasing definition and specialization to full maturity.

[1] From Line's *Investigation on the Eduction of Relations,* p. 211.
[2] *Cf.* p. 211, para. 3.
[3] See Burt, Appendix III, *Report of Consultative Committee on the Primary School,* p. 265 *ff.*

Hence quite young pupils, particularly if intelligent, may be given exercises requiring some reasoning, provided that the terms are familiar and the situations represented are not too complex and abstract.

STEPS IN THE DEVELOPMENT OF REASONING-ABILITY IN CHILDREN

It is convenient to summarize the levels of development in reasoning. They seem to be :

(a) An event x is experienced as related to an event y. The situation, ' x followed by, or related to, y,' is repeatedly noted.

(b) x is presented, together with the belief ' same as before.' Thereupon y is expected and looked for.

(c) The process represented in (b) is verbalized and carried on mentally. This can happen only after the child is capable of some degree of abstraction.

(d) The terms related and the relations involved are analysed into finer characterization, and more subtle relations.

(e) Experience shows that some inferences are false. This difficulty calls attention to the reasoning-process itself which thereby becomes explicitly conscious.

(f) The nature of reasoning is investigated systematically and the various modes of valid reasoning reduced to formulæ and classified.

In the majority of pupils the development stops at level (d). Only after specific training in logical reasoning at the adolescent period does the development advance to level (f).

OBSERVATION

Of the powers which the lay public demand that the teacher shall cultivate in the pupils next in importance after intelligent action is the ability to observe.

Observation is usually treated together with sense-perception and sense-training as though it were merely a function of perception. Actually observation depends as much (probably more) upon imagination and reasoning as upon sensory discrimination. Most readers will have heard· of Sherlock Holmes's famous phrase, " Watson, you see ; I observe."

We can infer the conditions of effective observation from the theoretical principles already discussed. They are as follows:

Acuity of sense-organs

This trait permits of fine sensory discrimination so that more precise analysis of characters of objects is possible. It is unlikely that a physician can become a first-rate heart-specialist unless he can hear well enough to distinguish fine differences in heart-murmurs.

However, good sensory acuity is not sufficient for good observation. As Holmes implied, there is more in observing than mere seeing. In any given situation, other things being equal, superior ability in observation will depend upon the following *psychological* conditions:

Familiarity with the situation observed

Frequent contact with the same situation produces facilitation and makes the discrimination of characters and relations more easy and rapid.

Knowledge about the situation observed

The more characters and relations already known and memorized, the more significant correlates is the observer likely to educe mentally and then search for in the actual situation. The importance of such knowledge is demonstrated every time an intelligent expert is compared with an equally intelligent novice. The owner of a car may have seen his engine many more times than the expert motor-mechanic, but he usually observes a good deal less about it when it goes wrong.

One very important feature of the knowledge about a situation is the possession of a battery of names. As we have seen, the names assist the systematic exploration of the situation, and items which would otherwise remain implicit and unnoted emerge into explicit clearness.

Interest in the situation and alert attending

Explicit attending and directing mental activity are essential in observation. The interest will depend upon the observer's need—practical or theoretical. In the absence of interest, even familiarity with and knowledge about the situation will not guarantee good observation, since the person concerned *will not be seeking for anything*. Therefore he will not attend with any concentration to the details. This is another instance of the law of least action. We never observe what has no interest for us. People do not count the number of steps in the stairs up and down which they may have gone thousands of times. Neither do they count the eyelets in their shoes nor the buttons on their coats. Usually they have no need of this information.

Thus interest in, familiarity with, and knowledge about the situation are essential for effective observation. The blind man's superior observation of sound and touch details is due to interest in them and concentrated attending. Having lost his eyesight, he *needs* sound and touch impressions for his personal safety and as a means of gaining further knowledge. This superiority of the blind person is not in sensory acuity but in nicety of interpretation.

These conditions are significant for teaching-practice : To foster good observation we must

> Keep the pupil in good health, take care of his sense-organs, and avoid fatigue.
>
> Provide a rich and varied first-hand knowledge of the environment together with an accurate dictionary of names.
>
> Stimulate interest in the situation—*make the observations worth while to the pupils.*
>
> Direct alert attention to significant items in the situations observed, and train the pupils in *systematic ways of exploring* the situations.

The second and fourth of these conditions are emphasized by an experimental investigation undertaken by Fox.[1]

A number of university graduates were shown lantern slides depicting suits of armour and instructed to write down every item they could observe. The results were marked and the group divided into two sets of equal average ability as shown by this first test.

One set, N (=not lectured), was dismissed. The other set, L (=lectured), had a lecture on the structure of a typical suit of armour, the various parts being pointed out and the corresponding technical terms written on a blackboard. The students made notes and sketches, and were allowed a week in which to memorize the details.

At the end of the week both sets were shown another lantern slide of a suit of armour and again they all wrote down as many items as they could observe.

The lectured group showed an improvement over the unlectured group by some 57 per cent.

---

[1] " A Study in Preperception," *British Journal of Psychology*, Vol. XV, Part I. See also Fox, *Educational Psychology*, Chapter III. Note the connexion of this investigation with the exploratory function of language.

In interpreting the results, Fox suggests that as a result of the preperceptual system organized by the lecture- and the learning-period, the trained group was capable of 57 per cent. more separate, definite acts of attention. By having a set of experiences organized with reference to a set of corresponding names, *which were learnt by heart,* the noting of details in a similar object presented afterwards was facilitated. The reports of the students on their experiences during the experiment show that the lectured group armed with the memorized system of names, *set out to explore the slides in the second test actively,* to discover whether parts corresponding to the names they had learned were present in the figures. Moreover, they *saw* the details more quickly and confidently than the other group in the second test.

One point of considerable interest for teaching-practice emerged in the preliminary tests. Several groups had been tried before a satisfactory experimental procedure was finally decided upon, and in one case the set L was given the lecture and told the names of the typical portions of a suit of armour as these were shown, *but was not given the opportunity of learning the names by heart.* The second test was given soon after the lecture.

In this case the lectured group was little if any better than the unlectured group in the final tests.

The reason seemed apparent from the reports of the students concerned. They found themselves concentrating upon the names, and endeavouring to remember them. They were confused by this effort to recall the names imperfectly known, and attended to this process instead of to the details of the armour.[1] The distraction introduced by the imperfectly learned names hindered the observation. It seems therefore that names will assist observation only when they have been made habitual by use. No effort of recall is then necessary, and the energy aroused is nearly all available for the work of observation. This fact should act as a warning against the tendency to believe that as soon as a clear and systematic exposition has been given by the teacher to a class of pupils, the subject-matter so treated will be perfectly well known and ready to function in future perception. The material needs to be repeated and worked over by the pupils themselves until it is consolidated as it were, and made habitual. Half-learned names and half-organized experiences are likely to interfere with, rather than help, future observation. In addition, the feeling of frustration

[1] *Cf.* Conditions of Attention, p. 216, para. 4.

and annoyance due to the distraction, will further dissipate the energy available and will produce a loss of confidence.

A note of warning is indicated here. The more systematic and specialized is the observer's knowledge, and the more habitual his names, the more is his observation likely to be limited to items within his apperceptive systems. Thus systematic well-grounded knowledge, while it makes us better observers within our own field, tends also *to make us psychically blind to other fields of experience.* The chemist will observe as a chemist, the engineer as an engineer, the lawyer as a lawyer. This explains why an intelligent classical scholar may sometimes note a good deal more about a neutral situation, or even a scientific situation, than a scientific observer who approaches the situation with certain academic scientific assumptions and preconceptions strongly active. Hence the value of observing with an ' open mind.'

SOME PRACTICAL APPLICATIONS OF THE PSYCHOLOGY OF OBSERVATION

The more we introduce manipulative and experimental activity into school-work, the more important will a knowledge of the conditions of good observation become. The application of the principles discussed in the section on observation to routine science-work in the laboratory, as well as to the successful showing of pictures and models is sufficiently clear. We must organize an anticipatory interest ; connect the situation to be observed with previous knowledge (and, if the necessary knowledge is not available, organize it first) ; arrange a correct mental ' set ' for interpretation purposes ; and provide a battery of names. Moreover, particularly with younger pupils, no act of observation can be taken for granted. It is necessary to direct the mental activity of the pupils specifically to whatever items in the situation are relevant to the purpose in view. This direction can be accomplished by pointing, or demonstration, or by instructions to observe, and these measures need to be followed up by some kind of test to ensure that the observation has been made, and made correctly. Students-in-training are apt to take far too much for granted in the pupils they teach.

The importance of these principles of observation has been emphasized still further by the introduction of school-excursions and field-work, and by the growing use of the cinema-projector and wireless-set in teaching. So much of the educative value of these devices depends on their skilful employment. Casually used they are merely expensive ways of wasting time. Hence a brief discussion of these teaching-devices in relation to the psychology of observation will be included here.

ORGANIZATION OF SCHOOL EXCURSIONS AND FIELD-WORK

In working out a satisfactory piece of field-work, or school excursion, three phases are essential—a preparatory phase, the actual field-work, and a follow-up phase.

Preparatory Phase

The function of this is to organize an interpretative background relevant to the situation to be observed, and to create an anticipatory interest. It is essential that the pupils shall seek for some definite objectives and not merely gaze around. Hence the preparatory phase should consist of:

(*a*) A talk about the general situation to be visited or explored.

(*b*) A clear indication of the purpose of the visit, the points to be looked for, and their connexion with previous and possible future work. Each excursion should have a clear, definite, and limited aim.

(*c*) Working out a ' plan of campaign ' with the co-operation of the pupils. If necessary the programme may be noted down in small exercise-books which can be carried easily.

In some cases it is useful to divide a class into small groups, each of which is given a special problem to investigate. In this way, not only is the objective restricted but an element of rivalry is introduced which is an added incentive to take sufficient care with the work.

During the preparatory phase any essential technical terms and their significance should be given to the pupils (*cf.* Fox's lectured group).

During the actual field-work, assistance and direction can be given as required by the pupils.

Follow-up Phase

(i) From notes and rough sketches made during the excursion, pupils should present reports. These may quite conveniently take the form of brief lecturettes and blackboard demonstrations. Incidentally this provides excellent practice in clear exposition and speech.

(ii) The reports may be considered critically by the teacher and the other pupils. Errors of observation can be corrected, misplaced values reduced to correct proportion.

(iii) The results of the observations may be collated, organized, reviewed, and correlated with the problem or project originally proposed, as well as incorporated within the broader subject development.

(iv) Finally, pupils may make some permanent record of the work.

It may be objected that this takes too long. The answer is that one well-conducted and well-followed-up excursion will be richer in real educational results than ten desultory pointless afternoons-out. In some cases the preliminary orientation and the follow-up can be done during term-time, and the field-work during an intervening vacation. For less ambitious projects the field-work can be allocated to evenings, or week-ends. In boarding-schools, such directed activity may provide healthy and stimulating occupations for pupils who are unfit for, or who dislike orthodox organized games.

USE OF WIRELESS PROGRAMMES

Wireless lessons fall into two main groups :

(i) Expository lessons on specific topics, *e.g.*, science, literature, history.

(ii) Background lessons, *e.g.*, travel talks and dramatizations of historical episodes. These aim more particularly at interest, stimulation, broadening the sympathies of the pupils, and linking up school-studies, such as geography and history, with everyday life and general social or economic problems.

The function of the wireless is not to supersede the teacher, but to provide a range and variety of intellectually stimulating experiences for teaching-purposes which would be unattainable otherwise by the pupils. Therefore the wireless lessons must be *co-ordinated skilfully with the main body of school-work.* They should be part of a properly organized school-course.

Since the appeal of the wireless is exclusively to the ear, and since pupils, particularly juniors and the more backward seniors, are most prone to misinterpretation of spoken sounds, the wireless lesson needs careful preparation, and follow-up.

In this connexion the wireless is at a disadvantage compared with a speaker actually in the classroom. The wireless voice is to some extent impersonal. No aid to interpretation is provided by facial expression and gesture. Moreover, the wireless speaker cannot see his audience and therefore cannot tell how they are responding. The teacher talks to a living class whose responses he can follow from moment to moment. The wireless speaker talks to a microphone.

The wireless lesson to be fully effective (particularly with younger pupils) must be prepared for in advance. The teacher should give some indication of the topic which will be treated, and how it is likely to connect up with (a) previous lessons in the same wireless series, and (b) the general mental background of the pupils. This indicates a careful study of the printed synopses issued for the use of schools in connexion with the series of talks.

During the presentation *any necessary visual aids* must be provided by the teacher. These include :

Atlases or specimens indicated by the wireless speaker.

Printed synopses, such as those issued by the British Broadcasting Corporation. Each child should have a copy of the synopsis and pictures for reference during the talk.

Writing on the blackboard any unfamiliar names and phrases not likely to be intelligible to the pupils.

Making a brief blackboard summary of the main points touched upon.

After the talk there should be a follow-up. This should include :

Questioning in connexion with specific points of importance.

Correction of errors and filling in gaps in perception.

Summing-up to ensure that the pupils *comprehend the talk as a whole* and its relation to other subject-matter.

Some form of synopsis (*e.g.*, a summary) to be entered, when desirable, into pupils' note-books as a permanent record. This is more necessary for definite expository lessons than for general travel, history, and civics talks, but it may be an advantage also for the latter on occasion.

Some form of application either suggested by the speaker, or devised by the teacher. Such application might be the preparation of drawings or maps ; study of a suitable text-book or reader ; making of models ; visit to a pond, or a walk in the countryside to look for specimens ; experiments in the laboratory, domestic science centre, or school-garden.

It is interesting to note that some American secondary schools used weekly evening broadcast talks in a series, " You and Your

Government," as homework assignments for senior pupils in social studies. The pupils were expected to listen, make summaries, and be able to discuss in class the talk given on the previous evening. The teachers organized listening groups for pupils who had no wireless sets.

This experiment suggests useful possibilities in connexion with subjects like history, economics, public health, international politics, world affairs, and appreciation in literature and music.[1]

Mass entertainment media encourage attitudes of passive un-critical attending. A radiogram or transistor set, for example, is often a constant accompaniment of indoor and outdoor activities (even of school homework). It is possible (in 1969) to hear a twenty-hour, non-stop daily programme of 'pop' music. These attitudes of passive acceptance can accompany also film and television and transfer from home to school. If, therefore, serious educational benefit is to be derived from the use of mass media in schools, attempts must be made to train habits of critical alert attending.

Not *all* radio, film, or television items need to be made too strictly instructional. Popular programmes may be used, particularly with less academically-inclined pupils, to stimulate informal discussion as a first step to more critical educational attending later.

This brings us to the instructional management of cinema and television programmes. (See also the section on educational technology, p. 408 *ff.*)

USE OF CINEMA FILMS

Cinema films should be presented as a general rule in five steps or phases. These are:

(i) *Introduction or Preparation*

(*a*) Preparatory lessons leading up to the film are required, to organize in the pupils' minds an adequate background for the correct interpretation of the significant elements presented in the film.

(*b*) An introductory talk just previous to the first presentation of the film is indicated. This should deal with:

General purport of the film.

Special points of importance to be looked for.

Difficult technical terms (in sound film exposition) explained and written on blackboard.

Problems which can be solved by observation of the film.

---

[1] *Educational Broadcasting* 1936 (Proceedings of the First National Conference on Educational Broadcasting), Washington, Dec. 1936, University of Chicago Press.

(ii) *First Presentation Film*

The film should be presented *without a break*.

(iii) *Follow-up*

This will include:

Questions about significant facts to emphasize the important points.

Correction of errors.

Further explanation of difficulties revealed by the follow-up.

Discussion emphasizing *comprehension of film as a whole,* and correlation with previous work.

Redirection of attention to weak points in observation revealed by the follow-up.

(iv) *Second Presentation*

This is a most important step.

Now that the general purport of the film has been grasped, attention can be concentrated upon difficulties revealed in the follow-up stage. For this purpose it may be desirable to stop the film at some points, reverse the machine, and re-present specific portions (in *silent* films).[1]

(v) *Final Follow-up*

This will include recapitulation, final summing-up, making some permanent record, and appropriate applications.

It is essential for success that the teacher shall be well prepared. For this purpose a pre-view of the film must be made. Once the film has been seen, its general purport must be clearly grasped, difficulties analysed and noted, and possible applications devised.

TELEVISION

The invention of television has provided the educator with another source of vivid substitute experience. There are obvious difficulties in the systematic use of television in teaching—fitting the television sessions into school time-tables, for example. However, in America large-scale experiments have already been organized, and some significant claims have been made for it. It would mean separating the functions of exposition and demonstration from those of promoting pupil-participation—discussing the television lesson, questioning, recapitulating, making a permanent record in the form of notes. In this connexion it is claimed that the ablest

---

[1] Sound films cannot be stopped and reversed.

expositors and demonstrators could be used for the television session ; that the television teacher, being released from the more routine teaching processes, could spend much more time on preparation—getting special working models, expensive apparatus, rare specimens, quite out of reach of the normal school. It would be economical, since these special services could be concentrated into one television session received on the sets of quite a large number of schools. It has also been claimed that teachers of average competence or less could, and actually do, continue their training and improve their methods by studying those of the television experts. Moreover, the television camera can enable many viewers to see microscopic processes simultaneously. It can introduce them to situations otherwise impossible to observe. An educational television service might help to mitigate the difficulties caused by a shortage of teachers.[1]

Television would appear to offer valuable assistance in infant-school work and in teaching backward children. In a survey of the effect of television on child audiences it was claimed that backward children derived more benefit than brighter children from the medium.[2]

Exercises

1. Suggest some tests by which the preferred imagery of a number of pupils could be estimated.

2. Analyse some pieces of descriptive prose or poetry, classify the images used into visual, auditory, tactile, motor, etc., and from your classification estimate the probable preferred type of imagery of the author.

3. Study the spontaneous play-activities of a number of children. What insight does the study provide into the predominant hungers and interests at that phase of development ?

4. Study the spontaneous choice of books and other reading-material made by children of a given age. Compare the type of choice at different phases of development.

5. Repeat Exercises 3 and 4, but with children's spontaneous drawings.

6. Study some children of the artistic type and others of the mechanically minded, scientific type. Compare and contrast their play-

---

[1] These possibilities and some American experiments were described in an article by John Wellens, " Teaching by T.V.," in *The Observer*, December 11, 1960. A series of articles on education by television up to university level was included in *The American Psychologist*, Vol. 10, No. 10, (October 1955).

[2] See H. T. Himmelweit, A. N. Oppenheim and P. Vince, *Television and the Child* (printed for the Nuffield Foundation by the Oxford University Press).

activities, reading-interests, preferred studies, special abilities, and also their aversions and special disabilities.

What special modifications in teaching, curriculum, and school-organization seem to be necessary for each type ?

At what age do the differences in type become noticeable ?

Can you find any cases in which a child appears to belong to one type at one period of development, and to the other type at another period ? Can you find any children with both types of interest strongly developed ?

7. Analyse as clearly as you can all the mental processes involved in :

   (i) Solving a cross-word puzzle.
   (ii) Solving a mathematical problem.
   (iii) Arranging a meal for a party.
   (iv) Choosing new clothes.
   (v) Making a dress.
   (vi) Finding why your car has stopped when it ought to be going.

8. Analyse the conditions which seem to be involved when you ' get an inspiration.' What bearing has your analysis upon the work of teaching art, music, mathematics, English composition, science, and practical manual work ?

9. Consult a standard text-book on logic and make a list of fallacies : (a) formal, (b) material.

For each fallacy collect examples from newspapers, political speeches, advertisements, children's statements and essays, your own beliefs and assertions, scientific text-books, etc.

10. Compare the mental processes involved in translating a Latin ' unseen ' passage of some difficulty, and making a qualitative chemical analysis.

11. Compare and contrast the mental processes and logical methods involved in (a) a mathematical argument and (b) a theological argument.

12. Collect some instances of reasoning by analogy from (a) children, (b) uneducated adults, (c) scientific works in different subjects, e.g., physics, biology, anthropology ; (d) books on educational theory.

In each case examine how far the ' reasoning ' is determined by (i) ignorance, (ii) complacence, (iii) wish-fulfilment, (iv) practical convenience.

13. Study the spontaneous assertions of a group of infant- and junior-school pupils. Pick out any cases of reasoning you can find. At what age does reasoning of any kind appear to begin ?

14. Collect observations from a number of fellow-students who have observed the same situation, e.g., a play, musical opera, cinema film. (Mutual discussion must be avoided before recording the observations.) Compare the replies, and note how the observations are related to

previous knowledge, special interests, special abilities of the students concerned. Note not only correct observations but omissions and distortions. Note also the prevailing character of the observations recorded.

15. Repeat Exercise 14 with a group of children. What is the bearing of your results on methods of presentation in teaching ?

16. Organize a field-excursion or educational visit.

For infant-school teachers such a visit may provide much realistic experience upon which to base speech-training, reading and composition lessons, drawing, and modelling.

17. Observe a wireless broadcast talk, or a film demonstration given to a group of children. Follow up by oral or written questions. Collect and analyse the answers. Note the following points :

(i) What parts are most readily noted and interpreted by pupils of given ages in a particular district.

(ii) What parts are least readily noted, etc.

From your analysis decide what measures are necessary for children of a given age in :

(i) Preparation for the lesson.

(ii) Helps during the lesson.

(iii) Guidance and follow-up after the lesson.

18. Observe critically a broadcast talk, educational film, or television feature. Discuss its educational excellence (or failings) with respect to the following :

(i) Suitability of material for pupils of a given age.

(ii) Selection and order of presentation of material.

(iii) Artistic interest.

What modifications, if any, seem to be indicated ?

Books for Further Reference

Bartlett, F. C. : *Remembering* (Cambridge University Press, 1932).
—— : *Thinking* (Allen and Unwin, 1958).
Cohen, M. R., and Nagel, E. : *An Introduction to Logic and Scientific Method* (abridged edition, Routledge, 1947).
Dewey, J. : *How We Think* (Harrap, 1933).
Faraday, M. : *Experimental Researches in Electricity* (Everyman's Library, Dent, 1940).
—— : *The Chemical History of a Candle* (Dent).
Fox, C. : *Educational Psychology* (Kegan Paul, second edition, 1950).
Galton, F. : *Enquiries into Human Faculty and its Development* (Everyman's Library, Dent). See particularly " Mental Imagery," pp. 57–105, and " Generic Images," pp. 229–233.

JEPSON, R. W. : *Clear Thinking* (Longmans, fifth edition, 1954).
MCDOUGALL, W. : *Outline of Psychology* (Methuen, 1949).
MONTMASSON, J. M. : *Invention and the Unconscious* (Kegan Paul, 1931).
POINCARÉ, H. : *Science and Method* (Nelson, 1914). See particularly Chapter III : " Mathematical Discovery."
ROSS, J. S. : *Groundwork of Educational Psychology* (Harrap, second edition, 1935).
STEBBING, L. S. : *Thinking to Some Purpose* (Pelican Book, 1939).
TYNDALL, J. : *Fragments of Science* (Longmans, 1871). See essay on " The Scientific Use of the Imagination."
THOULESS, R. H. : *Straight and Crooked Thinking* (Hodder and Stoughton, 1930).
WERTHEIMER, M. : *Productive Thinking* (Enlarged Edition, Social Science Paperbacks, Tavistock Publications, 1966).

SPECIAL BIBLIOGRAPHIES

BROADCASTING
Books :
CANTRIL, H., AND ALLPORT, G. W. : *The Psychology of Radio* (Harper and Bros., New York, 1935).
MARSH, C. S. : *Educational Broadcasting* (University of Chicago Press, 1936).
Pamphlets and Programmes :
Central Council for School Broadcasting, 12 Portland Place, London, W.1.

CINEMA
Books :
DEVEREUX, F. L. : *The Educational Talking Picture* (University of Chicago Press, 1936).
BRUNSTETTER, M. R. : *How to use the Educational Sound Film* (University of Chicago Press, 1937). Contains detailed directions for teaching techniques.
CONSITT, F. : *The Value of Films in History Teaching* (published for the Historical Association by Bell, 1931).
DALE, E. B. : *Audio-Visual Methods in Teaching* (Harrap, 1947).
GEORGE, W. H. : *The Cinema in School* (Pitman, 1935).
MARCHANT, SIR JAMES : *The Cinema in Education* (Allen and Unwin, 1925).

SUMNER, W. L. : *Visual Methods in Education* (Blackwell, 1951). A comprehensive treatment, including an introduction to the psychology of perception, visual devices for use in teaching and learning ; visual methods and apparatus for visual projection ; extensive bibliographies.

LONDON COUNTY COUNCIL : *Report on Experiments in the Use of Films for Educational Purposes* (P. S. King and Son).

Sources of Information :

British Film Institute, 81 Dean Street, London, W.1.

Central Office of Information (Films Division), Hercules Road, Westminster Bridge Road, London, S.E.1. Distributes films and visual units made for the Ministry of Education, Central Council for Health Education, and other Government Departments.

Central Film Library, Government Building, Bromyard Avenue, London, W.3. Catalogues available.

Central Information Bureau for Educational Films, 7 Baker Street, London, W.1.

Catalogue of Films of General Scientific Interest. Published by Aslib, 3 Belgrave Square, London, S.W.1.

Educational Foundation for Visual Aids, 33 Queen Anne Street, London, W.1.

National Committee for Visual Aids in Education, 33 Queen Anne Street, London, W.1.

TELEVISION

HIMMELWEIT, H. T., AND VINCE, P. : *Television and the Child* (Published for the Nuffield Foundation by the Oxford University Press, 1958).

The American Psychologist, Vol. 10, No. 10 (October, 1955). Report on " Film and Television in Education for Teaching." British Film Institute (address, see above).

Additional Sources for Films and Filmstrips

British Instructional Films, Ltd, 2 Dean Street, London, W.1.

Central Film Library (Wales), 42 Park Place, Cardiff.

Contemporary Films, Ltd, 14 Soho Square, London, W.1.

Educational Foundation for Visual Aids, Foundation Film Library, Brooklands House, Weybridge, Surrey.

Gaumont-British Film Library, 1 Aintree Road, Perivale, Greenford, Middlesex.

National Coal Board Film Library, Hobart House, Grosvenor Place, London, S.W.1.

Royal Institute of Chemistry, 30 Russell Square, London, W.C.1 (Inquiries to Education Officer). Scientific films (chemistry).

Scientific Film Association, 3 Belgrave Square, London, S.W.1.

Scientific Film Review (bi-monthly magazine), Journal of the Scientific Film Association, 3 Belgrave Square, London, S.W.1. Articles and reviews of contemporary films.

CHAPTER IX

TRANSFER OF THE EFFECTS OF TRAINING AND PRACTICE—CREATIVITY—PRODUCTIVE THINKING

I. Transfer of the Effects of Training

THIS is a most important problem for education and teaching, possibly the most important in a period of rapid social, economic, and intellectual change. It may be that civilization itself, as we know it, depends on solving the problem in schools.

I. THE PROBLEM STATED AND ITS IMPLICATIONS FOR EDUCATION

The general problem is—what effect has material already learned, how it was learned, and the attitudes engendered by the learning on future learning? So far as schools and teaching are concerned the problem may be stated thus : to what extent, if any, does training and practice in one type of subject-matter carry over (transfer) to some other type of subject-matter in which there has been none or a minimum of previous experience, training, and practice? Further, to what extent does what is learned in school carry over to the learners' experience outside school?

A subsidiary problem is—what is the difference between training and practice?

The implications of the problem for education and schooling are obvious. If learning one type of subject-matter, Latin or mathematics, does facilitate learning other subjects, such as science or geography or economics, then concentration on teaching and learning Latin or mathematics will make the effort of learning other subjects easier. Still more, if learning Latin or mathematics not only facilitates the process of learning *generally*, but also *develops an aptitude for learning*, then it would seem logical to organize the curriculum around the subject-matter having the most general and most educative effect.

Even more important nowadays is the relation between what is learned in schools and what is required in the later careers of the learners. To what extent does four or six years' work in school and three or four years in college affect the learners' competence in a profession or industry? Does a course in educational psychology improve the competence of a future teacher? Are, for example, all educational psychologists exceptionally competent teachers? Apparently, not necessarily! It depends on what kind of psychology is learned and whether the learners *perceive any relation* between the psychology and their work as teachers.

In a stable, unchanging society if a student learned classics at school, continued to learn it at college, later became a schoolmaster and taught classics to the next generation in the same way as he had learned it himself, then that type of schooling would be a satisfactory preparation for his vocation. The same principle applies to any situation in which the future needs for knowledge, habits, and attitudes are the same as or similar to those acquired in schools and institutions of higher education. However, in rapidly changing economic conditions a classical scholar might be asked to teach English or German or Russian or navigation. What then would be the situation? Would his classics help him to perform with equal competence in these other subjects? That was the case in English grammar schools in the post-Tudor period. One problem nowadays is this—can the graduate in mathematics, engineering, or medicine react competently in the conditions which he will have to meet in, say, twenty years' time? If the answer to these questions is ' Yes,' then the schools and colleges need not change their curricula and teaching methods ; if ' No,' then either they must reform or their students will not be fully competent later.

Owing to the impact of science and invention, and the enormous and ever-increasing output of new knowledge, changes in industry and technology are happening at a continuously increasing rate. A glance at the ' wanted ' columns of newspapers and journals will reveal advertisements for specialists in activities which were unheard of thirty years ago. Obviously, then, if schools and colleges are to produce the experts of the future they must *educate for change. Even so, they must attempt to educate for changes which cannot at the present be accurately foreseen.*

It is often said in educational conferences that the schools must educate for life. Unfortunately we cannot envisage what life will be even as far ahead as the next generation. Thus the only effective education for life is developing in the present generation of pupils and students attitudes of expecting change, of willingness to deal

I

with change when it comes, and the abilities to apply as successfully as possible the knowledge and skills they have acquired to the changed conditions in which they will have to work. Flexibility is essential. Only too often one finds a strong tendency to stereotype the traditional. In some educational circles, for example, even though this country depends for its material standards of living on technology, the study of technology has been and still is regarded as educational slumming; something to be done only if one's intellectual grade is below average.

Even if we believe that there are certain constant absolute values independent of time and circumstance—religious, ethical, moral—the educated person is still faced with the problem of discerning clearly these constant absolute values when they are disguised in the bewildering varieties of experience of the daily course of living. The educated person must also be capable of applying the constant absolute values (in so far as they may be deemed to exist) to the rapidly changing economic and social conditions of the twentieth and subsequent centuries.

We find a similar problem in contemporary teaching. The same technology which is regarded with dismay by some people has provided teachers with many new teaching helps and devices—audio-visual aids, language laboratories, programmed learning. Thus we are faced with a situation in which, although the ways of learning—by experience, by various modes of association, by forming concepts, by the use of speech forms—are much the same now as they were centuries ago, the methods and devices by which the learning processes can be facilitated and made more efficient are very different. The teachers' problem is to adapt new devices and arrange new methods the better to promote learning in individual pupils.

In short, schools and colleges must teach for transfer and not tradition in so far as teaching for transfer is possible. It is essential, therefore, to find out whether, to what extent, and in what conditions knowledge, skills, and attitudes do transfer and what teaching methods seem most likely to maximize effective transfer—that is, maximize the applicability of past experience and contemporary learning to future conditions.

This is the problem to be discussed in this chapter.

2. AN HISTORICAL REVIEW

In one form or another this problem of transfer of the effects of training has intrigued philosophers, psychologists, and schoolmasters since time immemorial. Three main aspects have been dominant :

   (a) Whether or not transfer is a fact.
   (b) If a fact, in what conditions is it greatest ?
   (c) How can the fact of transfer be explained—what are the mechanisms which would account for it ?

   As early as 400 B.C. the Greek philosopher and teacher Plato took it for granted that reasoning ability exercised by the study of geometry would spread to intellectual ability generally. So did some medieval philosopher-psychologists and schoolmasters. They justified their belief and practice by a doctrine of mental faculties. The mind was supposed to include certain faculties or powers or unitary operators, each of which was responsible for all mental activities of a particular kind. Just as the eyes are responsible for all acts of seeing, the ears for all acts of hearing, the muscles for all acts of moving, so, it was assumed, there must be a faculty or organ for all acts of memorizing, and imagining, and reasoning, and willing. It was further assumed that just as the muscles could be developed and strengthened by any sort of exercise sufficiently prolonged and strenuous, so could these hypothetical faculties of the mind. Any sort of memorizing, imagining, observing, reasoning, deciding, ought to raise the efficiency of the faculty by improving the mechanism. If this be so, training and exercise would fulfil two purposes : promote the acquisition of useful information and skills and develop the power of the faculties ; make the faculties more efficient ' engines ' for doing any kind of work.

   This belief has been prevalent up to the present day. It was adopted by renaissance schoolmasters and academicians to justify the teaching of Latin in schools and universities when the world outside was clamouring for modern languages, mathematics, military engineering, geography, astronomy, and navigation. As we saw in Chapter I above, grammar schools at that time were endowed for the sole purpose of teaching the classical languages : schoolmasters were trained for precisely the same work. When the grammar schools could no longer supply what the changing society needed the faculty doctrine was most apt as a justification for opposing any change in the schools. If the doctrine were correct it was much more important to exercise and develop the faculties than to provide specialized knowledge and skills. The knowledge and skills might very well be useless in some particular set of conditions, but the developed faculties could be applied generally. Since the study of Latin was supposed to exercise all the major faculties—*e.g.*, observing, reasoning, memorizing, judging—and since it was sufficiently difficult to need concentrated attention and the will to persist in the face of frustration, the powers thus developed by this particular study would encourage the competence necessary for success in any situation in which a student might find himself later.   In other words, activity was the essential factor in learning ; what was learned, the content of the subject-matter, was relatively unimportant.   The educational value of subject-matter was the *difficulty* of learning it, not its usefulness for any particular purpose.   This point of view has been expressed very precisely by a schoolmaster, Tarver.   " My claim for Latin," he wrote, " is simply that it would be impossible to devise for English boys a better teaching instrument . . . the acquisition of a language is educationally of no importance ; what is important is the process of acquiring it . . . the one great merit of Latin as a teaching instrument is its tremendous difficulty."

To judge by appearances, one result of the tremendous difficulty of learning Latin has been the development of a determination on the part of many victims to escape as soon as possible from the scholastic grind of school, and a lifelong resolve never on any account in the future to open a Latin text or turn the pages of a Latin dictionary.   Whether or not the content of a language is educationally not important, when a country depends for its standard of living on its exports, the production of sufficient salesmen and commercial representatives competent in the languages of consumer countries most certainly is.

The same essential opinion was expressed by the biologist Professor T. H. Huxley.   " A liberal education," he said, " should make the intellect into a clear, cold, logic engine . . . ready, like a steam engine, to be turned *to any kind of work*."   Nowadays, I suppose, he would have specified the diesel engine or electric motor.

This doctrine of formal training (practising the forms and neglecting the content of subject-matter) had its critics.   John Locke (1632–1704) believed that the intellect consisted of elementary sensations or impressions which were organized by the mind's activity of reflection into ideas and generalizations.   Herbart (1776–1841) believed that the intellect and the will consisted of ideas which, somewhat in the manner of electro-magnets, attracted and repelled each other and thus organized themselves into systems.

Obviously, if the intellect did, in fact, consist of elementary sensations, impressions, or ideas, the faculty doctrine must be false. Any educational principles founded upon it must be, if not completely wrong, at best misleading.

The faculty doctrine was, and still is, plausible. Latin was a useful subject in those regions of Western Europe which had been part of the Roman Empire. Therein political power and the practice of government were the prerogatives of an hereditary aristocracy, while industry and commerce were managed by quite different and supposedly less important social groups. Greek and Roman society was aristocratic. The predominant interests of the Greek and Roman upper classes were in public affairs, law, diplomacy, and military enterprise. Much of the classical literature was devoted to the theory and practice of politics, law, and government. Hence, in spite of the views of schoolmasters like Tarver, the *content* of classical learning was directly relevant to the interests of the governing classes.[1] A classical training for an upper-class boy *if he pursued it to a relatively advanced level* was a direct preparation for a political career. This view was aptly expressed in an article " The Making of an M.P. " in an issue of the *Sunday Times* Magazine. The M.P. in question said :

> My education was entirely classical and because of this, one was pre-conditioned to the ancient idea that politics was a natural profession toward which, or for which, people should be prepared. This may sound odd but I think it has made its mark. I've forgotten all my Latin and Greek but I think with this sort of education there is a bias toward public life. It is so much at the centre of all the literature we have about Greece and Rome. If you are being brought up in it you are being prepared too.

The author might have added that in many cases there was a tradition of public service in many of the families from which these boys were recruited which was an even more powerful conditioning influence than Latin and Greek texts.

It has been suggested that Charles II seriously considered banning the study of the classics in Restoration grammar schools because it had encouraged subversive trouble-makers like Cromwell, Hampden, Pym, and their colleagues.

The classical tradition was taken over to the United States by the early settlers, but it did not suit frontier conditions. The frontiersman had to be farmer, craftsman, and tradesman as well as

[1] See also the comments on pages 11–13, Chapter I above.

magistrate and governor. While, as governor, he may have been able to get some guidance in political theory and legal principles from the classics, if his cows suffered from contagious abortion, or his sheep from foot-rot, he would need some knowledge of animal husbandry *applicable in North American conditions*. He was not likely to find it in Virgil's *Georgics*.

Thus the pressure on the grammar schools in the United States was for information of a kind directly applicable to agriculture, manufacture, and trade in frontier conditions. It is not altogether an accident, therefore, that a systematic attack on the faculty doctrine and the belief in formal training came from that country. An American psychologist, E. L. Thorndike, proved to his satisfaction that the effects of the study of Latin (as it was carried on in American schools) did not spread to other subjects to any useful extent ; that, generally speaking, there was little or no transfer. Therefore it was the business of the schools to concentrate upon the kinds of subject-matter which could be employed directly, to good purpose, in industry and commerce.

Thus educational psychology and educational theory have been distracted by a perennial conflict of opinion backed by dubious speculation while educational practice has been determined by the contemporary needs of dominant classes in the various communities. We are driven, therefore, to seek answers to the questions at the beginning of this section : what reliable objective evidence is there for transfer ; what conditions favour it if it exists ; how to explain it ; and what are the implicatons for teaching methods ?

3. EVIDENCE FROM OBSERVATION

(i) *Positive transfer. Previous learning may facilitate learning*

Whether or not transfer was found depended to a marked extent on who looked for it, and whether the result agreed or not with the prevailing climate of opinion and socio-economic conditions of the area. If conditions needed transfer its presence was taken for granted ; if conditions required specific practice in some particular aspect of knowledge and skill no transfer worth noting happened. This bias on the part of observers in different conditions is noticeable in the experimental investigations which will be described later. The presence of this bias is, in fact, evidence itself of transfer both positive and negative. The observers have approached the problem already influenced for or against the fact of transfer due to their own previous knowledge, attitudes, and needs.

Common observation, in the absence of some particular bias, seems to reveal positive transfer in abundance. In fact, it would appear to be the rule rather than the exception if the topic is considered apart from the special case of the influence of one type of subject-matter on other sections of the school curriculum.

What follows will serve to recapitulate some of the discussions in the earlier chapters of this book.

When we recognize some object, or event, or situation, we feel with more or less confidence that we have experienced that object, event, or situation previously. Moreover, the more often we have had contact with what is recognized, the more readily and confidently do we judge—' same as before.' In the early stages of learning, recognition either is absent or is hesitant, and subject to error. This is obvious in younger children. As experience increases, recognition is more prompt and more accurate. There seems little doubt that the recognition of shapes—for example, circles, triangles, quadrilaterals—has to be learned and that it is learned by looking at, tracing outlines, manipulating the shapes concerned, naming them all the while. Thus previous training, instruction, and practice do improve recognition.

Exercises in using items of information make recall more easy, prompt, and accurate. From not knowing arithmetical tables, telephone numbers, formulae in physics and chemistry, facts in geography, and dates in history, repeated recall and use renders such information more easily recallable, less liable to error. By repetition associations are strengthened as in learning poetry and vocabularies.

Similarly, in the development of skills : by instruction and practice in reading, writing, and calculating we read, write, and calculate more rapidly. Through efficient training and practice in any kind of skill unsuitable responses are discarded, errors are eliminated, and various partial responses are organized into more complex patterns. In typing, or Morse signalling, for example, the operator first learns the responses for single letters—i n r e p l y t o y o u r l e t t e r o f t h e ... With further practice separate letter habits are organized into word habits :

in reply to your letter of the . . .

Still later, word habits are organized into habits of phrases or whole sentences :

inreplytoyourletterofthe . . .

with great increases in speed.

Practice makes estimations more accurate. A butcher can estimate the weight of a joint ; a grocer can cut off a pound weight of cheese ; cattle judges can estimate the weight of an animal within narrow margins of error. Practice makes discrimination more critical. An expert musician can detect the presence of individual instruments in an orchestra ; practised individuals can detect very small differences between colours, tastes, smells, of which the naïve observer is quite unaware.

What has been called ' cross-education ' is a case of positive transfer. Handwriting is an example. We learn to write with the dominant hand (right or left). Frequently repeated word habits such as the signature become stereotyped. Thereupon they can be repeated with the other hand without specific practice. More convincing, perhaps, is the fact that if the signature is traced with the toe of either foot, in sand, the characteristic pattern is reproduced. The scripts made by the non-dominant hand or with the toes without practice are not perfect copies. Nevertheless the resemblance to the original is evident. A *pattern has been transferred* in the absence of previous specific practice.

As a variant of this exercise one can try to write a word upside down, with the left hand (if right-handed), with the eyes shut. One of my experiments in this type of transfer is shown in Fig. 14. My first attempt was ' psychology ' (see (*a*)). That seemed too easy. The next word was ' anastomosis,' chosen at random, a word I had never seen, spoken, or written before. The diagram for this is shown at (*b*). At a third attempt I tried to write ' anastomosis ' not only upside down but backwards (see (*c*)). This last attempt is interesting in that it reveals a frequent feature of serial learning— namely, the first and last items are more accurately recalled than those in the middle. This diagram shows the tendency to confusion in the middle of the word. The shapes are not good approximations, and at least one letter has disappeared altogether. Nevertheless there is some evidence of carry-over from normal writing. Here, then, is an example of the spread of practice to activities which have never before been practised—indeed, never before experienced in that particular context. What has been transferred in this case is a *pattern*. Incidentally, the exercise illustrates the participation of mental images in the process of transfer. While writing I was aware of a visual image of letters reinforced by sub-vocal speech. By repeating a letter in internal speech the visual image could be kept in the focus of attention.

(a)

(b)

(c)

FIG. 14

Equally important for social intercourse, we learn likes and dislikes, attitudes of approval or disapproval, prejudice, bias, emotional associations which persist and spread. For some reason, probably due to the interest in transfer through academic subject-matter, this emotional aspect of transfer has not received the notice it deserves. Socially as well as educationally, it is supremely important ; how important is revealed by problems of racial antagonism and industrial conflict. Psychoanalytic studies of child development indicate how a single frightening or nauseating experience will affect the victim for years and will spread to situations which, at first sight, appear to have little or no connexion with the original experience. A person may display quite unconventional attitudes ; may become socially difficult, a self-conscious, self-proclaimed aggressive rebel in conflict with any kind of authority. He may produce quite subtle logical or philosophical justifications for this attitude. Nevertheless analysis may reveal an early revolt against parental domination, a causative factor of which the individual is quite unaware explicitly. Also, pleasurable experiences may and do persist in the form of a generally optimistic outlook, feelings of confidence and security which may be at variance with the realities of a situation.

There seems, then, no lack of instances of the effect of previous learning on present and future experience. Transfer is the rule rather than the exception.

(ii) *Negative transfer. Past experience may interfere with present learning*

Common observation and controlled experiment confirm the fact of negative transfer—that is, the *interference* of previous knowledge and habit with correct apprehension.   Not only previous experience, training, and practice but also mental attitudes induced by instruction and suggestion at any particular moment will influence perception.   In an experiment conducted by Carmichael, Hogan, and Walters a series of diagrams was shown briefly to two groups of observers who were asked to draw from memory, after the series had been displayed, what they had seen.   At each exposure one group was told that the diagram displayed represented a familiar object which was named; the other group, that the same diagram represented a different named familiar object.   After the display, the observers in each group tended to reproduce *not the shape actually shown but the shape of the object named by the experimenter*.   (See Fig. 15.   See also pages 160–165, Chapter VI, above.)

Thus, what we observe is markedly influenced by our vocabulary as well as previous experience.   We tend to observe what we have names for or happen to be thinking about at the moment (occasionally at the risk of serious error).   Speaking generally, our acts of attending are determined by predominant interests, experiences, *and prejudices*.

Ask a fisherman, a Rugby footballer, and a crane-driver to respond to the word ' tackle.'   If an urban engineer, a farmer, and a geologist walk through a stretch of countryside and are later asked to recall what they have observed it is usual to find that each recalls, mainly or exclusively, those aspects of the scene with which he is most familiar and which accord with his experiences and interests.

In reading we often misinterpret what should be quite obvious : in proof-reading, for example.   If we are looking or listening intently we may ' see ' or ' hear ' what is not there, and quite fail to note what is.   Recently I read a notice of a book the title of which was printed in italics.   Later, having forgotten in which journal the notice was printed, I looked intently through numerous notices several times for the *italicized* title.   I failed to find it.   Later,

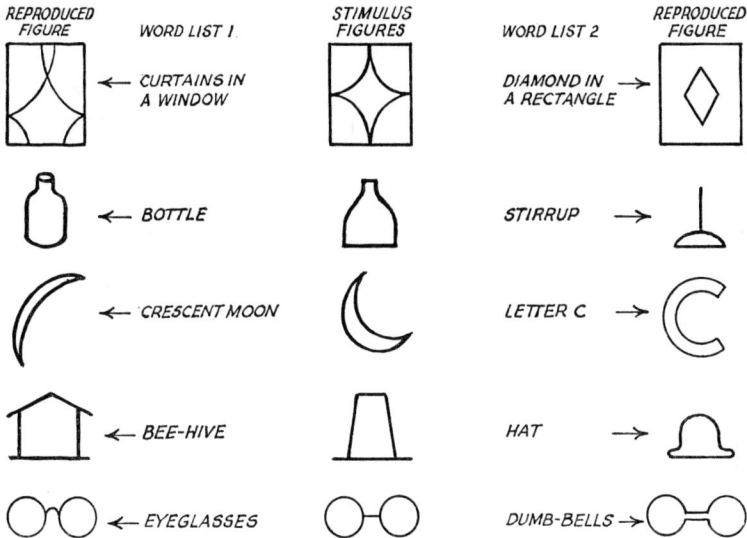

REPRODUCED FIGURE	WORD LIST 1	STIMULUS FIGURES	WORD LIST 2	REPRODUCED FIGURE
	← CURTAINS IN A WINDOW		DIAMOND IN → A RECTANGLE	
	← BOTTLE		STIRRUP →	
	← CRESCENT MOON		LETTER C →	
	← BEE-HIVE		HAT →	
	← EYEGLASSES		DUMB-BELLS →	

FIG. 15

Examples of how a Verbal Label affects the Reproduction of an Ambiguous Figure. Subjects in one group were told that the first stimulus figure looked like "curtains in a window," while subjects in the second group were told it looked like "a diamond in a rectangle." Note the differences that appear in the figure reproduced by each group. (Adapted from L. Carmichael et al., *Journal of Experimental Psychology*, 15, 73—86, p. 80.)[1]

having lost the obsession for italics, I chanced upon the missing title.   It was printed in bold-faced type in letters a quarter of an inch high.   Nevertheless I had ignored it !

The restrictive effect of past experience is clearly shown in new inventions.   The earliest motor-cars were pure horse-carriages.

[1] Sarnoff A. Mednick, *Learning*. © 1964.   Reprinted by permission of Prentice-Hall, Inc., Englewood Cliffs, N.J.

The horses and shafts were removed and the equivalent horse-power packed under the driver's seat. Any mechanically propelled vehicle at that period had to be preceded by a man with a red flag. The earliest motor vehicles were preceded by a man with a red flag. The first inventors of flying machines tried to make aeroplanes with moving wings after the manner of a bird in flight. The first paddles on steamships were water-wheels in reverse. Instead of a water-wheel driving machinery, the machinery drove the wheel through the water.

New discoveries in science have been aggressively attacked or ignored completely by contemporary scholars. Galileo's discovery of the satellites of Jupiter was ridiculed by his academic colleagues in Padua. Harvey's discovery of the correct model of blood circulation was opposed by medical experts of his period. The Abbé Mendel's essay on heredity was published in 1866, but did not attract any notice until 1900.[1]

Interference by already established habits of perceiving and thinking happens only too often in schools. What appears to a teacher to have been a perfectly clear statement on his part may reappear on a test-paper in a surprisingly different form. Each pupil or student brings to the interpretation of the teacher's words a lifetime of previous habits, vocabularies, word-meanings, specialized experiences, and local prejudices through which what is seen or heard may be grossly distorted. To make the situation more difficult there may be as many different distortions as there are pupils. For this reason it is always desirable to have testable responses from individuals to discover what errors in perception have occurred. This is particularly necessary in a socially mixed neighbourhood, and in teaching history !

[1] In the introduction to his treatise on the motion of the heart and blood Harvey writes : " Some chid and calumniated me and laid it to me as a crime that I had dared to depart from the precepts and opinions of all anatomists . . . others have essayed to traduce me publicly."

With regard to Mendel's theory of heredity, one scientist of some reputation, Karl Nägeli, a botanist, was aware of the publication, but he was not impressed. Mendel was far in advance of all his contemporaries . . . but no one paid any attention to his work. See A. Hook (Ed.), *The Origins and Growth of Biology* (Pelican Book, 1964).

An American scientist, R. Goddard, wrote a paper in 1910 on " The Possibility of Navigating Interplanetary Space." It was considered such a wild idea that the editor of a popular-science journal refused to publish it. Goddard had invented a multistage rocket model by 1914. Nevertheless he had to close down his laboratory owing to lack of funds. The Russians had not launched a potential atomic-bomb-carrying sputnik at that time !

It seems that we are compelled to envisage new knowledge in terms of what we already know. Scientific theories which are imaginative models of reality are usually expressed as analogies with familiar situations. Chemical atoms were first thought of as very tiny hard balls ; later they appeared more like miniature solar systems ; what they are like now is more obscure—something like disembodied spirits ! Radiations of light are conceived as waves or particles according to the apparatus used to reveal them. Faraday imagined magnetic forces to resemble elastic tubes. In psychology the brain has been thought of as a miniature telephone exchange. Now it is more fashionable to think of it as a computer. The Freudian psychologists have envisaged the ' mind ' as a series of layers superimposed one over the other—unconscious, fore-conscious, conscious ; id, ego, superego ; like strata in a geological formation. The danger is, of course, that these analogies taken over from the world as observed, and applied to situations which cannot be observed directly, may be accepted as fact instead of analogy. Even philosophy, which is commonly supposed to be pure wisdom, goes in fashions, the origins of which can be traced to social-class conditioning, economic necessity, or political expediency coupled with temperamental endowment and personality characteristics of the philosophers—idealism and pragmatism, for example.

Some motor habits transfer at the cost of efficiency. Hockey is not a good preparation for golf. The action patterns are different. If one learns to drive in one type of car, then transfers oneself with the acquired habits to another car with a different arrangement of controls, there is some confusion at first. Accents of speech fixed in childhood tend to persist through life. If for social reasons people strive to modify accent to a more socially approved pattern it seldom disappears entirely no matter how carefully the new accent is practised. When the speaker is tired, excited, or angry the early speech patterns reappear. Occasionally, by way of over-compensation, the new accent is an odd artificial hybrid. If one types in English for some time, then transfers to a foreign language with a markedly different alphabet or sentence structure, the speed of typing is slowed down considerably until new associations have been established. Similarly in spelling.

(iii) *Cases in which transfer does not occur when it might be expected*

The study of formal grammar may not spread beyond the grammar periods. It may not eliminate grammatical errors in other situations, neither does it necessarily eliminate ungrammatical speech, particularly in the case of pupils from homes and neighbourhoods where ungrammatical speech is prevalent.[1]

Some children can be observed stumbling with little success through a transcript of the local dialect they will use with idiomatic ease in their own conversations soon afterwards.

It has been demonstrated that a child can recognize a word in one context and a few moments later meet the same word in a less familiar linguistic setting and assert that he has never seen it before and does not know it.[2]

One can meet a friend whose appearance in a familiar situation evokes instant recognition. One can meet the same friend unexpectedly in a strange situation and, quite unintentionally, ignore him completely.

There is no guarantee that the effects of practice in routine arithmetical calculations will transfer to the solution of arithmetical problems. An analysis was made of scores in a Moray House standardized arithmetic test by 2088 pupils at the 11+ stage in a mixed-language area in Mid-Wales. The primary object of the analysis was to find whether, and to what extent, problems expressed in English were detrimental to the performance of predominantly Welsh-speaking pupils. The test in question is set in two sections—routine calculations and problems. In general, it might be expected that ability to work routine calculations would transfer in a high degree to the solution of problems.

The results did not support this. The overall average score of the Welsh-speaking pupils in problems was 22 per cent. less than that in calculations. For the English speakers the drop was 16 per cent. Thus, while some 6 per cent. of the fall could be ascribed to the difference in the language, *some 16 per cent. was common to both groups.*

It seemed that the change-over from routine calculations to problems had introduced a difficulty in addition to that specifically due to the Welsh-English factor. The extent of the disability can be seen in Table 1, in which are shown the scores in problems made by the group of pupils *returning the highest marks in calculations* :

[1] After a lesson on the undesirability of saying, for example, " He hadn't ought to do this " one pupil, on being asked what he had learned in the lesson, replied, " Sir, you didn't ought to say ' had ought '."

[2] J. F. Reid, *Acta Psychologica*, Vol. XIV, No. 4, 1958.

TABLE 1

In *calculations*	The following scored in *problems* :					
out of 743 pupils scoring 36–40 marks :	51–60	41–50	31–40	21–30	11–20	0–10
	284	239	146	54	20	—
out of 433 scoring 31–35 marks :	54	114	120	93	45	7

Thus in pupils scoring high marks in calculations there was a wide variation in the ability to solve problems.[1]   The problems involved the same formal rules as did the calculations ;   the actual calculations were in most cases simpler ;   yet some pupils *in the top grades in calculations* did very badly in problems.   The most probable explanation for the failure to transfer is lack in some pupils, both Welsh and English, of adequate ability in reading comprehension.   The fact that the predominantly Welsh-speaking pupils, although bilingual, were affected by the language difference itself is an example of the interference of one set of speech habits in a second language.

There was some evidence that teaching-methods were involved. Wide differences in average scores were returned between schools of similar type and size.   In some cases the average scores in problems were equal to or greater than those in routine calculations.   The form of instruction may hinder transfer.   In addition, this analysis suggests that one way of improving pupils' abilities in solving arithmetical problems is to improve their ability to read.[2]

This instance is instructive for the consideration of transfer. We shall see later that the amount of transfer, when there is any, diminishes with the degree of similarity between the training and test situations.   The *change of context* from calculations to problems itself introduces a difficulty.   The statement " $9 \times 7 = ?$ " may appear to be a different matter altogether when embedded in the sentence " How many times can seven be taken from sixty-three?" Factors of discrimination and analysis also enter.   The instruction " Add the smallest of these fractions to the second largest "

$$7/8, \ 16/17, \ 1/6, \ 1/34, \ 2/5, \ 18/19$$

---

[1] Full marks in calculations were 40 ; in problems 60.
[2] See A. Pinsent, in *The Teacher in Wales,* January 1965.

requires an appreciation of the nature of a fraction, ability to discriminate the difference between 16/17 and 18/19, as well as the ability to add 1/34 to 16/17. The fact is, as we shall see in more detail later, that any transfer that occurs is *not necessarily automatic*. It has to be achieved (and negative transfer prevented) by taking thought.

4. EXPERIMENTAL STUDIES OF TRANSFER OF TRAINING

Enough has been said to indicate that there is transfer in abundance. In some cases it facilitates subsequent performance ; in some cases it interferes ; in still other cases it does not happen when it might reasonably be expected. In what conditions, therefore, is positive transfer maximized ?

For this purpose controlled experiments are necessary. In view of its importance for education and teaching in a rapidly changing world a great deal of experimental work has been done on transfer. Some typical examples will now be considered.

The first experiment was performed by the American psychologist, William James.

He memorized 158 lines of Hugo's poem, ' Satyr,' the total time required being 131 minutes. He then practised memorizing, about 20 minutes daily for 38 days, learning by heart the whole of the first book of *Paradise Lost*. After this practice he memorized an additional 158 lines of the ' Satyr,' and this time he required 151 minutes. The result was just the opposite to that which would have been expected by hypothesis.[1]

This particular experiment had no great value as evidence, since it was not controlled with sufficient accuracy. However, it stimulated further investigation.

Most of the experiments had a similar type of organization. First came a test for the subject's ability in some kind of performance. Then followed a period of special training with a *different* type of material. Lastly, a second test similar to the first was given and the two test results compared. The kinds of performances and training may be gathered from a few typical examples :

(*a*) Thorndike tested the influence of training in estimating areas, lengths, and weights of a certain shape and size, upon the ability to estimate other areas, lengths, and weights similar in shape but different

---

[1] See *Principles of Psychology*, Vol. I, pp. 666–667.

in size ; different in shape but similar in size ; different in both shape and size.

(b) Several investigators studied ' cross-education '—that is, the improvement in performance with the left hand following training of the right hand.

(c) Ebert and Meumann investigated the influence of memorizing nonsense-syllables upon efficiency in memorizing series of numbers ; series of letters ; series of nonsense-syllables learned by a different method ; series of unrelated words ; series of hieroglyphics ; German-Italian word-pairs ; stanzas of poetry ; and paragraphs of prose.[1]

(d) Other experiments were concerned with influence of training in perceiving words containing ' e ' and ' s ' on efficiency in perceiving words containing ' i ' and ' t,' ' s ' and ' p,' ' c ' and ' a,' etc. ; influence of training in perceiving English verbs on efficiency in perceiving other parts of speech ;   influence of training in distinguishing different inten-sities of sounds on efficiency in distinguishing different shades of grey.

(e) In one study, practice in crossing out ' e's ' and ' t's ' on a page of prose hindered the cancellation of nouns, verbs, prepositions, pronouns, and adverbs.

In this case it seems likely that the perceptual ' set ' of searching for ' e's ' and ' t's,' carried over from the practice, induced the observers to cancel only those nouns, verbs, etc. which contained ' e's ' and ' t's.'

EXPERIMENTAL RESULTS

Generally speaking, the following results emerged from a mass of experimental work :

(a) There was some evidence of positive transfer of ability from the practice to the tests.   Working the tests was facilitated by the practice in some cases.

(b) *The amount of transfer was surprisingly small,* and occurred only when the practice material *resembled* the test material *very closely.*

(c) Increasing the difference between practice material and tests caused a *very rapid decrease* in transfer of training effects.

(d) Transfer might be negative as well as positive—*i.e.,* practice in one kind of performance on some occasions was found to hinder efficiency in other performances, even though the two performances appeared, on inspection, to be very similar.

The mainly negative results of the first experiments were re-ceived by the general public and by many teachers with horrified

---

[1] For details of these experiments see Thorndike, *Educational Psychology,* Vol. II.

incredulity. The results were so contrary to common expectation that they did not seem possible.

Actually, the methods used for carrying out the earlier experiments were rather crude and the statistical control of the conditions left much to be desired. However, in an outstanding series of experiments on memory-training from which the objectionable features of the earlier work had been removed, Dr W. G. Sleight confirmed the negative findings.

A number of London school children were chosen for the tests. They were given, first, ten tests in various kinds of memory-work. On the basis of these tests they were arranged into four groups of equal average memory-ability, A, B, C, D.

Each of these groups then had a different treatment. Group A had *no* special training over and above their ordinary school-routine. Group B received daily, special practice in memorizing poetry ; group C, in memorizing ' tables ' ; and group D, in memorizing the gist of prose passages.

At the end of the first training period all the four groups were given a second series of ten memory tests comparable in form and difficulty to the first tests. Then a second period of training was pursued by groups B, C, and D, after which *all* the groups took a third series of ten tests similar to series 1 and 2.

Precautions were taken to ensure that groups B, C, and D had equal training opportunities, and the same methods of treatment.

As a result it was found that :

(*a*) There was some improvement in the tests as a result of the practice.

(*b*) The improvement occurred only in those tests which were similar to the practice work.

(*c*) *In some respects the unpractised group* A *improved as much as the practised groups* B, C, *and* D, showing that the experience gained in working the tests themselves was as powerful in its effects as the special training.

(*d*) There was *no* indication of any *general improvement* in memory-ability as a result of the special training. This implied that there could be no general faculty of memory responsible for all the various kinds of memory-ability.

(*e*) There were indications of the presence of negative transfer.[1]

[1] " Memory and Formal Training," *British Journal of Psychology*, Vol. 4, pp. 386–457.

In the case of *simple dexterities*, later carefully controlled experiments have also confirmed the results of the earlier investigations.[1]

Other experiments have revealed more positive transfer. In learning lists of nonsense-syllables by human subjects and running mazes by rats it takes longer to learn the first list or the first maze in a series than is necessary to master subsequent similar tasks. In one experiment with verbal materials sixteen successive lists were memorized. The number of trials for a specified successful recall decreased from 38 to 14. The subjects must have *learned how to learn* the successive lists more efficiently.[2]

Learning how to learn was investigated by H. F. Harlow in a series of tests with monkeys. For each test a raisin was hidden under one of two blocks. The blocks differed in appearance, and the left-right positions of the rewarded block varied according to a predetermined order. The test involved *learning a rule* which indicated under which of the two blocks the raisin was hidden. Eight animals were tested.

344 problems involving 344 different pairs of stimuli were presented, the first 32 problems for 50 trials, the next 200 for six trials, the last 112 for an average of nine trials. Each monkey was allowed to look under one block on each trial. The pairs of objects were changed from problem to problem. If the animal chose the wrong block in the first trial it had the opportunity to alter its choice in subsequent trials.

At first the guesses were little better than chance. As the experiment proceeded, however, the correct choice was made increasingly often, until, in the problems 257 to 312, 97 per cent. of correct choices were made at the second trial.

Later the monkeys were given a series of discrimination-reversal problems. In these, after seven, nine, or eleven trials the correct (rewarded) object was changed in the remaining eight trials. Thus the object at first correct became incorrect and vice versa. Having discovered in the first reversal trial that the previously rewarded response was wrong, the animals learned to reverse their choice on the next trial.

Here was transfer from one discrimination problem to the next in the series, and from reversal to reversal problem. There was

[1] Langdon and Yates, " Experimental Investigation into Transfer of Training in Skilled Performances," *British Journal of Psychology*, Vol. 18, p. 422. See also Industrial Health Research Board Report, No. 67.

[2] L. B. Ward, *Psych. Monog.*, Vol. 49, No. 220, 1937.

also transfer from the original problems to the reversal problems. Moreover, the rate of learning in the latter, presumably more difficult problems was much more rapid than in the original series.

It would appear that the animals in this experiment were *learning rules for choosing*. They *learned how* to deal with a series of problems successfully. They had to learn which of the signs in each trial was correct. They learned to respond not to the *position* of a block, but to the *pattern* inscribed on it. They learned also to *vary their responses*. If they picked the wrong block on the first trial they did not try that response again.

Thus they acquired a ' learning set '—*a general rule for choosing* —which carried over from one problem to the next in the series.

Similar results were obtained in tests with children.[1]

5. HOW TRANSFER HAPPENS

(i) *The Presence of Common Components*

The experimental studies have shown that transfer does happen. It may be small in amount and negative. In some cases it is quite considerable. In any case, the amount decreases rapidly as the difference between the training and test situations increases ; the greater the difference, the less the transfer.

The next question is—how does the transfer happen? It has been suggested that transfer is due to the presence in the training and test situations of certain common components. These may be :

(*a*) Identical items of information.

(*b*) Identical stimuli or patterns of stimuli.

(*c*) Identical habits or very similar methods of work.

(*d*) Similar rules of procedure ; general principles.

(*e*) Similar methods of presenting the training and test situations ; similar contexts ; similar instructions.

(*f*) Identical attitudes—*e.g.*, proceeding with due care ; working conscientiously ; persevering in case of difficulty ; approaching both tasks with similar interests and intentions.

---

[1] H. F. Harlow, " The Formation of Learning Sets," *Psych. Rev.*, 56, No. 1. Readers may ask, why use animals ? The reason is that in the case of human subjects it is difficult or impossible to be certain that they have not had experiences of the same type before, in which case any carry-over may not be due to the experimental practice. In the case of Harlow's monkeys it was known for certain that they had had no previous laboratory learning experience.

(g) Identical nerve elements in the central nervous system and
   their patterns of connexion with sense-organs, muscles,
   and glands.

(ii) *Objections to the Doctrine of Common Components*

The supposition that the presence of common components in
the practice and test situations is the sole or even sufficient reason
for transfer of ability is open to serious objections.

It can be demonstrated that in many cases *no transfer of ability
takes place when identical common components are present in the
training and in the test situations.*

Components of complex perceptual situations are not mechanical
units in a mechanical aggregate. Such components cannot be removed from one setting to another without some degree of *qualitative*
change. If a grey vase is viewed first against a scarlet background,
and then against a green background, it will not appear to have the
same colour in both cases. A sheet of black paper can be made to
appear lighter than a sheet of white paper by arranging the conditions under which the two are viewed. The same physical thing
may appear to be several different perceptual objects according to
the context in which it is observed, and *according to the observer's
own mental condition at the time.* Thus the common objective
components of content in two or more different situations *may not
be recognized as common perceptual components* by the observer. In
this case no transfer will occur.

There seems no better case for the supposition that transfer is
caused by the operation of the same components of the central
nervous system in both the training and the test situations.

Lashley, an American authority on the anatomy of the nervous
system, has shown that if rats are trained to run a maze, and then
deprived by surgical operation of various parts of their upper brains,
they can still run the maze successfully although it may be traversed
" by a method of progression which involves no patterns of muscular
movement that can be recognized as identical with those utilized in
learning."[1] The author goes on to say that, in the doctrine of
common elements which has been so widely used to explain the
transfer of training,

> It is held that the stimuli may be diverse, but certain elements
> of each stimulus activate the same sensory paths exciting identical

---

[1] *Foundations of Experimental Psychology*, p. 544.

nerve cells and so eliciting the same reactions. The conditions of visual stimulation [in certain experimental studies of transfer in rats] seem absolutely to preclude any such common nervous elements, and it is equally difficult to find them in many cases of motor transfer. . . . *The common elements in transfer are not common neurons.*[1]

The common components need not be common movements. It was suggested by the behaviourist psychologist J. B. Watson that what rats learn in running a maze is a series of mechanical leg and body movements. This suggestion was tested by first training rats to run a maze without error. The maze was then filled with water. The rats swam. Next a floor was put in an inch below the water-level. The rats waded through, again with little or no confusion or hesitation. Obviously, here was a case of successful transfer in which the common components were not movements.[2] The common component in this case was a pattern—a map of a route.

The common components need not be common stimuli. It is easy to show that transfer does not occur in cases where there are common perceptual components in abundance. Look at the letter R. Few people recognize the letters P and D in it, although they enter physically into its constitution. Similarly, no F is recognized in E. The I is not noted in R, P, F, E, or D, although it is definitely a part of those letters. One can look at this diagram time after time without noting that it contains a figure resembling a letter E.

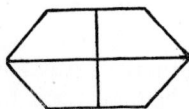

In Fig. 16 a careful search is needed to identify the shape (*a*) in the patterns (*b*), (*c*), and (*d*). Some observers fail completely to locate the shape (*a*) in the complex configurations, although they have been told that it is there. An amusing example of perceptual blindness is shown (Fig. 17) in the ambiguous figure of the Bride and the Mother-in-law.[3] There the whole configuration is common, yet it is difficult to see one figure rather than the other. Success in sorting out the components from the overall pattern depends on knowing that they are there and *making an active search*. Even the active search may be unsuccessful.

---

[1] Work cited, p. 545.   (The italics are mine.)
[2] See S. A. Mednick, *Learning* (Prentice-Hall, New Jersey), p. 4.
[3] From Boring, *American Journal of Psychology*, No. 42, 1930. Can you see the *two* women portrayed in the sketch ? When one emerges the other disappears.

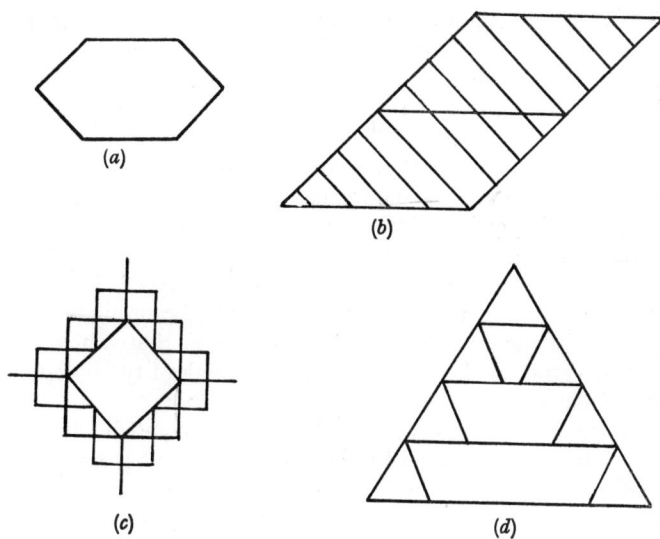

(a)

(b)

(c)

(d)

FIG. 16

FIG. 17

Thus transfer is not due merely to the presence of common components in the various situations between which transfer is desired or expected. There may be common components in abundance without any guarantee of transfer.[1] A perceptual pattern is not a mechanical aggregate to which items can be added or from which they can be subtracted without a change in their significance. How any particular item in a perceptual context appears depends not only upon its intrinsic qualities but also on the influence of the total pattern. The same word as a pattern of letters can have different meaning in different sentences. The word ' rose,' for example, may mean a flower, the perforated head of a watering-can, or the past tense of the verb ' to rise ' according to the context, and a reader concerned with the flower will not think of the past tense of ' to rise '—a common item but no transfer.

Transfer is not automatic. Any common components must be searched for, made explicitly clear, discriminated from the background, abstracted, and thus *made usable*. Transfer must be *achieved*. This poses another problem—*how to make the common items usable*. This brings us to the problems of teaching for transfer. In preparation for this we need to consider mechanisms of learning and transfer.

6. MECHANISMS OF LEARNING

Learning and the processes involved in intellectual development —getting experience directly at first hand and indirectly through the medium of languages, that is, the content of experience, and the processes of analysis and synthesis by which this content is organized into knowledge—have been discussed from the point of view of intellectual development in Chapters VI and VII above. It is desirable now to discuss them from the point of view of transfer of training. How, in fact, does transfer happen? What are the learning mechanisms involved?

Here a digression into more recent attempts to account for transfer seems to be indicated. Some acquaintance with learning theory helps to understand what is involved in transfer. To this we must now turn.

Theories of Learning.   Theories as Models

Learning, the process, must be distinguished from *performance*, the result. Experience is acquired at first hand through trans-

---

[1] See the accounts of experiences with the Pitman Initial Teaching Alphabet, p. 305 below.

actions with the environment—the receipt of impressions and the responses made to them. The learner is active, reacts to the physical environment; enters into communication with the social environment through the medium of speech. What can actually be observed are more or less permanent *changes in performance*. These are the outward indications that learning has taken place.

The fact that corresponding internal changes somewhere, somehow, within the learner cannot be directly observed, but only inferred, is a challenge to curiosity and the hunger for explanation. How, we feel drawn to ask, does learning happen? What are the ' mechanisms ' involved? Psychologists are forced to conjecture. They elaborate theories of learning.

The nature of theory has been touched upon previously (*cf.* p. 182 above). Theory may be the name for a set of established general principles which account for observations—the wave theory of light, the electronic theory of matter, for example. Alternatively, a theory is a name for a *model*—that is, an imaginative construction based on some known analogy which, if correct, will account for a set of observations. Readers of ' thrillers ' will be familiar with ' theories ' of a crime. From observations at the scene of the crime (fingerprints and other circumstantial evidence), from police records of similar crimes, from inferences which seem warranted by the observations, the police try to construct an imaginative ' picture ' or ' model ' of the crime as it might have been committed. In so far as the, theory (or model) is correct, it affords a guide to further action.

In much the same way imaginative ' pictures ' or ' models ' of mental activity have been constructed from the data of experiments and by conjecture. These, if correct, provide some understanding of the processes of learning and a guide for further research.

The Faculty Model

One such model of learning was the ' faculty ' theory already mentioned.

Sleight's experiments on memorizing raised some awkward doubts about the validity of this faculty model. If there is a faculty of memory responsible for all acts of memorizing, then there should be a close connexion between all types of memorizing. It might reasonably be expected that practice in committing a map to memory or memorizing the gist of prose passages would have some effect on the faculty as a whole. The improved ' machinery,' as it were, should then be evident in an all-over improvement in any memory performance whatever. Sleight's experiments showed that practice in one type of memorizing had little or no effect on other memorizing activities. Different types of memorizing were more independent than identical with each other.

Similar arguments apply to other so-called mental faculties. There seem to be different ways of imagining—reproductive, fantastic, constructive. Doubts have been raised about the identity of inductive and deductive reasoning, and reasoning by analogy. People competent in any one of these are not necessarily or always equally competent in the others.

There may be more than one type of ' intelligence.' A person may be intelligent in the production of analogies or in the ordering of a series, or in classification, in planning, in logical argument, or in solving practical problems. Few people seem to be equally competent in all these activities. Purely logical abilities may not be highly correlated with what have been called ' creative ' abilities, such as thinking of a number of possible uses of a barrel, paper-clip, tin of boot polish, brick, or blanket ; or writing down as many meanings as possible for ambiguous words like ' bit,' ' bolt,' ' duck,' ' sack,' ' tender ' ; or drawing sketches to illustrate the title ' ZEBRA CROSSING.'[1]

The available evidence does not support the traditional faculty model.

It has been found in analysing the results of thousands of mental test scores that *all* mental performances show some degree of positive correlation. Moreover, in addition to this overall correlation, certain activities, such as verbal-educational and spatial-mechanical, correlate more highly within the type than with activities outside it. So far as a general factor of ability is concerned, it would be surprising if there were no overall correlation. The various performances are all produced by the same person. His experiences, training, practice, interests, attitudes, and dispositions are all involved in all his activities. Many tasks are similar in form. What is done in any particular case is determined by the nature of the task as well as by the aptitudes and abilities of the individual concerned. Some correlations between performances may be due to positive transfer, similar environmental conditions, similar instructions, similar purposes, similar temperamental

[1] See L. Hudson, *Contrary Imaginations* (Methuen, 1966) ; J. P. Guilford, " The Structure of Intellect," *Psych. Bulletin*, 53, No. 4, 1956.

characteristics. This is not equivalent to supposing that the faculty model of learning is correct. Recent researches seem more and more to indicate that the *whole personality* and not a number of independent operators or organs or faculties is involved in any learning process.

Thus, if the traditional faculty model of the learning mechanism is doubtful, what alternative models are available? There are two main models (theories) at the time of writing. These are by no means perfect and, indeed, are in process of being modified. Nevertheless, although only approximate, they do afford some basis for understanding transfer, and as such they are introduced here. They are behaviourism (which is a form of associationism) and Gestalt psychology.

Alternatives to the Faculty Model of Learning. Behaviourism and Gestalt Psychology

Associationism as a model of learning has been fashionable since Aristotle at least (384–322 B.C.), probably earlier. He had worked out certain rules of association which have been current down to the present day.[1] The fact of psychological associations is obvious by reference to one's own experience. We acquire knowledge in the form of percepts and movements. These, together with feelings and desires, are the raw materials of learning. They are organized and extended through various forms of association. Seeing a photo reminds us of the actual person or place. The sound or sight of the word ' white ' suggests a snowfield, a snowdrop, a white flower, a white dress, something ' pure ' or pleasant. ' Black ' suggests night, a funeral, mourning, ink, thunder, something threatening, and so on. By means of associations we recall vocabularies, poetry, speeches we have heard, stories we have read. How often do we hear and say " That reminds me "? In one form or another mechanisms of association underlie the organization of our raw experiences into systems, particularly through the medium of associations of things and processes with words, and of words with words.

So far so good. The question arises—how are all these associations formed? What is the nature of the connexions?

Until comparatively recently it was supposed that the associations were between *ideas*, and that they occurred through similarity

---

[1] See J. C. Flugel and D. J. West, *A Hundred Years of Psychology* (University Paperback Edition, Methuen, 1964).

and contiguity. Ideas recalled or suggested similar ideas ; what had been experienced together or in sequence was recalled or suggested together or in sequence (contiguity). That this doctrine was sufficient to explain all psychological associations was open to doubt. There seemed to be no satisfactory mechanism to account for the associations. As knowledge of the nervous system and its operations increased, so did the belief that the missing links were *connexions* between various types of neurons in the brain *acquired in the course of experience,* or were organized patterns of neurons *given in the inherent structure of the nervous system itself*—or, of course, something of both. In any case, physiological models of the processes of perception and association have superseded idea models as explanations of the processes of learning. Behaviourism is a model of connexion between neurons which the behaviourists believe are due entirely to experience. They decry any recourse to instincts or inherently organized systems of neurons. The Gestalt psychologists, on the other hand, believe that patterns of innately organized neurons are given in the structure of the brain, these patterns being progressively modified by experiences. In fact, there is some justification for believing that both models co-operate. Neither is complete. What concerns us here is that both behaviourism and Gestalt psychology have contributed to the understanding of transfer.

Some Definitions

Before going on to a brief description of these two learning models some definitions of terms in common use may be useful. We shall be concerned mainly with reflex, reflex action, neuron, stimulus, percept, image, concept, conception, response, and feedback (response-produced stimulus).

Referring to a dictionary of psychology,[1] we find :

Reflex, the direct and immediate response of a muscle or a gland, or group of muscles and glands, to the stimulation of sense-organs.
Reflex arc, reflex action, sensory-motor arc, the working unit of the nervous system ; a connexion between sense-organs, glands, and muscles, or a connexion between the situation with which an organism is faced and the movement (motor response) which the organism makes. The arc consists of two or more structural units of the nervous system (neurons), one sort, the afferent neurons,

---

[1] See J. Drever, *A Dictionary of Psychology* (Penguin Reference Books).

conducting the nerve impulses from the receptors (sense-organs) to the central nervous system, the spinal cord, and brain ; the other sort (efferent) conducting the impulses from the central nervous system to the effectors, *i.e.*, muscles and glands.

Neuron, a single nerve-cell with its extensions (axon and dendrites).

Stimulus, any change of energy which excites a sense-organ.

Perception, the process of becoming immediately aware of something. The term is applied usually to sense perception when the thing of which we become immediately aware is the object affecting a sense-organ.

Percept, the mental result of the act of perceiving.

Image, a revived sense experience in the absence of the sensory stimulation, *e.g.*, ' seeing with the mind's eye.'

Conception, that type or level of cognitive process characterized by thinking of qualities, aspects, and relations of objects by which, therefore, comparison, abstraction, generalization, and reasoning become possible and of which language is the main instrument.

Concept, the product of the process of conception normally represented by a word.[1]

Response, the activity, muscular or glandular, of an organism as a result of stimulation.

The meaning of *response-produced stimulus* will emerge as the discussion proceeds.

BEHAVIOURISM.[2]   LEARNING AS A PROCESS OF CONDITIONING

Behaviourism is an aspect of psychology which emerges from the study of animal behaviour. Previously, psychology had been concerned primarily with the ' mind ' and its activities by the method of introspection—that is, a method of observing what appears to be going on in one's ' mind ' in the form of sensations, percepts, images, ideas, and feelings. This method is useless in the case of animals. They, lacking speech, cannot report their introspections even if they have any. Moreover, we are not aware in ourselves of every sort of mental activity. Some of it is ' unconscious,' and introspection can be misleading.

For these reasons, and encouraged by the progress in knowledge of the physiology of the nervous system, interest changed from percepts, images, ideas, to reflex actions—to stimulus-response psychology.

---

[1] *Cf.* pp. 190–209 above.

[2] For a useful, objective survey of modern ' schools ' of psychology see J. C. Flugel, book cited.

The experimental study of reflexes began in Russia as early as 1880 in the laboratories of Bechterev and Pavlov. Reflex psychology was taken up in America and popularized in the name of Behaviourism by J. B. Watson.[1] The Behaviourists wanted to develop psychology as a science similar in form to mathematical physics. For this purpose they can admit to their theories only those aspects of behaviour which can be directly observed and measured. So they cannot admit in their model any reference to consciousness, percepts, images, ideas, thoughts, or feelings. As I understand it, they do not deny, categorically, the existence of these mental processes. In view of the universal testimony of philosophers, scientists, other psychologists, biographers, novelists, and dramatists of repute, as well as laymen, such denial would be absurd. For their purpose these processes beyond the reach of direct measurement are irrelevant because not directly measurable.

We may say, then, that Behaviourism is the study of behaviour as it is manifested in the form of directly observable and measurable stimulus-response associations in reflex action. As such it has a contribution to make to the theoretical models of learning and the mechanisms of transfer, which is the justification for introducing it here.[2]

The overall plan of behaviour is exemplified in everybody's personal experience. In its simplest form sense-organs are affected by stimuli, that is, changes in the external environment as well as inside our bodies, which we interpret as sensations of light, sound, touch, taste, smell, muscular strain, movement, posture, pain, temperature, pressure. These stimuli set up activity in the central nervous system, accompanied or followed by movements of muscles and secretion by glands. In everyday experience stimuli are present

---

[1] See his book *Psychology as the Behaviourist Sees It*.

[2] Some strict Behaviourists insist on supposing that their theories are the one and only complete explanation of behaviour. Recent work on the nature and development of language is raising serious doubts about the generality of strict Behaviourism. See, for example, Chapters 4 and 5 in E. H. Lenneberg (ed.), *New Directions in the Study of Language* (M.I.T. Press, Cambridge, Massachusetts). It may be added that if and when strict Behaviourists cannot avoid reference to the unmeasurable and therefore unmentionable aspects of behaviour they call them by other names. So far as I am concerned, I have no doubt whatsoever that I am conscious at least part of my time ; that I experience percepts, images, thoughts ; that images aid my thinking and planning. I make no apologies, therefore, for introducing percepts and images, and thinking by name, whenever they appear to be relevant to the discussion of problems of transfer.

in complex patterns which appear to us as objects, events, situations. The responses also are most frequently complex organizations of nervous, glandular, and muscular action. This reflex arc—stimulus, connexions in the central nervous system, and response—is the Behaviourists' fundamental unit of behaviour.

An ambiguity in the meaning of ' response ' has led to much confusion in psychological discussion. There has been a persistent tendency to limit the response to movements and glandular secretions. The position and function in the reflex arc of percepts, images, thoughts as a series of part-reactions has too often been left undefined or ignored altogether. It is desirable, therefore, to look more closely into what exactly a response is and how much ' mental ' activity should be included in it.

The stimulus is essentially a physical change which affects one or a number of receptors. The full response is very complex. Certain aspects of it have been discussed in Chapter III above. In more detail we may note the following :

The effect of the physical impact of stimuli on sense-organs has been traced in the form of electrical impulses from sense-organs along nerve-fibres to centres in the mid-brain and outer cortex. The first effects of stimulation happen automatically without the awareness or the volition of the person—for example, the pupils of the eyes expand or contract ; sweat may be secreted ; changes occur in breathing and pulse-rate ; various glands secrete. Before the person is actually aware of what is happening muscle systems bring sense-organs into the most favourable positions to receive further stimuli. Gross body movement and breathing are suppressed. The eyes and head turn towards the apparent source of stimulation. This is what is meant by attending (see p. 79 above).

Frequently these unconscious involuntary adjustments are sufficient to meet the changing situation. Then nothing further happens. In many ways these subtle, involuntary reflex processes of adjustment are going on all the time whether we are awake or sleeping. If the involuntary aspects of the reflex arc fail to achieve a satisfactory adjustment, awareness supervenes. The person is alerted ; feels uncertain, confused, anxious meanwhile ; then attends voluntarily with concentration to the changing situation ; is aware of objects and events and their relationships as they are embedded in the immediate experience. Thereupon follow processes of recognition, perception, discrimination, and interpretation. Past experiences relevant to the developing situation are recalled, often in the form of images of various types, also in the form of words and phrases. Possible future changes are anticipated. With these reactions come feelings of pleasure or unpleasure, fear or anger, confidence or diffidence, elation or depression, desire or aversion, together with judgments of approval or disapproval. Usually, subsequent to these cognitive (knowing) and affective (feeling) experiences, there will be some overt act, observable, that is, by another person. The behaving individual moves with respect to the present and probable future situation.

A sudden intense stimulation, such as the sound of an alarm clock on a half-awake person, is followed by a ' startle ' response. The person ' jumps ' ; the heart misses a beat ; confusion occurs, followed by curiosity, a feeling of ' what's up now,' and exploratory activity if the situation is strange (such as waking up in a strange bedroom).

Stimuli may be verbal or symbolic. People react to the sounds of words or to printed and written words, then to their significance. Responses may be made in words or in writing. Language and communication is an enormously complex system of stimuli and responses which can be activated in the absence of perceptual experience and which facilitates discrimination, generalization, and abstraction and plays a very important part in transfer.

This description of a typical reflex-action system is intended to emphasize the fact that the total response is much more complex than any overt reaction immediately noticeable by an external observer. It is not too far-fetched to suppose that the real response begins in the sense-organs themselves immediately following the initial impact of the incoming physical stimulus. In any case, it is impossible to give a complete account of the facts of externally observable behaviour unless due account is taken of the mediating cognitive and affective aspects of the reflex act—in other words, percepts, concepts, meanings, images, plans.

An image can act as a stimulus and lead to a response. Who has not felt the emergence, while reading or day-dreaming, of an image, visual, auditory, or verbal, acting as a reminder of some promise not kept, some duty not done. This image-stimulus may be followed by image-responses indicating that the matter is not urgent, whereupon no overt action follows ; or the matter is urgent and overt action happens. Images can evoke emotional-affective aspects of response—sexual or frightening images, for example.

Feedback, or response-produced stimulus

A further complication of the complete reflex acts of which too little account has been taken is the response-produced stimulus. In muscles, tendons, and glands there are *internal sense-organs* which are *stimulated by the activities of the response itself.* Each response signals back to the central nervous system information about the ongoing action. Resulting from this feedback information, the central nervous system can control and modify subsequent responses, making them either competently adaptive or bringing the action to a close when no further response is indicated. This feedback of information from responses in action is the basis for the ability of an animal or human being to maintain a continuously competent adaptation of behaviour to a changing situation. The process can be observed in a predatory animal's pursuit of prey or in an expert games-player's responses to the continually changing demands of a game. Each stimulus from prey or ball leads to a response which *anticipates the next move of the objective.* Here, in fact, we have an example of a *continuous process of transfer from the accumulated stored experiences of the actor to anticipation of the next move in the game or pursuit.* A dialogue or discussion is another example of the same principle. Each speaker in a serious discussion not only responds to the words immediately spoken by others ; he is *continually planning ahead, choosing words to express thoughts in anticipation* of the probable course of the argument. He is planning to react to an imaginative situation which has not yet happened in fact.

Thus an adequate description of the fundamental unit of behaviour must be :

Stimulus→internal response (*a*) involuntary physiological adjustments of muscles and glands, followed by (*b*) an alert, perceptual, imaginal, feeling, evaluating condition→external response, *i.e.*, some action→feedback, *i.e.*, response-produced stimulus→central nervous system→a more or less permanent modification of nervous organization ready for future action. All this, and not the familiar and misleadingly simple S-R (stimulus-response) formula, seems to be indicated.

How behaviour can be elaborated and modified

We derive our experiences—percepts, images, thoughts, feelings —ultimately through stimulation from the outside world and the activities of the internal environment, the organs and tissues of the

K

body (*cf*. Chapter VI above).   Memories accumulate ; reserves of information and skilled actions increase.   At the same time images, memories, motor responses, are organized into increasingly complex systems through various processes of associations.

The counterparts in the central nervous system of these developing systems of knowledge and skill must be organized patterns of neural activity (called by various authorities ' schemas ').[1] What these schemas are, in fact, is a matter for conjecture.   They must be activated patterns of neurons which have sufficient stability to maintain an overall configuration while accommodating modifications in detail.

Thus it would appear that there are three main regions in which behaviour can be modified—namely, in patterns of stimuli as they impinge on the central nervous system ; in the schemas within the central nervous system ; in patterns of overt activity.   It is within these three regions that we must seek the mechanisms of transfer.

The processes of association called conditioning

(i) Classical or respondent conditioning

In the early years of this century the Russian physiologist Pavlov noted changes in the arousal of salivary secretion in dogs. He was interested primarily in processes of digestion, but he observed that his experimental animals secreted saliva not only when food touched the salivary glands, but also at the *sight or sound of the attendant who fed them.*[2]

This observation was followed up in a series of carefully controlled experiments.   Hungry dogs were harnessed in a stand in a sound-proofed room.   Shortly before the dogs were fed some signal—a light, a sound, a shape—was displayed.   After some repetitions of the signal-food sequence the display of the *signal alone* would activate the salivary reflex.   The food was called the ' unconditioned ' (*i.e.*, native, original) stimulus ; the associated signal, the ' conditioned ' stimulus.[3]

---

[1] See the works of Sir F. C. Bartlett, Sir Henry Head, Jean Piaget, and D. O. Hebb.   References in bibliography, p. 413.

[2] In one university veterinary department a tame old horse was used to demonstrate to students how to estimate a horse's age by looking at its teeth.   In time this well-disposed animal opened his mouth wide as soon as anybody in a white overall approached him !

[3] Strictly speaking, this should be ' unconditional ' and ' conditional.' The usual, less accurate description seems to have been introduced through some confusion in translation.

This process of association is called classical or respondent conditioning. It plays an important part in the elaboration and spread of behaviour.

Conditioning begins soon after birth. The bottle-fed baby makes sucking movements when a teat touches its lips. It will later make sucking movements at the sight of a bottle, the feel of a bottle in the hand, the sound of preparation of a bottle, and so on.

Responses connected with any primary and secondary hunger can be conditioned. Think of all the various stimuli which act as signals for food, for drink, for sex satisfaction, for the response of smoking or social climbing or danger. When some particular stimulus has been associated with a certain response other stimuli associated with the original conditioned stimulus will themselves evoke the conditioned response. Words will act as conditioned stimuli. The baby learns to react to the sound of the word ' bottle ' in the absence of the actual object. He will later react to any object which he learns to call a bottle. This is a case of transfer of a response to a generalization associated with a word.

A conditioned association can be extinguished by presenting the conditioned stimulus repeatedly without the native unconditioned stimulus. If a conditioned animal gets the customary signal—light or sound or whatever—without the unconditioned stimulus it begins to ignore the signal. The signal, we should say, changes its meaning. This process of extinction can be observed when travelling by train. As the train approaches sheep and cattle in the near-by fields the young animals gallop away furiously ; the older ones continue to graze quite unperturbed. In the control of children promises or threats, if not fulfilled, are soon ignored.

There was a tendency in the behaviourist camp to suppose that all associations of stimuli were due to respondent conditioning. Evidence has been reported that stimuli can be associated by contiguity alone without the help of conditioning, if they are presented sufficiently often simultaneously or in close sequence, and if the observer can be induced to attend sufficiently intently in the absence of the unconditioned stimulus. This appears to be the case when people hear the sound or see the sign ' rose ' and think of the shape, size, colour of a rose, or when the expert hears or sees ' Betty Uprichard,' or when an actual rose is perceived and the name recalled. A situation once experienced at all vividly may be re-called as a configuration. Later, a stimulus which evokes a particular aspect of the configuration will evoke other aspects, or the whole pattern. It is not necessary to *condition* each stimulus separately.

(ii) *Operant conditioning. Instrumental learning*

This process can be observed in a comparatively simple form in animals. A rat is put into a cage in which a lever is displayed. The creature is hungry, curious, and restless. It explores the cage. Sooner or later it will move the lever. Thereupon a pellet of food is delivered and eaten. This successful response is said to be reinforced (rewarded) by the satisfaction induced by the food. The reinforcement increases the probability that the successful response will be especially noted and repeated. Before long as soon as the animal is put into the cage it will go directly to the lever and press it. Eventually it may do this even if not hungry—just for the fun of it, as it were.

In another arrangement, rats were put into a cage having a wire-gauze floor. On the wall of the cage, within reach, was a wheel. The floor could be electrified. When this happened the animals made various evasive responses in the attempt to avoid the unpleasant shock, finally turning the wheel. This cut off the current and stopped the unpleasant stimulus. On subsequent occasions the animals learned to turn the wheel as soon as the gauze was electrified.

Young babies cry if hungry or uncomfortable. Usually they will be fed or taken up and made comfortable. Crying soon becomes associated with feeding and being cared for. Later it becomes a demand for food or comfort. The baby then cries to attract notice.

Thus responses can be *selected* by rewarding (reinforcing) those which are successful or socially approved and ignoring or punishing the others.

This process is called *operant* conditioning. As distinct from respondent conditioning, the response in this case must be made *before* the reward is given. Animals and young children soon learn to associate a particular response with the subsequent reward. The action is then repeated intentionally in order to get the reward. This is *instrumental learning*. The learning is instrumental in getting the reward or avoiding punishment.

This process lends itself to self-control. A successful response is its own reward if the objective is valued. Successful responses are noted and repeated ; unsuccessful responses are eliminated. The performer sets a self-standard and works towards it. By means of response-produced stimuli, information about success or failure is fed back to the schemas in the central nervous system. These are modified to a closer approximation to the end to be achieved.

A feature of respondent conditioning, very useful in teaching, is what has been called the schedule of reward. It is not necessary to reward the approved response on every occasion. If a pupil is praised indiscriminately the praise loses its incentive value. It is taken for granted. A more efficient method of control is to give the reward occasionally. Why make any special effort if any sort of behaviour is praised? If praise is given only for some better than usual performance, effort is more likely to be used for improvement, and is maintained at a relatively high level. If a gambler has won once he keeps on plunging in the hope that the success will be repeated in spite of a series of blanks—sometimes until he is ' broke.'

Summary. Associationist models of learning

We have indicated three ways in which knowledge and skills can be increased and organized through the mechanisms of association of stimuli and reflex connexions—namely :

(*a*) Associations of stimuli by contiguity or similarity ; by experiencing them simultaneously or in close sequence without the benefit of respondent conditioning.

(*b*) Associations between conditioned and unconditioned stimuli. In these cases previously neutral stimuli acquire a signal value. They direct attention to a sequel ; they indicate the probability that some hunger will be satisfied or some aversion aroused. These associations are organized in increasing complexity in the service of various primary hungers and secondary motives.

(*c*) Associations of responses with subsequent rewards and punishments leading to the repetition and strengthening of rewarded responses and the elimination of unrewarded and punished responses in development of skilled habits.

Gestalt psychology. A configuration model of learning

The second main alternative to the faculty model is provided by Gestalt psychology. Gestalt psychologists have been concerned almost exclusively with studies of perception ; the formation and modification of schemas in the central nervous system. From the point of view of transfer, the Gestalt model is particularly relevant to the processes involved in problem-solving.

Gestalt is a German word for a pattern or configuration. Gestalt psychologists reject the view that Associationism either of ideas or reflexes is an adequate account of mental activity and therefore of learning. W. Kohler expresses the views of this ' school ' as follows : " According to the most general definition of Gestalt, the processes of learning, striving, thinking, actions, emotional attitude, recall, may be included as subject-matter of Gestalt theory *in so far as they do not consist of independent elements but are determined by a situation as a whole.*"[1]

Some examples of *gestalten* were given on p. 188 above. It was suggested that some cases of the perception of movement could not possibly be due to the association of elementary sensations. In actual life we perceive whole objects of particular shape, size, and position, not elements such as the associationist doctrines assumed.

> In the configurations of perception, it is useless to consider the parts in isolation. A change in one part inevitably changes the whole. On the other hand, the *whole can persist when all the parts are changed* as when the same tune is played in different keys. Animals show clearly by their behaviour that they perceive in ' configurations ' and not in terms of elementary sensations—as is shown in a celebrated experiment in which an animal is taught to seek food in a medium-grey box in distinction from another box of light grey ; when a *dark*-grey box is substituted for the light-grey one the animal now goes to the new *dark*-grey box—and not to the medium-grey box as it should if it were judging by the absolute colour of the food-containing box rather than by the total situation.[2]

The influence of pattern on perception can be experienced by looking at the diagrams in Fig. 18. The configuration in (*A*) can be seen as groups of four ; groups of six, nine, or twelve ; horizontal or vertical lines of squares ; columns or rows of pairs of squares while the patterns change apparently spontaneously. The configuration in (*B*) is dominated by the cross of circles. The pattern resolves itself into the cross of circles and four groups of nine squares, and it *strongly resists modification*.

The lines in (*C*) are perceived as four close pairs. It requires concentrated effort to view them as three wide-spaced pairs and two odd lines outside. Even if one can envisage this arrangement it

---

[1] W. Kohler, *Gestalt Psychology* (Bell, 1930), p. 149. My italics.
[2] J. C. Flugel, book cited, p. 205. (The italics are mine ; they indicate one condition for transfer.)

persists only for a very short time, and the four-pair pattern re-appears.   If a slight spatial modification is introduced as in (*D*) it is now very difficult *not* to see three inside pairs with two odd lines out.   If the spaces are completely enclosed as in (*E*) this configura-tion is made even more dominant.   The influence of total con-

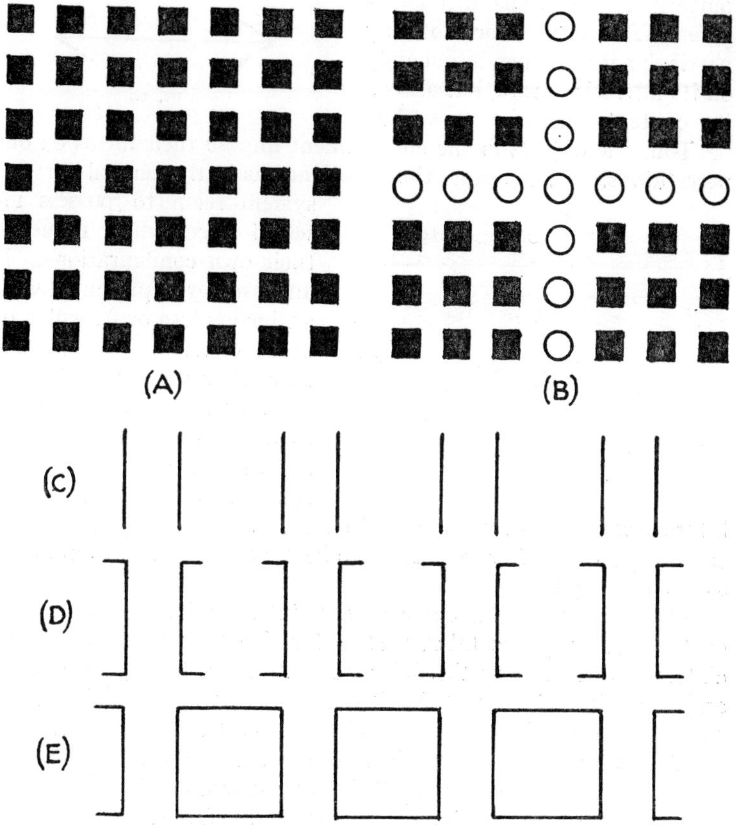

FIG. 18

(A) Arrangement of forms which permits alternate organizations while being observed (after Schumann, 1900). (B) Arrangements in which one dominant organization resists modification. (C) The nearness factor predisposes the observer to organize the lines in groups according to proximity. (D) The continuity factor counterbalances nearness, favouring grouping of less proximal lines. (E) Closure eliminates the possibility of grouping near parts of separate figures. From C. E. Osgood, *Method and Theory in Experimental Psychology*, New York: Oxford University Press, 1953.

figuration on the embedded details is exemplified in the illusions depicted in Figs. 19 and 20. The two horizontal lines in Fig. 19 are in fact equal in length. The long lines in Fig. 20 are in fact parallel. Items in a perceptual pattern are not mechanical aggregates. The significance of any particular item depends not only on its intrinsic nature, but also on its context, pictorial or verbal.

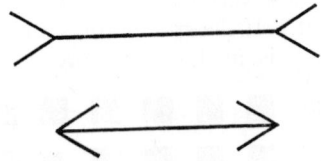

FIG. 19

Thus the objects in the environment impose their forms on our perceptions. At the same time the schemas in the central nervous system seem to possess internal forces which influence their own configurations. If an observer is presented with an incomplete or irregular or unsymmetrical figure, subsequent reproductions from memory will show tendencies to complete the figure, eliminate irregularities, or restore symmetry. Examples of this

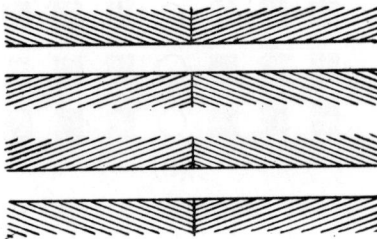

FIG. 20

internal change may be seen in Fig. 21. Shapes such as those in column (a) tend, after some time, to be remembered and reproduced as in column (b).

In addition to the external and intrinsic influences on perception, learning also takes part in forming the schemas. Young children have to learn the difference between a triangle, a square, and a circle. If presented with a form board containing these shapes a child will try to force a circle into a triangular inset.

Experiences, particularly in the first instance, are for the most part vague over-all patterns. Objects must first be discriminated— separated perceptually from a background. Later, details within the objects are discriminated and inter-related. This discrimination of figure from background and of details within the figures depends in the first place on the physical development of sense-organs and nerves. It is improved by repeated alert attending to details ; by practical manipulation ; by instructions to attend ; by descriptions of what to seek ; by pointing : by questions.

The original vagueness of perception in young children and the development of schemas are illustrated in the drawings on pages 199–200 above.   A bear, a monkey, and a human being all appear to look very much alike to the very young.   Nevertheless characteristic over-all patterns can be discerned lacking details.

The development of the schemas is assisted by the response-produced stimuli and feedback mechanisms.   As the internal con-figurations become more stable they in turn impose their forms on incoming stimuli.   They give meaning to otherwise meaningless perceptual patterns.   They are associated with names ; a name

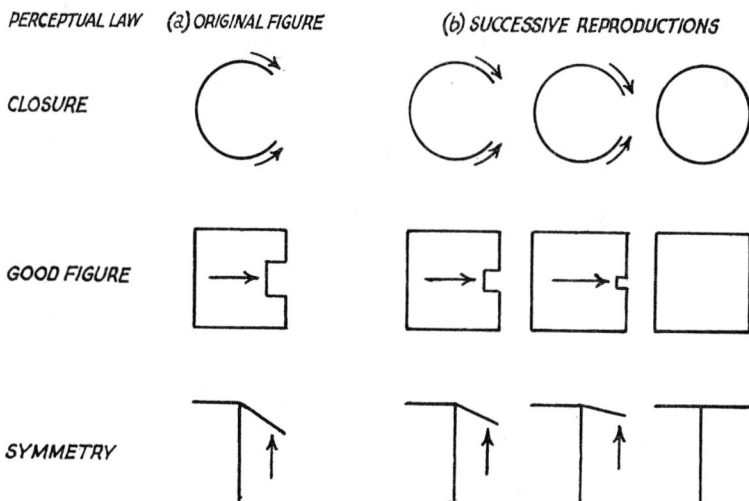

FIG. 21

Progressive Changes in Memory Traces predicted by the Perceptual Laws. Direction of predicted change is indicated in each case by an arrow. (From C. E. Osgood, book cited above.)

will evoke a schema, which is why we experience what we are ex-pecting ; what we have names for.   Amusing examples of the in-fluence of names and their associated schemas on the interpretation of neutral drawings are shown in Fig. 22.   A is supposed to rep-resent a soldier and his dog passing a gap in a fence ; B, a char-woman washing a floor.   One can look at C dozens of times and see a pattern of lines.   If, however, we are told it represents a bear climbing a tree it looks quite different.   The suggested concept im-poses its structure on the previously neutral pattern.

Bartlett made a number of experiments in serial recall. An Indian folk-tale expressing concepts different from those customary in Western cultures was read to a subject in a Cambridge laboratory. This subject then repeated his version from memory to a third subject, who repeated his to a fourth, and so on. The content and the form of the original tale were progressively modified as the series progressed to fit the experience and the concepts of those taking part in the experiment. Details were omitted ; concepts condensed ; the pattern distorted until the last reproduction was widely different from the original. A clear case of negative transfer.[1]

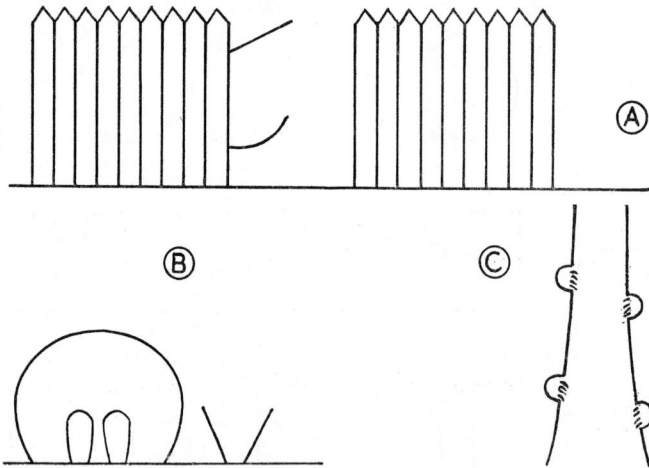

FIG. 22

Summarizing again, we have noted four mechanisms of learning : three forms of association—namely association by contiguity, and similarity, classical or respondent conditioning, and operant conditioning—and the formation of schemas (*Gestalten*) in the central nervous system. We have now to consider how these may enter into the processes of transfer.

7. MECHANISMS OF TRANSFER

We need to know how the products of training and practice can be applied to new situations. These descriptions of learning models indicate some possibilities.

---

[1] *Cf.* F. C. Bartlett, *Remembering* (Cambridge University Press, 1932).

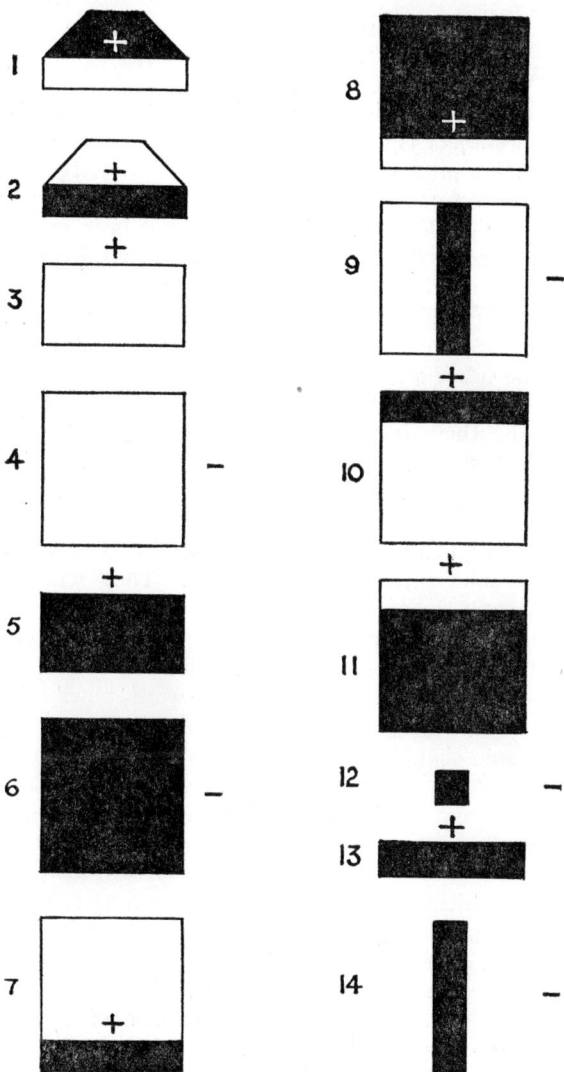

FIG. 23

Equivalent Stimuli for a Habit of jumping in the Rat. Animals were trained to jump to a platform having the appearance of 1, seen against the background of the room. The following figures were then presented in succession. The + sign indicates the position to which the animals jumped promptly; the —, failure to jump in five minutes. (K. S. Lashley, "Nervous Mechanisms in Learning," in C. Murchison (ed.) *Foundations of Experimental Psychology*, p. 543, Clark University Press, 1929).

Stimulus Generalization

In respondent-conditioning experiments it has been found that if an animal subject is conditioned to some particular stimulus—a note of a certain pitch or a particular beat of a metronome—it will respond *without further conditioning to stimuli sufficiently similar to those already conditioned.* If an animal has been conditioned to switch off a current (by turning a wheel or depressing a lever) at a sound of, say, 500 vibrations per second, it will switch off the current after sounds of 490, 480, 510, 520, etc., vibrations per second. However, when the sound is sufficiently different from the original, no action will be taken although the unpleasant shock continues.

K. S. Lashley trained rats to respond to the shape 1, Fig. 23. The creatures thereafter responded without further training to variations 2, 3, 5, 7, 8, 10, 11, and 13, but not to 4, 6, 9, 12, and 14. The horizontal white or black rectangle was the dominant stimulus pattern.

People who go to a meal at the sound of a gong will do so on hearing any sufficiently gong-like sound. They will not move, even if hungry, if they hear just clangs or crashes.

I have before me an advertisement for paint. Displayed therein are twenty-one hues to each of which, in my colour naivety, I should respond without hesitation with the word 'blue.' Other hues in the display are intermediate between greenish blue and purplish blue. At these I should hesitate, unable to make up my mind.

K. S. Yum investigated variations in response to similar patterns of stimuli in human subjects. Fig. 24 shows a series of diagrams having different degrees of similarity. The original patterns in the first column on the left were each associated with a word of three letters. The subjects were practised in responding to each pattern with the corresponding word. Twenty-four hours later diagrams in columns 2, 3, 4, and 5 were displayed in turn, and the number of times subjects responded with the word associated with the original diagram was recorded. The average number of correct recalls varied directly, without exception, with the degree of similarity.[1]

Similar results were obtained using nonsense syllables and words as examples of varying degrees of similarity.

Readers can test for themselves this effect of stimulus generalization—that is, the spread of transfer in proportion to the similarity

---

[1] In R. F. Grose and R. C. Birney, *Transfer of Learning* (Insight Book, D. Van Nostrand Co., New Jersey, 1963).

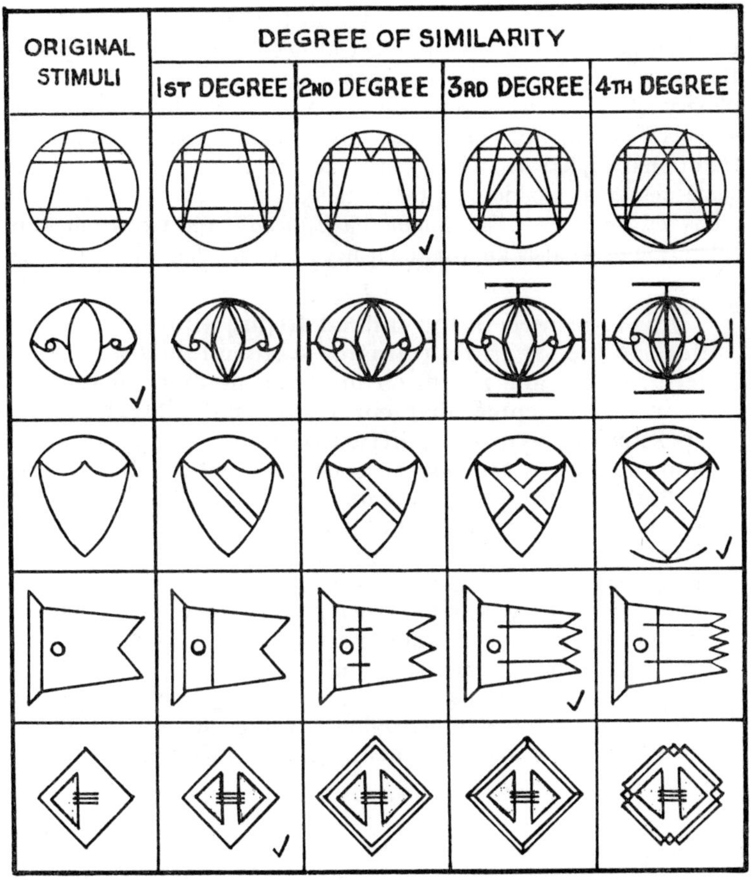

ORIGINAL STIMULI	DEGREE OF SIMILARITY			
	1ST DEGREE	2ND DEGREE	3RD DEGREE	4TH DEGREE

FIG. 24

of perceptual appearance. If presented with a passage of prose printed in the Pitman Initial Teaching Alphabet most readers will read through it without much difficulty but at a reduced speed (unless already habituated to the i.t.a.). This form of print presents varying degrees of difference from the traditional alphabet. If a reader's responses are timed it will be found that the hesitations vary according to the degree of difference between the two forms, the greater the similarity (mainly, but not entirely) the quicker the recognition and response (Fig. 25).

A survey of the use of this i.t.a. in teaching reading to young children has revealed both the fact of negative transfer in spite of the presence of identical common components ; and the complexity of the transfer process.[1] Groups of children in matched schools were taught to read, some through i.t.a. ; some through the traditional alphabet. The groups taught through i.t.a. were in some respects superior to those taught through the traditional alphabet. However, as might have been expected from consideration of what is known about negative transfer, when the i.t.a.

ſhis is printed in ſhe iniſhial teeｄhiŋ alfabet (i.t.a.) desiend bie sir jæms pitman. sⓞn aull ｄildren will lern tⓦ reed and riet ｝hrⓦ ſhis nue meedium, becaus it is nou acsepted ſhat our tradiſhonal alfabet and spelliŋs hav been mœst difficult for ſhe yuŋ beginner, and ſhe caus ov tⓦ slœ prœgress, and ov muｄh fæluer.

ſhœs uest tⓦ ſhe œld wæ mæ fiend it hard tⓦ beleev, but it is trⓦ, ſhat ｝haŋks tⓦ i.t.a. ſhe very yuŋ beginner lerns tⓦ reed and riet muｄh mor eesily, and cums very muｄh sⓞner tⓦ enjoi reediŋ and rietiŋ: hee ſhen (surpriesiŋly, wiſhout effort!), transfers aull ſhat noledƷ, enjoiment and sucsess tⓦ reediŋ and rietiŋ in our convenſhonal caracters and spelliŋs œnly.

ſhis is ſhe beginniŋ ov a mœst eksietiŋ bræk-｝hrⓦ— wiſh eduecæſhonal and sœſhial implicæſhons ov græt importans, ｝hrⓦout ſhe hœl iŋgliſh speekiŋ wurld.

FIG. 25

groups were changed over to the traditional alphabet there was some difficulty (although mainly temporary) during the transition period.

The i.t.a. groups were first tested on a version of Schonell's Graded Word Reading Test (a test of word recognition). When these pupils were tested later on the *traditional alphabet version of the same test* some curious results were noted. There was a considerable though by no means perfect relationship between correct recognition and the degree of similarity between the two versions. Analysis of the errors showed that, on the whole, the greatest

[1] See *The i.t.a. Symposium*, National Foundation for Educational Research, 1967. Also Downing and Jones, *Educational Research*, Vol. VIII, No. 2, 1966.

differences produced most errors. Nevertheless (and this contradicts the simple assumption that transfer is due to identical common
components), *some words which appear to an adult observer to present
very similar appearances produced the greatest number of errors* ;
more, in fact, than did other words which appeared much more
unlike. For example :

In i.t.a.	In traditional alphabet	Number of errors
orcestra	orchestra	95
canaery	canary	90
ieland	island	67
noledz	knowledge	95
nevue	nephew	71

Even a minor change like adding a serif to the d in ' applaud '
produced 72 errors.

It is obvious that what is implied by ' similarity ' and ' difference ' from the point of view of transfer needs a good deal more
careful investigation. And it raises in an acute form the problem
of what, in detail, is involved in teaching young (and more backward
older) pupils how to read. For example, do all pupils learn to read
in the same way ? Is the process of transfer the same for everybody ? In a comment on the results of the survey in question, Sir
Cyril Burt said,

> Most of us pay no attention to spelling unless it is faulty ;[1] the
> general appearance of the visible word, or of the phrase taken as a
> whole, directly suggests its meaning without any analysis into letters
> or sounds. Many children, particularly those who are visualisers,
> learn to read in this way from the very start. . . . Some, however,
> seem almost devoid of visual imagery. Of these many are audiles ;
> and their natural method of tackling a new word is to translate it
> letter by letter into its component sounds. There is, also, a third
> type of child less commonly recognised, the motile. For him, what
> the teacher calls ' sounds ' are really the movements needed to
> produce the sounds or the ' mental images ' of such movements.
> Pure types are rare. The majority of pupils are mixed types with,
> usually, one of the three main forms predominant.[2]

Thus, it seems likely that there are not only different degrees
of similarity but different types of similarity. In transferring

---

[1] He might have added, as we have noted elsewhere, " and sometimes not
even then."

[2] Book cited, p. 103.

from i.t.a. to the traditional alphabet, success may depend upon how one reads the printed words. Words having different shapes may have similar sounds ; or similar shapes may be associated with different sounds. Both, again, may have other relations with motor-speech habits. Some of the success or failure to transfer may be due to the fact that the reader has understood, or failed to understand, the purport of the passage and, on that account, can or cannot guess what word, irrespective of shape, sound, or movement, is necessary to fill the gap in order to make sense of the passage.[1] One may find positive and negative transfer processes going on at the same time. One may hesitate on account of a difference in perceptual shape (negative transfer), but succeed in translating the word correctly by similarity of sound (positive transfer). Previous experience and innate aptitude may also be factors affecting transfer.[2]

Rearranging the disposition of familiar letters without altering their shapes will cause some hesitation in responding. For example,

GESTALT PSYCHOLOGY

leavingotherconsiderationsasideitisnotpossibletobeable

und erth espre adin gches tnutt reeth evil lagesmi thys tood

If readers will take a card and cover first the lower then the upper halves of a line of print, they will find that the lower is more difficult to interpret than the upper half. This happens because most readers fixate the upper rather than the lower outlines in normal reading. (It is desirable to choose a line for the test which has not previously been read.)

Response Generalization

Responses in the form of motor habits transfer. Faced with a new situation, one tends to respond with an already practised

---

[1] See later discussions on differences in preferred methods of learning and the educational folly of treating every pupil in the same way.

[2] If it had done nothing else, this i.t.a. experiment would have been worth while for the questions it has raised with respect to the problems involved in teaching reading and learning to read. Further work is needed to discover ways of modifying the Initial Teaching Alphabet to improve the process of transfer ; and methods by which teachers can facilitate the transition period.

habit-pattern carried over from previous experience. The new situation may be a problem in mathematics, or plumbing, or teaching. In any case the first attempt at a solution will be one which has proved successful in apparently similar situations before. If this fails a search will begin for alternative solutions. One of Kohler's chimpanzees, seeing a banana beyond reach and no stick available, would use a piece of stiff cardboard, a branch off a bush, a piece of wire, or the brim of an old straw hat as a substitute. All movable objects long or oval in shape became sticks in the purely functional meaning of tools.[1]

A report of a mountaineering party trapped in a fall of snow in New Zealand described how one ingenious individual, lacking a knife, broke the lenses of a pair of spectacles and, with the fragments, cut through the canvas of a tent and escaped. In this case the transfer involved the realization that if no knife was available the lenses of a pair of spectacles offered a potential cutting edge. Cases of response generalization can be observed when a finger of the dominant hand is injured. Habitual movements of the other fingers are modified in order to make good the defect. Other instances are improvisations of tools, methods, and materials in practical constructions.

The instruction " Describe all the uses you can think of for a barrel, a brick, and a blanket " is a challenge to generalize the possible functions of the object in association with various situations.

Imagery plays a significant part in this process of response generalization. When a familiar motor response is unsuitable one asks in inner speech, " What can I do (use)? " or " How can I contrive instead ? " Thereupon a store of memories is scanned and alternatives recalled in imagery. Some of these appear immediately unusable. Others are tried out in practice, the trial-and-error process continuing until success is achieved or the operation discontinued.

It is desirable at this point to distinguish between at least two different uses of the term ' generalization.'

(a) When stimulus generalization and response generalization are mentioned in connexion with transfer, reference is intended to a process of association by which a response evoked in a learning situation *spreads* by reason of some degree of similarity from an

---

[1] W. Kohler, *The Mentality of Apes*, p. 35.

already experienced situation to a new one, the greater the degree of similarity the more probable the transfer. Any sufficiently green colour may be equivalent to a permission to proceed.

(b) On the other hand, a logical generalization—for example, a classification, a formula, a rule of procedure, a serial order, a scientific or ethical principle—is an *invariant* component of a number of situations in which the generalization can be discriminated in one situation, abstracted mentally, and *transposed* to other situations which are *logically* similar though superficially quite different. A number of colours can be arranged in the same serial order of intensity (brighter, louder, heavier) as a number of sounds or of weights. This generalization refers to a ' structure ' or pattern of relationships.

This distinction is relevant to our next topic.

Schemas. Configurations

In these cases we deal in similar configurations, similar ' frameworks,' outlines, or structures. The common features involved in the transfer are shapes, arrangements of series, rules of procedure, concepts.

Some examples have been mentioned—a tune played in many keys, on many different instruments, at different tempos ; signalling in Morse code by means of a variety of movements and a variety of instruments. Other instances are analogies :

Hat is to Head as   ?   is to Foot.

or rules of procedure :

To divide by a fraction invert the dividing fraction and multiply.

or general principles in physics and chemistry :

Objects attract each other with a force directly proportional to their masses and inversely proportional to the square of the distance between them.
Acids neutralize alkalis or vice versa. (Useful to know if a student has swallowed some.)
If any object is immersed in any liquid the loss of weight of the object is equal to the weight of the liquid displaced.

or rules of syntax :

Nouns and adjectives must agree in number, gender, and case.

or mathematical formulae :

$$(a+b)^2 = a^2 + 2ab + b^2.$$

It matters not what the details are : any number, any fraction, any acid, any alkali, any noun, adjective, object, or liquid relevant to the generalization or rule is covered. The details may be widely different ; the *relationships* must be the same. In the case of speech the same meaning can be expressed in quite different sets of words.

Similarly, in grading or ordering in a series. Here we have an apt illustration of the difference between what is ' specific ' and what ' general ' in connexion with transfer. It is impossible to transfer the sensory quality of red to blue or yellow ; or of a colour to a sound or taste or smell. Each sensory quality is peculiar (specific) to itself. Yet it is quite possible to arrange colours, sounds, tastes, smells, pressures in a given *order* or *grading* from more to less intense, for example. The sensory qualities are specific, but the order or set of gradations represents relationships which are general, that is, common to any similar order or gradation.

By the nature of things, transfer can never be total except possibly in a case of complete identity. Specific factors in both observer and situation must be taken into account. In teaching one can realize and understand a principle. This alone will not guarantee competence. I have known graduate students in a professional training examination to contradict, in a question about practical teaching methods, principles they had correctly stated in a theory paper. The book may say : Organize the subject-matter to suit the stage of development and interests of your pupils. The book may describe the characteristics and probable interests of each stage. To apply these generalizations in practice, however, one must learn from first-hand observation in the case of each individual pupil what is his stage of development and what his particular interests. The book may say : Choose illustrative examples from the experience of the pupils. What examples will be most appropriate for pupils in an expensive preparatory school, or a city slum school, or a remote village school can be decided only by first-hand observation in that situation. The book may tell the prospective teacher what to look for. It cannot tell him precisely what he will find.

Similarly, one can learn that $(a+b)^2 = a^2 + 2ab + b^2$, but that, by itself, may not guarantee success in answering the question, " A

number has the form $a+b+c$. What is the form of its square?"
Or, " Write down without multiplication the square of $\frac{1}{p}-\frac{2}{q}+\frac{3}{r}$."

In these cases success requires that the expressions given in the questions must be restructured, that is, written in the form of a general formula $((a+b)+c)^2$.

Formal Discipline. Formal Training

These terms have been used in discussions about transfer, often without adequate definition. From the descriptions of mechanisms of transfer we have indicated how transfer can happen—namely, through stimulus generalization, response generalization and the transposition of configurations, conceptual ' frameworks,' or mental ' structures.' These are the *forms* implied in formal training or formal discipline. Some parties in the transfer controversies have directly or by implication denied the possibility of formal training. All training, they suppose, must be direct and specific. If competence is desired in any particular subject, then training and practice is necessary in that particular subject. Transfer is so small as to be negligible. This, however, is too one-sided. Generalizations can be and frequently are transferred. The original mistake was to assume that the ' forms '—*i.e.*, rules, formulae, analogies, general principles, order in a series—would transfer automatically. As we have seen, they do not. In other words, the forms must be abstracted from details, memorized, and recognized in the new situations as applicable. *The forms must be made usable.* Here we approach the real problem for teaching—how can we make the forms usable?

8. METHODS OF MAXIMIZING TRANSFER

As well as the ' formal ' aspects of transfer we have to take account of subsidiary processes in making the forms usable, such as discrimination, registration, recall, recognition, attending, abstracting, ' set ', vigilance, language.

Discrimination

As we have seen, perception, the raw material of intellect, is at first vague, undifferentiated. This is revealed not only in drawings, but in the process of naming. One child is reported to have used the word " moo-i " for the moon, then for other round objects and for circles drawn on paper. Another used " wow-wow " for a dog, later for a squeaking doll, a fur-collar with buttons on it, and for the buttons on a coat (*cf.* the drawing of a lady by a child aged 4 years 7 months on p. 200). One child said " tee " for a cat (kitty), then used the same sound for cows, dogs, sheep, and horses. A big St Bernard dog was called " hosh " (=horse).[1]

From this early stage in the learning process development is due to two conplementary processes—analysis and synthesis. Analysis leading to the discrimination of detail and consequent recognition of difference is mediated partly by active manipulation and exploration, *partly by social communication.* Alert attending is essential for discrimination. The child attends to what it touches. Hands and eyes are occupied simultaneously. Objects are hard, often unyielding. They oppose intentions. They demand reactions. As the child notices, manipulates, explores, meets difficulties, attends again, tries more manipulation, the responses are fed back to the central nervous system, and there registered. Meanwhile all this activity goes on *in a social setting.* The young learner points to a dog and calls it " hosh." Parent or older sibling says, " No ! That's a dog." Later, if a horse is called a dog, the error is again corrected. Often this is followed up with a display of pictures or toys and the request " Show me the dog, the cat, the horse, the monkey," etc. More errors are corrected. *More successes rewarded.* By this process of operant conditioning objects which were formerly confused are now sorted out, recognized, and correctly named. The process is one of stimulus, response, reward, or rejection, feedback to the developing schemas, further perception, response, reward, feedback—a continuous circular process ; what was confused or ignored becomes clearer, is individualized, separated out, abstracted, *the abstraction fixed by a name.*

Meanwhile the complementary process is going on. The child is told to call a toy a ' dog.' The household pet is introduced as a dog different in detail from the toy. Other creatures are called dogs. They may vary in size from a Yorkshire terrier to a St Bernard or Great Dane. They differ in colour, details of shape, hairiness, friendliness, but they are *all called ' dog.'* Attention is

---

[1] M. D. Vernon, *The Psychology of Perception* (Penguin Books). H. Werner, *Comparative Psychology of Mental Development*, Second edition (International Universities Press, New York, 1948). M. M. Lewis, *How Children Learn to Speak* (Harrap, 1957).

now directed to outline ; details are cancelled out. A shape, configuration, mental structure, is developed—the schema. This again is helped by exploration and by social communication. A concept is formed and associated with a name.

Now, positive transfer can be made. A new creature with the characteristic ' shape ' having details never seen before is correctly labelled ' dog.' Similarly, schemas are developed for numerous other objects and processes and relations. A major factor in these processes of discrimination and concept formation is *the developing language.* Moreover, the associations between names, objects, qualities, relations, processes, must be *repeated, practised, learned thoroughly, and made readily recallable,* thereby available for use and for transfer. Differences in detail must be discriminated from the matrix of stimuli presented by the various situations and recognized. Recognition of pattern is necessary at the expense of detail.

Training for Discrimination

One essential aspect of enlightened training is the development of the ability to discriminate clearly and recognize details and patterns in both training and test situations. Several methods are available for this purpose :

(*a*) *Motivation.* The trainee must be sufficiently interested and concerned to learn. Discrimination will not happen in the absence of adequate motivation. Suggestions for arousing and maintaining interest have been given in Chapter V. Care must be taken to avoid arousing excessive interest, *particularly excessive anxiety.* Too much causes confusion and error. Motivation in medium intensity is most favourable for success. The rule is : enough interest to induce alert attending ; not sufficient to impel the learner to rush through the work or to fear the consequences of error. Too intense a motive leads to guessing ; taking a chance ; hoping for luck.

(*b*) Making comparison and contrast easier by bringing objects or situations closer together in space and time. This allows more rapid direction of attention to the aspects to be discriminated— whether details or outline.

(*c*) Instructing the observer to look or listen or touch with due care ; to suppress irrelevant or distracting events in self or in the immediate environment. The observer can be shown how to improve his posture, position, attitude, use of instruments or apparatus. This amounts to teaching the learner how best to attend.

(*d*) Directing the learner *where* to look by telling or pointing ; describing in words or by drawings *what* to look for ; *giving previous practice in hearing a sound or seeing a shape in isolation* before attempting to identify it in a matrix of sounds or visual stimuli.

(*e*) Making the components in the training and test situations more clearly discernible by using colours or emphasizing relevant lines (as in geometrical drawings) ; by directing the learner to draw or manipulate shapes.

(*f*) Dissecting the training and test situations ; drawing attention to each common component ; *allowing time for assimilation* ; then referring the learner again to the test situation to which transfer is desired.

(*g*) Rewarding (reinforcing) each successful act of discrimination. Even to accept the response as correct is rewarding. A word of commendation—" Good," " Well done "—occasionally, encourages the learner, supports his self-confidence, makes him willing to try again. On the other hand, errors should not be passed over. In this case, instead of an aloof, censorious reproof, which usually frightens or irritates the learner, it is sufficient to refer him back to the conditions of the problem with one or other of the suggestions (*d*), (*e*), or (*f*) as a help.

(*h*) Above all, in a new situation, *associating discriminated details or configurations with names* (*cf.* the vivid description by William James of the discrimination between the tastes of claret and burgundy on p. 204). In this connexion it is found that highly skilled workers in occupations dealing with colours and tastes may be no better than average in making fine distinctions (unless they have been specially selected for sensitivity to fine gradations of colour or taste). Learning a vocabulary of names for particular hues and tastes improves ability to identify the experiences from memory. In an experiment with a population of American college women each subject was shown four colours simultaneously for three seconds. After a half-minute delay she had to find these colours in a chart in which 120 shades of colour were arranged in order. When the observers were asked how they solved this problem the answer usually given was that they named the original four to themselves, then used the remembered names to make the choices on the test-card.[1] If one is presented with a diagram such as ( ) and

[1] Brown and Lenneberg, *Journal of Abnormal and Social Psychology*, Vol. 49, 1954.

later asked to say which of a series of incomplete figures most closely resembles the original diagram, it helps if one has described the gap as one-eighth of an inch.

It should be noted that the process of naming acts in reverse. If different objects are given the same name or symbol they tend to produce the same response. Children practised in calling a series of red, orange, and yellow lights by the same nonsense syllable responded by pressing the same button to all three lights even though they were trained originally to press the button in response to the red light only (a case of stimulus generalization and negative transfer).

The effectiveness of naming in improving discrimination depends on the association between name or symbol and discriminated feature *being thoroughly learned* (*cf.* Fox's experiments with suits of armour, p. 244). Half-learned associations are more likely to hinder than help discrimination. If the associations are not readily recallable the students will be searching for the names instead of attending to the details to be discriminated.

In this connexion it is useful to refer to the survey of teaching reading through the medium of i.t.a. (p. 303) above. Several commentators made the suggestion that the temporary retardation due to the transfer from i.t.a. to traditional alphabet might be minimized if teachers were familiar with the conditions of transfer and adopted methods of promoting discrimination instead of hoping that the transfer would happen automatically. Professor A. S. Artley (University of Missouri) said that preliminary studies in the use of i.t.a. with adult illiterates indicated the value of *pointing out similarities and differences between words written in i.t.a. and the same words in traditional alphabet on very early levels.* In this way the learners were making gradual and almost unconscious transfer to the traditional alphabet from the very outset. Whether or not some modification of this approach would work with young children is an interesting question.[1]

Learning ' Set '

This is a name for a very potent feature in transfer, both positive and negative. It is the name for a tendency for a particular habit of perceiving, thinking, or acting to persist through a series of situations. ' Set ' occurs in making a search. My experience in looking

---

[1] Book cited, p. 99. My italics.

intently for a book-title in italics and missing it in bold-faced type is a typical example. A golfer looking for a lost ball tends to keep an image of a small round white object in his ' mind's eye,' and reinforces this by repeating in inner speech (among other words !) ' white,' ' ball.' The result only too often is the false identification of any small white object with the lost ball—a case of negative transfer.

' Sets ' can be established by previous learning (cf. the mistakes so often missed in proof-reading).[1]

' Sets ' are established by intention and expectation ; by the nature of the task to be accomplished ; by instructions. The same subject will act in quite different ways if told to respond to a series of stimulus words by giving synonyms ; opposites ; the first word which comes to mind ; a word beginning with the same initial letter ; wholes in response to parts ; parts in response to wholes, etc. The instructions may be directions for procedure. Responses to a series of number pairs—e.g., 9, 7—will be quite different if the instruction is add, subtract, multiply, divide, or if the context is Cartesian geometry. So long as any particular request holds, the subjects will continue to add, subtract, multiply, or divide. When it changes from ' add ' to ' multiply ' the subjects will immediately respond with products (if they can multiply).

The effect of suggestions on what to expect was shown in the Carmichael experiment on naming neutral diagrams. Similar results have been obtained with displays of words. Groups of letters such as ' sael ' and ' wharl ' were shown very briefly. One group of observers, told that the ' words ' represented boats, reproduced them later as ' sail ' and ' wharf ' ; another group, told they represented animals, reproduced ' seal ' and ' whale.'

' Sets ' can be established by contexts. After reading through a series of nonsense syllables I found myself saying DAK-WAR rhyming with BAR, and having no connexion with WAR—i.e., conflict—until the nonsense-syllable context (set) had been dispelled.

' Sets ' are determined by the concepts (schemas) which happen to be dominant in the observer for the time being. If the stimulus word is LIGHT and the instruction is to respond with words having the same or a similar meaning, then if a concept relating to vision is activated the responses will most likely be ' colour,' ' white,'

[1] See p. 161 above.

'dark,' 'sun,' 'lamp'; if it relates to weight the responses are more likely to be 'heavy,' 'feather,' 'cork.' If the concept—'quality of behaviour'—is dominant the responses may be 'flighty,' 'irresponsible,' 'immoral,' 'untrustworthy' (light-fingered).

The influence of learning 'sets' in directing the process of attending and activating particular configurations of meanings and responses emphasizes the need for having *and stating* clear aims in teaching. Not only should the teacher have a clear aim ; the aim should be made clear to the pupils either by a statement of intention, or a question or a problem. It serves to evoke concepts relevant to the topic which will be necessary for interpreting and assimilating the new subject-matter or practical experience. Irrelevant ideas are suppressed. Attention is less apt to wander. If there is a clear aim in view there is less likelihood that some bright pupil will find himself knowing the meaning of every word the teacher has uttered, but quite unaware of what he was supposed to teach.[1]

'Sets' may persist for a short time, being dominant in a particular context, giving way to other 'sets' as a situation changes. They may also be relatively permanent. In that case they become attitudes or interests and affect broad fields of experience and action —professional, political, social, religious attitudes and interests, for example. These have the advantage of controlling responses and making actions predictable, a matter of considerable importance in social intercourse and communication. At the same time they impose severe restrictions on a person's adaptability to new situations and his willingness to accept facts which do not fit his presuppositions. This can be a serious obstacle to co-operative action —Socialist, Liberal, Tory ; Capitalist, Communist ; Catholic, Protestant ; Behaviourist, Gestaltist, Psychoanalyst. Attitudes can cause unfortunate amounts of negative transfer. A teacher from a middle-class social and intellectual culture may have difficulty in dealing with working-class children. Their attitudes may be incompatible.

The influence of 'set' on problem solving has been demonstrated very neatly by A. S. Luchins.[2] Subjects were presented with a series of water-jar problems (Table 2). " Using only the given jars which will hold exactly the amounts specified in column 2, how would you get the amounts of water required in column 3 ? " In problem 1, A holds 29 pints, B 3 pints ; how would you measure

---

[1] *Cf.* Westaway's example, p. 543.
[2] " Mechanization in Problem Solving," in *Psych. Monog.*, Vol. 54, 1942.

out 20 pints? In problem 2, *A* holds 21 pints, *B* 127 pints, *C* 3 pints ; how would you measure out 100 pints ? "

The solutions for problems 1 and 2 were given. In problem 1, filling *A*, then filling *B* three times from *A*, will leave 20 pints in *A*. In problem 2, filling *B*, then filling *A* from *B* leaving 106 pints in *B*, then filling *C* twice from *B*, will leave 100 pints in *B*. The subjects were then told to work through the remaining problems. Readers are invited to repeat the exercise and note their reactions. To give away the answers will spoil the experiment for our purpose. Do the problems first, then refer to the end of the chapter for the results and their bearing on this topic of learning ' sets ' and transfer.

TABLE 2

No. of problem	Given the following empty jars as measures			Get the undermentioned amount of water
	A	B	C	
1	29	3	—	20
2	21	127	3	100
3	14	163	25	99
4	18	43	10	5
5	9	42	6	21
6	20	59	4	31
7	23	49	3	20
8	15	39	3	18
9	28	76	3	25
10	18	48	4	22
11	14	36	8	6

Learning ' sets ' enter into performances in intelligence tests. The form of a standardized test may be quite different from that of the usual school work. If the pupils understand the purport of the test items the answers, even if they are in fact correct, may look wrong to some children. Some previous guidance with questions in the new forms is desirable to familiarize pupils with what to expect and give them confidence in responding. Formerly, intelligence tests were assumed to be ' culture-free,' not influenced, that is, by routine schooling and neighbourhood experience. It is now beyond question that previous experience, particularly in language work, vocabulary, and sentence structure, affects the responses of pupils to verbal tests. Ideally, before performances on tests can be fairly compared, all the testees should have had similar previous experience and training. Since this is often lacking, care must be exercised in interpreting intelligence-test performances.

Vigilance

Clearly, learning ' sets ' may be as much a hindrance as a help in learning and transfer. They may appear as automatic habits or as dominant schemas. In the one case the learner is quite unaware of his particular ' sets ' and applies them blindly. In the other case the schemas are transposed to situations which they do not fit. We have said that discrimination is essential for transfer. At the same time we have to recognize that a particular form of discrimination may become habitual, therefore automatic, therefore as likely as not to lead to error. For maximizing productive transfer some controlling, correcting mechanism is necessary. This we will call *vigilance*.

Vigilance, as used in this context, refers to a constant alertness to the possibility of change ; to a critical attitude of self-examination to check that one's discriminations and schemas are really applicable to the new situations to which they are applied. Vigilance is a ' set ' to control ' sets.'

Some methods for inducing an attitude of vigilance are available :

(*a*) Putting the learner into a variety of situations ; varying routines to encourage expectations of change ; providing new experiences ; arranging discussions with persons having different backgrounds, different habits, attitudes, opinions, particularly if the backgrounds are very different.

This is one argument for comprehensive schools. It is certainly one aspect of a ' liberal ' education. If it means anything at all, ' liberal ' does *not* mean providing a verbal type of curriculum, even if classics are included. It means, rather, liberating pupils (and adults) from habits and attitudes which prevent them from regarding their world with realistic accuracy, justice, and mutual toleration ; freeing them from the narrow restrictive ' sets ' of purely self-interest and local influence.

(*b*) Issuing challenges to learners to justify statements, attitudes, opinions. The challenge may be for the definition of a term ; for more clarity in expression ; for resolving ambiguities. If somebody asserts that democracy is impossible (or desirable) it is necessary to be clear about what is meant by ' democracy.' If the assertion is that Negroes are less intelligent than whites evidence should be produced which can be objectively tested.   It is possible to accustom students to challenge themselves before making assertions.

In an admirable little book by the late Sir John Adams[1] there is a verbatim report of a ' Socratic ' dialogue which illustrates this process of training in vigilance.   After a warning against giving learners too great a shock to their self-image Sir John went on to say, " A class will frequently cease altogether to answer when it finds all its answers turned against itself and made ridiculous."[2] At the same time, the first stage is necessary to lead to a desire to know the truth.   The pupils, however, may quite well be led to see the incompleteness of their answers without being humiliated. Stimulation may be made to take the place of the shock if the pupil is made to feel that he and the master are engaged in the same hunt for truth.   The following example—a verbatim report of an actual lesson—shows how the method can be used without repelling the pupils.

TEACHER.   Is the breath hot or cold ?
PUPIL (*confidently*).   Hot, sir.
T.   I have seen boys blowing on their soup at dinner-time.   What do
      you think they do it for ?
P.   To cool the soup.
T.   What cools the soup ?
P (*hesitating*).   The breath.
T.   But didn't you say the breath was hot ?
P.   Yes, sir.
T.   And the breath cools the hot soup ?
P.   Yes, sir.
T.   So the breath can't be hot, then ?
P.   No, sir.
T.   But I have seen cabmen blowing into their joined hands.   What do
      you think they do that for ?
P.   To warm their hands.
T.   What warms their hands ?
P (*hesitating*).   Their breath.
T.   But I thought you said the breath was not hot.
P.   Sometimes it's hot ; sometimes it's cold.

In the end it was agreed that the breath is hotter than some things, and colder than others.   That is all that can be said unless people

---

[1] *A Primer on Teaching* (T. and T. Clark, Edinburgh).   Now, unfortunately, out of print.
[2] Socrates, it will be noted, was judicially poisoned.   The Athenian ' Establishment ' regarded him as a subversive public nuisance !

know what they are speaking about, yet the breath is always the same.

In this example each statement is challenged and compared with earlier statements. Contradictions are brought to light. Pupils are referred to conditions and made to consider their answers and note the ambiguities.

An example of teaching for vigilance is reported in a volume *Recent Soviet Psychology*.[1] The question was asked: Which teaching method is more efficient—allowing pupils to discover a rule by their own efforts or stating the rule first, then by problems and questions directing attention to all the conditions of the problem and the implications of the rule? The Soviet authors favour the latter. They believe that it saves valuable time, prevents chance errors becoming fixed, and is at least as efficient educationally.[2] The pupils involved were of less than average ability in geometry or had had no previous geometrical training.

The procedure was as follows. A definition was stated by the teacher—*e.g.*, " Two straight lines meeting at a common point form an angle." Pupils were shown diagrams, some correct, some incorrect. Sometimes the problems were posed without a diagram. Pupils were allowed in preliminary stages to make drawings representing the rule.

Then a question would be put: " Two lines meet in a common point. What sort of a figure is formed? " If the answer is " an angle " the pupil is referred back to the rule and the corresponding drawing. " What," they are asked, " are the precise conditions specified in the rule? " If there is no response two curved lines meeting at a point may be shown and compared with the drawing and the rule. In this way attention is directed to the essential condition : the lines must be straight. Only if this condition is fulfilled is the answer correct.[3]

In another instance the rule given is : " The bisector of an angle divides it into two equal parts."

The question is then asked : " How can one recognize the bi-

---

[1] N. O'Connor (ed.).   See P. Y. Gal'perin, p. 247.   See also P. Y. Gal'perin and N. F. Talyzina, " Formation of Geometrical Concepts and their Dependence on Directed Participation by Pupils."   Book cited.

[2] It also fits their ideology—the supremacy of *collective* activity.

[3] The authors do not mention the fact that ' angles ' made by intersecting curved lines can be measured.   The statement in the text is adequate at the stage of development implied here.

sector of an angle ? " Pupils make suggestions to show whether they realize the relation between a diagram and the rule.

A problem is then posed : " From the apex of an angle a line is drawn dividing the angle into two parts. Is this line a bisector of the angle ? " No diagram is shown.

If the answer is " Yes," then :

TEACHER. " Why ? "
PUPIL. " The angle is divided. Therefore the line must be the bisector."
T. " Why ? "
P. " It divides the angle into equal parts."
T. " Does the problem say so ? " A drawing is made.

The pupil in this encounter had repeated the rule correctly in the first place. The last question directs the pupil's attention specifically to the conditions stated in the problem, then to a drawing, and to the conditions implied in the rule.

In this way the author believes that the correct concept can be developed by teacher and pupil working together ; the pupil's active participation is encouraged ; time is saved and errors corrected before they can be fixed. For our purpose the example serves to show how vigilance—the active, alert attending to the precise conditions of problem and rule—can be aroused and maintained. Each problem and question is a challenge to attend and discriminate ; to realize implications.

The principles of discrimination, ' set,' and vigilance apply in literary as well as in scientific and mathematical contexts. Creative writing in poetry and prose is to a great extent a process of regarding familiar situations from a new point of view. Details habitually ignored are revealed ; learning ' sets ' and stereotyped habits of thinking and feeling are reconstructed ; meanings clarified. Methods of questioning, challenge, and response apply. In a recent book on the teaching of English in secondary schools the first chapter is headed " The First Year. The Rediscovery of the Familiar."[1] " One has the feeling", the author says,

> when dealing with fourteen- and fifteen-year-olds that much adolescent inarticulateness has its roots in visual incapacity or at any rate in blunted sensibility ; children appear to grow up without really seeing anything, or to put it more accurately, perhaps, only

---

[1] J. W. Patrick Creber, *Sense and Sensitivity* (University of London Press, 1966), Chapter I.

seeing what they want to see. Thus, adolescents are allowed to bury half their experience without ever realising its significance ; perception becomes channelled and stultified with the cliché, a common feature not only of their expression but also, and more seriously, of their mode of thought.

Again :

> The problem of concreteness, of accuracy over detail, having thus been raised, we have to lead the children to discover just how much there is to say about familiar objects and experiences. . . . In all exercises of this kind—at any rate for the first two terms—the teacher should prompt them not by suggestion but by shrewd questioning, pausing after each question, leading the children to recreate in their minds all the details of familiar scenes and experiences and to bring them into sharper focus.

The author adds that occasionally a child will have his imagination fired by some very ordinary question, and his whole physical attitude will change.

Before their schooling ends pupils and students should have been made explicitly aware of the need for vigilance. They should be familiar with some logical tricks ; some methods of persuasion ; some forms of bias and their effects on judgments of affairs ; some of the insidious suggestions of mass advertising and political special pleading. To know what to expect in the form of propaganda and how to deal with it is of more value than memorized information that lies dormant or disappears when examinations have been passed (or failed). Occasionally exhortation may be useful. In Luchins' experiment with the water-jar problems one group of subjects was told to write " Don't be blind " on their papers when they had finished problem 6. Their results were distinctly better than a comparable group not warned.

Vigilance, even when emphasized by a particular teacher, *may not be generalized. It may be associated with one teacher in one subject usually taken in one classroom.*[1] In the ideal case it should spread to any subject and, indeed, to any situation, in school or out. For

---

[1] In one experiment a dog was trained *in one room* to secrete saliva in response to a bell and to withdraw a paw in response to a light. *In another room* the animal was trained to do exactly the opposite—secrete saliva in response to a light and withdraw a paw in response to a bell ! What happens in one context may not happen in a different context. N. E. Miller in Lindzey and Hall, *Theories of Personality. Primary Resources and Research* (Wiley, 1966), p. 428.

this to happen, the desirability, theoretical and practical, of an endeavour to achieve objectivity and get at the truth has to be encouraged and an attitude of vigilance developed.   Much depends on the example of vigilant teachers for whom pupils and students have respect.

9. TRANSFER IN PROBLEM SOLVING

Working to Rule.   Arranging.   Rearranging.   Restructuring a Gestalt

We have found that with respect to simple dexterities little or no transfer in the form of *spread of effects* occurs.   Practice improves performance, but the improvement is restricted rather precisely to performances identical with, or very similar to, those practised. Even in not so simple dexterities such as school subjects, where transfer might be expected, it may not occur, or occurs in only small amounts even in the case of Latin and English (as taught by traditional methods).

Some transfer of a quasi-automatic kind occurs in the form of stimulus—and response—generalization.   This may, as often as not, lead to errors.   Children who have learned to say ' boo ' to a goose may thereafter say ' boo ' to swans and ducks or to any birds resembling swans and ducks.   At the same time, transfer by stimulus generalization can be useful.   If one associates green with safety and red with danger any sufficiently green colour will evoke the go-ahead response ; any sufficiently red colour will signal caution.   In these cases the stimuli are associated with needs, hungers, fears. They have a signalling value ; they evoke anticipatory ' sets.' [1]

Of greater importance, both practical and theoretical, is the transfer involved in problem-solving, and it is in this connexion that Gestalt psychology provides the most useful model of learning.

What is a Problem ?

' Problem ' is very much a ' portmanteau ' word, the purport of which we are apt to take for granted.   For understanding processes of transfer it is useful to ask what is the nature of a problem and whether there are characteristic problems of more than one kind.

Broadly speaking, a problem is a situation in which stereotyped habits of thinking and acting will not achieve a desired result.

---

[1] This statement needs qualification.   The red or green colours have a signalling value only in situations where signals are expected or are customary. One would not associate red with danger in a plush Victorian drawing-room or green with liberty to go ahead on a Cambridge college lawn.

L

Again, broadly speaking, problems can belong to two groups—closed-system problems and open-ended problems. Some examples will make the distinction clearer.

Closed-system Problems

In these cases an initial and final situation is specified in advance by material conditions in the environment; by instructions; by rules stated or implied. The solution consists in *bridging the gap* between the immediate situation and the objective specified. The gaps can be closed by:

(*a*) *Interpolation*

    (i) Foot is to Ankle as   ?   is to Wrist.

The *relation* between the first pair must be discriminated and transposed to the second pair.

    (ii) Complete the following series:

       1, 2, 4, 8, ?, 32

In this case the relation between successive items in the series must be recognized, abstracted, and applied.

(*b*) *Extrapolation*

Write down the next two items in the following series:

    3, 6, 5, 10, 9, ?, ?

    L, O, M, P, N, ?, ?

    Farmer is to greengrocer
      as cutter, weaver, cloth, tailor, halter.[1]

Which two words best express the same relation?

In these cases a rule or set of relations must be discriminated and applied to other details. Problems of this type have been used extensively in standardized tests of ' intelligence,' on the assumption that ' intelligence ' is highly saturated with formal logical aptitudes. This practice has been criticized. Such problems, it is argued, admit of only one answer. They discourage 'creative' thinking and theoretical or practical ingenuity. The solver must work to rule or fail.

(*c*) *Rearrangement and/or reinterpretation*

In this type of solution no *general* rule is involved. The gap must be filled by the use of various alternatives in materials and

---

[1] See V. Serebriakoff, *I.Q.*, *A Mensa Analysis and History* (Hutchinson, 1966), p. 175.

methods determined by conditions in the particular situation. Examples :

(i) Crossing an unfordable river having no bridge, or boat, or ability to swim.   In this case the solution depends on a search for substitutes having the *same function* as a bridge or boat.   Also, anticipation is needed.   A log will float, but makes an inconvenient boat.   It has a persistent tendency to turn over and throw off the traveller—a subsidiary problem which can be solved by making several logs into a raft.   This again needs materials to fasten the logs together.

Problems of this kind invite ingenious substitutes for a traditional bridge to meet special difficulties—*e.g.*, suspension bridges, primitive and modern ; pontoon and ' Bailey ' bridges.   Materials and methods must be reinterpreted ; looked at ' in a different light '; a 'set ' or ' sets ' must be dissolved.

(ii) Crossing a river according to specified conditions—*e.g.*, the familiar problems such as three missionaries and three cannibals with a boat which holds only two.   This is a problem of arrangement.

(iii) How could you arrange three nines to equal eleven ?

(iv) Games of chess : problems of arrangements governed by a set of rules which allows a great variety of moves.

(v) Erecting a building.   Certain conditions are given—size and shape of site, upper limit of cost, accommodation required. Between the initial conditions and the completed building the designers must arrange, possibly rearrange, details.   Shortage of certain materials forces a search for substitutes, *some of which may not have been used or even thought of before.*   Shortage of labour and a time limit require adjustments and new methods—prefabrication, for example.

Problems of this type can be introduced in schools in the form of projects which will exercise the ingenuity of pupils.   Some pupils who do not ' shine ' in solving logical problems may be quite ingenious practically.

Inventions, theoretical and practical, require a process of restructuring a Gestalt—*e.g.*, the Copernican model of the solar system with the sun in the centre instead of the earth ; the sewing-machine needle ; the formula for benzine.   Transfer is involved in all revolutionary inventions.   The process is often ' unconscious.' The solution comes during reverie or a dream ; occasionally it seems to ' pop up ' when the thinker is occupied with other matters.[1]

[1] See H. Poincaré, *Science and Method* (Nelson, 1921), Chapter III.

Logical justification comes after the 'hunch.' Educationists, by and large, obsessed with the assumption of formal discipline and dominated by academic tradition, *have over-emphasized logical operations and working to rule, and underrated variety of first-hand experience and encouragement of original thinking.* In a hurry to get results they have given too little time for contemplation and discussion.

Open-ended Problems

In these cases a contemporary situation is found to be unsatisfactory. The objective is to modify the situation in some way which appears at the moment likely to make it more tolerable. What exactly the final condition will be cannot be forecast.[1] There are too many undiscriminated and uncontrolled variables. The solutions in such cases—*e.g.*, economics—are usually a series of successive approximations. One has to deal with a material Gestalt— a system of forces and pressures such that any modification in one aspect is followed often by quite unforeseen changes in other aspects. These introduce sub-problems which must be solved anew, and again these part-solutions may create their own problems. It is a case of change producing change in an infinite series. It has been supposed, for example, that more leisure would bring Utopia. More leisure, however, leads to new wants, new habits, new attempts to satisfy the new conditions, and instead of Utopia we get destruction, sudden death, and chaos on the roads.[2]

In all these cases mechanisms of transfer already indicated take part—observation, 'set,' vigilance, restructuring; regarding situations and materials and methods 'in a new light.' All the time there are tensions between desire for change, or the challenge of actual change, and the resistance to change by old-established attitudes and 'sets' which hinder restructuring. The moral for education seems to be that if we are to train pupils and students for life in a changing environment they must have sufficient experience

---

[1] Wallach and Kogan, authors of the book *Modes of Thinking in Young Children*, to which reference will be made later, say (p. vii) : "The work proceeded as a kind of bootstraps operation wherein the outcome of the early phases determined the nature of the later phases. . . . We could not know at the beginning exactly where we would arrive at the end."

[2] The application of drugs in medicine and agriculture is another case in point. A drug may cure some specific disability, but create others not clearly foreseen. Recent examples have been penicillin, thalidomide, lysergic acid, and various insecticides.

with these open-ended problems where ingenuity, foresight, and 'creative' abilities are more valuable than formal logic.   Whether it will be possible to invent examinations and tests which will encourage and assess these abilities is as yet another unsolved problem.
   This is not to say that tradition has no value.   Pupils and students must learn some facts, must be able to recall and apply rules; must have some regard for logic.   What we need is due regard for permanently valuable elements in tradition together with training in mechanisms of transfer, with opportunity and time for contemplation and ingenuity.

Summarizing

   In problem-solving transfer may happen, in favourable conditions, in considerable amounts.   The 'mechanisms' involved are :

   (a) Transposing relationships—eduction of relations and correlates (see pp. 192, 209, 324 above).
   (b) Arrangement of items in a series.
   (c) Substitution of items judged to be equivalent in function.
   (d) Restructuring a material or conceptual Gestalt—*i.e.*, regarding familiar things and situations 'in a new light.'
   (e) Recall of stored impressions in the form of images and words and rearranging them mentally.

Some Examples of Problem-solving by restructuring a Situation

(i) *Finding the Areas of Irregular Figures*

   The area of a parallelogram can be found by converting it into a rectangle (Fig. 26 (a)).
   The area of an irregular figure can be found by converting it into triangles (Fig. 26 (b)).
   A more difficult case of restructuring : Find the *sum* of the areas of the square ABCD and the parallelogram AECF.[1]   The solution depends on visualizing the figure as two triangles (Fig. 26 (c)). Operations of Gestalt reorganization are made difficult by traditional habits of thought and action.   One reason why revolutionary changes in scientific outlook occur slowly is that they have to be made against the resistance of strong, well-articulated concepts.[2]

[1] M. Wertheimer, *Productive Thinking* (Harper Bros., London, 1945).
[2] Wertheimer, book cited, Chapter VII.

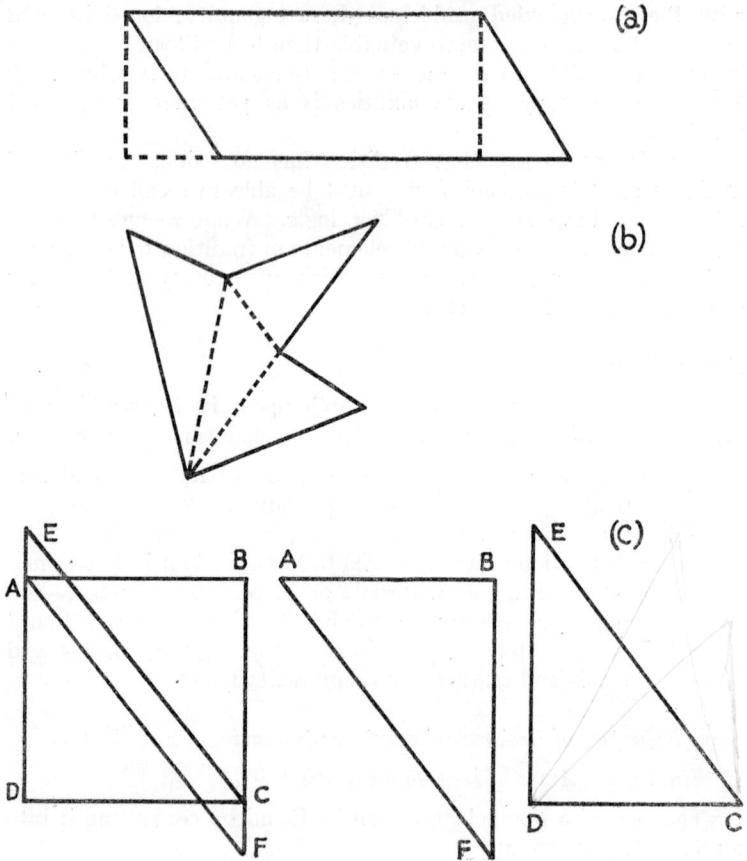

FIG. 26

(ii) *A Gimlet Problem*[1]

Subjects are shown a table on which lie three cords, two screw hooks, and a gimlet. A board is attached to a near-by wall. The problem is to hang the three cords, separately, from the board. In one variant of the display three holes are already bored. In another no holes are bored.

[1] See K. Duncker, " On Problem Solving," in *Psych. Monog.*, Vol. 58, 1945, p. 86, and W. S. Ray, " Complex Tasks for Use in Human Problem-solving Research," in *Psych. Bull.*, 52, No. 2, 1955. Contains descriptions of twenty-nine problems.

The solution depends on the subject's ability to regard the gimlet as a substitute for a screw hook instead of a boring tool.   It is more difficult when no holes are already bored.   The gimlet is used by the subject to bore the holes.   This establishes a learning 'set'—a strong predisposition to emphasize the boring function of the gimlet. That is how it will appear in this context, not at all like a support for the third cord.   When three holes are already bored it is an invitation to insert the screw hooks first.   This operation establishes a 'set' for supporting cords.   The third hole suggests that the gimlet should be inserted as a third support.

(iii) A Box Problem

The subjects in this experiment were shown a table on which was displayed an assortment of objects : drawing-pins, buttons, bits of wire, paper-clips, strips of paper, string, pencils, tin foil, old pieces of apparatus, ash-trays, together with three small candles and three pasteboard boxes the size of matchboxes.

The problem was to support the three candles side by side on a door at eye-level ' for visual experiments.'

The problem could be solved by ' seeing ' the boxes as platforms instead of containers.   A drawing-pin could be pushed through the side of a box thus fastening it to the door.   A candle could then be set upright on the bottom of the box (see diagram).

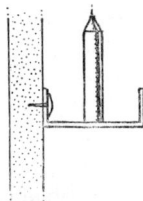

This experiment illustrates an aspect of transfer. Three variants of the display were used : (a) the boxes were shown empty, scattered among the other objects ; (b) the boxes were filled with drawing-pins, buttons, and other odds and ends ; (c) the boxes contained drawing-pins, matches, and candles.   When the boxes were filled with the drawing-pins, matches, and candles, twelve out of one group of twenty-nine subjects solved the problem.   When the boxes were shown empty, twenty-four out of twenty-eight subjects in that group were successful.

Obviously, more than the presence of common components is needed for transfer in problem-solving.   The mental ' set ' with which the problem is approached has more influence than common components, and the ' set ' can be established by the way in which the problem is presented.   In this example, the filled boxes suggested containers ;   the empty boxes were more easily regarded as possible platforms.   Moreover, the problem was more easy to solve if boxes, pins, and candles were shown in close proximity.

(iv) *A Pendulum Problem*

A pendulum consisting of a cord and a weight was to be hung from a nail which must first be driven into a board.   The solution depended on using the weight as a hammer and ignoring for the time being its use as the bob of a pendulum.   In this case all the items in the problem as presented appeared in the solutions, yet not everybody solved the problem.

It may be thought that these ' problems ' are highly artificial, reeking, as it were, of the psychological laboratory.   In fact, they often arise in actual life.   On one occasion I needed a screwdriver. That started a search among the tools in view.   No result.   Next a visit to another room.   Again no result.   Back again to the bench. Another search.   The hidden screwdriver was now revealed ; much time wasted.   Right in front of me almost beneath my hand was a pair of ' footprint ' pliers.   One arm of this tool was tapered off to be used as a screwdriver on occasion.   While I was obsessed with the normal shape of a screwdriver I completely failed to see the available substitute.

In all these examples the transfer necessary to solve the problem cannot occur until the situation has been restructured.   Original Gestalts must be reorganized in opposition to their tendency to persist.   *The reorganization may be hindered or helped by arranging the situation in different ways, by additional information, by suggestions from outside sources.*   Duncker reports that for many of his subjects who failed it was as if the scales had fallen from their eyes when the solutions were pointed out.[1]

The ' moral ' of all this for teaching seems to be that whether or not a problem will be solved depends very much on the way in which it is presented.   A problem can be made much more difficult by the presentation.   Thus failure is in some cases due more to the teacher than to the ' stupidity ' of the unsuccessful pupil.

10. TEACHING FOR TRANSFER

(i) *Distinction between Training and Practice*

In what follows examples of teaching-methods likely to encourage

[1] Book cited, p. 88.   Examples of transfer by restructuring a situation are described in S. R. Laycock, *Adaptability to New Situations* (Warwick and York, 1929).

transfer will be described. The transfer must be achieved ultimately by the learner with the help of the mechanisms of transfer—discrimination, generalization, naming, learning ' sets,' vigilance, *together with guidance* from teachers or teaching-devices—*e.g.*, radio, television, text-books, programmed learning.

We can now distinguish between mere practice and enlightened training. In practice, as such, habits and learning ' sets ' are established more or less mechanically by frequent repetition. In training, properly so called, practice is needed, but it must be undertaken with a clear view of its purpose, and with guidance in efficient methods of learning. Learners must *learn how to learn efficiently* if maximum transfer and adaptability are desired. They must analyse both training and test situations, realize how they are related, deliberately seek opportunities for transfer, and maintain a vigilant look-out for possible inappropriate learning ' sets ' and bias.

(ii) *Stimulus Generalization and Discrimination aided by Naming*

In an experiment reported from Leningrad children aged from twelve to thirty months were shown small boxes—red containing a sweet, green empty. The problem—select the box with a sweet. At first no name was mentioned. Choice was found to be difficult. A correct association between a red colour and a sweet was established only after many trials ; it was easily forgotten and had to be established afresh at the next practice.

The experimenter then named the colours of the two boxes. The correct association was acquired much more quickly and persisted much longer. Even the younger children associated the word ' red ' with the colour and the sweet. The correct response spread from the red boxes to any red object or material—cup, cardboard, cloth, paper.

In this case the word represents a stimulus (colour) generalization. The correct response was made to any object of a similar colour called by the same name.

In more complicated problems such as distinguishing between triangles and oblongs, transfer to triangles and oblongs different in shape and size was helped by learning a name *while feeling around the edges and looking at the objects. Names were associated with movements.* These generalized in association with the names. Extraneous details like colour, specific shape, and size were ignored.[1]

---

[1] A. R. Luria, *The Rôle of Speech in the Regulation of Normal and Abnormal Behaviour* (Pergamon Press, 1961), p. 60.

(iii) *An Experiment in Touch Discrimination*

Pieces of several different kinds of cloth—velvet, cotton, wool, silk, etc.—were put into a bag. Children (aged about ten years) were invited to put a hand into the bag, choose a remnant, feel it, and say what they supposed it was before bringing it out. This aroused high and sustained interest. All were eager to have a go. An exercise in discrimination and feedback.

(iv) *Experiments in Guidance. Suggesting an Answer without giving it away*

Sir F. C. Bartlett in his book on " Thinking " describes some problems about filling a gap. The first was :

" Look at the terminal words in the following arrangement, then fill up the gap in any way you think may be indicated."

A, BY, ... HORRIBLE.

This proved difficult. Only two successes were recorded out of more than two hundred attempts. Another item of information was then added :

A, BY, COW, ... HORRIBLE.

This produced more successful efforts in one respect, if not both. It appeared that (*a*) each word must begin with the next letter of the alphabet and (*b*) each word must have one more letter than its predecessor. Condition (*a*) was more readily discriminated.

Another item of information was added :

A, BY, COW, DOOR .... HORRIBLE.

By this time most subjects could solve the problem.

This is a case of learning a rule and generalizing. When the rule has been guessed the gap can be filled with any of hundreds of different words provided the rule is obeyed—alphabetical order of initial letters ; one additional letter in each successive word.

The next problem required extrapolation according to a similar but not identical rule. The words :

afterward, kit, entry, effort, mantle, i, overthrow,
gap, motor, cost, outcome, get, cowslip,
enter, quicksilver, o, potluck, quietness

were given together with three items of information :

GAP

I

KIT

The problem was to complete the series with items chosen from the given word list.

Subjects who had guessed the correct rule in the first problem were helped to transfer their ' set ' to this example—each word in either direction from the letter ' I ' must have two letters more and must begin with alternate initial letters—*e.g.*:

.... entry gap

i

kit motor ....

For our purpose, the interest in these examples lies in the fact that learners may be helped to a solution and *kept actively seeking the solution by the successive addition of more information* (giving guidance about direction and order) without telling them the answer. They show also how a generalized rule can itself be generalized.[1]

(v) *Transfer in Technical Situations*

(a) *A Study by J. W. Cox of Transfer in the Acquisition of a Manual Skill*

In addition to direct confirmation of the transfer of training-effects, this work indicates very clearly the type of teaching-method which produced the transfer. It is, therefore, of particular interest to teachers of handicraft, physical training, and games.[2]

The subjects of the investigation were groups of adults and of schoolchildren, both male and female. They were practised and tested in various elementary dexterities involved in the assembly of an ordinary electric-light-bulb-holder. The gist of those parts of the investigation dealing directly with the problem of transfer of training is given below.

The author begins by making a very significant distinction between ' practice ' and ' training.'

By ' practice ' is meant the mere repetition of routine exercises at maximum speed for a given time, *with no instruction of any sort concerning how the exercises might best be performed.* The ' practised ' workers were left to their own devices.

---

[1] See also Laycock, *Adaptability to New Situations*, for experiments in promoting transfer by guidance through the use of additional information, and examples.

[2] *Manual Skill, Its Organization and Development.* See particularly pp. 30–37, 141–146, 162–177.

By ' training ' is meant exercise together with an organized course of instruction about good methods of procedure.[1]

Hence the problem of transfer can now be reduced to two separate subsidiary problems :

(a) Do the effects of *practice* transfer from the mechanical operations practised to other mechanical operations in which there has been no practice ?

(b) Do the effects of *training* transfer from mechanical operations in which there has been training to other mechanical operations in which there has been no training ?

PROBLEM (a)—TRANSFER OF PRACTICE-EFFECTS

The assembling work was divided into six specific mechanical operations which we will label *a, b, c, d, e, f*. The workers were tested for their initial ability in all the six operations. They were divided into five groups. Four of these groups then each practised *one only* of the operations *a, b, c,* or *d* intensively during eleven daily working periods. The fifth (control) group had no special practice. At the end of the practice periods all five groups were given a second test in all six operations.

The tests showed that, as in Sleight's experiments, while the practised groups showed some improvement in the unpractised operations *e* and *f*, this was *nowhere significantly greater than the improvement in operations ' e ' and ' f ' made by the unpractised control* group. Cox states that nowhere was there any significant evidence of practice at one operation bringing about improvement in another operation.[2]

PROBLEM (b)—TRANSFER OF TRAINING-EFFECTS

For this problem a new set of workers similar to those used in the practice experiments was collected. They were tested as before for initial ability in the six operations *a* to *f*. Instead of the pure practice periods, eleven daily training periods of the same length were substituted. These had the form of eleven lessons, the aim of which was to *impart knowledge of certain general principles of skilful handling of material.* These general principles were then applied by the trainees in a series of exercises involving *one* assembly operation only. The training exercises were of five types :

(i) *General methods.* These dealt with such matters as the arrangement of parts on the work-bench ; the order of assembly ; manner of holding the parts, etc.

---

[1] *Cf.* Woodrow's experiments (p. 388).
[2] Work cited, p. 146.

(ii) *Eye-observation exercises.* The trainees were instructed to *look* carefully and *pay specific attention to* aspects of shape, and relations between them.

(iii) *Finger-observation exercises.* In these the trainees were instructed to *pay specific attention to feelings in the fingers* as the movements were carried out, and to note carefully certain aspects of these experiences. *Just exactly what to notice was made clear in each exercise.*

(iv) *Exercises in control of attention and effort.* The trainees were told how these could most economically be employed throughout the operation.

(v) *Application exercises.* In these the trainees practised the application of the exercises in method of procedure (i to iv above) to the one assembling operation chosen for practice, under normal working conditions.

Each lesson opened with a brief verbal revision of the chief points already dealt with. Attention was then directed to the point of the next exercise. This was explained and demonstrated by the instructor. Next, exercises were carried out by the trainees, special attention being directed to the point in question. Each exercise was repeated several times, the whole process being treated as an observation exercise rather than as one of mere speed. After all the exercises had been completed (in eight to nine days) the remaining lessons were devoted to revising the chief points, and dealing with bad methods observed in various individual trainees during the course of the learning.

Thus the training consisted of talks and exercises based upon *one* operation only, together with eighty-five repetitions of this operation. The former subjects in the practice experiments, who constituted the control group, had had 440 repetitions of the operation.

Finally, the trainees had a second test of ability in all the six operations *a* to *f*. The individual workers in the trained group were paired off with individuals in the practised groups of the first experiment, who had the same initial ability.

Cox's experiments showed quite clearly :

(i) That repetition without enlightened instruction in methods of work produced no significant transfer effects.

(ii) That when enlightened training was substituted for routine practice, then,

(*a*) The trained workers were much superior in all the six operations to corresponding members in the practised group having the same initial ability.

(*b*) The trained workers showed a more rapid rate of improvement.

(c) The rate of improvement of the trainees was much greater than was expected from the general run of improvement shown in the previous experiment.

(d) The trained group excelled from the first day of practice and maintained a higher rate of progress afterwards.

This investigator sums up the results of these two experiments as follows :

Skill developed by the mere repetition of one manual operation confers little advantage in the performance of other operations that may subsequently be undertaken. Where, on the other hand, repetition is replaced by suitable instruction, the skill thus developed at no additional cost in time tends to transfer to other operations over a fairly wide range of manual activity. . . . These results appear of great practical significance wherever work requiring manual skill is involved, especially when it is remembered that the limits of proficiency to be attained by training may far exceed those attainable by uninstructed repetition. The results indicate the wastage that must be produced by the customary practice of allowing beginners . . . to drop into the work as best they can. They suggest that a very real advantage would follow from the replacement of this current crude procedure by a short course of systematic training in the general principles underlying manual control, illustrated by specific examples from manual operations. A like procedure may frequently be adopted with advantage in other forms of manual activity, such as the work of our scholastic manual-training centres, and ' coaching ' for games, where the so-called instruction offered resembles ' practice ' rather than ' training.'

(b) Transfer of Technical Skills

An experiment in teaching for transfer of technical information and skills in the U.S.S.R. is reported by E. A. Milerian.[1]

The author begins by stressing the need for transfer and adaptability in modern engineering practice. New conditions need workers who must not only master a wide range of knowledge in mechanics, electronics, and industrial technology, but be able to apply the knowledge to a variety of industrial problems. It is desirable that schools should teach for this purpose.

The object of the experiment was to study transfer of knowledge and skill in working a lathe to the operation of drilling and milling machines.

[1] " Transfer of Technical Skills in Older School Children," in : B. and J. Simon (eds.), *Educational Psychology in the U.S.S.R.* (Routledge and Kegan Paul, 1963).

27 pupils aged 15–16 years were divided into two matched groups, 10 controls, 17 experimental. None had had any experience of working metallurgical machines. In the first task pupils mastered skills required in working a lathe ; later, when some degree of efficiency had been achieved, they were set to carry out operations in milling and drilling.

The *control group* practised on a lathe " in the way usual in Russian schools." They were told about the structure of the machine, introduced to its management, then used it to perform seven tasks increasing in complexity. These being accomplished, they were asked to prepare, independently, components for task eight, which included milling planes and drilling holes in a horizontal direction using milling and drilling machines.

The *experimental group* first recapitulated their knowledge of physics, metal-work, and carpentry. This served to recall general technical principles of using such tools as plane, chisel, drill, saw, file, hacksaw. The experimenter set problems requiring the pupils to investigate the general properties of the tools and describe principles of use. Later they were required to apply these principles in designing a machine for making cylindrical components.

This experimental group were not yet familiar with the lathe. They began without reference to the final task proposed. They made models, sketches, and working drawings which were discussed and assessed by the tutor. Finally they drew the scheme of the lathe in which the main features of the machine were represented, then came in turn to a lathe and identified the parts represented in their working drawings. The structure of the lathe was explained, and they were allowed to work with it.

After this training period the experimental group worked at the same tasks as the control group.

The visual aids and practical preparation helped the experimental group to analyse and compare properties of tools, and to try out methods of working in practice.

Both groups tried at first to apply their practice on the lathe, without modification, to the drilling and milling machines, but when in difficulties the experimental group began to recall and apply their previous studies. They selected features of both practised tasks and tests to find what aspects of the training could be applied to the new work. *The skills which transferred most successfully were based on understanding general technical principles.* The control group were less successful in making the transfer. Seven out of ten controls transferred successfully from lathe to drilling machine ; sixteen out of seventeen of the experimental group did so. The transfer from lathe to milling machine was achieved by fifteen out of the seventeen experimental trainees ; by only two out of ten controls.

(vi) *Transfer in Memorizing.   Learning how to memorize*

In an investigation on " The Effect of Type of Training on Transference " Woodrow tried to find whether the *kind* of training given had any influence on transfer.[1] He begins his report by referring to the fact that Sleight had shown that practice in one kind of memorizing failed to produce any facilitation of other kinds of memorizing, and then asks,

> Does this mean that the same conclusion is valid *no matter what type of practice is used* ?   Does it hold for practice accompanied by explanation of methods, and illustrations of how these methods should be applied in the performance of tasks other than the one in which the individual is drilled ?[2]

The author adds, " May not the general problem . . . be stated s the problem of the difference with respect to the resulting transfer [of training] between unenlightened drill, and intelligent teaching." This statement of the problem brings the whole issue very closely into relation with the principles of teaching-method.

Woodrow's experiments were designed to investigate *the possibility of teaching some general methods* of memorizing. The object was to show that " training in memorizing can be given in two such widely different ways that in the one case the individual will benefit little, or not at all, and in the other case, enormously, when he turns to *new* kinds of memorizing."

One hundred and eighty-two university students were used for the experiment.   They were arranged into three groups—the Control group (106 students), the Practice group (34 students), and the Training group (42 students).

All the students were given initial tests for ability in (1) learning poetry by heart, (2) learning prose by heart, (3) remembering facts, (4) memorizing a Turkish-English vocabulary, (5) memorizing historical dates, and (6) immediate memory for consonants.   Note that the initial ability of the Training group was *less* than the initial ability of the Practice group in all the tests except memorizing prose.

---

[1] *Journal of Educational Psychology*, Vol. 18, 1927, p. 159.
[2] Place cited, p. 159.

The Control group had no special practice. They merely tried the initial and final tests in order to provide a measure of the effects upon the second test of doing the first test, apart from the effects of special practice.

The Practice group spent 177 minutes, divided into periods of about 22 minutes, twice a week for four weeks, in routine memory practice with poetry, and nonsense syllables. They had 90 minutes' practice in poetry, and 87 minutes' practice in nonsense syllables. Their instructions were to *learn by heart as well as they could. Nothing more was said to them.*

In the case of the Training group, the same period of 177 minutes was divided up as follows : for a total of 76 minutes they listened to an exposition on rules for effective memorizing and *illustrations of how the rules could be applied in practice* ; for 76 minutes they practised memorizing poetry ; and for 25 minutes they practised memorizing nonsense syllables.

Thus, with the Training group, an attempt was made to give them a thorough grasp of some economical methods of memorizing, and all their practice was done *with the explicit purpose of applying the rules which had been discussed and illustrated.* They had 76 minutes *less* practice than the Practice group. Their practice material was the same as that used by the Practice group—namely, poetry and nonsense syllables. The difference between the Training group and the Practice group was in the instruction received by the Training group *in general methods of efficient memorizing.* So far as initial ability in the tests and the time allowed for actual memorizing were concerned, the advantage was decidedly in favour of the Practice group.

After all the students had completed the second series of six memory tests the following results emerged :

(*a*) The Practice group improved sometimes more, sometimes less than the Control group. In two cases the practice periods had interfered with the results in the second test.

(*b*) The differences between the Practice and the Control group were insignificant in all but one of the six tests.

(*c*) In spite of the disadvantages already referred to, the Training group decidedly *excelled* the Practice group in *every one of the six tests.* The average net improvement (*i.e.,* after the effects of the first test had been allowed for) of the Practice group was 4·5 per cent. The average net improvement of the Training group was 36·1 per cent. The actual degree of improvement varied from 17·5 per cent. to 51·8 per cent.

The investigation shows in a convincing way that transfer may happen, not by mere practice in memorizing, but by practice *informed by general methods of sound procedure* which have been explicitly abstracted and deliberately used by the learners. In the case of the Training group the improvement in ability to memorize, due to training in poetry and nonsense syllables *only*, was positive and *general*.

(vii) *Effect on Transfer of acquiring a Specialized Vocabulary*

A description of this experiment by Fox can be found on pp. 244–245 above.

(viii) *Teaching a General Principle by the Use of Examples*

Dr G. Katona conducted a series of experiments in transfer in order to show the difference between learning by memorizing and learning by understanding.[1] The topic is treated according to the principles of Gestalt psychology. The author believed that learning by understanding involves the same process as does problem-solving—namely, the discovery of a principle or rule, and that both problem-solving and meaningful learning require changing (re-organizing) the material—in other words, restructuring a Gestalt.

The author asks, " Of what significance are the elements ; must the elements in practice task and test be identical, or must the principle be identical ; must the principle be verbalized and under-stood to guarantee transfer ? "   " What methods of teaching and learning result in the greatest measure of applicability ? "   " By what methods can the transfer effect be increased ? "   " How can methods of teaching and learning be improved ? "[2]

Dr Katona proposes two criteria for the best learning method : (*a*) retention after eight days or more ; (*b*) inducing the largest number of subjects to solve the greatest number of tasks which have not yet been practised.

The problems used were a series of matchstick patterns to be rearranged according to certain conditions.

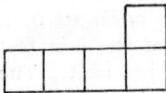

FIG. 27

" Here are five equal squares. Make four squares out of the five by changing the position of three sides. The new figure must be made up of equal squares of the same size ; no matchsticks must be taken from the table ; each new square must have only four sides—no duplication " (Fig. 27). The following teaching and learning methods were used :

---

[1] *Organising and Memorising* (Columbia University Press, 1940).
[2] Book cited, p. 55.

Learning Method I. *Result demonstrated.*

Task 1. Practice.

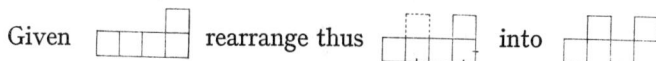

Given ⬚⬚⬚⬚ rearrange thus ⬚⬚⬚ into ⬚⬚⬚

Task 9. Test.

Given ⬚⬚⬚ rearrange thus ⬚⬚⬚ into ⬚⬚⬚

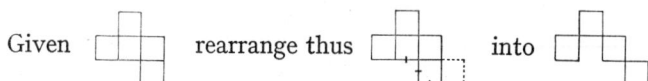

In Method I the training was :

(a) *repeated demonstrations* ; three sticks cross-hatched in the diagram were removed by the tutor several times and a new square formed ; the subjects looking on meanwhile (see Task 1).

(b) *solution demonstrated and the procedure memorized in words—* " Take lower match from second square from left and two matches from fourth square on left and make new square on second square from left."

No subjects who had these types of training on Task 1 could solve the similar test Task 9. Forgetting happened quickly. Of four subjects retested one week later, only one solved Task 1 again in two minutes. A few were successful by chance without understanding. They could not explain how they arrived at the result.

Learning Method II. *Principle taught.*

Here Task 1 was displayed and the solution demonstrated. The display remained in view while a principle was stated : " Here are five squares composed of sixteen equal lines. These five squares must be changed into four similar squares. Since we have sixteen lines and want four squares, each square must have its four independent side-lines which should not be side-lines of any other square at the same time. Therefore all lines with a *double function*—that is, limiting two squares at the same time—must be changed into lines with a single function—that is, limiting one square only."

This method of demonstration and verbal statement of principles helped a few subjects. The majority, however, *could not apply the principle to either Task 1 or Task 9.* In their cases Method II was less efficient than Method I. Again, the presence of common components failed to guarantee transfer. *The statement of the principle was not understood* and could not therefore be applied. The principle does not indicate which sides should be removed. Again we see the difficulty when a Gestalt must be restructured against the resistance of the present ' set.' The trainees could not regard the original pattern in any alternative way.

Supplementary practice with a partial process

At this stage a partial process was introduced. *The visual principle required in restructuring was demonstrated by easy examples.*

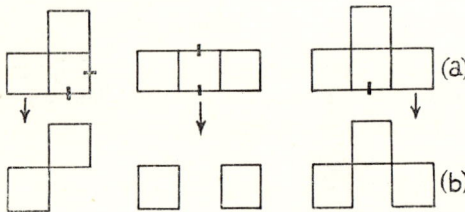

FIG. 28

By moving the cross-hatched sides in line (*a*) (Fig. 28) the arrangements in line (*b*) are obtained.

These examples illustrate certain rules for rearrangement: corner squares and centre squares can be destroyed by removing two sides; inner centre squares by removing one side. Instead of a verbal statement, the original principle is now exemplified in terms of squares and holes. In the finished task the squares are either attached by their corners or separated completely.

Now the demonstration and practice in the subsidiary structural rearrangement can be applied to the original tasks. As the author says, " Instead of teaching the principle abstractly in words, the subsidiary practice with the new method *helps the subject to develop the principle from a series of concrete examples.* The order in which the examples are presented can be chosen in such a way that the subjects are led from easier to more difficult tasks." This is a process of opening the eyes of the trainees to structurally important qualities. To supplement still further the practice, outline drawings were made by the trainees and practical manipulation of paper squares was introduced.

This is learning by discovery, or, in the cases of subjects arriving at the solution with the aid of hints from the tutor, learning by discovery through help.

The following conclusions seem to be justified :

(*a*) Teaching by memorizing is not an efficient method.

(b) Teaching by stating a principle verbally may help in some cases, but is limited in value.   It does not necessarily lead to transfer.

(c) Teaching by examples and help is much superior.

(d) Ability to solve a problem can be acquired without stating the principle in words.

(e) Success is due to learning *by means of* examples, not by learning the examples.   They help in discriminating and abstracting relationships and qualities in the practice and test situations.

(f) Understanding the principle leads to longer retention of the solutions in memory.

Readers may be interested in making a transfer to the following problem : With sixteen matches set up a five-square formation (see diagram).   By moving only two of the matches form four squares, each touching another, instead of five.

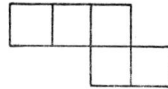

(ix) *Teaching Geometry with Help.   Discrimination, Availability of Information, Transfer*

One of Duncker's problems was geometrical.[1]   In a triangle ABC, AF, BE, CD are drawn from A, B, and C as perpendiculars to the opposite sides.   The points D, E, F, are joined.   Prove that the angles, DEF, EFD, and FDE are bisected (Fig. 29).

This proof could be demonstrated formally as follows :

Since $\angle$CFO and $\angle$CEO are right angles, points CEOF are concentric.   Therefore $\angle$COF$=\angle$CEF (angles at the circumference on the same chord).   Similarly, $\angle$AOD$=\angle$AED.   Because $\angle$COF $= \angle$AOD (angles formed by intersection of two straight lines), $\therefore$ $\angle$CEF$=\angle$AED $\therefore$ $\angle$FEO$=\angle$OED.   The proof could then be memorized.

A better way for understanding and transfer would be the following :

1. Read the problem.
2. Look at the figure.   What information are we given ?
3. Write the items down.
4. What have we to prove ?
5. How shall we begin ?   Any suggestions ?

[1] Book cited, p. 36.

6. If no response say : Look at the angles at E. What must be proved ? $\angle$FEO = $\angle$OED.

7. How could this be done? By proving $\angle$CEF=$\angle$AED. Why ?

8. Any suggestions ? If not : Look at the points C, F, O and C, E, O. Notice anything? (The discrimination can be reinforced either by outlining the area in a different colour or by drawing it separately.)

9. What now ? What are the angles CFO and CEO ? Refer to the conditions given. What can you remember about angles in a semicircle ? So, what can we draw around C, E, O and C, F, O ? Therefore, what can we say about the points CEOF ?

10. Can you tell me anything about the angles CEF and COF ? Why ?

11. Now look at the figure AEOD. What can you tell me about that ? Why ?

12. So, what do we know now ? Write it down. $\angle$CEF= $\angle$COF. $\angle$AOD=$\angle$AED.

13. Can anybody suggest the next step ? $\angle$COF=$\angle$AOD. Why ?

14. Now finish off the‾proof.

Similarly, the angles at F and D can be treated.

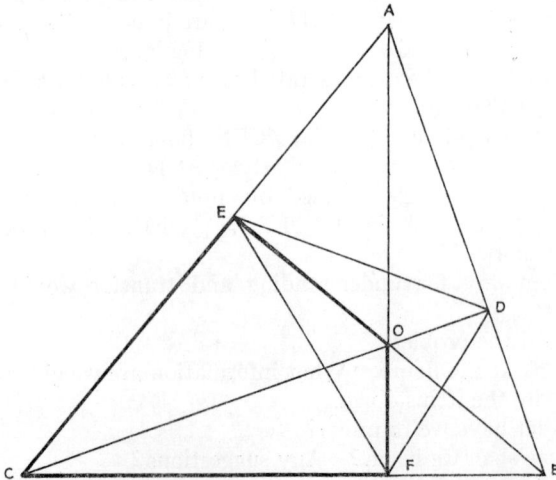

FIG. 29

This method of reinforcing discriminations, and help in the form of suggestions and instructions where to look, and what to look for, may not be necessary for very bright pupils. It is certainly useful for the not-so-bright. It represents a co-operative effort of tutor and taught. It keeps the pupils actively searching. It emphasizes the conditions of the problem. It prevents frustration. Above all, it teaches the pupils how to attack a proof. They are learning how to solve a geometrical problem. It offers them the opportunity to complete a step in the proof if and when it occurs to them.

In addition, it emphasizes the rule that in geometry it is more profitable to *memorize theorems than proofs*. It also emphasizes the fact that if the theorems are to be of any use for transfer they must be readily recallable at need. If they cannot be recalled they cannot be applied. *Hence the need to over-learn the items of information—principles, rules, associations, relationships which facilitate transfer*.

Readers might now work out these rules for facilitating transfer in the case of subject-matter in which they are personally interested.

(x) *Transfer through Consciousness of Method*

G. P. Meredith set out to find what influence *consciousness of method* exerted on transfer of ability to define meanings of words.[1]

Sixty boys, aged thirteen to fourteen years, in a Leeds elementary school were first given a test of general intelligence. In addition their intelligence was estimated by their teachers. On the results of these two estimates they were divided into three comparable groups of twenty each, *A*, *B*, and *C*, of equal average intelligence.

All the boys were then given the first test to determine their ability to define ordinary words. The test consisted of twenty nouns in common use. The instructions were : " Define the following words ; that is, say what they mean." The scores were reckoned in *errors* of definition, so that a lower score indicated improvement in ability.

Group *A* formed the control group. They received no special training. Groups *B* and *C* were then given three lessons in experimental magnetism. Each lesson included five experiments which were performed by the boys themselves. In the case of both groups *B* and *C* a few minutes at the beginning and ten to fifteen minutes at the end of each lesson were devoted to discussion of the experiments

---

[1] " Consciousness of Method as a Means of Transfer of Training," in *Forum of Education*, Vol. V, No. I, February 1927, p. 37.

and the inferences to be drawn from them.   In the case of group C, however, *the question of definition itself was explicitly discussed in each lesson.*   The question arose naturally out of the first lesson, in which the properties of magnets were discovered, since it was necessary to state in precise terms what things were magnets and what were not.

Before they began their experiments the boys in both groups B and C were told to write down their definition of a magnet.   These definitions were collected and discussed in the next lesson.

At the end of the first lesson some pupils were asked how they had defined a magnet.   Their definitions were discussed to find how far they agreed with the facts discovered in the experiments.   In group B the discussion stopped at that point.   In group C it was continued to a further stage when the *form of a definition was analysed and its essential features explicitly noted.*

The experiments in the second lesson dealt with the strength of magnetic influence, thus introducing the notion of a unit of magnetic force.   With group C the subsequent discussion about the definition of a unit carried the analysis of the characteristics of a correct definition a stage further.   The third set of experiments introduced the problem of defining a semi-abstract term such as ‘ magnetic induction,’ leading in the case of group C to a further and final analysis of the form and characteristics of a good definition, the various items being written down on the blackboard.

Hence both groups B and C performed the same experiments, and both had practice in defining various types of scientific terms. But in group B the practice was incidental and *no explicit reference to definition as such* was made.   On the other hand, group C were trained in the process of correct definition by means of practice in defining, *a critical analysis of actual definitions*, and, finally, formulation of the essential characteristics of a good definition.

At the end of the series of three lessons all the groups A, B, and C were given a second test in which they were required to define another twenty words in common use (not scientific terms) comparable in difficulty with the first test series.   It was found that group B had made an average *increase* of 3 errors as compared with the control group A.   This difference was only twice as great as its probable error, indicating that there was *no more than a chance difference* between the two groups.   The incidental practice had produced no transfer effect on the members of group B.   Group C made an average improvement (decrease in number of errors) of 12 as compared with group A.   This difference is eight times its

probable error, indicating that a difference as great as this is likely
to be due to pure chance only once in many thousands of trials.
Hence the *explicit* training in definition leading to a *consciousness of
the correct method of defining* produced a marked degree of transfer
of ability from the science lessons to the definition of common words.

II. TRANSFER OF MEANING. THE INTERPLAY OF LANGUAGE

The function of language in intellectual development was
discussed in Chapter VII above. Processes of discrimination
(analysis) which provide the learner with progressively clearer, more
detailed percepts ; and classification, conception, and generalization
(synthesis), which organize the accumulating details into orders and
groups which make logical thinking and problem-solving possible,
are helped to a very high degree by the development of a spoken and
written language. Details are discriminated by active exploration
in play or work, and by social communication—*i.e.*, instructions,
question and answer, desire to give information, desire to receive it.
As the details emerge from the background of experience they should
be named. As the associations of discriminated details with spoken
and written words are reinforced and learned thoroughly *the words
can act as representatives of practical situations.* They become
effective stimuli which free the learner from dependence on actual
experiences. Thinking is thus made more flexible, more easily
manageable. At the same time, names and definitions act as
vehicles of generalizations. They represent abstracted concepts.
By learning a language *along with the associated first-hand experience*
the mental manipulation of concepts (generalizations) is helped ;
problem-solving, planning, and transfer are facilitated.

It is possible to solve some problems, to plan, and to transfer in
the absence of a developed language. Nevertheless thinking
processes are apt to remain at a comparatively primitive level if the
language equipment of the learner is inadequate. All the now
numerous investigations into the intellectual development of
deprived children agree in finding the greatest retardation to be in
language abilities. Language, in this context, is meant to include
charts, graphs, and symbols such as are used in mathematics, the
physical sciences, symbolic logic, history, geography, and economics,
for example.

We now wish to discuss in some detail a type of transfer to which
new studies in psycho-linguistics are directing attention—namely,
transfer of thoughts and meanings.

What is to be understood as the meaning of ' meaning ' depends, as usual, on the particular psychological model (theory) to which the theorist has been conditioned.   For our purpose here, ' meaning ' will be the objects, relations, concepts, situations to which words and sentences refer, together with the intention of the speaker or writer. Thus ' rose ' may mean (that is, refer to) a class of flowers, the perforated head of a watering-can, the past tense of the verb ' to rise,' as well as dozens of variations and analogies.   Which of these many ' meanings ' is intended in any particular case is determined by the context in which the word is used.

Distinction between thought and language

This is important for clarity.   Language is the system of words and symbols in which thoughts must be incorporated in the effort to communicate with other people.   ' Thought ' is the meaning, the intention, the purpose, which one *strives* to express in words and symbols in the process of communication.

The distinction is easier to understand by reference to tests which involve matching ' proverbs.'   The same thought or meaning can be expressed in quite different sets of words.   " You must have got out on the wrong side of the bed this morning " is equivalent to saying that the person concerned appears to be irritable, in a bad temper.

Similarly in the case of fables :

" A cock scratching in a farmyard turned up a jewel.   He said, ' You may be a very fine thing no doubt to those who like to wear jewellery, but I prefer a barley corn.' "   What single word best describes this cock ?   He was .... what ?[1]

These examples indicate the distinction referred to.   In the fable test one *strives* to find the required word.   One hesitates.   In some cases possible descriptive words emerge only after active search. Even then there is a process of testing, comparing, rejecting, until finally we arrive at a description which satisfies us and fits the context set up by the words of the fable.   There is no doubt about the fact of striving.   The fable sets a framework, as it were, which has to be filled.   It sketches in outline certain ' personality ' qualities of which one is aware as a feeling, a tension not yet verbalized.   From somewhere, somehow, we have to find a word whose

[1] A. F. Watts, *The Language and Mental Development of Children* (Harrap, 1944).   See particularly Chapter I and pages 325 and 337.

meaning fits this context. As possible words emerge into explicit awareness they are accompanied by sets of qualities associated with themselves. The experience of striving for the required word is that of fitting the emerging suggestions over the outline suggested by the fable, a process which ends when the tension is allayed ; we feel relief, the striving then ceases, and satisfaction supervenes. In some cases we are not satisfied. Nothing seems to fit. We give up the struggle, being left with the frustration of defeat.

A similar process—that of striving to put meanings into appropriate words—can be observed in a speaker who is trying to explain a difficult, abstract concept to a lay audience. His speech consists of a series of phrases and sentences *interrupted by hesitations*. During the hesitation period he is planning his next statements. He is seeking the phrases which will best convey his intention *to his audience*.[1] In order to ' get his meaning across ' he must choose from his own resources *those examples, those phrases, which will be best understood by the audience*. He must use examples out of their own experience. Writing for a general population of readers is a struggle with words ; a struggle to change the writer's learning ' sets ' and speech habits into those which the readers are most likely to bring to the interpretation of the words.

Here is another type of transfer. The past experiences, habits, learning ' sets,' attitudes, and bias of the speaker or writer determine the forms in which his meanings and intentions are available for communication. If the communication is to be successful his meanings and intentions must be modified to fit those of hearers and readers before they will transfer. A common ground of meaning must be sought.

This is a perennial problem in teaching. The apprentice teacher, fresh from university or training college, thinks in terms of advanced-level subject-matter, and speaks in the forms appropriate to the junior common room and his own cultural background. It is difficult not to think and speak in these habitual ways when facing a class of pupils. Before there can be any intellectual rapport between teacher and pupils the teacher's thoughts must be reorganized to fit the various backgrounds of experience, learning ' sets,' and attitudes which the pupils bring to the classroom.

---

[1] See Frieda Goldman-Eisler, " Discussion and Further Comments," in : E. H. Lenneberg (ed.), *New Directions in the Study of Language* (M.I.T. Press, Cambridge, Mass.).

It has been suggested that general principles and rules are best 'put over' by means of appropriate examples. The only appropriate examples in teaching are those culled from the pupils' own experiences. Therefore explanation in teaching demands knowing how the pupils think; what is their background of experience; their idiosyncrasies. Moreover, understanding cannot be taken for granted. Responses are necessary from the pupils to find whether or not, and how, they have understood correctly; whether the meanings and intentions of the teacher have in fact been transferred successfully. If not, another attempt must be made to seek more appropriate examples and forms of words.

The essential feature of transfer of training is the application of practice to new situations in which there has been no previous practice. Teachers may find themselves in this situation quite frequently. They may have to adapt thoughts and speech habits into forms of expression they have never used, never even thought of before. In addition the competent teacher is not satisfied until the transfer has been shown to have been successfully achieved.

12. SOME NEGLECTED ASPECTS OF TRANSFER. BIAS AND PREJUDICE

Interest in transfer as an educational problem arose originally out of claims that certain types of subject-matter were the most efficient media for encouraging transfer of the effects of training. In particular, it was assumed that mathematics and classics were the media *par excellence* for what was called a 'liberal' education. Inevitably, 'liberal' education has been identified with an abstract verbal and pure mathematical training to the exclusion of anything remotely concerned with vocation, technology, and craft skills.

In this preoccupation with academic subject-matter two aspects of transfer have been neglected—namely, bias and prejudice. This is most unfortunate since in dealing with bias and prejudice we most nearly approach the very essence of a 'liberal' education. As we understand it, a 'liberal' education is one which will 'liberalize'— that is, free the individual from the restricting effects of bias and prejudice; from intolerance of any attitudes and opinions other than his own; from preconceived, purely traditional or customary attitudes which preclude a rational objective appraisal of a situation, whether abstract or practical, and from dependence on purely mechanical habits and specific facts.

To do justice to the concept of a liberal education in all its generality would need a critical discussion of definitions which would take us beyond the bounds of our present topic into a treatise on the philosophy of education. It must suffice to say that to ' liberalize ' means here to develop in pupils and students freedom from constraints imposed by *mere* tradition, custom, established authority ; freedom to consider any proposed changes—religious, social, economic, political, intellectual, or moral—with an open mind, on their merits, from the point of view of public good rather than private self-interest. Not all change is necessarily good. Change for the sake of change may end in chaos, the very condition most likely to lead to the superimposition of an authoritarian regime in which individual freedom is regarded as the ultimate evil and any deviation, even by a hair's breadth, from the official party line, in thought as well as deed, equivalent to blasphemy or treason.

The ultimate freedom is psychological—an attitude of mind. Education can and does contribute to either totalitarian or co-operative attitudes, and transfer of training is a factor in both. In view of the aim envisaged here we need to consider to what extent the influence of tradition, custom, and established authority can stereotype attitudes in opposition to any kind of change, however desirable it may appear to be, and to what extent teaching and educational organization can mitigate tendencies to negative transfer and maximize positive transfer, to what, from our point of view, would appear to be desirable attitudes.

In this connexion we need to distinguish between bias and prejudice. By bias we mean the limitations which the normal family and neighbourhood must inevitably impose on the intellectual and emotional development of individuals. We are all biased to some extent, in some respect ; bias due to selective imitation, suggestion, local group pressure. Some bias we pick up incidentally. Other bias is due to temperamental dispositions, to selection of information, propaganda, unintentional error. Prejudice, on the other hand, is, psychologically, more deep-seated. It is a condition in which judgment is warped by feelings of inferiority, reinforced by feelings of inadequacy, fear, hatred, and aggression; the attitude of the 'chip on the shoulder,' of individual helplessness against a malignant fate; the vindictive, malicious, sadistic attitude which leads to lynch law and mob rule. Against bias education may be effective. Against prejudice it has less influence. It may intensify rather than reduce it. Changes in social organization as well as in education are necessary to combat prejudice.

Bias

It may be said with some justification that bias begins at birth. The baby is conditioned to respond to stimuli characteristic of his home environment. Conditioned responses are made to a variety of stimuli similar to those in the original situation. Stimuli followed by rewarded responses are more likely to attract the learner's attention subsequently ; non-rewarded stimuli are ignored.

The earliest random reflex movements of the baby are operationally conditioned. Emotional and motor responses approved by parents and relatives in some particular socio-economic environment will be reinforced (or punished).

Thus early in life the infant modifies his behaviour to conform to what is approved in his neighbourhood. Later, as speech develops, he learns a particular language with its implications for opinions—intellectual, social-class, moral, religious (or agnostic). Piaget, the Swiss psychologist, has shown by clinical methods how younger children accept and repeat the beliefs of parents and older children whom they respect and *with whom they identify themselves.* Later spoken opinions become interiorized—that is, become habitual in inner speech and habits of thought.[1] Meanings are specialized. The intellect and the emotions are structured in specialized patterns ; the individual is sensitized to signs in the environment which accord with the learning ' sets ' ; other signs, equally matters of fact, are ignored. If the description of a response on p. 291 above is correct *no response is ever purely intellectual.* Emotional and feeling components are evoked as part of the total perceptual configuration— liking, disliking; approval, disapproval; satisfaction, annoyance—all of which are assimilated within the schemas leading to the selection of some and rejection of other experiences available in the environment.

This specializing process is continued in schools : Public schools, grammar schools, technical schools, modern schools, Borstal schools, all impose their style, subject contents, habits of speech and thought, on their pupils and students. These persistent learning ' sets ' are carried over to every subsequent experience, too often to the detriment of open-mindedness. Any kind of change is liable to be opposed automatically, or if the individual has been conditioned to change, any sort of change, whatever its merits, will be welcomed ' on

---

[1] J. Piaget, *The Moral Judgment of the Child* (Routledge and Kegan Paul, 1960).

principle.' Bartlett and others have shown how powerfully the learning ' sets ' can act in selecting and structuring new experience. Anything new will be viewed as a variant of what is already known. If it cannot be assimilated in this way it is ignored.[1] Historical studies are interpreted by authorities, text-books, teachers, and students in accord with national prestige and Party advantage. To Protestants, Mary Tudor will appear as ' Bloody Mary '; to Catholics she will be an Angel of Light. News is selected according to the political bias of owners, editors, and readers. Judgment is inevitably warped in a particular direction. A great deal of education is the very opposite of ' liberal,' even though it may be classical in form and content.

The effect of group opinion on individual judgment has been revealed by experiment. Some people in a group have been asked to judge which of two lights is brighter ; which of two lines is longer ; which of two squares is bigger. If they say A is greater than B other members of the group who are surreptitiously co-operating with the experimenter will thereupon declare with sublime confidence that B is greater than A. As a result the waverers in the experimental group quite often reverse their first estimates. One side-issue of opinion polls is their influence on the ' floating ' voters in the direction of agreeing with the majority opinion.

There is a strong tendency to conform to majority opinion. The normal individual fears isolation. Even scientific research is channelled by prevailing socio-economic or military-security climates of opinion. Space research, nuclear physics, and Behaviourist psychology are contemporary examples.

Thus bias of some kind is almost, if not quite, inevitable. Transferred to new situations it is liable to cause false judgments and misguided activity. As such it is undesirable in a free society. What can a ' liberal ' education do about it ?

The following methods can be tried :

(a) Errors in fact, incorrect definitions, bland assertions of biased opinions, can be challenged and correction requested (cf. the example of Socratic dialogue on p. 319).

(b) Students should be required to consult more than one source of information ; more than one authority (e.g., different newspaper reports of the same incident can be compared and discussed) ; correspondence columns of newspapers are most illuminating about

[1] Cf. Nägeli's attitude to Mendel's work on heredity, and the reception in the United States of Goddard's plan for interplanetary exploration !

gross differences of opinion concerning the same topic. History students should be referred, where possible, to a variety of original sources.

(c) Older students can be introduced to some elementary principles of statistics, including the effect of selection on sampling ; the way results can be influenced by the experimental methods used ; the need for control groups.

(d) Discussions *in a permissive atmosphere*, particularly when students from different socio-economic groups are able to express their points of view. These discussions are best carried on under the direction of a fair-minded tutor *who is known to be fair-minded and tolerant, and is respected by the participants*. This is a necessary condition for success. If the leader is biased the discussion is more likely to intensify bias than remove it. The leader must check intolerance ; allow expression of minority opinion ; demand clarity of definition ; insist on *testable* factual information. This is a case of learning how to learn methods of objective discussion ; tolerance ; good manners ; hearing both sides ; critical consideration of statements ; getting at the truth rather than making debating points ; suspension of judgment when the available facts do not warrant a conclusion. It has been found useful in training to practise the rules of objective discussion on neutral topics before going on to controversial problems.

(e) Learning to live and learn with people from different socio-economic and intellectual backgrounds. As a result of his investigations into the development of moral attitudes in children, Piaget finds that in societies of a segmented type (that is, characterized by close-knit clans or exclusive cliques) " Each social unit is a closed system, all the individuals are identical except with regard to age ; tradition leans with its full weight on the spirit of each. . . . To the increasing size of social groups and the ensuing liberation of the individual we can compare the fact that our children as they grow older take part in an ever-increasing number of local traditions. The marble-player of 10 or 12 years will discover that there are other usages in existence beside those to which he is accustomed ; he will make friends with children from other schools who will free him from his narrow conformity."[1]

This desirability of variety in background and the discouragement of cliques is one argument in favour of comprehensive schools

---

[1] Book cited, pp. 96–98.

and unstreamed classes. Intelligently managed by enlightened teachers, they may be effective in encouraging a liberal education.

(f) Rôle-playing. As a variant of the usual discussion, a problem can be stated and students asked to discuss it from particular points of view—e.g., take part as Germans, French, Russians, Americans, Welsh, as well as English. In preparation they should be able to consult authorities in translation, if not in the original language.

It must be acknowledged, of course, that success in curing bias is not inevitable. In addition to procedures such as these, some *concern* in the students for objective truth and determination to achieve it is necessary. This may be encouraged by methods of teaching and guidance. It is more likely to be secured by example ; by identification with teachers who are known to be relatively free from bias, just, and fair-minded. In teaching for liberal attitudes teachers must above all practise what they preach. Lip-service is deadly.

This influence of bias on value-judgments, particularly with respect to people outside one's own neighbourhood or national group, is particularly important educationally and socially in a period of international tension, conflict, and upheaval such as is characteristic of the world in the second half of the twentieth century. It is not too much to suppose that on the alleviation of the more extreme and intolerant types of bias the very future of civilization depends. Here we have an example of the unfortunate effects of transfer— transfer of restrictive attitudes and value-judgments which begin early in life.

The problem has been discussed in an article by Henri Tajfel, who describes a series of surveys of the development of national attitudes in children.[1] The author suggests that :

> nationalism is an attitude, a way of feeling and a mode of thinking. . . . shared by millions of people in a large variety of cultural contexts. It seems unlikely that this compound of beliefs, value-judgments and emotions springs fully into existence in adolescence or adulthood without some background process of growth. This is certainly so in the case of awareness of racial differences ; there is good evidence that such awareness exists at a very early age. . . . A good deal of work has been done on the development in children of a capacity to manipulate abstract

---

[1] " Children and Foreigners," in *New Society*, June 30, 1966. Mr Tajfel was at the time of writing University Lecturer in Social Psychology in the **University** of Oxford.

M

concepts but very little of this work has been concerned with concepts which are rooted in strongly entrenched value judgments. National stereotypes, as has often been shown, are shot through with affective or emotional valuations ; they are early learned, widely used and subject to very slow change. . . . Attitudes toward large-scale human groups affect behaviour even when they are not rooted in personal knowledge of individuals representing these groups.

In the surveys discussed children of various ages were asked to rank their preferences for various named nationalities. There were variations in the degree of national bias, but some degree was almost universal. This seems to be an example of the spread of an attitude by conditioning and the transfer of conditioned fears and dislikes to a wide range of cases. As was suggested above, in the obsession of educationists and teachers with problems of transfer in academic subject-matter, this aspect of transfer has been persistently neglected to the detriment of a real ' liberal ' education. The educational problem is presented by the difficulty of extinguishing a conditioned emotional response, or of restructuring a stereotype. It is difficult, for example, for the biased nationalist to realize that he, himself, is an alien to people of another nationality ; that he is at least as odd in appearance to them as they are to him. Here is a challenge to teachers and schools who are concerned with history, geography, and current affairs in a context of liberal education. The author of the article in question says :

> The most important implication which emerges from [the studies discussed] can be summarised as follows : thinking about large human groups in a rational and adequate manner is a complex conceptual achievement made even more difficult by the early intervention of emotional biases of various kinds. Many of these biases are introduced in the school curricula themselves. We do not expect a child to be able to learn without help the intellectual skills involved in most subjects taught at school. Yet, somehow or other, we assume that he is able to learn to deal rationally with a complex human problem by some kind of autonomous magic which he is supposed to evolve without any systematic educational support. Both on the basis of common sense and of the sort of evidence we were able to gather, this is obviously an untenable assumption. The policy of educational laissez-faire in this field is just as untenable —particularly in primary schools.

One difficulty, of course, in this as in other aspects of transfer is to find the teachers. Just as in the case of transfer between academic subjects the teacher must be sufficiently aware himself of the transferable components and of the techniques for maximizing transfer to other activities, so, in the case of bias, the teacher must himself either be free from bias (a very difficult attitude to achieve) or be aware of and in control of his own biases.

Prejudice

It has been suggested that bias is mainly a case of specialized attitudes and ' sets ' due to living and learning in restricted social groups and neighbourhoods. Prejudice, on the other hand, is due to deep-seated emotional fixations against which the procedures suggested in the previous section may be quite useless.

Writing about experience in the United States, P. H. Mussen suggests that children's prejudices are not usually based on their own experiences, but appear to be reproductions of adult attitudes, the results of direct or indirect teaching.[1] Prejudices, he believes, arise either through identification with intolerant and bigoted parents or they are expressions of profound feelings of general hostility related to parent-child relationships and personality structure. Mothers of prejudiced, intolerant children tend to be highly critical, rigid, and authoritarian in their disciplinary practices. Prejudiced children are basically frightened and frustrated. Superficially, they conform to authority, but they harbour deep-seated feelings of hostility and destructiveness. They admire all that is strong, tough, and powerful, but fear weakness in themselves.

> A prejudiced child lacks self-confidence ; is distrustful, uneasy and insecure in social relationships ; feels discontented about his status ; is bitter and hostile in his view of the world. When he feels frustrated, as he often does, he blames others, turning his aggression outwards, displacing it on to minority groups.

Professor Mussen describes an experimental attempt to reduce prejudice. Some hundred white New York City boys between eight and fourteen years old were given tests of racial attitude before and after a four-week vacation during which they mixed with Negroes. The attitudes of the whites changed. Some became more tolerant ; *others more prejudiced.* The latter showed strong underlying hostile feelings and strong needs to defy authority. They perceived the world as cruel, unpleasant, and exploitative ; they felt victimized by

[1] *The Psychological Development of the Child* (Foundations of Modern Psychology Series ; Prentice Hall, Inc., New Jersey, 1964).

others.   Boys whose prejudice diminished had more liberal attitudes generally and happier, better-balanced personalities.

Prejudiced individuals may have had their feelings of anxiety, fear, inferiority, conditioned by a few unfortunate experiences.   It is well known that responses due to fear are particularly resistant to extinction.   Failure at school, humiliation by an unsympathetic teacher or by school-mates, is enough, at times, to induce prejudice which may then transfer to anything even remotely connected with schooling and learning.

As for treatment, intellectual operations may be useless.   Some attempt to remove the fears and feelings of inadequacy are essential before other remedial treatment is likely to succeed.   In extreme cases admittance to a special school is necessary.[1]

Learning not to learn.   Learning how not to learn

This interpretation of prejudice as being due to conditioned fears, aggressiveness, inferiority, helps to make school phobias and resistance to learning more understandable.   Prejudiced children, particularly adolescents, literally learn not to learn and how not to learn.   They learn how to avoid learning, which is the opposite of what we hope the schools should teach.

In many cases the process begins in the homes.   Parents may be over-protective.   A child is allowed to do nothing independently ; everything must be done according to parental behest—" Do as Mother says because it is good for you."   Other parents may be over-demanding, harsh, and ambitious ; endeavouring to compensate for their own inadequacies by making their offspring successful in some way which contributes to the parents' self-regard.   If the child is not academically bright, failure at school is inevitable.   This reinforces the fear, inferiority, and feeling of inadequacy.   These negative feelings then spread by generalization to anything and everything resembling schooling.

Too many schools are geared too exclusively to abstract-verbal studies.   John Partridge, in a description of a secondary modern school, writes :

> For many of the boys in ' Middle School ' what they do here is quite meaningless ;   few really enjoy school work or show great

---

[1] See, for example, O. L. Shaw, *Maladjusted Boys* (Allen and Unwin, 1965). This topic is discussed in detail, with particular reference to racial intolerance, in S. Lowy, *Co-operation, Tolerance and Prejudice* (Routledge and Kegan Paul, 1948).

interest ; the older they get the more clearly they see how little relationship there is between the kind of things they are supposed to do here and what they will have to do when they leave school. . . . Such boys are then expected to knuckle down to formal, classroom-based education in which most weight is placed on mathematics, English and other academic subjects.   There is no choice of any subject for any of the classes and much of the instruction is watered-down grammar-school in style and content.[1]

The author goes on to say that some real effort is needed to relate the schooling to the outside world—new outlook, new methods, more choice of subject-matter, more obvious connexion between school and work.   This lack of interest leads to repressive discipline ; this in turn is opposed by " the rebels, the misfits, the emotionally disturbed, the hopelessly backward boys.   They drive the teachers to distraction and cause a mildly repressive system to degenerate into a harsh, cruel and uncomprehending one."[2]   A vicious circle with a vengeance.   This adds point to suggestions made earlier in this book—that school-work should be relevant (p. 15) ; that we should attempt to organize success and minimize the liability to failure, and make the work purposeful (Chapters IV and V).

In an outspoken book, *The Family, Education and Society*, Professor F. Musgrove reports the results of an attempt to discover the personal needs of a sample of young people between fourteen and twenty years old in a northern industrial region.   The author tried to find what were the predominant needs and satisfactions of this sample and to what extent they were met by home, club, school, and work.

Two hundred and fifty questionnaires were analysed.   Of these, 200 came from pupils still at school, 130 at grammar schools, 70 at ' modern ' schools.   Sixty-seven grammar-school pupils were in the sixth form.

Of the school replies the author says, " The main demand is for self-expression and self-direction : ' at school you should have plenty of chance to express your views ' ; ' at school you should always be able to feel that masters are not simply disciplinarians ' ; ' one should be recognised and treated as an individual.' "   To a large extent the nine grammar schools contributing to the research population appeared to be failing to meet this demand.   " ' At school you always feel like a little boy ' ; ' at school you always feel

---

[1] John Partridge, *Middle School* (Gollancz, 1966), p. 115.
[2] Partridge, book cited, p. 119.

disgusted with life ' (son of a schoolmaster) ; ' at school you always feel looked down upon by masters.' ''   Other pupils reported themselves as feeling neglected ; sick ; tired ; bored ; disgusted ; generally miserable ; down-graded ; a prisoner ; unimportant and hounded ; like a chicken being stuffed ! Pressure of work, aloofness, and authoritarian attitudes of staff are mentioned as well as the impersonality of the organization.

Not all the responses indicated complaints. Out of 600 statements from schools, 56 per cent. were positive expressions of satisfaction ; 52·3 per cent. negative expressions of dissatisfaction.[1]

To complete the picture we need to have reports from the teachers concerned. They have their professional and personal difficulties.

However, the evidence suggests that some schools at least induce negative attitudes in some pupils. These tend to generalize and spread to aspects of life outside school, not only with respect to further education but also to work, to authority, and to society at large. Schools can induce prejudices, and any attempt to treat them by purely intellectual measures seems more likely than not to fail. More drastic reorganization of curricula, organization, methods, and academic attitudes are indicated, even in grammar schools.[2]

This evidence is relevant to our concern with teaching-methods. The topic includes not only teaching techniques to maximize facility in learning and transfer ; it should include organization of curricula and management of the conditions in which teaching and learning take place.

13. TRANSFER, INSTRUCTION, TRAINING, EDUCATION

Review

So far certain aspects of the problem of transfer have been discussed—historical development ; evidence for transfer ; possible mechanisms of transfer ; methods available to teachers for maximizing transfer ; some hitherto neglected aspects of transfer, namely, bias and prejudice. As a result, certain broad principles have emerged :

---

[1] Some questionnaires contained both positive and negative responses—book cited, p. 114.

[2] See *Middle School* and R. F. Mackenzie, *Escape from the Classroom* (Collins, 1965), for some positive suggestions for reform. Also O. L. Shaw, book cited, for treatment of severe maladjustment.

(*a*) Transfer is quite a common process. In any but very young children transfer goes on during most of waking life. It may happen unconsciously, even during sleep, when a problem which has defied solution after a period of vain effort is solved, apparently spontaneously, on waking, or while one is occupied in some other routine work. It is doubtful whether, after the first few months of existence, we learn anything completely new, quite independent, that is, of experience and skills already acquired. In learning we build on what we know and can do already. Any new experience which cannot be interpreted and assimilated in terms of existing concepts and habits is ignored. This is why continuity is so very necessary in teaching.

(*b*) Transfer can be both positive and negative. It may help future learning ; it may hinder or prevent learning ; it may not happen in situations when transfer would seem to be inevitable. The problem in education and teaching, therefore, is to manage instruction and training so that positive transfer is maximized.

We can now go on to consider in more detail some implications of transfer for instruction, training, and education properly so-called.

Transfer is a complicated process

Earlier discussions of transfer were too simple. Attempts at explanation were determined by sociological pressures rather than psychological analysis and they depended on dubious models (theories) of learning. It is most likely that transfer is more complicated than even contemporary learning models indicate.[1] Transfer was assumed to be automatic and primarily intellectual. The influence of motivation, emotional conditions, the effects of teaching and training methods were largely ignored.

Some indication of the complexity of the transfer process may be gained by considering a translation of the passage printed in i.t.a. into traditional alphabet (Fig. 25, p. 304). Suppose the translation is to be made by a literate English-speaking person having no previous acquaintance with the Pitman alphabet. Allowing for variations in experience, preferred imagery, and training, something akin to the following is likely to happen :

---

[1] Readers wishing to follow more recent studies of learning in greater detail can find accounts and bibliographies in : R. M. Gagné, *The Conditions of Learning* (Holt, Rinehart and Winston, 1965) ; A. W. Melton (ed.), *Categories of Human Learning* (Academic Press, 1964) ; J. Deese, *The Structure of Associations in Language and Thought* (Johns Hopkins Press, 1965).

(i) A first glance reveals a mixture of familiar and strange shapes. The unfamiliar induces, first, arrest, followed by closer attending, then curiosity—the desire to investigate further (factor of motivation).

(ii) Discrimination, recognition : the letters both familiar and strange are seen as grouped into words (positive transfer by similarity from previous perceptual acquaintance with print). Some words will be recognized as English and the grammatical structure as English (positive transfer by similarity of structure).

(iii) *Expectation* (hypothesis, ' set ') : the passage is likely to convey a message in English in spite of unfamiliar details. Any interpretations, therefore, should probably be made in English. This ' set ' excludes foreign words and meanings (although there is just a possibility that the passage may ultimately be nonsense expressed in English phrases).

(iv) This restrictive ' set ' leads to closer attending, and further discrimination. Certain meanings emerge (transfer by similarity), *e.g.*, ' printed,' ' will,' ' children.' If the passage is pronounced *sotto voce*, or in inner speech, patterns unfamiliar in visual appearance become quite familiar in sound and motor-speech, *e.g.*, ' lern,' ' reed,' ' riet,' ' cums.' Here we have positive transfer by a mode of similarity, sound, reinforced by agreement with the possible meaning of a phrase overcoming negative transfer due to a mode of difference (visual appearance).

(v) By now, it will be supposed (hypothesis, ' set ') that the passage is concerned with teaching and learning : (lern) how to read (reed) and write (riet) in schools. This activates a concept (or concepts) associated with alphabet, spellings, books (positive transfer due to the availability of previously acquired mental structures—configurations, schemas), thus putting further limits on guesses at still more unfamiliar details.

(vi) When this over-all pattern has emerged the reader is likely to have felt an ' Aha ! I've got it ' response, together with removal of doubt, increased confidence, and satisfaction. Then will follow a renewal of attack on any still uninterpreted components.

(vii) If still more unfamiliar letter-shapes are encountered there will be further arrest, closer attending, evocation mentally of possible solutions, discrimination, evaluation, judgment ; in fact, a trial-and-error process *guided by the established* ' *set* ' until a solution congruent with the over-all meaning of the passage is reached.

(viii) By now, a reader who has translated some of the unfamiliar characters into traditional alphabet, thus learning some correct responses to new stimuli by solving simpler examples, particularly if he has been trained in methods of translation and has developed some *generalized ability* through practice with a variety of similar tasks, will begin to isolate (discriminate) certain shapes in i.t.a., now successfully associated with components of the traditional alphabet, and will apply these newly learned i.t.a.-traditional associations to more difficult items, if any, still not satisfactorily solved.   This is a case of transfer of a generalized method of attack from an already familiar pattern to a new problem (transfer of skill by similarity).

(ix) A trained reader will finally re-read the whole passage to make sure that all the part-problems have been correctly solved (transfer of *attitudes, e.g.,* conscientious working ; ideal of accuracy ; desire for perfection).   Also involved here may be certain factors of *motivation,* such as obsessions, dislike of failure, anxiety, guilt, derived from earlier experiences and training, together with factors arising from unconscious or partially conscious sources such as have been described by psycho-analysts.

Thus, we can discern positive and negative transfer proceeding concurrently, the end product being a resultant of the two.   Aspects of past experience are involved, *e.g.,* concepts (configurations, schemas) of varying range and depth ; meanings ; perceptual components ; motor-speech patterns ; generalized methods of problem-solving ; unconscious attitudes.   There are thought processes—hypotheses, guesses, ' sets,' vigilance, discrimination, recognition, trial and error, comparison, contrast, as well as dubiety, evaluation, judgment.   There are mechanisms of association, *e.g.,* stimulus-and-response 'generalization,' feedback.   Factors of training, practice, skill, ' intelligence,' ability are involved as well as motivation—curiosity, satisfaction, discomfort, hunger for achievement, reaction to a challenge (aggressiveness).[1]

In its most general form the problem of transfer can be stated thus : a learner with a given hereditary constitution, temperament, and motivation dispositions, with a given level of intellectual capacity together with experiences, knowledge, skills, attitudes, biases, prejudices, moral codes, aspirations acquired up to date, is

---

[1] Readers may find it interesting and instructive to analyse a process of breaking a secret code, or translating an ' unseen ' passage in a foreign language from the point of view of what is involved in the process of transfer.

Examples of the complexity of the transfer process are set out in S. R. Laycock, *Adaptability to New Situations* (Warwick and York, 1929).

faced with a relatively new situation. How, and to what extent, will his characteristics as a total personality affect his reactions to the new situation ? The personality and physical presence of the learner transfers to the new situation, not merely his acquired knowledge and skills.

Transfer occurs at different levels of intellectual abstraction and in various modes

It has been shown that the suggested explanation of transfer by reference to common components in different situations is inadequate. Examples can be found in which there are common components in abundance, yet no transfer. In any case one common component is always the learner himself. Again, even if transfer of a sort does occur it may be due to mistaken apprehension or unconscious bias and therefore conducive to error.

It is obvious that, ultimately, all transfer depends on some kind and degree of similarity between situations and experiences. At the same time, similarity (the presence of common components) is not a *sufficient* condition for transfer. Similarities must be discriminated, abstracted, and, at any higher than a primitive animal level, *named*.

This means that transfer must be achieved. Learners must be motivated to seek transfer ; they must be aware of different types and levels of similarity ; they must possess techniques for analysis and synthesis of experiences.

Types and levels of similarity (common components)

(i) Similarity of sensory quality.

If some stimulus—sound, colour, smell, touch—is associated sufficiently often with a glandular secretion or motor response, any other stimulus sufficiently like the original tends to produce the conditioned response. This transfer by stimulus ' generalization ' occurs at a primitive mental level in animals and young children as well as older learners (often without the benefit of speech).

Numerous examples can be observed in everyday life, particularly when combined with shapes and perceptual appearances. The effect may be negative as is the case when a small brown object elicits the same response as would a spider ; a damp, cold, slimy feel suggests a frog ; some unpleasant response aroused by an unfriendly teacher spreads to what he teaches. Another example is indicated by the saying " All is not gold that glitters."

(ii) Similarity of pattern or structure.

Examples of this type are transfer between a map and the geographical area it represents ; in general, between any diagram or plan and the corresponding object (*cf.* Fig. 6, p. 174).

A verbal pattern such as :

the cef gaxed the slow zuc

can be transposed into a number of sensible sentences having a different content but similar grammatical structure.

A melody can be recognized if played in different keys and tempos on different instruments.

(iii) Similarity of use.

Of this type there are two varieties :

(*a*) using different means or methods to achieve a similar result. Examples : Hannibal's elephants had a military function similar to that of modern tanks ; donkeys, mules, horses, elephants, steam, electric, and diesel locomotives, can all be used for hauling heavy loads ; a piece of broken glass may act as a substitute for a knife ; the edge of a tin can, a knife blade, even a strong thumb-nail can be used as screwdrivers in emergencies.

(*b*) using the same object or material to achieve different results.

This is another mode of transfer by similarity of function. It has been used as a test for fluency of ideas and flexibility of thinking. (*Cf.* the discussion of originality and creativity later.) The test is expressed as follows :

State as many uses as you can think of for a brick, a cap, a barrel, a paper-clip, a tin of boot-polish, a newspaper, a knife, a motor-car tyre, etc.

Both sorts (*a*) and (*b*) are examples of response ' generalization.'

Practical affairs such as ' make-do-and-mend,' first-aid to the injured, as well as technical work abound with improvisations based on transfer through similarity of function. It is noteworthy that many people, pupils and adults, with no more than average academic achievement or I.Q. (as estimated by a standard test of ' intelli-gence ') are very ingenious in working out improvisations. They do not always get, in schools, the opportunities or the credit their capacity for improvisation deserves.

(iv) Similarity of meaning.

The same or similar meanings can be expressed in a variety of words, *e.g.,*

It was an eloquent testimony to their organizing ability.
It spoke well for their power of getting things done.

For the educated all phenomena are interrelated.
Wise men tell us that everything which happens is somehow
connected with everything else.[1]

It is useful in teaching to be able quickly to express the same or
similar meanings in ways suitable for different learners.

(v) Conceptual similarity.

The following expressions differ in detail, but all refer to the
same number concept :

$$4 :: \;\; \equiv \triangle \; \triangle \; \triangle \; \triangle$$

four, pedwar, quatre.

(vi) Similarity of relationships.

Examples :

(a) $5 \times 8 = 10 \times ? = 26 + ? = 47 - ? = 80 \div ?$

(b) OBTAIN is to SEARCH as VICTORY is to
MANOEUVRE, TRIUMPH, SEIZE, DISCOVER.

(vii) Similarity of logical form.

Arguments may be inductive (particulars to classifications) ;
deductive (general principles to particulars) ; or forms of reasoning
by analogy.

Arguments of each type may be expressed in different words
embracing different details in different types of subject-matter.   An
argument in the form of a syllogism as it is shown in an introductory
text-book on logic may not be recognized when it appears disguised
in a political speech ; nor are the phrases of the speaker always
translated by the audience into a standard syllogistic form which
may more easily reveal some hidden fallacy.   This is one situation in
which transfer occurs less often than is desirable particularly when
education is the subject of debate.

The above are some of the main types of similarity through which
positive transfer can be made.   Educating for transfer means
providing learners with a working knowledge of the types, training
them in making transfers, and giving them sufficient practice with a
variety of examples of each type.

---

[1] From a test of matching sentences in A. F. Watts, *The Language and
Mental Development of Children* (Harrap, 1960).

General and specific factors in knowledge and skills

These examples of similarities illustrate two aspects of knowledge and skills, namely, general factors common to many situations and specific factors restricted to one particular situation. If positive transfer is to be encouraged the general factors must be emphasized rather than the particulars. Encourage the search for relationships, concepts, principles. Compare, contrast, associate. By all means, of course, attend to facts and details. Be accurate with respect to facts and details. However, facts can be collected and details memorized for much the same reasons as a miser hoards coins or an enthusiast collects stamps, namely, for pride of possession. The competent scholar values facts in so far as they can be used ; in so far as they exemplify relationships, meanings, implications ; in so far as they lead to principles, to solving problems, to artistic creativity.

Facts and details can be memorized and their implications ignored completely.

" Now, what I want is, Facts. Teach these boys and girls nothing but Facts. Facts alone are wanted in life. Plant nothing else, and root out everything else. You can only form the minds of reasoning animals upon Facts : nothing else will ever be of any service to them. . . . Stick to Facts, sir ! "

" Girl number twenty unable to define a horse ! " said Mr. Gradgrind. . . . " Girl number twenty possessed of no facts, in reference to one of the commonest of animals ! Some boy's definition of a horse. Bitzer, yours."

" Quadruped. Graminivorous. Forty teeth, namely twenty-four grinders, four eye-teeth, and twelve incisive. . . . Hoofs hard. . . . Age known by marks in mouth."

" Now girl number twenty," said Mr. Gradgrind. " You know what a horse is."[1]

Mr. McChoakumchild . . . and some one hundred and forty other schoolmasters, had been lately turned at the same time, in the same factory, on the same principles, like so many pianoforte legs. He had been put through an immense variety of paces, and had answered volumes of head-breaking questions. Orthography, etymology, syntax, and prosody, biography, astronomy, geography, and general cosmography, the sciences of compound proportion, algebra, land-surveying and levelling, vocal music, and drawing from models, were

---

[1] The joke being that girl number twenty's father was said to be a veterinary surgeon, farrier, and horsebreaker !

all at the ends of his ten chilled fingers. . . . He knew all about all the Water Sheds of all the world . . . and all the histories of all the peoples, and all the names of all the rivers and mountains, and all the productions, manners, and customs of all the countries, and all their boundaries and bearings on the two and thirty points of the compass. . . . If he had only learnt a little less, how infinitely better he might have taught much more !

No little Gradgrind had ever associated a cow in a field with that famous cow with the crumpled horn who tossed the dog who worried the cat who killed the rat . . . or with that yet more famous cow who swallowed Tom Thumb . . . it had only been introduced to a cow as a graminivorous ruminating quadruped with several stomachs.

Thus, Charles Dickens in *Hard Times*. In fact, what we really want is not facts, but facts in their proper relationships.

Techniques of analysis. Maximizing positive transfer by efficient instruction and training

(a) Transfer will be encouraged by an ample supply of stimulating first-hand experience. Moreover, as well as an ample supply there should be *variety* of experience. The greater the store of *usable* experience and the greater the variety, the greater will be the probability of positive transfer—the number and range of possible useful associations will be increased.

(b) Ultimately, positive transfer depends on the discrimination, explicit recognition, and abstraction of similarities and differences.

Failure to realize relevant similarities; failure to note misleading similarities leads either to no transfer where there should be transfer or to negative transfer and error. Positive transfer, therefore, at a higher than primitive intellectual level depends on effective discrimination. Many types of similarity essential for positive transfer are abstract—similarities of patterns, meanings, relationships, logical structures. These can be camouflaged by gross perceptual differences. Therefore they must be actively searched for.

Efficient search leading to clear discrimination needs:

(a) Sufficiently powerful motives on the part of the learner to attend with concentration and persist in face of temporary difficulties. Suggestions for inducing interest have been made in a previous chapter.

(b) Techniques—effective methods of observing and learning.

Pupils must be taught how to learn.   The average learner tends to work according to a law of least effort.   Attention and care will be given just enough to ' get by.'   Comparatively few people work at their optimum level of capacity.   Not only is stimulation needed but efficient methods and sufficiently high standards of performance.

In other words, learners need competent instruction and training in methods of work and models of good performance.   They can get these only from people who themselves have sufficiently high standards of knowledge, skill, and competence.

There is a fashion for praising self-activity, free activity, learning by discovery.   This is highly commendable—so far as it goes. One obvious weakness in this principle of education is involved however.   It is beyond question that for the most effective learning some active participation by the learner in his own learning-processes is necessary.   At the same time free activity alone is not sufficient.   Guidance by a more mature, competent person is essential.   Immature learners, particularly those below the highest grades of intellectual ability, are prone to be satisfied with too low standards and inefficient methods.   It is difficult to see how they can be otherwise unless they are introduced to higher standards and better methods and *actively encouraged to reach them.*

One productive source of stimulation and guidance is the challenge of discussion and questions.   We have already quoted from J. W. P. Creber on " The Rediscovery of the Familiar " in which he says that children appear to grow up without really seeing anything, or only seeing what they want to see ; that adolescents are allowed to bury half their experience without ever realizing its significance.   To offset this mental blindness Creber suggests prompting the pupils by shrewd questioning.   He says, " One of the main initial causes of vagueness is the children's tendency to (illicit) generalization.   They have to learn that attention to a particular object or experience is the essence of what we mean by accuracy."[1]   In other words, learners must learn to discriminate and it is the teachers' business to encourage them to do so.   Teachers cannot opt out of instructing

---

[1] *Sense and Sensitivity*, p. 26.
" We found that many witnesses, not excluding those who were intelligent and anxious to assist us, had been oblivious of what lay before their eyes.   It did not enter their consciousness.   They were like moles asked about the habits of birds."   Quoted from the judicial report on the Aberfan Disaster, *The Guardian*, August 4, 1967.

and guiding even in the name of free activity and learning by discovery.[1] If they do, each succeeding generation will contain more than its share of half-baked intellectual products. It is because competent instruction and guidance are essential in teaching for transfer that so much space has been devoted in this chapter to discussing them.

The importance of language abilities in the process of transfer

Some aspects of the part played by language abilities in intellectual development were described in Chapter VII above (*cf.* p. 203). It was said there that relationships, particularly subtle relationships, are elusive. To be abstracted and fixed they must be associated with appropriate words or symbols. Words, both spoken and written, have some of the stability and persistence of material objects. When habitually associated with things and relationships they can then represent the things and relationships. So, by mentally manipulating the words, new and more complex associations can be formed.

As well as acting as vehicles for meanings, words can act as probes. It has been shown that we tend to observe what we have names for. Armed with a wide-ranging accurate vocabulary a learner can more easily make the discriminations necessary for transfer when faced with an unfamiliar situation. The vocabulary guides his observations as well as records his discriminations.

Again, words facilitate classification and generalization. Similar objects, similar aspects, similar meanings can be called by the same name.

Thus, language is important for transfer. Indeed, for more subtle transfers of abstract complex concepts it is essential. For this reason, language training should not be restricted to linguistic subject-matter exclusively. It should be an intimate factor in all subject activities of the school, sciences and mathematics, practical and theoretical aspects included.

The purport of Chapter VII was written years ago. More recently sociologists and students of linguistics have emphasized the intimate connexion between language forms and intellectual potential. Basil Bernstein quotes Sapir as having introduced a new clarity and subtlety into discussions of the interrelations between language, culture, and personality. Language does not stand apart

[1] This topic will be treated further in connexion with ' traditional ' v. ' progressive ' methods of teaching and school organization. See Chapter X.

from or run parallel to direct experience but completely inter-penetrates it. People speaking different languages may be said to live in different worlds of reality in the sense that the language they speak affects to a considerable degree both their sensory perceptions and their habitual modes of thought.[1]

Many investigations of deprived children have stressed the fact that they are not only defective in ' intelligence ' as estimated by a standard verbal test but that they are usually markedly retarded in language development.[2] The same tendencies have been noted in studies of working-class children.

In the case of children in foster homes and remote villages these defects may be ascribed to lack of stimulation and poverty of experience. This is less likely to be the case among urban working-class pupils. Nor does it appear to be due entirely, if at all, to defects in sheer intellectual potential. In one experiment Bernstein gave a Mill Hill Vocabulary Test and a Progressive Matrices (non-verbal) Test of ' Intelligence ' to a group of day-release adolescents and secondary-modern school pupils. He found that their scores on the *non-verbal test of ' intelligence,'* particularly at the higher levels, were significantly better than their scores on the vocabulary test. In a group of Public schoolboys *making comparable scores on the Progressive Matrices test, the vocabulary scores kept pace with the ' intelligence ' scores.*

Thus, sheer intellectual defect did not appear to be the reason for the defect in the experimental group's verbal ability.[3]

Bernstein suggests that the relative deficiency in language scores on the part of many, particularly lower, working-class pupils is due not so much to defective intellectual potential as to their habitual forms of speech which curtail their powers of attending and perceiving, thus preventing them from making the most effective use of

[1] This is one serious cause of difficulty when teachers from middle-class backgrounds teach in working-class districts. See B. Bernstein, " A Socio-linguistic Approach to Social Learning," in *Penguin Survey of the Social Sciences,* 1965.

[2] See, for examples, M. L. Kellmer Pringle, *Deprivation and Education* and references in Chapter II above, pp. 35 and 36.

[3] In a sample of 618 subjects, if a Progressive Matrices Quotient of 116 (adopted from the parallel study of the sample of Public schoolboys) is taken as the lower limit for grammar-school entrance, no less than 80 of his 618 subjects would have qualified. In fact only six did so. An appalling waste of potential ability. See B. Bernstein, " Language and Social Class," *British Journal of Sociology,* XI, 3 ; " Some Sociological Determinants of Perception," *British Journal of Sociology,* XI, 2.

their experiences. Sensitivity to the structure of objects is a function of learned ability to respond to a perceived object as a matrix of relations. This is a sociologist's way of saying that informal restricted speech habits prevent fully efficient attending, accurate discrimination, and ordering of details.

Communication between members of intimate working-class groups (families, work-groups) depends very much on gesture, facial expression, body movement, tone of voice, rather than on elaborate verbal sentences. Speech is condensed, abbreviated, allusive; meanings are taken for granted instead of being made explicit; information is concrete and descriptive rather than analytic and abstract. Many working-class pupils have difficulty in ordering sentences. Sentences are short, often incomplete. Qualifying clauses are seldom used. These pupils, therefore, have difficulty in understanding concepts and abstract principles (and, by implication, in making effective positive transfer).

From the point of view of transfer and education this is important. In so far as Bernstein's suggestions are accurate they imply the action of a powerful environmental influence on the development of intellectual *potential*. Restrictive speech habits ingrained from early childhood can retard the growth of any innate ' intelligence ' to its full potential capacity as well as cause faulty perception and discrimination. This amounts to saying that one way of improving pupils' ' minds ' as well as their powers of transfer is to improve their speech habits.

Mastery is essential for optimum transfer

Transfer does not occur in a vacuum. It depends on an ample supply of *usable* mental resources. The operative word is ' usable.' Fox's experiments with suits of armour (*cf.* p. 244) showed clearly that effective transfer did not happen until the associations between the items to be discriminated and the appropriate technical terms had been sufficiently well memorized.

Facts must be observed; names associated; relationships discriminated, recorded, and systematized; theorems memorized; principles understood. These are the resources necessary for transfer. But all this needs time, and effort, on the part of the learner. For a high degree of competence much time and effort is needed.

Discovery, by itself, is not enough. The learner must have sufficient determination to attend with due care; to observe accurately ; to record, arrange, and systematize. The learning must be sufficiently thorough. This requires persistence and practice. Usually the learner (even the advanced student at high intellectual levels in research work) has to face temporary failure and tolerate some degree of frustration. Boredom is not unknown. As we shall see in the next section (on creativity) academic achievement and a high I.Q. alone will not guarantee future success. More depends on what the learner is prepared to make of his potential.

For our immediate purpose, the point is this—fully effective transfer needs intellectual discipline.

Incidentally, this explains the educational value of the classical languages. Competently taught to a sufficiently advanced level, *to students with the necessary interest and flair for the subjects*, the study of Latin and Greek did encourage the development of intellectual discipline. The mistake made by extremists like Tarver was to suppose that an intellectual discipline in the modern world could be developed in no other way.

Again, the learner, particularly the less intellectually able learner, needs constant encouragement as well as guidance ; and occasionally, be it said, some judicious pressure. One main source of encouragement (and pressure) is parents and teachers. Effort is further encouraged by an environment of educational opportunity and intellectual stimulation with sufficiently high standards of aspiration and competence. Learners tend markedly to gravitate to the level of their environment.[1]

Transfer and specialization in studies

In Chapter I above (p. 24) attention was drawn to possible definitions of a general education. The term can mean (*a*) the study of one or a few abstract theoretical subjects like pure mathematics or physics, both of which contain concepts of extreme logical generality, or (*b*) the study of a wide range of different subjects such as is done by a pupil who offers some eight, nine, or ten subjects at ' O ' Level in the General Certificate of Education examinations.

Neither of these alternatives is, necessarily, sufficient for a general education properly so-called. The concepts in mathematics and physics may have a wide range of logical generality, but that does not, of itself, mean that these concepts are related to other

[1] See later in connexion with the ' Comprehensive ' organizati on of secondary schooling.

subject-matter, or to more practical affairs in everyday life. The abundance of different subjects offered at ' O ' Level by some pupils does not, of itself, guarantee a general education. The subjects may be studied as so many separate collections of information for examination purposes. They need not be functionally associated either with each other or with affairs out of school.

A true general education of any type requires that the subject-matter has been analysed and *its concepts interrelated* both within the subject itself, with other academic subject-matter, and with practical problems in everyday affairs. In other words, a general education is one in which a high degree of positive transfer has been engendered.

This has a bearing on the problem of specialization in schools.

Knowledge is increasing so very quickly that it is difficult in one life-time to master more than a part of some one rapidly expanding subject, a science or economics for example. At some stage in a student's career some degree of specialization is inescapable. The error to avoid is undue specialization at too early an age. In these discussions on transfer, the supreme importance of a *variety of experience* adequately analysed has been stressed. In addition, at all stages of learning, the search for transferable items of knowledge and skills should be emphasized and the necessary techniques encouraged. Attitudes and techniques rather than subject-matter as such make the difference between an over-specialized and a liberal education.

One tendency about which a good deal of discussion has centred recently is that of selecting out very able pupils as early as possible and segregating them for specialized training in some specialized institution, preferably in some remote district away from any distractions. This apparently has happened in the U.S.S.R. One possibly unfortunate result of this specialization may be the production of a generation of specialists geared to the service of national defence in a competitive world and out of touch with the life of the rest of the community to which they should belong.

The limits of transfer

Transfer will seldom be complete. Even if pupils are competently trained the degree and range of transfer is likely to be limited by :

(a) The degree of logical generality of the subject-matter.

(b) The range and variety of experience available to the learner.

(c) The learner's sensitivity to experience, level of intellectual potential, and linguistic ability.

(*d*) The effectiveness of the learner's techniques for observation and analysis.

(*e*) The learner's degree of mastery of the subject-matter.

(*f*) The level of motivation and absence of bias and prejudice.

II. ORIGINALITY, CREATIVITY, PRODUCTIVE THINKING

For many years educationists and teachers have noted differences between learning as a process of collecting and memorizing facts and formulas, and learning as discovery, invention, problem-solving, and adventures with ideas. And since 1898 at least there have been attempts to invent tests for potential creative, original abilities. This activity, however, has produced relatively little effect on the curricula and teaching methods in the traditional schools. Psychological testing (of which, since Binet at the beginning of the twentieth century, there has been too much rather than too little) has been dominated by the invention of tests of intellectual aptitude for the purpose of detecting acceleration or backwardness in school work— the now familiar intelligence-quotient estimates. On the other hand, the search for originality of mind has been unwelcome to many education authorities who have equated originality with subversion, with social and political trouble-making.

Recently, however, there has been a change in the climate of professional and popular opinion. Psychologists, prominent in the field of mental testing, have compared early scores on tests of general intelligence with the later achievements of the tested subjects after school and college, and have found disconcerting deviations from what was expected on the evidence of the early test results. More shattering, perhaps, was the astonishing and successful launch of Sputnik I in 1957 by the Soviet Russians. This, with its implications for military purposes, frightened Anglo-Saxon ' Establishments ' out of their wits and seriously disturbed a smug, complacent belief in the superiority of English and American higher education— another shining example of the sociology of education !

As a result, emphasis is now on the importance of original, creative abilities and on the invention of tests to discover it as early as possible in the life of coming generations of pupils, coupled with the suspicion that I.Q. scores may not be the best indicators of future creative achievements.[1]

---

[1] Henceforward, in the interests of brevity, I.Q. will mean Intelligence Quotient as measured by standardized tests of ' intelligence.'

The topic is relevant to any discussion of school organization, curricula, and, particularly, of techniques of teaching. In our contemporary era of economic competition and military insecurity a single original idea or invention may tremendously affect standards of living and military security. Tanks, ballistic missiles, the internal-combustion engine, radar, jet propulsion, the atomic bomb, nuclear fission, are examples. Obviously originality is at a premium, although it is, perhaps, unfortunate that the search for originality may become a search for ' gimmicks ' in commercial advertising, and inventions in ' hardware ' for military purposes, at the expense of research for improvements in human welfare. Hence, for more than one reason, a critical examination of contemporary school business in the light of what we now know of the nature and nurture of originality is relevant to the purpose of this book. Further, the topic of originality and creativity is intimately connected with transfer of training. If these abilities can be discovered and encouraged in school, will the training transfer to after-school achievement ?

Creativity is more than originality.

It is desirable at the outset to note a distinction between creativity and originality. One can be original without being creative. Originality means producing new ideas ; planning new inventions ; seeing in imagination new economic plans and social policies ; plotting original stories ; making new discoveries and theories (models) in science ; envisaging existing knowledge in ways never thought of before. Creativity, on the other hand, means translating new ideas, new plans, new discoveries, into practice, applying them to some useful practical or theoretical purpose. If production of bizarre, fantastic notions were the test, some patients in mental hospitals would rank high in creativity. Many sane people imagine new theories, plans, inventions, but on account of diffidence or indolence or sheer bad luck never succeed in realizing their originality in practice. Creativity involves more than originality.

Doubts about the I.Q. as a Predictor of Future Achievement

Mental and other forms of testing have been used so insistently in the United States that popular resistance to the ' tyranny of testing ' has developed. The resistance has been sufficiently widespread and insistent to claim the attention of a Congressional Committee of Investigation, the proceedings of which were reported in a special issue of the *American Psychologist* (Vol. 20, No. 11, November 1965) under the title " Testing and Public Policy." It is not surprising, therefore, that much of the evidence to be summarized here comes from the United States and from the researches of psychological authorities distinguished for their work in the field of testing.

(i) *How Constant is the I.Q. ?*

It has been accepted frequently that the I.Q., as measured by what were hoped to be ' culture-free ' tests, would give a reliable estimate of a child's inborn potential intellectual aptitude. This was equivalent to assuming that instruction and practice could encourage the development of whatever factors are responsible for ' intelligence ' to the highest degree *compatible with innate endowment*, but that instruction and practice would not *improve* the innate capacity. On this assumption, intellectual development was to a great extent, if not altogether, dependent on the maturation, or ripening to full development, of the mental aptitudes concerned. Moreover, if the I.Q. was to be used to *predict* future levels of development and achievement *it must remain constant* from year to year throughout the length of school life at least.

Longitudinal surveys have discounted belief in the constancy of the I.Q.

Earlier in the history of intelligence testing it was supposed that the I.Q. was not only constant in amount, but indicated the upper limit of academic achievement which could be expected from any given pupil. Consequently, any manifest changes in the I.Q. in successive tests of the same pupil, or any ' over-achievement ' (that is, any case in which the academic achievement of a pupil was manifestly greater than might be expected in view of his I.Q.), had to be explained away as errors in the use of the tests or abnormalities in the testing conditions—ill-health, absence from school, anxiety, excessive demands for achievement by parents and teachers, systematic coaching in answering the tests.

Dr Nancy Bayley[1] organized a system of successive tests of development given to the same pupils at intervals from one month of age upward. She reported the amazement of the research team when they found no relation between the performances in the first few months and those at the end of the first year. " It is now well

[1] Presidential Address to the Western Psychological Association, U.S.A., May 1954.

established," she said, "that we cannot predict later intelligence from tests made in infancy. . . .   When the children were eight years old only a fifth of the survey group had maintained any stability in their relative status over the eight-year span."

Dr Bayley suggested that whatever is responsible for intellectual performance is not constant, but increases with age and experience. It is not a unitary factor, but consists of a variety of aptitudes, each of which has its own rate of development and does not operate equally well in all directions.   It is, rather, a succession of developing functions in which the more advanced and complex aptitudes form the different levels of a hierarchy depending on the prior maturing of earlier more primitive and simpler ones.[1]   In any case, as we shall see later, achievement in life depends on aptitudes which are to a considerable extent independent of what is measured by the I.Q.

(ii) *The Relation between High I.Q. and Later Achievement*

L. M. Terman, a distinguished expert in the standardization of tests of intelligence, has reported the results of a follow-up survey of adults whose I.Q.'s were measured in childhood.[2]   Fifteen hundred previously tested subjects were located.   Their average I.Q. was 150.   Eighty had I.Q.'s greater than 170 (the average I.Q. of the general population is 100).

This high-level group were much more productive of books, articles in professional journals, works of fiction, inventions, than the general population.   Tests of general intelligence given at six, eight, or ten years of age had given some indications about the capacity for achievement in later years, but they had not indicated in which direction the achievement would be, least of all about what personality factors would affect achievement.   *Nor did an exceptionally high I.Q. guarantee that the gifted individual would actually achieve success commensurate with the I.Q. level.*   Out of Terman's sample of high I.Q.'s two sub-groups were selected—150 men rated highest (group A) and 150 rated lowest (group C) for *achieved* success.   In I.Q. status the two groups were comparable.   Moreover, the members of the C group had I.Q.'s high enough to warrant brilliant work at university level.

[1] A. Koestler, in *The Act of Creation*, has expressed a similar explanation in considerable detail.

[2] Bingham Memorial Lecture on "The Discovery and Encouragement of Exceptional Talent," University of California March, 1954.

However, of the A group, 97 per cent. entered college, 90 per cent. graduated, and 52 per cent. achieved honours grades. Of the C group, 68 per cent. entered college, 37 per cent. graduated, and 14 per cent achieved honours. Analysis of the characteristics of the A group revealed that they came from more stimulating home backgrounds, and were rated higher than the C group on such traits as prudence, self-control, self-confidence, desire to excel, sensitivity to approval or disapproval, freedom from feelings of inferiority and inadequacy. All these, it will be noted, are predominantly volitional (having to do with decision-making) and conative (striving) traits of temperament and character rather than of intellect. Terman's verdict was : I.Q. and achievement in life are far from perfectly correlated. High I.Q.'s alone will not guarantee success. Other factors are involved.

(iii) *Academic Ability and Later Achievement*

If exceptionally high I.Q. does not guarantee later success, neither does academic ability as measured by traditional school and university examinations. Mackinnon's creative architects (of which there will be more later) were often undistinguished academically. Liam Hudson, in this country, reports that his evidence about the degree classes obtained at Oxford and Cambridge by groups of later distinguished people—Fellows of the Royal Society, Doctors of Science, High Court Judges, Cabinet Ministers—showed that quite frequently they got relatively poor degree classes. At Cambridge there was no relation between a research student's degree class and his chances, later, of becoming an F.R.S. or a D.Sc. Fully one third of the future F.R.S.'s at Cambridge had gained a second class or worse at some time during their university careers ; and the proportion among future D.Sc.'s was over a half.[1]

Similar discrepancies between high academic ability and later achievement are shown by State scholars, the *crème de la crème* of our grammar schools. Official reports on the later careers of State scholars for 1958 and 1964 revealed that about one in four had achieved a third-class honours or worse, or had failed to complete a university course. Supplementary State scholars showed similar results.

It would seem that neither I.Q.'s nor academic records are reliable indicators of later achievement. Some very distinguished

[1] *Contrary Imaginations* (Methuen, 1966).

men (including Darwin and Einstein) were not by any means distinguished in school and college.

(iv) *I.Q. not a Reliable Predictor of General Intellectual Potential*

Another Bingham Lecturer, J. M. Stalnaker, speaking of " Recognizing and Encouraging Talent,"[1] emphasized the need to develop fully our human resources. He went on to say :

> We psychologists are largely responsible for the over-emphasis which the public gives to the I.Q. Frankly, the I.Q. is over-rated. Parents and many teachers regard the I.Q. as an infallible and crucially significant index. As a result, they ignore the importance of many other characteristics which contribute to attainment. . . . The I.Q. is an empirically determined index which has certain practical values when used with appropriate caution. . . . Actually, it is a composite of a number of measures of different abilities. . . . The gravest danger of the I.Q. is that it gives a grossly over-simplified picture of the organisation of the mind and encourages parents, teachers and students themselves to under-rate the value of effort. The relationship between the I.Q. and productivity even in scholarly fields is not as high as is generally believed.

David Wechsler, the designer of several widely used tests for mental abilities, in an address on " Cognitive, Conative and Non-intellective Intelligence,"[2] said that general intelligence cannot be equated with intellectual ability, however broadly defined, but must be regarded as a manifestation of the personality as a whole. Nevertheless the I.Q. has been used not only to determine comparative mental endowment, capacity to learn, presence of special abilities and disabilities, and evaluation of degree of mental deficiency, but also as a basis for school placement, for vocational guidance, for psychiatric diagnosis, and for the prediction of adjustment potentials in a variety of situations from infancy to old age, including such areas as child adoption, juvenile delinquency, fitness for military service, college success, and old-age counselling. " On the other hand any bit of behaviour that seems concerned with or related to instinct, impulse or temperament is ipso facto considered to have no direct relation to general intelligence." The speaker concluded by saying, " To realise that general intelligence is a function of the personality as a whole and is determined by emotion

---

[1] At the Carnegie Institute of Technology, March 1961.
[2] Given at Denver, Colorado, September 1949.

and conative factors is just a beginning. We now need to know what non-intellective factors are involved, and to what degree."

Dissatisfaction with the I.Q. as a measure of intellectual potential is a feature of recent Soviet psychology. Soviet educational psychologists do not believe that intellectual development is solely a process of maturation. They believe that instead of limiting instruction to a level indicated by the I.Q., instruction should *precede* development. Children can acquire certain habits and skills with the aid of parents and teachers which they will be able to apply, by themselves, at a later stage. These psychologists believe that problems solved by a child without help indicate only the stage of development he has actually reached. Such problems do not test what the child can do with the aid of imitation, demonstration, and other forms of instruction.

The late L. S. Vygotski[1] writes about a zone of potential development :

> It is an empirical finding frequently verified and indisputable that learning must be congruous with the level of child development. . . . We may, therefore, confidently take as a starting point the incontestable and basic fact that there is a relation between a given level of development and potentiality for learning.
>
> Recently, however, attention has been drawn to the fact that when attempting to define the actual relation of the process of development to potentiality for learning we cannot confine ourselves to only one given level of development. We must determine at least *two levels of a child's development* otherwise we fail to find the correct relation between the course of development and potentiality for learning in each specific case. The first of these we call the *level of the child's actual development*. . . . This, however, does not indicate with any completeness the present state of the child's development. Let us suppose that we have tested two children and found that both have a mental age of seven. When we set these children further tests, however, essential differences come to light. With the help of guiding questions, examples, demonstration, one child easily performs the tests, passing his level of actual development by two years ; the other can do only tests which advance him by half a year. Here we meet directly with the central concept necessary for estimating the zone of potential development.

---

[1] See his article on " Learning and Mental Development at School Age," in B. and J. Simon (eds.), *Educational Psychology in the U.S.S.R.* (Routledge and Kegan Paul, 1963).

Again, " with the help of imitation in collectivity under adult guidance the child does much more than he can do with understanding, independently. The divergence between the level of performing tasks which are accessible with adult help and the level of performing tasks accessible to independent activity defines the zone of the child's potential development."[1] In another place the author declares that the only good teaching is that which outpaces development.[2]

The Canadian psychologist D. O. Hebb has suggested that there may be at least two aspects of intelligence :

> One (A) is an innate potential, the capacity for development, a fully innate property that amounts to the possession of a good brain and a good neural development. The second (B) is the functioning of a brain in which development has gone on determining an *average level of performance* or comprehension by the partly grown or mature person . . . two different meanings of intelligence . . . what we actually know about an intelligence-test score is that it is primarily related to intelligence B rather than intelligence A.[3]

If this assumption is correct (it certainly seems reasonable), then it follows that ' intelligence ' as measured by a mental test (the I.Q.) is a function of experience as well as of innate capacity. Therefore any person's manifest ' intelligence ' will depend on the kind and amount and variety of experience and instruction to which he has been exposed. That this is so is suggested by the different performances on intelligence tests of normal and deprived children. It follows that *innate potential for development is no guarantee that the development will occur*, which amounts to saying that an estimate of I.Q. by itself is not likely to be a completely reliable basis for predicting later achievement.

Professor P. E. Vernon goes one better. He suggests the term ' Intelligence C ' to refer to actual test results—*i.e.*, to the particular sampling of Intelligence B which an intelligence test provides. This implies that whatever ' intelligence ' may be, it is complex. It

---

[1] *Loc. cit.*, p. 28. Italics in original.

[2] *Idem*, p. 31. For my part this doctrine seems to be a plain invitation to teachers to " hammer in the facts " now, whether or not they are comprehensible, in the hope that when development has caught up with them they will then be used intelligently. Instruction should drive on regardless. I wonder.

[3] *The Organisation of Behaviour* (Wiley, 1959).

will not work with equal efficiency in every direction. Its products will depend on the kind of test used to measure it.[1] Instead of thinking of intelligence as

> ... a definite entity, an autonomous mental faculty which simply matures as children grow up, we have to think of it in terms of a cumulative formation of more and more complex and flexible schemata ... which develop through interaction between the growing organism and its environment. They depend both upon environmental stimulation and *on active exploration and experiment*; they are formed and organised by use.... They also depend on personality and motivational factors, organic and social drives, curiosity and interests; and they are channelled by family, cultural and educational pressures. Intelligence, then, refers to the totality of concepts and skills, the techniques or plans for coping with problems, which have crystallised out of the child's previous experience. Most representative of these are the thinking skills *which have been overlearned and which are transferable to a wide variety of new situations.*[2]

The upshot of all this is *not that the I.Q. is useless, but that it is not by any means a complete indication of a person's potential for achievement. Some aspects of intellect and personality necessary for creative achievement are not measured by the intelligence test as it has been constructed and standardized hitherto.* In many cases intelligence tests have been checked for validity by reference to success in academic subject-matter in schools. If used for diagnostic purposes as an indication of a pupil's standing relative to the general population in certain verbal, numerical, logical, and memory abilities the I.Q. is as good an indicator as we have at present. At the same time it cannot be used to make infallible long-term predictions about future achievement.

The Search for Originality and Creative Thinking

We are faced with a problem. Economic competition, military security, and human welfare all make originality, inventiveness, and creative thinking urgently desirable. At the same time neither high I.Q. as measured by existing tests nor high academic ability as revealed in school or university is a reliable indicator of later creative achievement. Can originality be detected relatively early in life?

---

[1] " Ability Factors and Environmental Influences," Bingham Memorial Lecture, Purdue University, April 1965.
[2] *Loc. cit.* My italics.

If so, how can it be fostered ? What conditions appear to encourage it ? How is it revealed ? What are the characteristics of creative people ?

Two methods of approach to these problems suggest themselves : (*a*) by way of theory—what is the nature of creative thinking ? (*b*) by way of practical investigation—what are creative people like, and can the creative traits be detected by tests ?

The Theoretical Approach

The first approach, by way of theory, has been tried by an American psychologist, J. P. Guilford, with the aid of factorial analysis.[1]

Broadly speaking, factorial analysis is a mathematical procedure by which the correlations between scores on a series of tests can be analysed into a number of aspects or factors of intellect or personality. Guilford reported that his experiments and analysis of productive thinking operations revealed two new factors which generate new information from already known and memorized information. These, following a suggestion made some years earlier by the American psychologist R. S. Woodworth, he has called ' convergent ' and ' divergent ' thinking.

He identifies convergent thinking with intellectual operations which concentrate (or converge) upon one unique answer, or upon the most correct or best-fitting answer to a problem. Examples of convergent thinking are definitions of words, analogies, eduction of relations and correlates, completion of serial orders—the type of thinking required, in fact, by the usual test of intelligence. Examples have been given above (see p. 324). Divergent thinking is identified with intellectual operations required by open-ended problems and tests. Here, thoughts go in different directions. The thinker seeks a variety of responses, particularly uncommon responses. No single correct or best answer is required ; the emphasis is on a number of different answers.

Guilford suggests that divergent thinking is evoked by tests of :

[1] " The Structure of Intellect," in *Psych. Bull.*, 53, No. 4, 1956. " Three Faces of Intellect," Bingham Memorial Lecture, Stanford University, April 1959. " Implications of Research on Creativity," in C. Banks and P. L. Broadhurst (eds.), *Stephanos. Studies in Psychology* (University of London Press, 1965). See also article in S. Wiseman (ed.), *Intelligence and Ability* (Penguin U.P.S. 5), pp. 218–237.

(*a*) word fluency—think of as many words as you can which begin with ' s ' or end in ' tion.'

(*b*) ideational fluency—think of as many things as you can which are round and edible.

(*c*) spontaneous flexibility—think of as many different uses as possible for a brick, a barrel, a piece of paper, etc.

(*d*) associational fluency—think of words which have the same or similar meanings as ' good ' ; or are the opposite to ' hard.'

(*e*) expressive fluency—a facility for the rapid forming of phrases and sentences.

(*f*) adaptive flexibility—solving problems with matchsticks.

(*g*) originality—thinking up clever titles for short stories ; writing ' punch ' lines for cartoons ; producing ' catchy ' advertisements for cosmetics, detergents, or beans !

Guilford's divergent-thinking factor has been identified with originality, and, correctly or not, it has been tacitly assumed in many quarters that these open-ended tests can be used to detect original thinkers who are, more likely than not, to be creative persons in later life. The alacrity with which these identifications have ' caught on ' arouses the suspicion that just as ' intelligence ' has been operationally defined as what the intelligence tests test, so creativity may be defined operationally as what is revealed by responses to " Think of as many words ... ; as many uses ... ; as many synonyms ; etc." before it has been proved beyond question that pupils who excel at these operations will be the creative writers, artists, engineers, and scientists of the next generation.

The connexion of fluency of ideas and flexibility of thinking with originality had been suggested by several authorities previously. Galton supposed that " extreme fluency and a vivid and rapid imagination are gifts naturally and healthfully possessed by those who rise to be great orators or literary men."[1] Binet said that intellectual activity is revealed most clearly by an abundant flow of ideas. Sir Cyril Burt followed up Binet's suggestion by designing tests. He found indications of a factor for productive imagination or inventiveness after the influence of general intelligence had been allowed for. He went on to say that most experienced teachers seem strongly of the opinion that fertility of imagination is by no means an automatic result of high intelligence ; that it is often shown by

[1] *Inquiries into Human Faculty*, 2nd Edition (Everyman, 1951), p. 147.

pupils with comparatively low I.Q.'s and may be absent in many whose intelligence is exceptionally good.[1] In studies of London school-children Hargreaves found a factor which he called 'fluency.' Tests for factors of 'fluency' and 'flexibility' had been devised by research workers in the late Professor Spearman's department (University College, London) in 1930.[2]

The Practical Approach.   What are Manifestly Creative People Like?

An American psychologist, D. W. Mackinnon, organized an investigation into the characteristics of people who have realized *their creative potential in actual performance*—writers, architects, mathematicians, industrial researchers, physical scientists, and engineers.[3] Mackinnon's results, summarized here, refer to creative architects.

Architectural experts in the U.S.A. nominated a number of what they considered to be the most outstandingly creative architects at the time of the investigation : forty of these agreed to be tested by means of " problem-solving experiments ; tests designed to discover what a person does not know or is unable or unwilling to reveal about himself ; by tests and questionnaires that permit a person to manifest various aspects of his personality and to express his attitudes, interests, and values ; by searching interviews that cover the life history and reveal the present structure of the person ; and by specially-contrived social situations of a stressful character which call for the subject's best behaviour in a socially defined role." These were Architects I.   By way of comparison, two other groups comparable with group I in age and location of practice—Architects II, who had worked for at least two years with Architects I, and Architects III, who had never worked with members of the first group—were studied.

Mackinnon's criteria of creativity were three in number :

[1] See " The Structure of the Mind," in S. Wiseman (ed.), *Intelligence and Ability*, p. 201.

[2] See R. B. Cattell, *The Scientific Analysis of Personality* (Penguin, 1965), p. 104 ; P. E. Vernon, *The Structure of Human Abilities* (Methuen, 1950), pp. 50–53.

[3] Investigations carried on between 1956 and 1962 in the University of California.   See " The Nature and Nurture of Creative Talent," Bingham Memorial Lecture, Yale University, 1962, reported in the *American Psychologist*, Vol. 17, p. 484, and " Personality and the Realization of Creative Potential," *American Psychologist*, Vol. 20, No. 4.

(a) Production of a response or an idea which is novel, or at least very uncommon.

(b) Mere novelty or originality is not sufficient—the creative person must have produced work which is usefully adaptive ; it must serve to solve a problem ; fit a situation ; accomplish some recognizable objective.

(c) The creative person must sustain the original insight, evaluate it, elaborate it, develop it to the full. In other words, the originality must be practically realized.

Mackinnon rejected the so-called tests of creativity which ask for unusual or uncommon responses. These may reveal infrequent or original ideas in response to specific test items, but " fail to reveal the extent to which the subject faced with real life problems is likely to produce solutions that are novel and adaptive and which he will be motivated to apply in all their ramifications."

Concerning the differences found between the more and less creative groups more will be said later. For our immediate purpose two results are significant :

(a) We have found within our creative samples essentially zero relationship (between intelligence and creativeness) and this is not due to a narrow restriction of the range of intelligence. Among creative architects who have an average score of 113 on the Terman Concept Mastery Test (1956) individual scores range widely from 39 to 179 yet scores on this *test of intelligence* correlate —·08 with rated creativity. Over the whole range of intelligence and creativity there is, of course, a positive relationship between the two variables. No feeble-minded subjects have shown up in any of our creative groups. It is clear, however, that above a certain required minimum level of intelligence which varies from field to field and in some cases may be surprisingly low, being more intelligent does not guarantee a corresponding increase in creativeness. It is just not true that the more intelligent person is, necessarily, the more creative one.

(b) As a result of a test of word association it was found that the unusualness of mental associations given by the creative group was one of the best predictors of creative ability. This applies to unusual as opposed to rare, bizarre, or remote associations.

There is, therefore, some practical justification for the use of these association tests.

Mackinnon suggests, further, that in selecting students for special training of their talent the importance of intelligence may have been over-emphasized by requiring too high an I.Q. regardless

N

of other factors. " If a person has the minimum of intelligence required for mastery of a field of knowledge, whether or not he performs creatively or banally . . . will be crucially determined by non-intellective factors." More attention should be paid in schools and colleges to non-intellective traits of temperament and motivation.

Again, it was found that, on the average, these creative architects earned about B grades in academic work in school. *When they were interested* they could turn in an A performance but in courses which failed to strike their imagination they were quite willing to do no work at all ! Consequently, they were not easy to teach. Nor were they all popular with their teachers.

A similar conclusion has been expressed in a review of a book *Cradles of Eminence* :

> Many people find it difficult to accept that eminent persons can be highly opinionative ; have failure-prone fathers ; are from both troubled and not-so-troubled homes ; experience considerable psychological discomfort during childhood and dislike school. Many of them took time off from school and this seemed to serve as a key to future achievement. Many were regarded by their teachers as mentally retarded. Some were outstanding in one field and neglected others. Many of their teachers apparently confused conformity with achievement ; these children were learning much on their own but not in the schools' way.[1]

Karl von Frisch has been described as one of the greatest experimental zoologists of his time. Among other achievements he succeeding in interpreting the ' dance language ' of honey-bees. Yet,

> He was never good at school ; had no gift for languages or mathematics, and it was touch and go whether he would be able to matriculate. Such a boy would probably fail to gain a university place in England today[2]—as indeed would Darwin, a sobering thought for those concerned with university organisation and admission. All Karl's youthful energies were given to collecting animals and plants in his mountain home ; nothing else seemed worth while.[3]

---

[1] Authors of the book are V. and M. Goertzel. Published by Little, Brown, Boston, U.S.A., 1962. See *Contemporary Psychology*, XI, January 1, 1966.

[2] He would, probably, have failed the 11 + selection test and have finished up in a secondary-modern school (unless, of course, his parents could afford to pay high fees for private schooling).

[3] W. H. Thorpe, F.R.S., in *The Guardian*, June 23, 1967.

Hudson[1] states that evidence from his own as well as the investigations of others indicates not that the general factor theory of intelligence is mistaken, but that for many practical purposes it is irrelevant. " The crucial fact is that a knowledge of a boy's I.Q. is of little help *if you are faced with a form full of clever boys*. The boy with the lowest I.Q. in the form is almost as likely to get top marks as the boy with the highest." The academically successful boy is distinguished, not by his intellectual apparatus, but by the use he sees fit to make of it. " Somebody with an I.Q. of 170 is more likely to think well than someone whose I.Q. is 70, but the relation seems to break down when one is comparing two people both of whose I.Q.'s are relatively high."[2] He says, further, that the intelligence tests cannot be discarded, that they perform perfectly well the functions for which they were conceived—namely, the rapid and impersonal assessment of intellectual ability in the population as a whole.

> Over a wide spectrum of ability the intelligence test gives quite a good indication of a child's ability at school. Difficulties arise only when the I.Q. is thought of as a precise measure of mental horse-power. It is nothing of the sort . . . it does not follow that all boys of I.Q. 110 will do better at ' O ' Level than all boys of I.Q. 90 . . . above a certain point a high I.Q. is of little advantage.[3]

Hudson believes that for success in science a high I.Q. is of little advantage above 125. (The average I.Q. for the whole population is 100.)

A similar condition seems to mark the probability of success in practical teaching. In 1933 I made a survey of the records of some 760 students in a university professional training department. Records were available for intelligence, academic achievement, previous teaching experience, and marks gained in the professional examinations at the end of the training year. In this group the correlations between intelligence, academic-degree status, theory marks, teaching experience previous to the professional training year, and the marks for practical teaching competence at the end of the training year, were all low ; too low to justify using any of them to predict later teaching competence.

[1] Book cited, p. 108.
[2] Book cited, p. 30.
[3] Book cited, p. 105. This book should be made compulsory reading for all Heads and teachers in grammar schools.

The table of correlations shows that there is not a single factor dealt with in this analysis which, taken by itself, could be used as any sort of reliable guide to future teaching success or failure. In addition, the men and women provide two separate problems ; criteria which might be useful in the one case would afford practically no guidance in the other. Pre-college teaching experience of at least one year duration of the uncertificated assistant type in the case of men and academic record in the case of women are the only factors in this sample of students which might be used as a possible guide to future success and the predictive value of these is not high. All the evidence suggests that given a minimum of academic ability and intelligence, success in teaching is most strongly determined by qualities of personality, temperament and character for which, as yet [in 1933], there are no very adequate tests. There seems to be a limit beyond which the possession of a pleasant personality, force of character, sympathy and tact will not compensate for intellectual defects but this limit seems to be well down in the intellectual scale, at least for primary and probably a good deal of secondary school work.

The clearest differences between the very good and the relatively poor practical teachers were those related to strong and attractive personality, enterprise, self-confidence, initiative, resourcefulness, industry, energy, and adaptability, all characteristics which have later been shown to be related to creativity.[1]

Summarizing : Evidence from different investigations shows that the relations between I.Q., as measured by standardized tests and academic status, on the one hand, and creative success later, on the other, are complex. Neither I.Q. nor academic ability by itself affords a reliable criterion of future creativity.

Processes of Association as Tests for Creativity

Guilford's factor analyses of intellectual abilities led him to postulate the identification of divergent thinking with factors of fluency and flexibility of mental associations. Rightly or wrongly, it has been assumed that divergent thinking can also be equated with originality and creativity. Mackinnon found that his highly creative architects made higher than average scores on his word-association tests. Moreover, from the reports of highly creative people about their own thought processes, it is obvious that

---

[1] A. Pinsent, " Pre-college Teaching Experience and Other Factors in the Teaching Success of University Students," in *Brit. Jnl. Educational Psychology*, Vol. III, Parts II and III, 1935.

fluency of associations has been a factor in their work. Thus Einstein has said in answer to a questionnaire about his working methods :

> Words or language as they are written or spoken do not seem to play any role in my mechanism of thought. The physical entities which seem to serve as elements of thought are certain signs and more or less clear images which can be voluntarily reproduced *and combined* . . . this *combinatory play* seems to be the essential feature in productive thought.[1]

Samuel Taylor Coleridge, poet and philosopher, author of *The Ancient Mariner* and *Kubla Khan*, said that facts which sank at intervals out of conscious recollection drew together beneath the surface through the almost chemical affinities of common elements. Poincaré, the eminent French mathematician, describing processes of mathematical discovery said that :

> it does not consist in making combinations of mathematical entities already known. . . . Discovery consists precisely in *constructing combinations* that are useful, an infinitely small minority . . . discovery is discernment, selection. . . . Mathematical facts worthy of being studied are those which, by their analogy with other facts, are capable of conducting us to the knowledge of a mathematical law. . . . They are those which reveal unsuspected relations between other facts long since known but wrongly believed to be unrelated to each other. . . . The most fruitful combinations are those formed of elements borrowed from widely separated domains.[2]

In another passage he describes how " a host of ideas kept surging in my head ; I could almost feel them jostling one another until two of them coalesced, so to speak, to form a stable combination."

Thus descriptions of creative thinking refer again and again to processes of playing with images and ideas ; to making new associations ; to breaking up already known idea-systems and re-combining them in associations not previously thought of ; to an upsurge of ideas.

It is not surprising, therefore, that various forms of association tests have been widely used to detect creative potential in studies of the relation between intelligence and creativity.

---

[1] Quoted by Koestler in *The Act of Creation*. My italics.
[2] *Science and Method* (Nelson), pp. 50–51.

The Relation between Intelligence and the Results on Tests of Association

Two American psychologists, Getzels and Jackson,[1] asked whether creative ability can be identified in advance before there has been creative achievement in later life. The I.Q., they say, has been used as if it measured the totality of the human mind and imagination. Common observation indicates a difference between memorizing, and discovering and inventing, which seems to have been ignored in the rush to apply intelligence-test procedure to everything from grouping children in the kindergarten to selecting students for graduate work. I.Q. is not necessarily synonymous with creativity. The ability to define words or memorize digits backwards may indicate very little about ability to produce new associations or restructure stereotyped situations.

The authors wondered, therefore, whether it might be possible to select groups of pupils, one high in I.Q., another high in creativity, and compare their characteristics. They invented or adapted five tests for creativity :

(i) Word association—think of as many definitions as possible for certain common, ambiguous stimulus words—*e.g.*, 'bolt,' 'bark,' 'sack.' The scores here were (*a*) the absolute number of definitions, and (*b*) the number of different classes into which the definitions could be assigned.

(ii) Uses for things—think of as many different uses as possible for common objects—*e.g.*, a brick, a paper-clip, a toothpick. Again the scores depended on the number and the unusualness of the responses.

(iii) Distinguishing hidden shapes in complex designs.

(iv) Unfinished fables—subjects were presented with fables, of which the last line was missing. They were told to supply three different endings : moralistic, humorous, and sad.

(v) Make up problems—four complex paragraphs were presented, each containing many numerical statements. The subjects were told to make up as many mathematical problems as possible from the information given. They were not required to solve the problems, not even to know how to solve them. The test was for an ability to *see* a problem in a complex situation. It is often more important to be aware of a problem than to be able to solve it.

[1] *Creativity and Intelligence. Explorations with Gifted Students* (Wiley, 1963).

Getzels and Jackson worked on the assumption that there are two types of personality and two types of thinking process—that measured by the standard I.Q. test and that measured by their tests of divergent thinking. Accordingly they hoped to identify two groups of pupils—one high in I.Q. and one high in ' creativity ' (more accurately, perhaps, a group scoring high on its divergent-thinking tests). Their survey was carried out in a private school near Chicago. The parents of the testees were mainly in university, professional, managerial, and ' white-collar ' occupations. The average I.Q. of the pupils was high.

292 boys and 241 girls were tested. From the total population two sub-groups were selected :

(i) The High Creative Group—these were in the top 20 per cent. in scores on the creativity tests, but *below* the top 20 per cent. in I.Q. (fifteen boys, eleven girls).

(ii) The High I.Q. Group—in the top 20 per cent. on I.Q. scores, but *below* the top 20 per cent. on the creativity scores (seventeen boys, eleven girls).

The results were, perhaps, surprising. In I.Q. the average of the whole school was 132 ; that of the High I.Q. Group was 150 ; of the High Creative Group 127 : *a difference in favour of the High I.Q. pupils of 23 points.* In academic achievement the school average was 49·9 ; that of the High I.Q. Group 55 ; that of the High Creatives 56. Here then was a group of pupils considerably lower in I.Q., the usually accepted criterion of academic ability, who were at least equal if not superior *in academic status* to the High I.Q. Group.

As the authors say :

The members of the high I.Q. group possess the demonstrated ability to perform with excellence in the type of problem-solving tasks common to the conventional intelligence test. They do not, apparently, possess the ability to perform with the same excellence on the type of cognitive tasks included in the ' creativity ' instruments. They may be able to define the word ' homunculus ' with ease, or to supply quickly the unique missing digit in a number series but they have less facility with problems requiring them to think of several novel uses for a stereotyped object like a brick, or a new ending to a familiar fable.

The reverse is true for the members of the high creativity grou p They do not do as well as the high I.Q. subjects on the intelligence-test problems. But their performance is very striking indeed on tasks calling for inventiveness and originality. Although they may not be able to give the meaning of the word ' homunculus ' or to complete a number series with the same precision and rapidity as the high I.Q.'s they are able to think with surprising facility of using a brick as a bed warmer, a weapon, or, if necessary, as a paper-weight, and they are able to create novel twists to fables almost at will.[1]

If these differences are not restricted to pupils of exceptional ability, but can be found, if only to a lesser degree, in the general population, then they present a challenge which must be taken seriously.   If the schools are to pick out and develop the pupils with ' creative ' gifts as well as those with high I.Q.'s it would seem necessary not only to invent and apply ' creativity ' tests as well as I.Q. tests ; it would seem necessary also to consider carefully the whole question of school organization, curricula, and, particularly, methods of teaching.

Moreover, if teacher ratings of superior students and the standards of university-selection committees are heavily weighted in favour of the higher I.Q.'s and academic achievement, as they undoubtedly are, then some at least of the pupils and students who possess the now desirable creativity abilities are being passed over in the competition for places in institutions of higher education.   That this danger is real has been indicated in several investigations.   Teachers, by and large, prefer to have the academically good, higher-I.Q. pupils and students in their classes.   They are more conforming, less disconcerting, and therefore easier to manage.   They do not ask so many awkward questions.

Getzels' and Jackson's results were confirmed in the case of children in a selective private school, four primary schools, a public high school, and two samples of graduate students.[2]

Some Doubts

These results are so contrary to much traditional educational thought and practice that it is easy to misinterpret them.   Apart from the question of the relation between these divergent-thinking tests and later real creative achievement, other queries arise in connexion with Getzels' and Jackson's work.   For example :

(a) Do the differences noted above occur only in the cases of
      exceptionally gifted children ?

[1] Book cited, pp. 20–21.
[2] See E. P. Torrance, *Education and the Creative Potential* (University of Minnesota Press).

(*b*) Could the results have been affected by the way in which the tests were administered ?

(*c*) Are we dealing with a general factor of creativity which is independent of intelligence ? In other words, are *all* the high I.Q.'s deficient in creativity, or is it possible to find individuals who are high in creativity as well as in I.Q. ?

My own experience with respect to these creativity tests may be pertinent here.

I cannot resist a challenge. Just as a mountaineer must climb every mountain he sees, I cannot resist the challenge of a test. It is always intriguing to find what is one's standing on some new type of test. If one succeeds it contributes to one's self-enhancement ; if one fails one can always blame the tests.

Anyway, I couldn't resist trying the tests used by Getzels and Jackson, and Torrance. The result was appalling. My creativity was approximately zero. However, other evidence might suggest that my creativity was not quite so conspicuously absent as the tests indicated. So it did seem possible that there were some defects in the tests or their administration.

(i) The tests were timed. Getzels and Jackson state that although no time-limit was set in the instructions, subjects required approximately 15 to 30 minutes to complete the test. In one case $3\frac{1}{2}$ minutes were stipulated. Some wit has said that the human brain starts to work at birth, if not before, but it stops working as soon as one stands up to speak in public. If I am told " You have *x* minutes in which to be original " my brain stops dead. I need time to think. I found that I could produce plenty of common associations fairly soon. Then the supply dried up. The more uncommon and, in this case by definition, original responses did not appear until in some cases hours or even days later.

The Getzels and Jackson tests were given to a *group* of pupils at the same time. Now, many examinees must have experienced that sinking feeling in the pit of the stomach when other people begin quite briskly to hand in papers, when they themselves are still sweating blood to think of some elusive answer. Even though no time-limit was prescribed, the conditions of administration suggested a limit. If creativity is to be equated with speed, then a time-limit is legitimate. But is it ? Many of the most creative products in the history of human thought have been a long time maturing—weeks, months, even years.

(ii) Some of the responses in the unusual-uses test—what could you do with a brick, a barrel, a piece of paper?—seemed altogether too frivolous—indeed, too crapulously silly for words. For myself, I have to get into a silly mood in order to produce silly answers. It seemed to me that this particular ' creativity ' test was measuring not real creativity of thought, but personality traits due either to innate factors of temperament or to the influences of home and social culture. If the psychoanalysts are to be believed some associations lie so deeply repressed in the ' unconscious ' that a special technique is necessary to bring them to the surface. And, in people with conventional attitudes, some uncommon uses for a barrel, a cap, or a piece of paper would be rejected as too perfectly shocking as soon as they appeared in consciousness. The point is— does divergent thinking indicate a certain irresponsibility, a gay insouciance which produces a superficial wit but not highly useful creative products? One also wondered whether the separation suggested by Getzels and Jackson between intelligence and ' creativity ' was as wide, or irrevocable, as they implied. Is it possible to find people with high I.Q.'s who are *also* high creatives and vice versa? Would these ' creativity ' tests pick out a set of cheerful, blatantly unashamed punsters or some offensively jolly, self-confident ' smart alecs '? It is true that Getzels and Jackson gave credit for *uncommon* responses as well as for the total number of responses produced. However, the criterion for uncommonness was uniqueness : a response was uncommon if it emerged only once or not more than a specified number of times in the whole test group. Thus ' to steal ' was one uncommon response for the use of a watch ! On another occasion an answer to the question " In what ways are milk and meat alike ? " was " They are both Government-inspected." If uncommonness alone is equated with creativity these two responses would get equal credit, which seems unrealistic unless one is searching for creativity in crime. It would appear that a fairer estimate of a creative response should be based on uncommonness and *appropriateness* for some worth-while purpose.

On the other hand, it may be argued that the greater the absolute number of associative responses, the greater the likelihood of a really useful creative response emerging. Some of the really creative ideas in mathematics, science, economics, and military hardware, for example, have seemed to contemporary opinion as too wild for words ; certainly too wild and preposterous to be entertained seriously by intelligent people. It would seem then that to encourage creative productivity a permissive atmosphere is essential when the ' censor ' is for the time being taken off and anything goes. Later, the unusual associations can be evaluated and the promising ones sorted out and used.

Further Investigations

Fortunately for my sadly mutilated self-image, further investigations have answered some of my queries. M. A. Wallach and N. Kogan undertook a survey of *Modes of Thinking in Young Children*, a study of the creativity-intelligence distinction.[1]   They began with the question—is there a general factor of creativity independent of a general factor of intelligence ?   And is it justifiable to speak of creativity *and* intelligence as if the two variables were independent ?   They suggest, rather, that the two found by Getzels and Jackson are related.   The correlation among their several tests of creativity is positive but low ;   so is the correlation between any of the creative tests with I.Q.   The correlation between any of the creativity tests and I.Q. is as big as the correlation of these tests among themselves.   It is not justifiable, therefore, to speak of a general factor of creativity which is independent of I.Q.   It is more realistic to think of different creative abilities each representing different mental operations having in common only what is involved in intelligence.   Therefore it is desirable to study a population as a whole rather than specially selected groups of highly gifted individuals.   Are ' convergent ' thinkers necessarily uncreative ?

Further, Wallach and Kogan object to timed tests.   In fact, they dislike any situation likely to appear to be a test or an examination.   They suggest that " in order really to discover how able a person is at the production of unique associates it is necessary to allow the person a great deal of time.   In fact it may well be desirable to allow the person as much time as he wants."   The authors quote experiments which indicate that in certain situations it has been found that the *lower the rate* of production of associative responses, the *greater the number* of responses that were produced.   Also, that later appearing responses are more remote and unusual than earlier ones.[2]   Again, there must be a relaxed and permissive atmosphere if the creative abilities are to have the maximum encouragement to appear.   The reports of creative individuals

[1] Published by Holt, Rinehart and Winston, Inc., New York and London, 1965.
[2] Book cited, p. 18.

about their own thought processes show the fact of a certain freedom from evaluation ; they suggest " that the associative processes possess some degree of functional autonomy from the observer, rather than being under his control. Critical faculties, censors, are to some extent stilled when the generation of cognitive elements is to be encouraged. The tendencies which direct a person toward selecting a single correct answer are replaced by a non-directive *carte blanche* attitude that provides a license for production of a freer kind." These suggestions about the necessity for ample time for contemplation, for a relaxed permissive atmosphere, and for the absence of *destructive* criticism are immensely important for the encouragement of creative responses in school work.

Wallach and Kogan believe that the condition most likely to encourage productive thinking is a stimulating situation *resembling play* rather than an examination or testing situation. Their research workers were introduced informally to the children to be studied as visitors interested in children's games some time before the investigation began, and the ' tasks ' were proposed to the pupils, individually, as part of a game. No precise requests were made for cleverness, unusual responses, or originality. All communication was oral ; no writing was required. The ' games ' were as follows :

(a) Instances : name all the round things that you can think of ; things which will make a noise ; square things ; things that move on wheels.

(b) Alternate uses : name all the different ways you could use a newspaper, knife, cork, shoe, key, etc.

(c) Similarities : tell all the ways a potato and a carrot, milk and meat, etc., are alike.

(d) Pattern meanings : children were shown some line patterns and asked to tell all the things each complete drawing could be.

(e) Line meanings : tell all the things the lines make you think of.

In addition, tests for I.Q. and academic achievement were given.

In this investigation the creativity measures correlated relatively highly among themselves ; so did the I.Q. tests. The correlations between the creativity and the I.Q. measures were relatively low. The authors claim, therefore, that they provided a working definition of creativity independent of intelligence *as measured by I.Q. tests.*

On the evidence of scores in the two types of ability, Wallach and Kogan were able to distinguish four groups of children :

(a) Those with high I.Q. and high creativity.
(b) Those with high I.Q. and lower creativity.
(c) Those with lower I.Q. and high creativity.
(d) Those with lower I.Q. and lower creativity.

The remaining sections of the investigation dealt with the characteristics of these four types and their behaviour in school. For our purpose the major interest and importance of these results is in the fact that there are children with high I.Q. and correspondingly lower creativity, and children with relatively low I.Q. and high creativity.[1] High creativity—that is, a high degree of fluency, mental flexibility, and inventiveness—can occur with both higher and lower I.Q. ; low creativity can be associated with both higher and lower I.Q. If, therefore, the schools are to detect and foster creativity as defined by these measures it will not suffice to pick out those who excel in I.Q. and academic work only.

Can Originality and Creativity be Trained ?   If so, how ?

If, as now seems to have been established, originality and creativity as defined by these tests of fluency, mental flexibility, and inventiveness can be detected in school pupils, the question arises—can these abilities be improved by training ? If so, how ? Further, will the improvement transfer from the training situation to other activities ?

This problem has been studied notably by Maltzman and colleagues.[2] They take up a Behaviourist standpoint and propose to use the process of operant conditioning as the means of encouraging originality. It will be remembered from the discussion about mechanisms of learning that in operant conditioning, when a response has actually been made, the probability of its happening again can be increased by rewarding it. Maltzman argued that if some means could be found to stimulate the production of original responses they could then be rewarded (reinforced) and thus encouraged. A response cannot be rewarded until it has happened. By definition

[1] Relatively low I.Q. As Mackinnon said, " No feeble-minded subjects have shown up in any of our creative groups."

[2] " On the Training of Originality," in *Psych. Review*, 67, 4, 1960. " Experimental Studies in the Training of Originality," in *Psych. Monog.*, Vol. 74, No. 6, Whole No. 493, 1960.

an original response is an unusual or an uncommon response. It may not happen in any given situation. At best, it will happen only infrequently. The problem of training by operant conditioning is, therefore, the production of original responses in the first place. How can this be done ?

Reference to other studies suggests that the technique of word associations might be effective. Consider Maier's two-string problem. Two lengths of string are to be tied together, but they are set so far apart that a person holding one string cannot reach the other. The only other object in view is a screwdriver. The problem can be solved by tying the screwdriver to string A, making a pendulum which can then be made to swing. When it is swinging in a wide arc the operator can hold the string B and the swing of the 'pendulum' will bring the end of string A to hand (see Fig. 30).

FIG. 30

Maier's problem had been offered to two groups of subjects. The first group were told to solve the problem, no aid being given. A second group had preparatory training during which they learned lists of words, some containing all three words 'rope,' 'swing,' and 'pendulum,' some two of the words, some one, some none. It was found that the subjects who learned the lists which included the suggestive words solved the problem more successfully than the untrained group.

In another series of trials the two strings were displayed together with a heavy screwdriver and a piece of very light balsa wood. Some subjects read lists of unusual uses, or lists of possible uses, for a screwdriver, balsa wood, and string (not directly applicable to the string problem). Some subjects had no preparatory training. The group trained with the word lists solved the string problem more successfully than the untrained group. Thus it seemed reasonable to suppose that word lists could be used to stimulate the production of unusual responses.

The experimental method in the training for originality series resembled that used in transfer trials :

(i) A first list of 25 words was presented to all the subjects with the instruction : respond as quickly as possible with the first word which comes to mind.

(ii) A training period ; different techniques for different sub-groups.

(iii) A second list of 25 words different from the first list. Same instruction. All subjects.

(iv) After the second word list all subjects had an ' unusual-uses test ' : give as many uses as you can think of for a motor tyre ; a key (to open a lock) ; a safety-pin ; a watch (to tell the time) ; a button (fastener) ; a pair of spectacles.

During the training period the following procedures were used. The subjects, 292 psychology students, were divided into five groups :

(i)   Control group C1 had the first list once only.

(ii) Control group C2 had five additional presentations of the first list. They were told to give the *same response each time* to any given stimulus word.

(iii) Experimental group E1 had a single presentation of the first list, followed by 125 common words, and the same instructions.

(iv) Experimental group E2 had a single presentation of the first list, followed by 125 uncommon words, and the same instructions.

(v)   Experimental group E3 had five additional presentations of the first list with the instruction to give a response to each word *different from any previous response.*

The results of interest to our present discussion were :

(*a*) The three experimental groups produced more responses to the second list of 25 words. They also produced more uses in the unusual-uses test than the two control groups.

(*b*) The experimental group E3, who had practised giving a *different* response to each of the five additional presentations of the first 25-word list, was more successful in producing unusual (*i.e.*, original) responses on the second 25-word list than the control group, which had practised giving the *same* responses on the five additional presentations of the first list.

(*c*) The experimental group E3 also produced the most unusual responses on the unusual-uses test, which, it should be noted, had been given to all groups *without any preliminary practice* in unusual uses. In other words, the practice in giving *different* responses to each of a number of presentations of the same training list of 25 words not only improved performance on the second (test) list of 25 words, but it *transferred to another operation different in kind from the training operation.*

The most probable explanation of this result is that the instruction " Give a different response . . . " set up a learning ' set ' which favoured the search for more original responses, and checked the tendency to produce stereotyped responses ; and that this ' set ' carried over to a different operation.

With respect to the influence of reinforcement, some of Maltzman's subjects were rewarded with a " Good " at intervals from the experimenter. Surprisingly, from the Behaviourist point of view, some of the subjects in the successful experimental group E3 did as well without any apparent reinforcement. The author, concerned to save the Behaviourist appearances, suggests that an original response is its own reward. In the first place, thinking of a different response for each of five separate presentations of a stimulus word can be a difficult, frustrating, indeed painful, process. The production of a different response, therefore, is equivalent to a release from tension, an escape from an unpleasant situation; that is a reward. It seems equally likely that the production of an original response satisfies the desire for achievement, enhances the self-image of the producer, raises his confidence level. Nothing succeeds like success—a principle continuously to be borne in mind in teaching.

Implications for Education and Teaching

It remains to state some of the implications of the work on originality and creativity for schools and teachers.

1. There are more ways than one of being clever.

There are, it would seem, two different types of intellectual operations for which the names 'convergent' and 'divergent' thinking have been suggested. Note, however, that these terms refer to intellectual operations, and *not* to persons. It is possible for the same individual to think divergently as well as convergently. Which he will do in any particular case will depend on mood, on the task in hand, and on the situation. It is still more important, schools and teachers being what they are, to note that *some pupils think divergently more easily and proficiently than they think convergently.*

Convergent thinking is predominantly academic—verbal, abstract, formally logical : good for success in the orthodox, standardized intelligence test where the emphasis is on one unique, correct, or best possible answer. It is good also for academic success. Strongly convergent thinkers tend to play safe, to favour the conventional, conformist type of behaviour, to seek the one correct answer.

Divergent thinking is more characteristic of the inventive, flexible person, fluent in associations of ideas, spontaneous, not always strictly logical ; of the person whose intellectual interests and operations go in different directions, bringing knowledge and skills together from different types of subject-matter : curious, enterprising, clever in different ways—*e.g.*, literary, musical, dramatic, constructive design. Predominantly divergent thinkers are much more likely to produce uncommon and unusual associations between ideas. They break up habitual associations, reshuffle them, play with images and ideas, recombine them into fruitful new suggestions. They are open to experiences, more interested in the meanings and implications of observations than in mere facts. They are sensitive to new problems, seeing problems where none were suspected before. Creative divergers are more than usually self-confident, self-assured, non-conformist, unconventional, witty and playful in their dealings with ideas. They are more adventurous, willing to 'have a go,' more independent of other people's standards, values, and opinions. They are guessers rather than gleaners.

In school they may be misfits, something of a nuisance in the classroom, less than normally interested in routine academic work and therefore apt to be undervalued by the teaching staff. This is unfortunate, since it is from the predominantly divergent thinkers that original ideas and creative enterprise are more likely to appear. Professor Musgrove's schoolboy correspondent who felt in school like a chicken being stuffed was probably a diverger. The replies to

Musgrove's questionnaires are particularly interesting in the light of the investigations into convergent and divergent thinking.

Schools and teachers, by and large, have tended to prefer and promote the more docile converger above the more turbulent diverger. In view of the need for creative achievement in modern affairs it seems desirable to restore the balance.

2. What can be done to encourage originality and creative achievement in schools?

In making these suggestions we are well aware that many schools and schoolmasters are more conventional than creative: geared very closely to examinations; judged by examination results. Only too often the material conditions of schools—buildings, size of classes, lack of a sufficient amount and variety of books and apparatus—interfere seriously with any attempts to create a context favourable to creative achievement. It is desirable, however, that the conditions favourable to originality and creative achievement should be known and organized whenever opportunity arises. The following suggestions are offered with the above qualifications in mind.

(i) Promote a permissive atmosphere in the classroom.

This does *not* mean permitting tomfoolery. It *does* mean allowing opportunity for self-expression. To quote Professor Musgrove again in connexion with his survey of satisfactions: " It is," he says, " in its expressive rather than its instrumental rôle that school falls far short of demand. The major expressive demand is for freedom and self-direction : *freedom to put your own point of view*, to be treated as an individual. . . .[1] The great demand is for self-expression and self-direction . . . ' At school you should have plenty of chance to express your views ' "; not always to feel a prisoner or like a chicken being stuffed. The permissive atmosphere is one in which any original suggestion by a pupil, or any original piece of prose or poetry, is accepted as something to be discussed and considered ; not dismissed with aloof superiority or cold disdain, certainly not with ridicule. One experience of that sort is likely to suppress any original work for the rest of a pupil's school life. Koestler has said that Copernicus refused to publish his heliocentric theory, not because he feared an unfavourable reaction from the

---

[1] Book cited, pp. 112, 114, 115. My italics.

ecclesiastical authorities, but because he feared the ridicule of contemporary astronomers. Caldwell Cook, who made experiments in creative education, has said :

> The development of personality demands freedom of expression and every opportunity for the exercise of originality. . . . The teacher must take care not to thwart natural inclination and yet at the same time insure that the efforts of his pupils do not run away into fantastic conceits, blind imitation, affected novelty or sheer tomfoolery. He must know a good thing when he sees it and must neither let pass unchallenged any work which the author could improve, nor reject as unfit anything which has life in it and true inspiration however feebly showing. He must be ready to set aside all convention in method, all blind rigidity or discipline and pin his faith on no stereotyped formulae. There is a different way every day.[1]

In fact, good teaching for originality needs a touch of genius in the teacher.

(ii) Originality and creative work need time for contemplation, for incubation.

Hughes Mearns, an American who has done much for the encouragement of creative writing in schools, compared what he called product-education and creative education :[2]

> A vast difference between the two systems is that each has its own notion of the use of time ; and one must regard this difference, otherwise disappointment and depression are sure to follow those who set up to practise the new way. The standardised curricular education requires ' results ' each day, each week, surely each month, with an accumulated measurable outcome at the end of each term ; creative education thinks in terms of years, and even in spans of years. . . . After reading an enthusiastic book on the creative side, or hearing a modern school lecturer, some teachers go forth to their classes, rap for order, explain the idea, then with the best intentions assign a lesson in ' creative work.' They are disappointed when they do not get a roomful of results the next day. ' Fraud ' they are apt to cry and give up forever.

Creative work needs time to develop. The reports of creative writers, inventors, mathematicians, indicate quite clearly that much

[1] See Hughes Mearns, *Creative Power*, 2nd Revised Edition (Dover Publications, 1959), p. 39.
[2] Book cited, p. 34.

of the ' creative work ' during the incubation period goes on in the ' unconscious depths ' of the mind, in fantasy, in day-dreaming.[1]

(iii) Provide a stimulating situation.

This means, first, providing to the greatest degree possible in the circumstances a variety of first-hand experience. Associations do not grow in a vacuum. They grow on the basis of observation, exploration, manipulation, experiment. One feature of predominantly divergent thinkers, noted by all the investigators of creative thinking, is their ' open-ness to experience.' Not experience merely, but a *variety* of experience is desirable. Some teachers, and a few education authorities, have organized residential courses for urban pupils. R. F. Mackenzie, in *Escape from the Classroom*, tells the story of an attempt made by a school in a Scottish mining area to take over a shooting-lodge in the Highlands. Some extracts from the report of one teacher who took part in the enterprise make interesting reading in the context of our present topic :

> Most of the children who came in this party were about fifteen years old and had never been farther north than Perth. The journey was, therefore, rather like a fairyland trip for them. Lunch on Loch Tummel-side was somewhat protracted since it was difficult to drag them away. Some children noticed that some of the trees were growing under water and asked how this could happen. We then explained about the damming of the loch for the hydro-electric scheme and the subsequent water-level rise. This was done briefly but it was *raised again one evening by one of the children* so we discussed, at length, hydro-electric schemes, the grid system, the tremendous number of uses of electricity, the ruination of scenery by pylons and the flooding of some Welsh villages.
>
> This was typical of all the teaching done at Rannoch. *An observation, a comment, and then, after the children had time to ponder on it, further discussion* usually in the evening to leave the days free to observe. In this way we covered forestry commission work, bracken prevention, soil erosion and forest clearance.
>
> On one of our many expeditions we noticed that one region of the forest seemed to have a great many dead trees and most of these looked as though they had been struck by lightning. This led to a multitude of questions. What was lightning, why did it strike things, what did it strike, where did it come from ?[2] ... Stray

---

[1] See A. Koestler, *The Sleepwalkers*, a study of original thinking.
[2] Book cited, p. 16. My italics.

remarks sparked off discussion. As I was reading a newspaper I made a remark about Foster Dulles' illness. Who was Foster Dulles ? What did he do ? What was a Foreign Secretary ? What did people in Government offices do ? A complete evening was spent discussing various items of news. The Notting Hill racial problem, the racial problems as seen in Little Rock and similar situations were discussed. Many of the children had little or no idea of recent events. The causes and background were talked about as long as time allowed. . . . Newspapers became more than pieces of paper with cartoon strips and racing tips. *Since our return to school* many of the children have come to me and made some comment on an article or asked for an explanation of a situation.

As a description of divergent thinking it would be difficult to improve on this extract. There was no unique subject or unique answer. An observation would start off *mental explorations in a number of different directions.* Discussion led to associations. Observations stimulated questions and led to further observations. Moreover, knowledge from a variety of very different fields was included—nature study, elementary science, forestry, foreign affairs, economics. And the ' set ' to inquire spread to the school situation later.

It is necessary to add that not all was sweetness and light. There were some sporadic outbursts of bad behaviour ; some instances of initial lack of interest in the new surroundings. Nevertheless the effect of this permissive atmosphere and the stimulation of new and varied experiences is most instructive for our purpose here.[1]

In addition to variety of first-hand experience, substitute experience in the form of illustrations, films, and television is now available. Further, all schools ought to be provided with a variety of reading matter.

(iv) Reward original work.

As we have noted, operant conditioning is a process of rewarding (reinforcing) a response as soon as possible after it has been made. In this way a similar response is more likely to be made in the future. To quote Mearns again :

" We produce excellent creative work," my friends tell me often, " but it reaches a certain stage and stops. . . . Tell me why ? "

---

[1] See also Sybil Marshall, *Experiment in Education* (Cambridge University Press, 1963).

My invariable answer is that *I so manage the controls that the highest approval goes solely to that work which bears the mark of original invention.* . . . No matter how crude the product judged by the usual standards of adult perfection, the work with the individual touch is given the place of distinction and there it is kept for all to see. Not that other contributors are neglected or made needlessly to feel their lack ; there are many easy devices for the encouragement of those who have not yet found their native tones.[1]

Further :

Those teachers who know how to keep their praise for the good thing just a step in advance of the moving group are agreed upon one other interesting and puzzling phenomenon. The results each year are better than the year before. A new class arrives ; seemingly, one should begin at the beginning ; on the contrary, the immediate product is in advance of last term's beginning. . . . A certain expectation is set up in advance.[2]

A possible explanation may be that recognition of original work does increase the probability of more original work ; it stimulates the desire for achievement ; it organizes a ' set ' for seeking more original responses, which is capable of transfer to other situations.

(v) Mark the distinction between specific facts and skills and general facts and skills.

As we have seen, perceptual patterns, rules, formulae, and generalizations can be transposed from one situation to another. Emphasize them, therefore. Encourage the search for transfer. Stress similarity, analogies, similes, metaphors. Encourage exercises in imaginative play. Bring together and compare ideas from different aspects of knowledge and skill. Associate, connect, associate—not bare facts, but meanings, suggestions, implications. Look for connexions. Avoid being one of what the late T. H. Huxley contemptuously called the hodmen of science—people who collect facts but fail to do anything with them ; the uninspired pedants.

(vi) Present some at least of the subject-matter in mathematics, science, history, geography, and current affairs as problems for discussion and solution rather than as facts to be memorized.

---

[1] Book cited, p. 37. My italics.
[2] Book cited, p. 40. *Cf.* Mace's experiments with a moving average (p. 150).

Encourage self-initiated learning ; provide opportunities for enterprise and ingenuity.[1]

(vii) *Respect* as well as allow suggestions and questions from pupils.

Do not ridicule or freeze them with cold disdain. Remember that most of the really creative ideas in the history of human thought have been ridiculed by so-called scholars and experts, or opposed in anger and their producers ostracized or destroyed ! Don't be an intellectual ' Blimp.'

(viii) Promote hobbies. Encourage early interests and talents.

It has been found in the studies of creative individuals that special interests and talents are better indicators of future creative achievement than either I.Q. or academic status.

Before leaving this problem of training for creativity and originality it is desirable to stress one principle which seems to be forgotten or ignored by some writers on the reform of teaching methods. It is this : creativity and originality do not happen in an intellectual vacuum. Problems cannot be solved in the absence of relevant information, instruction, and knowledge of principles. Originality is not a process of producing ideas out of ignorance. It means putting together in a new combination ideas and principles which have not previously been combined. To be original, it is not necessary—indeed it is not possible—to discover everything by oneself from the very beginning. Facts must be experienced ; theorems memorized and made readily recallable ; generalizations understood. Discovery methods are valuable but they need to be combined with other activities including instruction. Reading can be an activity when one reads in search of information. Moreover, some pupils need guidance and stimulation. Left to themselves they lack initiative and direction. They accept too low standards of efficiency or excellence. They lose confidence, become frustrated or apathetic.

Of this, more later.

Finally, one cannot do better than conclude with Mackinnon's description, on the basis of his studies of creative individuals, of the optimum conditions for creative development. In the following passage read ' teacher ' for ' parent ' and ' school ' for ' family ' :

[1] See, for example, *Science in Secondary Schools* (Ministry of Education Pamphlet No. 38, H.M.S.O.) ; *Mathematics in Primary Schools* (Curriculum Bulletin No. 1, H.M.S.O.).

An extraordinary respect by the parent for the child, and an early granting to him of an unusual freedom in exploring his universe and making decisions for himself ; an expectation that the child will act independently but reasonably and responsibly ; a lack of intense closeness between parent and child so that neither over-dependence is fostered nor a feeling of rejection experienced ; in other words the sort of interpersonal relationship between parent and child which has a liberating effect upon the child ; a plentiful supply in the child's extended social environment of models for identification and the promotion of ego-ideals ; the presence within the family of clear standards of conduct and ideas as to what is right and wrong ; but at the same time an expectation, if not requirement, of active exploration and internalization of a framework of personal conduct ; an emphasis on the development of one's own ethical code ; the experience of fragment moving within single communities or from community to community or from country to country which provides an enrichment of experience both cultural and personal . . . the possession of skills and abilities which though encouraged and rewarded are nevertheless allowed to develop at their own pace ; finally, the absence of pressures to establish one's professional identity prematurely.[1]

Addendum I

THE LUCHINS WATER-JAR PROBLEMS

Two variations of the problems were included in the table. Problems 1, 7, 8, 9, 10, and 11 could be solved by the use of a formula $A-3B$ for problem 1 ; $A+C$ or $A-C$ for problems 7, 8, 10, and 11. Problems 2 to 6 needed the formula $B-A-2C$. Problems 7, 8, 10, and 11 could also be solved with this formula.

It was found that students shown the solution of problem 1, and who then went on to problems 7 to 11, used the $A+C$ and $A-C$ formulae. Students shown the $B-A-2C$ solution for problem 2, who then tried problems 3 to 6, continued to use the $B-A-2C$ formula for problems 7 to 11, due to the carry-over of the learning 'set' induced by the practice on problems 2 to 6. They failed to see the easier solution. Problem 9 cannot be solved by using the $B-A-2C$ formula.

[1] In " Personality and the Realization of Creative Potential," Presidential Address to Western Psychological Association, Portland, Oregon, April 1964.

One group of students who had worked through problems 2 to 6 was told to write ' Don't be Blind ' on their papers before attempting problems 7 to 11. They succeeded in changing from formula B—A—2C to the A+C, A—C formulae more quickly than those who were not warned to be vigilant.

Elementary, secondary, college, and adult subjects all showed this effect of learning ' set.' This may console readers who did the same.

The experiment shows very neatly how, in the absence of vigilance, a learning ' set ' will carry over to the detriment of efficiency. It also shows how vigilance may be reinforced by an instruction and a warning.[1]

Addendum II

VARIETIES OF CREATIVE WORK

Originality and creative achievement in schools may take any one of several *types* and *levels*—music ; painting ; modelling ; wood and metal work ; writing stories, poems, and essays ; ingenuity in various forms of design ; illustrations in line or colour for stories ; planning experiments in science ; suggestions for explanations in science, history, and geography ; planning in project work ; making models for demonstrations in ancient and medieval history—houses, weapons, transport, and dress ; making proofs in mathematics more elegant. The characteristic to look for and *reward* (reinforce) is *originality*, the uncommon or unusual response which is at the same time *adaptive—i.e.*, relevant to some objective : uncommon or unusual, as distinct from the stereotyped, merely imitative, response. Nor must the ideas or products be judged by adult standards. Even younger children may produce creative—*i.e.*, uncommon or unusual—adaptive ideas, without having the skills to express them practically and without adult elegance in theoretical form. For example, a boy of six years made, quite independently, the same observation as led Archimedes to his work on buoyancy, and on

[1] Readers may try the following for testing transfer : Two friends were presented with an 8-gallon cask of beer. They had only a 5-gallon and a 3-gallon measure in addition to the cask. How could they measure four gallons each ?

another occasion speculated on the possibility of ultimate atoms of matter while cutting up bits of paper. Another, not yet five, after learning the 2, 5, and 10 tables, discovered that he could make up other tables from the information available. He had realized and applied the principles according to which the tables already learned were built up.

With regard to *levels* of creativity and originality, it has been suggested by an American, Irving Taylor,[1] as the result of a survey of many definitions and examples of creativity, that it can occur at five levels :

(a) Expressive creativity in spontaneous drawings and writing —creativity at a primitive level.

(b) Productive creativity exemplified in improving techniques.

(c) Invention and discovery—flexibility in perceiving new, unusual connexions between previously separated parts.

(d) Innovation—modifying the basic foundations of some art or science.

(e) Emergent creativity—finding and stating a new principle— *e.g.*, relativity or the quantum theory, or theories of evolution. A few highly gifted individuals at the sixth-form level do occasionally reach this level, particularly in mathematics.

With the contemporary emphasis on ingenuity in advertising and military hardware—rocketry, for example—it is easy to ignore or deprecate creativity in human relations—new plans in factory management, industrial relations, international relations ; even creating a home in which future creative individuals are encouraged to develop to maturity.

Creativity in human welfare is urgently needed.

EXERCISES

1. Collect instances where some transfer of the effects of training has occurred. Some typical examples are recognition of analogies. (*Cf.* the spread of word-meanings in colloquial speech—*e.g.*, when a person has had a stroke of good fortune he is said to be ' in clover.' Or we speak of a locomotive ' running '; ' running ' water ;

[1] See Moya Tyson, " Creativity," in B. M. Foss (ed.), *New Horizons in Psychology* (Penguin Books).

' running ' a business concern. Examine the nature of the transfer in these and similar cases.)

2. Collect instances of (a) lack of transfer in cases when it might be expected to occur (e.g., in presence of common elements of knowledge or skill) ; (b) negative transfer—i.e., where training in one branch of knowledge or skill interferes with the learning of a second branch. (Consider, for example, training in hockey and training in golf.)

How can the lack of transfer or the negative transfer be avoided or minimized ?

3. What bearing has the principle of transfer of the effects of training upon the problem of the person whose " mind exists in watertight compartments " ? How can such people's mental activity be freed ?

4. What bearing has the discussion in this chapter upon the true function of university training ?

5. Examine the bearing of the discussion upon the theory and practice of examinations—e.g., entrance-scholarship examinations, school-leaving certificate examinations, university degree examinations.

Is it possible to train a pupil for a specified examination and educate him at the same time ? If so, how can it be accomplished ?

6. Has an intelligent study of the classics any value for a future scientific specialist ?

7. What bearing has the doctrine of transfer as developed in this chapter upon the problem of explaining present-day civilization in terms of the past ?

8. Of what value is a study of the history of education for the modern practical teacher ?

9. The author of the Book of Ecclesiastes asserted that there is nothing new under the sun ! What does this assertion mean, and is there any foundation for it ?

Apply your answer to the history of educational theory and practice.

BOOKS FOR FURTHER REFERENCE

I. *Transfer of Training*

> OSGOOD, C. E. : *Method and Theory in Experimental Psychology* (Oxford University Press, New York, 1964). An excellent review of learning theories with applications to

transfer.   For more advanced students.   Not easy reading, but very much worthwhile.

BARTLETT, SIR F. C.: *Thinking* (Allen and Unwin, 1958). Experimental studies of thinking, problem-solving, and transfer.

CARROLL, J. B.: *Language and Thought* (Foundations of Modern Psychology Series, Prentice-Hall, New Jersey, 1964).   Chapters 6 and 7.

DUNCKER, K.: " On Problem Solving," *Psych. Monog.* 58, No. 5, Whole No. 270, 1945.

FOSS, B. M. (ED.): *New Horizons in Psychology* (Penguin Books, 1966).   Chapter 15: Operant Conditioning.

GAGNÉ, R. M.: *The Conditions of Learning* (Holt, Rinehart, and Winston, 1965).   Chapters 5, 6, 7, 8.

GROSE, R. F., AND BIRNEY, R. C. (EDS.): *Transfer of Learning* (Van Nostrand Co., New Jersey, 1963).   A collection of reprints of original papers on transfer.

GREEN, D. R.: *Educational Psychology* (Foundations of Modern Psychology Series, Prentice-Hall, New Jersey, 1964).   Chapters 4 and 5.

HAMLEY, H. R.: *British Journal Ed. Psych.*, Vol. VI, Part III, 1936.

HARGREAVES, S.: " The Faculty of Imagination," *British Journal Psych. Monog. Supp.*, 1927.

HUNTER, I. M. L.: *Memory: Facts and Fallacies* (Penguin Books, 1957).   Chapter 4.

JAHODA, M., AND WARREN, N. (EDS.): *Attitudes* (Penguin Books, 1966).   A collection of original papers.

KATONA, G.: *Organising and Memorising* (Columbia University Press, New York, 1940).   Experimental studies of transfer.   Applications to teaching methods.

LAYCOCK, S. R.: *Adaptability to New Situations* (Warwick and York, Baltimore, 1929).   Experimental studies of transfer.

LURIA, A. R.: *The Rôle of Speech in the Regulation of Normal and Abnormal Behaviour* (Pergamon Press, 1961).

LENNEBERG, E. H. (ED.): *New Directions in the Study of Language* (M.I.T. Press, Cambridge, Mass., 1964).

MEDNICK, S. A.: *Learning* (Foundations of Modern Psychology Series, Prentice-Hall, New Jersey, 1964).   Chapters 3, 4, and 6.

MEDNICK, S. A., AND FREEDMAN, J. L. : " Stimulus Generali-
sation," in J. R. Braun (ed.), *Contemporary Research in
Learning* (Van Nostrand, New Jersey, 1963).

MUSSEN, P. H. : *The Psychological Development of the Child*
(Foundations of Modern Psychology Series, Prentice-Hall,
New Jersey, 1964).   Chapters 4 and 6.

PEEL, E. A. : *The Psychological Basis of Education* (Oliver
and Boyd, 1956).   Chapter IV.

SLEIGHT, W. G. : *Educational Values and Methods* (Oxford
University Press, 1915).

SPEARMAN, C. : *The Abilities of Man* (Macmillan, 1927).

——— *The Nature of Intelligence and the Principles of
Cognition* (Macmillan, 1923).

——— *Creative Mind* (Nisbet, 1930).

SIMON, B. AND J. (EDS.) : *Educational Psychology in the
U.S.S.R.* (Routledge and Kegan Paul, 1963).

SPENS REPORT : *Secondary Education* (H.M.S.O., 1938).
Chapter III, Part II, and Appendix IV and V.

THOMSON, R. : *The Psychology of Thinking* (Penguin Books,
1959).

THORNDIKE, E. L. : *Educational Psychology* (Vol. II)
(Teachers' College, New York, 1921).

——— *Educational Psychology* (Briefer Course) (Teachers' College, New York, 1917).

VERNON, M. D. : *The Psychology of Perception* (Penguin
Books).

——— (ED.) : *Experiments in Visual Perception* (Penguin Books).

VINACKE, W. E. : *The Psychology of Thinking* (McGraw
Hill, 1952).

VYGOTSKI, L. S. : *Thought and Language* (M.I.T. Press,
Cambridge, Mass., 1962).

WERTHEIMER, M. : *Productive Thinking* (Harper and Bros.,
New York, 1945).

II. *Creativity*

ANDERSON, H. H. (ED.) : *Creativity and Its Cultivation*
(Harper and Row, New York, 1959).

BARRON, F. : *Creativity and Psychological Health* (Van
Nostrand, New Jersey, 1963).

Foss, B. M. (Ed.) : *New Horizons in Psychology* (Penguin Books, 1966). Chapter 8.

Getzels, J. W., and Jackson, P. W. : *Creativity and Intelligence* (Wiley, New York, 1962). Explorations with Gifted Students.

Guilford, J. P. : " Implications of Research in Creativity," in Banks, C., and Broadhurst, P. L. (Eds.): *Stephanos. Studies in Psychology* (University of London Press, 1965).

Hebb, D. O. : *Organisation of Behaviour* (Wiley, 1949).

Hadamard, J. : *The Psychology of Invention in the Mathematical Field* (Dover Publications, 1954). Chapters on " How Creativity is Tapped in Science " ; " The Unconscious Mind and Discovery " ; " Creative Techniques of Einstein, Pascal, Wiener, and others."

Hudson, L. : *Contrary Imaginations. A Psychological Study of the English Schoolboy* (Methuen, 1966).

Koestler, A. : *The Act of Creation* (Hutchinson, 1964). An historical and psychological study.

Mackenzie, R. F. : *Escape from the Classroom* (Collins, 1965). An experiment in a ' divergent ' curriculum.

Montmasson, J. M. : *Invention and the Unconscious* (Kegan Paul, 1931).

Thomson, R. : *The Psychology of Thinking* (Penguin Books, 1959).

Torrance, E. P. : *Guiding Creative Talent* (Prentice-Hall, New Jersey, 1962).

—— *Education and the Creative Potential* (University of Minnesota Press, 1963).

Wallach, M. A., and Kogan, N. : *Modes of Thinking in Young Children* (Holt, Rinehart, and Winston, 1965). A study of the creative-intelligence distinction.

III. *Creative Writing*

Creber, J. W. P. : *Sense and Sensitivity* (University of London Press, 1966).

Holbrook, D. : *English for Maturity* (Cambridge University Press, 1964). English in the secondary school.

—— *The Secret Places* (Methuen, 1965). Essays on Imaginative Work in English teaching.

MEARNS, HUGHES : *Creative Power* (Dover Publications, New York, second revised edition, 1958).   Education of youth in the creative arts.

MARSHALL, S. : *An Experiment in Education* (Cambridge University Press, 1966).

PRACTICAL TEACHING

CHAPTER X

TRENDS OF CHANGE IN SCHOOL ORGANIZATION, CURRICULA, AND TEACHING METHODS—COMPREHENSIVE SCHOOLS—NON-STREAMING—PROGRESSIVE v. TRADITIONAL—PROGRAMMED LEARNING

I. Be Prepared for Change

THE most powerful factors in educational organization and practice are not educational theory, or philosophy, or even psychology, but menaces to national security, economic crises, wars, foreign competition. Of these since 1900 Britain has experienced an abundance ; neither have we lacked prophets of doom (backed by Russian sputniks, Japanese shipbuilders, and American atomic hardware) demanding that we reorganize the educational system or perish.

New fashions in teaching and school organization develop, are welcomed by some people with uncritical enthusiasm, and spread in the belief that they are the final absolutely correct solutions to all educational problems. A few pioneers establish experimental schools to the accompaniment of much publicity. Meanwhile established educational institutions show a persistent resistance to any changes. The new enthusiasms wane. The new fashions are absorbed by the 'establishment.' Some modifications in practice may follow or affairs may revert to normality like ripples subsiding in a pond until another fashion appears. One can recall the Herbartian lesson plans ; centres of interest ; the Montessori Method ; the Dalton Plan ; the Project Method ; Sanderson of Oundle and applied science ; A. S. Neill ; not to mention Rousseau, Pestalozzi, Froebel, Dewey, and Activity Methods generally.

Educational reform, so far, has made most progress in infant schools, one reason being, of course, that they are least hidebound by university-entrance requirements with their backlash effects on secondary grammar schools, and, via the 11+ selection tests, on the junior departments of the primary schools.

More recently, particularly since the Education Act of 1944, traditional curricula, school organization, and teaching methods have been subjected increasingly to criticism from two sources—psychological investigations into the extent and variety of individual differences among children and young people at school, and socio-logical surveys of the effects of environmental influences on the development of ' intelligence ' and consequently on the fairness or otherwise of selection procedures for secondary and higher education. Recent official reports have both stated and implied that grammar schools are not providing satisfactory curricula or treatment for some pupils in them. Too many pupils leave school before completing a secondary-school course. Much valuable talent is thereby wasted, a loss the nation can ill afford.

Thus there is in the second half of the twentieth century increasing public interest in school organization and teaching-method. Yet the aims and methods of many schools and teachers differ very little from those characteristic of the Tudor period or even earlier.

This state of affairs presents a problem to a writer of a text-book on teaching-methods. It seems logical to approach the subject through what is known about the nature of learners and their modes of learning. Teaching, in practice, however, does not occur in a vacuum. It is carried on in certain conditions—for example, predominant educational values and aims ; existing knowledge (or, rather, the knowledge which is prescribed in examination syllabuses) ; economic and social-class pressures ; buildings (often generations out of date) ; available books, apparatus, equipment. Theoretical principles must be adapted to these conditions. The relevance of this for our purpose should be obvious. If it is difficult in a period of rapid change to know with any degree of certainty for what sort of life we should prepare children now at school it is equally difficult in a period of changing values and methods to predict the conditions in which students now in professional training and younger practising teachers will have to teach, say, in even twenty years' time. Some may find themselves in traditional schools teaching classes in traditional ways for examination purposes ; others, in new schools using individual methods, or teaching small groups with curricula widely different from the traditional grammar-school subject-matter.

The final chapters in this book deal with certain aspects of

O

teaching practice—for example, recapitulation, revision, memorizing, and ' lesson ' development. These may be anathema to some ' progressives.' Not all schools are progressive, however. Even in progressive schools with progressive methods some habits must be formed ; some facts ingested and stored ; some general principles and theorems not only understood but memorized and made easily recallable. Moreover, even in progressive schools and certainly in higher secondary and technical education, it may be economical of time and energy, as well as efficient, to impart information to groups by means of lectures. If facts and principles are not readily recallable they are not readily transferable. Without efficient techniques, original ideas cannot be translated into creative work. It is sometimes implied that epoch-making scientific discoveries—radioactivity or penicillin, for example—are accidental. It must be remembered, however, that the ' accidents ' happened in the observations of men who were experts in their science and who were so accurately familiar with what might be expected to happen that the unexpected was immediately obvious and constituted a problem to be investigated. A lay observer would not have noticed that an ' accident ' had happened. There is a place, therefore, for discussing some rules of efficiency in learning and suitable methods of teaching for efficiency. In this connexion readers will recall the views of the Head of the Rugby Day Continuation School noted above (p. 60). The same principle has been stated with admirable clarity by Mrs Sybil Marshall, who cannot by any means be called a traditionalist :

> A teacher should realise that his function is still to teach. I apologize for making such an obvious statement but it must be said. We have passed, quite rightly, from the era of being taught to the era of learning for oneself. This is perhaps the very essence of modern education and the two following sections of this book will, I hope, convince anybody who reads it that I am wholly in favour of it. But it does not and cannot alter the function of the teacher . . . the teacher is not in school just to mark the register and to see that the children teach themselves. He is there to see that they learn.[1]

This present chapter is intended to bridge the gap between some more theoretical aspects of learning and teaching, and practice in actual conditions. In particular, suggestions of possible future developments in school organization will be made so that they can

[1] *An Experiment in Education* (Cambridge University Press, 1966), pp. 24–25.

be at least considered and their implications for teachers' aims and attitudes discussed.

II. Some Probable Changes

The fate of most predictions is to be falsified by events. Nevertheless there does seem to be some justification for the following suggested directions of change in the not-too-distant future :

(a) *Changes in School Organization*
(i) In favour of comprehensive secondary schools.
(ii) Against rigid streaming.

(b) *Changes in School Curricula*
As we have stressed elsewhere, schooling should be *relevant* : it should accord, that is, with national welfare and public interest on the one side and with pupils' interests and needs as growing individuals on the other. Thus in periods of rapid change curricula (the subject-matter taught particularly at secondary-school level) will need periodic revision and revaluation. New economic conditions, new modes of industrial organization and production and new inventions, demand new types of academic knowledge and skills. Changes in the mathematics and science required in industry since the nineteen-forties are cases in point.

Again, new school organizations—*e.g.*, comprehensive schooling with its introduction of greater diversity of interests, abilities, and talents, will require not only that new subject-matter be introduced, but also that existing subject-matter be regarded and taught according to new values, attitudes, and purposes in line with the changed conditions.

So far as pupils' needs and interests are concerned, observers in close touch with adolescents agree that as they approach school-leaving age they become increasingly interested in and pre-occupied with after-school careers. Thus, as the compulsory school-leaving age is raised to sixteen years or even later, pressures for changes in content and methods of teaching subject-matter will arise from the older pupils themselves.

We must be prepared, therefore, for changes in curricula.

(c) *Changes in Teaching Techniques.* ' *Progressive* ' *versus* ' *Traditional.*'

(d) *Increasing importance of educational guidance.*

(e) *Shortage of qualified teachers. Use of mechanical teaching aids. Programmed learning.*

To the consideration of these trends, particularly with respect to their implications for changes in attitudes and methods, we can now turn.

I. CHANGES IN SCHOOL ORGANIZATION AND CURRICULA

(a) ' Comprehensive' Secondary Schools. Why reorganize ?

To understand the trend towards ' comprehensive ' secondary schools it is necessary to realize the extent to which (to quote again from the Spens Report) education (in England) has been envisaged in terms of social classes—one education for the least affluent class, another for the middle classes, and a third for the upper classes. There has been no machinery for passing from one grade to another, although a boy of exceptional ability might occasionally succeed in doing so. In other words, schools in England have been, and still are, organized according to a system called ' Apartheid ' in South Africa and ' segregation ' in the United States. Some religious sects have sorted humanity into two groups—the elect and the damned. We separate our secondary-school population into the private sector and the State sector ; the latter into grammar and secondary modern, grammar implying the academically elect, secondary modern the academically damned.

Prior to 1944 secondary schooling in England was a jumble of institutions having little or no effective connexion with each other— county and municipal secondary schools ; selective and non-selective central schools ; junior technical schools ; trade schools ; higher tops of all-age schools. The Act of 1944 was an attempt to co-ordinate this shambles. It proposed that every Local Education Authority must provide schools sufficient in number, character, and equipment to afford for *all pupils* opportunities offering such *variety of instruction and training* as might be desirable in view of their different ages, abilities, and aptitudes, including practical instruction and training appropriate to their respective needs.

Not a word, it should be noted, about any particular types of school. That issue was prejudged with sublime confidence in a White Paper on Educational Reconstruction (July 1943) in which it was decided that " such, then, will be the three main types of secondary schools to be known as grammar, technical and modern schools." Nor was it altogether surprising that soon after this the Norwood Committee discovered, on very dubious evidence be it said, that there were three types of intellectual ability which exactly fitted the three types of secondary schools ordained by the authors of the White Paper. It is not surprising because both the authors of the White Paper and the members of the Norwood Committee came from the same social class and the same educational background ; and both were conditioned by and accepted the same centuries-old educational assumptions and values.

Thus, with that persistence so characteristic of English educational tradition, we had what was, in effect, the same essential structure disguised by a different set of names. There were, of course, the usual platitudes about the need to facilitate the interchange of pupils from one type of school to another, and pious hopes that the different types of school would, eventually, achieve parity of esteem in public estimation.

Since 1944 there has been a growing distrust of this educational Apartheid for several reasons :

(i) The hoped-for parity of esteem has never been realized ; most probably it never will be. The grammar schools have been for centuries and still are the main avenues of approach to the universities and to professional careers. Technical schools and colleges of technology in our academically snob-ridden society are held to be tainted by contact with industry and trade ; deemed suitable by the best people only for second-rate academic ability or worse. The secondary-modern schools, whether or not with any justification, have been and still are regarded as institutions for the mentally and academically sub-normal ; for all educational purposes, dead ends.[1] Consequently the competition for grammar-school places is fierce. Not a few parents have regarded their offspring's allocation to a secondary-modern school as something of a disgrace to be avoided at all costs. On the other hand ' passing ' into a grammar school was an occasion for a celebration ! Similar values are accepted by many teachers.

(ii) The provision of grammar-school accommodation varies considerably between neighbouring counties, from less than 10 per cent. to more than 40 per cent. of the 11+ population. Whether a pupil enters a grammar or secondary-modern school may depend not on ability or attainment but on which side of a county boundary he

---

[1] In Wales the secondary moderns have been known as the ' *twp* ' schools. *Twp* is Welsh for ' dull and backward,' alternatively ' simple ' or ' daft.'

or she happens to have been born.   Chance, that is, not merit, may be a deciding factor.

(iii) The criterion for allocation at 11+ has been, for the most part, a test in attainment (arithmetic, English, Welsh), together with, in some but not all cases, a standardized test of intelligence, usually verbal.   It must be acknowledged that very great care has been taken by Local Education Authorities, assisted by educational psychologists, to make these 11+ tests as objective and free from bias as possible.   Nevertheless it has become increasingly obvious that as *selective* devices these tests are by no means perfect.   In a report on *Procedures for the Allocation of Pupils in Secondary Education*[1] it is said that " by almost any method of allocation to different types of school the five or ten per cent of pupils clearly suitable for grammar-school education are identified, as are the sixty or seventy per cent who are clearly unsuitable for it ; the real problem lies at the borderline.   *It is also true that no method is without error at the borderline.*"[2]   Again, " under any of the arrangements outlined above (as used by L.E.A.'s for selection) there is a margin of error which *in the most favourable circumstances cannot be expected to be less than 5% on either side of the borderline.*"   This means, of course, that in the whole of the country some thousands of children in this obscure border area are likely to be allocated to the wrong type of school *every year.*   This might not be so serious if adequate facilities for transfer were available.   In fact, the proportion of transfers is almost negligible and seldom, if ever, from grammar to secondary modern.

(iv) It has become increasingly obvious that even allocation by means of standardized objective tests (from which as much subjective bias of judgment as possible has been removed) favours pupils with good home backgrounds.   Children with comparable native ability but who lack the stimulation of a favourable environment, particularly with respect to the development of language and reading skills, are at a disadvantage in any form of academic test.

(v) Cases are known of late-developers who do not reach their full intellectual potential until after they have tried and failed the 11+ test.   Some of these achieve positions of distinction, even academically, later in life.

(vi) In areas where the provision of grammar-school places is

[1] Published by the National Foundation for Educational Research, London, 1963.

[2] Book cited, p. 23.   My italics.

inadequate, secondary-modern schools have organized successful courses for the Ordinary Level Examinations of the General Certificate of Education. Nevertheless, such is the prestige of the grammar schools that when it is known that these successful candidates were trained in a secondary-modern school they are apt to be compared unfavourably with grammar-school products, although, as we have seen, if the allocation procedures had been more reliable, or if luck had favoured them, they would have been in grammar schools.

It was asserted by the propagandists for the three separate types of schools to serve three supposedly differentiable types of mentality that it would be in the best interests of the pupils concerned to be given instruction and training best suited to their type and needs. This is suspiciously like a piece of special pleading. The evidence is against the assumption of clear-cut types. Children *vary in all sorts of ways, not neatly according to three types.* Nor do we know, at present, with any high degree of precision what sort of training and instruction is most likely to suit individual pupils at different periods of their secondary-school careers. The same pupil may require different treatment at different ages.

It has been asserted that allocation to the secondary-modern school causes disappointment and frustration in children. In some cases this is undoubtedly true. However, in what proportion of the 11+ population so allocated, and how intensely, it is the case we do not precisely know. At the same time one fact does appear to be generally true. Both children and adults tend to adapt themselves to the level of aspiration and achievement characteristic of their environment. A pupil, once allocated, whether or not correctly, to a grammar or secondary-modern school is likely to stay therein during the remainder of his school life. It may very well be, therefore, that the pupil who settles down to a career of comparative academic mediocrity in some secondary-modern environment might have achieved a higher standard in a more stimulating situation. In other words, the allocation to grammar or secondary-modern schools at 11+ may be what has been called a self-fulfilling prophecy.[1]

Thus for social more than purely educational reasons there is a growing demand for reorganizing secondary education on comprehensive principles. This trend represents a determination to secure for as many pupils as possible some approximation to equality of

---

[1] That is, a prediction which tends to produce the conditions which encourage its fulfilment. See, for example, D. H. Hargreaves, *Social Relations in a Secondary School* (Routledge and Kegan Paul, 1967).

opportunity in education. The difference between 1943 and 1965 may be seen by comparing Circular 10/65 (July 12, 1965) with the White Paper of July 1943. Circular 10/65 on *The Organisation of Secondary Education* states that :

> It is the Government's declared objective to end selection at eleven plus and to eliminate separatism in secondary education. The Government's policy has been endorsed by the House of Commons in a motion passed on 21st January 1965 : " That this House conscious of the need to raise educational standards at all levels and regretting that the realisation of this objective is impeded by the separation of children into different types of secondary schools, notes with approval the efforts of Local Authorities to reorganise secondary education on Comprehensive lines which will preserve all that is valuable in grammar school education for those children who now receive it and make it available to more children . . and believes that the time is now ripe for a declaration of national policy." The Secretary of State accordingly requests Local Education Authorities, if they have not already done so, to prepare and submit to him plans for re-organising secondary education on Comprehensive lines.

Readers cannot fail to have noticed that this motion of 1965 represents about as many pious hopes and assumptions as did the White Paper and the Norwood Report of 1943. The pressure for comprehensive education is social rather than educational. The 1965 declaration of policy seems to imply that a grammar-school education is superior to any other alternative. It does not define what part of it, if any, is valuable for the children who already receive it, and it blandly assumes that what is supposed to be good for the pupils already in grammar schools is equally good for every-body else. As we shall suggest later, some at least of these assumptions are very much open to question. If, as seems to happen very often in practice, the grammar-school curriculum is geared closely to the Ordinary and Advanced Levels of the General Certificate of Education and to university entrance, and if we can judge by the Report of the Central Advisory Council for Education on *Early Leaving*, by Professor Musgrove's surveys of school satisfactions, by Mackinnon's studies of his gifted architects, and by the by no means distinguished university careers of some 25 per cent. of State scholars, not to mention the almost complete divorce which has existed between the grammar schools and technology, industry and trade, it would appear that the education provided by the grammar schools is not exactly well suited to some of the pupils already receiving it—so much so that it cannot be taken for granted that it would be advantageous for others who are not.

Comprehensive education may help to establish a closer approximation to equality of educational opportunity for many pupils. It will not, of itself, solve any educational problems. Rather, it will make some. Some teachers are genuinely apprehensive about the educational efficiency of comprehensive schools ; others regard them, for social reasons, with suspicion ; still others, with contempt. For reasons which, we hope, will become clearer as this discussion proceeds, if the comprehensive schools are to become educationally successful new attitudes, understanding, and sympathies as well as new methods will be needed. This is why the trend towards comprehensive reorganization concerns us here. Whatever their opinions may be, some students now in professional training may find themselves teaching in comprehensive schools during their professional lifetime, and their attitudes and values will affect the success or otherwise of the reorganization. Some consideration of the educational problems involved is desirable therefore.

(b) What is a Comprehensive Secondary School ?

This question is asked and answered in a *Report on London Comprehensive Schools* (1966) issued by the Inner London Education Authority. The authors stress the danger of misconceptions :

> The comprehensive school is in danger of becoming something everybody knows about but few understand. Many misconceive it as a multi-lateral school, talking about ' grammar ' and ' technical ' streams ; some argue that it merely substitutes selection within the school for selection between schools. There is the deceptive over-simplification that it provides a ' grammar-school education ' for everybody—or for at least as many as want it—*whereas its true aim should be to provide something educationally richer and more varied than the separate grammar school is able to do.*[1]

To be really comprehensive a school should include representatives in due proportion of all social classes, grades of ability, and varieties of talent in the general population. It should be noted, of course, that while some parents can afford to buy places for their offspring in private schools and choose to do so, no State school can

[1] Publication E. 80, County Hall, London, S.E.1, 1967. My italics.

be fully comprehensive. Moreover, while there are slum districts there will not be fully comprehensive schools. The socio-economic and cultural level of a neighbourhood will itself act as a selective agency, scholastic as well as social and cultural. A comprehensive school in a more affluent residential district will be different from a comprehensive school in the middle of an urban slum. Each will present its own set of educational problems. Some educational problems will not be solved until the economic level and material culture of a neighbourhood are altered.

Nevertheless, with these provisos, a comprehensive secondary school is one to which the majority if not quite all of the children in a neighbourhood will go, irrespective of ability and attainments and social class ; all, that is, except educationally sub-normal and physically handicapped children—deaf, blind, spastics for example—who need very specialized treatment.

It follows that, in order to fulfil its proper function, the comprehensive school must *offer a wide range of courses at different levels of difficulty* ; and along with variety must go opportunities for choice to a greater extent than the traditional grammar school has provided.

(c) *Some Problems of Comprehensive Secondary Education*

As we have suggested above, comprehensive schools will not, by themselves, solve any educational problems. On the contrary, they will raise some new ones. At least three difficulties can be predicted : there will be a very wide range of ability ; a wide variety of talent, interest, motivation, and cultural background ; a variety of need both intellectual, emotional, *and vocational* which will require drastic revaluation and reorganization of traditional secondary-school curricula and methods. In addition, during the period of transition, *many grammar-school and university-trained teachers will need to revise their attitudes, values, and methods of approach to the educational problems of the comprehensive schools.* As we noted in the previous chapter, transfer of training can be negative and obstructive, particularly when it is rooted in bias, prejudice, and ignorance.

(i) If the comprehensive school is not to be a rehash of the grammar, technical, and ' modern ' system of Apartheid some methods need to be worked out whereby, *socially, the school population can be integrated into a community*, while different levels of ability, different upper limits of academic and practical achievement, different rates of learning, different preferred methods of learning, different talents and interests, are given due opportunities, encouragement, and treatment. It may be that the arrangement whereby a group of some 25 to 30 pupils remains together as a group for all school purposes is on its way out. For some purposes pupils may be grouped into relatively homogeneous ' sets,' any given pupils being in ' sets ' at different academic levels. For other purposes, much larger groups can profitably be taken together. Already in 1968 experiments are being made in the internal design of school buildings, making more flexible groupings for different purposes possible. In any case, much more attention must be given by specially trained teachers to backwardness in reading and in oral and written language. These skills are the foundations on which all general educational progress depends.[1]

(ii) The evidence summarized in the section on creativity is particularly relevant to the comprehensive school. We may note :

(*a*) Increasing dubiety about the absolute constancy of the I.Q. and its value as an overall *predictive* device for future success. It seems certain that qualities of personality not measured by the standard tests of intelligence in their present form are at least as important for creativity and productive thinking as the qualities of intellect that are so measured.

(*b*) Investigations have shown that the I.Q. depends not solely on innate aptitude, although that undoubtedly is a factor ; it also depends markedly on the stimulating qualities of the environment, particularly with respect to variety of experience, training in language habits, and motivation.

(*c*) Academic achievement has been overrated with respect to after-school success. High academic performance *above a certain minimum* seems to bear little relation to future productivity.

(*d*) The typical grammar style—abstract, logical, linguistic— is by no means the only way, nor is it necessarily the best way, of learning and thinking. Different people have their own preferred ways of learning. The same people may adopt different methods of learning and thinking at different times ; the rule seems to be— different tasks, different methods of attacking them. Several investigations have indicated two broad methods of thinking—what may be called the logical and the associative. These may co-exist at different levels of efficiency in different individuals. If the I.Q.

---

[1] For suggestions about organization, classification, timetables, etc., see the I.L.E.A. *Report* mentioned above.

is a measure of logical thinking, and tests of flexibility and fluency of ideas are measures of ' creativity,' then what is very important from the point of view of comprehensive education is the discovery that high I.Q. may be accompanied by high creativity ; high I.Q. by moderate or low creativity ; and, even more important, *moderate I.Q. can be accompanied by high creativity*. In other words, I.Q. and formal academic achievement have been traditionally, and still are, overrated in grammar-school estimation at the expense of other forms of creative talent.

Not only are there more ways than one of learning : there are more ways than one of being creative.   Professor P. E. Vernon says :

> There certainly exist both children and adults of mediocre 'g' (*i.e.*, general intelligence) and educational attainment who develop outstanding talents in the fields of art or scientific invention or become leaders in business, politics, warfare for example.   Such talents can to some extent be attributed to the possession of strong group factors but personality influences, drives and interests are probably more important.[1]

The principle is sufficiently important to merit more detailed illustration.   The example of Sir Francis Galton has already been noted (p. 111 above). Flugel says of him :

> In his wealth of novel ideas Galton is indeed without a parallel in the whole of modern psychology but his genius was of a roving rather than a persevering order.   His insatiable curiosity constantly attracted him to new problems. . . .   Galton was, from the start, interested not so much in the general laws governing the mind as in individual differences.

Significantly for our purpose, Flugel compares Galton with Wundt, a noted German psychologist :

> By Pearson . . . we are asked to look upon Galton as one whose claims as a founder of a new method in psychology are no whit inferior to Wundt's.   So far as originality, ingenuity and versatility are concerned, there is much to be said in favour of this contention. If his work proved less immediately fruitful and inspiring it was probably because the wide dispersal of his energies did not allow him time or patience to follow up the clues that he himself provided . . . he was a wanderer in the realms of science . . . so far as immediate utilisation was concerned his discoveries were at a disadvantage

---

[1] *The Structure of Human Abilities* (Methuen, 1950), p. 36.

compared with those of Wundt whose chief interest was psychology throughout his life, who founded an institute and worked there for forty years.[1]

Here is a vivid description of the versatile, flexible, adventurous thinker as compared with the more concentrated, theoretical one-track personality. There are indeed more ways than one of being creative.

David Livingstone is yet another example of the ' divergent ' personality. If I may quote myself, I said in 1946 :[2]

> We still have to seek some principle of unity in practical life which does not involve to any great extent the capacities for grasping logical and aesthetic forms of generality, and the importance of this kind of integration increases as pupils' powers of mastering abstract-logical and aesthetic generality decrease to average, or less. This emphasises the importance of what may be called purposive, associative integration.
>
> In the preoccupation with abstract ' pure ' knowledge and logical unity, schoolmasters seem to have under-rated, sadly, the integrative function of a practical purpose which is emotionally satisfying to the learner. Items of experience can be organised not only by reason of their logical connections and (or) aesthetic interest, but also because they all share the common qualification of being a means to some end which has value for the learner. Some people show this purposive associative interest to a high degree. A. L. Rowse in *The English Spirit* gives a vivid description of Livingstone, the missionary-explorer. He seems to have had an extraordinary passionate curiosity which drove him to learn everything he wanted for his purpose. As a young lad in a cotton factory he fixed a book on a spinning jenny so that he could catch sentences as he walked to and fro. He studied botany, zoology and geology. He was observant and thorough at gardening, carpentry, mechanical work and native languages. He learned from a ship's captain during a voyage to the Cape how to use a quadrant and make navigational observations. While on holiday at the Cape he studied practical astronomy with the Astronomer Royal. Livingstone's encyclo-paedic knowledge reminds one of Rabelais' notion of a Gargantuan curriculum.
>
> I know that logical analysis and understanding entered into Livingstone's mastery of this wide-ranging and varied knowledge.

---

[1] *A Hundred Years of Psychology* (Methuen, 1964), p. 110.
[2] " What is General Knowledge ?", *Sociological Review*, Vol. XXXVIII, 1, 1946, p. 36.

He was, probably, something of a logician, scientist, philosopher, and theologian. My point is that his interests were pre-eminently in practical achievement rather than theoretical system. I cannot see that we are justified in comparing the Livingstone type with the academic scholar or the creative artist to the detriment of the former. Society has need of all, surely. The types are complementary rather than exclusive. Moreover, many more pupils who will come into our future secondary schools may achieve effective participation in school and society which is essential for their full mental and moral development through the enthusiastic pursuit of practical ends than will achieve it through logical analysis or artistic creation. This, I think, is the justification for due recognition of practical projects, even of vocational interests in the curricula of our future secondary schools. It is sometimes forgotten that abstract knowledge and power of logical analysis are in fact direct vocational interests of the learned clerk.

The principle with which we are at the moment concerned has been described in other words by Mr H. R. King[1] as a result of his experience as Head of a London comprehensive school. As a result of such first-hand experience the description has particular relevance here. " The consequence," he says,

of segregating children into three types of school has become obvious and palpable ; it is to produce three types of ' misfit'. It is realised that with a tripartite set-up, the more the schools conform to type the more misfits they will produce. . . . Instead of the sterile notion of three types it now appears more serviceable and illuminating to develop the idea of two polarities in the approach to the whole field of curricular content. For the sake of definition we might call them the disciplinary and the empirical : they correspond with what has been imagined as the typical approach to learning of the grammar and the modern school respectively. . . . At one pole there is the systematic building-up of the subject as a logically coherent system of thought step by step from the fundamentals : at the other pole the organisation of a livelier field of awareness expansively around a centre of interest . . . at one pole there is the pursuit of knowledge for its own intrinsic interest, the ability to inter-relate ideas, the capacity for analysis and abstraction ; at the other pole, knowledge in use, relevant to present experience and applicable to a job in hand. In the one case the stress is upon theory, in the other upon practice. With the other they work at projects which give them a grasp of the integral situation, the concrete.

---

[1] " Conclusion—The Changing Face of English Education," in *Inside the Comprehensive School* (Schoolmaster Publishing Co., 1958), pp. 133–135.

All children, whatever their ability, acquire knowledge *in all these ways* . . . no pupil's education revolves entirely round one pole. For a balanced development, elasticity and variety of approach are called for. It is a matter of adjusting the approaches for each pupil, in his various studies, between the two polarities. The child's abilities and bents determine which modes he should exploit. *Our job as teachers is to discover these and make the adjustments as the pupil develops : not to pre-determine them at eleven plus.* Hence if we are to fit the educational curriculum to the pupil and not create misfits by attempting the opposite, we should have at our disposal the *widest possible range and variety of provision, approaches and methods*.[1]

We have dealt in some detail with this principle—namely, that there are more ways than one of learning, and more ways than one of being clever. Both from the point of view of the pupil's optimum development and of the nation's urgent need of a variety of talents and skills, this principle of preferred ways of learning is most important. Under the pre-1966 organization of schools we were not only creating misfits, but were wasting much valuable ability the nation could ill afford to lose. Evidence for this can be found in the statistical sections of recent official reports.[2]

One objection to comprehensive schools which many people consider final and unanswerable is—the introduction of pupils of lower-grade academic ability will drag down the academic standards of a whole school. In the first place, it should be noted, this indicates an obsessive concern merely with scholastic attainment. Little importance is attached by these objectors to any other aspect of education.

Unfortunately it is difficult to get quite reliable evidence in this respect. Perhaps the most significant, up to date, comes from Stockholm.[3] There were, up to the mid-nineteen-fifties, three types of secondary-school organization, in which pupils were streamed into groups according to academic ability and attainment : (*a*) streamed

---

[1] My italics.
[2] *E.g.*:
" Early Leaving " ;
" 15–18" (The Crowther Report);
"Higher Education" (The Robbins' Report);
" Half our Future" (The Newsom Report).
[3] See N. E. Svensson, " Ability Grouping and Scholastic Achievement " (report on a five-year follow-up study in Stockholm), *Educational Research*, Vol. V, No. 1, November 1962.

at 11+ ; (b) streamed at 13+ ; and (c) comprehensive schools, in which streaming did not occur until 15+.

10,958 pupils at 11+ in 1954–55 were tested subsequently at 13+, 14+, and 15+. Teachers' qualifications, size of classes, home background, level of ability, and spread of ability within classes were taken into account.

Educational progress was estimated in terms of scholastic attainment. The Report lists the following conclusions which seem to be justified by the evidence :

   (i) Attainment of pupils in the more academically biased classes
       was not correlated systematically with the type of previous
       schooling. A slight tendency towards superiority in
       early-streamed classes had disappeared by the age of
       15+.
  (ii) Localization of classes in five-year, three-year, and compre-
       hensive schools had no significant bearing, in the long run,
       on achievement.
 (iii) In cases of pupils in less academically biased classes, age of
       streaming had no demonstrable effect on attainment.
  (iv) Socio-economic background had some effect.

The study suggests that early transfer of talented pupils to separate schools or classes had no significant effect on their attainment levels at 15+. There was some evidence in this, as in other surveys, about the effects of segregation—that less able pupils did better in unstreamed than in streamed groups, an effect, possibly, of more stimulation and a higher level of aspiration and motivation. In cases of low-ability pupils the total scores in attainment tests were highest in the mixed groups. Classes of varying homogeneity were approximately equal in attainment. This casts doubt on the assumptions that attainments of a class are closely related to its degree of homogeneity.

The main matter for our purpose is this—namely, that the pressures in favour of comprehensive schools are mainly social ; that whether we like it or not the comprehensive principle is on its way in ; that some of the allegedly educational objections are not borne out by more objective research, and that the success or other-wise of the comprehensive principle of organization will depend on a radical revaluation of many teachers' attitudes to secondary education.

(d) Raising the Compulsory School-Leaving Age. Need for Revision of the Secondary Curriculum. Integration of Secondary with Further Education

Raising the compulsory school-leaving age to sixteen years is now official policy. When this happens many pupils in the secondary schools will be, in fact, young adults, not children, and they will expect to be treated as such. In addition *their major interests will be concerned, increasingly, with after-school careers.* If they are to be reconciled to staying longer in school, and if the lengthened school period is to be maximally fruitful, the school must appear to them to serve a useful purpose. We are likely to find, therefore, increasing demands for reorganized curricula with closer connexions not only with university entrance and the professions as was the case up to the nineteen-sixties, but with technology, commerce, craft skills, and the arts. Again, new valuations and new attitudes on the part of teachers will be necessary. Whereas previously all the able pupils were *expected* to take courses leading to the Advanced Level of the General Certificate of Education, while technical, art, and craft courses were considered suitable for the below-average to near-morons to occupy their time in school until they arrived at the compulsory leaving age, in the future these technical, more artistic and practical courses must be given parity of esteem up to and including sixth-form level. This is not only educationally important, it is an economic necessity. It is already happening in French schools. In an article " Lessons from the French " the author[1] writes :

> The French educational planners envisage that by 1970 at age 16, some 40 per cent of all pupils will be attending a *lycée* : 23 per cent will follow a classical or modern course and 17 per cent. a technical one in this type of school. What strikes the English observer is that the *lycée*, like the new Swedish *gymnasiet*, is in effect a sixth-form college, *that technical education is possible in it, and that some of the brightest children will opt for it*—unlike the situation in England where it is held to be for the second-raters.[2]

Again, to risk a prediction, we are likely to see closer approximations in the future comprehensive schools to a variety of courses such as the following (not, be it said, in any descending order of educational or academic importance) :

[1] Dr W. D. Halls, Lecturer in Education, Oxford University.
[2] *Where*, No. 28, November 1966. My italics.

  (i) More formal : abstract theoretical mathematical, scientific, and linguistic studies for those pupils whose ' bent ' is in that direction.

 (ii) More general humanistic : literary, environmental studies— *e.g.*, economics, social studies, history, human geography.

(iii) More technological : technical, applied science, industrial organization.

(iv) More commercial : with strong emphasis on foreign languages and business organization.

 (v) More applied biology : *e.g.*, in pre-nursing, pre-medical courses.

(vi) More creative arts and design : art, music, drama, crafts (including housecrafts).

In all the above, adequate attention must be given to training in language, both oral and written, *as a medium of communication and expression*, rather than exercises in formal grammar merely.

One objection frequently made to comprehensive schools is that they are too big. This ignores the obvious truth that only in a comparatively large school is it possible to organize successfully the wide variety of courses which will be necessary to satisfy the variety of abilities and aspirations of future generations of pupils, and meet the needs of the nation's economy for a variety of new types of talent and skill.

(e) *Academic Achievements in the Comprehensive Schools*

Any *significant* comparisons of academic achievement as between comprehensive and grammar schools are difficult to make. Comprehensive schools are comparatively new foundations. They have not the traditions nor, as yet, the public esteem of the older-established grammar schools ; tradition and esteem, however, are factors in achievement. The comprehensive schools are faced with much more complex problems of organization and method than the selective—often highly selective—grammar schools. Many comprehensive schools—such, for example, as those described in the London Report—are working side by side with very selective county grammar and independent schools which take in a high proportion of the top grades of academic ability. Moreover, it has been shown beyond doubt in many recent surveys that social-class level and home background are at least as influential in academic achievement as the I.Q. and in this respect the comprehensive schools are often handicapped in comparison with the highly selective county grammar and independent schools.

Not everybody will agree that examination successes are, or should be, the major criterion of *educational* efficiency. At the same time, in a modern competitive commercial and industrial society, examination successes are important career qualifications.

With these considerations in view the examination results in seven London comprehensive schools are at least interesting if not statistically significant for purposes of comparison. The following Table shows the number of passes at the Ordinary and Advanced Level of the General Certificate of Education gained by pupils in the I.Q. levels indicated in the first column who entered these seven schools in 1957 and 1958 :[1]

TABLE 3

G.C.E. EXAMINATION RESULTS IN 7 LONDON
COMPREHENSIVE SCHOOLS—1957 AND 1958 INTAKE

I.Q. at 11+	Numbers gaining ' O ' Level passes in					' A ' Level passes in		
	1	2	3	4	5 or more subjects	1	2	3 or more subjects
110 and below	264	151	114	118	231	74	26	31
100 and below	137	54	34	24	53	25	6	5
95 and below	76	28	14	9	16	12	1	0

If the Table shows nothing else, it does show that given the opportunity some pupils who would have failed the 11+ selective test can pass both O and A Level examinations and gain what is considered to be a good certificate, even though in some cases they were below average intelligence as indicated by the usual 11+ tests. And, by implication, these results suggest that our present so-called tripartite system of secondary schooling is causing more waste of potential ability than the country can afford.

Before leaving this topic of secondary school organization one further consideration of importance should be noted. For the benefit of pupils who will continue to leave school at the age of

[1] Report cited, Appendix 21, p. 138.

sixteen there should be a close co-ordination between the secondary schools, Colleges of Further Education, and improved apprenticeship schemes.   Otherwise much of what may be gained by extending the age-limit will be wasted by lack of adequate opportunity for further education.

2. *Opposition to ' Streaming '*

' Streaming ' is the practice of arranging a school generation into approximately homogeneous groups, A, B, C, D, etc., according to estimated academic ability and/or attainment.   In small schools with a one-form intake, streaming in the meaning of the term as it is used here is impossible.   A class may be divided for certain studies into smaller groups, but these are re-assembled for other activities. In streaming properly so called, a year's intake may be divided into two or more classes.   Each such class, A, B, C, D, etc., is then kept together as an administrative group and taught together for most, if not all, school activities.

In larger schools streaming has been an almost universal practice. In a survey of 660 schools of 108 different Local Education Authorities in various parts of England and Wales in 1962, 96 per cent. of the schools were streamed.[1]   In 50 per cent. of the schools involved, pupils were already streamed on arrival from the infants' department.

The practice of streaming is supported by a majority of primary-school teachers for the same ostensible reason as the segregation of children at 11+ into grammar and modern types : it is easier to treat the children according to their needs.   One suspects, however, that it is less troublesome to teach an academically homogeneous group.   There is also a strong tendency for teachers to aspire to teach the A streams, coupled with an equally strong aversion to teaching the C, D, or lower streams—a case of academic respectability and prestige.

Several attempts have been made to discover, by experiment, whether the segregation of children into supposedly homogeneous groups for teaching purposes is educationally more or less efficient than non-streaming.   Up to the time of writing few if any of these investigations had produced significantly reliable results.   It has been found impossible either to justify criticisms of streaming or to prove that streaming is desirable and effective.   The difficulty has been to ensure that the subjects of the experiments have been suffi-

[1] Brian Jackson, *Streaming: An Education System in Miniature* (Routledge and Kegan Paul, 1964).

ciently numerous and representative of the general population and sufficiently well matched for sex, age, initial ability, ' intelligence,' and home backgrounds. In addition it has been difficult to ensure that they were taught with equal confidence and competence and according to the same syllabuses and methods.[1]

Perhaps the nearest approach to a satisfactory experimental design was organized by J. C. Daniels.[2] He compared the results on standardized tests of intelligence and attainment in two three-class-entry junior schools, in which streaming was practised on entry from the infant department ; and two three-class-entry junior schools approximately equal in size, distribution of I.Q.'s on entry, age-range, and socio-economic status, in which the children were not streamed. In both sets of schools syllabuses and teaching methods were comparable.

Daniels found that there was some evidence that non-streaming raised the average I.Q. of these junior-school children by some 3 points, and that it *reduced the spread of variation of attainments*. In other words, the ' tail ' represented by the lower streams was to some degree removed. This implies that the backward were helped by non-streaming more than the brighter children. It may be, however, that more individual attention was paid to the backward children in the unstreamed schools, or that in the streamed schools the lower streams, as is only too frequently the case, were taught by less competent or less enthusiastic teachers. And, other things being equal, it may be easier for the lower-placed children to improve compared with those who are already high on the attainment scales.

Brian Jackson, by matching 81 unstreamed with 81 streamed children in reading ability at the end of their first junior-school year, found at the end of their second junior-school year that " in the unstreamed class the obviously able children had done rather better ; the weakest children had improved remarkably and the average attainment of the class had been raised." He admits, however, that this evidence is suggestive rather than convincing : the numbers involved were small and not enough was known about the children apart from their attainments in reading.

Educationally, then, the case for or against streaming is not proved either way. Jackson believes that unstreaming can help

[1] See, for example, A. Yates and D. A. Pidgeon, " The Effects of Stream-ing," *Educational Research*, Vol. II, No. 1, 1959.

[2] " Effects of Streaming in Primary Schools," *British Jnl. Educ. Psych.*, XXXI, Part 2, 1962.

to abolish the C-stream tail.   Otherwise there is, academically, little difference between the two methods.[1]

The evidence from the Stockholm survey is relevant here.

The main objections to streaming, like those to segregation at 11+, are mainly social.

(i) Streaming is often done on the basis of teachers' estimates, or on early attainments in number, reading, and language.   These estimates, as is the case at 11+, may be unreliable, particularly at the borderlines between streams.   Nevertheless, once allocated to a particular stream it is the rule rather than the exception for a pupil to remain in that stream for the remainder of the junior-school period, with differential effects on success at the 11+ test and allocation to a grammar or secondary-modern school.

(ii) Socio-economic status and home background are powerful selective factors in deciding into which stream a child will go.   The proportion of pupils from the homes of semi-skilled and unskilled workers in the lower streams is higher than would be expected by chance.   In Mr Jackson's sample six times as many eleven-year-old children of unskilled manual workers as children of professional and managerial workers finished in the D streams of 228 four-stream schools (32 per cent. as against 5 per cent.).

(iii) Another and unexpected selective factor is date of birth. Children may enter infant schools at the beginning of each autumn, spring, or summer term.   They are all moved into the junior school and streamed at the end of the school year in July.   Children born in autumn, therefore, may have spent some six months or more longer in school and are correspondingly more advanced in attainment than summer-born children, although they may be comparable in native ability.   They are that much more likely to go into an A stream and *remain there*.   Jackson gives details of eleven-year-old children in 228 four-stream schools grouped according to dates of birth.[2]   He found the following :

TABLE 4

Children born between	A Stream	B Stream	C Stream	D Stream
	%	%	%	%
September 1st and December 31st .	39	30	28	22
January 1st and April 30th . .	35	37	33	36
May 1st and August 31st . . .	26	33	39	42

[1] Book cited, p. 119.   [2] Book cited, Table 12, p. 26.

Thus, in this sample from 228 schools, about twice as many summer- as winter-born children finish up in D streams at the end of the junior-school period. It is most unlikely that the distribution of innate aptitude corresponds with this distribution into streams. Similar trends are found if children are streamed at 7, 8, 9, or 10 years of age. When it is realized that a higher-than-average proportion of children in A streams are allocated by the 11+tests to grammar schools we are forced to conclude that chance factors—socio-economic status, home background, and date of birth—as well as ability and attainment help to determine secondary-school selection and later careers.

(iv) Brian Jackson was an experienced teacher and had first-hand knowledge of A, B, and C streams. One comment of his is significant in view of what was said about creativity in a previous chapter. " Teaching streamed children was a puzzling experience if only because the roots of their problems lay far outside the classroom. It was perplexing to encounter creative children in ' C ' classes and tidy-minded but less enterprising children in ' A ' classes."[1] This suggests another possible objection to rigid streaming, one we have already noted in the case of 11+ segregation in secondary schools. Even if streaming according to early academic attainment were more reliable than, in fact, it is, a group which is homogeneous with respect to attainment in arithmetic, reading, and language may be still far from homogeneous in all other respects—e.g., in personality, motivation, rates of development, modes of thinking, ' creativity.' Moreover, it is most likely that there will be considerable overlap at the borderline between two streams. Some children at the top of a B stream might have performed better than some at the bottom of an A stream had they been reallocated. One meets here the factors of stimulation, motivation, level of aspiration, and adaptation which have been noted in connexion with secondary-school segregation.

The practice of streaming is not restricted to primary schools. In *Culture and the Grammar School* a former Head of the High Pavement Grammar School in Nottingham[2] believes that larger grammar schools, while able to offer wider varieties of treatment, are open to criticism on account of their addiction to ' streaming ' :

[1] Book cited, p. 121.
[2] Harry Davies, later Director of the Institute of Education, Nottingham University.

Many schools arrange pupils in ability groups according to their performance in the selection examination even though repeated experience must show them how unreliable this is. By the end of the second year, and sometimes earlier, a C or a D form and an A form are clearly sorted out and apart from a few exceptional cases the pupils will stay in these ' streams ' until the end of their fifth year in the school. Thus the process is at work by which the bright interested boy who entered the school at 11 degenerates into the bored rather loutish young tough of 15 who seems to be getting very little out of the school.[1]

As the author says, not all children can be top of their form. All these, however, were deemed suitable for an academic education at 11+ and their abilities should not be wasted ; otherwise they become discouraged, uninterested, maybe embittered. A school creates its own bottom stream and its own bottom-stream mentality.[2]

In his school streaming was abolished. At the end of the third year four entirely new forms were arranged with courses biased according to individual pupils' major interests—science, language, history, geography together with technical drawing, art, metalwork, and woodwork.

A clear distinction must be made between ' streaming '—that is, segregating pupils at the beginning of their secondary-school period on the evidence of some academic test—and arranging courses at a later stage, biased in the direction of pupils' talents and interests. Again, in view of what has been said about ' creativity ' it is interesting to note Mr Davies' attitude to non-academic activities. Arts and crafts, he believes, are underestimated in importance in most boys' grammar schools. Consequently, the creative abilities of many pupils remain undeveloped :

> A deep satisfaction can be obtained from painting a picture, writing a poem, modelling in clay, making something in wood or metal, a satisfaction which has great therapeutic value. The conquest of the material, the judgment of the finished product by one's own standards, the feeling that one has created something can more than make up for failures or disappointments in the academic sphere and in other activities, and can generate self-reliance and poise.[3]

---

[1] Book cited. Published by Routledge and Kegan Paul, 1965. See p. 38.
[2] See also D. H. Hargreaves, book cited, Chapters 8 and 9.
[3] Book cited, p. 47. The whole chapter on " Curriculum and Teaching Methods " will repay serious study.

One further objection to rigid streaming in any type of school is the attitude of many teachers. It is considered *infra dig.*, even an insult to one's intelligence, to be asked to teach a C or D form. Thus the pupils most in need of skilled guidance tend to get, instead, the youngest, least experienced, least adventurous teachers. This helps to confirm their C or D status. Again we are faced with the conclusion that as well as reforming traditional curricula to meet the changed conditions of a modern industrial community, *new values and attitudes* as well as methods are essential if the schools of the future, whether grammar or comprehensive, are to deal fairly and effectively with the variety of personality and talent the schools will collect and the nation will need.

2. 'PROGRESSIVE' VERSUS 'TRADITIONAL' FORMS OF ORGANIZATION AND TEACHING-METHOD

Another trend of change at least as old as J. J. Rousseau has spread more recently with increasing rapidity—namely, the change from 'traditional' to 'activity' methods of learning, a change which seems likely to accelerate in the future. This trend, particularly as it was advocated in America by John Dewey, was due as much to the growing influence of the scientific temper and technical pressures of the early twentieth century as to any established educational principles. It is true that the educational principles had been outlined by Froebel, Pestalozzi, the Edgeworths, and Herbert Spencer, for example, but the principles needed the pressures of a scientific and industrial era before they began, significantly, to affect the practice of the schools. Even so, the effects were apparent most clearly in the infant schools which were least dominated by the conservatism of the older universities, with their classical traditions and examination requirements.

'Traditional,' as the word is used here, refers to the curricula and teaching methods of the medieval grammar schools. As we said earlier in this book, the sole business of those schools was teaching the grammar of the classical languages, mainly Latin, in preparation for university studies in philosophy, theology, and law. The content of the curriculum was authoritarian, fixed by holy writ and by the grammar and style of classical authors. There was no thought of discovery as we now understand it. All that need be known had been either revealed or determined by the grammarians, theologians, logicians, and lawyers. Academic learning consisted for the most part, if not entirely, of repetition, imitation, memorizing.

Scholarship meant book-work—forms of words which as time went on had less and less connexion with changing conditions outside the schools and universities.

Thus ' tradition ' has meant verbal repetition, grammatical style, abstract logic, justified, as we have seen, by the seventeenth-century schoolmasters as exercises in mental-gymnastic and formal discipline ; a process of training the ' faculties '—arguments rendered doubtful if not completely false by later experimental investigation.

There is no doubt that this verbal tradition did not suit every learner even in the Middle Ages. Folklore describes the schoolboy who crawls unwillingly to school and is skilful in avoiding work when he gets there. It has been taken for granted (it still is in many cases) that corporal punishment is unavoidable as an incentive to learning. There is also a good deal of evidence that many pupils, trained by methods of memorization, imitation, and verbal repetition, fail completely when they are required to adapt what they have learned to new, even slightly different situations. They cannot think independently or make any transfer. Mr Harry Davies in the book already cited sums up some criticisms of the traditional curriculum.

> Since facts can be more easily examined than ideas and general principles, facts matter most ; they can be noted down, learned off by heart, frequently tested and ultimately regurgitated in the appropriate place on the examination paper. Teaching in certain subjects can be reduced to the business of filling so many receptacles to the brim with information as if a school were a petrol station. The need to think, to understand, to be critical is minimised . . . all that the pupil has to do is to repeat second-hand opinions. Is it any wonder that so many pupils are utterly bored, and overworked since the learning process is long and laborious ? Their own interests remain unstimulated ; they are not trained to work out things for themselves ; their will to learn is ruined and their curiosity killed.[1]

---

[1] Book cited, pp. 41–42. It should be noted that it was precisely because the medieval student was discouraged from thinking things out for himself that this type of curriculum and teaching-method was held in high esteem. We tend to be dissatisfied nowadays with the vestigial remains of medieval aims and methods. We now need students to think out things for themselves —at least some things ! Even nowadays the original thinker is not always welcomed with open arms even by contemporary scholars ; certainly not by some politicians and ecclesiastical authorities.

It is possible, of course, to justify this deadening of schoolboy and student interest on Tarver's principle that what is most valuable in education is not what is learned, nor how it is learned, but how difficult it is to learn it.[1]

Since this medieval content and method of education has become increasingly divorced from the requirements of many present-day careers (whether or not this can be justified philosophically), the opposition to the ' traditional ' in education has increased. In fact, some educationists with quite uncritical enthusiasm have gone to an opposite extreme. Everything traditional is necessarily bad. ' Tradition,' ' imitation,' ' repetition,' ' memorizing,' ' lessons,' ' tests,' ' records ' are derisory words. Away with such reactionary practices. Change everything forthwith and all will be perfect. Thus some ' progressives.' On the other hand ' progressive ' has become a synonym for praiseworthy, modernistic, educationally sound. The emotively correct terms now are ' discovery,' ' understanding,' ' interest,' ' self-activity,' ' transcendental freedom ' ! After listening to some ' progressives ' one may be forgiven for supposing that to be educationally progressive all that is necessary is to rearrange the seats in a classroom.

That more than this is involved is obvious from the warnings of innovators like Caldwell Cook, Hughes Mearns, and Mrs Marshall. The latter, emphatically, thinks so :

> Those to whom what I have just written seems patent and unnecessary must count themselves enlightened beings ; because for every one of them there are still fifty who worship at the shrine of the fixed and dependable ; of the scheme, the record and the time-table. To such all that I have said will be sheer heresy. If they stick to their stalls long enough, however, they may find that their methods, like an old coat, will come back into fashion. If that is so, it will have been caused by a revolution against those greater enemies of real modern education, the people who embrace anarchy in the name of freedom and who find it convenient to believe that no time-table and no record-book means, in effect, no work. Let no young teacher reading this get any false values from it. To control a class in freedom, to learn with each child instead of instructing a passive class . . . is the most exhausting way of all of doing a teacher's job.[2]

---

[1] One suspects that that argument, also, was sociologically determined rather than educationally well founded.

[2] S. Marshall, book cited, p. 42.

Thus, as in the case of grammar versus comprehensive schools, of streaming versus non-streaming, so in the case of ' traditional ' versus ' progressive ' we find even in the second half of the twentieth century two completely opposite sets of values and opinions.

What has research to say about the controversy ?

In 1956 a longitudinal study of 250 children attending two junior schools in the Midlands was begun.[1]   From the age of seven onward various aspects of their intellectual, educational, emotional, and social development were explored by means of repeated tests, interviews, and other measures, supplemented by reports from teachers and parents.   By the end of the school year in 1960 some hundred different assessments had been made to chart their progress in relation to *two very different school regimes*—namely, one predominantly ' progressive,' that is child-centred, the other mainly traditional, that is subject-centred.

The schools were called Parkside (progressive) and Townsend (traditional).   The Heads of the two schools had their own very definite ideas about the theory and practice of education, and, convinced of the value of their different approaches, both had attracted an able enthusiastic staff who shared their views.

In the Townsend (traditional) school, children were streamed on entry at the age of seven.   From then on tests and examinations were a regular and prominent feature of the school life.   Formal class teaching was the main method of imparting information.   The value of achievement was stressed, and learning took place in a deliberately competitive atmosphere.   Parkside, on the other hand, adopted a progressive approach.   The children were not streamed except in the final year before 11+ selection.   All classes were mixed in ability.   There was no formal timetable.   Most of the school work was done in projects by children working together in small groups.   Learning had an exploratory bias with much scope for self-expression both as free-writing and a wide range of creative art forms.   *A striking feature of the school was the wealth and high quality of art work on display.*

In 1960 the children surveyed in the two junior schools were transferred to four neighbouring secondary-modern schools and at the age of fifteen a sample of 81 pupils, consisting of those in the

---

[1] See *Four Years On* by S. Gooch and M. L. Kellmer Pringle, National Bureau for Co-operation in Child Care, Research Report No. 1.   Later published by Longmans.

original population whose reading attainment at the end of the junior-school period had been average or below, was followed up.

The final results are almost as contrary to some widely accepted opinions as those of the first experiments on transfer of training. After certain reservations about the small numbers of the sample and other conditional factors the authors venture the following conclusions :

The boys as a whole and the more intelligent girls did better in a traditional framework, while girls as a whole and the less intelligent boys performed best in the progressive framework.

The survey confirms the findings of other studies—namely, that bright children tend to get brighter and dull children duller with increasing age.

Attempting a cautious generalization, it appears that the traditional approach favours the brighter child, while the progressive regime benefits the duller child. Boys in general benefit from a traditional framework, while girls in general benefit from the progressive environment.

Since the sample was small, only tentative conclusions are justified. Nevertheless the authors suggest :

> Two conclusions emerge quite clearly and each has far-reaching educational and psychological implications. First, that questions such as whether streamed or unstreamed schools, or whether a child-centred or a subject-centred approach achieve better results are so broad as to be almost meaningless. Instead it need be asked which aspects of a child's learning and progress are affected in what ways by different theoretical, organisational and teaching approaches ; as well as what are the differential effects on boys and girls respectively and on children of different ability levels and from different socio-economic home backgrounds. In short, the task is to examine the differential effects of different ' educational ' treatments not only on different groups of children but also on individual children. The implications of our study are that to ensure the optimal development of all pupils the educational system needs to become not only more varied so that guidance according to individual need can become a reality ; but also that greater breadth and flexibility are needed in teaching methods rather than more uniformity and rigidity to ensure the continuation of the growth of slower-learning children as well as the fullest social and moral development of all children. . . .
>
> *It may well be that fostering emotional and social potential may prove more conducive to improving a child's rate of learning than concentrating more directly but narrowly on educational progress itself.*

The authors conclude that in the population studied the brighter child did better under the traditional approach, to some extent at the expense of the duller child, while the duller child did better under the progressive regime at the expense of the brighter child.

> Which of these two results is the more desirable is a social and political rather than scientific question. . . . If one's aim is the production of ' experts ' the traditional approach will be commended. If one believes that dull children must be given an equal or more than equal chance the progressive system will be favoured. From a broad point of view neither the progressive nor the traditional system is satisfactory. Both waste undeveloped potential. Neither fulfils the dictum ' to each according to his needs.' It would seem that *at least two approaches to education must co-exist if a just and rational system is ever to come into being.*[1]

There is also the question of identification of a teacher with a particular type of child from particular home and neighbourhood backgrounds. Possibly teachers who favour ' traditional ' methods prefer the brighter academic child ; ' progressive ' teachers feel more sympathy with duller children. This tendency to identification would reinforce differences found in this follow-up study.

It may be argued that the survey from which we have just quoted need not be taken seriously. It involved only a relatively small sample of pupils in one particular area and may, therefore, be dismissed as no more than a special case. Evidence from other sources, however, points in the same direction.

Miss D. E. M. Gardner (formerly Reader in Child Development, University of London Institute of Education) has described an investigation in which children in a number of ' progressive ' and ' traditional ' primary schools were compared at the age of ten years with respect to attainments in various types of subject-matter and activity. In the cases to which reference is made here, the *experimental* pupils had attended ' progressive ' schools continuously from the ages of five to ten years. Results from twelve pairs of schools, matched ' progressive ' and ' traditional,' are summarized in Table 5. To secure accuracy of comparison the following precautions were taken :

(*a*) Children in the two types of schools were paired for age, intelligence, sex, and social background ;

---

[1] My italics.

(b) In the opinion of the Head Teachers the children had been taught by competent teachers throughout their primary-school life ;

(c) The same person tested both groups of children in exactly the same way ;

(d) When results could not be marked exactly—as in art and original composition—the work was submitted to three independent assessors who did not know from which schools the specimens came ;

(e) Any differences were checked for statistical significance.

TABLE 5

COMPARISONS OF ATTAINMENTS OF 10-YEAR-OLD PUPILS IN TWELVE MATCHED PAIRS OF SCHOOLS

Subject	Progressive school undoubtedly superior	Progressive school slightly superior	Traditional school undoubtedly superior	Traditional school slightly superior	No difference	Total
Handwork Neatness	4	3	—	2	3	12
Handwork Ingenuity	6	1	—	4	1	12
Drawing and Painting	6	1	1	—	4	12
English I	6	1	—	2	3	12
English II	5	2	—	—	5	12
Composition	4	2	1	1	4	12
General Information	2	4	—	—	6	12
Totals	33	14	2	9	26	84
Reading	2	3	1	1	5	12
Handwriting	2	3	1	—	6	12
Arithmetic Mechanical	2	—	4	2	4	12
Arithmetic Problems	2	1	2	3	4	12
	8	7	8	6	19	48

Thus, the superiority of ' progressive ' or ' traditional ' methods depends partly on subject-matter. In what may be called the more æsthetic subjects the progressive schools were superior in forty-seven comparisons, the traditional schools in eleven ; while in twenty-six comparisons there were no significant differences. In the more formal subjects progressive schools were superior in fifteen comparisons ; traditional schools in fourteen ; while no differences were found in nineteen comparisons.

Thus, so far as attainments are concerned, the Birmingham survey is confirmed. Differences depend in part on the type of subject-matter. In no less than 45 comparisons no significant differences were found—26 cases out of 84 (31 per cent.) in the æsthetic subjects ; 19 cases out of 48 (39 per cent.) in the more formal subjects. Since the children were matched for sex, intelligence, and social background ; had been taught (so far as could be ascertained) by competent teachers, and may be supposed to have started at the beginning on equal terms, the implication is that, apart from progressive or traditional methods, the quality of the personal relationship between teachers and pupils, and factors of temperament and personality (extrovert-introvert ; convergent-divergent), are involved. Some children will thrive better with traditional treatment, others with progressive treatment, irrespective of the subject-matter. Some teachers are more comfortable and confident in a ' progressive ' regime ; other teachers are neither comfortable nor confident—the ' progressive ' methods seem so very unsystematic, and untidy ; too many loose ends.[1]

In a review of some American investigations into the educational treatment of emotionally disturbed children the reviewer noted the spread of a tendency to use therapy methods in a school environment.

> In part, this was due to an assumption by educators that the therapist was a kind of present-day John Wellington Wells whose stock in trade was indeed magic and spells. As a result, schools which attempted to educate emotionally disturbed children began trying modified play-therapy in small un-structured groups. *Some of these succeeded in some cases with some children ; others were notably unproductive of change, while still others served to confound the problem and the child further.*[2]

The authors of the book being reviewed tried providing emotionally disturbed children with

> a reasonably planned program where individual attention was possible. The classroom atmosphere and program were structured and directive. Classroom routines were fully planned and carefully carried out. At first very specific and limited tasks were assigned. These were later extended and elaborated as success and

---

[1] D. E. M. Gardner, " Does Progressive Primary Education Work ?", *Where*, No. 29, January 1967. See also the same author's *Experiment and Tradition in Primary Schools* (Methuen, 1966).

[2] My italics.

progress in the tasks were achieved. At all times the teacher maintained and promoted the expectation that the children were there to work. Mistakes were corrected, sloppy work redone, incomplete work completed. At all times what was prescribed and required was fair and reasonable for the child.

Emotionally disturbed children who had presented serious and protracted problems were selected and placed in one of three groups :

Group I   was given a highly structured programme ;
Group II   was kept in regular classrooms and all known techniques to help the children were employed ;
Group III had a permissive programme in a special class.

On the evidence of tests of academic achievement and behaviour ratings it was found after a period of six months that Group I with the planned highly structured programme were more constructive and tractable in the classroom and the home ; were academically more proficient and behaviourally better organized with much less meaningless random behaviour. Another somewhat unexpected result from the point of view of ' progressive ' methods.[1]

As we have suggested before, there seems to be no one absolutely correct and most efficient method of teaching or learning or school organization. It is, rather, a question of who teaches what to which particular pupil or pupils for which particular purpose in which particular environment. In the American experiment the effective factors seemed to be, not teacher-centred or child-centred, nor directive or permissive organization, but (a) classes small enough to allow individual attention to each pupil ; (b) careful adjustment of the tasks the children were required to do to their capacities, needs, and progress—in other words, *organizing success*, thereby promoting confidence and expectation of success ; increasing motivation to learn ; raising levels of aspiration.

One more comment, this from Mr George Leith at a Conference on " School of the Future " (1966) :

I want to say a few words about another issue, the issue of discovery. I have had a team working on this over a couple of years and we have got this far. We find that discovery works with some

---

[1] Review in *Contemporary Psychology*, VIII, February 2, 1963, by E. M. Bower, of a book *Educating Emotionally Disturbed Children* by N. G. Haring and E. L. Phillips (McGraw-Hill, 1962).

P

kinds of material for some children at certain ages but formal instruction works for other children with the same and other materials at the same ages. In effect we are not completely confident about this yet but it looks as though what is required in working out how to teach people is to diagnose the stage which a pupil has reached in his learning. If a child has not had much experience within a certain subject area ; if he is lacking in certain foundations of experience then he must have a period of discovery to be completely successful. *If he is well versed, then giving more discovery is rather inclined to put him off. He learns best by well-organised direct instruction because he has gone through all the discovery processes necessary. This tends to be the pattern we are finding in a number of researches.*[1]

The speaker went on to say that the real problem is to find what each pupil needs at that particular stage in his development. Different personality types may need different forms of instruction— on the one hand individual ' personalized ' teaching ; on the other, mass teaching. Some children may welcome the opportunity to answer back ; ask questions ; criticize. Others may not react well to this environment.[2]

Let me try to make my intention quite clear. I do not suggest that we go back to the excessively strict, narrow, authoritarian organization and methods of the nineteenth and early twentieth century, some of which, unfortunately, have persisted and are still practised nowadays. In fairness to the teachers, many of whom were humane, it must be recognized that much of that authoritarian ' atmosphere ' has been made inevitable by the material conditions of primary education, unsuitable buildings, enormous classes, absence of didactic material and apparatus, as well as by the prevalence of certain political, social, and religious prejudices and values. At the same time it is not at all necessary to go to an opposite extreme and in the name of progressive education " embrace anarchy in the name of freedom," as Mrs Marshall puts it, " and find it convenient to believe that no time-table and no record book means, in effect, no work." Whether we opt for traditional or progressive methods, let us agree that, ultimately, the children are in school to learn, but, *that different pupils learn best in different ways.* Traditional or

---

[1] In this connexion readers are referred back to Chapters VI and VII above. See particularly pp. 201 and following. My italics.

[2] Mr Leith was at the time of writing Deputy Director of the National Centre for Programmed Learning, Birmingham University. See *School of the Future* published by the National Union of Teachers, Hamilton House, London, W.C.1.

progressive, the unforgivable educational sin is to treat every individual in exactly the same way. Educational health means treating each individual pupil, so far as is practically possible, according to his needs and this can be done by a competent perceptive teacher even in a traditional environment, provided that the group taught is not too large.

What is valuable in the trend from ' traditional ' to ' progressive ' is the change in emphasis in the educative process from passive listening by the pupils to active participation. Pupils are now encouraged by the use of assignments, job-cards, Discovery Books, and programmed learning to teach themselves. So far, so good. Nevertheless, in whatever type of classroom organization (or its absence) and no matter how efficiently the assignments, job-cards, Discovery Books, and programmes are written, sooner or later, depending on temperament and mental ability, some check on the progress being made by individual pupils will be necessary and some systematic records must be kept. What have the pupils made of their reading and their experiments ? How have they interpreted their instructions ? To what extent have they organized their learning or understood its purport correctly ? Have they realized the connexions between different types of subject-matter ? Can they transfer ? Do they need help ? If so, in what particular difficulty ?

These questions can be answered only by discussion with a more mature person, a competent teacher. The teacher cannot stand aloof from the learning-process whether it is organized traditionally or progressively. Indeed, one of the main advantages claimed for the newer methods is that they relieve some of the routine work of teaching, thereby enabling teachers to do their real work more effectively. They are not teacher-substitutes, however.[1]

Finally, common observation indicates that some personalities are so constituted that they will produce their best efforts only as the result of some judicious pressure. Otherwise, they are too easily satisfied with mediocrity. They tend to equate freedom with licence. Not all human nature is perfect, even in a progressive organization.

Some, at least, of the controversy involved in ' progressive ' versus ' traditional ' is due to ambiguities in the meanings of the

[1] See D. Unwin and J. Leedham, *Aspects of Educational Technology* (Methuen, 1967), Chapters I, VII, and VIII, for evidence of superior efficiency of teacher plus programme over programmes alone.

terms concerned which have not been discriminated as clearly as is desirable.   The results noted above need not be so surprising if these implications are sorted out.

' Progressive ' may mean :

(i) Moving forward in *what is defined as* a positive direction.

(ii) Favouring educational, social, or political reform.

(iii) Improving in character, morality, or efficiency.

The implication being that the movement represents what in the speaker's or writer's opinion is a change for the better.

It may also mean :

(iv) Proceeding step by step in some logically necessary order of development or argument as in mathematics or theoretical science ; or proceeding step by step from easier to more difficult ; from simpler to more complex tasks.

One can ' progress ' by exploration, by discovery, by invention, by solving problems, by applying theory to practice, or by checking theory by the feedback effect of practical experience.

One can progress by being creative and original.   One can also progress, in fact at times must progress, by imitating, by being instructed, directed, advised, controlled.

The words most characteristic of the traditional educational system are ' instruction,' ' instructions,' ' to instruct,' ' to imitate,' ' to direct.'   These carry implications of overbearing authority, of passive obedience, of fixed routines which preclude individual variation or initiative.   One tends to think of traditional teaching as exclusively oral or through the medium of the printed word ; of the master ordering, directing, commanding, demonstrating, controlling what is to be learned and how it is to be learned by everybody without exception.

These terms, however, both ' traditional ' and ' progressive,' tend to arouse emotive attitudes, exclusive all-or-none separation, rather than critical awareness.   In fact, nobody's intellectual development is exclusively one or the other.   Some kinds of knowledge to be functionally adequate must be obtained by first-hand experience via the sense-organs ;   by active exploration of the environment. Other kinds of knowledge cannot be learned in that way.   They consist of arbitrary associations, settled by custom which varies from one locality or country to another.   These can be got only by imitation or instruction and in no other way, no matter how progressive the educational system may be.   Such, for example, are the names for objects, qualities, processes, relationships ;

conventional numerals ;   conventional sequences (the alphabet, for example) ;   conventional shapes of letters ;   conventional spelling. These arbitrary associations cannot be understood in the same way as can a logical relation or a relation of similarity.   In many cases there is no such relation.   Thus in the absence of instruction, direction, demonstration, or imitation some kinds of learning will not happen at all.   Words and symbols without the experiences to which they refer are not functionally adequate, but neither are experiences without the words and symbols with which to describe them and manipulate them mentally.

Learning cannot be regarded as two exclusive processes, exploration, self-activity, discovery, on the one side, and instruction, direction, imitation, memorization, on the other.   The two must be combined in different proportions at different periods of development and for different purposes.   The young learner must acquire ample first-hand and substitute experience together with the customary names, forms of speech, and techniques of reading and writing.   Here exploration, observation, manipulation, self-activity, are fundamental.   Even so, most children need suggestion, direction, guidance, demonstration, along with the first-hand contact with the environment.   Later, information, knowledge at second-hand, become increasingly important.   The research scientist must keep himself informed about developments outside his own laboratory by attending conferences, reading journals, searching in abstracts and bibliographies.   Indeed, an essential part of an adequate scientific training is not only acquiring experimental techniques, but knowing how to gather information from authoritative sources when it is required and how to estimate its validity.   The manager of a complex industrial enterprise keeps experts to supply him with information which he may have neither the leisure nor the expert skill to get for himself.   His function is to assess the value of this information with reference to the policies he wishes to pursue, then make his decisions accordingly.

This principle of dual function in learning is aptly illustrated by an experiment in teaching described by Mrs Marshall in the book already mentioned.[1]   Although familiar with Ordnance Survey maps, the children had difficulty in understanding the significance of contour lines.   As they lived in a flat East Anglian countryside, their experience did not include hills and valleys.   A practical demonstration was needed.   This was arranged by making a

[1] See p. 56.

miniature landscape with a hundredweight of clay. This was moulded into " hills and valleys and cliffs and beaches and promontories and harbours and peaks and estuaries (*learning all these geographical terms as we went along*)." Then, with the aid of a stretched wire, slices were cut horizontally off this landscape, laid on a flat sheet of tough paper, and an outline drawn around them until all the levels were treated.

In this way the pupils' attention was directed from the object to the symbol ; from the symbol back to the object. Words, lines, and experience at first hand took on mutual significance.

This would be called an activity method. To call it self-activity would not be strictly accurate. It was, in fact, a co-operative effort involving activity of both teacher and pupils. It is doubtful if, left to themselves, those Fenland pupils would ever have invented that method of illustrating the significance of contour lines. Apart from the teacher's instructions, the very problem itself might never have arisen. The exercise involved manipulation, discovery, information ("learning all these geographical terms as we went along "), directions, instructions, memorizing. The important matter for our purpose was that *the exercise called for active responses by the pupils. They looked and compared and manipulated as well as listened.*

The same principle is true for Froebel's ' gifts,' Montessori didactic apparatus ; Cuisenaire rods ; the Dienes mathematical blocks ; the Dalton Plan ; the Project Method. None of these represents pure self-activity on the part of the pupils. The apparatus and the method are devised by the ingenuity of a teacher for a specific purpose. The method demands and, in so far as it is efficient, it produces an active response from the pupils. This is one of the important factors in the so-called teaching machines and programmed learning. Pure self-activity is found only in spontaneous play. The difference between that and the teaching apparatus and methods mentioned above can be imagined, if not experienced, if children were given complete freedom to play with the didactic apparatus as they pleased. The results, in many cases, would be quite different from those intended by the inventors !

As we have said, all educative process involves elements of instruction, direction, information, memorizing, imitation, as well as exploration, manipulation, and discovery. Success in teaching and learning depends on (a) combining these in due proportion according to the needs of the learner in any particular situation, and (b) timing.

The real objection to instruction, direction, or information is that it may be introduced without reference to a pupil's need or purpose ; and without reference to his readiness to receive it.

This brings us again to the problem of readiness in learning. Readiness depends on several factors :

Maturational readiness—the general level of physical and neural development.

Intellectual readiness—the working level at which the learner is able to think.

Apperceptive readiness—whether or not an effective background of experience and information exists by means of which the learner can interpret and understand new experience and information.

Motivational readiness—the readiness of curiosity ; the need to know ; the realization of a problem and the desire for a solution.

Some of these factors depend (Hebb's intelligence A, for example) on innate endowment. Others depend on experience, stimulation, instruction, opportunity.

Intellectual readiness can best be understood by reference to the researches of the Swiss psychologist Jean Piaget. As a result of presenting children with problems, asking them questions, and noting their responses at different ages, he suggested that, broadly speaking, intellectual development passes through four main phases or stages—namely :

A *sensory-motor phase* when experience is derived entirely through play and active contact of the infant's sensory-manipulative apparatus with the environment.

A *pre-operational phase* when the child learns to connect things with words and symbols and can think of and talk about things in their absence, a representational phase.

A *concrete-operational phase* in which more systematic thinking is carried on in terms of practical activity aided by concrete imagery.

A *formal-operational phase* in which thinking can proceed through the medium of abstract logical relationships.

Piaget distinguished various sub-phases which need not concern us here. Our concern is that in these phases of intellectual development, experience and information proceed together, a mutual assimilation of actual experience and verbal (symbolic) elaboration.

Thus no useful educative purpose is served when a pupil is required to ingest information of a formal abstract logical nature if his intellectual development is still at the concrete-operation phase of development. It is not necessary to suppose that any given pupil goes abruptly from one phase to the next. There are transitional periods. At the same time there must be some degree of intellectual readiness before more advanced instruction and information can profitably be introduced.

Apperceptive readiness we have already dealt with in preceding chapters. It means that new experience, new information, new instruction, can be *understood and assimilated only by reference to a background of already existing knowledge*. Hence care must be taken in whatever method of teaching and school organization we adopt, to ensure that necessary preliminary experience and knowledge is established securely before new material is introduced, particularly in subject-matter with a logical structure. It is not useful practice, for example, to try to teach the method of long division in arithmetic until children can recognize numerals, add, subtract, and multiply with some degree of mastery.

Effective teaching and learning needs adequate organization and good timing.

Finally, there is the readiness due to the occasion or situation— a problem to be solved ; a practical difficulty to be overcome ; the emergence of a need or desire to speak, to write, to draw, to observe, to discover, to be informed,[1] to create something.

In summary we may say that the objection is not to instruction, direction, information as such, but to instruction, direction, information which seems to have no appreciable purpose ; which is badly timed ; for which there is insufficient or no readiness ; which is forced on to the learner by methods out of line with his own preferred ways of learning ; which is entirely teacher- and subject-determined, no exceptions being allowed, no questions, no discussion, no time for contemplation or creation. On the other hand, the objections to self-activity are to activity without a purpose, just busy work without direction. Thus no clear distinction can be made between ' traditional ' and ' progressive,' and what research has been done suggests that what is good for some pupils may not be so good for others.

---

[1] Problems can be solved by hearing or reading instructions—how to use a subscriber trunk dialling telephone system, for example, or reload a camera !

3. INCREASING IMPORTANCE OF EDUCATIONAL GUIDANCE

The need for educational guidance was noted in an earlier chapter (p. 64). The trends of change discussed in the present chapter will make guidance more rather than less necessary.

As we have seen, the main ' stream ' of secondary education since 1902 has moved via the traditional grammar type of schooling to the university. All other varieties of secondary schooling have had much less esteem. Selection for this stream has begun as early as entry into the junior primary schools, the basis for selection being scholastic attainment in arithmetic and language, combined in some cases with a standardized intelligence test.

More recently a tendency has developed against rigid streaming and in favour of comprehensive secondary schools. Both tendencies mean, in fact, bringing together into the same class or school a variety of individual differences.

Again, the spread of ' progressive ' child-centred schooling in place of ' traditional ' methods means the replacement of class teaching by methods of dealing with small groups or individual pupils according to their individual needs.

Thus the *main feature of most, if not all, the modern trends in the schools is the increased importance ascribed to the individual pupil.* In so far as this is psychologically sound it implies that curricula and teaching methods must be adjusted to the individual, not the individual to the curricula and teaching methods.

Another trend has been noted—namely, the suspicion that the I.Q. and scholastic achievement by themselves have been over-rated as indicators of future creative potential. Other factors of intellect, temperament, and personality generally may be at least as important as if not, in fact, more so than the I.Q. and scholastic attainment. Further, it appears that as the age of pupils increases, special abilities and talents increase in importance in relation to general ability.

Educational guidance has two important functions to perform in any future educational organization :

(i) To produce reliable tests not only for different aspects of intelligence and scholastic aptitude, but also for levels of development and intellectual function ; for qualities of personality and temperament (introversion, extroversion, aggression, anxiety, level of aspiration, self-image, emotional maladjustment), as well as for potential creative talents in art, music, crafts, technical skills. The early

discovery and encouragement of creative talent is important for economic and technical reasons. It is also
important psychologically. Creative activity is emotionally satisfying. The early discovery of emotional
maladjustment and conflict is important not merely for
the satisfaction of the sufferer, but because there is a close
connexion between emotional maladjustment and scholastic progress. As the authors of *Four Years On* said,
" It may well be that fostering emotional and social
potential may prove more conducive to improving a
child's rate of learning than concentrating more directly
but narrowly on educational progress itself."[1]

(ii) To discover in much more detail than is known at the time
of writing *what types of curriculum and teaching methods
will best suit the needs of particular individuals*. It is
naïve to assume (as the Circular 10/65 appears to do)
that we ought to extend the grammar-school type of
education to children who do not at present receive it.
It may not suit everybody even though all pupils attend
the same comprehensive schools.[2]

The functions of educational guidance have been stated very
clearly in the pamphlet on *Procedures for Allocation of Pupils in
Secondary Schools*. Extension of the comprehensive type of
secondary organization or an adoption of the eight- or nine-year
common school will not eliminate the need for guidance. Differences
between individuals and the consequent differences in educational
needs . . .

> . . . increase steadily in importance as children grow older—this
> will occur, one may safely predict, even if all environmental ad-
> vantages can be eliminated. The supreme educational injustice is
> to treat all children in an identical way. . . .
> Guidance is a process dependent upon three things : diagnosis
> of the child's present status, strengths, deficiencies and needs ;
> knowledge of the directions that this growth appears to be taking ;

---

[1] See also M. L. Kellmer Pringle, *Deprivation and Education*, Chapter 8
" Learning and Emotion " (Longmans, 1965); J. B. Biggs, *Anxiety, Motiva-
tion and Primary School Mathematics* (National Foundation for Educational
Research, Occasional Publication No. 7).

[2] The question we should be asking is—are the grammar schools as they
existed up to, say, 1960 worth keeping ? The answer may be ' Yes,' but it is
by no means a foregone conclusion. It remains to be proved.

and predictions about likely outcomes of different kinds of educational provision for him. . . .

If we accept that guidance is our aim (not selection, which implies a limitation below the level of demand of certain types of education), then the information described above has to serve the purpose of making the best possible choice for each child ; one which will lead to his maximum self-realisation. . . .

Finally, the predictions, modified by knowledge of the directions which growth appears to be taking, should provide an estimate of minimum targets or expectations which skilful adaptation of educational methods would attempt to exceed.[1]

It is obvious that efficient guidance will need special training and expert knowledge.   This is another argument in favour of secondary schools sufficiently large to make possible the appointment of a teacher or teachers with special responsibility for guidance.   It is equally obvious that the other members of the teaching staff should be aware of the reasons for guidance and *be prepared to work in close co-operation with* the guidance officers or teachers responsible.

A system of this kind has been established in France.   Dr W. D. Halls in the article mentioned above[2] says :

> Basic to the reform is the concept of 'guidance.'   Throughout his secondary career—and before—the child is systematically observed and detailed records kept.   The 'common school' from 11–15 is officially termed the 'phase of observation and guidance.'   The pupil's file contains records of attainment, class positions and test results ; interviews with parents and child ; medical history ; reports by social workers where applicable.   Once a month at least, the form teacher calls together all subject teachers and, in the presence of the headmaster, the progress of each pupil is assessed and recorded.[3]

4. PROGRAMMED LEARNING.   TEACHING BY MACHINES
Another Fashion?

We have already noted how fashions in teaching and school organization arise from time to time, flourish, and wane, due, fundamentally, to economic and sociological conditions, though the advantages claimed may be psychological and educational.

---

[1] *Loc. cit.*, p. 19.
[2] " Lessons from the French," *Where*, November 1966.
[3] At the time of writing training courses have been established at Keele and Reading Universities.

At the time of writing the latest fashion is the introduction of what have been miscalled ' teaching machines,' the purpose of which is to promote individual learning as opposed to mass teaching.

These ' gadgets ' have aroused the usual uncritical emotional attitudes of enthusiasm or rejection. If only every pupil in every school and every student in every university, training college, and institute of technology had his own teaching machine the educational millennium would be just around the corner. On the other hand, particularly among professional teachers, there is suspicion of yet another ' stunt ' and the belief that for teaching there is no substitute for teachers.

This new trend, however, needs serious consideration for several reasons :

(i) Britain, the United States, and under-developed countries particularly are faced with a critical shortage of teachers. It is estimated that in Britain, by the time the compulsory school-leaving age is raised to sixteen years, there will be some 120,000 too few teachers. In the U.S.A. the shortage is likely to be nearer a million !

(ii) There is an ' explosion ' of knowledge as well as of population. The demand for more varied and highly specialized knowledge and skills in industry, commerce, and the Armed Forces is increasing faster than experts can be trained to teach them.

(iii) There is an increasing tendency for pupils to remain at school, voluntarily, after the compulsory leaving age. In education opportunity helps to create demand.

(iv) The trends towards comprehensive schools, against rigid streaming, towards more ' progressive ' methods, all involve recognizing and catering for a greater variety of individual differences, wider ranges of ability and rates of learning in groups of the same chronological age. Consequently, more provision will be necessary for individual work at all levels of schooling. Even if there were enough teachers to deal with all the classes in our present schools the same number of teachers could not deal adequately with the pupils as individuals.

(v) There is increasing dissatisfaction with traditional classroom teaching—at secondary school and higher levels typically a talk or lecture supplemented in some cases by blackboard, pictures, diagrams, and summarized by dictated notes. It has been said that the only place in the modern world in which an ancient Greek could feel at home would be in a secondary-school classroom. Yet it has been known for some time that oral methods of instruction are not conducive to efficient retention. Some experimental results may be found in Chapter XI below on Rates of Forgetting (*q.v.*). In a more recent American investigation[1] the listening ability of several thousand students and hundreds of business and professional people was tested for retention. They listened, as they believed, with concentration. Nevertheless, on average, only about half the information was recallable immediately after the talk ; about a quarter after a short period. One-half to two-thirds had been forgotten within eight hours. As any listener knows from experience, attending fluctuates ; casual associations lead thoughts away from the main discourse, the trend of an argument is lost, and boredom sets in. The amount recallable depends on previous knowledge of the subject-matter, its degree of difficulty, one's interest and purpose in listening, as well as on differences in aptitude for memorizing.

The pass lists in public examinations are not encouraging. At the Ordinary Level of the General Certificate of Education on the average somewhere between 55–60 per cent. of students pass ; at the Advanced Level about two-thirds. In National Certificate Examinations in 1961 at the Ordinary Level 18,000 out of 40,000 passed ; at the Higher level 11,000 out of 18,000. Results such as these would not be tolerated in any efficient industrial organization.[2]

Attempts have been made to supplement oral methods of instruction by the use of epidiascope, cinema films, and television, all of which are, incidentally, ' teaching machines.' The practical difficulty is to incorporate extrinsic devices, films, radio, and television into the normal school timetable. The schools cannot control the timing of these programmes, and by no means all schools possess either film projectors or television sets.[3]

It is in these circumstances—chronic shortage of teachers, increasingly insistent demands for new types of subject-matter and skills, and growing dissatisfaction with oral methods of instruction—that the use of teaching machines or, to be more precise, programmed learning has spread. This is another example of the way in which educational practices and sociological conditions interact. S. L. Pressey, an American psychologist, invented a mechanical device in

---

[1] Nichols and Stevens, *Harvard Business Review*, September–October 1957.

[2] This is relevant to the intention expressed in the Circular 10/65 to extend the benefits of grammar-school education to pupils who do not now enjoy them. Examination results are not, of course, the only criterion of grammar-school efficiency, but they are the usual ' yardstick ' by which it is estimated.

[3] In 1966.

1926 which would automatically check students' responses in revision tests at the college level. He found that not only did the machine mark responses on multi-choice-type questions, it also increased the students' learning efficiency as the result of making the responses. Here, it seemed, was a device which would not only relieve a teacher of much of the drudgery of routine marking ; it could also be used as an aid to teaching and learning.

At that time, however, circumstances did not favour the use of such a device. There was no serious shortage of teachers. There were no insistent demands for new types of specialist technical knowledge such as had arisen during and after the Second World War. Industry in 1926 was not organized to mass-produce the machines. And neither psychologists, the teaching profession, nor the general public were ' conditioned ' to accepting so apparently revolutionary an invention as a teaching machine. Consequently the proposal lay dormant until another American psychologist, Professor B. F. Skinner, published in 1954 a paper suggesting that methods he had found successful in teaching pigeons to play a caricature of a game of ping-pong could be applied to the teaching of children in schools. By 1954 the time was ripe for introducing mechanical teaching devices. Automation had become a familiar concept in industry ; so had operant conditioning in psychology.[1]

A NEW LOOK AT LEARNING AND TEACHING PROCESSES

The theoretical foundations of the Skinner proposals are the principles of operant conditioning and reinforcement. These have already been discussed in the section on mechanisms of learning in Chapter IX. Readers will recall that after a particular behavioural act has been *emitted* that response is made more probable on a future occasion if it is *immediately reinforced* by some form of satisfaction—for example, food—or the removal of an unpleasant stimulus. By reinforcing each of a sequence of responses all tending towards some appropriate form of behaviour Skinner said that it would be possible to control (to ' shape,' as he called it) the learning process in any direction decided upon by the trainer. Moreover, by the judicious use of reinforcing rewards, motivation could be kept at a sufficiently

[1] Professor Skinner's paper on " The Science of Learning and the Art of Teaching " was presented at a conference on Current Trends in Psychology and the Behavioural Sciences in Pittsburgh in 1954. It is reprinted as Chapter 2 in W. I. Smith and J. W. Moore (eds.), *Programmed Learning* (Van Nostrand, 1962).

high level for long periods of time. As he said, in all this work the species of organism had made surprisingly little difference. Comparable results had been obtained with pigeons, rats, dogs, monkeys, human children, and human psychotic subjects. Why then should not this operant conditioning and reinforcement technique be applied to such fields as perception and thinking? In learning arithmetic, for example, children acquire many verbal responses—speaking and writing certain words, figures, and signs which refer to numbers and arithmetical operations. Hence the business of teaching is to 'shape up' these serial responses by appropriate reinforcements into the processes we know as arithmetical calculations. How he proposed to do this will appear later.[1]

Thus the question arises : can some teaching processes be carried on efficiently by a mechanical device? If so, which processes, and how?

This is an invitation to reconsider what is involved in instruction and education. Learning involves :

(a) Gaining a variety of experience *at first hand* by means of transactions with the environment in active free play, exploration, manipulation, discovery, *in which all the sense-organs are in use*. In the same transactions sensory-motor habits are formed and developed into increasingly complex skills.

(b) Along with this activity goes the acquisition of arbitrary associations by 'conditioning' and instruction—learning to speak, read, write, calculate. Much of this arbitrarily associative learning must be consolidated and made readily recallable by revision, repetition, and practice.

(c) As the result of the activities in (a) and (b) complex intellectual skills develop—for example, attending, observing, discriminating, classifying, generalizing, reasoning, problem-solving. Here again practice in a variety of situations promotes efficiency and transfer.

(d) There remain certain more intangible results which distinguish education properly so called from instruction—the development of manners, social behaviour, moral codes, ideals, standards of judgment, aesthetic tastes, as well, incidentally, as biases and prejudices. Instruction plays some part in these developments, but

---

[1] Professor Skinner appears not to be interested in any conditions *within* the learning organism. All he is concerned with is which responses follow which stimuli. If I have understood him correctly he seems to imply that education is concerned solely with the production of correct—*i.e.*, socially acceptable—verbal responses to particular stimuli.

the results arise as much or even more through the pupils identifying themselves with models—parents, teachers, characters in biography and fiction, film stars, television stars, leaders in politics, society, sport.   Also, attitudes are 'picked up,' unwittingly, from the 'tone' of the social environment.   This aspect of education is fostered by discussion, debate, argument, criticism, question and answer; by the free exchange of opinions in social situations.   Mrs Marshall says :

> Good conversation is an art in itself and one that I have always thought well worth acquiring . . . the children talked freely not only in front of me but with me and to me.   They began to realise that a good discussion was as exciting as any other sort of contest.   They had to obey the rules of good conversation which meant listening while others talked, keeping to the subject under discussion, and saying only those things they were prepared to back by further argument, if necessary.   Discussions ranged far and wide over many different subjects but nearly always came round, in the end, to questions of religion, ethics and morals.[1]

Again, this time the Head of a grammar school, who says :

> Sixth form work at its best involves a close relationship between student and tutor in which the one helps the other to do his own work. As Plato said " Intellectual progress does not take place when the teacher is laying down the law and the pupil is memorising.   Teacher and pupil must work together to bring the pupil to a rational answer to the question before him."   The best methods of education are criticism, question, discussion and debate.[2]

We have noted also in Professor Musgrove's survey of school satisfactions the desire on the part of students for self-expression ; for opportunities to state their own views.

It would seem, therefore, that at the beginning of each phase in the rhythms of educative process there must be first-hand contact through free play, exploration, manipulation, active observation between learner and environment.   Moreover, in discussing creativity and productive thinking, we noted the importance of the *free play of imagery and concepts during periods of browsing and contemplation when new associations are formed and novel responses take shape.*   Throughout the educative process, direct social intercourse between teacher and learners, and between the learners themselves in various forms of co-operative (and competitive) activity, is essential for full personal development.   And in view of what has been said about comprehensive schooling and non-

---

[1] Book cited, p. 131.   [2] H. Davies, book cited, p. 57.

streaming, it should be noted that practical activity, creative imagination, collective discussion, argument, debate, is not the exclusive prerogative of high scholastic achievement. Pupils at different levels of purely academic ability can be included in the same co-operative activities. Creativity and scholastic achievement are by no means perfectly correlated. This is one conclusion about which most, if not all, writers on creative activities are agreed.

Between these two aspects of the educative process—namely, the accumulation and organization of first-hand experience and social and creative activities—there are instruction, regulation, direction, revision, repetitive practice, testing, and marking, much of it routine work which might easily lend itself to mechanized treatment, thereby relieving teachers for more creative, educative work.

HOW CAN INSTRUCTION BE MECHANIZED? PROGRAMMED LEARNING

This is where self-correcting, didactic apparatus, and programmed instruction enter.

Behaviourist psychologists, operant conditioning, and systems-engineering notwithstanding, the notion of self-correcting, didactic apparatus and programmed instruction is by no means new. It has not been talked about, however, in specialist technical language. The abacus in various forms has been used for performing and teaching processes of numerical calculation for centuries. More recently we have had the Montessori apparatus, the Dalton Plan, Discovery Books, the mathematical materials of Cuisenaire and Dienes (to name only two of the best known).

The Dalton Plan is particularly instructive for our purpose. It was a method of organizing individual work in a small rural school where the mistress, Miss Helen Parkhurst, had to deal with a wide range of ages and abilities in the same group. Instead of presenting the syllabus orally to several sub-groups in turn, Miss Parkhurst wrote out ' assignments ' calculated to keep a pupil occupied for a fortnight or a month. Each pupil undertook to complete each set of assignments before going on to the next set. Thus each pupil was guided by instructions, directions, references to books, atlases, experiments, problems, and exercises and *was made responsible for his own learning*. He could go at his own pace, within limits, and could, if he wished, spend most time at his weakest subjects. Thus these assignments constituted a series of programmes of instruction.

A variant of this programmed instruction has been devised by A. W. Rowe and called the 'job-card' method. This has proved successful in dealing with slow-learning children.[1]

The more recent types of programmed instruction are, in fact, extensions and refinements of these assignments, job-cards, and Discovery Books. The term 'teaching machine' is a misnomer—a product of inaccurate popular journalese. The teaching part of the device is the 'programme,' a set of instructions, directions, and questions to be answered. This, of course, is conceived and set out by a human teacher or technological expert. The machine is a box of some sort in which the programme can be displayed and which incorporates an anti-cheating (or rather anti-peeping) arrangement. Illustrations of these mechanical devices can be seen in the books referred to in the bibliography (p. 494).

TYPES OF PROGRAMME

There are five types of programme in common use at the time of writing : Linear, Multi-choice, Branching, Ruleg, and Scrambled Books. Short examples only can be given here. For fuller details see references in the bibliography.

(a) *Linear Programmes*

These are associated with the name of Professor Skinner. In them *the subject-matter to be learned is divided into a sequence of very small steps.* Each step is enclosed in a separate 'frame' and *requires an active response* from the learner. As each frame is answered a mechanical device propels the programme one frame forward. This reveals the next question and the correct answer to the immediately preceding frame. In this way, according to the theory of operant conditioning, learning at each step is *reinforced immediately by knowing the correct result,* thereby making the retention and reproduction of that correct answer more probable on subsequent occasions. In programmes of this type the answers (responses) must be 'constructed '—that is, written down.

The following example shows a sequence of five frames in a Skinner Linear programme on operant conditioning.[2]

[1] See Helen Parkhurst, *Education on the Dalton Plan* (Bell, 1930) ; A. W. Rowe, *The Education of the Average Child* (Harrap, 1959). Also Chapter XII below.

[2] See M. Goldsmith (ed.), *Mechanisation in the Classroom* (Souvenir Press, 1963), Appendix A, p. 211.

1. Performing animals are sometimes trained with ' rewards.' The behaviour of a hungry animal can be ' rewarded ' with ——	
2. A technical term for ' reward ' is reinforcement. To ' reward ' an animal with food is to —— it with food.	1. Food.
3. *Technically* speaking, a thirsty organism can be —— with water.	2. Reinforce.
4. The trainer reinforces the animal by giving it food —— it has performed correctly.	3. Reinforced NOT rewarded.
5. Reinforcement and behaviour occur in the temporal order (1) —— (2) ——	4. When, if, after.
6.	5. (1) Behaviour (2) Reinforcement.
	6.

And so on through a set of thirty frames. The student can write his answer in the space provided in each frame. The correct answer is given, one frame later, in the column on the right.

There are various ways of displaying linear programmes. One comparatively simple form is shown in Fig. 31, page 472. The box has perspex covers for the completed frame and the corresponding answer. By turning a knob or moving a lever the programme can be advanced by one frame and one answer, making possible immediate comparison between the two. Note the very short steps into which the programme has been divided and the way in which the concept involved is repeated in different contexts. Programmes of this type can be designed for different types of subject-matter at various levels of difficulty from junior primary school up to university level.

Multi-choice Programmes

Instead of ' constructed ' answers such as those illustrated above, Pressey has used multi-choice programmes in which several possible answers are provided and the pupil must indicate in some way which he believes to be the correct one. For example, in a science programme on ' The Atmosphere ' for top Juniors and lower Seniors are two such multi-choice frames :[1]

79. When you squeeze a sponge what happens ? A. It gets bigger. B. It gets smaller. C. It stays the same.	
80. What happens to the holes in a sponge when it is squeezed ? A. They get bigger. B. They get smaller. C. They stay the same.	79. It gets smaller.
	80. They get smaller.

Branching Programmes

It has been felt by some investigators that the Skinner linear type of programme may be too restrictive—too closely controlled and likely after some time to induce boredom. Not all learners may need to go and some may not want to go at the pace dictated by so many and such short steps. As an alternative, ' branching ' programmes have been suggested by A. N. Crowder. These may be arranged in the form of a ' scrambled ' text-book. In this case a student is allowed more freedom, and more opportunity to make mistakes. So long as his answers are correct the learner is referred forward to more problems. If he makes a mistake he is referred back to one of several sections (according to the nature of the error) which explains why he is wrong. Attention is directed to the precise conditions of the problem, and he is invited to try again. If now he is correct he is referred to a section which explains how the correct answer is obtained.

The following is an example from a branching programme in text-book form on introductory probability devised by Professor J. R. Dixon for engineering students :[2]

On p. 17 (of the programmed text) we find this problem :—
Suppose there are three balls in a box ; two green, one red. You

---

[1] See J. Leedham and D. Unwin, *Programmed Learning in Schools* (Longmans, 1965).
[2] See " Programmed Instruction in Engineering " in M. Goldsmith (ed.), book cited, p. 176.

are told that the balls are drawn out one at a time and kept out. What is the probability that a red one was drawn at the first try ? Easy, you say, 1/3. Right. Now, however, suppose you are told that a green ball was drawn on the *third* try. What is the probability now that a red ball was drawn on the first try ?

If your answer is 0, turn to page 20.
If your answer is 1/2, turn to page 23.
If your answer is 1/3, turn to page 29.
If your answer is none of the above turn to page 32.
If you can't get an answer, turn to page 35.

On page 20 we find :

Your answer is 0. You are wrong. You must have your reds and greens mixed up. Go back to page 17, and read the problem carefully.

And so on. On page 23, the correct answer is given and an explanation of how it was obtained. A new multiple-choice question is then given.[1]

Experiments are in progress in the Universities of Sheffield and Aberdeen in which a combination of branching and linear programmes is used. So long as the student gives a correct answer he is referred forward in bigger steps to more material. If, however, he makes a wrong response, he is referred back to his last correct answer and from there has to proceed by a series of short steps in a linear programme until he has understood that particular section of the material.

Ruleg Programmes

These contain a combination of rules (or principles) together with illustrative examples. The rule may be stated first, followed by examples, or the examples can be given and a statement of the rule required. The following is an example from a ' Ruleg ' programme in High School Physics :[2]

3. Any object which gives off light because it is hot is called an *incandescent* light source. Thus, a candle flame and the sun are alike in that they both are (*a*)   sources of light.

---

[1] Note how the example given (from p. 20) resembles the Russian experimental method of teaching geometry, described above on p. 320.

[2] See M. Goldsmith (ed.), book cited, p. 216.

4. When a blacksmith heats a bar of iron until it glows and emits light, the iron bar has become an (b)................................. source of light.

5. A neon tube emits light but remains cool. Unlike the ordinary electric light bulb, then, it is not an (c)........................... (d).......................... of light.

6. An object is called incandescent when (e)...................................... ....

Item 3 above states a rule and an example. The word in 3a should be ' incandescent.'

Item 4 gives an example. 4b=incandescent.

Item 5 gives a negative example. 5c; 5d=incandescent; source.

Item 6 requires a statement of the rule. 6e="it emits light because it is hot."

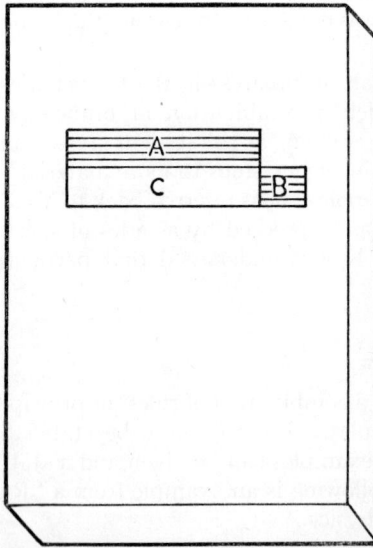

FIG. 31

Showing in diagram form the layout of a simple teaching machine:

A = Perspex cover for frame answered in C and advanced one step forward.

B = Perspex cover for correct answer to frame under A.

C = open space for next question and answer.

A lever conveniently placed is available for moving the programme one frame forward as required.

CRITICISMS OF TRADITIONAL TEACHING METHODS

The protagonists of programmed learning are very critical of traditional teaching methods. Some of their strictures appear to be aimed at caricatures of what really competent teachers actually do. Moreover, although some of the critics appear to be ignorant of the fact, some of their suggestions for reform are centuries old. Rousseau in 1762 made a vigorous attack on passive, merely verbal methods. Comenius more than a century earlier in *The Great Didactic* (1630) had suggested some of the rules according to which Skinner's linear programmes are designed: for example, proceed step by step; go from what is easy to what is more difficult; arrange everything to suit the capacity of the pupil; subjects should not merely be taught orally; errors must be corrected on the spot; every subject should be taught in definitely graded steps; books should be written simply and clearly and should give the scholars sufficient assistance to pursue their studies without the help of a teacher; introduce only one difficulty at a time; no-one should be assumed to understand anything without being able to express his knowledge in words; and so on. Comenius' theory was different from that of Professor Skinner, but his recommendations for teaching-method were much the same.

However, original or otherwise, the challenge of programmed learning has demanded a critical consideration of traditional teaching practice. The critics point out that :

(i) Oral teaching encourages passive listening. Frequent active responses from the pupils are necessary, both for retention and to maintain interest at a sufficiently high level.

(ii) Responses should be corrected as soon as possible after they have been made. Too long an interval elapses between response and confirmation, or correction (that is, reinforcement).

(iii) Too much material is presented at a time.

(iv) The aims of the teaching are not sufficiently precise.

(v) Not sufficient care is taken to ensure that each step has been sufficiently well mastered before further steps are introduced. (In other words, not enough care is taken to ensure full apperceptive readiness. This is particularly disconcerting in subjects like mathematics and physical science which have a logical structure.)[1]

---

[1] I have found, for example, pupils floundering about, trying in vain to solve problems in algebra before they had understood the rudiments of simple arithmetic.

CLAIMS FOR PROGRAMMED LEARNING

These may be summarized as follows :

(i) The pupil is actively engaged. He must make a series of *frequent active* responses. This ensures that adequate attention has been concentrated on learning.

(ii) The fact that the mechanical device provides for immediate self-correction ensures the maximum reinforcing effect of knowledge of results. Frequent reinforcement maintains motivation and interest at a sufficiently high continuous level.

(iii) Linear programmes particularly are designed to *reduce the likelihood of error to a minimum*. This maximizes the motivating effects of success, avoids frustration and feelings of aversion, raises confidence and levels of aspiration, particularly in the cases of slower-learning pupils normally depressed by too frequent failure.

(iv) Errors, if made, are not allowed to accumulate to the detriment of future understanding.

(v) Because the material to be learned is presented (in a well-designed programme) in a series of very small steps which follow each other in a correct sequence for understanding, and because all the information necessary for a correct response on each frame has already been introduced, apperceptive readiness is maximized.

(vi) Each pupil can proceed at his own pace.

(vii) If absent, time lost can be made up.

(viii) Mistakes, if made, are not publicized to the humiliation of the pupil.

(ix) Pupils learn faster by using the programmes.

(x) The mechanical device with its programmes can relieve the teacher of much routine work, leaving him with more time and energy to devote to productive teaching.

MAKING A PROGRAMME

Programmes are made in somewhat the same way as objective tests of intelligence and attainment are standardized.

First, a clear appreciation of the nature of the subject-matter to be presented is needed, and the kind of pupil or student for whom it is intended.

An experimental programme is then drafted. This draft is

checked and probably modified by teachers or technical experts other than the author of the draft.

The modified draft is duplicated and tried out on a sample of learners *comparable to the population for which the final programme is intended.* Performances on this trial are scrutinized for errors, and, by implication, faulty wording and sequence in the draft. Subsequent drafts may be reworded and retested until the percentage of errors is reduced to what is considered desirable by the designers of the programme.

Finally, this revised draft is duplicated or printed for general use.

The general use of these standardized programmes has its dangers. It is apt to be assumed that any printed programme must be universally valid irrespective of the circumstances in which it has been standardized. Moreover, the publication of standardized programmes is likely to become commercially profitable and encouraged by high-pressure sales methods. Any faults not discovered in the standardizing process may be spread abroad and school syllabuses and teaching methods determined by the printed programmes instead of the printed programmes being supplementary to the syllabuses and the objectives for which they are taught. There is no doubt that standardized tests of ' intelligence ' and attainment as well as public examinations have influenced what is taught and how it is taught irrespective of the needs of a locality and of individual pupils.

There is something to be said, therefore, for the practice of a group of teachers making their own programmes. To do this certain rules must be followed :

(i) The aim of the programme must be very clearly envisaged. What knowledge is to be acquired and what skills learned ?

(ii) The material must be presented in sufficiently small steps. Each frame should present *only one* new idea or one new difficulty at a time.

(iii) In subject-matter with a logical structure the frames must follow in correct sequence. All the necessary preliminary information or subsidiary skills must already have been mastered to make success on the next frame highly probable.

(iv) To ensure over-learning and ready recallability of information, frequent repetition is necessary. To avoid boredom and encourage transfer, the same item of information should be repeated in a sufficient variety of contexts. (See, for examples, the specimen frames already quoted above.)

(v) Knowledge must not be taken for granted. Whoever writes a programme should be well acquainted with the environmental background and previous schooling of the pupils for whom the programmes are intended. It does not follow that a programme suitable for urban children in district X is equally suitable in detail for rural children in district Y. The same proviso applies to children from different socio-economic backgrounds.

IS PROGRAMMED INSTRUCTION EFFICIENT ?

There seems to be no doubt that programmed instruction does work, *within limits*. At the time of writing what precisely these limits are is not clearly known. Some experimental evidence is favourable. Studies reported by P. Cavanagh in *Occupational Psychology*[1] in connexion with Navy, Air Force, and British European Airways personnel with programmes about elementary trigonometry and technical information indicated that when groups were matched for intelligence and initial knowledge of the subject, then :

(i) Achievement with the teaching machine was as good as that with conventional instruction.

(ii) Students learned faster by using the machines (this has been confirmed in other experimental studies).

(iii) Material learned through the use of programmes was retained longer than in conventional instruction.

(iv) The teaching-machine method was more effective from the point of view of learning-speed and retention than the scrambled text-book.

(v) The more able students are helped most by the machines. There may be a tendency in the absence of carefully controlled experiments to compare programmed learning in favourable conditions with traditional methods in by no means favourable conditions. The very novelty of the mechanical devices by stimulating curiosity and intensifying motivation may be a favourable factor in the situation whatever the merits of the programme. This may diminish in importance as familiarity with the ' gadget ' increases. Some writers have noted a ' pall ' effect after expanded use of the machines.

All types of programmes teach something. With respect to which is better—constructed responses, multi-choice responses, linear, branching or scrambled text-book programmes, there seems at present to be little reliable evidence for or against. As we have noted in

[1] Volume 37, 1963, p. 44.

other connexions, learning efficiency depends on the objectives in view in terms of knowledge and skills to be acquired, the purpose for which the learning is to be used, the age and idiosyncrasies of individual learners. Because the experimental investigations have, so far, revealed little or no significant differences it cannot be inferred that there are none. There may be, but the experimental arrangements have not revealed them. One possible reason may lie in the complex nature of the learning process itself. It is probably a *system* rather than a mechanical mixture. If that is so, it means that by altering one factor in the learning situation several other factors are thereby changed *at the same time*. For example, we may learn in one way when preparing for an examination and in quite another way in making a research, or in mastering a subject because we find it interesting and satisfying, intellectually or emotionally. Long-term learning is probably different from the rapid ingestion of a ' brief '—material which will be needed for one special occasion in the near future and thereafter discarded. Most experimental procedure attempts to alter only one factor at a time. This may be difficult to ensure in complex learning experiments.

Sufficient evidence has been found to suggest that for some types of instruction at least, programmed learning is worth further trial.

SOME QUERIES

Without being pernickety and wishing to denigrate programmed learning because it represents a departure from traditional practice, certain queries need to be kept in mind with respect to its general use as an educational medium.

(i) Does the Skinner type of linear programme exercise too rigid a control of the learning process ? It may be frustrating to some learners to proceed in such very small steps. Answering in single words or short phrases may induce active attending for the time being, but it may also be exasperating when the novelty wears off. Moreover, in normal reading the student may want to refer back to previous material or forward in anticipation of possible developments. There is such a process as adventurous exploration in learning and thinking which a too rigidly controlled programme may prevent to the detriment of the learner. This intellectual adventure may be an important factor in transfer and productive thinking.

What has been suggested previously about the importance of individual idiosyncrasies in learning may apply to programmed learning. In some American experiments in which the learners could control the sequence of steps in a programme, they chose a sequence different from that of the standardized product.   Further, when some adult learners were allowed to organize their own individual courses their training was achieved in 65 per cent. less time than in comparable cases in which a uniform pattern was imposed.[1]

This may not apply equally at every age nor at every level of intellectual ability.   Nevertheless, there does appear to be some danger that too many rigidly controlled programmes may adversely affect some learners, particularly those with the highest creative potential.

(ii) A programme can direct a student to other sources ; can require an essay to be written and presented to a tutor ; can give directions for conducting experiments.   It cannot, however, provide first-hand experience.   Consider the making of the clay island described on p. 455 above.   A programme could help a student by means of a succession of definitions, examples, and exercises to answer questions about contour lines on an Ordnance map.   It could not provide for children living in a flat plain some vivid three-dimensional imagery of what the lines on the contour map represent.   The necessary first-hand experience with the clay model having been obtained the concepts involved could be recapitulated, revised, and memorized by the aid of a supplementary programme.

It is possible that the maximum utility of programmed instruction will be found in connexion with the development of structured subjects such as mathematics and logic, and in assisting the learning of arbitrary associations—*e.g.*, technical details and vocabularies.

(iii) What, precisely, is reinforcement, and is reinforcement an essential factor in human learning ?

There is an element of mystery about this process of reinforcement.   The fact that knowledge of results is a help in learning has been demonstrated experimentally.   The fact that work should be corrected as soon as possible after completion has been known since the time of Comenius, if not earlier.   It does not follow that reinforcement in Professor Skinner's concept of the term is always and necessarily the most efficient method of promoting learning.   His principles, according to which much of the subsequent design of programmed learning has been due, were derived from experiments with animals *lacking a spoken language and consequently any capacity for inner speech as a factor in learning.*

[1] R. F. Mager and C. Clark, " Explorations in Student-Controlled Instruction," *Psychological Reports*, No. 91, October 1961.

Learning-processes in human students may be more complicated than those in animals, and it cannot be taken for granted that what holds good for pigeons in a Skinner box can be transferred without modification to human pupils in schools.

In the first place, Skinner's animals were hungry while being trained. Their learning was instrumental. They wanted food and they learned in order to get it. Food was satisfying. It is the satisfaction rather than the food which is rewarding and, therefore, reinforcing. An animal already fed to satiety will not exert itself (unless artificially stimulated) to get more food. It is more likely to go to sleep unless some aspect of the food situation arouses its curiosity. Even so, it will satisfy its curiosity rather than learn a new trick. Similarly, the correct answer to a question in a programme is not likely to aid learning unless the learner *wants to know the correct answer*. A sexually precocious young woman of fifteen-plus years whose interest is concentrated on a 'date' after school couldn't care less what is the correct answer to some academic question about arithmetic, or history, or grammar. Whether or not knowledge of results will be reinforcing depends on the interest of the learner.

Secondly, in operant conditioning it has been supposed that for learning to be reinforced the *act* to be learned must occur *before* the reward is given. In the case of human learners there is evidence that this is not essential. In a series of experiments in paired-associate learning (*e.g.*, learning vocabularies) learners were shown the correct answers *before* instead of after they had made the response. In other words they were prompted rather than rein-forced. No harmful effects were found. Instead there was a slight improvement.[1] Thus, *in some contexts* prompting can be as efficient in promoting learning as reinforcement (in Skinner's use of the term). Incidentally, this confirms suggestions made elsewhere in this book that two people working together as partners when learning vocabu-laries, or prompting by reference to the book as soon as hesitation occurs in memorizing poetry or prose passages, are both effective *methods* of learning.

Animal and human learning are not identical processes after a certain stage of development has been reached, one major difference being the spoken language which makes prompting possible. As the author of the report noted above said—what works beautifully in

[1] J. O. Cook, " Superstition in the Skinnerian," *American Psychologist*, Vol. 18, No. 8, 1963. Cook and Spitzer, " Prompting versus Confirmation in Paired-associate Learning," *Jnl. Exp. Psych.*, 59, 1960.

one learning context may not work so beautifully in another. It is not essential, therefore, in designing learning programmes to keep too closely to one exclusive theoretical model of the learning-process. A broader basis for experiment is desirable.

(iv) Skinner's linear programmes have been designed deliberately to reduce the making of errors to a minimum. We have noted elsewhere the desirability of organizing success and avoiding frustration due to undue failure. At the same time some degree of error may not be undesirable. A correct response does not always guarantee that a pupil has *understood* what has been ' learned.' He may be repeating a statement mechanically. He may have copied the answer. He may have made a lucky guess. On the other hand, an error is a sign that something is wrong which needs to be rectified. The error competently dealt with by a sympathetic teacher can provide an important feedback effect. To the pupil, it indicates where his understanding or his memory is deficient, thereby inviting closer attending and re-consideration. To the teacher, it indicates what is wrong with the pupil's learning-process and what needs further help. It also *indicates what may be wrong with his own methods of teaching and what faults need to be avoided on a subsequent occasion*. Some investigations have indicated that errors need not be detrimental if corrected quickly and *if the learner understands clearly where and why he is wrong*.

(v) It is doubtful whether any programme can emulate the flexibility of a really competent teacher. We have spoken previously of *rapport*, an affective as well as intellectual relationship between teacher and pupil. The teacher who knows his pupil as an individual can switch quickly from one explanation to another more in line with the pupil's background and methods of thinking. If one example fails he will suggest another. If a verbal report is not sufficient he will draw a diagram or make a sketch or refer the learner to a model. He may put a question in another way. Moreover, the sympathetic teacher is responsive to moods. These are, decidedly, factors in motivation and learning. It is true, of course, that some investigators are testing programmes controlled by computers— adaptive programmes—when the machine varies its questions and problems according to the students' previous responses. It is doubtful, however, whether the computer can be programmed to take account of moods. It is also doubtful whether students will identify themselves with a computer, and it would be interesting to know what would happen if they did.

(vi) Scanning the literature on programmed learning suggests one possible defect in the method if used too exclusively. It depends unduly on visual information, and particularly on verbal-visual stimulus. This may be satisfactory in the case of more senior students, but for juniors or for seniors beginning some new type of work manipulative activity involving the senses of touch, position, and muscular effort may be essential. This suggests that programmes are likely to be most effective if used in co-ordination with other teaching-devices and sources of first-hand experience.[1]

(vi) There is a place for group as well as individual activities. Not all children may wish to learn individually, at least not all the time. Some may prefer to work in a group and with a group in co-operative and competitive operations. This need not make programmed learning unnecessary. It does suggest, however, that it has a limited effectiveness. There is, moreover, still a place, on occasion, for a ' lesson ' or talk or lecture to a whole group.

(viii) The importance of discussion as an educational medium has been emphasized in the chapter on Transfer, and again in this section. It should be granted a place in this list of queries. In this connexion some comments in the Newsom Report are relevant :

> There are in any case some objectives which can and should deliberately be pursued through every part of the curriculum. Very high in this list we should place improvements in powers of speech : not simply improvement in the quality and clearness of enunciation, although that is needed, but a general extension of vocabulary and with it a surer command over the structures of spoken English and the expression of ideas. That means seizing the opportunity of every lesson in engineering or housecraft or science as well as in English to provide material for discussion— *genuine discussion, not mere testing by teacher's question and pupil's answer.*
>
> Discussion should be used to develop judgment and discrimination. This may apply to enjoyment in music or art or literature ; to taste and craftsmanship in the workshop ; to a sense of what is appropriate behaviour in a particular situation, which will generally involve some consideration of other people's feelings and points of

---

[1] " In general, where information is required, teaching machines work. In the acquisition of skills where the feel of materials and controls are important there may be little benefit from teaching machines however skilfully designed." O. G. Edholm, *The Biology of Work* (Weidenfeld and Nicolson, 1967), p. 179.

view ; or to an appreciation of what is relevant to the immediate task in hand.[1]

This comment is relevant to both the strength and weakness of programmed learning.   Programmes can contribute to the extension and increase in precision of a pupil's vocabulary, but less effectively to surer command over spoken English and expression of ideas ; to genuine discussion which needs a social situation with free expression of personal opinion.   It may improve certain aspects of judgment and discrimination.   It is less likely to enhance enjoyment of music or art or literature or social perceptiveness (*i.e.,* the consideration of other people's feelings and points of view).

The surest way of maximizing the usefulness of programmed learning is to find out by actual trial what it does most efficiently and use it for that purpose.

PROBLEMS OF ORGANIZATION

Apart altogether from the educative efficiency of programmes and mechanical devices, their use in schools raises problems of economics and organization.   Initial costs and costs of maintenance must be considered.   There will be problems of storage.   What is to be done with the machines and programmes when not in use ?   A variety of programmes in different subjects and at different levels of difficulty must be stored, numbered, recorded, and catalogued for easy access both for teachers and pupils.   Some supervision of completed programmes will be necessary to ensure that frames have not been left unanswered.   Records of programmes completed by each pupil will need to be kept.

If programmed learning is to be an important feature of future schooling, buildings will have to be designed for it.   One possibility is that each class should have two rooms, one for group activities, the other for mechanical devices.   Or, several classrooms may be arranged around a central area allocated to individual work.   Some of the care and maintenance of apparatus, cataloguing, and recording may be done by auxiliaries, freeing the trained professional teachers for more important educative work.   It is most likely that the rather cumbersome machines which have been used in the early days of programmed instruction will be superseded by much smaller and more easily manageable devices no bigger than a text-book.   Some

---

[1] *Half our Future*, p. 29.   My italics.

teachers have found it more satisfactory to use programmed books in place of machines.

EPILOGUE. SCHOOL OF THE FUTURE

This section can very well be introduced by a quotation from the Newsom Report, *Half Our Future*. The authors say :

> There is much unrealised talent especially among boys and girls whose potential is masked by inadequate powers of speech and the limitations of home background. Unsuitable programmes and teaching methods may aggravate their difficulties and frustration express itself in apathy or rebelliousness. The country cannot afford this wastage, humanly or economically speaking. If it is to be avoided, several things will be necessary. The pupils will need a longer period of full-time education than most of them now receive. The schools will need to present that education in terms more accep-table to the pupils and to their parents by relating school more directly to adult life and especially by taking proper account of vocational interests . . . Experiment is required both in the content of the school programme and in teaching methods. Finally, the schools . . . will need the tools for the job in the provision of adequate staff, buildings and equipment.[1]

In this chapter emphasis has been on change—change in school organization, teaching methods, teaching-devices, design of school buildings. Changes are already happening. They are likely to happen even more rapidly in the not-too-distant future. To meet the challenge which these changes will present, comparable changes in professional teachers' attitudes will be essential. Even if, for example, the new educational technology can provide genuinely useful aids for teaching and learning, their usefulness will be can-celled out if they are ignored, or used perfunctorily, or allowed to deteriorate through lack of adequate skill in maintenance. " Fore-warned is forearmed " applies to school-practice as well as to warfare and industry. It may be profitable, therefore, to consider what the school of the future may be like.[2]

Forecasts are legitimate if certain principles of development can be discerned in the past. This seems to be the case with respect to schooling. Undoubtedly, change proceeds on a very uneven front, rapidly in some directions, slowly, if at all, in others. Yet, taking a broad view, certain constant tendencies are discernible.

---

[1] Report cited, p. 3.   [2] See J. Vaizey.

(i) Schooling must, eventually, keep pace with economic and social needs and pressures. At one time, secondary schools taught little else but Latin. After the Tudor period the demands were for ' modern ' subjects. When the grammar schools failed to respond, private enterprise in schooling flourished to meet the demand. When industry needed science, scientific studies appeared sooner or later in the curriculum. Nowadays, economics, social studies, ' current affairs,' pre-vocational training are increasingly taught in schools in response to pressures for new knowledge. It is reasonably safe to predict, therefore, that as knowledge increases in variety and as technology develops, changes in the curricula of secondary schools will follow suit. Curricula, even at the primary stage, will become more diversified.

(ii) Methods of teaching respond to the capacities of technology and industry to provide teaching-aids. When books and writing materials were scarce, learning—in schools—was almost entirely by verbal repetition. The art of printing made readers and text-books possible. When paper became cheaper, even the poor were taught to write. The teaching of science depended to a great extent on the availability of apparatus. Modern technology has produced the flannelgraph, magnetic ' blackboard,' epidiascope, film-strip projector, overhead projector, radio, cine-camera, cine-film, film-loop, miniature film and projector, television, tape-recorder, record-player, language laboratory, teaching-' machine,' video-tape, computer—examples of all of which can be found in some schools at the time of writing. Closed-circuit television has already been adopted by some universities and Local Education Authorities. Again, it is safe to predict that more Authorities and schools will have more of these examples of educational technology as time goes on. Another tendency already apparent is the miniaturization of these devices, so that in the future it is probable that we shall see not one radiogram or one television set per school but miniature tape-recorders, television sets, record-players available for individual pupils to be used in conjunction with programmed learning-devices. Not a few pupils now at school own transistor sets (some no bigger than a pack of playing-cards), record-players, cine-cameras, miniature projectors, tape-recorders ; and they know how to use them. As sources of information these devices will supplement and, for some purposes, may eventually supersede text-books.

(iii) Formerly, schooling was restricted to certain social classes ; the others learned what they needed to know on the job. That arrangement has long been inadequate. Later we had compulsory schooling for a majority ; compulsory schooling for everybody ; compulsory leaving ages—ten, twelve, fourteen, fifteen years—to be raised in 1973 to sixteen. Meanwhile more pupils are remaining at school voluntarily, after the age of sixteen. It is possible that in the not-too-distant future the majority of pupils will remain in some form of secondary or further education till they are eighteen or more.

This extension of the period of schooling will, most likely, lead to three other changes :

(*a*) A tendency to envisage the whole period from five to sixteen-plus years as constituting *one continuous educative process* in a variety of stages to match real or assumed phases of physical and mental development : 5 to 8 or 9 years ; 8 or 9 to 13 years ; 13 years to 16+ years, as alternatives to the present 5 to 7 ; 7 to 11 ; 11 to 16+ years (an arrangement dictated as much by administrative convenience and former matriculation-examination requirements as by any psychological or educational principles).

(*b*) The present (1968) Ordinary Level tests for the General Certificate of Education will disappear. They were geared to university-matriculation requirements which no longer have any validity. The almost universal present-day university-entrance requirement is the Advanced Level Certificate. When compulsory schooling to sixteen-plus years is general, these Ordinary Level tests can be superseded with advantage by tests of secondary education for the non-university pupils ; tests much more in keeping with the less specialized studies suitable for more practically minded pupils, and more closely connected with their later careers. This change has already begun and is likely to develop more rapidly as the compulsory leaving age is raised.

(*c*) There is likely to be a much closer connexion between the curricula of the last years of secondary schooling and the conditions in industry, commerce, and social life in which the adolescent population will later live and work. The dichotomy between the so-called liberal and vocational aspects of training and education will be increasingly recognized and acknowledged for what it undoubtedly is, namely, a social-class prejudice rather than an educationally well-founded principle.

(iv) There was a time when a professor of philosophy was expected by virtue of his office to write a book on the theory and practice of education. In doing so he appeared to take it for granted that all learners were mentally and temperamentally like himself and that every student learned in the same way as he did—what might be called the ' inner-conscious ' theory of learning and education. Little systematic experimental study of learning and thinking appeared before the second half of the nineteenth century. In 1883 Galton published an investigation of mental imagery which revealed a variety of experience which, as he said, " amazed " him.[1] Since 1900, many experimental investigations of perceiving, concept-forming, generalizing, problem-solving, and more recent studies connected with the use of programmed learning, have shown that human learning is a very complicated process, much more complicated than the somewhat naïve, over-simplified, animal-based Behaviourist theories have implied. In fact learning is very much a matter of individual idiosyncrasy ;[2] a process which, as Piaget has shown, goes on in different modes in the same individual at different phases of mental development. There seems little doubt that psychologists have much more to discover about the details of learning-processes and it seems safe to suppose that what is discovered will emphasize the importance of individual attention and some freedom of choice in how a task may be learned. This knowledge will influence the design of learning programmes. It will also indicate that while mass methods of teaching may be useful for certain types of subject-matter, these must be supplemented by a variety of individual work. In the schools of the future, variety of individual work will be facilitated by the increased availability of the miniaturized devices described in section (ii) above, as well as by improved designs of school buildings.

(v) The absolute necessity for optimum mental development of direct first-hand experience via every sense-organ, particularly in the earlier stages of schooling, was stressed in Chapter VI above. Moreover, at any stage of development the interpretation of new experience and the understanding of words and symbols depends on accumulating a rich variety of first-hand experience. "No words without things ; no things without words" is an essential principle of mental development and learning.

More recent studies both of the nervous system and of behaviour have revealed other essential functions of first-hand or vivid-substitute experience.

---

[1] See Flugel, book cited, p. 107.
[2] See the quotation from Humphrey, p. 54 above. See also R. M. Gagné, *The Conditions of Learning* (Holt, Rinehart and Winston, 1965).

(a) It now appears that the effect of stimulation on sense-organs and the central nervous system is, broadly speaking, twofold. Stimuli (which are forms of physical energy) are conducted to the thalamus, one of the more primitive sections of the brain. There the stimulus effect divides, one part going to the outer brain cortex where it is decoded into conscious awareness as information ; the other part *acting as a generalized energizer keeping up a necessary level of activity or readiness in the nervous system itself.* If this activity level sinks below a critical intensity the efficiency of the brain is affected.[1]

It should be noted that excessive stimulation can also be deleterious. However, between these two extremes there is an optimum level of *intensity* and *variety* of stimulation necessary for satisfactory physical and mental efficiency. Evidence is available from experiments with young animals showing that if they are deprived of stimulation at certain periods of development (being kept continuously in the dark, for example) their capacity for certain aspects of perception may be permanently damaged.[2]

(b) The counterpart of this nervous activity has been studied experimentally in the form of behaviour.

In one series of experiments in sensory deprivation carried out at McGill University, student volunteers were paid an honorarium to do literally nothing ! The situation was arranged in such a way that all types of external stimulation and bodily movement were reduced to the very minimum. The volunteers simply did nothing ; or rather they tried to endure doing nothing. It was found that the lack of stimulation became quite intolerable. As one report states :

> They wanted stimulation so badly that they would ask to hear a recording of an old stock market report over and over again. . . . Most subjects could endure the confinement for only two or three days. . . . Many had peculiar experiences during the sensory deprivation period. At first they tried thinking about personal and intellectual problems but after a while they could not concentrate or sustain a train of thought. They had periods of confusion, irritability and stress.[3]

These studies in sensory deprivation show that *lack of adequate stimulation causes deterioration of behaviour ; makes the individual*

[1] See R. A. McCleary and R. Y. Moore, *Subcortical Mechanisms of Behaviour* (Basic Books, 1965). D. E. Berlyne, *Conflict, Arousal and Curiosity* (McGraw-Hill, 1960).
[2] See J. McV. Hunt, *Intelligence and Experience* (Ronald Press, 1961).
[3] See E. J. Murray, *Motivation and Emotion* (Prentice-Hall, 1964).

less efficient ; causes strong aversions.   It seems that sufficiently vivid and varied stimulation from the environment is necessary for the efficiency and stability of behaviour, and for the biological maintenance of the organism.

Some adverse effects of sensory deprivation were recognized long before these experimental demonstrations forced the attention of the psychologists to them.   Solitary confinement, particularly in dark cells with restriction on free movement, has been, almost universally, one form of dire punishment.   Most people have felt the intolerable boredom of having nothing whatever to do ; of being forced to endure a constant iteration of sound ; in fact any prolonged monotony.   There is, in other words, *a strong craving for stimulation, variety of experience, and free movement.*[1]

These recent investigations into sensory deprivation and its deleterious effects on learning and mental development have an obvious bearing on the introduction of teaching-devices such as those listed in section (ii) p. 484 above.   Traditionally, schools have catered almost exclusively for a verbal-minded, academically able minority.   Teaching and learning were carried on by oral instruction, reading, and verbal repetition.   Many times in the history of educational thought, observers have noted how much more quickly and readily children learned out of school, and have deplored the fact that so much and so severe punishment has been necessary to keep some pupils in school at their learning tasks.   These studies in sensory deprivation supply the explanation.   The traditional schooling lacked stimulation, variety, and positive activity.   For many children and adolescents schooling has been and still is associated with monotony, boredom, restriction, and exasperation, particularly in the cases of the not-so-academically-minded who now make up the majority of our secondary-school population.[2]

---

[1] See S. Cobb (ed.), *Sensory Deprivation* (Harvard University Press, 1961), D. W. Fiske and S. R. Maddi, *Functions of Varied Experience* (Dorsey Press, Illinois, 1961). J. Vernon, *Inside the Black Room* (Souvenir Press, 1963). When the notes on motivation for Chapter IV above were written some critics demurred at the use of ' Hunger ' in connexion with motive.   These recent studies in the effects of sensory deprivation seem to vindicate the accuracy of the description.

[2] The attitude of many adolescents has been pungently expressed in the quotation on Page 2 of the Newsom Report *Half Our Future.* " A boy who had just left school was asked by his former headmaster what he thought of the new buildings. ' It could all be marble, Sir,' he replied, ' but it would still be a bloody school.' "

Now, through recent advances in educational devices it is possible to introduce more vivid stimulation, more variety of experience, and more opportunity for movement into school business. We have to note, of course, that some people appear to welcome change for the sake of change, particularly if it is strikingly spectacular and conducive to publicity. Nevertheless, we realize that devices for making schooling and learning more vivid and more varied are psychologically soundly based if used efficiently. There is no doubt that the school of the future will incorporate more of these aids to learning, particularly for the encouragement of the less-verbally-minded majority. The teachers of the future need, therefore, to make themselves familiar with the use of these devices in connexion with their special subjects.

(c) Other recent studies of learning, particularly learning skills, have stressed the importance of ' feedback.' The learner must have a pattern of activity to imitate and a standard of efficiency to reach. The learner must then make some positive action with respect to the pattern to be learned and the standard to be reached. This positive effort usually falls short of perfection. The difference between the attempt and the standard reveals to pupil and teacher the extent and direction of the error. This information is fed back to the learner whose movements are also controlled by stimuli from his own *internal* environment—the senses of position, strain, movement located in muscles and other internal organs. When the learner is sufficiently intent on learning, the information (feedback) from the standard aimed at, and from the learner's own internal sense-organs, helps to correct the errors and bring the subsequent performances nearer to the desired objective. The purpose of active repetition is to reduce the error.

The effects of this feedback process can be enhanced by some of the newer teaching-devices. A clear example is to be found in learning a foreign language. Preliminary interest (motivation) and a standard of performance can be stimulated by a cinema film or television interlude showing some everyday situation in a foreign country. The repetition necessary for perfection of accent and speech-patterns can be monitored by means of tape-recorders. The learner's attempts at speech can be recorded on the tape and played back to him. Immediately after, the same speech-form previously made by an expert can be played back and compared with his own. This process of repetition can be repeated by the tape device as often as is desirable. In this way, it is possible to combine vivid, dramatic illustration with feedback repetition in the learning of a complex skill.

Thus, the use of the new technology is more than mere gimmickry or gadgetry. It is based on experimentally demonstrable principles of learning efficiency. This is the justification for the introduction of these modern teaching aids and the answer to doubters who believe that they will make teachers unnecessary. These mechanical devices are aids to more efficient learning. They can provide experience and stimulation and improve practice. They are analogous to aids for improving observation and calculations in scientific work—microscopes, telescopes, electronic amplifiers, mechanical calculators. These do not supersede the scientific workers. They do not make needless the correct design of experiments or the discovery of problems for research. They extend the range and accuracy of observations and make calculation more rapid (thus removing much tiresome time-consuming routine work). Understanding their possibilities and becoming expert in their use is a necessary aspect of a scientific training. Without a trained observer they are useless pieces of machinery.

Similarly, without a teacher who understands the educational and psychological value of mechanical teaching-devices as aids to more efficient learning and who is competent in using them, they also are so many useless pieces of machinery. Understanding their value and becoming competent in their use in schools will be a necessary aspect of professional teacher-training.

(vi) If the school of the future is to make the best use of available educational technology, school buildings must be designed for the purpose. Arrangements will be needed for large groups, for small groups or ' sets,' and for individual work. Also, as well as provision of more vivid stimulation, audio-visual aids, variety of experience and activity, provision will be necessary for quiet reading and study. Too much stimulation can be as frustrating as too little.

(vii) The school of the future with its wide range of personality differences, temperaments, abilities, and attainments will need members of staff trained in guidance and methods of diagnosis.

With its educational technology it will need members of staff with technical training who can service the devices. It is absurd to provide language laboratories, film-projectors, teaching-machines, television sets, and then find half of them temporarily unusable, in need of repair.

It follows that to meet the additional demands likely to arise in the future, schools will be built in bigger units. A big school need not be a disadvantage either academically or socially, provided that it is adequately staffed and intelligently organized.

So much for the school of the future. The purpose of this chapter has been to hazard a guess about future developments and to suggest the need for new attitudes, techniques, and experiments in teaching. Meanwhile, particularly in secondary schools, the examination system, university-entrance requirements, conservative attitudes, unsatisfactory buildings, and the fact that some teaching can very well be done by means of lectures and talks to larger groups will mean that traditional methods will persist for some time if not for ever. Even with all the new educational technology there will still be need for introductory comments, guidance, explanations of reasons for learning, motivation, continuity, integration ; functions which only a competent teacher who knows the pupils can perform. Moreover, lesson periods, time-tables, class methods of instruction will not vanish overnight. Therefore, the chapters on Recapitulation, Revision, and Repetitive Practice and on the Practice of Instruction have been retained (Chapters XI and XII).

Some permanent functions of a good teacher and a glimpse into one possible aspect of the school of the future may be gathered from an account of some experiments in teacher-and-machine co-operation described by Grant Noble.[1]

The author summarizes his own and other experimental results :

1. Programmes are more effective (and pupils' attitudes more favorable) when combined with teacher presentations.

2. Systematic oral summaries by a teacher combined with pro-grammes are more productive than either teacher or machine alone.

3. *A teacher should be responsible for motivation and for over-all control and direction of the learning system.* A steady decline (' pall-effect ') in interest toward programmed instruction has been noted after only one month of trial.[2] Reinforcement (reward) alone is not sufficient to maintain interest in the programme techniques. Thus, long-term programmed learning can be inferior to competent teacher instruction.

4. Not all children respond equally well to programmes. Some can use the machines on their own. Others need a teacher to stimulate and control the learning.

---

[1] See " An Experimental Attempt to Integrate Programmed Instruction with Classroom Instruction " in Unwin and Leedham, *Aspects of Educational Technology* (Methuen, 1966).

[2] Craving for variety, change in type of stimulus.

The author goes on to describe how teaching was combined with programmed instruction, thus giving a hint about one aspect of the school of the future. The class have their machines and programmes ready. The teacher goes to the class for the first five or so minutes of the period, gives a quick review of what is to be learned, and *explains how the knowledge can be used profitably in real-life situations* (motivation, purpose). He then goes away to deal with another class, leaving an auxiliary in charge. He returns for the last few minutes of the period and questions the children on what has been learned (introduction of variety, motivation, feedback, continuity with previous learning, summary, repetition, consolidation).

Using this arrangement one teacher with an auxiliary can deal with two or three times as many children by teaching for some ten minutes of a forty-minute period, then dealing with another class (or classes) meanwhile. This is one possible answer to the shortage of teachers, particularly to the shortage of specialists in certain subjects.

So competent teachers will still be needed for the most efficient results. In the future, however, they will have to know not only the children, and their subject-matter, but also how to make the best use of educational technology.

Books for Further Reference

I. *Reports*

> Central Advisory Council for Education: *Early Leaving* (H.M.S.O., 1954).
> Crowther Committee: *15 to 18*, Vols. I and II (H.M.S.O., 1959).
> Robbins Committee: *Higher Education* (H.M.S.O., 1963).
> Newsom Committee: *Half our Future* (H.M.S.O., 1963).
> National Foundation for Educational Research: *Procedures for the Allocation of Pupils in Secondary Schools.*

II. *Educational Change*

> VAIZEY, J.: *Education for Tomorrow* (Pelican Books, 1966).
> ——— *Education in the Modern World* (Weidenfeld and Nicolson, 1967).
> YOUNG, M.: *Innovation and Research in Education* (Routledge and Kegan Paul, 1965).

HUTCHINSON, M., AND YOUNG, C. : *Educating the Intelligent* (Pelican Books, 1962). A discussion of secondary-school curricula.

SIMON, B. (ED.) : *New Trends in English Education* (Mac-Gibbon and Kee, 1957).

YOUNG, M., AND ARMSTRONG, M. : " The Flexible School," *Where*, Supplement 5, Autumn 1965. A well-balanced practical discussion of ways of organizing comprehensive schools with unstreamed classes.

III. *Comprehensive Schools*

Political Quarterly, Vol. XXIII, No. 2, 1952, " Two Views on Secondary Education."

Sociological Review, Vol. XXXVIII, No. 1, 1946, " School and Society." See Chapter IX: " What is General Knowledge ? " and Chapter XIV: " The Multi-bias School as a Social Experiment."

SYMPOSIUM : *Inside the Comprehensive School* (Schoolmaster Publishing Company, 1958).

SYMPOSIUM : *London Comprehensive Schools* (London County Council, 1961). A survey of sixteen schools.

CHETWYND, H. R. : *Comprehensive School. The Story of Woodberry Down* (Routledge and Kegan Paul, 1960).

PEDLEY, R., AND OTHERS : *Comprehensive Schools To-day. An interim survey* (Councils and Education Press, 1955).

PEDLEY, R.: *The Comprehensive School* (Pelican Books, 1963).

YOUNG, M., AND ARMSTRONG, M. : " The Flexible School," *Where*, Supplement 5.

SAMPSON, ANTHONY : *Anatomy of Britain Today* (Hodder and Stoughton, 1965). Chapter 12: " Schools."

IV. *Streaming*

SIMON, B. (ED.) : *Non-streaming in the Junior School* (P.S.W. (Educational) Publications, 1964).

JACKSON, B. : *Streaming. An Education System in Miniature* (Routledge and Kegan Paul, 1964).

DOUGLAS, J. W. B. : *The Home and the School* (MacGibbon and Kee, 1964). Chapter XIV: " Streaming by Ability."

DAVIES, H. : *Culture and the Grammar School* (Routledge and Kegan Paul, 1965).

PARTRIDGE, J. : *Middle School* (Gollancz, 1966). Chapter 4 : " Shades of the Eleven Plus." Chapter 5 : " What Effect Does Streaming Have ? " Chapter 6 : " Discipline and the Motive to Work."

YOUNG, M., AND ARMSTRONG, M. : " The Flexible School," *Where*, Supplement 5.

ROWE, A. W. : *The Education of the Average Child* (Harrap, 1959). Organizing individual work by means of ' job cards.'

V. *Progressive versus Traditional*

MARSHALL, S. : *An Experiment in Education* (Cambridge University Press, 1966).

PARTRIDGE, J. : *Middle School* (Gollancz, 1966).

GOOCH, S., AND KELLMER PRINGLE, M. L. : *Four Years On.* National Bureau for Cooperation in Child Care, Research Report No. 1. Now published in book form by Longmans. A follow-up study of children formerly attending a traditional and a progressive junior school.

BIGGS, J. B. : *Anxiety, Motivation and Primary School Mathematics.* National Foundation for Educational Research, Occasional Publication No. 7.

VI. *Programmed Learning*

(*a*) Introductory sources :

Aspects of Programmed Instruction I to IV, Educational Research, Vol. V, No. 3, 1963. Four short critical assessments.

BORGER, R., AND SEABORNE, A. E. M. : *The Psychology of Learning* (Pelican Books, 1966). See Chapter II : " Programmed Learning." A concise, useful summary.

HOLDING, D. H. : *Principles of Training* (Pergamon Press, 1965). See Chapter 8: " Programmed Learning." Illustrated.

GOODMAN, R. : " Programmed Learning and Teaching Machines," *Where*, No. 13, 1963.

LEEDHAM, J., AND UNWIN, D. : *Programmed Learning in Schools* (Longmans, 1965). A good practical account. Illustrated. Sources of information.

(*b*) More specialized sources :

AUSTWICK, K. (ED.) : *Teaching Machines and Programming* (Pergamon Press, 1964). Six essays. Illustrated. Bibliographies.

GOLDSMITH, M. (ED.): *Mechanisation in the Classroom. An introduction to Teaching Machines and Programmed Learning* (Souvenir Press, 1963). Nine essays. Specimen programmes. Illustrated. Bibliography. Sources of information.

SMITH, W. I., AND MOORE, J. W. (EDS.): *Programmed Learning. Selected Readings in Theory and Research.* An Insight Book (D. Van Nostrand Co., Princeton, N.J., 1962). Sources of information. Mainly American.

UNWIN, D., AND LEEDHAM, J. : *Aspects of Educational Technology* (Methuen, 1967). A collection of 43 papers read at a programmed-learning conference in April 1966. Includes accounts of experiments with programmed learning in primary, secondary, technical, and higher education. Processes of writing, validation, and production of programmes considered. A comprehensive survey of programmed learning in the United Kingdom and elsewhere up to 1966. Bibliographies. Illustrated.

SOURCES OF INFORMATION : Department of Education and Science, London. National Centre for Programmed Learning, University of Birmingham.

VII. *Experimental Syllabuses and Activity Methods in Science and Mathematics*

Mathematics in Primary Schools, Curriculum Bulletin No. 1, the Schools Council (H.M.S.O., 1965). Bibliography. Suggestions for Assignments.

A School Approach to Technology, Curriculum Bulletin No. 2, the Schools Council (H.M.S.O., 1966).

Science in Secondary Schools, Ministry of Education Pamphlet No. 38 (H.M.S.O., 1960).

BASSEY, M. : *School Science for Tomorrow's Citizens* (Pergamon Press, 1963). Bibliography.

CHAPTER XI

RECAPITULATION, REVISION, AND REPETITIVE PRACTICE

A. Recapitulation and Revision

MEMORY AND HABIT

The human organism possesses a primary retentivity—the capacity for registering and retaining the effects of experience and movement. On a subsequent occasion images and ideas can be recalled, and movements repeated. Memory is the name we give to the process of registering and recalling images and ideas. Habit is the name given to the process of registering and repeating movement-patterns and performing mental operations automatically. Some psychologists refer to the recall of images and ideas as true memory, and the reproduction of movement-patterns (including speech-movements) *in the absence of imagery* as habit-memory.

It is not always possible to distinguish in practice between memory and habit. The two represent the opposite ends of a series and it is often difficult to say when memory ends and habit begins. In many cases both are intermingled in one complex process.

POSITIVE EFFECTS OF THE TIME-FACTOR IN LEARNING

The passage of time plays an essential part in learning.

1. It has been shown already that no complex perceptual experience is completely apprehended at the first presentation. Perception is not comparable to photography (except in the one similarity that some more or less permanent effect accrues in both cases). Perception is selective. On the first presentation, certain details only are apprehended in the total situation. To make the

perception *clear* and *adequate* the situation must be re-presented, often several times. At each subsequent re-presentation the learner notes more details, filling in the gaps left at the earlier presentations.

2. It has been shown that the relational elements in a complex experience are not fully analysed and abstracted at the first presentation. They may remain dormant for long periods before being analysed clearly and abstracted. Before the relations emerge from obscurity into clear consciousness the related characters and relations must be attended to specifically, compared, contrasted, and reflected upon. After each re-presentation and period of reflection the relations become clearer and attain to a greater degree of abstraction. At the same time relations between relations in an order of increasing complexity are apprehended, enabling the learner to organize his experiences into a complex knowledge system which is the basis of understanding. *The approach to understanding is a process of evolution in which time is an essential factor.*

3. Sensory-motor learning leading to the acquisition of skilled habits is also a process of evolution. We begin with elementary sensory-motor reflexes provided for in the build of the human body. These must be co-ordinated into new movement systems needing perfect timing and co-operation between the component elements. It is not sufficient for the performer to be able to envisage, merely, the complex movement pattern required for a highly-skilled performance. The elements must be shaped into the pattern by repeated practice during which successful responses are selected and conserved, and unsuccessful responses eliminated.

NEGATIVE EFFECTS OF TIME-LAPSE IN LEARNING

Learning may be considered to be a resultant of two antagonistic tendencies. On the one hand, experiences leave residual effects whereby we add to our knowledge and skill. On the other hand, lapse of time in the absence of re-presentation and practice tends to wipe out the effects of the original experience. If an original experience is vivid, striking, and accompanied by intense feeling-tone it may produce an effect upon the learner which remains throughout his lifetime. Mild experiences, particularly if not noted with concentrated attention, soon fade beyond voluntary recall.

The studies of medical psychologists concerned with patients in a hypnotic trance, and reports of individuals after very intense emotional crises, seem to indicate that no experience once appre-hended is completely lost with lapse of time. However, for practical teaching-purposes it is sufficient to realize that both ideational and sensory-motor items may fade with lapse of time beyond the voluntary recall of the learner.

FREUD'S THEORY OF FORGETTING: REPRESSION

The assumption that the fading of experiences and sensory-motor habits beyond voluntary recall is due entirely to lapse of time and disuse has been questioned by Freud. He has pointed out facts which indicate that the mechanical explanation of forgetting is too simple to account for all the observed instances of forgetting.

Freud noted the significant fact that *forgetting appears to be selective* in many cases. All past experiences are not equally recoverable at will.

Some ideas seem to spring spontaneously into consciousness with no effort on the part of the thinker. Other ideas are recoverable only by concentrated attention to their associations (*e.g.*, recovering the forgotten address of a friend by thinking hard about the appearance of the friend, or of his house, or of the circumstances in which we last wrote to him). Even in these cases, disuse and lapse of time cannot account completely for the difference in power of recall since some events spontaneously remembered may have happened many years ago, while others difficult to recall may have happened only a few days ago. Differences in the concentration of attention at the time of perception do not completely explain differences in power of recall.

Still other events appear to be forgotten so completely that they do not reappear in consciousness spontaneously, and *cannot be recalled by any effort of will, however concentrated or prolonged.*

Freud startled the psychological world by asserting that these experiences had not disappeared; that on the other hand they were extremely active, and reappeared quite often *but only in a fashion so distorted or disguised that the thinker in question could not recognize them.* He suggested that the events which were forgotten so completely, were events of which the person was ashamed, the recall of which would interfere with his self-esteem, and set up painful conflicts. These events were not *forgotten* by a passive process of disuse and lapse of time, but were actively *repressed*, that is, thrust out of consciousness by the thinker and kept out.

Freud supposed that mental activity could be thought of as stratified into three levels—conscious, fore-conscious, and unconscious. The fore-conscious level was supposed to contain all the experiences temporarily forgotten, but possible to recall. The unconscious level contained the experiences beyond voluntary recall. It was the repository of our dark and shameful secrets Guarding the egress from the unconscious to the fore-conscious there was, according to Freud, some faculty or operator which he called the *censor*, whose function it was to keep our ' skeletons ' in their proper cupboards. A repressed experience could ' dodge the censor and emerge into consciousness once again only if it were so disguised as to be unrecognizable by this watchful Cerberus who kept the gates of the mental nether regions.

The Freudian theory of forgetting has been clothed in such fanciful terms that its real importance has been neglected. It has served to call attention, however, to the inadequacy of the explanation of forgetting by disuse and lapse of time only. *Motive is a powerful factor in remembering and forgetting.*

We remember most readily what is most satisfying and convenient for our purposes to remember. We forget most completely what we do not wish to be recalled. Both the factor of motive, and the time factor need to be kept in mind when considering the economy of learning.

The Freudian theory of repression applies to sensory-motor degeneration as well as to the forgetting of ideas. For example, many cases of paralysis have been studied in which no organic disease can be traced in the affected limbs. The *capacity* for co-ordinated movement still remains although the *ability* has lapsed. This is known as *functional* paralysis. It is just as though the limbs in question retain their capacity for movement but the patient has *forgotten how to move them*. This is suggested by the fact that during dreams, in hypnotic sleep, or in moments of intense excitement, the patient temporarily recovers (recalls) his normal power of movement. Many instances of paralysis due to shell-shock were of this kind and the Freudian theory of repression was a valuable guide in suggesting methods of medical treatment.

This theory of forgetting is very significant for teaching-practice. It indicates that if we wish pupils to remember we must not only present the material to be learned, vividly and clearly, and take care that it is repeated sufficiently often. We must also make the process of learning pleasurable to the learner. We must make the material worth the effort to learn it and take care that the learner has *no reason for wishing to forget it.*

R

RATE OF FORGETTING

Experiments have been carried out to estimate the rate of forgetting due to lapse of time.

The material to be learned may include both logical meaningful material such as passages of prose and poetry, and nonsense-material. This latter consists of nonsense-syllables (syllables of three letters specially composed so that they can be pronounced, but which do not resemble common syllables, *e.g.*, zik, naf, yun), hieroglyphics, digits.

The purpose of the nonsense-material is to prevent, as far as possible, the formation of secondary associations. These are associations of similarity or meaning between the material to be learned and already established ideas.

In memorizing a car registration number such as XY4378, one may do so by repeating the letters and digits in their presented order time after time until the performance has become a sensory-motor speech-habit. This is like memorizing by brute force. It depends on primary associations.

On the other hand, we can assist the recall of the number by *associating it with other ideas of long standing.* XY recalls the familiar designation of lines in geometry or axes of reference in co-ordinate geometry. They are the letters immediately before the last in the alphabet. Inspection of the numbers reveals that 4 plus 3 equals 7, which is one less than 8. The last digit is double the first. 3 is 4 less than 7. These are secondary associations and by means of their aid it is often possible to *reconstruct* the whole series when one item only can be recalled.

The experiments are usually conducted as follows : The material to be learned is repeated by the learners until it can just be recited correctly twice. The repetition is then stopped and the learners' attention diverted to other matters so that no further repetitions will be made. At the end of a given time the learners are required to reproduce as much of the material as possible. The difference between what is reproduced, and the original material, represents the loss due to forgetting.

The results show that the normal rate of forgetting is extremely rapid, *particularly in the period immediately after learning.*

Of nonsense-material more than one-third is normally lost in the first twenty minutes ; more than one-half in an hour ; nearly two-thirds in nine hours; and more than two-thirds in twenty-four hours.[1]

[1] Pyle, *Psychology of Learning,* p. 167.

Of meaningful material, one-third is lost in two days ; one-half in seven days ; and three-fourths in thirty days.

These facts are extremely significant for teaching-practice. Thirty days is about a third of an average school term. Thus, even if the presented material is intelligible, the normal pupil is likely to have forgotten by the second half of the same school term *more than three-fourths of what was presented in the first half of the term* in the absence of systematic revision. Further, if the presented material is new, and abstract, it approximates for the child to nonsense-material. In that case the normal pupil may forget by the end of a thirty-five to forty-five-minute period *something between a third and a half of what is presented during the first fifteen minutes*. This emphasizes the absolute necessity of recapitulating not only at the end of the lesson and revising in subsequent lessons, but also of recapitulating *during the course of each lesson.*

In a previous chapter we have seen how the correct interpretation of new material depends upon ideas already clearly apprehended. Therefore, in a lesson dealing with abstract material arranged in logical form, if significant items presented at the beginning of the lesson are forgotten, what is presented towards the end of the lesson cannot be correctly interpreted. Hence confusion and frustration will supervene and the pupil will develop a distaste for the material which will add the factor of repression to the effect of lapse of time.

Truly, in teaching, to hurry is the best way to waste time.

THE PURPOSE OF RECAPITULATION AND REVISION

For practical teaching-purposes a distinction should be drawn between recapitulation and revision. The processes serve different aims.

According to the *Oxford Dictionary* ' recapitulation ' means " to go over the headings of ; summarize ; go quickly through again (with the implication that the previous doing was deficient or erroneous, or now requires alteration, improvement, or renewal)."

The primary purpose of recapitulation is to facilitate a clear, accurate grasp, by the learner, of the material to be learned, as a whole ; to give a conspectus. Recapitulation should aid understanding rather than memorizing as such. In so far as it aids understanding it also aids recall, but the latter is not its main purpose.

The recapitulation of a lesson or lecture should bring clearly to the notice of the learner, and emphasize, the *significant* elements to be learned. In recapitulation these significant items are recalled, or re-presented if necessary, (a) to test whether apprehension and understanding are adequate, and (b) to enable the learner to correct errors and fill in gaps in the previous learning. Thus the pupil is able to select these significant elements, abstract them more clearly, and by grasping their inter-relations weld them into a unity.

Recapitulation is essential both in a single lesson and in a series of lessons, because it may happen that the full significance of the first parts of the lesson or series cannot be grasped adequately until the material as a whole can be envisaged. It is necessary to return and contemplate the first parts in the light of the whole. This is frequently the case in studying a book. Too often, mechanical revision of *all* the presented material is substituted for intelligent recapitulation. If adult students would do more intelligent recapitulation and less mechanical revision they would economize their time, and examiners would find less cause to deplore the parrot-like detail and precision of many quite irrelevant answers to questions.

Revision, on the other hand, should aim at *memorizing* the selected material after its inter-relations have been grasped. Revision plays the same part in ideational learning as practice plays in the acquisition of skill. It off-sets the loss due to lapse of time, secures long retention, and facilitates accurate speedy recall on subsequent occasions. One important result of revision is the establishment of motor-speech (*i.e.*, word) habits.

METHODS OF RECAPITULATION AND REVISION

Recapitulation may be accomplished in several ways :

By question and answer.

By pupils' reports and discussion.

By making a summary which is then examined to stress inter-relations.

By application of the material learned to the solution of problems, theoretical or practical.

The problem reveals the weak points in understanding and forces the learner to reconsider the lesson material with an active searching attitude.

By making a map, diagram, drawing, time-chart, or by constructing a model. This method of recapitulation and summary is particularly useful in history, geography, and biology. The map, diagram, or model if well constructed displays the significant elements visually and emphasizes their mutual relations.

It is bad practice to leave all recapitulation till the end of a lesson, particularly when the material presented is unfamiliar or consists of many details. It is better to use a progressive-part method of treatment (see p. 522). In this method, the material to be presented is divided into convenient sections (the more complex and unfamiliar the material the shorter the sections). Section I is presented and then recapitulated before passing to section II. At the end of section II both sections I and II are recapitulated together. At the end of section III, sections I, II, and III are recapitulated, and so on. By this method the significant elements of the lesson material are *carried forward continuously* and the pupils find it easier to grasp the significance of the material as a whole.

It may be objected that this method will be tiresome and will destroy interest. This is doubtful. If the material is difficult the most potent element in interest will be a feeling of mastery over the lesson as it proceeds. If each portion of the lesson is recapitulated judiciously, the pupils, with memories refreshed, will carry along with them all the relevant information at each stage of the exposition. They will therefore be in a position to interpret and comprehend the later stages of the exposition. The mastery thus gained will enhance the interest. On the other hand, if vital information given at the beginning of the lesson is forgotten, the pupil is apt to spend the remainder of the time in painful confusion which is the reverse of interesting, and which makes the learner strongly averse to further attention.

Revision may be accomplished in the following ways :
Repeating after the teacher.
> This method is suitable for very young pupils whose reading- and writing-habits are not fully established. The repetition can often be organized as a game.
Silent re-reading.
Reading aloud.
> Many people whose visual imagery is weak find this method useful since the pronunciation of the words aids the formation of stable motor-speech habits. For this

reason it is *not* desirable to insist that all pupils shall revise silently.

Reciting without consulting the copy.

This is more effective than merely re-reading since it requires active effort to recall, and it reveals precisely the places where memorizing is weakest. These weak places can then be attacked intensively without wasting time in repeating what is already well established.

In reciting without copy it is necessary to have the copy available for reference as soon as the recall fails. Thus *the correct version can be obtained immediately and errors are not repeated*. It is a good plan to allow pupils to revise in pairs, one reciting while the other follows the copy, prompts when recall fails, and corrects any errors as soon as made. Working in pairs adds an element of rivalry to the procedure and brings in a social factor, both adding to the pleasure and zest of the enterprise. In addition both partners will be actively learning, which is more effective than passive repetition.

By writing down or re-drawing.

This method is valuable for pupils with well-developed visual and motor imagery. Also the motor-habits of writing reinforce the motor-speech habits. Writing or drawing is *not a useful method of revision until writing and drawing habits are well established*. Otherwise the attention of the pupil will be directed to making the movements of writing and holding pencil or pen, instead of being concentrated exclusively upon the material to be learned.

By answering a series of questions which demand for answers the items to be memorized.

Frequent short tests of the 'quiz' type are very valuable in revision, since they demand active recall by the pupil, *reveal losses, and provide a measure of progress*, particularly if a record is kept of marks gained in each test. Here again an element of rivalry can be introduced. (See p. 151, para. 5.)

By using the items to be revised in order to attack new work.

This is a useful method of revision in any subject-matter which has a cumulative or logical order, *e.g.*, foreign language, or mathematics. When memorizing arithmetical tables of multiplication, in addition to specific oral practice in tables, the pupils can revise the separate items by using them to work out multiplication and division calculations. This revision by application relieves the monotony of specific practice, and it encourages active learning.

TIME FOR REVISION SHOULD BE INCLUDED WHEN PLANNING A SYLLABUS

In planning school-work, whether for a single lesson or for a whole term, it is essential to include sufficient time for adequate recapitulation and revision. This is particularly the case in learning foreign languages when new sets of speech-habits must be established. Further, the revisions should be spaced over the whole term. Nothing can possibly be worse from an educational point of view than the practice of leaving revision to one frenzied week of concentrated repetition immediately preceding the terminal examinations.

The proportion of time required for revision will depend upon such factors as age and ability of pupils, amount of previous knowledge, nature of the subject-matter. Generally speaking the more the subject-matter involves arbitrary details not amenable to logical arrangement, the more frequent should be the revisions, and the more time allocated for that purpose.

B. HABITS AND HABIT-FORMATION

ADVANTAGES AND DISADVANTAGES OF HABIT

There has been a strong tendency for school-work to settle into a routine of mechanical repetition. There are several reasons for this tendency. In the medieval schools, books were extremely scarce and writing materials a luxury possible only to the wealthy. In the grammar schools the main subject was Latin, which was commenced, often, before the pupils could read English fluently. Oral repetition and catechism were, therefore, the only methods of conducting school-work. Later, in the early days of public elementary education, the classes allocated to each teacher were so enormous,[1] and the supply of books and writing-materials so

[1] Some elementary school teachers were responsible for classes containing more than 100 young pupils, while classes of 60 to 100 were relatively frequent.

meagre that, again, the teachers were forced to adopt methods of mechanical oral mass repetition. Individual treatment of pupils was almost impossible in such conditions.

The mechanical routine became extremely tiresome and monotonous and produced a profound boredom in the pupils. It is not surprising therefore that there have been, from time to time, furious protests by educational reformers against this form of drudgery. It has been asserted that school-work must be made interesting, and extremists have gone so far as to claim that children should not be required to do any work which is intrinsically uninteresting. In other words, there have been attempts to remove all forms of drill from school-practice.

Further, the disadvantages of habit have been emphasized. Habit is mechanical, stereotyped, and therefore not adaptable to changed circumstances. The creature of habit fails to respond intelligently to changed conditions in which the habits do not fit. Habit has been opposed to intelligent behaviour as if the two types of behaviour were mutually exclusive. Rousseau went so far as to say that the only habit a child should be allowed to form is that of learning no habits, and some ultra-modern educational reformers have tried to put this extreme suggestion into practice. This is another example of the way in which people revolt from an unsatisfactory state of affairs by going immediately to the opposite extreme.

However, in spite of the vociferous claims of extremists, unbiased observation of mental development shows that extreme informalism does not work satisfactorily in practice. Ideas cannot be expressed clearly without grammar and a good vocabulary, particularly in a foreign language. One cannot reason accurately without knowledge of facts, calculate correctly without knowledge of tables, nor use a dictionary effectively without knowledge of spelling, and of the alphabet. However much we may value intelligence, it cannot function as a purely formal process. We can only be intelligent in practice in so far as we use knowledge and tools intelligently.

It may be argued that there is now no need to learn to spell, nor to memorize facts and tables. Have we not dictionaries to supply words, books of tables and ready-reckoners to supply answers, laboratories in which to discover facts ? This may be so. Yet, in the first place life is too short, and practical needs too urgent to allow us to be continually turning over dictionaries ; looking up vocabularies and books of tables ; performing experiments to give us half-baked results which have already been correctly established by experts years ago. In the second place, *we cannot even use these aids to knowledge with precision and speed unless we have established some habitual skill in using them.*

The plain fact is that well-established habits are necessary for our peace of mind and sanity, as well as mental development. It is desirable, therefore, to emphasize the positive value of habituation.

(1) Habituation increases accuracy and speed of performance.

(2) Habituation makes complex movements more automatic, less and less dependent upon concentrated attention.

Hence, habits are great savers of energy, and the energy thus saved is freed for work on new and more important problems.

Consider a pupil who has never learned the multiplication tables. He is presented with a problem in arithmetic which itself demands concentrated and sustained attention. If the pupil must needs turn up a set of tables and search for every individual item he requires for his subsidiary computations, it is obvious that the energy needed for the intelligent solution of the problem will be frittered away in exasperating searches for items of information.

It is often asserted that a good education should make pupils think. It is just as reasonable to assert that a good education should free them from the necessity for thinking. The ideal education makes the pupil *selective in his thinking.* It enables him to decide when constructive thinking is necessary, and when it is better to memorize and become habituated. The position may be summed up by saying that memorizing and habituation capitalize the results of experience and render them more readily available for quick and accurate application.

We should not hesitate, therefore, to make fundamental knowledge and skills habitual in our pupils, and *for this purpose some drill is essential.* It may be objected that drill is identical with drudgery. This is not necessarily so. In the first place drudgery is unremitting repetition which is *forced upon a pupil without his realizing the purpose which the drill will serve.* In the second place it is well established by the observation of children in free play, and leisure occupations, that instead of avoiding repetition they engage in it spontaneously, particularly *when it enables them to achieve some end they desire.* Many childish games are mostly rhythmic repetition. The repetition is welcome in so far as it **develops ability and mastery, thus inducing a feeling of confidence** and success, and satisfying the hunger for self-enhancement. Drill ceases to be drudgery when its useful purpose is clear to the pupil. If it is impossible to make a pupil of a given age realize the purpose of drill, the drill should either be discarded as unnecessary, or postponed to a later, more mature phase of development. But some drill at some time is unavoidable.

THE FUNCTION OF REPETITION IN HABIT-FORMATION

One fallacy which seems to be inherent in the arguments against drill, is the assumption that repetition is nothing but a mechanical process in which constructive observation and thought play no part. This assumption is not accurate, particularly in the early formative stages of habituation. Then, repetitive practice is never purely mechanical. It is invariably selective. No two repetitions are quite identical. Actually a trial-and-error process goes on, during which the learner modifies his movements or his ideas in such a way as to make the performance approximate more and more closely to some standard of correctness and speed which is kept in view throughout the learning-process. In economical learning the intelligent and well-instructed learner is not repeating either ideas or movements mechanically. He is aiming at a goal—a standard of good performance.

No complicated skill is achieved at the first trial although we may have a clear idea in advance of what we ought to achieve, and how we must attempt it. *Actual trial reveals to the learner (and to his teacher) how far his present ability falls short of the standard, and in what respects his performance differs from the standard.* In other words practice is a device which indicates to the learner a measure of the results of his efforts. Knowing the standard aimed at, and then discovering by trial how far he can approximate to the standard, the learner can, at the next repetition change his responses in an intelligent way so as to correct his mistakes and approximate more closely to the standard. Repetition enables the learner to *select the more successful trials and reject the less successful.* This indicates another reason for providing the learner with good standards, and keeping him acquainted with his results.

In this connexion we must note the importance of *successful* trials. One successful performance which brings a measure of elation and enhances self-valuation is of more value in establishing a habit than dozens of failures. Hence the desirability of encouraging success as early as possible in the learning-periods.

Apart altogether from any ' stamping-in ' effect, repetition is essential for *shaping* the performance into a correct copy of the standard.

Using an apparatus which enabled them to show, or withhold, at will, the result of an action, Elwell and Grindley tested the effect of knowing one's results on improvement in skill. They found

No improvement in accuracy of performance without knowledge of results.

Improvement with knowledge of results.

Withholding results after acquiring skill leads to a degeneration of the skilled habit.

They suggest the following reasons for their findings :

Knowledge of results enables the learner to repeat successful actions.

It has a *directive* effect in that it enables unsuccessful trials to be corrected.

It sets up a conscious attitude or mood conducive to accurate performance. Withholding results dissipates this mood.[1]

The third reason seems to indicate the growth of a feeling of confidence and mastery to which reference has been made previously.

THE LEARNING-CURVE

The course of progress in acquiring some form of skill can be studied conveniently by reference to typical learning-' curves.' A learning-curve is a graph obtained by plotting some measure of the proficiency attained by the learner, against the length of time occupied in practice, or against the number of practice periods.

Inspection of such graphs reveals two interesting features :

(1) Reversals of progress.

(2) Plateau-periods.

The first feature is illustrated by the graph in Fig. 32.[2] The curve was obtained during an investigation of the course of improvement in typewriting. It shows that *on the whole*, there is a rise in speed of typing roughly proportional to the number of lessons. The day-to-day progress, however, is uneven. On some days the learner's speed shows a rapid increase over previous performances. On other days there are just as pronounced reversals of efficiency. Thus there is, in the case illustrated, a serious drop near the

[1] *British Journal of Psychology*, Vol. XXIX, Part I, p. 53.

[2] Reproduced by Blackburn in *The Acquisition of Skill. An Analysis of Learning Curves*, Industrial Health Research Board Report, No. 73 (H.M. Stationery Office), p. 19.

twentieth lesson, the learner showing no greater efficiency then, than at the tenth lesson. Near the fortieth and fiftieth lessons there are rapid spurts followed again by severe reversals.

These spurts and reversals are due to several factors among which are, enthusiasm with which the practice is attacked ; complacence and less effort after a rise in efficiency ; determination to make up a loss in efficiency ; weather-conditions; room-temperature and ventilation ; subjective feelings of cheerfulness or despondency induced by circumstances not connected with the learning (*e.g.*, illness or bad temper of a member of the family) ; the learner's own state of health ; presence or absence of fatigue.

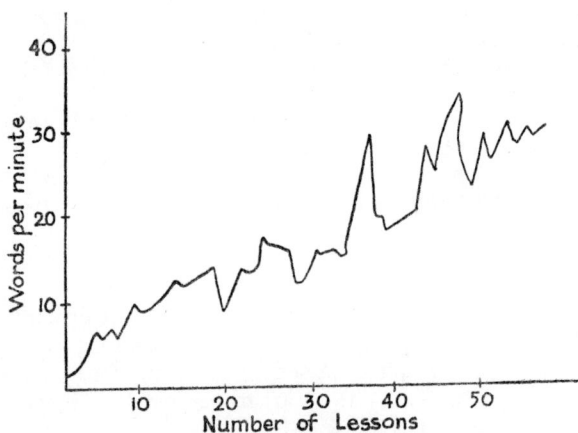

Fig. 32

Showing curve of progress in typewriting.

A good example of plateau-periods is shown by the graph in Fig. 33. It represents the course of improvement in tool-skill of a group of good elementary schoolboys. It shows rapid improvement during the first term's work, almost no further improvement in the second term in spite of continued practice, a second spurt beginning half-way through the third term, and then a long period of no improvement lasting for approximately three terms, followed by a third spurt.

It was supposed that these plateau-periods were inevitable in learning. This view is no longer held. It has been shown that some of the plateaux reported by earlier investigators were due either (*a*) to the conditions in which the experiments were conducted, or (*b*) to the mathematical procedure employed to estimate the rate of improvement.[1]   Further, curves have been obtained in which no plateaux are apparent. *e.g.*, the typewriting curve in Fig. 32 and the curve obtained by Mace for progress in arithmetical addition (Fig. 34).[2]

After eliminating plateaux caused by experimental conditions and methods of calculating results, however, true plateaux are

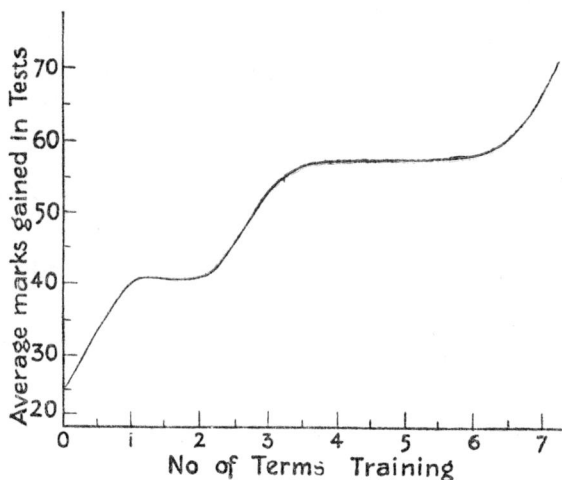

FIG. 33

Graph showing course of improvement in tool-skill of a group of good elementary school boys.[3]

found in learning-curves.[4]   These periods of no improvement may be due :

(*a*) To factors *external to* the learning-process.

(*b*) To factors *inherent in* the learning-process.

Chief among the factors in class (*a*) are falling off in enthusiasm and interest ;   onset of fatigue and staleness ;   accidental conditions causing bodily and mental discomfort ;   bad attitudes, *e.g.*, belief by the learner that the limit of improvement has been reached, or complacence owing to the rapid attainment of a too-low standard

[1] Blackburn, Report cited, Chapter IV, p. 27.

[2] *Cf.* p. 151.

[3] From James and Dixon, *Creative Handwork*, Chapter XIII. " An Experiment in Testing," p. 60.

[4] Blackburn, report cited, p. 30–33.

of work, etc. These factors are also mainly responsible for the reversals already noted in a previous paragraph.

The factors in class (b) are found to occur in the learning of *complex skills in which many component habits must be shaped into a co-ordinated pattern.* Such factors include :

(a) Paying attention to one component of the skill only, to the neglect of other components, *e.g.,* in typewriting it is essential for speed that the learner's attention should be given to the ' copy ' to be written and not to the keyboard. The learner's tendency is to attend to the keyboard and neglect the ' copy.' Then there is an oscillation of attention between the copy and the keyboard which prevents the attainment of high speeds.[1]

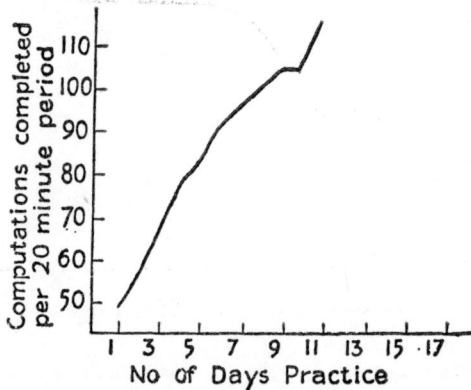

FIG. 34[2]

Showing increase in efficiency in arithmetical addition with practice.
(Group of boys, average age = 11 years 5 months.)

(b) Forming simple ' lower-order ' habits which persist unchanged and thus prevent the perfection of ' higher-order ' habits. A familiar example in school-work occurs when young pupils copy a passage of prose into an exercise book. The child's natural tendency is to copy letter by letter, or word by word, instead of reading several words at one glance and then transcribing from memory. If the learner persists in using the simpler habit (because it is more easily mastered at first) he may soon achieve some skill in the performance, but the limit *for that habit* is quickly reached,

---

[1] The same difficulty occurs in learning to play the piano.

[2] Adapted from Mace's Fig. III, p. 21, Industrial Health Research Board Report, No. 72 (H.M. Stationery Office).

and further progress is impossible until a more complex but more efficient habit has been substituted.

(c) Changing the methods of performance during the learning-period. One instance of this is the bad co-ordination of the different stages in the teaching of arithmetic.

Suppose that a pupil has been taught multiplication by using the digits of the multiplier from right to left, i.e., in ascending order of place-value. In that case the computation will be set out as follows:

$$1249 \times 371$$

$$
\begin{array}{r}
1249 \\
371 \\
\hline
1249 \\
8743. \\
3747.. \\
\end{array}
$$

This method of setting-out has the disadvantage that the partial product of greatest significance is dealt with last. When the pupil reaches a more advanced stage, and begins to learn to do 'approximation,' methods of calculation, this order of working must be exactly reversed. Hence if the first habit has been thoroughly practised in the elementary stages of instruction, there will be a temporary cessation of improvement in calculation when it is necessary to learn the 'approximation' habits. The two sets of habits conflict.

This brief survey of learning-curves gives some useful hints for teaching-practice. Children must be habituated in certain fundamental skills, such as reading, writing, transcribing, arithmetical computation. Our aim should be to conduct the learning so that the pupils' progress is:

As rapid as his mental and physical capacity will permit.
Free from reversals of progress.
Free from plateau-periods.

To secure these results we must keep in mind the two sets of factors, external and inherent. To control the first we can do the following:

Make the classroom conditions bright and cheerful, and as hygienic as circumstances permit.
Avoid fatigue due to too prolonged practice at each sitting.
Remove distractions.
Keep the pupils' motives strong and persistent by a judicious organization of incentives.

Suggestion 4 has already been dealt with in detail in Chapter **V.** Particular attention should be given to the setting of *as high a standard of attainment* as the pupils' powers permit ; to informing pupils clearly and regularly about the results of their practice ; and to the prescription of definite achievements to be aimed at in each practice.[1]

To control the factors inherent in the learning-process itself we must carry out the following procedures :

1. Practise partial habits in the way they will be required at a later phase of learning.

Children do not require multiplication tables *en bloc*, but only specific items. If a pupil learns a table in serial order—one two is two, two twos are four, three twos are six, and so on, he may find it very difficult to say what seven twos amount to, without beginning at the first line and repeating the series until the item ' seven twos ' is reached. Therefore as soon as a multiplication table has been demonstrated, and its ' build ' understood by the pupils, they should be practised, not in memorizing the table as a whole in serial form, but in memorizing the separate items in haphazard order (or disorder !), as they will have to use the table in practice.

Similarly, it is better to teach the process of multiplication in a form favourable to the ' approximation ' phase, from the very first lessons. Thus, instead of using the setting described on p. 513, we should use this alternative :

$$1249 \times 371$$

$$
\begin{array}{r}
1249 \\
371 \\
\hline
3747 \cdot\cdot \\
8743 \cdot \\
1249 \\
\hline
\end{array}
$$

beginning to multiply with the digit of highest place value.

In all elementary teaching we should keep in view not only the immediate future, but also the requirements of the ultimate stages of skill. A well-taught pupil *will have as little as possible to unlearn* at a later date.

2. Wherever possible aim at practising the complex co-ordina-

[1] *Cf.* p. 148. It is interesting to note that the curve of improvement in arithmetical addition obtained by Mace (Fig. 34) in which there is no plateau, and an almost complete absence of reversals, was obtained with boys of $11\frac{1}{2}$ years of age (on the average) using the method of prescribing a moving standard of achievement.

tion of habits from the commencement of learning rather than at perfecting one partial habit at a time.

In teaching young children to transcribe, encourage them from the very beginning to look at a word or a phrase, as a whole, and then transcribe it from memory. Discourage the natural tendency to copy one letter, or one word, at a time. Similarly in teaching typewriting, modern instructors require their pupils to practise typing from the copy as soon as they begin to practise. Looking at the copy and then finding the keys by looking at the keyboard is discouraged. The first alternative may be more difficult at first, but it produces a much greater skill later.

If, as often happens, some particular phase of the process presents special difficulties, this will have to receive special attention and special practice. This special practice, however, is best undertaken *after* the learner has been able to get a *general view of the whole process*. Then, the *need* for the special practice is more apparent. In addition, the connexion between the particular phase receiving attention, and the whole pattern of the skill, is clear. The general outline of the whole process should be grasped *first* before any partial habits are intensively practised.

In all sensory-motor learning a good *demonstration* of the skill habits to be acquired is most important. Demonstration is much superior to verbal instruction. The learner must have in view as clear as possible a picture of the skill to be acquired from the commencement of the practice.

Some Conditions of Effective Practice

A great deal of experimental work has been done to discover the most effective conditions for habituation. The following sections deal with some of the results particularly relevant to normal school-practice.

OVER-LEARNING

If thorough mastery of subject-matter or of skill and long retention are desired, the learning-process must be continued *well beyond the critical point at which the material learned can just be recalled, or the task just accomplished with effort*. In the early stages of learning there is usually a lack of confidence and a feeling of insecurity. The material to be remembered seems to be just beyond recall, and the task just too difficult to perform. If the learning is continued, the feeling of insecurity begins to give place to a feeling of mastery. Practice must be carried on beyond this stage, until the performance can be accomplished with a minimum of effort. Carrying on the learning-process well beyond the critical stage of bare achievement is known as over-learning.

ACTIVE LEARNING 'VERSUS' PASSIVE REPETITION

Learning will be most effective when the learner adopts an active attitude towards the process.

This principle is very well exemplified in the conduct of memory-investigations. Suppose we wish to find out how many repetitions are needed to commit a poem to memory. The investigator can collect his subjects together, and read the poem through while they listen. If a number of groups take part in the experiments he may read the same passage several hundred times. It often happens that although the investigator may be a better memorizer than his subjects he is unable to repeat correctly what he has read many times, while the subjects require only a comparatively few repetitions.

The investigator is not required to recall correctly what he has read. Therefore he is not interested in the attempts to recall. His listeners, on the other hand, will be trying very hard to memorize.

This active attitude will be guaranteed by interest in the material, and interest in the learning-process. It may be encouraged deliberately by requiring the learner to try to reproduce, without the aid of the copy, as early as possible in the learning-process. For example, in learning a poem, after it has been read through a few times ' to get the hang of it,' one should discard the copy and attempt to repeat from memory. As soon as memory fails glance at the copy again to pick up the correct clue, then proceed without the copy. When teaching children tables, geometrical or other proofs, formulæ, etc., let them *apply* the material as soon as they have grasped the general outline of the connexions.

Passive repetition carried on with an attitude of indifference or boredom is very inefficient and every endeavour should be made to avoid it.

WHAT IS THE BEST LENGTH FOR A LEARNING-PERIOD

By a learning-period is meant any period of time during which the learning is carried on continuously.

Economical learning requires active interest and effort. Boredom and fatigue prevent effort. Hence learning-periods should be stopped *before* the onset of boredom and fatigue. For concentrated learning, short periods are indicated.

The periods should not be too short, however. Measurements of output have proved that normal learning-periods have three phases :

(i) *A ' warming-up ' phase*

The learner usually begins slowly and requires some little time to " get into the swing " of the task.

(ii) *A phase of full output*

Having got a good working ' swing ' the learner continues for some time at his best, until he arrives at

(iii) *A slowing-down phase*

This begins with the onset of fatigue or boredom. Output diminishes slowly at first then more rapidly. If a definite task must be completed, or a definite period has been allotted for the learning, there is usually a spurt when the end is in sight.

Represented graphically, the output curve is somewhat like this :

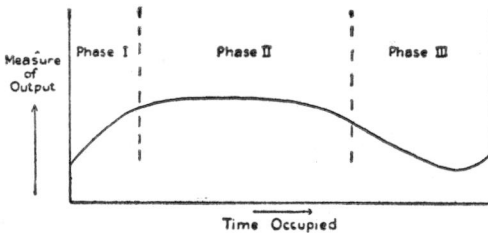

FIG. 35

Hence, if the working-period is to be filled most economically, phase II must be as long as possible in comparison with phases I and III. If the periods are made too short the working-time is finished before phase II runs its full course, or, in extreme cases, before it has really begun.

For senior pupils and adults the best length for a learning-period is about thirty-five to forty minutes. This is an average time and will vary according to the individual learner's power of concentration and endurance, and the nature of the task to be learned. The more difficult the material the shorter[1] should be the learning-period. Shorter periods are necessary for younger pupils, since they are more easily fatigued.

[1] Within limits suggested by the output-curve.

THE DISTRIBUTION OF LEARNING-PERIODS

Another problem in economical learning relates to the frequency with which we ought to practise. Is it better to 'mass' the learning-periods close together with only short intervals between them, or is it better to space them out by allowing a greater interval between successive practices ?

In this connexion we must first note some further characteristics of the learning-process :

(*a*) First impressions are rapidly forgotten and need early and frequent revision. (*Cf.* p. 500).

(*b*) Retroactive inhibition.

This is the name given to the interference caused by intense mental effort exerted *immediately after* a learning-period has been completed. The effect of the interference is indicated by the following experiment.

A group of learners is tested for memory-capacity and learning-ability. The group is divided into two sub-groups of equal average ability. Both sub-groups are required to memorize the same material such as prose, poetry, or tables. At the end of a given time the learning is stopped. Sub-group *A* is required to commence immediately, some further intellectual work demanding close attention. Sub-group *B* is allowed a complete rest. At the end of this second period both sub-groups are required to reproduce as much as possible of the material first learned.

It is found invariably that sub-group *B*, the members of which have been rested after the learning, can reproduce more than the members of sub-group *A*. The further period of intellectual effort undertaken by the latter interferes with the previous learning.

Experimental tests indicate that the maximum amount of retroactive inhibition is produced when the second activity is very similar in form to the first.[1]

This inhibition is undoubtedly one factor in reducing the efficiency of a learner who extends his learning-periods over too long a time. After an optimum period (which is probably from thirty-five to forty minutes for the average adult) the effect of continuing the effort to learn is equivalent to taking up another similar kind of intense intellectual work. What is attempted in the later portion of the long learning-period not only adds nothing of value *but positively cancels out part of what has already been accomplished.*

---

[1] See T. G. Foran, "Retro-active Inhibition," *Journal of Educational Psychology*, Vol. XXVIII, September 1937, p. 460.

It should be an invariable rule, particularly with children, that after they have been occupied in concentrated learning they should either (i) have an opportunity for complete relaxation, or (ii) take up another kind of occupation which is *different in form from what they have been doing, and easy to accomplish.*

REMINISCENCE

It has been shown by Ballard [1] that the effect of lapse of time is not a simple one-way loss of what has been learned. While there is a loss of some items, *other items are actually recovered* after a lapse of time.

A class of schoolboys was given thirteen minutes in which to memorize the poem, " The Loss of the Royal George." At the end of this period they were required to write down as much as they could remember of the poem. The precaution was taken to exclude from the experiment any boys who were at all familiar with the piece. Of the remainder, *one* boy wrote down all of the 36 lines, the average for the class being 27·6 lines.

After an interval of two days, during which no opportunity for revision was allowed, Ballard gave the same class a second, *unexpected* test and obtained a rather striking result. *Eight* boys wrote out the whole poem of 36 lines, and the class average rose to 30·6 lines, an increase of rather more than 10 per cent.

This result was confirmed by further experiments on subjects of varying ages. In addition the investigator found that:

The more comprehensible and interesting the material learned, the greater the reminiscence.

Some reminiscence occurred even with nonsense-material.

The younger the pupils the more marked was the reminiscence.

There were considerable individual differences with respect to the power of reminiscence.

The process appears to be most active *in the case of the older and better established associations of ideas.*

The most favourable interval for maximum reminiscence is about two days.

Ballard considered that the most satisfactory way of accounting for this interesting phenomenon was to suppose that the initial learning-process stimulated growth in the actual nervous system of the learner, and that this increased growth, once stimulated, continued under its own momentum (so to speak) for some time after active learning ceased.

[1] " Obliviscence and Reminiscence," *British Journal of Psychology.* Monograph Supplement, Vol. I, No. 2.

Consideration of the phenomena of retroactive inhibition and reminiscence seems to suggest that there should be a definite advantage in spacing out (or distributing) learning-periods. This rule is now generally accepted. Two learning-periods of fifteen minutes each, one in the morning, one in the afternoon, are more effective than one period of thirty minutes. Starch has shown [1] that for a total period of 120 minutes of practice in substituting numbers for letters according to a key, the greatest progress was made by a group of learners doing two ten-minute practices each day for six days. A group doing one twenty-minute practice per day for six days did less well, and the worst result was shown by a group doing 120 minutes' continuous practice.

However, the general rule that spaced practice is most effective needs some qualifications of which the following are important :

(i) There must be obviously a lower limit beyond which it is not economical to sub-divide the learning-periods. (*Cf.* p. 517).

(ii) In view of the very rapid disappearance of nonsense-material, and of items of information with a minimum of logical connexion, such as dates in history; geographical data; vocabularies; it seems desirable in those cases *to revise frequently at short intervals as soon as possible after the initial learning.* When the pupils approach the condition of over-learning, the successive practices or revision periods can be spaced out at rapidly increasing intervals.

(iii) In the acquisition of skill it is essential for success that the pupil shall *acquire correct and economical habits as soon as possible* in the learning-process. If bad habits acquired in early practices are repeated they will persist at the expense of more efficient habits, and they will need much time and care to eradicate them. Therefore, it is often advantageous in learning skills, to ' mass ' the practice-periods at the beginning of the learning until the pupil has acquired some degree of proficiency in the correct habits. After that, the learning-periods may be spaced out.

(iv) In acquiring complicated skills it is difficult for a learner to make much progress until (*a*) he has discovered a general principle of procedure (in other words, has found the ' knack ' of it), and (*b*) has established a good rhythm of operation (*i.e.*, has got into a good ' swing '). The sooner these two results are attained, the sooner will the learner make good progress. Hence in learning complicated skills there may be a definite advantage in ' massing ' together the practices in the early part of the course.

[1] *Journal of Educational Psychology,* Vol. 3, 1912.

CRAMMING

By ' cramming ' we mean what may be called brute memorizing by means of prolonged and concentrated effort. Cramming is to a learner what forced marches are to an army. The question arises, does cramming ever pay ? The answer depends on our purpose in learning. There are two alternatives.

1. We may try to learn a set task with the *fewest possible number of repetitions*, and learn it with the *intention of remembering it for the longest possible time*. If this is our purpose then *spaced* learning is by far the more advantageous process.

2. We may be obliged to memorize information in the *shortest possible time*, for use on one particular occasion *after which we shall not need to recall the information again*. A student may be required to pass an elementary test in Latin, not because he is interested in it, nor because he will require the knowledge later, but because an examination syllabus prescribes it. For this purpose concentrated practice is often necessary on account of the time-limit imposed.

For general teaching-purposes when the material is valuable and likely to be needed for a long time, cramming should be avoided. It is very fatiguing, arouses strong aversion for the subject-matter, and what is learned in this way is soon forgotten.

WHOLE *v.* PART LEARNING

There has been a good deal of controversy about the advisability of learning a poem (a) by repeating a large portion of it as a whole each time, or (b) by repeating it a line at a time. In many schools formerly, pupils learning a hymn would say the first line over and over again until they knew it by heart. Then they would treat the second line in the same way, and so on to the end of the first verse. Then the verse would be repeated as a whole.

The disadvantages of such a procedure are obvious. In the first place, what may be an interesting piece of poetry with a thread of meaning running clearly through it is broken up into a large number of comparatively meaningless phrases. The superior memory-value of the logical associations is thus destroyed. Secondly, the mechanical associations are not learned in the form in which they must be reproduced. In normal use, the last word of any line must be associated with the first word of the *succeeding* line. By learning one separate line at a time, the last word of the line is associated with the first word of the *same* line in a continuous cycle.

It was found by experiment that many subjects could learn a piece of continuous prose or poetry by heart much more economically by the ' whole ' method, and this has been advocated as the best method for learning in all cases.

This statement needs qualification, however. It has been shown by Pechstein [1] and Gopalaswami [2] that for learning complicated motor associations, such as running a maze, or mirror drawing, what is called " a progressive-part method " is more economical than either the whole or part methods. This was found to be true both for rats and human beings in learning to run a complicated maze, and for human beings in learning nonsense-material.

The progressive-part method consists in dividing up the task to be learned into several short portions. The learner masters the first portion thoroughly. Then he masters the second portion. Next he *repeats portions one and two together until they have been learned as a whole.* The third portion is then mastered, followed by the repetition of portions one, two, and three together. This progressive method is followed until the whole task has been accomplished successfully. This method is the more advantageous the more difficult the material to be learned. (*Cf.* recapitulation, p. 503).

THE ' MIXED ' METHOD OF LEARNING

The whole method of learning makes it possible to use any logical sequence or ' plot ' to advantage. However, even with logical material it is found that some portions are more easily mastered than others. We usually find what are called ' refractory associations.' If we adopt the whole method and continue to repeat the piece from beginning to end until we have mastered it, it is obvious that we shall repeat the easy associations as often as the refractory associations. This is a waste of time. Therefore a ' mixed ' method is best. The following procedure is recommended for *logically connected* material.

Read through the whole piece, noting the plot, the sequence of events, and the connexions involved.

Repeat this several times until the material as a whole begins to feel familiar.

Turn the copy over, and attempt to recall it actively, prompting

---

[1] *Psychological Monographs*, 1917, No. XXIII ; *Journal of Educational Psychology*, 1918, No. IX.

[2] *British Journal of Psychology*, Vol. 15, 1924-5.

at each hesitation by referring to the copy. Active recall is always better than passive repetition, and, by prompting at each hesitation *we avoid repeating errors.* This active recall also indicates what are the refractory associations. Having noted these, concentrate upon each in turn, practising it until thoroughly mastered. Then connect it with its immediate context.

Read through the piece as a whole and repeat until mastery has been achieved.

C. Manner of Presentation in Relation to Long Retention and Effective Recall

We may summarize the discussion so far by stating three fundamental conditions for long retention and effective recall. These are (a) Motivation, (b) Frequency, (c) Recency.

Motivation

Other things being equal, the greater the zest for learning, and the more definite the intention to remember, the longer are we likely to retain the effects of an experience and the more readily can we recall it.

The principles of motivation have been discussed in Section II, which should be revised in connexion with the present chapter.

Frequency

Other things being equal, the more frequently an experience has been repeated, the longer will its effects be retained and the more readily will it be recalled.

Recency

Other things being equal, the more recent the experience the more readily will it be recalled.

Recapitulation ensures recency of experience; revision and repetitive practice ensure frequency of the experience. The best conditions for recapitulation, revision, and repetitive practice have been indicated in the present chapter.

To these three conditions we must now add a fourth :

Vividness and Impressiveness of Stimulation

Other things being equal, the more vivid and impressive the experience the longer is it likely to be retained and the more readily recalled.

In school-practice, vividness and impressiveness of stimulation can be enhanced by the manner in which the material to be learned is presented to the pupils. The most important conditions which favour vividness and impressiveness are as follows :

1. Stimuli must be clear, adequate, and free from distraction. Therefore attend to lighting and accoustic conditions (*e.g.*, use clear deliberate speech loud enough to be heard comfortably by all pupils and free from distracting noises).

Maps, pictures, diagrams, models should be large enough to be seen easily and free from unnecessary detail.

2. Mild stimuli may need several repetitions before they are fully noted.

3. Impressiveness of stimulation is increased by using several correlated sense-organs at the same time.

Material should be presented in such a way that as many sense-organs as possible are stimulated together. Vision, motor-speech, practical manipulation must be used to reinforce aural impressions. For most children visual and motor stimuli are more vivid than aural stimuli.

Hence :

Use colours to emphasize distinctions.

Use pictures and models to reinforce oral description.

Use demonstrations rather than oral description in introducing *processes*.

Note importance of moving pictures and working models.

Use the blackboard to reinforce oral exposition.

Note the importance of graphical devices for presenting relations.

Graphical devices are particularly useful for representing comparative statistics in economics, geography, history, science, etc. Compare the vividness of the output-diagram with that of the verbal description of variations of output in the course of a learning-period (p. 517).

In this connexion note the fact that the cinema can be used for presenting not only moving pictures but also *moving maps, charts, and diagrams, e.g.*, the successive phases of an invasion or growth of an institution ; variations in volume of imports and exports, etc. In other words, the cinema film and screen can be used to develop a moving blackboard.

Examples of devices for using several co-ordinated sense-organs are :

Writing a new word on the blackboard, pronouncing it for the pupils, requiring pupils to pronounce it aloud, requiring them to write it down.

Allowing pupils to repeat material to be memorized, aloud, with appropriate gestures.

Dramatizing historical and literary scenes.

Using manipulative methods in the teaching of arithmetic and science.

4. Grouped data are more impressive than isolated data. In presentation, data may be grouped:

By close spatial proximity.

According to similarity.

By logical association, either in a series or a system.

By artificial devices, such as mnemonics or rhyming verses.

In presenting any factual details, such as occur frequently in history, economics, geography, language, it is desirable to group associated data together, and emphasize logical relations between them. Make secondary associations whenever possible and, in doing so, associate new material with *old, familiar, and well-established knowledge*.

Emphasize in the pupils the attitude of seeking for relations, and grouping data in systematic summaries.

Where a series of arbitrary details must be learned, mnemonic devices are sometimes useful. Years ago the writer had to learn by heart the battles of the Wars of the Roses. The following mnemonic was suggested: All Boys Never Will Mention All Those Hateful, Horrid Battles To Bosworth. Here the initials are also the initials of the names of the battles in question, namely, St Albans, Bloreheath, Northampton, Wakefield, Mortimer's Cross, St Albans, Towton, Hedgeley Moor, Hexham, Barnet, Tewkesbury, Bosworth.

The mnemonic has some recognizable logical form and is much easier to retain than the list of names.

5. Experiences may be made more impressive by arousing interest in them. The pupils are then more alert, attention adjustments more quickly made and more effective.

In this connexion note particularly:

(i) Emphasis on the value and use of the material to be learned.

Material which serves a felt need, and the purpose of which is clearly recognized, will be the more readily apprehended and retained (*cf.* discussions on motivation, Chapter V).

(ii) Preparation of an expectant attitude in the pupils.

A reasonable amount of what may be called 'showmanship' is valuable in teaching. Its purpose is to increase the attractiveness of the presented material, to 'intrigue' the pupils and arouse an expectant attitude.

Compare the attractive value of the following procedures for presenting the fact that chlorine gas is a bleaching agent:

Instructing pupils to read a statement of the fact.

Stating the fact orally to the pupils.

Merely showing an experiment to demonstrate the fact.

Showing an experiment in the following way :

The teacher takes a jar of chlorine gas, and mentions that the gas will act as a bleaching agent.

He then takes a sheet of paper and writes on it in *ink*, " Form III boys are clever." Underneath this he writes in *pencil*, " Form III boys are not clever."

The sheet of paper is shown to the class with the suggestion that the jar of chlorine gas will act as an oracle and deliver judgment. The paper is then dipped into the gas.

The ink marks are rapidly bleached and disappear, leaving the pencil marks still showing clearly.

In a case like this the presentation not only arouses a strong expectant attitude in the class, but it also intrigues them and the pupils will discuss it later, spontaneously. This ensures recall and repetition in imagery.

Further, the experiment is so arranged that the result leads directly to a discussion about the reason why the ink marks and not the pencil marks are bleached, and thence to an inquiry into the conditions in which chlorine acts as a bleaching agent.

D. Teaching Pupils how to Study

Generally speaking, very little attention has been given in schools to the need for teaching pupils how to study. Without expert guidance few individuals succeed in realizing their full learning-powers. Much time and energy are wasted daily by university students for the simple reason that no instruction in methods of economical learning and study has been given to them in their secondary-school careers. Sufficient is now known about the best conditions for learning, to enable any teacher to organize his work and guide the learning-habits of his pupils efficiently. If only a fraction of the knowledge available were systematically applied a very considerable improvement in teaching and learning would be gained. It is even more important that as pupils approach the senior stages of school-life, the more obvious rules of economical learning should be explained to them as occasions arise, and these methods *made explicitly conscious*. If the adolescent is interested in his mental processes and their conditions he will be the better able to carry on his own further education when he leaves the tutelage of his school.

From replies to questions, one gathers that the secondary-school tuition of some students has consisted to a great extent of verbal exposition in the form of a lecture by the teacher, followed by hurried dictation of notes. The pupils contribute little or nothing to this process beyond passive listening and bad writing. When such students pass into university institutions where some degree of independent work is expected, they are helpless. Their one aim in life is to make verbatim copies of lectures or books and then hurry off to memorize their notes. This condition of affairs is by no means limited to one country. In their *Elementary Principles of Education,* Thorndike and Gates assert that " it requires considerable time and much guidance to develop skill in learning from books. Many university students of the present generation have amazingly little skill." [1]

As books multiply, and find their way in increasing numbers into all types of schools, and as more importance is given to ' individual ' methods of school-organization, the more is it necessary to train pupils in the art of reading. The following habits intelligently used will make reading more profitable :

Read the book (or article) through rapidly at first to get a conspectus of the general plan, the main and subsidiary problems treated, and the author's point of view.

Review the first reading from memory and endeavour to re-construct the general lay-out of the argument, putting the topics treated in some order of importance.

Read subsequently *with definite problems in mind* for which answers are sought.

Endeavour to separate main principles of importance from illustrative material and subsidiary detail.

Associate the facts learned with other facts already known.

Compare what is read with material gathered from other sources. Make definite references from one book to another and from the book to personal practical experience.

Recapitulate frequently what has been read, and actively relate it to the present reading.

Think out possible ways in which the information gathered can be applied.

Test the assertions of the book by reference to specific facts in the reader's own experience. If a text-book on educational psychology asserts that the average child behaves in such and

[1] Book cited, p. 244. The authors have American students in mind.

such a way, think of some normal children in actual life and endeavour to find out how far the assertion is true in their particular cases.

Make short summaries of main principles for convenient reference and revision later.

Pupils in secondary schools need practice in making *their own notes and summaries* both from verbal exposition and from books. From an *educational* point of view the dictation of notes by the teacher is a veritable plague and should be avoided as such. Only in cases where some formula or statement must be learned in precise language should the practice of dictating be used. Pupils who are inured to dictation soon fall into the habit of ignoring the preliminary lecture, knowing full well that in due course they will be able to copy down just what information they are expected to learn. To pay any attention to the exposition is clearly superfluous, in their opinion.

E. Fatigue

Fatigue is an important factor in causing loss of efficiency in learning. Psychologically it consists first in feeling a loss of interest in, then aversion to, the activity being performed, accompanied by desire for change. If the worker persists in the activity, definite localized, organic sensations arise. Headache, aching of the limbs, and in extreme cases pain on movement are felt. When very tired we feel an intolerable aversion for any further movement. In extreme fatigue co-ordination both of thinking and muscular action fails. Ideas are disjointed and movements jerky.

In an earlier chapter it was suggested that successful activity depends upon the maintenance of certain internal constants. It is known that any nervous and muscular activity is accompanied by chemical changes in the tissues. The energy for the work is derived from the decomposition of complex, organic substances, and by-products are secreted into the blood as a result. The by-products include carbon dioxide, lactic acid, and toxins derived from the destruction of cells. Normally these are removed as fast as they are formed, fresh fuel and oxygen are supplied to the working parts and the cycle of physiological activity continues. It would seem that the physiological causes of fatigue are mainly (a) the excessive production of toxic substances faster than they can be removed, and (b) lack of fresh fuel and oxygen necessary for rebuilding the exhausted tissue. It is well known that after illness, during malnutrition or oxygen deprivation, fatigue sets in very quickly, and the amount of work possible is small.[1]

It seems desirable to note a distinction between *local* and *general* fatigue. In writing, for example, the muscles immediately involved begin to tire and the act of writing becomes painful. One turns from writing to general movement such as walking or playing tennis, with relief, and the local fatigue passes away. Probably the increased general circulation helps to remove the local physiological conditions of fatigue. Similarly, one turns from continued study of one kind of subject-matter to a different kind with a renewal of interest and vigour. In such cases a change of occupation is equivalent to a rest.

Native, or old-established habitual activities are less easily fatigued than newly acquired habits. For this reason, practice-periods in all *new* skills should be short, particularly for young children.

There seems no reason to distinguish between mental and muscular fatigue. Both appear to be due to similar physiological causes. Provided that the fatigue is not excessive we can turn with interest and pleasure from mental work to muscular activity because the fatigue is local. However, if the fatigue is excessive, whether mental or muscular, it spreads throughout the system, and if we are thoroughly tired we cannot do any more work efficiently whether physical or mental. People who are thoroughly tired after an examination for example, do not perform muscular activity with either efficiency or pleasure. This is important, for it is sometimes assumed that excessive demands for physical activity may be made upon children without reference to their mental work and *vice versa*.

When fatigue becomes general, the only effective remedy is complete rest and sleep.

If continuous work is required, then care should be taken to *adjust the rate of work so that it is well within the worker's capacity*, and periods of relaxation must be allowed between periods of strenuous activity. It is probable that both adults and children adjust themselves more or less automatically to an *optimum* rate of work. This optimum rate represents a condition in which the energy output is approximately equal to the input of fuel and rate of restoration. In walking, for example, the body adjusts itself to a comfortable pace at which walking is a pleasure. At this pace the walking can be kept up for a long time. If the pace

[1] See A. V. Hill, *Living Machinery*, Chapter II.

is faster than this, fatigue sets in rapidly and although it appears that a better result is obtained at first, the final result is less than if the pace had been favourable. At the optimum rate of walking, there is time for short periods of relaxation between the instants of intensive effort. What applies to walking, applies equally well to mental work. Over-driving at school gives the appearance of rapid progress, but the pace cannot be maintained without damage to the pupils. Teachers should aim at an *optimum* rate of progress, *not the fastest rate* at which they can drive the pupils to work.[1]

Note that interest diminishes fatigue. Interest may be considered as a sign that energy is being freely supplied.

Also, children show great differences in fatiguability. Some tire much more quickly than others. Allowance needs to be made for this.

Conflict of motive, worry, anxiety are all powerful causes of fatigue.

DAILY VARIATIONS IN EFFICIENCY

Experiments have shown that efficiency of work varies fairly regularly during the course of the day. Beginning at 9.0 A.M. the rate of work tends to rise to a maximum between 10 A.M. and 11 A.M., then decreases to a minimum between 1 P.M. and 2 P.M. Thereafter follows a second rise in efficiency till about 3 P.M., followed by another decline. The differences are not great, but sufficient to be worth noting. Hence it is desirable to arrange the most difficult work during the second part of the morning session. Any tests requiring concentration may be assigned to this period : routine exercises to the afternoon session, and games to the last afternoon periods.

In making time-tables attention must be paid to the need for sufficient change of occupation, and the inclusion of rest-pauses.

BOOKS FOR FURTHER REFERENCE

BOOK, W. F. : *Economy and Technique of Learning* (Heath, 1932).

MACE, C. A. : *The Psychology of Study* (Methuen, 4th ed., 1955).

STILLMAN, B. W. : *Training Children to Study* (Harrap, 1928).

THORNDIKE, E. L. : *Educational Psychology*, Vols. II and III (Teachers' College, New York, 1921).

VALENTINE, C. W. : *Introduction to Experimental Psychology in Relation to Education* (University Tutorial Press, 5th ed., 1953).

---

[1] Hill, book cited, Chapter VI.

CHAPTER XII

THE PRACTICE OF INSTRUCTION

A. PRESENTATION, GUIDANCE, DIAGNOSIS OF DIFFICULTIES, AND LESSON-DEVELOPMENT

I. SOME PRELIMINARY CONSIDERATIONS

This chapter is intended primarily for students-in-training who have had but little actual practice in teaching.

The most effective methods of teaching can be inferred from the principles of motivation and of intellectual development already discussed. However, it is one thing to have a theoretical knowledge of mental development, yet quite another to be able to apply the principles in the very varying conditions in which teachers may have to practise. In this chapter therefore we shall consider two main problems: (*a*) the organization of a unit of work; and (*b*) the variations which must be made in order to do justice to different types of subject-matter.

THE PRACTICAL TEACHING-SITUATION

We will suppose now that we are confronted by a class, in size somewhere between twenty-five and forty pupils. In general, the pupils may vary in age from about five up to about eighteen years, but we shall assume that we have a reasonably homogeneous class, and that the pupils are at the secondary stage of schooling. The principles we have discussed hitherto are general in their application and cover all phases of education. Nevertheless, differences in organization are required for different age-groups.

In the five-to-eight year age-groups the teaching needs to be informal, giving opportunity for plenty of free movement and play-activity.

The characteristic emphasis in this period is upon first-hand experience of the environment; development of sense-perception;

and of the fundamental tools of learning, namely, the motor habits, first of speech, and later of reading and writing.

In the eight-to-eleven year age-groups, while the organization should still allow as much as possible of free movement, the emphasis becomes more matter-of-fact and realistic. The pupils continue their first-hand contact with the environment and extend it over a wider area on account of their greater strength and physical independence. At the same time they can supplement this experience by information gained through reading. This is the period for perfecting the habits of speech, reading, and writing, and using them in the extension of the pupil's intellectual universe. Towards the end of this period comes a gradual transition to more formal studies, *e.g.*, the first rudiments of grammar, and mathematical work (including elementary mathematical concepts in physical geography and surveying, *e.g.*, position, time-measurement).

In the eleven-plus period, again without any abrupt change, the characteristic emphasis passes to the more formal, abstract, and systematic aspects of learning. The pupil keeps on gathering more first-hand experience. His intellect increases in breadth, but the facts are now seen to be related by general principles in the systematic branches of knowledge we call subjects. This is the time when full abstraction approaches, and when the interrelatedness of experience makes possible more efficient observation and reasoning. The intellect increases correspondingly in depth and subtlety.

It is with this secondary period that we shall deal in detail here.

In addition to our class, we shall have some more or less definite syllabus of work to cover, possibly in one year only, but more frequently in a period of four or six years. Our practical task is to *introduce this syllabus to the pupils* in such a way that they *assimilate* it and it is incorporated within their mental and physical development in the form of *living knowledge and skill*.

Working by the light of nature, so to speak, in the absence of any definite professional training, we may adopt two extreme ways of organizing the teaching. We may call these the *recitation* plan, and the *heuristic* plan. The former is usually the choice of the pedants ; the latter of the originators—artists, scientists, literary creators, and craftsmen.

In the recitation plan the pupils repeat a form of words after the teacher, or read one from a book, until they have memorized it ' by heart.' Then they recite it to the teacher who checks it from his own memory or from the book. Whether or no the pupils *understand* the significance of the form of words is not a matter of great consequence. The plan may be modified into a catechism, the teacher asking questions and the pupils responding with the appropriate form of words.

The extreme form of this plan produces intellectual death through suffocation. The pupils' mental activity is smothered in a heap of words. (*Cf.* p. 176).

The heuristic plan goes to an opposite extreme. The pupil is put into a laboratory or a workshop and given some apparatus and tools ; or he is presented with a copy of Virgil and Plato in the original classics. Thereupon he is told to teach himself. Alternatively, according to a more modern version of the plan, he is encouraged to roam at will and pick up what information and skill he may, at any time, and in any way that happens to suit him at that moment.

In the case of a young genius this plan may succeed and produce striking results. However, such geniuses are relatively rare, and the usual result is intellectual anæmia and malnutrition. A good hearty meal of steak and chips with a pint of ale may be excellent for a robust adult, but it merely makes a baby sick, and he will starve on such a diet, if it is continued.

Somehow we must steer a common-sense, middle course between these two extremes. This the scholarly and efficient teacher can do because he knows both the subject-matter *and the pupils* and he can *adapt the subject-matter to their needs.*

It is this process of adaptation that we shall attempt to indicate in detail.

Most beginners in teaching are obsessed with the subject-matter and forget the pupils, and the higher their academic honours the more complete seems to be the forgetting. We would invite readers for the moment to forget their academic specialized subject-matter and concentrate upon the pupils.

IMPORTANCE OF CLEAR AIMS IN TEACHING

The first consideration in approaching our class must be—*what aims do we expect to achieve by the teaching?* From the point of view of *intellectual* development our general aims should be :

Clear grasp by the pupils of significant knowledge (characters and relations).

Skilful habits of work.

Interest and satisfaction in the possession of knowledge and skill.

Ability to use the knowledge and apply the skill—that is intelligent adaptation through transfer.

High standards of aspiration.

IMPORTANCE OF EFFECTIVE CONTACT BETWEEN TEACHER AND PUPILS

Having set himself a clear aim, the teacher's next task must be to establish a *vital personal contact* with his pupils. This contact has two aspects :

Social

The social aspect of contact implies the existence of a *community of feeling and interest* between teacher and pupils.

On the part of the pupils there must be sentiments of respect and admiration for the teacher's knowledge, skill, personal integrity, and standards of conduct. Some degree of self-abasement is essential in the pupils. They must have the attitude of disciples towards a master (or mistress) or they will not be willing to learn. This attitude is not servility but reasonable acceptance. It is essential on account of the spread of interest and aversion by conditioning. The pupil's feeling-tones and emotional moods transfer from the teacher to what he teaches.

On the part of the teacher there must be sympathy, *courtesy*, patience, kindly encouragement, and an *interest in each individual pupil*. The pupils must be treated as persons and their personalities respected. This does not exclude firmness when it is indicated. Pupils prefer firmness tempered with justice to an easy, slovenly familiarity. They prefer their teacher to be dignified.

This social aspect of the contact is the foundation for good motivation. It inspires in the pupils the will to work before they are capable of full voluntary control.

Intellectual

The teacher must maintain effective *intellectual* contact with his pupils. This means that he must be aware of the following factors :

Their degree of maturity and general intelligence.

Their special aptitudes and interests.

Their mental background and intellectual difficulties.

This intellectual awareness marks the difference between the mere scholar, and the scholarly teacher. It requires a knowledge of child-development ; observation of individual pupils' responses ; familiarity with the general cultural background of the school region, the immediate local environment, and each individual pupil's educational attainment.

Knowledge about the cultural background—rural or urban ; English, Welsh, Scottish ; prevailing religious beliefs, political prejudices, social attitudes — can be obtained by the teacher through his own contact with the school-region and the immediate local environment. Such knowledge is essential if the pupils' deep mental background is to be correctly estimated.

Educational attainment can be discovered by studying the syllabuses supposed to have been covered in previous years. There should be collaboration between the staffs of secondary schools, and of the junior schools from which their pupils come. There is, even now a great diversity in methods of teaching (e.g., decimals) and unless this is taken into account by the secondary teachers the disturbance in development consequent upon the change of schools will be unnecessarily lengthened and intensified. Specialist teachers ought also to know what their colleagues are doing in cognate subjects. English, Latin, and modern foreign languages ; science, mathematics, domestic science, handicraft, gardening, physical geography ; humanistic geography, history, economics and civics—each of these groups contains many common elements both of content and procedure. If the specialists in charge of each subject are not fully alive to the interrelations of their own with other cognate subjects, and to what their colleagues are actually doing at any given time, there is bound to be overlapping, unnecessary repetition, and, perhaps worst of all, confusion and lack of explicit awareness in the pupils' minds. Instead of realizing the fundamental connexions, the learners are aware only of isolated and often meaningless items. Thus transfer and adaptability are smothered.[1]

In addition to knowing the syllabuses already covered, the secondary teachers should explore, systematically, the attainments of the new pupils by means of oral discussions, questions, and written tests. It is important to discover what the pupils do

---

[1] This lack of explicit awareness of the interrelatedness of subjects is the most disturbing feature of our present over-specialized, over-mechanized, examination-ridden epoch. Nor will conditions improve until professional teachers awake to their educational responsibilities and get a scholarly grasp of their own and cognate subjects before they try to teach them.

not know, or know only imperfectly, since new knowledge must be interpreted in terms of what is already known. Hence gaps and distortions in knowledge exercise a cumulative effect upon future intellectual development.

Such preliminary information about the pupils must be supplemented by *continual careful observation* of their activities, preferences, and responses. This intellectual contact cannot be maintained directly since thoughts are not usually, if at all, transmitted by telepathy. The teacher must *infer* the pupils' states of mind, and difficulties in understanding, from their responses, *particularly from their wrong responses*. By this systematic observation of right and wrong responses, both oral and written, it is possible to estimate with reasonable accuracy how fast to proceed with the syllabus, and what parts of it need to be repeated.

Hence, a golden rule in all teaching is—*observe the pupils*. Watch their reactions closely and attempt to infer what is going on ' inside their heads ' so to speak. This is every bit as important as exposition and use of teaching-devices.

ORDER IN PRESENTATION

Teachers may not be able to choose their own syllabus of work, but they are completely in control of the order in which the material to be studied shall be presented, *i.e.*, set forth for the attention of the pupils.

Good order in presentation is indicated by our analysis of intellectual development. Certain types of order were there revealed which we can summarize briefly :

The Natural Rhythm of Intellectual Progress

(*a*) Knowledge is based first of all upon the fundamental characters of things apprehended through first-hand contact of the sense-organs with the physical environment.

Therefore at any stage in intellectual development the first step must be the analysis by observation of these fundamental characters and the provision of a corresponding vocabulary.

(*b*) Founded upon this first-hand knowledge of characters is explicit awareness of their *relatedness*. This gives to the characters their significance.

We have noted how relations emerge into full explicit awareness. First come the lower-order relations between the characters themselves, then higher multiple-order relations of greater complexity and subtlety.

Hence we must build upon the lower orders of relations, introducing them first and then working out relations between relations.

Our order in presentation must be, therefore, first-hand experience, first-order relations, multiple-order relations, at each stage developing a vocabulary flexible enough to enable the intellectual advances to be described, stabilized, and applied.[1]

If the pupils have already had ample first-hand experience and have organized a certain degree of relatedness, we need not begin again at the beginning. We can use this knowledge as a foundation and proceed to build upon it.

This order of presentation is aptly summarized in some of the rules of order set out in former text-books on method, *e.g.*,

Begin with the concrete and proceed to the abstract.

Begin with the familiar and proceed to the unknown.

Begin with a broad general view of a topic as a whole and proceed to more and more detailed analysis.[1]

These rules of order hold good for literary, descriptive, and scientific material. We should not commence the study of grammar until the pupils have already acquired a vocabulary and some practical skill in description. We should not begin a study of literary criticism and prose or poetic styles until the pupils have a good working acquaintance with *actual works of literary art*. In the same way we should not begin the study of chemical formulæ and atoms until the pupils are acquainted at first hand with a variety of chemical substances and the ways in which they react with each other. In geography and history, how well the pupils will appreciate what happens on the other side of the earth, or what happened a thousand years ago, will depend upon how well they have grasped the significance of what they have observed in their own neighbourhood and generation.

We can summarize this natural rhythm of intellectual progress as follows :

Analysis leading to clearly apprehended and abstracted characters and simpler relations.

Synthesis leading through association to systematization and generalization.

By comparison, contrast, reflection, complex relations between relations are elaborated.

[1] *Cf.* Line's experimental results, p. 210–212.

Application or creation.

Systematized knowledge is applied to the solution of new problems or to the production of original work.

Like waves on the ocean, this rhythm reveals itself in various periods, short periods superimposed on longer periods. The whole of life is one long cycle: analysis in early youth, synthesis in adolescence, creation in the adult period. Shorter periods are revealed in each of the scientist's new investigations, the author's new novels, the artist's new pictures, or the craftsman's new inventions. For each new endeavour the material must be collected, analysed, reflected upon and systematized, then applied. Whatever the period, however, the same fundamental order is followed.

Within this general rhythm of intellectual progress certain details of order are important for good presentation. These are :

Order of Interpretation or Apperception

Each new presentation to be fully intelligible to the observer must be interpreted or apperceived in terms of already existing knowledge. Therefore we can test whether the order of our presentation of items of lesson material is satisfactory at each step in the development, by asking : *Is this new material, now to be presented, likely to be interpreted adequately and therefore to be intelligible to the pupils?* If this criterion is not fulfilled, then before that item is presented we must first *organize a place for it* in the pupils' intellectual system.

Thus it is useless to talk about lines of latitude and longitude, equator, axes of reference, and so on until the pupils are acquainted *at first hand* with the idea of locating the position of a given object by referring it to a fixed system of lines. This notion must first be worked out in detail in simple cases in the classroom before lines of latitude and longitude can be intelligible to the pupils.

Logical Order

In any exposition involving an argument a logical order must be obeyed, in addition to the order of interpretation.

The pupils must first be familiar with the characters and relations involved, so that the actual terms in the argument are intelligible. In addition, however, the exposition must present the various propositions in the argument so that *all the necessary antecedents (or premisses) are clearly presented before a conclusion is asked for.*

A logical argument is like a chain composed of links. All the links must be sound, and all must be present in the correct order, otherwise the chain is useless. In the same way a logical argument must proceed step by step. If one step is omitted, or if the steps are presented in a wrong order, the argument becomes unintelligible to the listeners.

ILLUSTRATION AND GUIDANCE

Before proceeding further we must make a careful note of two processes which should *pervade* the presentation. These are illustration and guidance.

Illustration

Good illustration will make intellectually dead presentations come to life. We have already discussed the value of substitute-experience, *e.g.*, models and pictures. We wish at this point to call attention to the value of *verbal illustrations* such as simple stories and analogies.

We have noted that many apparently different situations have the same underlying logical form. Hence, if the similarity in form becomes explicitly recognizable, the significance of a familiar example can be transferred by the learner to the interpretation and understanding of an abstract new situation.

The function of verbal illustration was most aptly used by Professor John Hilton in a lecture which he gave to a lay audience on ' Credit.' The speaker began by saying how elusive and complex the problem is, and to what a degree the real nature of credit has been obscured by controversial arguments and special pleading. He then went on to give the example of a small girl who was sent by her mother to the butcher's shop for a pound of the scrag end of neck of mutton " on the nod till Saturday." He proceeded to analyse this homely example, and showed that it expressed in a simple and accurate way all the essential factors and relations in this complex problem of credit.

This method of teaching, as well as aiding understanding, has another great advantage. It aids the memory and *stimulates self-activity in the learner*. Many of Professor Hilton's audience knew little of abstract economics and a text-book exposition would have conveyed nothing but technical terms devoid of significance. But everyone was perfectly familiar with " on the nod till Saturday." Now, whenever the topic of commercial credit is mentioned, those listeners will immediately call to mind the homely illustration and *from it will proceed to work out anew* its implications, which can then be used as analogies with which to attack the much more complex problems of banking and state credits.   Thus the good illustration gives the knowledge which is power.

Some of the most brilliant examples of the use of verbal illustrations in the English language are the well-known " Parables of the Kingdom " in the New Testament.   There, a most abstruse and subtle system of relations implied in the phrase " the Kingdom of God " was brought out with special clarity, for the benefit of uneducated peasants and work-people, by the use of homely analogies taken from the immediate social environment with which they were all perfectly familiar.   Apart from their spiritual significance, these parables are worth studying for their pedagogic value.

Note that the illumination given by a good illustration works in two ways.   Not only does the homely illustration bring out clearly the implications of the abstract subject-matter studied, but the general principles contained therein illuminate the homely environment and give it a significance not before suspected by the learner.

Note also how the mastery produced by the good illustration enhances the interest of the subject-matter.

Hence, every teacher must regard a collection of good illustrative stories and analogies as an essential part of his professional stock-in-trade.   This, again, emphasizes the need for a close study and intimate knowledge of the local environment of the pupils.

Guidance

The mere act of presentation is not sufficient for good teaching. We have seen how it is usual for even important characters and relations to remain implicit—buried in the material details of the situations presented.   These characters and relations must be brought clearly to light by a process of analysis.   This consists essentially in concentrating the mental activity upon the characters and relations in question.

Again, methods of procedure in thinking and in practical work may remain bound up in the material situations without being explicitly realized by the learners.   (*Cf.* experiments of Woodrow, Cox, and Meredith).

How then can the pupils' alert mental activity be directed

specifically to the characters, relations, and procedures in question ? This is the work of guidance.

It can be accomplished by such devices as :

Pointing by the teacher.

Instructions from the teacher to look, listen, point out, touch some particular item in the presented material.

Instructions to compare and contrast specific items and say what is noted.

Providing problems and organizing difficulties which have the effect of producing *mental arrest* in the pupils, thereby intensifying the conative factors in mental activity. (*Cf.* the Socratic dialogue.)

Providing good standards of taste ; models of workmanship ; and methods of procedure.

This guidance is most frequently neglected by students-in-training.

II. ORGANIZING A UNIT OF WORK : LESSON-DEVELOPMENT

We can now turn to the practical task of organizing a unit of work, keeping in mind the considerations already noted about contact, order in presentation, illustration, and guidance.

It has been customary to think of teaching as giving lessons. This term ' lesson,' however, is misleading. In the first place a lesson is apt to be identified with a given time-table period, and it is assumed that the material presented and the pupil activities concerned must just fill a period of thirty-five or forty minutes and then cease. In the second place, a lesson has become identical in traditional schooling with a verbal exposition by the teacher.

Both these associations are purely accidental. A logical section of the syllabus may extend over only a part of one time-table period, or over a term's work.

Also, modern teaching-practice has veered away from the verbal exposition method of teaching. In the Dalton Plan, and the plan adopted by the Parents' National Educational Union,[1] the ' lessons ' are not verbal expositions by the teachers but typewritten or printed assignments by which the pupils are directed to source-books and problems and thereby enabled to carry on their work by individual study. These two plans are rather like correspondence courses— the teachers write out directions for study and problems for solution, and the pupils return written answers.[2]

[1] Initiated by Miss Charlotte Mason.
[2] See Helen Parkhurst, *Education on the Dalton Plan.*

In another modern form of teaching-practice—the so-called Project Plan—the ' lessons ' are problems to be solved, both theoretical and practical, by the co-operative work of teacher and pupils. The Project Plan lends itself particularly well to science-work, handicraft, practical geography, mensuration, and dramatic work in literature.[1]

Both these plans require drastic modification of the traditional time-table and do not admit of teaching in orthodox lessons. For this reason it is better to speak of organizing ' units of work ' than of teaching lessons. However, the term ' lesson ' is so familiar in educational literature and practice that we shall use it for convenience, it being understood that lesson means a unit of work, *i.e.*, a logical whole or thought-unit.

The practical arrangements fall into three sections :
An introductory section.
The main body of the unit.
A rounding-off section.

Introductory Section

Organizing a favourable mental set.

In a class of thirty pupils each with a different mental set, a variety of different interpretations may be placed upon the same object or word presented to them, and all these interpretations may differ from that of the teacher. Therefore it is desirable to organize a similar mental set in all the pupils.

The organization may be accomplished in several ways :

(*a*) *By ' suggestions.'*

Note the difference in the interpretation of an equivocal drawing, such as *B*, Fig. 2 (p. 158), (i) with no special preparation, (ii) after the suggestion, " Here is a picture by a modern artist," (iii) after the suggestion in the title, " A Week-end out of Doors."

Suggestion (iii) calls up images of holidays, picnics, and the usual arrangements for an open-air meal. Thus a preliminary schema is organized in connexion with the object presented, which determines a given interpretation.

(*b*) *By telling a story or giving a description which calls up and organizes appropriate ideas.*

(*c*) *By recapitulating at the beginning of each lesson the salient points of previous lessons relevant to the new material.*

(*d*) *By stating the aim of the coming lesson.*

[1] See Bibliography at the end of this chapter.

A clear statement of aim serves three purposes. It calls up relevant ideas, it excludes irrelevant ideas, and it specifies a definite objective to aim at which helps to increase the interest. Lessons with no clearly stated or implied aim are most tiresome. Pupils are confused. They wonder what it is all about and try first one alternative and then another, quickly losing any grasp and any interest. The words used by the teacher may all be comprehensible, and the presentation logical, yet if the aim is not clear to the pupils the lesson may be a failure. Westaway records the case of a bright boy who said at the end of a science-lesson, " I am awfully sorry, sir, but although I was easily able to follow Mr X in everything he said, I do not understand at all what he meant to teach us." [1]

The aim can be indicated in several ways. The most direct is a plain statement of the objective of the lesson, *e.g.*, " In our last lesson we studied the position and physical features of Australia. To-day we will find what sort of climate Australia has, and how it compares with our own." By this means the objective is indicated, knowledge of climatic conditions in general recalled, and interfering systems of ideas banished.

In science-teaching the best introduction in many cases is a series of questions which indicate quite clearly a problem to be solved.

Instead of telling junior secondary schoolboys that to-day they will learn about the Principle of Archimedes, it is better to indicate the aim as follows :

" When you are washing your hands with a big cake of soap, does the soap feel heavier or lighter when you hold it under the water, than when you lift it out ?

" How many of you swim in the baths ? Have you noticed, that after you have been in the water for some time, when you walk up the steps to come out of the baths, your body seems to feel heavier and heavier as you get farther out of the water ?

" When you dip a bucket into some water in a river or a tank, what do you notice about the weight of the bucketful of water as you pull it out of the river (or tank) ? How does it feel if you lower it back again ?

" Does an object really weigh less in water than it does in the air ? This is what we want to find out.

" How can we find out ? "

In this way the pupils are made explicitly aware of a problem arising out of common experience, and a definite objective is suggested.

---

[1] *Science Teaching,* p. 65. The whole of Chapter VI, *A Common Cause of Failure,* in Westaway's book is most instructive.

It is often desirable to indicate the scope and aim of each lesson and of larger sections of the syllabus by means of what some American writers have called "The Orientation Lesson."

Thus, in history, the course of events can be sub-divided into periods which have predominant characteristics. Such are the prehistoric, ancient, medieval, and modern periods. In introducing the modern period a lesson should be given in which the scope and the predominant characteristics of the period are sketched in broad outline, and compared with those of the medieval period just completed. Again, each sub-division (*e.g.*, the Renaissance in Northern Europe, the Tudor period in England, the Industrial Revolution) should have a preliminary orientation treatment.

The Main Body of the Unit of Work

Having made a suitable introduction, we pass to the main body of the unit. In this we present new material and guidance.

The manner of presentation will vary in detail according to the source of the experience. We may have one or more of the following :

Directing observations in field-work or educational visits.

Use of specimens in classroom.

A demonstration by teacher or selected pupils.

Individual study of books by pupils.

Narrative, description, exposition by teacher or selected pupils.

Use of epidiascope, cinema, wireless.

Directing practical work by pupils in laboratory or workshop.

When sufficient content has been supplied and grasped clearly, it must be systematized.

The main body of the unit includes the phases of analysis and synthesis. The purpose and method of these phases has been indicated in Chapter VII.

During the presentation of the main body of the lesson it will be necessary to sub-divide the work into convenient short sections, recapitulating at the end of each section.[1] If the pupils' responses show that the significance of that section has not been thoroughly grasped, it will be necessary to repeat some or all of the section with special emphasis on the weak places revealed in the recapitulation.

[1] Refer to Chapter XI for details.

Rounding-off Section

Final Recapitulation

When the end of the presentation has been reached, a final comprehensive recapitulation is indicated.

Its purpose is to weld the various sections of the work into an understandable unity. The pattern of the arrangement, the logical relations involved, and the relative value of individual items can be stressed.

Permanent Record

Some permanent record of the new gains should be made by the pupils as an aid to future revision.

These may take the form of :

Notes, drawings, summaries.

Collections of typical examples of work of literary or pictorial art. These can be gathered by pupils to build up a scrap-book, or anthology.

Collections of specimens mounted and labelled.

Notes and summaries should represent the pupils' own work as far as is possible. Younger pupils will need guidance in making notes and summaries, but the aim of the teacher should be, continually, to train the pupils in making their own notes and summaries.

A decent standard of neatness, accuracy, and order should be demanded, and if necessary, enforced. In the reaction against the copper-plate copybook perfection of drawing and writing which was the ' be-all and end-all ' of some former elementary education, there has been a rather deplorable tendency to allow slap-dash, untidy, written work. This tendency has been strengthened by the overloading of scholarship and secondary-school syllabuses for examination-purposes. In consequence many pupils pass out, from secondary schools particularly, with bad habits and low standards of workmanship.

Occasionally, specialist teachers adopt the attitude that this part of the work does not concern them. Their business is to teach science or geography or literature and not writing or neatness. This attitude is thoroughly unsound. In the first place, standards of neatness, accuracy, clear expression cannot be divorced from subject-matter. Secondly, if the attitude is tolerated it becomes nobody's responsibility to make sure that pupils are effectively trained to adopt and maintain decent standards of work.

Exercises

Exercises fall into two main types :

Exercises for routine practice.

These are essential if the new knowledge or skill is to be retained permanently, and if a high standard of facility is required.

Creative exercises.

In this type the pupil is required to apply his newly acquired knowledge or skill to the solution of problems, or to express his own ideas and feelings in some simple (and, for him, original) example of craftsmanship.

It is now generally agreed by expert teachers of ' appreciation,' that lessons which aim primarily at æsthetic enjoyment should be followed by opportunities for the pupils to compose simple melodies, make pictures, or write stories, poems, plays, or descriptions. Successful teachers of appreciation seem to be unanimously agreed that many pupils, in fact a surprisingly large number, find pleasure in such exercises and show a spontaneous desire to try them.

In the absence of creative exercises of any kind, the educative process degenerates into a dull, purposeless and therefore lifeless routine of memorization and habituation.

Exercises serve two purposes :

(i) For the pupils, they provide :

(a) Practice which strengthens the knowledge and skill gained, and enhances the degree of æsthetic enjoyment. It is probable that full appreciation is not attained until pupils gain some insight into the craftsmanship of art, and realize its difficulties.

(b) A means of self-examination.

The need for application of knowledge and skill reveals weaknesses which cannot be glossed over. Each pupil then can attack his own special weaknesses. It also reveals strength and with the realization of strength comes enjoyment in the exercise and a desire for further advance.

Thus the exercises are a valuable factor in continuous motivation.

(ii) For the teacher they provide definite responses which indicate the extent and the adequacy of the pupils' learning. This brings us to a very important aspect of teaching, namely, following-up the work done, diagnosing and correcting errors.

NO IMPRESSIONS WITHOUT EXPRESSION

This is a very valuable educational slogan popularized by William James.[1] It means that any impressions presented to the pupil in the course of teaching should be followed up by requiring the pupil to react appropriately with respect to them. This overt response by the pupil is essential because :

It provides a corrective agency for the pupil himself, *enabling him to compare his own performance with some standard or model which is accepted as correct.*

It provides the only possible means by which the teacher can find out how the pupil's internal mental organization is progressing. It is essential, therefore, for the practice of mental hygiene, which is just as much a part of the teacher's work as is instruction.

The first point is important because, with regard to the sufficiency of our own beliefs, we are all such incorrigible optimists. For example, we look at a motor-car or a horse. We note a general vague outline and some (often inconsequential) details. When we see a similar object a second time we recognize it sufficiently well for our everyday needs and fall into the comfortable belief that we know all about it. If, however, we are required to draw a sketch of the object from memory (*i.e.*, to express our impressions) we then realize with a shock how inadequate our grasp of the impressions really is. Similarly, the best way to realize the weak points in our grasp of a logical argument is to work out the argument from memory or attempt to apply it to another problem.

ERROR AND DIAGNOSIS

However clear the presentation may have seemed to the teacher himself, he can never take for granted that either verbal or concrete practical material has been correctly interpreted and assimilated by any one of his pupils. He must therefore take steps to find out what actually has happened. *Every presentation must be followed up systematically to detect and correct possible errors.* Omission of this follow-up procedure is one of the main sources of incompetence in teaching. Good follow-up work is an essential distinction between teaching and preaching or lecturing. It is the more necessary in proportion to the immaturity, paucity of experience, and lack of intelligence of the pupils.

[1] See *Talks to Teachers*, Section V, " The Necessity of Reactions."

As with recapitulation, the follow-up may alternate with sections of the presentation if the topic is extensive. In no case, however, should a follow-up be allowed to spoil the logical or æsthetic continuity of the work. This tends to kill interest and produce a feeling of frustration and irritation in the pupils. A systematic follow-up should *follow the completion* of each section of the work, but not necessarily immediately afterwards. With older and more intelligent pupils a period of reflection may be given. During this period difficulties not at first apparent may become clearer to the learner himself.

The main sources of error are:

1. Lapses of attention. The pupil fails completely to note some significant part of the presentation.

2. Distorted interpretations

(a) A pupil may fail to note some part of the presentation, and the gap makes the rest of the work unintelligible. In this case the pupil may try to fill in the gap by imperfect correlate-eduction or reproduction, in such a way as to make the whole sensible to himself. Such additions may, however, have no connexion with the actual facts as presented.

(b) Some part of the presentation may be noted, but at the same time be obscure to the pupil. In that case he may interpret the experience in terms of some crude and false analogy. Children make use of the most absurd analogies, *e.g.*, butterflies make butter; butter comes from buttercups; grasshoppers make grass; kittens grow on the pussy-willow.[1]

3. Lapses of memory.

4. Poor methods of working.

The aims of the follow-up process must be to reveal the precise nature of the error; to ascertain the cause of the error; and to correct the error.

It is not sufficient to find out the actual errors, and correct them perfunctorily by repeating the relevant parts of the presentation. The fact that an error has been made may be a symptom that the mental background, which is the medium of interpretation and assimilation, is itself badly organized. Merely to repeat some part of the presentation may appear to effect a superficial correction of a pupil's difficulty, but it is just as likely that *the repetition itself will be wrongly interpreted again*. The ultimate aim of the follow-up

[1] " The Contents of Children's Minds on Entering School," Stanley Hall, *Aspects of Child Life and Education*.

process must be to *reveal defects in the pupils' mental backgrounds and to discover lack, or weakness, of specific aptitudes.*

The absolute importance of good following-up is evident when we consider that the effects of wrong interpretation are cumulative. An error made to-day and allowed to remain unchecked will itself be the cause of further errors to-morrow, and these again on the next day, and so on.

THE PROCESS OF DIAGNOSIS

In this following-up work a teacher is comparable to a physician. The physician is concerned with the physical health and hygiene of his patients, the teacher with the mental health and hygiene of his pupils. Their methods of approach to a problem of disease are also comparable. When a patient with some obscure internal complaint consults his physician, the latter's problem is to discover the nature of the complaint and *locate its cause.* How can this be done ? The physician cannot see inside his patient. He cannot proceed forthwith to cut the patient to pieces to discover the cause of difficulty. Instead of this drastic method of investigation, he applies certain tests, *the purpose of which is to produce a response.* The physician knows what should be the response of a healthy person to each particular test. He applies the tests systematically until he finds an *abnormal* response. From the nature of the abnormal response he must then infer the cause of trouble.

If the physician cannot see directly into the ' innards ' of his patients, still more is the teacher unable to see directly into the minds of his pupils. He also must apply tests which *call forth definite responses* from his pupils. The teacher knows (or should know) what constitutes a healthy response to his test. Then, when he finds abnormal responses, or no responses, he must suspect mental difficulty and try to infer the cause.

What kinds of tests will elicit the responses necessary for the teacher's diagnosis ? There are :

Questions about matters of fact to which a verbal or written reply can be made.

Requests to pupils for verbal or written reports on matters of fact, opinions, conclusions, etc.

Exercises and problems which can be solved correctly only if the relevant knowledge has been correctly assimilated (*e.g.*, problem questions in arithmetic, geometry, physics).

Instructions to pupils to make models, sketches, diagrams ; to perform practical experiments (including experiments in art-expression).

It is useful to note that for diagnostic purposes *the wrong responses are more valuable than correct ones*. If the pupil makes a correct response to a test question or exercise, it is highly probable [1] that his impressions have been adequate and his interpretations correct. The teacher can then pass on to further work. If the response is wrong it reveals a difficulty which must be treated.

Now suppose a pupil makes no response or a wrong response to a test. Two alternatives are implied :

(*a*) The impressions presented to the pupil have not been received at all, owing to momentary lapses of attention, or to distracting conditions in the classroom at some instant. Another pupil may have sneezed, or dropped a book with a loud bang, just as an important statement was made by the teacher. If this case is suspected (*e.g.*, by taking into account the usual level of attentiveness and intelligence of the pupil) the relevant information can be repeated, or the pupil's attention re-directed and then the test applied again.

(*b*) The impressions have been received, but misinterpreted. In this case the difficulty is most probably due to a faulty mental background. Mere repetition of the impression will not correct the mistake. Supplementary questions and tests *each demanding specific responses* must then be given until the root of the difficulty is isolated.

In framing diagnostic questions and tests, one must make certain that each test is concerned with *one point of difficulty only*.

Suppose we find that a pupil cannot do correctly a long division sum. It is a futile waste of time to give him more long division sums in the pious hope that after he has worked through many examples, the light will dawn in him spontaneously. It is better to note the specific ways in which it is possible for the pupil to go wrong. Can he add simple numbers correctly ? Can he deal with carrying figures ? Can he subtract correctly ? Can he multiply ? Does he know all his multiplication tables correctly ? Can he deal with remainders ? Etc., etc. For each of these possible difficulties a specific test can be applied which involves that particular difficulty *and no other*. When the actual difficulty has been revealed, it can be treated.[2]

---

[1] Note that it is not absolutely certain.

[2] See Schonell's diagnostic English and Arithmetic tests for examples.

This may sound a formidable programme. However, the time spent in diagnosis is more than regained later, since the teacher's knowledge of individual pupils is so much more certain and precise, and the correction of the difficulties more radical and effective. Further, after some experience, it will be found that certain difficulties frequently recur in many pupils. A working-knowledge of these common difficulties makes diagnosis more rapid.

TO WHAT EXTENT SHOULD A TEACHER PERSIST WITH THE FOLLOW-UP TREATMENT?

This depends upon the circumstances of the teaching. If a group of pupils is engaged in individual work, then it is desirable to take each individual and continue the diagnostic treatment until the difficulty has been overcome. Meanwhile the other pupils have their own work to keep them busy and interested. In class-teaching, however, we must not lose sight of the welfare of the class as a whole. In this case, after each subsection of the presentation has been made, one can ask for responses from certain pupils. If distortion has occurred and is not serious, it may be corrected quickly and the presentation resumed. If the distortion appears to be general among the pupils, the presentation can be repeated, possibly *using another method of approach.* If, however, there appears to be some serious difficulty with one or a few pupils only, it is not desirable to persist there and then with the complete correction of these few. The remainder of the class will be bored by the interruption and lose interest. In this case it is more desirable to proceed with the presentation, give the majority of the class some further work, and then, at the first opportunity, treat the few mistaken pupils individually.

SUMMARY

The practical stages in the organization of a typical unit of work may be summarized in the table on p. 552. It must not be supposed that all the details in the second column will be included in every unit. The exact procedure in any given case will depend upon the logical structure of the unit. Thus in some lessons no generalization or definition is arrived at. In such cases that item will not appear in the 'lesson notes.'

The variations in procedure according to the logical form of the subject-matter will be indicated in a later section of this chapter.

TABLE SHOWING IN SUMMARY FORM THE PRACTICAL STEPS IN THE
ORGANIZATION OF A UNIT OF WORK AND THE CORRESPONDING
PSYCHOLOGICAL RESULTS.

1. Introductory Section	Organization of favourable mental set in relation to new material for study. Statement (or other indication) of the aim to be realized by the unit of work.
2. Main Body of Unit	Presentation Setting forth the new material to be studied. (Or working out a project or assignment.) Guidance Analysis—leading to clearness of apprehension. Abstraction. Synthesis—leading to system and culminating, in cases of inductive development, in formulation of general principle, or definition.
3. Rounding-off Section	Final recapitulation. Permanent record. Follow-up process—Diagnosis of error. Remedial measures. Application (a) Exercises for practice—Consolidation of results. (b) Exercises for creation.

This plan for the organization of a unit of work will apply to schools or classes working on the Dalton Plan, or the Project Plan. Under whatever plan the pupils work, the psychological phases through which their knowledge develops remain the same. Thus, in drawing up assignments for individual work according to the Dalton Plan an introductory section is necessary to organize the pupils' mental set and indicate the aim. The presentation will consist of (a) written references to sources of information, and (b) instructions or suggestions, the purpose of which is to guide the pupil through the processes of analysis, abstraction, synthesis, and generalization. When working on the Dalton Plan, the follow-up process is even more important than in the case of orthodox oral teaching, since the pupil is working silently during the ' body of the lesson ' and is therefore more liable to accumulate distortions in interpretation. Also it must be remembered that although individual work may be more efficient than *mechanized* class-teaching, at the same time there is no magic in the process. Immature pupils still require sufficient practice exercises to promote speed, accuracy, and skill in application.

The grave weakness of the Dalton Plan, in schools where each teacher must deal with thirty or more pupils, lies in the fact that the essential work of guidance and follow-up cannot be carried on so thoroughly as in good class-teaching. It is very largely a problem of time. If thirty pupils are to get the guidance and diagnosis they need, as individuals, it is obvious that each one can have only a small fraction of the time which would be available if groups of pupils are dealt with simultaneously. In practice, one usually finds that no matter with what uncritical enthusiasm the pure Dalton Plan is adopted in an ordinary primary or secondary school, before long, modifications have to be introduced in order to economize time and increase the guidance and follow-up work by teaching groups simultaneously.

Similarly, in organizing projects, the project or problem must be clearly indicated, and its bearing on other work discussed. During the development of the project guidance is necessary if the results of the work are to be educationally valuable. Finally, practice and follow-up work must be undertaken.

Like the Dalton Plan, the Project Plan has its own characteristic difficulties, the chief of which is a tendency to superficiality and lack of system and intellectual discipline. The project does not allow of sufficient time for the practice of fundamental skills, and the subject-matter may remain in the minds of the pupils as a collection of topics rather than a system of knowledge.

Actually, no kind of plan of school-organization, whether Montessori, Dalton, Project, Heuristic, and so forth, will make it unnecessary for the teacher to understand the essential psychological principles according to which the normal pupil develops. Usually, the more one departs from class-teaching the more thorough and scientific must one's psychological knowledge be.

ARTICULATING A SYLLABUS

Beginners in teaching frequently find difficulty in *articulating* a syllabus, *i.e.*, arranging beforehand how the work to be done shall be allocated in the time available.

For this purpose we need to take note of :

The number of periods per week allowed for the subject in question.

The length of the time-table periods.

The intellectual capacity of the pupils which determines the pace at which they can assimilate the work.

Having ascertained these facts the syllabus can be sub-divided into units of convenient length according to the logical form of the subject-matter. But, in estimating how much work is likely to be covered in a term or a year it is necessary to allow adequate time for recapitulation, for exercises, permanent records, revision, and diagnosis. Most beginners *overcrowd their work-periods with subject-matter* because they forget to take account of these other essential factors.

B. MODIFICATIONS OF PROCEDURE REQUIRED BY DIFFERENT TYPES OF SUBJECT-MATTER

We must teach something to somebody. Hence we must take account, not only of the psychological processes in the learners, but also of certain differences in the formal structure and value of the subject-matter itself. We can distinguish six main types of subject-matter, each of which will require its own special treatment. They are :

(i) Subject-matter mainly descriptive and informational, leading to increase in the learner's knowledge of his environment, and enrichment of his imagination. Examples are : literature ; descriptive geography and history (including biography and travel reports or stories) ; nature-study ; elementary mathematics, physics, chemistry.

(ii) Subject-matter mainly concerned with the inductive development of generalizations, leading to the systematization of knowledge. Examples are : grammar ; physical geography ; certain aspects of mathematics ; certain aspects of experimental science.

(iii) Subject-matter mainly concerned with deductive application of facts and principles already established. Examples are : formal geometry, advanced grammar, theoretical (particularly applied) science and mathematics ; critical studies in more advanced geography, history, economics, literature, and the fine arts.

(iv) Subject-matter mainly concerned with experimental investigation and scientific research.

(v) Subject-matter mainly concerned with the development of skill. For the sake of clearness and convenience we can take account of two types of skills :

(*a*) Practical skills, *e.g.*, shorthand, typing, handling craft-tools and scientific instruments.

(*b*) Mental skills, *e.g.*, observing, defining, generalizing, reasoning.

(vi) Subject-matter mainly concerned with the appreciation or enjoyment of literature, music, and pictorial art.

Limits of space prevent detailed illustration of the procedures necessary for each type of subject-matter. A general indication will be given and readers can work out specific topics in detail as exercises.

SUBJECT-MATTER WHICH IS MAINLY OBSERVATIONAL AND DESCRIPTIVE

With this type, the aim must be to present new experiences, directly or indirectly, in such a way that the pupil's knowledge of the environment is clarified and extended. The teaching should secure that objects and situations in the environment are analysed into basic characters and relations, which can then be abstracted and described accurately in words.

In lessons of this kind we are concerned mainly with the order in which the subject-matter is introduced, and it is in this respect that the student-in-training seems to find most difficulty. He will have studied his subject-matter at college in an abstract systematic way, usually by the aid of standard text-books. If he wishes to read more information about an unfamiliar topic he will go first to a text-book or encyclopædia and read through an abstract formal introduction which is then presented without modification to the pupils, often with the ' aid ' of abstract diagrams—plans, elevations, sections, etc. This is precisely the wrong order for teaching-purposes.

Information lessons should have the following general form :

An introduction to arouse anticipatory interest and indicate the scope and aim of the lesson to follow.

Presentation of the new material :

(*a*) If the pupils have not yet had adequate first-hand experience of the objects and situations to be discussed, this should be provided if possible.

If first-hand experience is not possible then the children's local experience must be supplemented by substitute-experience in the form of pictures, cinema-films, or models.

(*b*) In deciding upon the order in which to present the items of information we should ask ourselves in each case—*have the children already acquired a sufficient apperceptive system to interpret this particular item adequately and clearly ?* If the necessary interpretative system is not there it must first be organized. In a well-presented lesson, each new item finds an appropriate interpretative system already organized for it into which it fits intelligibly. If this rule is applied with a sympathetic insight into the pupils' available mental resources, the lesson-material cannot fail to be clear.

Much good use can be made of analogies, both verbal and material, drawn from the local environment. Thus in a lesson on the human eye we can utilize the fact that the formal structure of the eye resembles that of a box-camera—lens, diaphragm, sensitive film, and strong walls to hold these parts together. Even if bulls' or sheeps' eyes are dissected (as they should be in any case) the camera analogy is still useful as it represents a less complicated arrangement containing only the most essential features.

The teacher's aim in these lessons should be to bring out explicitly the significant characters and relations in the material presented. This can be done by directing attention specifically to these items. New names must be supplied as the characters and relations are explicitly realized and abstracted.

In these lessons there is no logical generalization, and strictly speaking no application. The aim is to increase clear experience of the environment. The presentation will be rounded off by recapitulation, permanent record, and follow-up for correction of errors.

SUBJECT - MATTER   INVOLVING   MAINLY   INDUCTIVE DEVELOPMENT

This type occurs frequently in grammar, geography, nature-study, geology, elementary physics, and chemistry. The aim of the lesson is to establish clearly a classification, or general principle.

The method of presentation will consist in setting forth a number of cases each possessing the significant character or relation in question, but differing in all other respects. In each case attention must be directed specifically to the significant common characteristic. This can often be made still more definite by presenting cases not possessing it. Thus in an elementary demonstration of capillarity it is customary to dip substances like sponge, blotting-paper, lamp-wick, unglazed earthenware into coloured water and show that in each case the liquid rises up within the substance. On comparing the substances it is made clear that all have a common character—porosity.

This character and its relation to the rise of the liquid can then be made more striking by dipping non-porous substances like a wax candle, solid glass rod, glazed paper, glazed porcelain into the same liquid. Now the water does not rise.

Another instance was shown on p. 237, where the function of the preposition was indicated by induction.

When sufficient cases have been presented, and the comparison and contrast made, the generalization can be stated in words.

After recapitulation, permanent record, and follow-up, it is desirable to apply the generalization to the elucidation of new cases.

At the secondary stage the pupils should be introduced specifically to the commoner fallacies of induction, *e.g.*,

Have the facts been correctly observed and stated ?

Have sufficient clear *representative* cases been noted to warrant a generalization ?

Have the cases noted been specially selected in any way in order to ' prove ' an already favoured hypothesis ? (Selection of cases to ' prove ' a prejudice is very common in history, economics, and political science.)

Can any negative cases be found ? The possibility of negative evidence must always be kept in mind in making inductive generalizations. One negative case has more value as evidence than several hundred positive cases.

Properly conducted, these inductive-development lessons can be made into a powerful medium for cultivating a cautious, critical scientific attitude.

SUBJECT-MATTER INVOLVING MAINLY DEDUCTIVE DEVELOPMENT

This will occur in the lower forms mainly in geometry. At the post-matriculation stage it is increasingly common in physics, chemistry, and the mathematical aspects of geography, geology, and biology.

Usually it takes two forms :

Demonstrating the proof of a theorem.

Solving a problem and then demonstrating the formal correctness of the proof :

The steps in the deductive development are as follows :

Demonstrating a Proof :

Enunciating a theorem.

Following up the enunciation to ascertain that all the key-terms are clearly understood.

Setting out the data.

The pupils should be required to state *exactly what has been given* in the theorem. This step is most important since beginners are very prone to take for granted just what they are required to prove.

Stating exactly what is to be proved.

Formulating the proof.

This should be done as a co-operative effort by pupils and teacher, the teacher guiding the pupils when they are in difficulties.

Recapitulation, permanent record if necessary, follow-up to check errors in apprehension.

Application of the theorem proved to the solution of further theoretical or practical problems.

Solving a Problem :

Enunciating the problem.

Follow-up to ascertain that the terms are clearly understood.

Setting out the data given, and the *exact conditions to which the solution must conform.*

Evolving the solution.

Here it is often useful to imagine the problem solved, analyse the conditions necessary for a solution, then reconstruct the solution formally. This is the well-known method of working backward.

Proving the solution.

Recapitulation, permanent record, follow-up.

As in inductive development, so here it is essential to bring the nature of the reasoning process itself, and the common fallacies likely to be met with, explicitly to the notice of the pupils. Deductive reasoning is a powerful *general* method which can be applied to many different kinds of material conditions if the process is explicitly realized.

SUBJECT - MATTER INVOLVING EXPERIMENTAL INVESTI-GATION

The essential formal steps in this type of development have been indicated in the report of Lavoisier's work on combustion (p. 239). They are :

Ascertaining the exact nature of the difficulty. This includes a preliminary test in some cases to make sure that the problem has been correctly stated. It may be found that the supposed problem has arisen from an error of observation or interpretation, *e.g.*, before investigating the appearance of a ghost, it is desirable to establish first that a ghost has actually appeared ! It may turn out that some frightened person has seen a scarecrow or a signpost in the moonlight. Such a fact disposes of the original problem.

Working out imaginatively possible solutions of the problem or explanations of the difficulty—this amounts to formulating a number of alternative hypotheses.

Stating the implications of each hypothesis in such a way as can be tested by quantitative experiment.

Making the experiments.

Considering the bearing of the results on the original problem.

These steps can be worked out quite easily even in lower form chemistry and physics. Consider, for example, the case of the Principle of Archimedes.

It would appear from casual observation that objects weigh less in water than in air. The problem is : Do they really weigh less in water than in air ? How can this be tested ?

This introduces a subsidiary problem, namely, how can an object be weighed while it is under water. There is scope for ingenuity in arranging some apparatus for this purpose.

When weighed in water, an object will be found to have lost weight. Therefore there is a problem to explain. What is the cause of the loss of weight ?

Now hypotheses can be stated, *e.g.*,

(i) The substance of the object itself has changed its nature on being submerged, and has not now the same *mass*.

(ii) The water displaced by the object when submerged is pushing it upward. (Incidentally this seems to have been the hypothesis which so excited Archimedes that he rushed into the streets without his shirt shouting ' Eureka.') [1]

Next the implications of each hypothesis must be stated in such a way that they can be experimentally verified. (Readers can work these out, in the present case, for themselves.)

At the completion of the tests, the whole topic can be recapitulated, a permanent record made, and details followed up.

Presented in this way to intelligent pupils science becomes an adventure, often quite exciting. Moreover, the pupils are

[1] Eureka, *i.e.*, I have found it.

familiarized with a most powerful general method of procedure. Again, the formal nature of the procedure, and the checks necessary to control it, should be made explicitly clear to the pupils.

It is not necessary that the pupils should do all the experimental work. At the junior secondary-school stage, practical laboratory manipulation can be overdone. Much exciting and intellectually valuable scientific work can be accomplished by a lecture-demonstration method. In fact for teaching scientific method as against training in routine laboratory manipulation, the lecture-demonstration method is quite valuable.

It should be noted in passing that many of the simpler scientific laws can be introduced to intelligent boys and girls in such a way that they actually rediscover the laws in question. The topics must be introduced *from the standpoint of the original investigator* and by following out his train of thought the *process* of scientific investigation is brought clearly to the notice of pupils as well as the results achieved. The results themselves often come as a surprise to the pupils and the whole becomes extremely interesting. This is what Sir T. P. Nunn has called, "putting the pupil into the skin of the scientific discoverer."

Too frequently, scientific principles are taught in quite the wrong way, simply as pieces of bookwork. In this case, the laws are merely stated by the teacher or set out in a text-book, and the experiments then become dictated devices for verifying the laws in question. Since the law is known already before any experiments are made, the element of rediscovery which is the essential intellectual factor in good science-teaching is completely missing.

Science taught in this way can be abominably dull and intellectually deadening. It is on a par with memorizing moral aphorisms out of the scriptures, or technical grammar rules in Latin. Good Latin, intelligently taught, will reveal to an able pupil far more about the reality of scientific thinking than any amount of stereotyped dictated experiments undertaken to verify already stated laws.

The procedure indicated above is very useful in organizing lessons in what might be called ' science-handwork,' *i.e.*, the design and production of simple machines and apparatus. In this case the problem becomes the production of a piece of apparatus to serve a specified purpose. Suggested designs are drawn out as rough sketches by the pupils. The designs are then criticized, and obvious faults in them discussed. When the design is suitably modified and seems likely to be successful, the pupil draws it accurately in detail. The constructional work is then carried out. Finally, the apparatus is assembled and tried.

Handwork organized according to this procedure, when pupils have some facility in the use of tools, affords much scope for ingenuity and inventiveness, and is highly interesting to ' mechanically minded ' boys. The same treatment is possible in domestic science and needlework for girls.

In connexion with the discussion on transfer of training, this investigatory method is capable of transfer to many other types of subject-matter. As an illustration let us consider its application to history. Suppose we were dealing with some specific topic with a good set of post-matriculation pupils, who had access to some historical sources. Let the topic be the Peasants' Revolt.

The scientific person would begin by asking a question. Was there *in fact* a Peasants' Revolt, or is the text-book account (a) an interpolation by some ingenious and romantic chronicler, or (b) a report of a widespread rumour ? Such a rumour is by no means an impossibility.[1]

Here then is a first-class problem. How can it be settled ? Where can we turn for evidence, and *what sort of evidence will be accepted as satisfactory.*

Thus the problem leads to an investigation of sources and a critical attitude to methods and results.

Having settled that there was a Peasants' Revolt, the next problem is to ascertain exactly *how* it happened. What were the facts of the case ?

Having the facts, it is then necessary to discuss causes. *Why* did it happen ? Here it might be a very educative procedure for the pupils if the asserted causes given in the text-book were treated as so many possible hypotheses and used as starting points for investigations.

It is agreed, of course, that such a method of treating history would not cover much ground in a short time, and it might not, therefore, be a good preparation for an examination. Also, it would require a class of intelligent pupils and an intelligent scholarly teacher. However, if only a few representative problems were thus treated it would provide a valuable element in a good general education, not only in history itself, but also in the scientific attitude and scientific method. Moreover, the training might spread to, say, newspaper-reports, advertisements, and other common

---

[1] Consider some of the fantastic notions that found their way into print during the Great War of 1914–1918. Medieval people seem to have been, if possible, even more credulous than the modern newspaper-reading public. Or it may be that their credulity expressed itself in rather different directions.

forms of propaganda. And it might make history an interesting subject.

LESSONS AIMING AT DEVELOPMENT OF SKILL

We can include here two types of skill :

(a) Mainly depending on muscular co-ordination, *e.g.*, physical exercises, games, athletics, practical handicraft, writing script, reading aloud, etc.

(b) Mainly depending upon the use of some logical, grammatical, or artistic method of operation, *e.g.*, use of the accusative-infinitive construction in Latin ; solving a problem in experimental science ; solving a problem in geometry by assuming it to be completed and working backward ; solving a quadratic equation ; writing an essay, or sonnet.

For this purpose we can proceed as follows :

Introduction

Encourage motivation by inducing a favourable attitude to the learning. This is best accomplished by showing clearly what purposes can be served by mastering the skill. If a child can see some use in learning a skill he is usually much more ready to learn, than if the learning has no apparent purpose.

Presentation

Demonstrate clearly by means of a good model exactly what is to be done.

Guide pupils' attention to the various phases of the demonstration and to points of special importance or difficulty. (*Cf.* Cox's experiments in manual training, p. 333).

Follow up by questioning pupils about the end to be achieved, and the special features of the demonstration. In all learning of skills it is essential that each pupil shall have as clear a notion as possible about what is to be accomplished by the practice, and how the practice must be carried out *before it is actually commenced.* Confusion about these points leads to bad-habit formation together with loss of confidence and interest.

Practice

Allow pupils to attempt to perform the process themselves.

Correct bad practice both by further demonstration to the whole class, and by individual treatment.

When the correct procedure has been grasped in outline, give exercises for repetition, making use of the rules for motivation and efficient learning already given (p. 146).

Application

Let pupils use the developing skill in order to accomplish some constructive work. In connexion with this application an interesting problem arises. Is it better to maintain the artificial routine-exercises in a particular form of skill until proficiency is established, or should pupils be allowed to undertake some constructive work as soon as they reach partial proficiency?

The objection to routine-practice alone is that it soon becomes tiresome and induces resistance to further practice, whereas the constructive work provides a change of occupation and a new purpose. In teaching pupils how to make a dove-tail joint in wood-work some practice in making dove-tail joints merely, is necessary as a preliminary. As soon as a fair proficiency has been attained, however, further practice is best induced by requiring the pupil to make a model incorporating dove-tail joints. If any special difficulty occurs, a further period of routine-practice dealing with that particular difficulty may be given. The pupil will do this more readily when he realizes that he cannot do the more interesting constructive work without it.

ÆSTHETIC APPRECIATION LESSONS

This topic raises fundamental psychological problems which must be decided, to some degree at least, before it is possible to discuss the organization of lessons in æsthetic appreciation.

In the first place, can æsthetic appreciation be taught, or is it something which depends entirely upon the person who is appreciating? This will depend upon the nature of æsthetic enjoyment.

Here we can give only a brief and possibly dogmatic treatment. Readers specially interested in the topic can follow up this introduction in books devoted specially to the problem.[1]

Appreciation, or, to be more exact, æsthetic enjoyment, *is a way of experiencing and knowing* different in some respects from what may be called intellectual and practical cognition, with

---

[1] *E.g., The Lesson in Appreciation* (An Essay on the Pedagogics of Beauty), F. H. Hayward. Contains a bibliography. *Training in Appreciation*, Edited by N. Catty.

T

which we have been mainly concerned hitherto. The significant difference seems to be in the attitude in which the experiencing person approaches the object or situation to be known or appreciated.

A simple example will show the difference implied.

Let the object be a hammer. In *intellectual knowing* we approach the tool in a detached critical attitude. To what class of tools does it belong ? What are its significant characters ? How are the parts mechanically related ? How is its function performed ? What mechanical principles are involved ? These are the types of questions we should have in mind. We approach the object as a thing in itself apart altogether from any relation it may have to ourselves (except, of course, the relation of knowing it). Our attitude is ' objective,' detached, impersonal. We have no interest in this particular hammer itself, but regard it merely as a concrete example of certain general mechanical principles. Nor have we any interest in any particular practical use to which we could put the tool.

In *practical knowing* we approach the hammer as an object which will serve a useful purpose. Our interest is in the purpose primarily, and in the hammer only in so far as it enables us realize the purpose. Usually we pay only perfunctory attention to the tool itself.

There is, however, a third attitude. A keen craftsman may inspect a number of hammers, and he notes one particular tool. He regards it with pleasure, takes it up, and balances it in his hand. The perfect balance of the instrument and the feeling of personal fitness which comes with handling it gives the craftsman a thrill of enjoyment. The satisfaction comes from contemplating and using the object itself. There is no specific consideration of its mechanical principles, nor interest in its immediate utility for any particular task. This is shown by the fact that the craftsman who finds a superlative tool will exclaim, " What a beauty ! " and use it on anything which happens to be at hand, not because any hammering is necessary but just for the joy of using it. Usually in such a case the proud possessor will call other people's attention to it saying, " Look at this ! Try it. What do you think of it ? " expecting admiration equal to his own.

In æsthetic enjoyment we experience pleasure in the contemplation (or use) of an object or situation for its own sake. Its beauty appeals to us. We feel thrilled and uplifted. The interest does not go beyond the object either to its utility, or its objective characteristics as such.

Æsthetic enjoyment is not identical with sensuous pleasure although the latter is usually an element in the enjoyment. We can experience sensuous pleasure without æsthetic enjoyment, as in experiences of savoury smells, sweet scents of flowers, bright saturated colours, and the massive feeling given by a warm bath when one is cold and tired.

For æsthetic enjoyment the sensuous pleasure must be accompanied by certain intellectual elements—apprehension of order, symmetry of arrangement, proportion, balance, harmony. This is shown by the fact that the same objects can produce both enjoyment and repugnance, according to their arrangement. A familiar example is a vase, with flowers either tastefully arranged or just pushed in roughly in a bunch. The intellectual elements just mentioned provide a major part of the enjoyment of certain mathematical patterns—including mathematical calculations and proofs. To a mathematician an exercise in the calculus is an object of enjoyment compared with an exercise in ordinary arithmetic which may arrive at the same result but in a roundabout, clumsy, *ugly* way. Here the sensuous elements are reduced to a minimum— a series of black marks on white paper. They have no particular beauty in themselves. The object contemplated and enjoyed is an arrangement of ideal order. Moreover, a mathematical proof may have no practical utility whatever. Yet it can produce in the mathematician a thrill of enjoyment comparable to the musician's delight in a concord of sweet sounds, and the artist's delight in a harmony of colours.

The intellectual elements, however, remain as a background in æsthetic enjoyment. They are apprehended in a synthetic way as part and parcel of the object contemplated. So soon as we pass from a contemplation of the beautiful object to an analysis of its specific characteristics, the æsthetic enjoyment ceases and we pass into the critical detached intellectual way of knowing.

This point is shown clearly in the case of literary passages :

> But now farewell. I am going a long way
> With these thou seëst—if indeed I go
> (For all my mind is clouded with a doubt)—
> To the island valley of Avilion ;
> Where falls not hail, or rain, or any snow,
> Nor ever wind blows loudly ; but it lies
> Deep meadow'd, happy, fair with orchard lawns
> And bowery hollows crown'd with summer sea
> Where I will heal me of my grievous wound.[1]

This passage might be used as a grammatical exercise for practising analysis and parsing. (It was thus that I first became acquainted

---

[1] Tennyson, *Morte d'Arthur.*

with the passage in school.) It might be used as an example of literary style, and the passage analysed for the purpose of discussing its poetic structure and characteristics, and the reasons why it may be called good poetry (or bad, as the case may be). These are instances of the intellectual attitude in knowing the passage.

It might also be part of the three hundred lines of poetry which together with knowledge of meaning and allusions were required by the 1875 code for the last year in the elementary school course. As lines to be memorized by heart for inspection purposes the passage above would be as good as any other equal number of lines. Here it fulfils a practical purpose, and would be approached primarily with a practical attitude.

In neither of these ways would æsthetic enjoyment be obtained fully. The intellectual or practical attitude interferes with the æsthetic attitude which seeks to know the passage for its own sake on account of the enjoyment produced in reading and contemplating it.

It is clear that in æsthetic enjoyment we are dealing with sentiments. Æsthetic sentiments are acquired associations between cognitive and feeling- plus-conative elements, in which the feeling-elements strongly predominate and the object of the sentiment is some form of beauty.[1] Thus æsthetic enjoyment can develop from crude experiences of sensuous pleasure in childhood to a refined and strengthened love of beautiful things and an ideal of beauty in later life. As the sentiment develops on its positive side as a love of beautiful things, it will develop on its negative side as a hatred [2] of ugly things.

Attunement and Absorption

The distinguishing character of æsthetic enjoyment as a way of knowing seems to be the more or less complete *absorption of the observer into a unity of being with the object or situation observed.* The more complete the absorption, the greater the enjoyment. The observer becomes one with the object and, for the time being, shares its nature. The beauty of mountains is in their grandeur and massive strength, and when the mountain-lover contemplates this beauty in a mood of æsthetic enjoyment he is absorbed within the scene and for the time being shares the grandeur and power.

Many mechanically minded people can be absorbed in the contemplation of a machine and experience a feeling of identity with the

---

[1] Compare with moral sentiments where the object is some form of moral conduct.

[2] *I.e.*, dislike reinforced by feelings of disgust and repulsion plus a desire to destroy the offensive ugliness.

machine and its power. Guns, aeroplanes, and other engines of destruction can inspire this feeling, and it is possible to feel a thrill and glory in their use and forget for the time being the dreadful consequences. This is a factor which many people who are trying to stop war fail to recognize sufficiently in assessing the causes of war.[1]

Teaching Æsthetic Enjoyment

If this analysis of the factors in æsthetic enjoyment is correct, we can answer the question, " Can appreciation be taught ? "

In so far as appreciation depends upon sensuous pleasures and certain forms of intellectual apprehension, a person cannot, by the nature of things, appreciate if he does not possess the specific or general aptitudes which make the pleasures and the apprehension possible. To the extent that the person's native endowment does not include these aptitudes, he cannot be taught to appreciate.

Hence the problem of teaching appreciation amounts to this. Assuming that the capacity for enjoyment is there, how can the teacher secure that the fullest possible degree of enjoyment will be realized ?

First we must note that since the enjoyment depends upon feelings which are peculiar to each person there will be very wide differences between individuals with respect to the enjoyment of any given object or situation. One man's meat may be another man's poison here as elsewhere. Therefore we cannot present objects of artistic merit to a class of pupils and demand that all shall admire and enjoy at the same time and in the same way.

However, a teacher can assist the process of appreciation in several ways :

1. Select objects worthy of appreciation and likely to be appreciated by pupils of a given age and condition. The teacher's wider range of experience enables him to bring to the pupils' notice many worthy objects which would not be available otherwise. Thus the teacher can arrange opportunities for appreciation and determine a worthy standard of taste.

2. Arrange quiet conditions free from material distraction during which objects and situations worthy of appreciation can be presented with some chance of their being appreciated.

3. Assist in the essential process of attunement or adjustment of the pupil, mentally, before the complete absorption required for full enjoyment is possible.

[1] This is a case where some effective substitute-satisfaction is needed.

4. Present the work to be appreciated in a way calculated to bring out its essential beauty in the clearest possible way.

5. Guide æsthetic discussion by the pupils after the presentation.

6. Provide opportunities for practice and training in æsthetic expression by pupils who show a desire for it.

A Procedure for the Appreciation Lesson

Enumerating what things the teacher can do to assist the pupils' appreciation indicates an outline of a lesson-formula. We have the following ' steps ' or phases :

    I. Preparation of Pupils.
    II. Presentation.
    III. Guidance.
    IV. Practice (or Creation).

I. Preparation of Pupils

This is probably the most important step of all in the practical teaching of appreciation, more important even than the introduction step in the intellectual or practical way of approach. It requires therefore a longer period and a greater measure of consideration and practical skill.

Its importance arises from the necessity that the pupils shall be *attuned to the object or situation presented*—poem, melody, picture —before they can become absorbed within it and apprehend its nature in the *direct immediate* way characteristic of æsthetic enjoyment.

The preparation of the pupils seems to include three aspects, all of which are necessary for full appreciation.

1. Organization of anticipatory interest

This has two subordinate phases :

(*a*) Removal of outside interests which may conflict with the appreciation—interests arising out of worry or excitement about events not connected with the coming appreciation lesson.

(*b*) Building up a positive anticipatory attitude, a readiness to pay attention to the object to be appreciated in the coming lesson.

Such an attitude may be encouraged by suggestions about the lesson in question, allusions to it, associations between items of interest in other lessons (*e.g.*, history, literature, grammar, nature-study) and the subject of the coming lesson in appreciation.

2. *Organization of an intellectual background*

Full enjoyment needs sufficient intellectual background to allow adequate interpretation of the medium in which the work to be presented is expressed. Without this background full apprehension of the significance of the work and therefore complete absorption in it is impossible. In this part of the preparation the aim is to remove any conditions which may cause frustration of full enjoyment. In appreciating a literary work, clear vivid imagery which conveys the exact significance of key words or phrases is essential for full enjoyment.

A quotation from Trench's *On the Study of Words* will illustrate this point. The author remarks that Coleridge said, " In order to get the full sense of a word, we should first present to our minds the image that forms its primary meaning." He then goes on as follows :

" What admirable counsel is here ! If we would but accustom ourselves to the doing of this, what a vast increase in precision and force would all the language which we speak, and which others speak to us, obtain ; how often would that which is now obscure at once become clear ; how distinct the limits and boundaries of that which is often now confused and confounded. It is difficult to measure the amount of food for the imagination as well as gains for the intellect which the observing of this single rule would afford us.

" Let me illustrate this by one or two examples. We say of such a man that he is ' desultory.' Do we attach any very distinct meaning to the word ? Perhaps not. But get at the image on which ' desultory ' rests ; take the word to pieces ; learn that it is from ' desultor,' one who rides two or three horses at once, leaps from one to the other, being never on the back of any one of them long . . . what a firm and vigorous grasp will you now have of its meaning ! A ' desultory ' man is one who jumps from one study to another and never continues for any length of time in one.

" Again, you speak of a person as ' capricious,' or as full of ' caprices.' But what exactly are caprices ? ' Caprice ' is from *capra*, a goat. If ever you have watched a goat you will have observed how sudden, how unexpected, how unaccountable, are the leaps and springs, now forward, now sideward, now upward, in which it indulges. A ' caprice ' then is a movement of the mind as unaccountable, as little to be calculated on beforehand as the springs and bounds of a goat. Is not the word so understood a far more picturesque one than it was before, and is there not some real gain in the vigour and vividness of impression which is in this way obtained ? "

Much of the enjoyment of literature consists in just the picturesque, vigorous, vivid impressions conveyed to the listener or reader by the words. If the words signify vivid accurate imagery one is able to enter into the situation portrayed directly and not " as through a glass, darkly," as is the case when the words convey nothing but confused impressions.

Note that what is desired is not the formal dictionary meaning of the word, but the *concrete imagery* of which the dictionary meaning is a second-hand description. If the pupils know the dictionary meanings of all the words in a poem by heart it will not guarantee that they will appreciate the poem. The very mass of their erudition may indeed prevent the appreciation. Given the vivid concrete imagery, however, they can get as it were through the words to their primary significance.

Hence, for this aspect of preparation, the teacher must familiarize himself with the work to be presented and understand it thoroughly. Each item likely to be difficult should be noted and these items rehearsed with the pupils in periods *previous to the appreciation lesson itself.* To interrupt the presentation in order to inquire into significance of words and allusions is to break asunder the artistic unity of expression and at the same time to translate the mood of æsthetic enjoyment into one of intellectual detachment and analysis, thus effectively preventing full appreciation.

3. *Inducing a suitable mood*

Immediately before the actual presentation it is desirable to induce in the pupils a receptive mood, ' coloured ' by the predominant feeling-tone expressed in the work to be appreciated—poem, melody, a picture—which may be sad, solemn, contemplative, or angry, excited, gay, etc.

This can be done to some extent by tone of voice and teacher's manner, by verbal suggestion or description. This process is sometimes called creating an appropriate atmosphere.

In this connexion it is not fantastic to suggest that some consideration be given to the relation between the ' atmosphere ' of the work presented and the actual conditions within and without the classroom at the time of presentation. A dark, howling, rain-soaked afternoon in late November is not quite the best setting for the successful appreciation of a poem on gay young lambs in a sun-drenched field in May !

It follows that preparation for the lesson in appreciation may occupy a fairly long period. For fullest success these lessons cannot be organized according to a rigid schedule—one lesson per week at the same specified time. Rather than risk taking many lessons for which adequate preparation cannot be made, it is better to take fewer but well done.

II. *Presentation*

It is essential that the presentation shall be continuous, in such a way as to enhance the unity of the work to be contemplated. All but the induction of an appropriate atmosphere and mood should have been completed in previous lessons, leaving the present clear for effective presentation.

III. *Guidance*

If the presentation has produced any vivid impressions, the pupils in a free and happy classroom atmosphere will usually comment spontaneously on their feelings, express likes and dislikes, ask questions, etc. Such expressions provide a basis for discussion.

Such discussion falls into two modes with different aims and prevailing attitudes—æsthetic and intellectual.

The æsthetic discussion will be occupied principally with the æsthetic feelings and values, comparing notes about individual responses to the presented work ; indicating items which have produced greatest enjoyment ; repetition of outstanding portions of the work, etc.

The æsthetic discussion is best taken soon after the presentation while the impressions are still vivid.

After the discussion the whole work or selected parts of it can be re-presented in the light of the discussion.

Note that this æsthetic discussion cannot be forced. Enjoyment is subjective and will not occur in obedience to a command from the teacher. It is necessary to ' feel ' the mood of the pupils and refrain from attempting by artificial teaching-devices to elicit expressions of opinion about non-existent enjoyment. Forced protraction of the æsthetic discussion soon becomes tiresome and defeats the purpose of the appreciation lesson. Moreover, some pupils are shy of expressing their feelings in public. Because a given pupil does not give vent to opinions it does not follow that there has been no appreciation. Appreciation is like a tender plant. It needs careful sympathetic cultivation rather than forcing.

Intellectual discussion can be left till a later period. It is more appropriate for senior pupils engaged in the study of music, literature, pictorial art, etc.

The object of the discussion will be :

To clarify still further meanings and allusions.

To discover how the artist has obtained his effects, leading to analysis of art forms, and formulation of principles of style and canons of taste.

The extent to which the intellectual analysis is carried must depend upon the interests, abilities, and needs of the pupils. For younger pupils, and for a general education, only such points as will serve to introduce the pupils to the elements of craftsmanship in artistic expression, and thereby enhance future enjoyment are needed. In literature, for example, such items as choice of words, poetic value of words, alliteration, repetition, contrast, metaphor, simile, rhythm, are interesting and helpful.

In so far as intellectual discussion deals with analysis, abstraction, and generalization, the rules for inductive development already given will apply.

IV. *Practice and Creation*

The abler pupils with some aptitude for artistic expression will desire to carry their studies to the stage of acquiring skill and trying to produce artistic work of their own. When skilfully taught it is rather surprising to find that the majority of the pupils desire to proceed to this stage and produce worthwhile results.

This phase of the process of training deals with the acquisition of skill and can be organized according to the rules for skill lessons.

EXERCISES

1. From the points raised in the discussion in this chapter, draw up a schedule for use in observing and criticizing a lesson.

The schedule should include suitability of the material selected for a given class of pupils ; amount of material ; effectiveness of the introduction, presentation, follow-up ; teacher's manner ; estimation of the degree to which the aim has been realized, etc.

2. Prepare a syllabus for a month, a term, or a year, in your special subject for typical classes (boys, girls, mixed) of a given age and ability, in a specified local environment.

Arrange the material in a suitable order, having regard to the attainments and ability of the pupils.

Consider the most effective places for recapitulation, summary, revision, and practice.

3. Study types of programmes for use at various levels, and in different types of subject-matter. Then try to write a programme for a specific purpose in which you are interested.

4. Repeat Exercise 2 for a Project Curriculum.

5. Write out lesson-notes for a specified class of pupils (stating sex, age, and previous knowledge assumed) in the following topics:

A medieval monastery.

Contours.

Measuring the height of a tree or church steeple by methods involving angles.

Proof that three angles of a plane triangle are together equal to two right angles.

Construction of a tangent to a circle from a given point outside it.

Introduction to quadratic equations.

Acids and alkalis.

The Preposition.

Analysis of complex sentences.

Milton's Sonnet on his Blindness.

The Parable of the Sower.

Capillarity.

Food-values.

Money.

The accusative-infinitive construction in Latin.

Construction of a mortice and tenon joint.

6. Select a pupil in school who fails to understand some process, *e.g.*, long division, simple equations, analysis of sentences, etc Diagnose the cause of the difficulty with appropriate tests and apply remedial measures.

7. Write a series of assignments according to the Dalton Plan suitable for ten- to eleven-year-old pupils in a small rural school.

8. Plan a series of projects suitable for slower learners in a secondary-modern or comprehensive school.

BOOKS FOR FURTHER REFERENCE

In many grammar and comprehensive schools syllabuses and methods will continue to be dominated by the requirements of O- and A-level examinations and university regulations. Methods, particularly in the higher forms, will still tend to follow the more traditional formal verbal exposition, illustration, notes, and exercises.

Nevertheless the spread of comprehensive-school organization ; the tendency to abolish streaming ; the increase in the numbers of working-class pupils and students with their own culture, values, and speech forms ; the increase in technical and further education with provision for day-release classes—all these changes are bringing into secondary and further education a range of abilities, attainments, and needs far wider than has been the case hitherto. The same changes are forcing teachers and administrators to reconsider drastically not only syllabuses and methods, but also the fundamental principles and values which, up to the time of writing, have been characteristic of secondary and further education in this country.

The most striking changes have occurred in English, mathematics, and science.

It is impossible to mention more than a few of the new books which now flood the market. The following is a selection of some of the more characteristic.

I. English

FLOWER, F. D. : *Language and Education* (Longmans, 1967). This is a very important and instructive work—an introduction not only to methods of teaching English, but also to recent investigations into general linguistic principles. It is concerned mainly with problems of English teaching in Further Education and Day-release Classes, but it is eminently applicable to secondary education generally. It should be compulsory reading for all teachers of English. Bibliographies. Suggestions for courses.

HOLBROOK, D. : *English for Maturity* (Cambridge University Press, 1961).

CLEGG, A. B. (ED.) : *The Excitement of Writing* (Chatto and Windus, 1964).

CORDER, S. P. : *The Visual Element in Language Teaching* (Longmans, 1966).

JACKSON, B. (ED.) : *English Versus Examinations* (Chatto and Windus, 1965).

CREBER, J. W. P. : *Sense and Sensitivity* (University of London Press, 1966).

MEARNS, H. : *Creative Power: The Education of Youth in the Creative Arts* (Dover Publications, 1959).

II. *Mathematics*

Report : *A Second Report on the Teaching of Arithmetic in Schools* (Bell, 1964). Prepared for the Mathematical Association.

Report : *Teaching Mathematics in Secondary Schools.* Ministry of Education Pamphlet No. 36 (H.M.S.O., 1958).

Report : *New Thinking in School Mathematics.* Organization for European Economic Co-operation (Paris, 1961).

Report : *Synopses for Modern Secondary School Mathematics.* Organization for European Economic Co-operation (Paris, 1961).

Report : *Mathematics in Primary Schools.* Schools Council Curriculum Bulletin, No. 1 (H.M.S.O., 1965).

HERITAGE, R. S. : *Learning Mathematics* (Penguin Education Series, 1966).

Report : *Nuffield Mathematics Teaching Project at Primary Level* (Penguin).

DIENES, Z. P. : *The Power of Mathematics* (Hutchinson, 1964).

—— *Building Up Mathematics* (Hutchinson, 1960).

—— *An Experimental Study of Mathematics Learning* (Hutchinson, 1964).

—— *Mathematics in the Primary School* (Macmillan, 1965).

DIENES, Z. P., AND JEEVES, M. A. : *Thinking in Structures* (Hutchinson, 1965).

Multibase Arithmetic Blocks and Algebraic Experience Materials for use with Dienes Manuals from the Educational Supply Association, Harlow, Essex.

BALLARD, P. B., AND HAMILTON, E. R. : *Fundamental Geometry* (University of London Press, 1935–53). 1st Series : Pupils' Books, 1, 2, and 3 and Teachers' Book ; 2nd Series : Pupils' Books, 1, 2, and 3 and Teachers' Books 1, 2, and 3. Introduction to elementary geometry by practical, discovery methods.

BRANFORD, B. : *A Study of Mathematical Education* (Oxford University Press, 1921). Essays on the development of mathematical concepts and methods of teaching.

WESTAWAY, F. W. : *Craftsmanship in the Teaching of Elementary Mathematics* (Blackie, 1931). Principles and methods. Covers secondary-school work up to sixth-form level.

III. *Science*

Report : *Science in Secondary Schools.*   Ministry of Education Pamphlet No. 38 (H.M.S.O., 1960).

Report : *A School Approach to Technology.*   Schools Council Curriculum Bulletin No. 2 (H.M.S.O., 1967).

The Nuffield Foundation Science Teaching Project.   Objectives—to make science intelligible and accessible to pupils of all kinds in schools of all kinds and to make science a more useful tool both intellectually and practically.   Details for five-year courses for pupils 11 to 16 years old :

Physics :   Teachers' Guides I–V.
             Guides to Experiments I–V.
             Pupils' Question Books I–V.

Chemistry: Introduction and Guide.
             Sample Schemes Stages I–III.
             Basic Course.
             Background Books.

Biology :   Teachers' Guides I–V.
             Texts I–V.
             Keys to Small Organisms.

For details, catalogues, apply to Longmans, Pinnacles, Harlow, Essex, or Penguin Books Ltd, Harmondsworth, Middlesex.

For details of apparatus required apply to The Nuffield Foundation Science Teaching Project, Mary Ward House, 5–7 Tavistock Place, London, W.C.1.

Association for Science Education Series. Science for Primary Schools. List of books and teaching aids. J. Murray, 50 Albemarle St, London, W.1.

BASSEY, M. : *School Science for Tomorrow's Citizens* (Pergamon Press, 1963).

ASHBY, E. : *Challenge to Education* (Angus and Robertson, Sydney and London, 1946).   Contains some stimulating articles on science teaching.

ARMSTRONG, H. E. : *Teaching of Scientific Method* (Macmillan, 1925).   A pioneer of the Heuristic Method.

ADAMS, J. (ED.) : *Educational Movements and Methods* (Harrap, 1930).   See article on the Heuristic Method.

WESTAWAY, F. W.: *Science Teaching* (Blackie, 1929).
Principles and practice. A comprehensive treatment.
See Chapter II : " A common cause of failure."

BROWN, J.: *Teaching Science in School* (University of
London Press, 1949). Suggestions for the Topic Method of
teaching.

HUMBY, S. R., AND JAMES, E. J. F.: *Science and Education*
(Cambridge University Press, 1942).

VAN BUSKIRK, E. F., SMITH, E. L., AND NOURSE, W. L.:
The Science of Everyday Life (Constable, 1938).

IV. *Topic and Project Methods*

COLLINGS, E.: *An Experiment with a Project Curriculum*
(Macmillan, 1924).

HOTCHKISS, E. A.: *The Project Method in Classroom Work*
(Ginn, Boston, 1924).

STEVENSON, J. A.: *The Project Method of Teaching* (Macmillan, New York, 1924).

STOCKTON, J. L.: *Project Work in Education* (Houghton
Mifflin, Boston, 1920).

MINISTRY OF EDUCATION : *The New Secondary Education*,
Pamphlet No. 9 (H.M.S.O., 1947). Notes on practical
activities, topics, and projects. Illustrated.

PARKHURST, H.: *Education on the Dalton Plan* (Bell, 1930).
How individual work in small rural schools can be organized.

V. *General*

ADAMS, J.: *Exposition and Illustration in Teaching* (Macmillan, 1923).

ADAMS, J.: *Modern Developments in Educational Practice*
(University of London Press, new edition, 1955).

JONES, A. J., GRIZZELL, E. D., AND GRINSTEAD, W. J.:
Principles of Unit Construction (McGraw-Hill, 1939).
Principles and methods of selecting and arranging subject-
matter for teaching purposes—subject-matter units,
centre of interest units, units of adaptation. Sample
units set out in various subjects.

DEWEY, J.: *How We Think* (Harrap, 1933). See particularly Chapters XI–XVI.

JAMES, W. T., AND DIXON, J. H.: *Creative Woodwork* (Pitman, new edition, 1947).

See also sections V and VI of the bibliography to Chapter I, pp. 29, 30.

CLEGG, A., AND MEGSON, B.: *Children in Distress* (Penguin Education Special, 1968). Survey of problems of child distress, with particular reference to intellectual and moral development and the impact on schools and education generally. What can schools do to help children in distress? Important little book.

HARGREAVES, D. H.: *Social Relations in a Secondary School* (Routledge and Kegan Paul, 1967). A carefully documented study of some unfortunate results of rigid streaming.

LAWTON, D.: *Social Class, Language and Education* (Routledge and Kegan Paul, 1968). Study of relations between language, thought, and social background. Useful survey of current psychological research.

VI. *Some Books likely to be Useful for B.Ed. Students*

BRUNER, J. S.: *The Process of Education* (Harvard University Press, 1966).

BRUNER, J. S.: *Toward a Theory of Instruction* (Harvard University Press, 1967).

GAGE, N. L. (ED.): *Handbook of Research on Teaching* (Rand, McNally Co., Chicago, 1967).

HILGARD, E. R. (ED.): *Theories of Learning and Instruction* Sixty-third Year Book of the National Society for the Study of Education, Part I, 1964 (Chicago University Press).

APPENDIX

NOTES ON DISCIPLINE AND CLASS CONTROL

Many students-in-training are apprehensive about discipline and class control, an essential aspect of practical teaching. The following notes are offered for guidance.

I. THE MEANING OF DISCIPLINE

The *Short Oxford English Dictionary* gives these suggestions :

> discipline (noun).   Mental and moral training ; order ; a system of rules for conduct ; control exercised over members of an institution.
>
> to discipline (verb).   To bring under control ; to train to obedience and order.

Thus the operative words are 'control,' 'obedience,' 'order,' representative of conditions which are essential for the success and smooth-running of any co-operative social enterprise, including school work. The problem, then, is to encourage these conditions in the practice of teaching.

The discussion here will be restricted to three aspects of the problem—namely :

(*a*) Interest in school work and loyalty to the school as an institution.

(*b*) Self-discipline and self-control.

(*c*) Class control.

Aspects (*a*) and (*b*) are long-term problems over which the individual teacher has only partial control. Aspect (*c*) is more immediate and to a greater extent within each individual teacher's control.

II. INTEREST AND LOYALTY

When pupils are interested in their school-work and school activities, either because these are intrinsically attractive and emotionally satisfying or because they are realizably instrumental as preparations for adult life and worth-while careers, then pupils will attend and put some effort into what they are required to do. If in addition the teacher is aware of pupils' interests and vocational aspirations, if the connexion between school work and aspirations is made sufficiently obvious, the pupils' will to work will be enhanced. In such conditions no difficulties of discipline or class control are likely to arise.

Moreover, as we have emphasized in previous sections of this book, success breeds interest, raises levels of aspiration, enhances confidence, and helps to maintain motivation at a sufficiently high level. Therefore organizing success tends to eliminate difficulties of discipline and class control.

In only too many cases, however, in grammar and secondary-modern schools, what is required to be done in school bears little or no recognizable relation to either intrinsic interests or after-school careers. Nor is it adapted sufficiently well to the pupils' levels of ability, talents, and rates of learning. That this is so is suggested by Professor Musgrove's survey of dissatisfactions and by the results reported in recent official publications—e.g., *Early Leaving* and *15 to 18*. In the latter report, out of a sample of grammar and technical-school pupils 78 per cent. of the boys and 81 per cent. of the girls did not want to stay at school any longer. The corresponding percentages for a sample of modern and all-age schools were 84 and 77 respectively. Out of the same sample of grammar and technical pupils, 24 per cent. of the boys and 33 per cent. of the girls either disliked school or considered they were not learning anything useful for future careers.[1]

In the cases of academically-minded convergent-thinking personalities expected to pass O and A Level examinations and proceed to institutions of higher education, the possibility of failure tends to inhibit tendencies to serious misbehaviour. For the not-so-academically-minded, divergent-thinking personalities, such restraining influence may be conspicuously absent. For the latter, nothing less than a drastic re-organization of curricula and teaching methods is likely to enlist their interests and stimulate their will to work. Attempts to drive these students forcibly into submission by oppressive measures usually intensify their will to resist ; they may lead to open defiance.

Hence the great importance for discipline and class control of suitable curricula and teaching methods.

[1] See *15 to 18*, Vol. II (Surveys), Tables 9*a*, 9*b*, and 10.

In the case of children and adolescents from working-class homes and neighbourhoods, their loyalties, more often than not, are bound up with their neighbourhoods, their gangs, and quite often their homes. To them the school is an alien institution. Too often their parents are indifferent, even actively contemptuous of the school and its values. Their experience is limited ; their vocabulary restricted. Their standards of taste are represented by ' pop ' music, ' pop ' dancing, ' pop ' radio, and ' pop ' television. Middle-class tastes and values leave them cold, or mystified, or contemptuous ; or arouse their hilarity. Any aloof, critical, ' snooty ' attitude stimulates resentment, ridicule, open defiance. The teachers who have been most successful in dealing with these pupils have (a) accepted them as they are ; (b) have started their teaching with the pupils' interests, standards, and tastes and advanced from there. There seems to be no other way. Such attitudes of acceptance are by no means easy. Not all teachers can deal successfully with these pupils. The effort, however, must be made if they are to be controlled.

A further consideration will increase in importance with the rise in the compulsory school-leaving age. Adolescents of sixteen years, particularly from working-class districts, are already young adults. They will actively resent and resist any attempts to treat them as children. Authoritarian pedagogues will create difficulties for themselves.

Hence the great importance of suitable attitudes and methods of approach on the part of teachers. Also the value of fostering co-operation between schools and homes.

III. SELF-DISCIPLINE AND SELF-CONTROL

Not all school work can be intrinsically interesting. Not all activity can be effectively supervised. The ideal objective of moral training and development is the individual who will attack a difficult piece of work ; who will persist until a task is finished ; who can tolerate a reasonable amount of frustration without resorting to anti-social behaviour or delinquency ; who, moreover, will do this when not under direct supervision ; who, in more traditional phraseology, is proof against temptation.

It is doubtful whether any normally emotionally well-balanced individuals will find any of the above aspects of behaviour intrinsically satisfying. Rather will they tend to avoid them. How then can this aggression in face of difficulty, persistence, tolerance of frustration, be generated? Some motivation stronger than the desire for an easy life is necessary. Psychologists seem now to be agreed that the deterrent is some degree of anxiety. More is involved than plain fear of detection and its consequences. That is not a sufficient deterrent when the individual is reasonably confident of evading detection. The ultimate deterrent is anxiety associated with and aroused by concrete examples of conduct, in the first place; later by accepted ethical principles. This association is developed by identification of the growing person with a model.[1] The first models are parents and near relatives; later, senior pupils in school, gang leaders, personalities in history, biography, television, cinema, politics, society, sport; even teachers! Which personality types are favoured will depend on temperament and physique. They will also depend on the continued influence of the earliest models—the parents. As the result of this process of identification, each growing child develops a self-image—the ideal type to which the young person is attracted. This self-image, by whatever name it is called—conscience, self-regarding sentiment, super-ego—is the ultimate arbiter of conduct. Any act contrary to the self-image arouses sufficient anxiety to act as a deterrent in the absence of other forms of supervision. At the highest level. the self-image is associated with a moral and social code and a system of ethical principles.

If schools and teachers stimulate the interest and gain the respect of pupils they can become models for identification, particularly with respect to standards of academic probity and intellectual honesty, as well as good manners in sport and behaviour generally. Hence the importance of suitable models for purposes of identification.

IV. CLASS CONTROL

The notes on curricula, methods of teaching, and development of a self-image refer to long-term processes. Of more immediate consequence for practical teaching is class control. Even in 'progressive' schools using activity methods there must be adequate control. Children can and do get excited; they can be aggressive; they can quarrel; they can 'show off.' In a 'permissive' classroom atmosphere the children are permitted to work—to work, that is, at their own pace and in their own preferred methods. They are

---

[1] *Cf.* Mackinnon's description (p. 410 above).

not to be permitted to play the fool. As Mrs Marshall so aptly said, the teacher is there to see that the children learn.

How then can class control be exercised without tyranny? Here are some suggestions :

   (i) Prepare thoroughly. Know in advance the objectives to be gained and the methods to be used. At the same time be ready with alternatives if conditions seem to need them.

  (ii) Have all necessary apparatus, books, pictures, writing materials, readily accessible at the beginning of each work-period. Nothing is so conducive to horse-play and lapse of interest as an awkward pause in the course of a teaching period to search for something which is needed but not immediately available.

 (iii) Keep the class busy.

 (iv) Introduce some variety into the treatment. Avoid monotony.

  (v) Organize success (see previous chapters).

 (vi) Watch the individuals in the class. Learn to read the signs of inattention, day-dreaming, boredom, incipient mischief-making. Deal with these gently, maybe, but if necessary firmly, before they develop. Prevention is better than cure.

(vii) Issue as few regulations as possible and *make sure that their purpose is understood*. Then, when regulations have been made *and discussed with the pupils*, make sure that they are obeyed.

(viii) If a request or a command is necessary make it in a mannerly fashion but expect to be obeyed and make sure that it is carried out.

 (ix) Avoid unnecessary threats. If, however, a threat seems indicated, make sure that it is carried out.

  (x) Remember the principle of operant conditioning. Praise behaviour or results which are really praiseworthy. Praise is sometimes more effective if given privately. Some children may be embarrassed if praised in public. They fear that other children may suspect favouritism and may ' rag ' them for being teacher's pets if they are praised publicly.

 (xi) Be scrupulously fair. No favourites. No nagging. No spite.

(xii) When assuming responsibility for a new class it is advisable to be more strict at first. Then when the class or group has settled down, relaxations may be allowed as rewards for good conduct or good work. If a teacher begins by being too easy-going and then finds it necessary to tighten up controls, the pupils are apt to resent what is taken to be an infringement of their rights and privileges.

(xiii) If you do not already know some of the more usual schoolboy and schoolgirl tricks and ' leg-pulls ' learn them and be ready to anticipate them. Nothing is more disconcerting for the school practical joker than to find his leg-pulls anticipated. Forewarned is forearmed in teaching as in other situations.

(xiv) In case of persistent trouble try to isolate and deal with the ring-leaders.

(xv) The qualities most likely to earn the respect of pupils are : good-humour ; fairness ; willingness to listen, to help, to explain ; patience ; firmness and consistency ; an equable temper. Also, children admire experts, people who can do something really well. Respect for a teacher's ability in games and athletics will often transfer to his authority in school work. Respect is an attitude which can and does spread from one context to others.

(xvi) Above all, cultivate a pleasant, friendly, helpful approach. Avoid the aloof, cold, disdainful, superior, ' snooty ' attitude. *Respect the personalities of the pupils.* To humiliate is the surest way to arouse resentment and active resistance.

Books for Further Reference

Argyle, M. : *The Psychology of Interpersonal Behaviour* (Pelican Books, 1967).

Wilson, J., Williams, N., and Sugarman, B. : *Introduction to Moral Education* (Pelican Books, 1967).

INDEX OF NAMES

INDEX OF TOPICS